TRAD DADS, DIRTY BOPPERS AND FREE FUSIONEERS

Popular Music History
Series Editor: Alyn Shipton, Royal Academy of Music, London, and City University, London

This series publishes books that challenge established orthodoxies in popular music studies, examine the formation and dissolution of canons, interrogate histories of genres, focus on previously neglected forms, or engage in archaeologies of popular music.

Published

Being Prez: The Life and Music of Lester Young
Dave Gelly

Chasin' the Bird: The Life and Legacy of Charlie Parker
Brian Priestley

Handful of Key: Conversations with Thirty Jazz Pianists
Alyn Shipton

Jazz Visions: Lennie Tristano and His Legacy
Peter Ind

The Last Miles: The Music of Miles Davis, 1980–1991
George Cole

Lee Morgan: His Life, Music and Culture
Tom Perchard

Lionel Richie: Hello
Sharon Davis

Mr P.C.: The Life and Music of Paul Chambers
Rob Palmer

Out of the Long Dark: The Life of Ian Carr
Alyn Shipton

Soul Unsung: Reflections on the Band in Black Popular Music
Kevin Le Gendre

Trad Dads, Dirty Boppers and Free Fusioneers: British Jazz, 1960–1975
Duncan Heining

Forthcoming

Gone in the Air: The Life and Music of Eric Dolphy
Brian Morton

In Search of Fela Anikulapo Kuti
Max Reinhardt and Rita Ray

An Unholy Row: British Jazz, 1945–1960
Dave Gelly

Trad Dads, Dirty Boppers and Free Fusioneers

British Jazz, 1960–1975

Duncan Heining

equinox

Published by Equinox Publishing Ltd.

UK: Unit S3, Kelham House, 3 Lancaster Street, Sheffield S3 8AF
USA: ISD, 70 Enterprise Drive, Bristol, CT 06010

www.equinoxpub.com

First published 2012

ISBN: 978-1-84553-405-9 (hardback)

British Library Cataloguing-in-Publication Data
A catalogue record for this book is available from the British Library.

Library of Congress Cataloging-in-Publication Data
Heining, Duncan, 1953-
     Trad dads, dirty boppers and free fusioneers : British jazz, 1960–1975/
     Duncan Heining.
         p. cm. – (Popular music history)
     Includes bibliographical references and index.
     ISBN 978-1-84553-405-9 (hardcover)
   1. Jazz–Great Britain–History and criticism. I. Title.
     ML3509.G7H45 2012
     781.65′50941–dc23
                                        2012011936

Typeset by JS Typesetting Ltd, Porthcawl, Mid Glamorgan.
Printed and bound in the UK by MPG Books Group.

Contents

Acknowledgements

The author wishes to thank all of the musicians and jazz activists who have contributed to this book. He also wishes to thank his partner of nearly forty years for her patience, support and advice. It has been a labour of love.

Two good friends and great servants of British jazz died while the book was being written. Michael Garrick and Graham Collier both made music that remains truly inspirational and, in their own different ways, they have helped to define British jazz. Since they both left town, the scene seems sadder and less beautiful. This book is dedicated to them and their achievements, and also to photographer Peter Symes, who died in 2011. We miss you.

Introduction

If you remember the sixties, you weren't actually there.   Grace Slick (attributed)

Quem deus vult perdere, dementat prius.
[Those the gods would destroy, they first make mad.]   Euripides

What begins life as a pithy, ironic comment on an epoch quickly becomes a cliché. The 1960s have already had their share of memoirs and social histories written both by those who were at the centre of events and by those who observed from the sidelines. Like most periods of social and cultural change – and those years were most definitely years of flux and transformation – what one sees has much to do with one's perspective. What is clear is that a variety of art forms were significantly affected by a sense of liberation and freedom. The development of British jazz between the early sixties and early seventies was a remarkable example of this process at work.

We might debate how much actually changed during those years. Some might see those years as a decade of sexual liberation and as ones that ushered in a classless society, where merit rather than (or as much as) birth determined the individual's life prospects. Others might suggest that in reality very little changed, and that Britain remained a class-bound society where money, power and privilege continued to rest with the few rather than with the many. At the same time, analysts, whether of the right or left or centre, do tend to agree on the themes that ran through the sixties and by which the decade could be characterized. One of these was most definitely class and privilege. Another was the rise of radical politics of left and right. Education was a constant theme, as were questions of tradition and modernization. Race and immigration became areas of contention, while demands for racial and sexual equality became increasingly vocal.

Sex was also talked about a great deal and more openly than in previous decades, and the use of recreational drugs was both more widespread and a cause for concern. There was much talk of freedom, though what this meant and how it might be obtained was often less clear. At the same time as these matters were contested, the arts became less obviously defined in terms of high and low culture, and instead more democratic and open. We could like the Beatles and Pink Floyd and discuss Stockhausen and Miles Davis. We could read the Liverpool poets, Wilfred Owen and T.S. Eliot, and enjoy Turner, Picasso and Andy Warhol. We could laugh at the Marx Brothers and the Boulting Brothers and ponder Ingmar Bergman and Fellini.

In most histories and documentary films about the 1960s, the same faces keep reappearing and have all acquired a near-iconic quality. There are the actors like Terence Stamp, Vanessa Redgrave, Julie Christie and Michael Caine. There are the models – Anouska Hempel, Twiggy and Jean Shrimpton – and the pop stars – the Beatles, the Rolling Stones, the Who and Jimi Hendrix. Then there are the politicians – Harold Macmillan, Alec Douglas-Home, Edward Heath and, most image-conscious of all, Harold Wilson, with his pipe and Gannex mac. And there is the Royal Family, notably Princess Margaret and Lord Snowdon. Jazz is at best a side-show in such accounts and, with the exception of an occasional photograph of a jazz band accompanying Campaign for Nuclear Disarmament (CND) marchers, was never part of the iconography of the period. One may find a mention of the "trad boom" and of "Ronnie Scott's Jazz Club in Soho", but little else. On the other hand, jazz histories that cover the period give scant space to events external to the jazz scene itself.

It may be the case that much of the main action was elsewhere, but the idea that any art form was unaffected by its times or had no impact upon them seems insupportable. History is, after all, written in the margins as well as on the pages themselves. British jazz might have been a smaller player on that stage, but its role was not without significance and it was, in turn, affected by trends evident elsewhere in Britain and the world. The aim of this history of British jazz is to locate the music within that broader social, political, economic and cultural context. Some conclusions we will reach may be tentative, others firmer and based upon a stronger evidential trail. It will also be clear that a particular perspective runs through this book. It is a socialist one, rooted within the ideas of Marx but aided also by those of later theorists such as Herbert Marcuse, Theodor Adorno, Walter Benjamin and Antonio Gramsci. It is underpinned by the understanding that to a significant extent events within society, including those of political and cultural activity, are dependent on economic relationships. Specifically, a view of class is both implicit and explicit throughout the text. This focuses not on status or wealth, though both are key secondary considerations, but on the dynamic relationship between individuals and groups with respect to the dominant mode of production.

British jazz underwent an important series of changes throughout the fifties, sixties and early seventies. It came of age and began to develop an identity of its own that was distinct from the original African-American template. Britain was one of the first countries outside the USA to do so, and the first to do it on such a scale and depth. Instead of a chronological or anecdotal history, the intention here is to write thematically using the issues of class, race, politics, and so on as reference points. This will allow us to assess their impact upon British jazz and how they might have shaped the music that came out of the period. We can then, with confidence, evaluate the contribution of British musicians to the development of British, European and world jazz.

1 Ancients and Moderns

Oh how quickly the glory of the world passes!   Thomas à Kempis

Historical accounts of periods of social and cultural change often characterize emerging trends and tendencies in terms of their newness or modernity.
Currents that defend or reflect the status quo are then defined as representative of tradition or defined as "old-fashioned". The "new" is seen to take on
the "old", or youth its elders, in a struggle to impose a "new" vision in place
of the "old" one. This is all too often a caricature of events. Our picture of
the sixties is just such a caricature. The reality, in Britain certainly, was one
of paradox in which traditional power refreshed itself and continued, while
adjusting to prevailing economic winds. In British jazz, tradition was also
seen to be set against modernity and was caught up in a Spenserian struggle
for survival. But this too was really just a partial and partisan view of what
actually occurred. The real story of British jazz in the 1960s is actually much
more complex and far more interesting. To understand it we also need to
understand the sixties.

As the clock turned from 1959 to 1960, the winds for jazz in Britain
seemed set fair. In its modernist form, the music had at least established a
foothold in the capital, and one or two outposts in the provinces. True, it
attracted nothing like the popular attention of its just slightly older, traditional sibling. There might have been one or two musicians and critics who
dared to suggest that *jazz moderne* was either a changeling child or at least
born the wrong side of the bed sheets. However, despite such slander, John
(then Johnny) Dankworth, the Jazz Couriers with Ronnie Scott and Tubby
Hayes, and the various Tony Kinsey and Tony Crombie Ensembles had
acquired a more than satisfactory degree of public recognition.

By comparison, traditional jazz had achieved much, much more. It had
succeeded in seeing off the rock & roll challenge, up to a point at least.

That this was so was, ironically perhaps, due in no small measure to the Musicians' Union (MU) "ban" on American artists, which was imposed in the mid-1930s, and which continued until 1956 for concert performances and until 1961 for club dates. This effectively stopped not only American jazz musicians but also restricted the main US rock & roll acts from playing and touring in the UK early in their careers. It is a moot question whether British audiences or those who monitored taste would have accepted Elvis Presley; and, of course, Presley never played the UK. Bill Haley's UK tour in 1957 had been met with mini-riots but, in many respects, his career was by that time already in decline. Jerry Lee Lewis visited the UK in May 1958 but was dogged by the scandal surrounding his thirteen-year-old bride. Along with Little Richard, these singers were the real deal and, though their records were available in Britain, fans largely had to make do with home-grown imitations. Denmark Street, London's Tin Pan Alley equivalent, and its core of mainly Jewish, often homosexual promoters, were bound up in the world of light entertainment. Pop music, in the sense of a separate youth-centred phenomenon, was at most an ephemeral side-show within that world.

As George Melly pointed out with regard to singer Tommy Steele and his agents Larry Parnes and John Kennedy in *Revolt into Style* (1970):

> As early as 1956, before he had even made Number 1 in the charts, he was taken away from the rock circuit, and was topping the bill in the Moss Empire variety theatres. Pantomimes and films followed (the British "Rock" films are a subject in themselves, a crucial stage in the "castrating" process of the middle and late 50s). All these factors contributed to Tommy's wider acceptance and the consequent alienation of his first public, the teenage rebels. (Melly 1970, 50)

Cliff Richard's first hit, "Move It", was written by producer Ian Samwell-Smith, whose name crops up again and again throughout the sixties and seventies. It had a genuinely authentic air to it, and the singer, with his sideburns, Elvis quiff and suggestive on-stage demeanour, had enough of that sense of danger to pass muster. His next record, however, was the execrable "Living Doll". He too was instantly booked onto the variety circuit and his Presley-derived style was further sanitized for mass public consumption by TV producer Jack Good for appearance on "Oh Boy!". The quiff was trimmed, the sideburns removed and the phallic guitar taken away (Melly 1970, 55).

Perhaps Billy Fury had the look and added a certain substance to the style. When allowed his own band in 1960, he took with him from the Parnes and Kennedy stable Georgie Fame on piano, Colin Green on guitar, Tex Makins on bass and, on drums, Red Reece. A handful of quite genuine rock & roll records did come out of Britain around that time, notably those of Vince Taylor and Johnny Kidd, but they were few in number. Otherwise,

Marty Wilde blurred into Mark Wynter, who dissolved into Johnny Gentle and Terry Dene. It was either a case of a pale, desexualized imitation of the American originals or pastiche that replaced the sexual charge of rebellion with innuendo and a nudge and a wink.

As Georgie Fame, himself one of the Parnes stable of singers and musicians, notes:

> Well, before the groups came along it was all just show business. There was a rock & roll element to that show biz, like Tommy Steele, Marty Wilde and Cliff Richard. When the groups came along that changed everything. Everybody wanted to be in a band.
> (Interview with Georgie Fame, April 2009)

Back in late 1959 and early 1960, jazz was part of show business. While the modernists grooved in their subterranean and nocturnal homes supported by bits of session work and dance band gigs, the fortunes of traditional jazz in particular in its more popular "trad" form (see pages 17–18 for the distinction) were booming. Pete Townshend, the Who's guitarist and songwriter, described the attraction of the style very neatly:

> We were all interested in traditional jazz at the time. There was a bit of rock and roll, which hadn't fully blossomed by that time basically because there was no radio platform for it in the UK. The "trad" jazz that we played was fairly pure. It was based on Louis Armstrong. It was "Willie the Weeper", "The Saints Go Marchin' In" – people like Kenny Ball, Ken Colyer, the Chris Barber Band, that kind of stuff. It was very authentic.
> (*An Ox's Tale – The John Entwhistle Story*, documentary)

John Entwhistle, the Who's bassist, played second trumpet with a traditional jazz-cum-dance band and would busk around the West End, just trumpet and banjo, playing the "trad" favourites of the day. Elsewhere, drummer Ginger Baker and bassist Jack Bruce also began their careers in traditional jazz groups. Townshend actually goes on to note that: "You hear some very weird shit in the Who's sound and some of it has got to do with the fact that we used to play a lot of 'trad' jazz" (*An Ox's Tale – The John Entwhistle Story*, documentary).

The reasons for the attraction of early jazz, whether in what was described at the time as its revivalist form associated with Chris Barber, Acker Bilk, Kenny Ball and others, or the more "authentic", "traditionalist" style pursued by Ken Colyer, were in some ways quite simple. It was lively and, compared with the more formal dance orchestras, unpredictable and exotic. When so much of cultural life in the late fifties seemed mired in Victorian and Edwardian expectations of good taste and appropriate behaviour, jazz of such kinds offered young people of all social classes an outlet. You could dance to it and, more importantly, invent your own steps or steal them from your friends. While parents danced sedately to the foxtrot and the waltz with the addition of an occasional, semi-risqué tango, their children danced to George Melly and the Mick Mulligan Band, Terry Lightfoot, Chris Barber and Ken Colyer.

Compared with modern jazz, traditional jazz was a style that could be picked up and played passably well with comparative ease by an amateur musician. No long apprenticeship was required and nor was any great skill. Playing it well was, of course, another matter altogether. Although the earlier style might in the main be less complicated in form and structure than much modern jazz, this is not always the case. Compare, for example, the modal approach used by Miles Davis on *Kind of Blue* with some of Jelly Roll Morton's arrangements. Early jazz and the British variants on it are also generally more straightforward in terms of use of harmony and rhythm. Its fairly consistent rhythmic structure is particularly important in terms of its function as dance music. It is therefore more easily assimilated by non-specialist listeners than the more complex harmonic and metrical structures of the post-Charlie Parker jazz played by the Ronnie Scotts, John Dankworths and Tubby Hayeses. What is more, being essentially repetitive, it stuck in the memory.

What other attractions did it hold? It certainly attracted a degree of scholarly attention, and not only from critics like the *Melody Maker*'s Max Jones, the *Telegraph*'s Philip Larkin, *Jazz Journal*'s Sinclair Traill and the Hon. Gerald Lascelles, the cousin of Queen Elizabeth II. To today's reader, the style of some of these writers might seem old-fashioned and even clumsy at times, but there can be no doubting either their commitment or enthusiasm. In fact, it was these writers, along with people like Joachim Berendt (Germany) and Hugues Panassié and André Hodeir (France), who laid the foundations of jazz studies and jazz discography. There was Brian Rust, who epitomized the perfect jazz discographer, so much so that the word "Rustian" was coined to compliment a comparable attention to detail. Then there was Marxist historian Eric Hobsbawm writing in the *New Statesman* under the *nom de plume* of Francis Newton. As he explained in the *London Review of Books* in May 2010:

> I owe my years as a jazz reporter to John Osborne's *Look Back in Anger*, which made the British cultural establishment of the mid-1950s take notice of a music so evidently dear to the new and talented Angry Young Men. When, needing some money, I saw that Kingsley Amis wrote in the *Observer* on a subject about which he obviously knew no more and possibly less than I did, I called a friend at the *New Statesman*. He arranged a meeting with the editor, Kingsley Martin, then at the peak of his glory, who said "Why

not?", explained that he conceived his typical reader as a male civil servant in his forties, and passed me on to the commander of the (cultural) back half of the mag, the formidable Janet Adam Smith. Her interests ranged from mountaineering to poetry, but did not include jazz. As "Francis Newton" (named after a Communist jazz trumpeter who played on Billie Holiday's "Strange Fruit"), I wrote a column every month or so for the *New Statesman* for about ten years.   (Hobsbawm 2010, 41)

More importantly, Hobsbawm (as Newton) wrote *The Jazz Scene* (1959), which was later published as one of the Jazz Book Club editions, and which was a rare attempt to offer a sociological analysis of jazz that was erudite without being at all dry. The Jazz Book Club series was a successful and, by present standards, bold attempt to provide authoritative writing on jazz for an information-hungry readership. The series was edited by Herbert Jones and began to be published in 1956; from then until its demise in 1967 it issued sixty-five volumes. As well as British writers like Newton/ Hobsbawm, Brian Rust, Sinclair Traill and Rex Harris, the Book Club made available texts by Hodeir, Panassié, Berendt, and American writers Martin Williams, Studs Terkel and Whitney Balliett. Veteran blues writer Paul Oliver's classic *Blues Fell This Morning* (1962) was one club edition, while autobiographies by Humphrey ("Humph") Lyttelton, Sidney Bechet, Wingy Mangone, Eddie Condon and Mezz Mezzrow offered remarkable insights into the world of jazz.

As for *Jazz Monthly*, edited by Albert McCarthy, some of its content would be almost unthinkable nowadays, in terms of its subject matter and length. For example, in 1963, the magazine published a very insightful piece by John Postgate entitled "Jazz and Race", which began:

> A sagacious and far-sighted writer once wrote in these pages: "As jazz lovers we are never far from the colour problem." For the purposes of this article I shall take it for granted that readers share my view of colour prejudice: that the mere existence of such prejudice makes me ashamed that my skin is white.
>   (Postgate 1963, 2–3)

Nor was this an unusual topic for *Jazz Monthly*. Its January 1961 issue had featured an article by Maurice Capel under the title "The Metamorphosis of Orpheus", which sought to address the debate regarding playing to segregated audiences in the American South, as well as the broader struggle for equality. Capel had highlighted "Jazz at the Phil" promoter Norman Granz's stance on the issue and his (Granz's) views on Dave Brubeck's cancellation of a tour of Southern universities due to their refusal to accept Brubeck's mixed-race quartet. Granz had pointed out that Brubeck was being praised for his stance when no mention was made that he was not – apparently – playing to non-segregated audiences. By contrast, Granz had clauses in contracts that allowed him to pull out of dates if the local promoter insisted on segregation. Where this resulted in financial loss to African-American musicians on the tour, Granz went to litigation and won. The magazine's G.E. Lambert (Lambert 1962) came to Brubeck's defence, which prompted a furious reply from Capel. He wrote: "Freedom is not a dream or an ideal: it is the structure for living. It is not a stand but a commitment. It is not an attitude but a passion (in the religious sense)" (Capel 1961, 26). This indicates a highly perceptive reading of and insight into the questions involved. *Jazz Monthly* also gave extensive space in autumn 1961 to an unusually forward-thinking piece on jazz, alcohol and drugs by Charles Winick, an American psychiatrist, who had treated the addictions of various musicians during his career (Winick 1961). Meanwhile, Christopher Whent pondered the "Phenomenon of Jazz" over the course of three issues in 1961 (Whent 1961). These are all fine examples of jazz scholarship and suggest that an important section of the jazz public was ready and willing to absorb such challenging writing about the music.

But there was also something about jazz that specifically excited the attention of young men beyond such rarefied discussion. Hours of harmless fun could be had from imagining how Buddy Bolden's band might actually have sounded or debating the relative merits of Armstrong's Hot Fives against those of the Hot Sevens. In a way it was all very earnest and innocent, and, to a modern ear and eye, it does sometimes sound rather awkward and self-conscious. That, nevertheless, may be our problem rather than that of the British jazz writers of the fifties and sixties.

Something of that rather self-conscious flavour pervades many of the Jazz Book Club tomes like Rex Harris's *Enjoying Jazz* (1960). Its final chapter, "Do It Yourself Jazz and Skiffle", begins: "Now – suppose you are interested in jazz and you want to join a jazz club. The best thing to do is find out if there is one in easy reach of your home, and then go along and see what it is like there" (Harris 1961, 123). Jolly sound advice, indeed. Harris's penchant for critical precision is demonstrated in his comment on clarinettist, Barney Bigard:

> Barney Bigard, the clarinettist from New Orleans, added a grace to the performances by his versatility, producing a shrill and exciting sound when necessary, but also providing throbbing sub-register work when the occasion demanded.   (Harris 1961, 87)

Such writing was not confined to Harris. Consider this from Charles Wilford writing on the chart successes of Lonnie Donegan, Humphrey Lyttelton's "Bad Penny Blues" and Johnny Dankworth's "Experiments with Mice" in *Just Jazz*: "And of these three, the first two groups were quite without resort to overt commercialism, while the Dankworth record was of real musical worth, though also presented with appealing slickness" (Traill and Lascelles 1957, 186). There is something of musty church halls, common rooms and campfire bonhomie about all this.

If one aspect of the attraction for British fans, and white audiences elsewhere, lay in the exoticism of "traditional jazz", then it is necessary to examine how this element was understood and experienced by the music's supporters. Its scene was certainly not all about cold showers, puritanism and intellectualization. There was a lot of sex about as well. With the exception of George Melly's *Owning Up* (first published in 1965), it just was not talked about in polite society. The BBC documentary *Smokey Dives* (2007) illustrates this very well. Interviews with individuals and couples who remember the era and the clubs are quite unambiguous on the matter. It also suggests a certain amount of cross-class fraternization, with jazz clubs in the late fifties and early sixties providing a mutually valued venue. This mixing of classes would increase as the sixties progressed, though the venue had by then shifted from the jazz club to the discotheque. As Colin MacInnes's unnamed hero notes in the novel *Absolute Beginners*:

> Now, you can think what you like about the art of jazz – quite frankly, I don't really care *what* you think, because jazz is a thing so wonderful that if anybody doesn't rave about it all you can feel for them is pity: not that I'm making out I really understand it *all* – I mean certain LPs leave me speechless. But the great thing about the jazz world, and all the kids that enter into it, is that no one, not a soul, cares what your class is, what your race is, or what your income, or if you're a boy, or girl, or bent, or versatile, or what you are – so long as you dig the scene and can behave yourself, and have left all that crap behind you, too, when you come in the jazz club door." (MacInnes 1960, 64)

With the opening up of higher education, the mixing of young people from different social backgrounds became more normal. The availability of scholarships to private schools in those areas that did not have grammar schools also played a part in reducing boundaries between classes. And there were open-air concerts in London parks, which had, since their inception in the Victorian era, maintained a certain egalitarian atmosphere, though access to upper crust events such as Royal Ascot, Henley Regatta or the "Coming Out" balls was not on a reciprocal basis. Whether this truly provides evidence of a genuine and fundamental social mobility or a move towards greater equality is perhaps another matter.

Fans interviewed on the *Smokey Dives* film recall an active sex life on the scene, which sometimes involved sexually transmitted diseases and unwanted pregnancies. There was clearly something in the music and, of course, the scene that surrounded it that contributed to a lowering of barriers, at least within that specific context. Sex was not, after all, invented in the sixties. What traditional jazz and its clubs provided in the fifties was a meeting point where people who shared a love of the music could mix outside the supervision of their elders and within which wider social codes did not apply, or were at least relaxed.

With regard to racial issues, it seems unlikely that the more general fan of "trad" considered deeply the question of how the "American Negro", to use the parlance of the period, came to create this music, or pondered the social and economic circumstances in which they did so. However, as we have seen, that certainly would not have been true of the readers of *Jazz Monthly*, and even the more populist *Melody Maker* was alive to racial issues.

Perhaps it was ironic that the supreme cultural achievement of an oppressed people should find such favour in the country that had first uprooted them from their home. This music came, after all, from people transported in British ships and those of other imperial powers across the Atlantic over several centuries as part of a pattern of trade that had made Britain one of the most economically powerful nations on the planet. Britain's empire provided it with income, raw materials, cotton, spices, gold and other precious metals and stones, but also with markets for the goods produced in British factories and with investment opportunities for the wealth that accumulated in British banks. It was never an equal trade, of course, whether those exploited lived and worked in India or were taken as slaves from west Africa. At the same time, Britain's empire acted as a shield against those economic winds that might have encouraged modernization of its industry and managerial practices. In fact, as both Eric Hobsbawm (1990) and C.R. Hensman (1975) reveal, the British economy was thoroughly enmeshed with those of its colonies and dominions well into the twentieth century. The implications of this were that its empire allowed Britain to continue as if it were business as usual long after its competitors had begun to adapt to a changing world (see Kemp 1985).

Britain's role as world power, trading nation and world financial centre continued during the inter-war years, and even to a degree after the Second World War. It had been and remained a cultural hub, perhaps not always or even often at the very heart of cultural developments, but as a point of confluence. Throughout Britain's imperial and later Commonwealth eras, trade in goods did bring with it new ideas, new forms of entertainment, new styles of dress and new forms of conduct. People came to Britain from all over the empire, as well as from North America. Others came from continental Europe to escape persecution. However culturally conservative Britain might have seemed under Victoria, and then her son Edward and grandson George, such impressions belie a number of artistic, social and political currents that were open and receptive to the new. Socialism established roots in Britain under Victoria. Notions about the relationship between art and society could be found in the work of William Morris and

Ford Madox Brown, and writers such as G.B. Shaw, John Ruskin and Oscar Wilde. The Aesthetic Movement drew extensively on influences from the Far East, while the Vorticists, artists like Paul Nash, Stanley Spencer and Dora Carrington, and novelists and poets such as D.H. Lawrence and Virginia Woolf embraced the avant-garde of Surrealism and Futurism. Psychoanalysis had already taken root in Britain after the First World War, long before Freud took up residence in Hampstead. Popular culture might have been swamped by patriotic fervour in 1914 but the music halls, its most obvious representative, also retained an independence from dominant middle-class culture.

In terms of modern British jazz, musicians from the Empire/Commonwealth would play a major role in its achievements in the 1960s. But, historically, Britain's openness to and receptiveness to jazz goes back earlier to the inter-war years, and perhaps even before 1914. In a way, empire may have created an awareness, however paternalistic or dismissive, of other cultures and maybe even a guilty pleasure in their otherness. There was arguably a greater openness with British society and culture than sometimes seems apparent. And one should never underestimate the power of the exotic or its erotic overtones. Jazz was risqué, and in appreciating it, truly appreciating it, one became a member of a special club. Not a stuffy Mayfair or Piccadilly club frequented by one's *pater* or the smoky, grimy, male-only working men's club of your dad. You had your own club, your own codes and your own friends, and it was jazz that bound you together, made you different from your parents and set your agenda. You could identify with Jimmy Porter from John Osborne's *Look Back in Anger* or Archie Rice's son Frank from the playwright's second play *The Entertainer*. Both were jazz fans after all, who identified with this music in a way that expressed their dissatisfaction with all the cant and hypocrisy of their parents' generation. One should also note that that the "school" of writers from Osborne and John Wain to John Braine, Philip Larkin and Kingsley Amis played no small part in promulgating jazz values, even if (in some cases) their political views veered to the right as youth was followed by the conservatism of middle age.

One writer who did seem to understand the appeal of jazz, and who wrote about the period and the coming of youth with panache, was Colin MacInnes. It was MacInnes as well who, in an article on Tommy Steele for *Encounter* magazine in December 1957, identified that Steele *et al.* signified something more than an ephemeral moment in show business: the arrival of a new generation. His novel *Absolute Beginners* succeeds in celebrating youth without condescension but retains its sense of brash self-awareness in a way that is rather charming. As noted, there were a number of writers who treated jazz seriously. There was Max Jones and musician–writer Benny Green and, perhaps the best of them all, Philip Larkin. Larkin's *Daily Telegraph* articles and reviews still stand up today. There is something quite charming about Larkin's rather grumpy prose and, perhaps surprisingly, he often seems unusually generous to music and musicians he obviously detests. MacInnes lacked others' knowledge of jazz or their authority, but somehow he captured the tenor of the time in a way that they didn't quite manage.

And perhaps one other reason why Britain was prepared for traditional (if not modern) jazz lies in our own musical traditions. In particular, this country has a strong brass band tradition. While saxophones and clarinets rarely feature in British brass ensembles, the tonal colours and harmonies of trumpets, cornets, trombones and tubas coupled with a solid, martial rhythm are sounds with which we are quite familiar. It is perhaps worth suggesting here that, however exotic traditional jazz might have sounded, it was not completely alien in its form to British ears.

The element in jazz that was certainly far less familiar to British audiences, or at least English ones, was its emphasis on improvisation. There is really nothing in British popular or classical music that might prepare us for this, aside from the occasional melodic embellishment that might be allowed in Baroque or early Romantic music. The exception lies in folk music, a form that had become less and less familiar as a vernacular music, to the English, at least. The majority of the urban population would only have had limited contact directly with folk music through BBC Educational broadcasts or Cecil Sharp's English Folk Dance and Song Society. Nevertheless, in some parts of rural Britain, as the folklorist A.L. Lloyd and broadcaster Charles Chilton were at pains to demonstrate before it was too late, folk music survived as a living oral tradition, particularly in the Celtic and Cornish fringes. Some of this music embodied a strong tradition of improvisation, both melodically and rhythmically, and a number of folk clubs existed in many areas of Britain. However, folk music as a developing form that allowed for extemporization was not something of which most English people would have been aware, though they would through the English *National Song Book* that was used extensively in schools and through church attendance be familiar with its melodies (Stanford and Shaw 1905). As Pete Townshend suggests above, "trad" jazz may well have gone some way to preparing British audiences for improvisation in music.

The history of the British reception of jazz is a fascinating one. Jim Godbolt's *A History of Jazz in Britain 1919–50* (1986) sets out how jazz took a hold in Britain in the period before, during and immediately after the Second World War. David Boulton also explored similar territory in *Jazz in Britain* (1958), albeit in less detail and with less in the way of oral history or intriguing anecdotes. Visits by the likes of Armstrong, Ellington, Bechet and, as early as 1919, by the all-white Original Dixieland Jazz Band certainly primed British audiences for this music. However, Alyn Shipton (2001, 33–5) suggests that the process of acculturation began even earlier. He notes that a number of orchestras playing ensemble ragtime visited Europe several years before and began the process of dissemination, while Rye (1990) notes the presence in Britain of the "cakewalk" musical show *In Dahomey*, and bands such as the Musical Spillers and Jamaican-born pianist Dan Kildare and his Clef Club Orchestra.

It should also be noted that the whole notion of the British Empire was very strong both prior to the First World War and during the inter-war years. We have come to understand imperialism and empire in very different ways; at that time it spoke to white Britons of more than just power, and rather as a means by which British and Christian values might be spread across the pink quarter of the globe. Many people went out to the colonies and brought back stories and experiences. Empires require communication and this can never be just one-way. In a sense, as suggested already, it can be argued that the British Empire prepared us to hear the new and exotic music coming from overseas.

As jazz became widely appreciated through the visits of African-American and white bands to the UK, there were noteworthy attempts to recreate the music played in the UK by these artists. As early as 1923, trombonist Lew Davis formed the Original Lyrical Five to play Dixieland jazz modelled on the Original Dixieland Jazz Band. Then, in 1927, Philippines-born pianist Fred Elizalde formed a band called the Quinquaginta Ramblers. The band began a residency at the Savoy on 1 January 1928 and Elizalde, unhappy with the calibre of some of his players, succeeded in recruiting five musicians from America, including the multi-instrumentalist Adrian Rollini. Boulton suggests that the sides they recorded for Brunswick "were undoubtedly the finest made in England during that decade" (Boulton 1958, 53). Their engagement at the Savoy came to an end in 1929 following disputes between Elizalde and the hotel's management over the extent of the jazz content in the group's performances. Put simply, the Savoy wanted less of it!

For a brief period in the early thirties, the music of Patrick "Spike" Hughes held sway. Although, following a period in New York playing with his idols in 1933, Hughes subsequently abandoned jazz, his compositions remain of more than historical interest. (Boulton 1958, 55–9; Godbolt 1986, 69–74). And there were others like Derrick Turner's New Dixieland Band and the group that featured on Crown Records under the pseudonyms of the Rhythm Rascals and the Swing Rhythm Boys (Godbolt 1986, 134) These names hid a group that included Scottish musicians George Chisholm on trombone and Tommy McQuater on trumpet. It was these players who were among those who recorded with American Benny Carter when he was in London in 1936. Yet, for all the space devoted by both Boulton and Godbolt to the subject, an impression remains that these examples were more high spots, and that much of what passed for jazz in Britain prior to 1940 was really just dance music that featured the occasional "hot" soloist such as trumpeter Nat Gonella. What is more, as Godbolt points out, while there was a procession of American artists passing through the UK between 1919 and 1935, records by key American jazz musicians were hard to come by in Britain. In fact, as he notes, the key sides by the King Oliver Creole Jazz Band featuring Louis

Armstrong and recorded in 1923 did not become available here until 1936 (Godbolt 1986, 132). And of course, from 1935, the British MU in concert with the Ministry of Labour imposed a ban on visiting American musicians, and that effectively halted the flow of US artists appearing in this country.

So, while some foundations may have been laid for the establishment of jazz in Britain before the Second World War, it was really during the war and immediately afterwards that we can identify trends that would coalesce to form and shape British traditional and revivalist jazz. It was in the forties that a number of key figures began to emerge, first of all around an amateur pianist called George Webb, and later around trumpeter Ken Colyer, who first gave shape and direction to jazz interest in the UK. Around 1941 (different sources give the date as 1942 or 1943), Webb began holding sessions at the Red Barn public house in Barnehurst. Born in 1915, Webb had been enthused by the few 78s of King Oliver and Louis Armstrong's Hot Five and Seven that had become available in the mid-thirties. Webb was working at the time at a local Vickers armaments factory, which remarkably also employed clarinettist Wally Fawkes and trombonist Eddie Harvey. With the addition of the twin cornets of Owen Bryce and Reg Rigden, Buddy Vallis on banjo, Art Streatfield on tuba and Roy Wyckes on drums, the band became George Webb's Dixielanders. As Humphrey Lyttelton, who would soon join the band on trumpet, recalled in his autobiography, *I Play as I Please* (1957), the Red Barn was soon packed to capacity every Monday night (Lyttelton 1957, 123) by studious, mainly young listeners. This was music to be heard with rapt attention and appreciated. When the BBC gave the band a broadcast on Radio Rhythm Club, it soon became clear that here was an underground phenomenon with the capacity to survive outside the confines of its small coterie of fans.

The renewal of interest in, or discovery of, the music of New Orleans, albeit as first recorded in Chicago, was not just a British trend. It had its parallels in the States around Lu Watters and Turk Murphy, and the arrival in Britain in 1947 of Graeme Bell's Australian Jazz Band marked a further advance in the music's popularity. If George Webb's Dixielanders (or perhaps its audience, or the landlord of the Red Barn) had discouraged dancing, Bell's group actively encouraged it.

If the first major event in the formation of British traditional or revivalist jazz can be attributed to George Webb's Dixielanders, the second came when Lyttelton left the Webb band to form his own ensemble. Like the Bell band, the trumpeter was less rigid on the subject of dancing and, by 1948, the Lyttelton Band and the Australians had established a base at the London Jazz Club in Great Windmill Street. Jazz had recovered its function as a music that deserved terpsichorean attention as well as intellectual evaluation. The third event in this area of the music's development in Britain was the formation of the Crane River Brass Band at Cranford in 1949. Ken Colyer was its leader and, along with his brother Bill, its ideologue. If Webb's aim was to recreate the jazz of New Orleans alumni Oliver and Armstrong, Colyer's went back further still. He was anxious to bring to Britain the sounds of contemporary 1950s New Orleans jazz as played by George Lewis, Bunk Johnson, Percy Humphrey and others. According to Alyn Shipton, his major influence in terms of his own sound was Mutt Carey's New Yorkers. For Colyer, what came afterwards might still be considered jazz but had been watered down by other influences and, in particular, by commercial considerations. In 1952, Colyer made his historic pilgrimage to Mecca and got to play with many of the musicians, including clarinettist George Lewis, still living and playing in New Orleans (see Shipton 2001, 630–1; Pointon and Smith 2010, 95–160).

For younger readers and modernists, the distinctions between "traditional", "trad" and "revivalist" jazz may seem arcane and confusing. It is, however, necessary in terms of what comes later to understand why this was important to Colyer, and to those who followed him, and why those who took a different course flourished and what this in turn meant for traditional jazz. Put simply, "traditional" went back to the roots of the jazz that had never left New Orleans or at least was seen to maintain that original approach and style. "Revivalist" jazz on the other hand included arranged sections and soloing with much greater emphasis on the individual or star musician. Traditional jazz was almost entirely "ensemble music". As George Melly noted in *Owning Up* (1974):

> What we expected a trumpet player to aim at was the early Louis Armstrong noise. Ken didn't sound anything like that. His wavery vibrato and basic melodic approach was based on Bunk Johnson. He sounded, and intended to sound, like an old man who had never left New Orleans when they closed Storyville. He played *traditional* not revivalist jazz.   (45–6; emphasis original)

Digby Fairweather in *Jazz: The Essential Companion* (Carr *et al.* 1987) makes a useful distinction between "revivalism" and Colyer's music:

> By 1950 – along with promising young revivalists such as Eric Silk and cornettist John Haim, who died early – three separate factions of British revivalism were clearly apparent: Freddy Randall (playing Chicago-style jazz at a North London venue, Cooks Ferry Inn), Humphrey Lyttelton, the classic trumpeter, who played the Armstrong/Bechet areas of jazz at the London Jazz Club, and – most intriguing of all – Ken Colyer, who (slightly to the dismay of Armstrong-based revivalists) played strict New Orleans jazz.
> "Trad", on the other hand, is a journalistic term to describe the commercial pop/jazz played by Acker Bilk, Kenny Ball, Chris Barber, Terry Lightfoot and others, though it should be stressed

that each of these also made some very acceptable revivalist jazz recordings. It is not unusual to find "Trad" used to describe the debasement of this music in the late fifties and early sixties as commercial considerations held sway. (Carr *et al.* 1987, 415–16)

As Fairweather again notes in defining trad jazz:

An abbreviation of "traditional" jazz and a curtailment of most of its essential values. This peculiarly European form of deviant Dixieland was influenced mainly by British bands, though it might be said to include the more commercial side of the Dutch Swing College Band and several French and German groups. The negative side of "trad" was that, after the popular success of "skiffle", there were a few hit parade singles by such as Chris Barber, Kenny Ball and Acker Bilk (which made the charts in both the UK and the US). As a result the music industry took notice and signed up all the potentially money-making groups, and the gigs which they had been filling were immediately taken over by decidedly inferior musicians all hoping to make the big time.
(Fairweather in Carr *et al.* 1987, 504–5)

(Note that the word "trad" has been used to refer in this chapter and elsewhere to the most popular form of revivalist jazz. While we have distinguished in certain contexts between the terms "revivalist" and "traditional(-ist)", the latter is used for convenience as a more or less generic name covering both.)

The final event of significance during this period of British revivalism was the arrival on the scene of trombonist Chris Barber. At first Barber worked with his own group, which included among others Dickie Hawdon on cornet and multi-instrumentalist Micky Ashman on bass. He then changed tack and joined with Colyer's clarinettist Monty Sunshine to prepare a band for Colyer's messianic return from New Orleans. With Lonnie Donegan on banjo, Jim Bray on bass and Ron Bowden on drums, everything was in place. Yet it was not long before Colyer and Barber fell out, with the trombonist taking with him what was essentially Colyer's entire group, replacing the Guv'nor with Pat Halcox on cornet. Colyer then set about forming a new band, which included Acker Bilk on clarinet, Diz Disley on banjo and Stan Greig on drums. If Colyer conserved a style and sustained an audience for classic jazz from New Orleans, then Barber was its first popularizer and in many ways the musician who most successfully developed traditional jazz within a British context. In addition, Barber's wider influence on British jazz and rhythm and blues (R&B) is incontestable, and, more than that, his own music has, along with that of Sandy Brown and Al Fairweather, shown the greatest variety within the format.

Chris Barber was an ex-public schoolboy and an ex-Guildhall School of Music And Drama student. He was also an astute businessman and one of the few in British jazz who contradicts the adage that the best way to end up with a million in jazz is to start out with two. Yet his financial success should not suggest any lack of integrity as far as the music itself is concerned. As George Melly has written about Colyer's music compared with that of Barber, "It wasn't exactly ugly, on the contrary it was quite often touchingly beautiful, but it was clumsy. It needed prettifying before it could catch on. Chris Barber was there to perform this function" (Melly 1974, 162). Perhaps this appears to suggest a level of calculation on Barber's part. Indeed, Melly describes his approach to the music a few sentences on from the quote above as "somewhat mechanistic". Yet he also notes that Barber's impact was enormous. Barber himself is happy to accept this. In his account, he had invented a style by accident and contrasts his approach with other bands who concentrated on imitating the New Orleans bands. "We were doing American black music but we weren't trying to sound like them. We particularly wanted to absorb the lessons about how it was done, but we weren't copying it" (interview with Chris Barber, February 2008).

In a sense, Barber is acknowledging the inevitability that this music would be changed through its transplantation to these shores. If Colyer was Calvin-like in his belief that there was but one route to the kingdom of jazz heaven, Barber was more broadly ecumenical and adaptable – more like the Church of England, perhaps. For Barber, the decision not to use piano but to replace it with the banjo and guitar was the key factor. This effectively became the template for "trad" jazz.

The band that Barber and Sunshine put together for Ken Colyer had made this decision de facto. Colyer had used Pat Hawes in the Crane River Jazz Band, but he did not add a pianist again to his bands after 1953 until Ray Foxley around 1956. The reason the Colyer band (and subsequently Barber's) dispensed with piano was because it greatly expanded the number of places in which they could play. Humph went the opposite way and dropped the banjo around the same time, first adding Neville Skrimshire on guitar and then dropping it altogether. But this restricted his venues to those that had a piano.

But Barber was also an evangelist in his own right. Along with his business partner, Harold Pendleton, he brought over to play with his band African-American blues and jazz artists such as Muddy Waters (1958), Champion Jack Dupree (1959), Sonny Terry and Brownie McGhee (1958), Sister Rosetta Tharpe (1957 and 1960) and Louis Jordan (1962).

> We tried very hard to educate our audience and [show them] that
> what we were playing was part of a much bigger music and that
> the greats of it were people like Louis Armstrong, Eddie Condon
> and so on. We made constant reference to those real people. So,

we were hoping to become by experience, good feeling, intensity and our love of the music real people ourselves – real jazz people ourselves, not just imitators.

(Interview with Chris Barber, February 2008)

Barber has always been committed to the blues. In 1954, he was introduced to Ottilie Patterson by fellow singer Beryl Bryden. Describing Patterson as a "great devotee of proper blues with an understanding of the proper meaning of the music", Barber says that it was working with her that taught his band how to accompany a blues singer:

And this showed when we brought over blues artists from America to play with us because even though they weren't accustomed to working with trumpets, etc., we knew how to play the music. And they enjoyed it, in fact. It was a change for them but we still played the blues.   (Interview with Chris Barber, February 2008)

Mention must be made here of the style of folk-blues known as "skiffle" that swept the UK in the mid- to late fifties. This simple form originated in the Southern States of America in the twenties, or possibly earlier. There is a suggestion that the word was just one coined to describe the rent parties that were common in rural and urban African-American culture at that time. It relied on primitive instruments like washboard percussion, tea-chest string bass, kazoos along with acoustic guitar (or with banjo), and its intro-duction to Britain came essentially through Ken Colyer in the early fifties. His then banjo player Lonnie Donegan would sing a few numbers in the interval between sets derived from the repertoire of Leadbelly, Josh White, Big Bill Broonzy or (later) Woody Guthrie. It was the subsequent success of Donegan's record "Rock Island Line", recorded during a break from a Chris Barber session, that launched skiffle in Britain. When Donegan left Colyer's group to go with Chris Barber's band, his place was taken by Alexis Korner. The skiffle craze lasted for several years and the ease with which it could be imitated with only the most rudimentary musical skills was the main cause of its popularity. It was important far more for its longer-term influence than its content. Many later beat and rock musicians started out playing skiffle and its success aided the dissemination of the "trad" jazz with which it was associated.

Barber might have had a finger on the popular pulse but it was his love of the blues that allowed him to adapt and change. Even if he remained largely consistent in style and approach, he used the blues as a way of opening his music out to other influences that emerged in the later sixties with rock and white electric blues. Some other artists, who began in traditional jazz in the late forties or during the fifties, chose to turn their music into a cabaret show for the "chicken-in-a-basket" circuit. Others, like Humphrey Lyttelton, Alex

Welsh and the Scottish pairing of clarinettist Sandy Brown and trumpeter Al Fairweather, adopted a more mainstream style based on the small American groups of the thirties and forties. In contrast, Barber decided early on to try and expand the range of his music while remaining true to its original impulse. It is also clear that he has always had a desire to leave a musical legacy of lasting value. Talking about his relationship with producer Denis Preston, with whom he recorded a number of albums, he notes with regret their different attitudes to posterity:

> I knew Denis Preston for a long while. He was a real record collector, an experienced producer, he loved Duke Ellington and everything else but he wouldn't take British traditional jazz seriously. Even though he was selling millions of it. If I asked to do another take on something we'd recorded, he'd say, "Don't worry about that Chris. It doesn't matter. In twenty years time, you and I will both be sitting around drinking brandy and playing our Duke Ellington records. Just play what the kids in the clubs like to hear." I wanted to record Big Bill Broonzy with Lonnie Donegan's skiffle group. Bill could have made a lot of money. Denis Preston wouldn't do it. He was very dismissive and put him with a group with Kenny Graham and Ronnie Ross. The record was awful, a waste of time. He did the same with Sister Rosetta Tharpe.
> (Interview with Chris Barber, February 2008)

Whatever else, Barber was concerned about making good music and not just with making money. He believed that he could do both and, in many respects, he was proved right.

* * *

"Bad Penny Blues" – Humphrey Lyttelton – that was an important record. I used to play a bit of boogie-woogie. "Bad Penny Blues" was just as important to me as Jerry Lee Lewis and Fats Domino.   (Interview with Georgie Fame, April 2009)

The "trad jazz boom" of the late fifties and early sixties saw a rise in popularity of a more commercial, popular style. The main bands that were seen to initiate the boom were those of Bilk, Ball and Barber, though others such as Terry Lightfoot's Jazzmen also became extremely popular and featured regularly in the pop charts. According to newspapers at the time and history books since, the "trad"/revivalist and modernist camps were separated by a deep ideological divide about what was and was not jazz. It was in Birmingham in 1953 at a Humphrey Lyttelton concert that irate fans, sensing a "sell-out" by their hero, unfurled a home-made banner directed at the band's new alto player, Bruce Turner. Famously, it read: "Go Home Dirty Bopper." The incident gave

Turner the perfect title for his autobiography, though sadly he chose *Hot Air Cool Music* instead. Humph's response was to call his autobiography, and a record of the period, *I Play as I Please*. That it actually happened does not alter the fact that the story has acquired an almost mythical status among British jazz fans as a kind of crystallizing moment when battle lines were forever drawn.

That there were big differences among fans of these different styles was evident. Some of it was good-natured and some of it less so. As George Melly acknowledged in the *Smokey Dives* documentary, there was a degree of rivalry between modern and "trad" musicians. Francis Newton wrote in 1959:

> Modern jazz had been on the American and European scene since the middle forties. Its sectarian appeal would no doubt have made itself felt earlier but for two facts: it was much harder to listen to than the older kind, and the bulk of the established critics and jazz intellectuals, formed in the school of the thirties, were bitterly hostile to it, for political and social reasons. What they cherished in jazz was a "people's music" – that is, both a music which appealed to ordinary people and which, in its nature, provided an alternative pattern of the arts to that of the esoteric minority culture of our age. Modern jazz seemed to them to sell the pass: a jazz version of esoteric *avant-garde* music which might have its own merits but they were not the ones they had come to jazz for.
>
> (Newton 1960, 255–6)

However, there was also a lot of contact between players to mutual benefit. Trombonist George Chisholm recorded *Chis* in 1956 (Decca; Vocalion) with a band that included modernists Jamaican altoist Joe Harriott, drummer Phil Seamen, pianist Alan Clare and vibraphonist Bell Le Sage. Harriott played regularly with Chris Barber and can be heard to fine effect on *Chris Barber at the London Palladium* (Columbia; Lake) and Barber still plays Harriott's tune "Revival" (see also Robertson 2003). Such pairings could prove inspired. Some of Denis Preston's ideas might wallow in the realms of bad taste. However, in 1968 *Blue Acker* (Columbia; Lake) brought Bilk together with Stan Tracey Big Brass and produced some of the most beautiful settings for Bilk's limpid clarinet on tunes such as Bilk's "Stranger on the Shore", "Royal Garden Blues" and Tracey's "Blues for this Year". It remains one of the highlights of British jazz of the period.

There were also a number of musicians who felt comfortable in any jazz setting. Welsh pianist Dill Jones seemed equally comfortable playing Dixieland, mainstream or modern jazz. Clarinettist and saxophonist Tony Coe began his career with Humphrey Lyttelton when revivalist jazz was still a significant part of the band's repertoire, and yet saw no reason why this should preclude him from playing with modernist composer Mike

Westbrook or free improvising guitarist Derek Bailey in the seventies and eighties. Colin Purbrook is another good case in point. The pianist was regularly featured with Kenny Ball's Jazzmen, the modernist Allan Ganley–Ronnie Ross Jazzmakers and the mainstream swing of the Al Fairweather–Sandy Brown Band. He played with both the Ronnie Scott Jimmy Deuchar Quintet, featured alongside Charles Mingus on the score for the film *All Night Long* and was an early member of the Don Rendell–Ian Carr Quintet.

In addition, quite a few musicians began their careers in "trad"/revivalist bands before moving into modern jazz. Bassist Jack Bruce started out with a Scottish "trad" band, while drummer Ginger Baker's first gig was with Terry Lightfoot's Dixieland outfit. Even more notable in this regard is trombonist Keith Christie. Starting out with Humphrey Lyttelton, he soon formed his own traditionalist group, the Christie Brothers Stompers, with his brother Ian on clarinet (and Ken Colyer on trumpet), but spent much of his later career playing with the likes of Tubby Hayes and Johnny Dankworth. In some ways, it is very hard to characterize the music played by Lyttelton, George Chisholm or the Fairweather–Brown Band as "trad" or traditional jazz. By the end of the fifties, their music could be just as easily be described as "mainstream", drawing as it did as much on the Kansas City and Harlem swing of the thirties and forties as on the music of New Orleans and Chicago. In fact, how else could one portray Sandy Brown's *The Incredible McJazz*, where tracks by Ellington and Mingus are to be found, while much the same must also be said for Lyttelton's *Blues in the Night* from 1960?

In practice, there seems to have been as much mutual respect as suspicion between musicians in the two camps. Scottish saxophonist Bobby Wellins remembers going to the 100 Club in Oxford Street with pianist Terry Shannon to catch Humph's band or Alex Welsh and makes this point very clearly:

> There was a little bit of anti-"trad", I suppose, with us. But as I say, we used to go down the 100 Club. There were one or two bands that I knew ... well, musicians I knew in those bands, who were class players. A lot of great piano players and drummers and you loved the characters of those days. Like Lennie Hastings, the drummer, and some very class bands playing that sort of music. As it turned out in the later years, Humph was a big champion of all the British players, with his jazz programme. He never failed to play new CD's, if you sent them to him and he championed all the boys including myself.
>
> (Interview with Bobby Wellins, September 2009)

Wellins played with the Fairweather–Brown Band and recalls Brown saying to him, "Just play like you play. I don't want you to do anything different. That suits us just fine." And he added, "And there was a great flexibility in what he did, which was wonderful." For Wellins the music derives from the same source. "I think one has a lot in common. If the music is good, that's all that matters. The era doesn't matter. I always thought, 'If it's good, do it!'" Sandy Brown clearly had no problems with modern jazz or its musicians; in fact, in 1969 he made the excellent *Hair At Its Hairiest* (Fontana; Lake) with guitarist John McLaughlin, trumpeter Kenny Wheeler, bassist Lennie Bush, drummer Bobby Orr and the omnipresent George Chisholm. Chris Barber, as well, remained extraordinarily open-minded about jazz:

> Yes, I knew some of them very well. I knew Ronnie [Scott] very well. Kenny Graham, I knew. I mean, I always liked modern jazz. When I started my first band and if you'd asked me what my favourite records were, I'd have quoted one from King Oliver, one from Louis Armstrong and Charlie Parker's "Cool Blues". I loved it. I've always liked all kinds of jazz.
> (Interview with Chris Barber, February 2008)

On a US tour in 1959, Barber was "dragged along" by his friend Modern Jazz Quartet pianist John Lewis to see Ornette Coleman, and was genuinely impressed:

> There was Ornette Coleman with Scott La Faro on bass, who was totally amazing, and Don Cherry. The thing was that when Ornette Coleman played free, Scott La Faro playing the bass followed him. So, you got the impression that they were really playing a tune together that you didn't know, not that they were all at sixes and sevens, like four guys shouting in different languages at the same time. It actually was music played together which could go anywhere they cared to take it. But they did it together and that for me is what jazz is all about.
> (Interview with Chris Barber, February 2008)

As for Acker Bilk, he admits that some modern jazz made him uncomfortable: "I wasn't all that enamoured with modern jazz. I didn't understand a lot of it – a bit far out some of it. Mainstream – I quite enjoyed a lot of that. As long as it's not too far out" (interview with Acker Bilk, February 2008).

With regard to Stan Tracey and their collaboration on both *Blue Acker* and Tracey's tribute to Duke Ellington, *We Love You Madly* from 1969 (Columbia), Bilk's comments are once more succinct: "Stan Tracey – I like Stan. We got on alright. Good arranger. Good player." Both Bilk and Tracey clearly enjoyed each other's company. However, any conversation between with these two quite laconic individuals would appear to have been on the brief side.

There is, however, a sense in which the use of the word "traditional" to describe the jazz that developed in New Orleans in the early part of the twentieth century is remarkably unhelpful. "Modern" in this context is only marginally more useful. It is a point well made by, Philip Larkin in *All What Jazz*. As he points out, "Jazz has gone from Lascaux to Jackson Pollock in 50 years … the term 'modern' when applied to art has a more than chronologi cal meaning" (Larkin 1985, 22–3).

If one takes the closing of Storyville in 1919 as the point where Dixieland became the definitive form of the music, and the experiments of Charlie Parker, Dizzy Gillespie and Thelonious Monk at Minton's Playhouse in Harlem, New York as the beginnings of "modern" jazz, then we note a period of just twenty-two years. It is true that jazz went through a very rapid series of stylistic changes in those two decades. However, in an historical sense, all jazz is, or at least was, at that point "modern". In fact, seen from a longer-term historical perspective, jazz from the 1920s onwards sits very neatly alongside other "modernist" artistic works of the twentieth century, be this in classical music, photography, literature, drama, film, dance or fine art.

Turning to Britain in the middle of the last century, we see the birth of British "traditional" jazz in the early 1940s at the Red Barn with George Webb's Dixielanders. Just six or seven years later, John Dankworth and Ronnie Scott opened Club Eleven in Great Windmill Street. In a very real sense, both the traditionalists and the modernists were dealing with very recent musical developments and transposing these from their African-American and white American contexts to the completely different social and cultural context of the UK of the 1940s. What was really a divide of stylistic preference became an ideological one that obscured the fact that both were actually exploring a set of musical practices and conventions derived from the same ultimate source material. How this became a matter of ideological positioning is quite obvious. That it was exacerbated by the position taken by Ken Colyer, his brother and their acolytes is equally clear. However much open-minded musicians in both camps crossed the divide to appreciate and play each other's music together, that divide remained enforced by jazz fans and critics, and, consequently, the music's promoters.

The modernists had their clubs – Ronnie Scott's in Gerrard Street, The Downbeat Club in Old Compton Street and the Flamingo in Wardour Street. The traddies had theirs like Humphrey Lyttelton's Club at 100 Oxford Street (from 1964 The 100 Club), the Wood Green Jazz Club, clarinettist Cy Laurie's at 41 Great Windmill Street and the Ken Colyer Jazz Club in Great Newport Street (Godbolt 1989, 249ff.).

Even the jazz festivals that had sprung up around the country, following the success of Lord Montagu in establishing the Beaulieu Jazz Festival in 1956, tended to have "trad"/traditionalist and modern acts on separate days, as Chris Barber points out:

> I've always liked all kinds of jazz but when you're touring with
> a band – a full-time professional band – you would never see

anybody else. You would only see other bands, modern or traditional, if you were on a gig together.

(Interview with Chris Barber, February 2008)

As he adds, the clubs in and around London tended to be either one or the other, as the audience was divided on those lines: "Generally speaking, that meant that when we were at a festival that would be a traditional day. There'd be other traditional bands there but no modern bands." Acker Bilk confirms this. Asked about whether he had any relationship or contact with the modern scene, he told me: "Well, we didn't have one really. There wasn't much of a relationship at all. They played different clubs from us. We never really saw each other. It was almost a race apart, modern jazz" (Interviews with Acker Bilk, February 2008).

The Marquee was an exception. It was established by Chris Barber and his business partner, Harold Pendleton, under the auspices of the National Jazz Federation (NJF) at 165 Oxford Street, under the Academy Cinema. The NJF must not be confused with the (by then moribund) National Federation of Jazz Organisations. Barber met Harold Pendleton at Foyles bookshop in Charing Cross Road in the late forties, going through the second-hand records looking for jazz and blues 78s. It would prove a powerful and significant combination not only for the jazz scene but later for blues and rock music as well. In many ways, the history of the Marquee club and its annual summer event, the NJF Jazz Festival, is the story of British music in the sixties, and it mirrors the changing and fluctuating fortunes of British jazz.

By the end of 1957, a number of jazz nights had taken place in the ballroom under the Academy Cinema, involving pianist Dill Jones, who ran the club along with his manager Peter Burman. The venture was not a success and was losing money. Jones and Burman approached Harold Pendleton, who took over the rental in April 1958. Barber had been interested for some time in having a regular club. "The Marquee Club really started up because by 1958 I was fed up. I didn't like the 100 Club and for me it was uncomfortable to play in and I wanted to find somewhere more suitable," he says. He and Pendleton were already involved together in running the magazine *Jazz News*, and having a jazz club was the next logical step. By the end of 1958, the club had added Friday nights to its programme featuring the Johnny Dankworth Orchestra, who would later take over the Sunday night slot. Under Pendleton's astute management, the Marquee became a success. In some ways, its success was its undoing, as far as jazz was concerned. For a few years, however, the Marquee reflected Barber and Pendleton's open-minded and pragmatic attitude to jazz. In 1961 or 1962, a typical week would feature modernists such as Joe Harriott's Quintet perhaps supported by Ronnie Ross's group and later Michael Garrick's Quartet on the Saturday night. Dankworth's band took the Sunday night with support from Dudley

Moore's trio, occasionally with touring guest singers from the States or UK, such as Anita O'Day or Bobbie Breen. Wednesdays were devoted to "traditional jazz". Sometimes it would be Chris Barber's Jazz Band with blues singer Ottilie Patterson and support from Wally Fawkes's Quartet. Other times it could be the Kansas City Jazzmen or Terry Lightfoot, or any of a number of others.

Although Pendleton had brought American bluesman Muddy Waters to Britain in 1958 and Waters had played at the Marquee, it wasn't until 1962 that the club started a series of R&B nights. On 10 May 1962, Alexis Korner began a Thursday night residency with his new band Blues Incorporated. Korner knew Barber well and had twice played in his band, between 1949 and 1951 and again in 1961. He had also been a member of Ken Colyer's Skiffle Group in the mid-fifties and had appeared on the BBC both as a broadcaster and performer. He shared with Barber a devotion to the blues, but took this further in the direction of electric Chicago blues. Both, however, could justifiably contest custody for the child that became British R&B. As Harold Pendleton noted in the *Melody Maker*:

> Alexis Korner is often hailed as the father of the British blues scene, but if that's the case then Chris Barber must be hailed as the great-grandfather. For Chris put together the band with Cyril Davies and Alexis and told them what to do. Chris is monstrously underrated for his contribution to the music scene in Britain.
> (quoted on Marquee Club website,
> www.themarqueeclub.net/chris-barber)

Korner's Marquee residency was to have a major impact in terms of a shift in popular musical taste, at least as far as the young were concerned. It would not be long before others would take up the mantle and soon R&B nights at the club would begin to dominate, first with groups like Blues By Six and Big Pete Deuchar's Country Blues, and then in 1963 by bands like the Rollin' Stones (the "g" was added later), the Yardbirds and Manfred Mann. It might not have been the death knell for British jazz but it was certainly indicative of the shape of things to come.

This point was not lost on Alexis Korner. Asked by Max Jones in the *Melody Maker* in August 1962 if he believed that British R&B could really overtake trad, Korner replied, "I don't think it can this year. But sometime next year, it may. If trad stays as it is, of course. I anticipate that there'll be a hell of a lot more R&B bands by the end of the year" (Jones 1962, 8–9). How right he was. Even more significantly, however, were the increasing references that would appear over the next few months to a new beat group from Liverpool, who had hit the top twenty in December 1962 with their first single "Love Me Do". As "Please Please Me" entered the *Melody Maker* charts at number two, the paper ran a short news item on page 3 of its issue of 16 February 1963 announcing the release of the record in the States, and that their first LP was finished and ready to be issued. Now, the writing really was on the wall.

Korner's comment that R&B would replace "trad", "if trad stays as it is, of course", is pertinent on so many levels. In a way, "trad" could hardly do anything else. That was what made it "trad" after all. Two very important questions have never been quite satisfactorily answered by the more traditional end of British jazz. First, how could traditional jazz change and develop artistically while remaining within the tradition? Second, how could it retain and expand the popular audience base it had established by the late fifties and early sixties?

There had clearly been a traditional/"trad" jazz boom in the late fifties and early sixties. "Trad" jazz had received support from the BBC, and artists appeared regularly on music and variety programmes on television. Its leading protagonists were working very regularly and commanding higher fees in the concert halls and in the clubs that had sprung up. In fact, the sheer scale of the support is hard to believe these days. As a couple of examples, in *Melody Maker*'s regular "Round The Jazz Clubs" column on 3 September 1960, it was announced that Brighton's "Chinese Jazz Club" now had 7,000 members. Two years later, there was an item in the magazine's "Raver" noting that Kenny Ball and his jazzmen had greatly enjoyed their "two-week residency at the 10,000 capacity Empress Ballroom, Blackpool". Though Ball also noted:

> But I found I had to be more careful in choosing programmes. Some nights we had to cut obscure numbers that would go well in jazz clubs. We had to watch our tempos – I found we could only get away with one really fast number per session. Often there were lots of youngsters standing around obviously wondering what was happening. At the other extreme was one old lady of 70 who sat in the balcony for almost every session.
>
> (*Melody Maker* 4 August 1962, 5)

Chris Barber notes that in the year Eddie Condon's band toured the UK, he had filled Newcastle Civic Hall on four previous occasions. Eddie Condon, with Humphrey Lyttelton's band in support, failed to do so. It is hard not to read more into Ball's words than they are intended to carry. An interview with Ball (and others on the scene) in the *Melody Maker* in December 1961 was given the title "TRAD – A Taste of Money", this being a direct reference to an Acker Bilk hit with a similar title. In it, Ball discussed his success and his earnings, as well as that of his band. In a short time, their position had changed dramatically. "'We used to play for a few bob years ago,' says Kenny Ball. 'Now, the boys in my band average between £40 and £70 a week'" (Coleman 1961, 3). It was not a king's ransom, even then, but it was very good money indeed, though it was not just about money and, anyway, who could begrudge hard-working musicians their place in the sun? Nevertheless, it is worth recalling the earlier quote from Digby Fairweather regarding the distorting effects that this success had on the scene. With the advantage of hindsight, his and Ball's comments and Barber's contrasting of his experience on tour with that of US star Eddie Condon also say a lot about the audiences that were attracted to "trad" jazz.

In the jazz clubs, Ball, Barber, Bilk and their peers met with the hardcore fans, though as Ball notes such bands were already pricing themselves out of this market (see *Melody Maker* 23 December 1961). They bought the records, devoured information about their heroes and knew something at least about the origins and history of the music. Then there were the "youngsters", perhaps the younger brothers and sisters of those hardcore fans. Their knowledge was perhaps limited to the hits or the music they had heard on the radio or on the various TV shows that featured not just jazz, but the full range of popular music of the time. Finally, there were the mums and dads for whom "trad" was just another part of that rich tapestry that was "light entertainment". To take a band from the steady, reliable work of the club scene to the ballrooms and a national stage required that broadening of audience to which Ball refers. However, such popularity is always a double-edged sword. Success breeds success only as long as the formula is consistently applied and only as long as it coincides with the fickle and changing nature of public taste.

Can a musical form be both popular and remain an art form? Perhaps for a short period it can. But popularity is most often bought by the compromises through which art suffers. We should not judge "trad" too harshly in this respect. Perhaps the Rhythm Clubs first established by jazz fans in the thirties and the earnest young men who continued to support them saw something more profound in the music. For many, including producer Denis Preston, in its British form at least traditional jazz was an ephemeral attraction. Despite critics like Sinclair Traill, Albert McCarthy and Philip Larkin, as well as musicians such as Chris Barber and Ken Colyer, the function of "trad" for much of its audience was not that of "art" but that of entertainment. It was primarily a music for dancing and one that brought with it a legitimized contact with the opposite sex.

Thanks to Roland Barthes and others, we have learned how to read the signs of popular culture and have come to question distinctions between "high" and "low" culture (Barthes 1981). Issues concerning the power to bestow on a form or a single work the status of "art" were not perhaps the primary concern for Barthes. Rather his focus was more on how, as artefacts, works of art or myths might be read and their underlying ideological assumptions understood. For those coming from a more conventional Marxist standpoint the emphasis is instead upon the power to impose such definitions, meanings and distinctions. Nevertheless, here we might still want to distinguish between the capacity of *any* song, piece of music, film, play or novel to signify meanings beyond its manifest content and the more limited potential that the very best examples of these have to speak to wider issues of social or philosophical concern, or of aesthetic endeavour, and to do so across historical epochs. That is, surely, one of the key differences between that which is and which is not "art".

The pressures generated within the music business to produce "hit" material have always been strong. If we look at the "trad boom" in terms of chart success, the picture that emerges is confusing. The two most successful artists in the singles chart were clearly Acker Bilk and Kenny Ball, and by a very long way. Between 1959 and January 1963 (pre-"Mersey/Beat boom"), these two artists accounted for eight top ten singles, with a further ten making the top thirty. Bilk's single success then dried up, while Ball had a further four records in the top fifty between 1963 and 1967. Barber's sole top ten was "Petite Fleur", which featured the clarinet of Monty Sunshine and Barber on bass rather than trombone, and which reached number 3 in February 1959, and he had a further two records that made the top fifty. As for the rest, Alex Welsh made the fifty once, Terry Lightfoot and Bob Wallis three times, and the Clyde Valley Stompers.

In terms of album sales, Bilk was by far the most successful with six chart placings. Barber had three albums in the top twenty, while Ball had one with his *Golden Hits* record. All three, of course, shared in the million-selling success of the "Best of" series put out by Pye to capitalize on the boom. It seems fair to assume that, as with jazz recordings in general, "trad" artists' LPs would continue to sell over time without actually charting, unlike much of the ephemera that is pop music. That there was a "boom" of sorts is clear but the information above suggests that it hardly compares with what would follow shortly with the arrival of the beat groups.

What is more, many of the records that did make the charts were hardly typical of the club work of the "trad" bands. Bilk's singles included the admittedly lovely "Stranger on the Shore", "White Cliffs of Dover" and "A Taste of Honey". Ball's offerings included "Green Leaves of Summer", "Midnight in Moscow" and "March of the Siamese Children" (from *The King and I*), records that connected only slightly with jazz. As for Bob Wallis, two of his three chart successes included "Everybody Loves Saturday Night" and "I'm Shy Mary Ellen, I'm Shy", while Terry Lightfoot reached number 49 with "Tavern in the Town" (see Melly 1970).

When the entrepreneurial Peter Leslie devised Acker Bilk's uniform of bowler hat and striped waistcoat, he tapped into something. It was an image that spoke simultaneously of riverboat gamblers on the Mississippi (its one tenuous connection to the origins of jazz) and the Britain of the Edwardian era. It was the latter that resonated most with the British public, tying traditional jazz forever in the public mindset as something somehow associated with the music hall. It was just that association that the Temperance Seven, and later the New Vaudeville Band and Bob Kerr's Whoopee Band, played upon, while the Alberts and the Bonzo Dog Doo-Dah Band traded on it to surreal comic effect.

But the upshot was that a lot of the albums made by "trad" bands at the time do not stand up to scrutiny. The problem was that their work was often compromised by commercial considerations. Musicians have to work, they and their families need a roof over their heads, and they need to eat. One can hardly blame them for wanting to take financial advantage of the opportunities presented by the "trad boom". In an interview for this book, Kenny Ball stated that in the early fifties, a day or two before he was hired by bandleader Sid Phillips, he was having to borrow money to feed his baby daughter. With Phillips his income increased from single figures to £30 per week, a very good wage. As he pointed out to me, selling a million copies of a record could change a musician's life.

> Do you know what my royalties were on "Midnight in Moscow"?
> A farthing – that is one quarter of one old penny. Not a lot, is it?
> But "Midnight in Moscow" sold a million copies and that's 25,000
> quid. That was a lot of money in 1962.
> (Interview with Kenny Ball, May 2008)

Ball's arithmetic might not quite add up but the point remains. For younger readers, a detached period cottage in the home counties back then might cost between £3,000 and £5,000. £25,000 could buy you something with a moat and drawbridge!

In judging "trad" aesthetically, we come up against a number of problems, one of which is most certainly the impact upon it of its commercial success. The recording of pop material or tunes that a broader audience would know in a jazz style was nothing new in jazz. But it becomes unreasonable for "trad" musicians to then complain if later listeners judge their work by "In a Persian Market", "Buena Sera" (Acker Bilk), "Peter And The Wolf", "Loch Lomond", "Scotland The Brave" (Clyde Valley Stompers), "Tavern in the Town" (Terry Lightfoot), "I'm Shy Mary Ellen, I'm Shy" (Bob Wallis) or "Samantha" (Kenny Ball) rather than those fine versions of "Dippermouth Blues" and "Muskrat Ramble" they might also have recorded. The second problem with British traditional jazz for the later listener is the incredible amount of recycling of material that went on. It seems as if there were certain tunes that every band had to record from the catalogue of King Oliver, Louis Armstrong, Bix Beiderbecke, Jelly Roll Morton and other heroes of New Orleans jazz. This brings us to the third problem, namely that this was a form that was hard to develop while staying reasonably true to the original template. As a consequence quite a few players who started out playing traditional jazz moved increasingly into more mainstream styles.

Listen to any compilation from the period and the abiding impression is that Ball, Bilk and Barber were successful because they had genuine talent. Both Humphrey Lyttelton and trombonist George Chisholm were similarly gifted. Bob Wallis and Alex Welsh and the bands they led were also musically strong, and Ken Colyer, if sometimes hard listening, clearly had both ability and vision. Trumpeter Freddy Randall's bands were excellent, and it is unfortunate that lung problems forced him out of the business from 1963 until his full-time return in the seventies. South African drummer Joe Daniels also produced some interesting music, often in a vein similar to the American musical humorist Spike Jones, and there was more to Terry Lightfoot than "Tavern in the Town". There were also one or two regional bands of note like the Avon Cities Jazz Band. Perhaps best of all was the Fairweather–Brown Band, co-led by trumpeter Al Fairweather and the brilliant clarinettist Sandy Brown. Groups such as Mick Mulligan's Magnolia Jazz Band with George Melly were great fun. But one also has to accept that there were some truly dreadful musical crimes committed in the name of "trad". It is sad that these musicians are often judged by those misdemeanours instead of some of the much better music that was produced.

In terms of "trad", revivalist and traditional jazz, these were musical styles for entertainment and dancing, and they certainly succeeded in those terms. Treated as pop music, this music has to be compared with what else was around at that time in the British charts. For every Ottilie Patterson there were a lot of Susan Maughans, and for every George Melly, Kenny Ball, Acker Bilk or Chris Barber there were many Eden Kanes, Mark Wynters and Adam Faiths. We may judge these musicians but not too harshly.

By the time the bubble burst with the arrival of the Beatles and then the Stones, many of these players had already moved into more mainstream jazz. Colyer inevitably stayed with the style he had pioneered. Ball, Bilk, Lightfoot and others stuck with the compromised form that had become British "trad" – a mix that allowed "West End Blues" to co-exist with the crowd-pleasing hit tunes their wider fan base expected. Not that there was anything wrong *per se* with drawing on the popular music of the present and past. Jazz has always done so, after all. It was just that much of the material smacked of the end of the pier and the holiday camp.

As to the "trad" or traditionalist records that bear scrutiny, Philip Larkin made an interesting point when reviewing Chris Barber's excellent *Battersea Raindance* from 1969 (Marmalade), another highlight of the period, but one that Larkin disliked intensely:

> I missed Chris Barber's *Battersea Raindance* (Polydor) when it first appeared, and was expecting something more exciting than this turned out to be. There is a tendency nowadays to praise

anything unlike an artist's usual run of work: because Barber is known as a traditional player, this mélange of souly samba-ish riffery was hailed as an advance.   (Larkin 1985, 264)

While I disagree with Larkin's assessment – and Barber's *Get Rolling* on Black Lion from the same period is even better – the poet does make an interesting point. With traditional jazz, it is perhaps the exceptional, in both senses of the word, that best withstands critical scrutiny. Acker Bilk's collaboration with Stan Tracey, *Blue Acker*, would be another such example, falling as it does closer to mainstream than to "trad" and outside much of the clarinettist's work. However, in Barber's case, he has always surrounded himself with fine musicians. Whether it was clarinettist Monty Sunshine in the fifties, trumpeter Pat Halcox, who stuck with him over the decades, or guitarist John Slaughter, who joined the band for *Battersea Raindance* and *Get Rolling*, Barber remains the maverick among the herd. A musician steeped in the blues, Barber's open mind has allowed him to enjoy everything from Eddie Condon and Big Bill Broonzy to the Modern Jazz Quartet (MJQ), Ornette Coleman and the Brotherhood of Breath, and even the improvising rock bands of the late sixties. Perhaps uniquely among traditionalist musicians, Barber seems always to have had a belief that traditional, New Orleans-derived music could both develop and remain true to the form. Both the records above work for precisely that reason, and the music Barber continues to make with his band retains an unusual capacity to excite.

Of Barber's more traditional records, the best is *At the London Palladium* featuring Joe Harriott. This and Colyer's *This is the Blues Volume I* (Columbia) represent the most completely satisfying albums in the style of the period. For the rest, the best music from erstwhile "trad" dads tends to be found in a more mainstream format. Alex Welsh's *At Home With ... Alex Welsh and His Band* (Columbia) is just such an example. Ellington's *It Don't Mean a Thing*, Gershwin's *I Got Rhythm* and Johnny Mandel's *The Shadow of Your Smile* may not suggest a great deal of adventure, but the music is played with such joy and such a relaxed feel that it is all immensely attractive. But then the band included, as well as Welsh, the hugely talented drummer Lennie Hastings and saxophonist Johnny Barnes, as well as that master trombonist, Roy Williams. Mention has already been made of Humphrey Lyttelton's *Blues in the Night* (Columbia; Lake), which moves effortlessly from "Basin Street Blues" and "Royal Garden Blues" to Ellington's "Creole Love Call" and Dizzy Gillespie's "The Champ". This shift from early jazz into the mainstream perhaps did result, as Francis Newton proposed, from "a vague malaise, a boredom with the traditional music whose limits they felt they had explored pretty completely, a desire to play something more interesting" (Newton 1960, 256). At the same time, these musicians seemed to make the transition effortlessly and without losing sight of the music that had inspired them.

By 1963, the Fairweather–Brown Band was as likely to offer their audience Benny Golson's "Blues March" or Mingus's "Wednesday Night Prayer Meeting" as "St. James Infirmary" or "Willie the Weeper". Those modernists who refuse to accept that anything good ever came out of the New Orleans Revival should give a long hard listen to Sandy Brown's *The Incredible McJazz* (Pye; Lake). Brown was also responsible for one of the period's ultimate oddities. Reissued by Lake Records in 2001 as *Work Song* (Lake), Sandy Brown and his Gentlemen Friends' *Hair at its Hairiest* should have been a total disaster. An obvious and deliberate attempt to cash in on the success of *Hair – The American Tribal Love-Rock Musical*, with its title and cover a pun on the incredibly hirsute clarinettist's face and body, Brown somehow transcends expectations to produce something that is both witty and much more than the sum of its parts. For the rest, it might not be great art but it was great fun.

Quite whether "trad" or modern jazz in Britain suffered most from the rise of the Beatles, the Rolling Stones, the Kinks, Manfred Mann and others is hard to gauge. Because of their success, the Beat Boom must have hit "trad" musicians harder in the pocket. After all, modern jazz always sat to one side of that whole pop/light entertainment scene. But it was not just pop music that was changing. Modern jazz was about to begin to move into whole new areas of development in Britain, as a new and differently educated generation of musicians would begin to make themselves heard.

2 Class Will Out!

England is the most class-ridden country under the sun. It is a land of snobbery and privilege, ruled largely by the old and silly.

George Orwell, *The Lion and the Unicorn*, 1941

When George Orwell wrote these words, he went on immediately to point out that despite, or even because, of our "class-ridden" society, Britain seemed to revel in a degree of unity that transcended "class". His own abhorrence of such distinctions based on privilege was genuine, and both intellectual and personal. In some senses, Orwell seemed to embody the contradictions of the British class system, and its contradictions run very deep indeed. Educated at Eton, though certainly not of the upper echelons of British society, a child of empire and at one point one of its officers, the writer's life and work could be read as one man's attempts to negotiate or obviate "class".

As the fifties turned into the swinging sixties, it seemed that all the absurdities of class would be swept away in Britain, as "working-class" or "lower-middle-class" figures such as the Beatles, Michael Caine, photographer Terence Donovan, Twiggy and others rose to prominence. It is quite true that class, like sex, got talked about a great deal in those years, and barriers between the "U" and "non-U" – to use Nancy Mitford's nasty little phrase – became more elastic. Opportunities did increase socio-economically for those from working- and lower-middle-class backgrounds, though just how much things changed is disputable.

Problems of definition arise immediately in considering the matter of class in British society, which is in turn affected by what exactly is being studied or considered, and why. After the Second World War, a strong sense had emerged in Britain that an individual's life chances were or had been overly influenced by the circumstances of their birth. There was an egalitarian spirit abroad that saw this as unfair and outmoded, and this seemed to coincide with a growing awareness that Britain's competitiveness in the new economic world ushered in by the 1944 Bretton Woods Agreement would be damaged if the best and brightest from whatever class could not rise to the top. We will see in Chapter 3 how access to secondary and higher education was opened up in the forties and fifties, and the word "meritocracy" began to be used to describe a society where ability rather than class might become the arbiter of success in life. "Class" began to be talked about less in terms of a fixed social caste within which each person would and should "know their place". Instead, the rise of figures from lowly backgrounds to wealth and status was seen as proof that "class" was a flexible and even transient identity from which the able and meritorious might ascend.

As such, class became more than just a socio-economic or sociological category. It (or rather changes within its structure) became a barometer for social mobility and change. It became a measurement of social integration to be considered positively when opportunity on the basis of ability was seen to dominate or of social division where privilege preserved its advantages. Even more so, it became something to be derided as "old-fashioned" and destructive when "class conflict", often in the form of industrial disputes, reared its head in 1960s and 1970s Britain. In this last context, class was, and continues to be, also a political category based upon a relationship of both the individual and the wider grouping of which they are a part to the means of production.

"Class" would intersect in various ways with British jazz in the sixties. It would even have implications for the emergence of a distinctively British jazz located within a specifically British social, economic and cultural milieu. In what follows, we will look at class in terms of the backgrounds and social positions of both British musicians and fans. In later chapters, we will return to the issue to examine how the class position of British jazz musicians influenced an emergent social and political content in or aspect to the music.

* * *

On 29 March 1962, photographer Terence Donovan was on a photo shoot for *Queen Magazine* in Trafalgar Square. The inspiration for the shoot lay in "A Great Day in Harlem", Art Kane's 1958 photograph of fifty-seven jazz musicians standing and sitting outside a brownstone in New York. Donovan and *Queen* had gathered thirty-nine British musicians for the spread, including Graham Bond, Dudley Moore, George Melly, Brian Dee, Ronnie Scott and Tubby Hayes. It should have been forty, but Joe Harriott arrived late (see pages 230–31 for the resulting photograph).

Donovan was a hugely talented working-class lad from Stepney, who left school at fifteen. By the time he was in his twenties, he was much in demand as a society photographer, and his pictures of actors like Terence Stamp, Julie

Christie and Sean Connery, and models such as Twiggy and Celia Hammond, have become iconic images of the period. Along with David Bailey and Brian Duffy, he captured, and in many ways helped create, the "Swinging London" of the 1960s; like Bailey and Duffy, Donovan socialized with actors, musicians and royalty, and became a celebrity in his own right. More than that, he was emblematic of a process of social change identified by journalists, commentators and pundits that was seen to occur in the sixties. Britain had suddenly become a "classless" society, one where an East End boy could end up photographing and hobnobbing with royalty, and where four young men from Liverpool could become the toast, not only of London but of New York, Paris and Rome. Turn again, Whittington!

Changes were certainly taking place for many in British society. Wages rose in the ten years from 1955–64 by almost twice as much as prices and the working week had become considerably shorter. Those within the broad middle-income bands had become increasingly better off. A shift in employment from manufacturing, in particular heavy industry, to service industries was already becoming evident. Production became increasingly specialized as automation within industries, including traditional ones, expanded. This pattern of social change might not have been entirely consistent across British society – some 2,000,000 people received an income that was one-fortieth of that of the 25,000 highest earners – but for many people, they really had "never had it so good!" (see Gregg 1968, chapter XVI).

What this meant in terms of class, attitudes, behaviour and voting habits was the subject for much research and discussion, most notably by liberal academics such as John Goldthorpe (Goldthorpe and Lockwood 1968, 1969) and A.H. Halsey (1972, 1978; Halsey *et al.* 1980). On the one hand, the working class might be becoming more affluent. On the other, as suggested by the work of Goldthorpe *et al.*, a more complex picture emerged of a modified but sustained class identity. Examining the place of class in British society in the post-war period up to and including the sixties, the evidence often appears contradictory. Perhaps this was, in part, because what constituted evidence came from sources that were themselves different in kind. An individual's class position might be objectively established by economic and social criteria but this might not be consistent with how they perceived themselves. It now seems clear that what sociologists, commentators and pundits were seeing was the unfolding of a much longer phase of social, economic and cultural changes that are still being played out. Yet the notion of "classlessness" had acquired a life of its own. It drew on images as much as economic and social facts and on a complex interaction between popular perception as represented by the media and individual perceptions of personal levels of affluence. Such impressions were not "wrong", but they were partial, and they also appear to have had a strong predictive element.

"The Frost Report", a satirical sketch show hosted by David Frost, ran from 1966 to 1967 on BBC television. Its best-remembered skit featured three men – John Cleese who represented the upper classes, Ronnie Barker who was middle class and Ronnie Corbett who was working class. Each in turn would respond to an issue of the day according to their class. Whenever it came to Ronnie Corbett's turn, he would always begin, "I know my place..." The joke came both from its familiarity but maybe also from the feeling that the rest of and the best of us were no longer so stuck in that world. At times, it almost seemed that the era was determined to conform to the kind of picture suggested by the following quotation:

> Although, like music, cinema, and theatre, the photography of the "swinging sixties" had its roots in the 1950s, it became much trendier and more visible in this decade, with magazines and – from 1962 – colour supplements its principal vehicles. Fashion photography, formerly represented by old masters like Beaton, John French and Norman Parkinson, was galvanized by the youthful working-class triumvirate of David Bailey, Brian Duffy and Terence Donovan who, working mainly in black-and-white, mingled fashion and documentary styles, the gritty and the cool. In his film *Blow Up* (1966), Michelangelo Antonioni forever fixed the image of the brash young photographer-about-town with his Rolls-Royce and apparently limitless supply of (also) sexually available models (the photographs in the film were by [Donald] McCullin). Meanwhile, Snowdon and Patrick (Lord) Lichfield bridged the gap between the new classless celebrity culture and England's entrenched traditional elite, including the royal family, to which they lent a new glamour.
> (Sadler undated)

In the seventies and eighties, issues around class again came to the fore in ways that might have seemed old-fashioned even to some sixties commentators, as economic downturn and crisis dominated the headlines. However, the expectations and aspirations of individuals and social groups in the 1960s were not just determined by objective economic facts but also by social psychological factors, including the sense of personal liberation and freedom conveyed in the term "classlessness". With hindsight, the optimism of the period was at odds with underlying problems within the British economy. In 1964, the Wilson government had inherited from the Tories a balance of payment deficits that was almost twice that which they had been led to expect, a pound that was heavily overvalued against other major currencies and levels of industrial productivity that compared unfavourably with Britain's competitors (see Morgan 1997; Glyn and Booth 1996, chapter 11). Yet, for several years, such worries had little impact on popular confidence or the sense of economic and social stability that characterized the decade and in its way infused British jazz.

That day in Trafalgar Square, Donovan was not photographing royalty or celebrities but jazz musicians. At the same time, he was also on an assignment for a fashionable magazine read by the wives and daughters, if not the husbands and brothers, of high society. How would they have seen these thirty or forty musicians? Would they see them as interestingly picaresque or decidedly "non-U"? Where would they locate Dankworth, Scott, Moore *et al.* in terms of the British class system? And how would they define those who followed this music?

It is impossible to identify with any certainty the class origins and place of British jazz fans. No comprehensive surveys were conducted and what information exists is anecdotal and inconsistent. It might be easier to determine the position in class terms of British jazz musicians but even here firm conclusions are problematic. There were no studies of their attitudes or beliefs, let alone their financial or social status. However, for the moment, staying within a definition of class based essentially on background or origin, we will try to uncover where we might locate musicians and fans within such a schema.

Writer and photographer Val Wilmer notes in her beautifully written memoir *Mama Said There'd Be Days Like This* that by the end of the fifties, "the jazz world was divided into two distinct, and often warring, factions." She continues:

> Sharp young working-class boys constituted the bulk of the "modernists", who listened seriously, without dancing, to the music known as bebop. The advocates of "trad" (Dixieland), on the other hand, tended to be middle-class tearaways, often from an art-school, "beatnik" background. The clubs they frequented catered for dancing – or jiving, as it was known (in an odd misappropriation of an African-American word that means something completely different). (Wilmer 1991, 31)

She goes on to point out that, whatever the class differences, in the main jazz fans had gender in common, jazz being "something that men did". Her point on class, however, is echoed by Steve Sparks, who in Jonathon Green's *Days In The Life* describes himself as one of the "original mods":

> Mod has been much misunderstood. Mod is always seen as this working-class, scooter-riding precursor of skinheads, and that's a false point of view. Mod before it was commercialized was essentially an extension of the beatniks. It comes from "modernist", it was to do with modern jazz and to do with Sartre. It was to do with existentialism, the working-class reaction to existentialism. (Green 1998a, 38)

Whether the "mods" were in fact "working-class" originally is also a matter of contention. Others locate their origins in the Jewish East End of London. Drawing on a number of "orally based" historical sources, Mary Anne Long suggests:

> It is easy to see how theorists of this era could assume this; as the Mod culture became popularized it moved out into the working class, and this assumption fits their structural ideology. First-hand accounts and contemporary theorists point to the Jewish upper-working or middle-class of London's East End and suburbs ... This background seems very appropriate for teens who had plenty of disposable income in part because of their early entry to the workforce.   (Long 1998)

Dick Hebdige in *Subculture – The Meaning of Style* (1980, 52–4) appears to lean more in Steve Spark's direction and relates the emergence of mod culture as the response of working class youth to the geographical proximity of immigrants from the Caribbean and to their own changing economic, if not social, circumstances. Donnelly in *Sixties Britain* (2005, 38–9) echoes this point, adding:

> Mods arrived in east London in the late fifties with an interest in modern jazz (hence the Mod title), continental fashions and some aspects of urban black immigrant culture ... The tribe spread to the London suburbs of Shepherd's Bush and Richmond in the early sixties and eventually reached the provinces, making Mods the dominant youth style of the time.   (Donnelly 2005, 38–9)

Despite Mary Anne Long's suggestion, on balance, a working- to lower-middle-class origin for the mods seems most likely, though she is perhaps right to highlight its origin in the East End and its Jewish connection, after all many of the early generation of modern jazz musicians like Ronnie Scott, Pete King, Harry Klein and others came from such Jewish backgrounds. The issue of disposable income that she notes is also crucial.

A 1959 study by Mark Alexander Abrams noted that real earnings of people aged fifteen to twenty-five increased 50 per cent between 1938 and 1958, which was double the increase for adults as a whole. Of even more significance was the pattern of their expenditure. Accounting for only 8.5 per cent of all personal income in Britain and only 6 per cent of total consumer spending, by 1957 they were responsible for 44 per cent of spending on records and record players, 26 per cent of cinema admissions, 24 per cent of cosmetics, 19 per cent of footwear and 16 per cent of women's clothing. By the 1960s, youth represented a particularly important niche market and, as a consequence, new businesses including publications and advertisers grew up to meet the demand. Significantly, Abrams also noted that the teenage market was "almost entirely working class" (the figure he gives is 90 per cent), as middle-class children remained at school (Abrams 1959, 13). There is some suggestion that Abrams exaggerated the extent of teenage consumerism. However, the general scope of his argument remains convincing. This would again seem to support Steve Sparks, as well as Hebdige and Donnelly's argument that the mods were essentially a working class youth subculture. Colin MacInnes's unnamed hero in *Absolute Beginners* (1960) – a clothes-obsessed, self-employed, jazz-loving nineteen-year-old photographer – seems to have been a kind of "proto-mod", whose concerns echoed those of Steve Sparks. At the same time, we must remember that as far as the early sixties are concerned "mods" were essentially a phenomenon of London and the metropolitan southeast, and should not assume that this picture applied across Britain. We will see later that their eventual desertion of modern jazz for R&B would have serious consequences for British modern jazz financially and for its connection with youth.

At the end of the fifties and even at the beginning of the sixties, modern jazz and modernism were indeed largely synonymous. Many of those who were later to connect in some way with the rock and pop worlds, either as promoters or managers or as couturiers to the pop elite and "Swinging London's" beautiful people, were involved in jazz. Harold Pendleton and Chris Barber would play a major role in the development of British R&B and later rock through the Marquee Club and the National Jazz Federation festivals at Windsor, Plumpton and Reading. Rik Gunnell, who started the weekend all-nighters at the Flamingo in Wardour Street, began his career promoting jazz and launched the career of Georgie Fame. Gunnell went on to manage Fame, Chris Farlowe, John Mayall, Zoot Money, Geno Washington, P.J. Proby and others. He also later ran the trendy rock venue, the Bag O'Nails in Kingly Street (now a regular jazz venue, The Spice of Life). Even Simon Napier-Bell, of Marc Bolan and Wham! fame, started out trying to make it as a jazz musician and worked as a band boy for the Dankworth Orchestra. But perhaps more than any other figure, Andrew Loog Oldham seems to define the time and its interface between the jazz and pop worlds and the classlessness that so obsessed pundits.

Loog Oldham is an intriguing character. Not only was he the one-time manager of the Rolling Stones and, briefly, with his Immediate record label, Britain's answer to Phil Spector, just about everything about him and his life speaks of the ambiguous, chameleon-like, possibility-rich period that concerns us. If anyone epitomizes the "classless society" it is surely Loog Oldham. His mother, Celia, though of eastern European Jewish extraction, was born in Australia and had estranged herself from her family. His father was a married US serviceman killed during the Second World War, before the young Loog Oldham came into the world in 1944. He grew up in London's West

End. Celia was hard-working, bright and beautiful, but it was not her work as a book-keeper for several small companies that would pay for her son's education at a public school. The source for that came from her boyfriend, a married man, who became to all intents and purposes Loog Oldham's father. The picture one gains from Loog Oldham's background is one of fluidity, of class being less a fixed, pre-determined state but rather one where one might rise or fall according to the extent of one's luck and degree of persistence and ambition.

Loog Oldham had certainly picked up on Elvis and rock & roll, but by the early sixties, out of school and scuffling round Soho, it is clear that his soundtrack and that of others was a mixture of black R&B and modern jazz. Inspired by John Cassavetes's TV character, Johnny Staccato – a private eye-cum-jazz pianist hanging out in New York's Greenwich Village – Loog Oldham gravitated to Ronnie Scott's Club in Gerrard Street. He was already working for fashion designer Mary Quant at her Chelsea Bazaar but, as he put it, "wanting in", he became the club's first waiter. In the words of Scott's business partner, Pete King:

> He was what we were, modernists. He was very pleasant, a guy dressed in a modern way from Austin's in Shaftesbury Avenue. Austin's used to get a small importation of the real thing – that's what Andrew liked, what we all liked. (Oldham 2000, 103)

And as Loog Oldham notes:

> The music I got to hear live at Ronnie Scott's was world-class – Ahmad Jamal, Les McCann, Dizzy Gillespie, Thelonious Monk – and one musician, who made a lasting stylistic impression. Harold McNair was an alto (and) flute player in his own quintet. He was so cool, he was super-cool, with a smooth American edge to him. He simply beamed. In his houndstooth suit he evoked Miles Davis posing in his raglan-sleeve one-button houndstooth jacket for a fashion layout in Esquire. Harold beamed, he was just there. He played so well and he knew how to handle the spaces. (Oldham 2000, 107)

And Mary Quant remembers: "When Andrew was working at Ronnie Scott's he would ring and let us know if some American jazz musician was in for the night. Alexander and I would leap out of bed and jump into a taxi" (Oldham 2000, 107).

Vidal Sassoon, hairdresser to just about everybody in the sixties, was another Scott regular, as was hard man John McVicar. One is reminded of Lenny Bruce's comment on jazz – he liked the "clothes and the attitude". In a sense, that is what modernism is about – the coalescence of style and substance – and fashion was hugely important, not in the flamboyant sense of the Teddy Boys but in a more understated, still fetishistic, sense. The young "mods" hung out at the Flamingo and the Scene, aand shopped at East End tailors, Austin's and later at John Stephen's Carnaby Street store. Even in their choice of clothing, there was an overlap between the sharp-suited Soho beboppers and these young "modernists". Suits had narrow lapels, were often made from mohair, shirts had pointed collars and ties were narrow. There was also a connection on another level – that of aspiration.

The Second World War was very much a "before and after" rupture in British history. In Britain, following the war, there was a determination that past errors, economic and social, would become consigned to history's dustbin. The sixties, and the changes that took place in all areas of the arts including jazz, were to some degree shaped by political decisions made by Labour and Tory administrations. And there was broad, cross-party agreement around the social welfare issues set out in the Beveridge Report of 1942, while the 1944 Education Act, which was introduced by Conservative politician R.A.B. Butler (and which provided for free secondary school education), began a process of extending higher education to working and lower middle class children. The establishment of the welfare state, alongside the nationalization of ailing, essential, but mainly, unprofitable industries both took place, as Britain struggled to recover economically from a war that had cost it dear. The high levels of pre-war unemployment and associated poverty, inadequate and deteriorating housing stock and the poor standards of health experienced by many people were significant motivational factors for politicians of left, centre and centre-right. There was also an expectation among those who had fought, worked for victory over the Axis powers and made enormous sacrifices that their reward should be a fairer and more socially and economically just society.

A Labour government was returned to power for the first time in 1945 with a significant majority and reflected this change in the popular mood. The rationing of foodstuffs, however, continued until 1954, though restrictions on clothing ended in 1949 and on petrol in 1950. Gradually, however, as restrictions relaxed and "full" employment was restored, productivity increased, though less significantly than was, with hindsight, needed to meet increasing consumer demand. Britain moved quickly – over the course of just a dozen years – from war-time privation and post-war austerity to become a consumer society.

Poverty continued to coexist with new-found prosperity. But even the concept and definition of poverty began to change to one based on a more relative set of standards as affluence spread across British society, albeit unequally so. In 1961, 22 per cent of households had no running water and in 1964 only 8 per cent had central heating. Yet, by the early 1990s, virtually no homes in Britain lacked a hot tap and few were without central heating.

Even those who were in their infancy in the fifties can recall the dramatic changes we have witnessed. As Rosen notes: "By the end of the twentieth century it had become possible to be poor and still have a telephone, a washing machine and a colour television. In 1950, this would have been out of the question" (Rosen 2003, 29).

On the other hand, such positive developments contrasted with other indicators within the infrastructure of the UK economy. Between 1945 and 1964, Britain's share of world trade in manufacturing goods declined from 30 per cent to 14 per cent, a trend that has continued. As a consequence, patterns of employment began to shift from manufacturing to the service industries. This was already becoming apparent in the sixties, as was a progressive trend to higher levels of unemployment. This ran at 1.67 per cent during the 1950s, rose to 2.3 per cent in the 1960s and then doubled during the 1970s (see Rosen 2003).

Nevertheless, for a time, levels of demand, production and consumption seemed to coincide, and this in many ways set the tone for the "Swinging Sixties", one that was at least reflected in changes in British jazz. Though it was neither the abolition of class nor its relevance in British society, there was a distinctive move from a blue collar to a white collar society from the 1960s onwards. There was most definitely a loosening of class barriers and the social mobility noted by Goldthorpe and Lockwood and by A.H. Halsey was very real and this process has continued to unfold. Educational reform in particular, following the extension of higher education, has had a very significant impact on the way in which class is understood in Britain. What is more the opening up of higher education has influenced the development of British jazz in several ways and this in turn has altered its position in social and cultural life in the UK.

While few of the traditional or modernist jazz musicians were old enough to fight – Lyttelton was one exception, serving with distinction at Anzio – many of them were coming of age in the late forties. Saxophonists Ronnie Scott and John Dankworth and drummer Tony Kinsey all turned twenty-one in 1948, drummer Phil Seamen and saxophonist Don Rendell a year earlier, and drummer Tony Crombie in 1945. The age differences for the traditional jazz players, who emerged at the same time, were not significantly different. Humphrey Lyttelton was twenty-five in 1945, whereas George Chisholm was thirty that year, but Ken Colyer was born in the same year as Dankworth and Scott. George Melly was, like Rendell, born in 1926, but Bilk, Barber and Ball were actually slightly younger than their bebop counterparts. Age, it seems, is not an indicator of a stylistic preference in jazz.

As to the "class" backgrounds of the traditional jazz musicians who came up in the fifties, a confusing picture emerges. Bilk, Ball and Colyer were working class, and George Chisholm, Ian Christie (clarinettist with the Mulligan band) and bandleader and trumpeter Freddy Randall were hardly upper crust. Pianist George Webb, the father of British Dixieland, was of a working-class background from Camberwell, London and worked on the assembly line at the Vickers gun factory during the Second World War. Sandy Brown attended Edinburgh's Royal High School (whose alumni include Sir Walter Scott and Alexander Graham Bell), before reading architecture at the city's university, while Mick Mulligan, George Melly, Humphrey Lyttelton, Chris Barber and Alexis Korner were all ex-public schoolboys. It is hard, therefore, to draw any firm conclusions about class from this brief survey of musicians' backgrounds.

We must also be somewhat circumspect in seeking to identify a predominant class element within the traditional jazz audience. Val Wilmer suggests that there was a distinctly "middle-class" aspect among such fans. By contrast, however, both Hilary Moore (2007, 60) and George Melly (1970) describe an audience that cut right across social strata, though both also suggest, in Melly's words, that it included "a surprisingly large minority of middle- and upper-class adherents" (Melly 1970, 26).

While Hilary Moore does look at the question of class in relation to Ken Colyer, she seems to lose focus here. Instead of considering class as a set of relationships to the means of production, she blurs the issue into one that is essentially cultural and social rather than economic or political. In linking this both to the destruction of working class communities, first by Hitler and second by post-war developers and government, and to the wider intellectual opposition to class differences, her analysis quickly becomes too generalized to be of much help to us (Moore 2007, 47–50). The only writer to examine the question of the class background of British jazz musicians and their audience in any degree of depth is Francis Newton (aka Eric Hobsbawm). Newton is a Marxist, so his interest in the issue does not surprise. He suggests that with the development of:

> ... a specific jazz public in the 1930's and forties, the ordinary professional dance band or variety musician formed an even more important component of jazz. Socially, in Britain at least, he came either from musical or show-business families, or more usually from a working-class background, with the usual admixture of bohemian ex-clerks and students. The working class background was inevitably strong, since the most obvious school in which the musician learned his trade was one which, both as a professional military and as an amateur civilian institution, has long been part of the British working class, especially the skilled part: the brass band.
> (Newton 1960, 224)

Despite the fact that Newton is writing of the pre-war period, much that he says about the importance of professional, dance band musicians for the emergent British jazz remains true for the post-war period. In fact, many of the modernists began or continued their careers in the bands of Bert Ambrose, Ted Heath, Tito Burns, Jack Parnell, Vic Lewis, Ivor Kirchin and others. One or two, like Ronnie Scott and Tubby Hayes, also had fathers who had been professional dance band musicians. Like Val Wilmer, Newton identifies the "jazz public" in the UK as being overwhelmingly young and male and estimates the audience for jazz in Britain as being in the region of 100,000. In his reckoning, this population divided into some 60,000 in London, another 20,000 in the other large cities and 20,000 in the rest of the country (Newton 1960, 236). However approximate this guess may be, it again rings true. In terms of its class composition, again referring to the pre-war period, Newton contrasts the situation in Britain with that in the USA and France, in both of which he suggests that the jazz audience was more markedly middle class and intellectual. In Britain, he suggests, the market for jazz came more from the lower middle classes – the sons of skilled workers, small business men, shopkeepers and the like.

> They were cultural self-made men. The respectability against which they revolted was that of the semi-detached suburban, three-bed, two reception house; but they also resented, and revolted against, the world of upper-class culture, as reached through the public school and 'varsity. (Newton 1960, 247)

Newton links this in turn to the outlook of the post-war "Angry Young Men", who "wrote jazz among many other rude words on their banners". Towards the end of the thirties, when Newton was himself at Cambridge, jazz had begun to make inroads into the universities and public schools, primarily among the left-leaning and romantically inclined. However, even with the emergence of revivalism in the forties and early fifties, Newton identifies the core of the jazz population as remaining within the lower middle classes (see Newton 1960, 252–3).

Essentially, Newton is referring to the "trad"/New Orleans/Dixieland/revivalist audience here. Superficially at least, his comments contrast with Val Wilmer's impressions that the modernists were sharp-suited working-class men, whereas the "traddies" were middle-class, art-school tearaways. Two other images of the period with regard to the traditional jazz audience are worth considering, one visual and the other written.

The first of these involves a short filmed extract from the *Smokey Dives* BBC documentary, of some youngish people jiving in a cellar club, while on the sidelines what appear to be "debs" dressed in fur stoles with Savile Row attired male escorts look on smiling. The image has an anthropological qual-ity to it, as if the debs are on a field trip planned to observe the lower orders and their courtship rituals. At the same time, there are no clear signifiers for the class of the jiving couples. What it does suggest is that the audience for "trad", at least, was quite heterogeneous and drawn across classes, and that jazz, in its traditionalist form at least, was a meeting ground for adherents of very differing backgrounds. Again, however, it depends how one chooses to read such impressionistic evidence.

The second image comes from writer/musician Jeff Nuttall's *Bomb Culture*. He describes how teenagers, while by no means the majority among the CND Aldermaston protesters of the late fifties and early sixties, gave the march its carnival atmosphere:

> The Colyer fans, now dubbed beatniks, although they differed from the Venice West originals in many important ways, appeared from nowhere in their grime and tatters, with their slogan-daubed crazy hats and streaming filthy hair, hammering their banjos, strumming aggressively on their guitars, blowing their antiquated sousaphones, capering out in front of the march destroying the wooden dignity of Canon Collins, Jacquetta Hawkes, Sydney Silverman and other celebrities who were the official leaders of the cavalcade. It was this wild public festival spirit that spread the CND symbol through all the jazz clubs and secondary schools in an incredibly short time.
>
> (Nuttall 1970, 47; see also Melly 1970, 59)

Even more to the point, discussing the Soho scene of the mid- to late fifties, Nuttall describes these "beatniks":

> Solemnly dedicated, grimly puritan, with their black jeans, shoulder-length hair, donkey jackets, the sexes only distinguishable by breasts and beards, they constructed a left-wing romanticism based on that patronizing idolization of the lumpen proletariat that only the repressed children of the middle class could have contrived. (Nuttall 1970, 40)

There are two possible conclusions we can draw here, neither of which are exclusive. First is that jazz provided a meeting ground between classes, one that represented at least a degree of equality in jazz. This is echoed in our earlier quotation by Colin MacInnes's nameless narrator in *Absolute Beginners* (MacInnes 1960, 64), though, at the same time, I note that another character in the book refers dismissively to the Beaulieu Jazz Festival, saying, "That garden party's for the ooblies and the Hooray Henries, anyway" (MacInnes 1960, 76). Paradoxically, one has to be aware of and acknowledge the relevance of class to attempt to dismiss or transcend it.

The second possible conclusion is that we need to think about the make-up of the jazz public, in particular the traditionalist audience, as consisting of several different groupings, which would include the art school beatniks and middle class layabouts as well as other less committed publics. The hardcore fans probably did come from the educated upper and middle classes, and included leftist intellectuals and students, and those who were among the first in their families to enter higher education. Records were, comparatively, far more expensive in the fifties and sixties than today (and, incidentally, relatively speaking far more expensive to manufacture than compact discs). In 1959, 22 per cent of the population in work earned between £50 and £250 per annum. Nearly 50 per cent of working people earned less than £500 per annum. By 1962, the figures were 18.4 per cent and 40 per cent, respectively (Halsey 1972, 92). Record prices were fairly consistent during the early sixties. In that period, a long playing record cost approximately 33 shillings (or £1.65), a single 6 shillings (30p) and an extended player around 13 shillings (65p). With rent, food, fares and other living costs taken into account, record collecting required commitment and a reasonable disposable income – not in itself an issue of class. As Mark Abrams and others like Colin MacInnes (1966) suggest, teenagers (including the young working class) had money in their pockets as never before. The point is that following jazz required commitment, including that of a financial nature.

After this grouping came the younger adults and teenagers, for whom "trad" jazz was the pop music of their day. Then there were those from privileged backgrounds taking a "walk on the wilder side" and various bohemian and déclassé types. Finally, there were the mums and dads. Various of these groups would desert "trad" in due course – working- and lower-middle-class teenagers for home-grown beat and R&B, the bohemians for other styles of jazz and experimental music, the mums and dads for more familiar, light popular music, and the privileged for music more fitted to their station. After the arrival of the Beatles, the audience for traditional jazz, at least, would continue to be drawn in the main from the hardcore fans and from the younger adults, who had picked up on it before or during the "trad" boom onwards.

Our witnesses – Newton, Wilmer, Melly, Nuttall and others – are therefore not consistent with regard to their assessments of the class backgrounds of members of the traditional jazz audience. Perhaps some of this confusion arises from the possibility that this audience was reflecting a situation of flux within and between what had been hitherto more rigid social boundaries. Between 1951 and 1961, the biggest single increase within employment came among white collar workers, and significantly among the higher and lower professions. This group increased by 1.5 million in those ten years. While the numbers of skilled manual workers increased slightly, overall there was a fall of over 400,000 among manual workers (see Glyn and Booth 1996, 176–7).

These changes were in turn reflected in wage/salary rates, and the desires and expectations of these new professionals. It is undeniable that pay and working conditions have improved for many in Britain. Essentially, there has been a shift in the UK and throughout the northern hemisphere from a capitalism based on manufacturing to one based on financial capital and consumerism. Changes within classes and the overall class structure of British society have taken place. In effect, we have exported our industrial proletariat to the Far East and elsewhere, to countries where labour and production costs are cheaper and where trade unions and indeed civil rights are less of an inconvenience. We even have a new word for it – globalization.

There is an alternative, Marxist, view of class that we need to introduce here, though surprisingly not one that Newton has used, and one which takes us momentarily away from the more specific issues that we have been considering. According to this view, class is defined primarily in terms of two main groupings – those who own the means of production or other forms of wealth-generating property and those who sell their labour, from which profit is in turn extracted. Those who do not own the means of production but are not engaged in any aspect of the productive process in turn form an intermediate class between the proletariat and capital, and are most often referred to in Marxist theory as the *petite bourgeoisie*. Some within this class might be professionals, the three main chartered professions being medicine, law and finance. Those in such professions who own their own companies or are directors of other companies would come within the capitalist class. Others in this group might work in ancillary professions to law or medicine, while others might be teachers, nurses, social workers, police officers, journalists, small traders, self-employed skilled workers, factory managers or supervisors. Marxists, however, are careful to distinguish between those who are actually workers whose occupations produce profit for their employers, such as white collar workers in the finance industry, and those whose work involves the provision of services to capital.

Within the *petite bourgeoisie* are a number of workers whose class position is ambiguous. They are not involved in productive work and their labour does not produce profit. Yet they sell their labour in much the same way as productive labourers. Some of these workers – teachers, journalists or social workers, for example – may not be engaged in the production of goods or services for sale, but they are engaged in what can be described as ideological or cultural production, what Barbara and John Ehrenreich call the "reproduction of capitalist culture and capitalist class relations" (see Ehrenreich and Ehrenreich 1979, 12). This means that they are involved in the production and inculcation of ideas and values that support the capitalist mode of production. The American Marxist theorist Erik Olin Wright uses the term "contradictory class location" to describe the position of such workers and distinguishes between two significant groups within these locations. First, there are the managers or supervisors. Second is the group that concerns us:

> [C]ertain categories of semi-autonomous employees who retain relatively high levels of control over their immediate labour-process occupy a contradictory location between the working class and the petty bourgeoisie.   (Wright 1978, 63)

Some of the "evidence" we have discussed regarding the class origins or position of British jazz musicians has been anecdotal or impressionistic. That does not make it irrelevant, of course. If nothing else it reveals the complexity and fluidity of the picture we are trying to bring into focus. It is, however, worth for a moment considering whether a more objective approach could be applied.

It must be noted that many jazz musicians in Britain, as elsewhere, often had dual careers. Lyttelton was a critic and cartoonist; Melly was also a critic; Sandy Brown was an acoustic architect. Many musicians were semi-pro rather than full-time professionals. Nevertheless, if we concentrate on their work and role as musicians as opposed to other trades and work, and using the UK Registrar General's model of social classes (which was used extensively by sociologists such as Goldthorpe and Halsey), our 1960s British jazz musician would probably find themselves placed in Social Class IIIN – Skilled Non-Manual. He (or possibly she) would sit alongside social workers, teachers and journalists. This might be appropriate given that the jazz musician is also involved in cultural production. Within Social Class III as a whole, they would be classed alongside carpenters, electricians and engineers. This might tell us little about the working life and social position of the freelance musician. However, from the previous discussion it will be seen that many of those in the Registrar General's Social Class III function within what can again be described as an ambiguous class position, one with a Janus face looking simultaneously towards the proletariat and towards capital.

Karl Marx's definition is by contrast delightful in its simplicity when it comes to the position of the artist, although we need to adapt it to the circumstances that applied 100 years later. Marx notes that Milton, in writing *Paradise Lost*, did so because it was "an activity of *his* nature" and that he later sold his work to a publisher for £5. He is therefore an "unproductive labourer". By contrast, the jobbing writer churning out copy for his publisher is a "productive labourer". The reason for this is that, in the case of the latter, "his product is from the outset subsumed under capital and comes into being only for the purpose of increasing that capital." Marx then gives a further example of immediate relevance to our inquiry:

> The singer who sells her song for her own account is an unproductive labourer. But the same singer commissioned by an entrepreneur to sing in order to make money for him is a productive labourer; for she produces capital. (Marx 1969)

As a corollary of this, the freelance musician can fall into either category. However, the band or orchestra leader, insofar as he or she employs other musicians and profits from their work, must by definition come within the capitalist class. In jazz terms, Benny Goodman or Artie Shaw, and perhaps

Duke Ellington, might qualify here, and perhaps someone like Dankworth or Barber. But it is hard to see how Mike Westbrook, Keith Tippett or Graham Collier might be considered in such terms. In these cases, the role was more that of gang leader than employer, foreman than contractor. Within British jazz during the sixties and early seventies, most bandleaders dealt with the headaches of organizing gigs, tours and recording sessions and did little better for their pains than those they employed, who in practice might well employ them in their own groups. The majority of British jazz musicians in our period would seem to fall within the *petite bourgeoisie*. In addition, it can be argued that they occupy a contradictory class position in line with Wright's use of the term. In fact, their position would at times be even more contradictory than that of other workers in this group as they were often employed directly in settings which would be seen as involving them in "productive labour", for example within the session or theatre worlds.

If we look at the situation of many British jazz musicians during these years, the accumulation of wealth was not really part of the plan. Many could quite probably have earned far better and more secure livings in a number of other occupations. However, from this perspective, their position in class terms is far from academic. Later, we will see how their "contradictory class location" was explored by several British jazz artists in developing a practice in the music that reflected a core set of ethical and aesthetic values that could be seen to be critical of the dominant culture and ideology within British society.

* * *

On balance, from the forties through subsequent decades, British jazz – traditional and modern – did represent a meeting place for people of different classes. It had acquired an egalitarian aspect that was extremely important in its progress musically and artistically, but also in terms of its access to its audience and of its audience's access to the musicians. This was more than just a shared enthusiasm, being a reflection of elements within the music itself that in turn derived from its history. In particular, the absence of such distinctions as class on the scene may well have allowed the music a greater freedom to develop than might otherwise have been the case. This does not mean that class in broader economic, social and political terms ceased to be relevant. However, at an everyday, working level within the language of the time British jazz could be said to be "classless" and, in this respect, was perhaps ahead of other areas of British society.

That audience members of differing class backgrounds intersected during our period can be clearly seen in the four jazz festivals that took place over the August Bank Holiday at Lord Montagu's estate at Beaulieu in Hampshire on the edge of the New Forest between 1958 and 1961. Such links may well have been generally positive for all such "adherents", but at Beaulieu in 1960 events took an interesting turn, which might suggest that at least some who were present were unaware that Britain had now entered a period of classlessness.

The first Beaulieu jazz weekend went ahead without any problems, though the one that followed in 1959 experienced a certain element of rowdiness, apparently from local youths unhappy at the incomers. For the 1960 festival, Montagu had requested "police assistance", but this had been refused due to "Bank Holiday commitments" (Brand 1960, 2–3). It was at the third Beaulieu Jazz Festival that a "riot" took place, an event as astonishingly un-British as it was fascinating. What made it worse, in the public eyes, was that the BBC had a live broadcast unit there to film the performers. Instead of jolly beat-niks jiving to the sounds of jazz, the viewers were provided with the shocking sight of rioting young people, many dressed strangely and clearly intoxicated. As Stuart Nicholson has pointed out, there was already, thanks to its con-struction in the media, an image of jazz that associated it in the popular mind with drugs and unruly, and even criminal, behaviour (Nicholson 2005). The story made the national newspapers, and the *Melody Maker*'s pages and letter column were filled with the issue. Yet, despite all this high-profile coverage, nobody seems to have asked the obvious question: to which class or classes did these "rioters" belong? This is unfortunate because it might have told us a great deal. But then, as sociologists like Stanley Cohen (see, for example, Cohen 1972) have noted, newspaper and TV coverage of the "disturbing" activities of young people rely extensively on an undifferentiated notion of "youth".

Stuart Nicholson's account in the *Observer Music Monthly* is essentially a factual one given the magazine's imposed brevity, though he does offer a limited analysis of the event. He locates the cause in the "schism" that had developed between the fans of traditional jazz and their modernist counter-parts. He notes that alcohol was also a factor and that the presence of TV cameras might have encouraged the rioters.

> As the lighting gantry collapsed somebody grabbed a microphone and demanded "free beer for the working man". A lone figure made it to the top of the stage, a converted merry-go-round com-plete with fairground horses, and once the crowd realised he was on television, a mass climb began to join him.   (Nicholson 2005)

And he continues:

> The trouble had been sparked initially by a modern jazz set by the Vic Ash/Harry Klein band. "Teenagers invaded the stand, danc-ing, shouting, pulling, pushing," Klein later told Melody Maker.
> Clarinettist Acker Bilk, whose "trad" band played for over an hour to pacify the protesters, later said: "They were phoney imita-tion beatniks. Real ones may be weird, untidy and excitable but

they're not hooligans." Bilk had in fact enjoyed a taste of what might happen when he had played Victoria Park in Hackney two months earlier. "It was uglier than Beaulieu, but police with dogs broke it up," he said. (Nicholson 2005)

Vic Ash, recalling the incident in his autobiography, *I Blew It My Way – Bebop, Big Bands and Sinatra*, supports Nicholson's description of the antagonism between rival fans:

> I was able to catch up with Kenny Ball and Terry Lightfoot but, whereas backstage we modern and traditional musicians would meet, share a drink and talk shop, there existed a sharp and sometimes violent dividing line between our respective audiences.
> (Ash 2006, 65)

The contrast between such backstage bonhomie with what followed could not be more sharply defined.

> The modern groups were continually heckled during the afternoon as the "trad" fans grew increasingly restless. We went on and there were soon screams of "WE WANT ACKER!" We played on. A few drunken fans tried to pull Harry Klein into the audience and then clambered onto the roof of the outdoor stage. We began to play Too Close For Comfort (an ironic choice) and things started to go badly wrong. I called out to the group: "Off!" And we just managed to get off-stage when the roof collapsed. There was then a total riot and this made sensational national press headlines the next day. It did not do the image of jazz any good at all and I know that Acker would have been very embarrassed by it. (Ash 2006, 66)

George McKay makes reference to press coverage of the story, noting:

> The combination of aristocracy and jazz madness was an outstanding story of English eccentricity run, literally, riot. The Battle of Beaulieu was in part a symptom of jazz purists' investment of their particular form: subcultural tensions between traditional jazz fans and modernists were evident. (McKay 2005, 76–7)

In considering the setting and Lord Montagu's position as a member of the landed aristocracy at a time when some of his "peers" faced financial ruin, McKay notes the presence of such elements of class in providing the backcloth to the drama. He also points out local resentment at the invasion of outsiders, quoting attendance figures for 1958 at around 4,000 rising to between 5,000 and 10,000 in 1959. However, he goes no further. Instead, he focuses on the issue of "carnival" and "transgression". Both he and Nicholson explain the event with reference to differences between "modernists" and "traditionalists". Sadly, their reading of the event is inadequate, and merely serves to mythologize the event and its place in British jazz history.

This is unfortunate because "class" was very clearly an issue, and two reports from the *Melody Maker*, one from 1961 and one from 1960, make specific reference to a different source of antagonism, one that lay in the presence of local, working class youth, who appear to have started the trouble. In addition, John Dunbar – the artist, art-dealer and co-founder of *International Times* – was at the festival that year, and he gives a similar account. Everything about the event, including the very English aspect of the lord of the manor opening his gates on special occasions to his social inferiors, speaks of class. Surviving BBC and Pathé footage shows young people, including Rod "the Mod" Stewart, arriving in the village and wandering around the estate. Much of the time, the camera focuses on the traditionalists, bearded, pipe-smoking, scruffily and eccentrically dressed. Iain Chambers describes their type in *Popular Culture: The Metropolitan Experience*, when he notes:

> The bohemia that hovered around the jazz clubs – the "beatniks" identified by the popular press on the Aldermaston CND marches ("Ban the Bomb") – usually adopted for the decidedly more English route of eccentric dress and manners.
>
> (Chambers 1993, 149)

For some commentators the riot has been understood as an issue between rival fans, with class, in McKay's account and that of Nicholson, at most a backdrop to the occasion. However, whether this antagonism was the cause of events is disputable. John Dunbar gives a very different description of the "battle":

> The Jazz Festival at Beaulieu, that was my first riot, that was good. All the teds suddenly wanted Acker. Poor old Lord Thing [Montagu] had flown in Little Fingers Montgomery 5,000 miles to play and these teds are going "We want Acker! We want Acker!" and it just got crazier and crazier. I remember him standing out on stage saying, "I say, could we have a bit of quiet?" "Get down, you fairy!" And bottles were coming down and finally a lighting tower collapsed. It was complete, mad devastation over absolutely nothing, over fucking Acker Bilk. Crazy.
>
> (Interview with John Dunbar, April 2011)

Dunbar is referring to "teddy boys", a completely different youth subculture – essentially working class and musically enthusiastic for rock & roll.
According to Dunbar the crowd at Beaulieu that year was a very mixed one
in terms of class and, interviewed recently, he confirmed that he saw quite a
few "teddy boys" in the audience and that they were the ones who initiated
the "riot".

> There were certainly a lot of quiffs in evidence there. The teds
> were into rock and roll but were also into Acker Bilk because he
> had a hit record. Acker was the closest thing to pop they had at
> Beaulieu. They were drunk and they got impatient. They certainly
> weren't serious jazz aficionados. That was really it as far as I could
> tell. As a schoolboy of seventeen, I just watched in wonder.
>   (Interview with John Dunbar, April 2011)

Pat Brand, writing in the Melody Maker the following week, gave a similar account. He very specifically blames working class youths from nearby
Portsmouth and Southampton.

> Well, I suppose you could say THEY'VE won. And it should have
> been obvious to all of us that, short of ringing the village with
> armed guards, empowered to search and turn back undesirables,
> THEY were bound to do so. And by THEY, we are not referring
> to jazz fans, nor even necessarily to the weirdies, some of whom
> do possess some slight appreciation of the music. THEY are the
> mobsters (more prevalent in the South than the North it seems)
> to whom this sort of event is an irresistible invitation to smash,
> loot, set aflame and generally destroy whatever lies in their path.
> In Beaulieu's case they are probably so familiar a sight around the
> docks of nearby Portsmouth and Southampton that their conduct
> is no longer news.   (Brand 1960, 9)

Beaulieu did take place the following year, this time with Lord Montagu
forced to fund a much higher level of security. From that point on, future
events were unsustainable. Tony Brown wrote at length on the problems
faced by the festival in the *Melody Maker* in August 1960. Brown suggests
that Fleet Street and lazy, inflammatory reporting of this and similar incidents such as the cinema riots that accompanied the film "Blackboard Jungle"
were one of the causes of mayhem at Beaulieu. In the piece, he bemoans the
way that jazz has become associated in the public mind with delinquency
and calls for fans to repudiate this slur. Intriguingly, Brown is articulating
a process that Stan Cohen would later define as a "deviancy amplification
spiral". However, like the People newspaper who referred specifically in its
coverage to "Teddy Boys", Brown also identifies the rioters in that way:

Call them Teddy Boys, call them jazzers, call them what you like. The fact is they were young hooligans inflamed by drink, doing what comes naturally to hooligans all over the world in all walks of life. (Brown 1960, 3)

From these accounts, it seems that it was Edwards rather than Hooray Henries who were responsible. Now this changes the class content of the incident somewhat. If working class youths caused the problems at Beaulieu, then that young man's cry of "free beer for the working man" ceases to be an ironic statement by middle class youth and becomes a rallying cry for working-class transgression. Either way, class remains a central feature of the "riot". It becomes less a subcultural contest between rival jazz fans, from whatever class backgrounds, that took place on lawns that were part of the 8,000-acre estate of Lord Montagu. Its timing, its context and its participants seem to suggest that the "Battle of Beaulieu" was a matter of class – a phenomenon that in Britain as elsewhere is not easily wished away.

However much politicians, editors of broadsheet newspapers, social reformers and commentators might have wished it, "class" did not vanish from the social and economic scene with the arrival of four cheeky, chirpy lads from Liverpool. And yet there are elements of truth in all the punditry. As we have noted, both living standards and social aspirations were rising among working and lower-middle class Britons, and in the metropolitan areas of the country, or in London at least, the determination of class position was becoming more fluid and, to an extent, allowed for definitions of social status that included celebrity, talent and newly acquired wealth. Historically, there was nothing new in this process. The rising bourgeoisie had married into the landed gentry throughout the previous 300 years, and talented and charismatic entertainers, from David Garrick to George Robey and Harry Lauder had been feted by the wealthy and aristocratic. Traditionally, there had been three routes out of the East End, the Gorbals and the mill towns of Lancashire for young working-class men – music/light entertainment, sport and crime. For young working-class women, there were just two – the entertainment industry and marriage.

The singer Cleo Laine is an example of the latter. Born Clementina Campbell in Southall, Middlesex to a black Jamaican father and white English mother, Laine attended local schools and worked as a hairdresser and librarian before taking up singing professionally. Her subsequent career has been phenomenally successful, artistically and materially, and was marked in 1997 by a peerage. If Laine exemplifies a pattern for young, talented working-class girls, then saxophonist and jazz club owner Ronnie Scott does so for young working-class men. Scott's origins lay in London's Jewish East End. He was the son of a dance band saxophonist and a young, hardworking sales girl. Scott's parents separated when he was a toddler and his father, Jock Scott (originally Joseph Schatt), was a shadowy presence throughout Scott's adolescence. Following his mother's remarriage, to a more dependable and solid character, the family moved out of Aldgate to more prosperous Stoke Newington. Yet Scott had already caught the bug and his way in life – like his wandering father – would be led by music and the saxophone (see Fordham 1986).

Laine and Scott were hardly untypical of their generation of modernists. Drummers Phil Seamen, Tony Crombie, Laurie Morgan, Bobby Orr, Allan Ganley and, later, Ginger Baker were all working-class lads. Pianists Tony Kinsey, Victor Feldman, Dill Jones, Bill Le Sage and, come the turn of the decade, Brian Dee and Gordon Beck were all early school-leavers and could be broadly be described as coming from working-class backgrounds. Of the saxophonists, the same could be said of Pete King (Scott's later business partner), Tommy Whittle, Ronnie Ross, Don Rendell, Tubby Hayes and Danny Moss. All embarked early in life on musical careers and many of them came from musical family backgrounds. Indeed, there does seem to be some truth in Val Wilmer's perception of modernism as more of a working-class phenomenon initially.

John Dankworth might perhaps have been an exception, though he was hardly born with a silver saxophone in his mouth. His father was a sales manager, and therefore, middle class. More significant in Dankworth's case was his attendance at the Royal Academy of Music (Chris Barber attended the Guildhall). As will later become clear, Dankworth certainly did not study jazz but he was, by the time he found his way to Archer Street, a "schooled" and formally educated musician. For most of his fellow modernists, music was learnt in the home from family, friends or a local teacher and the finer points of technique developed on the bandstand, from playing and, more importantly, from listening to colleagues and the few records that were then available. For a few, there was also Geraldo's Navy. As well as being a bandleader in his own right, following the Second World War, Geraldo (born Gerald Walcan Bright) ran an agency from his offices at 73 New Bond Street, London. He booked bands for theatres and hotels, and also placed musicians on transatlantic and cruise liners. Hence, the name – Geraldo's Navy. Such gigs were prized by nascent British boppers, not just for the wages but for the chance to hear Bird, Diz, Monk and Bud Powell on 52nd Street, New York.

It is not that their "schooling" was any less instructive or valuable than those who appear later in the decade. Put as prosaically as possible, who would one rather listen to: John Dankworth or Ronnie Scott? Dankworth – talented, educated and widely knowledgeable about jazz and classical music – or Scott – more instinctive and perhaps closer to the popular image of the jazz musician? Simply, why on Earth would anyone want or need to make such a choice? But learning on the job or in the classroom create differing sets of opportunities and musical possibilities, as will become clear. Jazz in Britain did undergo a whole raft of changes in the period (roughly) from 1964–70 and, as will be seen, one major factor in these changes involved the influx of a considerable number of musicians who studied music formally and/or who were graduates. While there is a tendency to see this as a "revolution" in style rather than part of a more natural progression, new entrants on the scene invariably built on the achievements of their predecessors. This is very important because one can observe in certain writers' work an assumption that British modern jazz in the fifties was conservative and a pale imitation of an American original. This is unfair and misunderstands the processes that function within the context of a non-mainstream art form. However, the influx of musicians post-1960 into modern jazz who had university backgrounds did presage a shift in the broader class make-up of British jazz and its audience. More significantly, it coincided with new developments within the music.

Two aspects of the question of class and its connection with British jazz in the fifties and sixties stand out. The first lies in the confidence and optimism inspired in musicians and their audience by the relaxing of social boundaries. The second can be found in the real social changes that were being initiated most notably by the opening up of secondary and higher education. A third aspect is less obvious and more complex and concerns class as a more political and politicized categorisation and its relationship through ideology to wider issues of art and culture. We will examine this in later chapters.

However, in terms of our discussion so far, it must be stressed that the Butler Education Act of 1944 did far, far more to blur Britain's rigid class boundaries in the longer term than all of the examples of working-class heroes from Lennon to footballer Jimmy Greaves and Twiggy put together. Previously, working-class parents might hope that their children would experience a life less marked by hardship and uncertainty than they had. However, such aspirations focused on the office rather than the coal face or factory floor (or, in rare cases, on sport, show business or crime). From the 1950s and 1960s onwards, there would be an additional route off the estate and out of the tenements – education.

3 Education, Education, Education

From the 1950s onwards, the British education system became a mechanism for social engineering. The 1944 Butler Education Act had grown out of the bipartisan, social welfare agenda that emerged during the Second World War. It created, for the first time in Britain, what could truly be described as an "educational system", one based on state funding and on standards set by parliament. It established a tripartite system of schooling with access to secondary education determined by an examination to be taken by all children at the age of 11 years. Based on their results, children would be allocated to the more academic education offered by grammar schools, the vocational education provided by secondary technical schools or training in practical skills and home economics at a secondary modern school. While parity of status for each educational was the intention, this was far from the case. Few technical schools were set up, most of the funding went to grammar schools and many bright young people were offered an education that was not commensurate with their abilities. Furthermore, provision of grammar school places varied greatly, there were more places for boys than girls and the 11-plus examination discriminated against working-class children in a variety of ways. In due course, these shortcomings would lead to the replacement of the tripartite system by comprehensive education for all.

The Wilson government formally issued instructions in 1965 to all local education authorities to implement plans for comprehensivization of schooling. However, by that point, many Local Education Authorities had already begun to move in that direction. In fact, the first comprehensive school was established in Anglesey in 1949, and several city and county authorities (including Leicestershire) had by 1965 already adopted a similar model. Yet, despite its obvious limitations, the Butler Act achieved several important changes in practice. It introduced moves towards a standard curriculum, its implementation did begin to promote a degree of social mobility and, most important of all, it firmly instituted the state funding of education providing free education for all to the age of 15. In respect of the latter, it significantly improved educational access for young women and working class children.

The musicians that we are concerned with in this book actually fall into three categories. There are those such as Ronnie Scott, Tony Crombie, Stan Tracey, Don Rendell, Tubby Hayes, Pete King *et al.* whose school education predates the Butler Act's implementation in 1947. Then there are those educated under the tripartite system. This group would include Mike Westbrook, Michael Garrick, Ian Carr, John Surman, Evan Parker and others. Finally, there is a slightly younger tranche – musicians like Chris Laurence, Frank Ricotti and Stan Sulzmann, for example – who experienced secondary education at a comprehensive school. It is reasonable to assume that the music that each group would produce would present different qualities and pose different questions. Indeed, we will see that access to secondary and higher education was a major factor in the development of and changes that took place within British jazz in the second half of the 1960s.

For the Scott–Tracey–Hayes generation – and their non-musical peers – access to secondary education depended on money. Their parents needed to be able to support them materially and actually pay for their schooling, should they wish to continue in education. The main options for working-class children in the period after the Second World War involved taking up an apprenticeship or finding employment, with the former being also dependent on family finances. If one wanted to become a musician, it was simply a case of finding a job with one or other of the groups or bands that were in demand from a public keen to find some emotional uplift in a Britain still under the thrall of the privations and losses of the Second World War. And this is exactly what they did – Ronnie Scott joined trumpeter Johnny Claes's octet in 1944 and then Ted Heath and his Music in 1946. Saxophonist and bandleader Kenny Graham was a few years older and began playing jazz and dance music in 1940. Stan Tracey began his career in bands entertaining forces personnel, as did Don Rendell, while Tony Kinsey worked in bands playing the transatlantic boats. Their education in that period was very much an ongoing one. As well as earning a living playing dance music, sometimes with a jazz tinge, these musicians were learning a trade and at the same time trying to get to grips with the demands of bebop. It is not unduly romantic to suggest that the bandstand was their classroom and their textbooks the very few 78s of Parker, Gillespie and Davis that they could obtain, with the additional resource of the occasional radio broadcast. Extending the metaphor slightly, jam sessions and bar-room discussions were their seminars, where their shared enthusiasm and interest allowed for the exchange of ideas, information and technique.

Asked whether musicians shared information about their musical discoveries, veteran pianist Stan Tracey puts more emphasis on a learning process that focused on listening to records by the bebop pioneers and by observing them on the stand, first in New York and later here:

> A small part of it was from each other. Sometimes the information we gave each other was wrong. The greater part was from recordings and, in the case of Ronnie and others in his clique and myself, we went on the boats and could listen to the music first hand and also buy records there that you couldn't buy here. But for the greater part it was from listening to records.
>
> (Interview with Stan Tracey, December 2009)

And once the MU ban was lifted:

> It created the same interest, as when we saw them live in New York. With regard to Ronnie's, we looked forward to working with those guys but whenever they were playing over here in concert you would try and catch them. I remember flying to Brussels to hear Stan Kenton – something I wouldn't do now, if he was alive! [laughing] But that was the enthusiasm that was around at that time, just taking any chance to hear them.
>
> (Interview with Stan Tracey, December 2009)

As he acknowledged, in the beginning his own and his peers' efforts were largely imitative: "At that time, it was about reproducing that music. You have to know what it's about before you can start messing with it. You had to find out about it first" (interview with Stan Tracey, December 2009).

Returning from that first trip to New York and filled by the sounds of Parker and Gillespie, these young musicians, arrived home to preach the new gospel. As John Dankworth notes: "Soon little groups of us banded together for informal jam sessions at each other's houses in the suburbs or, when we could afford it, in rehearsal rooms in central London" (Dankworth 1998, 59). Jazz, by its nature, and with its emphasis on improvisation, is an interactive music and, whatever aspects of it might be taught, its practice has to be learned on the stand playing with other musicians. Talking about his friendship with altoist Mike Osborne and his own early steps in jazz in the mid-1960s, saxophonist John Surman stresses how important the jam session continued to be. They had met when Osborne had auditioned for Mike Westbrook's band, of which Surman was already an essential part:

> [F]airly soon after that I got to know Mike really well because he had a gig for the CND at The Peanuts Club. It was an upstairs room in a pub in New Hall Street. That was Friday nights and I started to go up there with him in a quartet which would have been with Harry Miller and Alan Jackson and, of course, carrying

on with the Westbrook thing. Then we became very close friends and both of us were jam session crazy. If we couldn't find a jam session to go to we'd start one. We found a cellar below a music shop in Portobello Road, which smelt very heavily of gas and which may not have done us much good. [laughing] But we had jam sessions there and anywhere else we could find and really played a lot together. I didn't room with him or anything but we saw each other a lot at one point. I suppose almost on a daily basis there'd be something going on two or three times a week and we'd be playing for peanuts – what an aptly named club. That would be just for the door and playing and jamming.

(Interview with John Surman, November 2008)

It was just such a jam session in 1949 in a rehearsal room in Soho that led to the establishment of the legendary Club Eleven in Windmill Street. The musicians were approached by a young fan and wheeler-dealer called Harry Morris and it was his suggestion that they form themselves into two bands – the Ronnie Scott Sextet and the Johnny Dankworth Quartet – and use one of the rehearsal rooms in Windmill Street and turn it into a jazz club. In his autobiography, Dankworth recalled their first night:

As the evening went on it became obvious that young London had thronged to hear us, and during the ensuing months our once-weekly appearances were doubled and then tripled to satisfy the burgeoning demand. News of Club Eleven spread rapidly, first to the music papers, then to the record companies.

(Dankworth 1998, 62)

And later:

Over the months and indeed years that followed the Club Eleven became synonymous with progressive jazz thinking in Britain – a sort of jazz Bauhaus. Visiting musicians and critics from overseas dropped in to listen or jam. Saxophonist Spike Robinson, then resplendent in a US Navy uniform complete with bell-bottoms, was one. Another was legendary pianist-composer Tadd Dameron, whom I remember vividly as he gamely battled with the beat-up grand piano allotted to my quartet.

(Dankworth 1998, 63)

It is unsurprising that the first formal attempt at teaching these skills and techniques should have occurred in this period. In 1950, guitarist and teacher Ivor Mairants established the Central School of Dance Music in London. Among his teaching staff were John Dankworth, classical clarinettist Jack

Brymer, trumpeter Kenny Baker, guitarists Bert Weedon and Ike Isaacs, and composer–theorist Eric Gilder. Pianist Stan Tracey also taught there, as did drummer Alan Ganley. A number of British guitarists passed through its doors, and pianist and composer Michael Garrick studied with Tracey there (Heining 2006d; Cooper 1998). Despite Mairants's efforts, jazz continued to rely on more informal learning and study practices and it would be thirty years before a major music school in the capital would be willing to countenance the teaching of jazz within its sacred walls. In fact, it was Leeds College of Music in 1965 that was the first British educational establishment to offer such a course.

In his biography of Ronnie Scott, John Fordham conveys very well the impact for Scott and his peers of hearing Charlie Parker for the first time. It was on a Sunday in January 1947 at drummer – and later Esquire Records boss – Carlo Krahmer's flat. Present were Scott, drummers Tony Crombie and Laurie Morgan, guitarist Pete Chilver and bassist Lennie Bush.

> Out of the crackle and hiss came a sudden unison chorus. The tune they were playing seemed familiar, though far more urgent and driving than the idiom from which it had been borrowed and reforged. It swung easily, with that arrogant relaxation Ronnie Scott already knew as a trademark of American jazz. And at the end of the ensemble introduction arose something utterly different, and so bursting with life and tumultuous harmonic complexity as to be unlike any kind of saxophone playing Ronnie Scott had ever heard. (Fordham 1986, 33)

Its effect on Scott was to make him dissatisfied with his extremely well-paid gig with the Ted Heath band and determined to hear this music first hand in New York. He and Tony Crombie made it across the Atlantic that spring and Scott and a bunch of friends joined Geraldo's Navy that summer and again found themselves on 52nd St. On his return, Scott found a temporary home with Tito Burns's sextet. Burns and his group played a strange mixture of styles from old-style showbiz through dance music to jazz. Burns was also an excellent accordionist, whose records have a charm of their own and his instrumental skill was such that he had little difficulty adapting to the presence of nascent beboppers like Scott, Dankworth, trumpeters Denis Rose and Leon Calvert, guitarist Pete Chilver and drummer Tony Crombie. In fact, his group were the first British band to perform bebop on the BBC in 1947.

The important thing to note here is that Scott, Dankworth and the rest built a scene from scratch. As Laurie Morgan notes:

> Our jazz grew up in what you might call a greenhouse. There was nothing outside it that fed us. It was just little groups in Soho meeting up, playing feeding off each other. Nothing being fed

from the outside because we weren't presenting ourselves to the outside in that way. The Dixielanders appealed to ... we used to call them "mouldy fygges". You've heard that phrase. It appealed to the beer drinkers and so on. We had nothing except our own fascination with what we was doing and, when we played, we hired our own places, we did our own sound system, we did our own publicity, we did everything else. Before we even played, we had to set the place up.

(Interview with Laurie Morgan, March 2012)

Jazz is not unique, of course, in this respect. Since the 1950s at least, folk music, which was going through a revival at this point, has relied on both fans and musicians to create its performance spaces, and even its means of dissemination through publications and other media. Like jazz, its record labels' outlets often began with musicians and fans. For Esquire Records established by Carlo Krahmer on 13 December 1947, just substitute Topic Records. Originally set up by the Communist Party-led Workers Music Association in 1939 to sell Soviet and leftist music, by the late 1940s Topic had become a musician-led label pursuing a policy of releasing traditional English, Scottish, Welsh and Irish music. In a similar way, Transatlantic Records began in 1961 importing American jazz, blues and folk music to the UK, but soon branched out into recording artists such as Bert Jansch, John Renbourn and Irish close-harmony group the Johnstons. And as with jazz, folk music has had a similar relationship with the major labels – performers were picked up, if it were believed they would sell records, but dropped when this proved not to be the case.

In these respects and others, jazz and folk music in Britain established similar kinds of scene, often based around pub rooms with clubs run by local fans. They have both benefited from time to time from major label interest but this is not their lifeblood. With other areas of the music business such as pop, rock, light entertainment and classical, certainly in the sixties and at least until recent times, the relationship with the record business has been more or less symbiotic. In fact, the Beatles' success, in effect, created the modern recording industry and, in turn, the pop/rock aristocracy that dominated popular entertainment from the sixties to the mid-nineties. With jazz and folk, there has certainly been in Britain a very different relationship between the musicians and their audience, with the latter often developing the infrastructures for performance, publicity and recording.

The importance of the contribution of this tranche of British modern jazz musicians cannot be underestimated. They were picking up on a musical style from America that was still in its infancy. If one dates the birth of bebop in the USA to 1941/2, Ronnie Scott, Dankworth and others were beginning to fashion their own take on the new form just five or six years later. From the establishment of Club Eleven in 1948 at 41 Great Windmill Street to the opening of Ronnie Scott's Club in Gerrard Street in October 1959, these individuals created a modern jazz scene in Britain, based in Soho, London. Obviously, they were assisted by those like drummer Carlo Krahmer, who established Esquire Records, Emile E. Shalit, the proprietor of Melodisc, and producer Tony Hall of Tempo Records, and also by those various promoters and entrepreneurs, willing to turn a large fortune into a very much smaller one. But it must be stressed that the British modern jazz scene was their creation. It was also their university. And while its location was essentially London-based, those urban areas capable of supporting their own local scene had already begun to do so by 1948. For example, Bill Birch's history of jazz in Manchester, *Keeper Of The Flame: Modern Jazz in Manchester 1946–1972* (Birch 2010), notes that an array of swing-to-modern groups, including vibraphonist/pianist Victor Feldman's Quartet played the city's Astoria ballroom in 1948, while the whole of the Club Eleven line-up played Manchester in June and December 1949.

Dankworth's first record date took place when he was seventeen, Ronnie Scott's when he was nineteen. Kenny Graham had a slightly later start and first went into the studio with Nat Gonella when he was twenty-two, having served during the war. Tubby Hayes was just sixteen when he cut "I Only Have Eyes for You/I Can't Get Started" with Kenny Baker, while bassist Lennie Bush's first session was when he was nineteen. The majority of musicians, like Bill Le Sage, Tony Kinsey, Phil Seamen and Tony Crombie, who came through from 1945/6 to the early fifties, had been playing for several years before making their first recordings in their early twenties, with one or two like Stan Tracey and drummer Bobby Orr being, for various reasons, a little older. These were young men, who had several years behind them in music but they were also taking up a style of jazz they had had no part in developing and to which their access was limited. They were learning on the job.

Listening to the records they made, as they took their first steps into modern jazz, is inevitably a mixed experience. In a way, they were seeking to acquire a second language that came from a very different cultural background to their own. Intriguingly, they were doing so at pretty much the same time that Barber, Webb, Lyttelton, Colyer and others were exploring an earlier dialect of that language. One might read Ken Colyer's sojourn in New Orleans and Lyttelton's trip to Nice in 1948 to hear his heroes in person as a parallel to the engagements of Scott, Tracey and others on the transatlantic boats. Charly Records' four-volume set, *Bebop in Britain*, provides a valuable insight into the attempts of the groups of Dankworth, Scott, Kenny Graham, Tito Burns and Vic Lewis to grasp the new vernacular. One can already hear a number of musicians beginning to develop a style of their own and perhaps one or two writers just beginning to find their compositional voice.

The earliest tunes on the record – "Lady Be Good", "What Is This Thing Called Love?", "Boppin' at Esquire" and "Idabop" by the Esquire Five with Ronnie Scott on tenor, Pete Chilver on guitar, Ralph Sharron (later to work for Tony Bennett) on piano, bassist Jack Fallon and Carlo Krahmer on drums – were recorded in January 1948. The latest tracks – this time featuring the Ronnie Scott Orchestra and including drummer Tony Crombie, Scottish trumpeter Jimmy Deuchar, bassist Lennie Bush and altoist Derek Humble – were released in summer 1953. In a way, comparing those early efforts with the music coming out of the jazz clubs in New York misses the point. The 52nd Street crowd reign supreme. These early British modernists need to be judged instead on the progress that they were making, both as imitators and in developing a local approach to the music. This is, after all, a work in progress. But jump just five or six years further to 1957 and listen to Dizzy Reece's appropriately titled *Progress Report* (Tempo; Mosaic) and any head-master would surely speak well of his charges.

Reece came to Britain in 1948 from Jamaica having studied at that fine musical academy in Kingston, the Alpha Boys School. Reece also spent quite an amount of time playing in Europe, in particular in Paris, with various visiting or expatriate Americans like saxophonist Don Byas and drummer Kenny Clarke. He was gifted with a strong, full tone and was capable of daz-zling flights of melodic ingenuity. He moved to New York in 1959, where his subsequent fortunes proved to be quite mixed. By most accounts, he was not an easy individual to work with and was quite scathing at times of some of the British musicians he played with. In the sleevenotes to his US LP from 1962, *Asia Minor*, he complains: "I always had trouble with rhythm sec-tions over there though. Rhythm sections are supposed to accompany and I don't think they were always aware of that." That caveat aside, the music on *Progress Report* and also his previous album for Tempo, *A New Star* (Tempo; Jasmine) reveal the extent of Reece's rapid advances and those of his British colleagues. Compare Reece's version of Parker's "Scrapple from the Apple" with Bird's 1947 original. It does not have that easy, loping groove of the Parker's band, but it swings and has a harder edge, more in common with the emerging hard bop of Blakey, Cannonball Adderley and Lee Morgan. Ronnie Scott plays on this tune and both he and Reece sound confident and assured. Listening to the version of "Now's the Time" (also a Parker tune) from *A New Star*, the ensembles do sound slightly ragged, but the interplay between Reece and Tubby Hayes is exceptional in quality and there is an excellent solo from drummer Bill Eyden. This track was apparently taped at the end of another session and was essentially a jam where producer Tony Hall had allowed the tape to keep running. Better yet is the version of "Yardbird Suite" from *Top Trumpets* (Tempo; Jasmine), with a strong rhythm section featur-ing Terry Shannon, one of the most underrated pianists of the period, Lennie Bush on bass and Phil Seamen on drums.

Ronnie Scott's *Presenting the Ronnie Scott Sextet* (Fontana), recorded early in 1957, shows a similar advance in competence and confidence. As well as standards such as Ellington's "It Don't Mean a Thing", "Polka Dots and Moonbeams" and "All This and Heaven Too", there are four tunes by trumpeter Jimmy Deuchar, who also took care of the arrangements. It is not by any means an Earth-shattering set but the playing is increasingly assertive from a very strong front line of Scott on tenor, Deuchar and altoist Derek Humble. The record owes a lot to Deuchar's writing, who later moved to Germany, as did Humble, to work with and arrange for the Kurt Edelhagen band. "Pittsburgh Opener" and "Bass House" are two fine pieces by Deuchar with some very fine playing, while "It Don't Mean a Thing" is performed at a furious pace with some bold, forthright solos from Scott, Humble, Deuchar and Seamen. As for Scott's ballad feature, "All This and Heaven Too", this provides further evidence of his growth as a musician. These two albums were by no means exceptions. Dankworth's 5 *Steps To Dankworth* (Parlophone; Vocalion) from 1957 gave clear indication of his growing assurance as a bandleader and composer but also, in the small group settings of trumpeter Dickie Hawdon's Quintet and trombonist Laurie Monk's Quartet (a piano-less group), of his skill as a soloist. The lovely "Somerset Morn" remains a glorious example of his ability as a performer. Even though tenorist Don Rendell was to become an even mightier musical prospect in the sixties and seventies, *Don Rendell Presents The Jazz Six* (Nixa; Vocalion) recorded in 1957 is by any standards a very good record, with powerful performances from Canadian trumpeter Kenny Wheeler and baritone saxophonist Ronnie Ross. Rendell's *Roarin'* (Jazzland; BGP) featuring Graham Bond on alto from 1961 is even better, with Bond's wild, aggressive playing a dynamic foil for Rendell's beautifully graceful approach to the saxophone.

But perhaps the most popular group in Britain in the late fifties was the Jazz Couriers. Run jointly by Ronnie Scott and Tubby Hayes, the Couriers released three albums – *In Concert* (Tempo), *The Last Word* (Tempo) and *The Couriers of Jazz* (London). All three, in particular *In Concert*, come highly recommended, and the majority of tracks the group recorded can be found on CD. Perhaps the music they played – like that of their peers – remained subservient to an American model, but it was developing and beginning to show that it could find its own voice. More than that, real problems arise if the argument that British jazz of this period was a more or less slavishly copied, perhaps misunderstood, form removed from its cultural and socio-economic roots is pursued too rigorously. Taken *ad absurdum*, we would be obliged to continue to dismiss later British jazz in the same way and conclude that it could never be anything more than the sincerest form of flattery. However, if we accept that British jazz did make major progress in the sixties and developed a local style of its own, then we need to account for that development. Did British musicians suddenly discover the secret of making modern jazz? Did some revolution take place or another generation simply arise that was able to do justice to British jazz? Such assertions simply do not hold water. Here, a developmental process, with success building upon success, with the acquisition of new knowledge gained through experimentation and experience and through closer contact with the originators of this music and their successors is more than enough to account for the progress made by Dankworth, Scott, Hayes, Tracey and others.

On the other hand, if we argue in favour of the validity of British jazz as an inevitable development in the music and of its continuing internationalization, we still need to address issues regarding its aesthetic content compared with the African-American original. And it would be ridiculous to suggest that British musicians and the records that they made in the fifties were the equal of those of Parker and Gillespie. But a careful and fair hearing given to records made by Ronnie Scott and Tubby Hayes, Dankworth, Dizzy Reece and Tony Kinsey in the early fifties reveals more than just youthful enthusiasm. Furthermore, catch those same artists a few years later and the progress that they made is quite astonishing.

With hindsight, the most important breakthrough in British modern jazz came with a series of records that Joe Harriott made for Denis Preston in the early sixties. Arguably, Harriott's advances were not seen as such at that time in all sections of the jazz community. The saxophonist's career is considered in more detail later. However, the enormous strides he made around the turn of the decade need to be considered here. As Alan Robertson (Robertson 2003) points out, Harriott elaborated his own ideas about creating a free form of jazz while in a sanatorium recovering from tuberculosis. Coleridge Goode, bassist with the Joe Harriott Quintet, remembers hearing him play for the first time:

> I joined Tito Burns and one of the first gigs I did with Tito was a concert at St. Pancras Town Hall. We were the main band and in the interval this other band came on and in it was a saxophonist who was playing terrific stuff in the style of Charlie Parker and we had never heard that before. They were a band from Jamaica and the name Joe Harriott came up. I didn't actually meet him then but the impression he made was very solid indeed.
> (Interview with Coleridge Goode, May 2008)

A short while later that Harriott sat in with a group involving pianist Alan Clare, Coleridge Goode and drummer Bobby Orr. It was after this meeting that Harriott asked the bass player, and also Orr, to join the group he was forming. As Goode emphasizes, not only was what Harriott proposed with his notion of free form jazz revolutionary, the fact that it worked as it did owed much to the calibre of the musicians in the quintet.

> I couldn't imagine how this could possibly work. I had no idea and I remember when I was driving him to a gig in Frankfurt, he put this idea to me and I said I couldn't see how the bass would work with this and his reply was more or less, "You could always play diminished runs". I remember thinking, "You mean I'm going to

have to spend my life playing diminished runs?" (laughing) Once, he brought the draft of his first composition like this I began to hear more or less what was required and so did all the others because they were all wonderful musicians. The sum total of our experiences in music gave us the chance and the way to find a way to do it.

And he adds of the experience:

It was exciting. I mean you were actually the composer at the same time because the ideas came entirely from you being suggested by whatever else was happening in the group. We were constantly supplying each other with what to play next. It demanded absolute concentration and ability. People can play their instruments but when they need to do something off the cuff, can they just do it? This is what was demanded by that music.

(Interview with Coleridge Goode, May 2008)

Hilary Moore in *Inside British Jazz* (2007) makes the same point. Her book is in fact a fine, scholarly read, which uses sociological terminology sparingly and only where necessary. And it offers remarkable insights into its subject, and in particular, Joe Harriott's music:

This performance of roles must not be mistaken for the predefined role playing of traditional jazz. The percussion is not the timekeeper. The bass and piano are not providing the harmonic underlay. The piano's chords, far from offering a traditional harmonic base, add colour in counterpoint to the harmonic implications of the other instruments. The horns are not providing the melodies. Their roles have been carved more freely and with more equivalence. Coleridge Goode uses Bach as an analogy to explain the concept. The five instruments, while providing different flavours from different directions at different moments, are in counterpoint with one another rather than harmony. There are five melodic instruments, all providing rhythmic and harmonic impetus. The roles are both different and equal.

(Moore 2007, 75–6)

It is generally accepted in some quarters that Harriott evolved his "free form" concept autonomously from that of Ornette Coleman in the USA (Litweiler 1990; Robertson 2003). Coleman's records were not readily available in the UK until after Harriott's *Free Form* (Jazzland) was recorded in 1960 and Coleman's *Free Jazz* was made a month later than the Harriott album. Moore makes a distinction between the two records that is potentially helpful in this context:

It will become clear that Coleman's structuring of *Free Jazz* champions the individual's right to complete musical freedom, while Harriott develops a method of spontaneous composition that is arguably more communally-minded.   (Moore 2007, 70)

In a complex argument, Moore locates these differences in the contrasting ideological conditions in which they were both made. She makes a number of points that will be re-examined later but, briefly, she contrasts the situation of African-Americans involved in, at times, a life or death struggle for basic civil rights with that of black people like Harriott, Goode and the group's trumpeter, Shake Keane, who had emigrated from the Caribbean islands to the UK, as centre of the British Commonwealth. She does not ignore the pernicious and sometimes virulent racism of many white British people that was expressed towards such immigrants. But she emphasizes that there are marked differences between situations of formal and enforced segregation and the informal, everyday prejudice encountered by black people. She also, without "psychologising" Harriott, notes aspects of his personality that stood him apart from both mainstream white society and the Caribbean community of London. As she implies above, Coleman's *Free Jazz* in one sense paralleled the assertion of African-Americans of their right to the same dignity and individual freedoms guaranteed to white Americans. For Moore, Harriott's *Free Form* is simultaneously his claim to be seen as an original artist and thinker and, unconsciously maybe, an expression of a longing for belonging and community (Moore 2007, 79–80; Goode and Cotterell 2003, 120).

However, the argument that Harriott evolved his approach without any regard for that of Ornette Coleman is not accepted by all scholars. Alyn Shipton, for example, offers a somewhat different take on this matter:

The biggest event in contemporary jazz was Coleman's debut in New York on November 17, 1959 and it was widely reported. I can't imagine Harriott not being aware of it, as his ear was close to the ground. My view is that Harriott would have been aware of what Ornette was doing. He may not have heard much of it but I wouldn't mind betting that it was the rumours coming from L.A. and then NY that prompted that conversation with Coleridge in the car from Frankfurt. So, at one level, you're probably right about independent "development" but I think it was not something that happened in complete isolation.

The point here is that the album *Free Jazz* is not the place to look in Ornette's work for parallels with Harriott. The double quartet format, the experiments with playing in time between Haden and LaFaro, the conjunction of Cherry and Hubbard, the jousting of Ornette and Dolphy are about something different – similar territory to that explored by Coltrane in *Ascension*. The place to look is in the quintet with Paul Bley, whose role is similar to that of Pat Smythe and the quartet sessions from *Tomorrow is the Question* onwards. Ornette's quartet was underpinned by musical theory. I have discussed racism with Ornette and he has linked it to aspects of his early career and his decision to adopt the alto rather than the tenor but whenever we talked of the quartet – and the same is true of my discussions with Charlie Haden – he has always discussed it in terms of musical theory.

(Interview via e-mail with Alyn Shipton, May 2011)

Such differences of opinion as to its "originality" or "independence" aside, the music on *Free Form* is exquisitely beautiful. There are few sounds in jazz as achingly touching and expressive as that of Harriott's alto, but this record is so much more than leader plus sidemen. There is an intricacy to the performances that does, as Goode has suggested, recall Bach, and it seems to fit together like few other free jazz sets. There is a shared recognition that "abstraction" in this context does not mean "without form" but rather it replaces pre-arranged or pre-determined form with emergent form. To explain his ideas, Harriott referred to painting. In the liner notes of *Free Form*, he states, "We are attempting to paint sounds, colours, and effects." In those for its successor, *Abstract* (Columbia), he expands on this theme:

It is best listened to as a series of different pictures – for it is after all by definition an attempt in free improvisation to paint, as it were, freely in sound. My contention is that the pictures thus evolved should be taken as the audience hears them, not in relation to anything else.

Free Form was the first genuinely distinctive and ground-breaking British jazz release. It heralds a music that speaks on its own terms and, as both Robertson and Moore suggest, Harriott himself saw it as a challenge to an American dominance in jazz. Featuring, as well as Harriott and Goode, trumpeter Shake Keane, drummer Phil Seamen and Scottish pianist Pat Smythe, it has that perfect ebb and flow of great art. There is also more than a hint of the musical styles of Harriott's Jamaica. It is most obvious on "Calypso", but is also present in the bubbling, skipping style of the opening track, "Formation". Perhaps Brubeck, George Russell or even Lennie Tristano might have come up with the perverse angularity of "Coda" with its gorgeous piano solo from Smythe and the way the horns hover like a Greek chorus from time to time. However, there are few other jazz musicians from America who might have come up with something that so clearly owes its inspiration to European art music. Elsewhere, the fast bop-derived lines of Keane's trumpet on "Abstract" over Goode's liquid, flowing bass and amazingly loose drumming from Seamen, dissolve quickly into Harriott's declamatory alto before the brief entry of Smythe's piano. Nothing lasts. Nothing is fixed. Its allusions to bop are oblique and almost ironic and at times there is an almost burlesque quality to these pieces. This is incredibly confident music played with rare skill. As for "Calypso", it recalls Harriott's earlier piece "Revival", which had been recorded by both Harriott and Chris Barber, in its roots in Caribbean popular and folk forms. But it also represents an advance on the earlier tune. The playing is looser with the form and structure guiding but not determining the performances. Smythe's role is no longer that of comping behind the front line, who improvise singly and together. His choice of chords and notes is much more open and interesting being no longer limited to those suggested by the harmonic sequence of the track. Seamen's role has shifted from time-keeping and at times it is almost as if he is now part of the front line. As for Coleridge Goode, he seems to imply the pulse rather than state and restate it for the other musicians. In fact, it is his playing alone that provides the sense of linear progression on "Calypso". He provides the gravitational pull while the others orbit around him.

This track is significant for other reasons, namely in its use of non-African-American folk forms. It allows for the possibility of jazz styles that are derived from other sources. The Swedish baritone saxophonist Lars Gullin had already begun to use Nordic folk music as the inspirational foundation for his music in the 1950s. Django Reinhardt's music had also combined jazz and gypsy styles to great effect. And Harriott was not alone in this respect in the UK. We have already noted Chris Barber's desire to move beyond the imitation of New Orleans jazz and create something that reflected its situation in a British context. But pianist Michael Garrick, who would later use both Harriott and Keane in his sextet, expresses a very similar point:

> I wasn't born in Chicago or New Orleans but in Enfield. What's our background? Maybe It's Because I'm A Londoner? (laughing) I thought, "Well, I love some English Folk Music." So, I did little arrangements of these English Folk Songs.   (Heining 2003a)

Garrick's point is well made, and echoes Chris Barber's wish to create an authentic British jazz. Jazz is, after all, a music that has always concerned itself with authenticity. While the impetus or demand for this has sometimes come from critics and fans (often white), it has also come from musicians, both black and white. Jazz is a music that has at least some of its roots in traditional folk forms, both African and European. If, as seems supportable by evidence, Britain was one of the first countries outside the USA to develop its own style and approach to jazz, then it was partly because its musicians grasped this imperative. What is more, assuming this to be the case, Britain was unusually well placed to do so.

Britain had experienced several folk revivals. Interestingly, the first of these took place between 1890 and 1920, and involved, as well as British

Joe Harriott with the Chris Barber Band, 1959. Left to right: Chris Barber (trombone), Pat Halcox (trumpet), Graham Burbidge (drums), Joe Harriott (alto sax), Monty Sunshine (clarinet). Photograph © Terry Cryer (tac).

composers Ralph Vaughan Williams and George Butterworth, musician and researcher Lucy Broadwood and musicologist Cecil Sharp, the American professor of music Francis James Child and the Australian composer Percy Grainger, both of whom were resident in Britain during this period. Vaughan Williams – like other composers influential in the development of a British pastoral style of classical musical such as Gustav Holst, Charles Wood and Geoffrey Shaw – was taught by Sir Charles Villiers Stanford. It was Stanford who, along with his pupil Geoffrey Shaw, compiled the 1905 *National Song Book – A Complete Collection of the Folk-Songs, Carols and Rounds suggested by the Board of Education* (Stanford and Shaw 1905). This became the *New National Song Book* in 1938 and remains in print today. It was hugely influential in the teaching of music in primary and secondary schools well into the 1960s. In fact, in many schools, it provided the sole subject material for music lessons. This book and the 1959 *Penguin Book of English Folk Songs* compiled by Vaughan Williams and singer and musicologist A.L. Lloyd have both had a profound influence on music in Britain.

Baritone saxophonist John Surman is just one British jazz musician for whom indigenous folk music has been a significant influence. Interviewed for *Jazzwise* in 2009, while he was working on a new project in Norway, where he now lives with his partner singer Karin Krog, he acknowledged this point:

> Yes, you could say that my roots are showing. (laughing) It's not been a conscious move but it's a fact of life that I was brought up on the English National Song Book and those kind of folk melodies and I've been listening to them again over the last couple of days in Rainbow Studios. When my back is to the wall, what am I going to play? I start to hear these lyrical, rather English-sounding folk songs. They may be bit Scottish or a bit Irish but that is the music that I came from and it's not surprising. Equally, it's not surprising that somebody who comes from Chicago plays blues. That is their music. That's what they've heard and that's ingrained in their soul and I think that other stuff is ingrained in my soul. It's just the jazz form, that kind of improvised collectivism, that I got introduced to that gave me the opportunity of expressing that music.   (Heining 2009c)

What we are seeing is a coming together of distinctive trends and imperatives. The desire to forge a new British jazz was one of these but, in order for the musicians to achieve that, they must look to other sources of reference, ones which would draw on native sources such as British folk songs. With Harriott and others coming from the Caribbean and elsewhere in the Commonwealth, other forms were available as material from which to fashion a British approach. Obviously, Britain was the centre of the Empire and, after the Second World War, of the Commonwealth. After the war, Britain saw several fresh waves of immigration from different parts of the Commonwealth, but even prior to that people had come from India, Africa and the Caribbean to work and study in England. Coleridge Goode was one example of the musicians and entertainers from Jamaica and elsewhere who had settled in the UK (Moore 2007). Within a decade or so, Britain had "welcomed" workers from all points of the globe and they had brought with them their social customs and their culinary, musical and literary arts. Britain's history and culture was different from that of the USA. It was inevitable, therefore, that its own folk traditions and those of the countries of the Commonwealth would affect the way it interpreted and developed the form that jazz would take here.

Returning to our theme of education, we have seen that the Scott/Hayes generation of British modernists were, in the main, largely self-educated in jazz and music. This reflected their educational and class experiences to a very large extent. Their access, pre-Butler, to secondary education was limited, and they left school at the earliest opportunity. Harriott's group of musicians provide an intriguing contrast to this. Harriott himself was educated at the Alpha Boys School in Kingston, Jamaica. Although established as a "school for wayward boys" in 1880, it gave its pupils an amazing musical education, and its alumni include Harold McNair, Dizzy Reece, Rico Rodriguez, Cedric Brooks and numerous reggae stars, including four founding members of the Skatalites. However, three of the musicians in his quintet were university educated. Coleridge Goode studied electrical engineering in Glasgow, pianist Pat Smythe was a law graduate and ex-solicitor who had studied at both Oxford and Edinburgh universities, and Shake Keane came to Britain to study literature at University College London. In this respect, the group was quite different from others in terms of the educational level of its members and, in a way, it had more in keeping with some of the groups and artists who would begin to come through later in the decade.

One such group was the rightly feted Don Rendell–Ian Carr Quintet. Formed late in 1962, the quintet's first album *Shades of Blue* (Columbia; BGO) was not issued until 1965. An earlier recording made in January 1964 remained unissued until 2000, when Spotlite Jazz released it with additional live tracks from the group's 1968 Antibes Festival performance. The Rendell–Carr Quintet's first pianist was John Burch, who was followed by Colin Purbrook. Purbrook left in 1964/5 and was replaced by Michael Garrick. It was Garrick's arrival that helped the group discover its own style, with a personnel that included one of Britain's finest ever rhythm sections in bassist Dave Green and drummer Trevor Tomkins. Don Rendell is quite clear that his group's distinctive sound was a consequence of a distinctive combination of musical personalities.

> It was really quite unique and quite brave in a way because we had so many originals with Michael Garrick writing, Ian writing and me writing. It was just amazing how we suddenly found that we'd gone a whole concert without using a standard. It was not designed you understand. It just happened. I think you've got to say that it was because we were all such mixed personalities. I mean, I'd been a professional musician twenty years because I turned professional at the age of sixteen in 1943. I was like the senior statesman of the band and Ian and Michael were both of a similar age and both university people. Dave Green was much younger and so was Trevor Tomkins and they weren't university people. They were just grammar school boys. I felt the university influence, I felt that from Ian Carr and Mike Garrick. It was like

five pretty different people pitched together and I think a lot of chemistry came out of the conflict of personalities.

(Heining 2004b, 14)

Rendell's comments are incredibly insightful. Garrick and Carr brought the influence of a university education to the group. Though they had not gone on to further study, Tomkins and Green were beneficiaries of the Butler Act and its provision of secondary education, unlike their older statesman boss, who left school at fourteen. Education does not just teach one how to spell experience. It provides a framework within which to interpret and understand it. Noting this takes nothing away from Don Rendell or from Scott, Hayes or Stan Tracey. If anything, it makes their achievements all the more remarkable. Yet, as Rendell suggests, the coming of a new, formally and more broadly educated generation of musicians brought with it new ideas and perspectives that would help to change British jazz. The impetus to create a distinctly British jazz was already present in the generation of musicians who came through in the fifties. The source material that would allow it to emerge was to be found partly in British musical traditions but also in the musics of the Caribbean, the Indian sub-continent and Africa that could now be heard in the UK as a result of post-war immigration.

The group's second album, *Dusk Fire* (Columbia; BGO), was many things. It showed a group coming of age and revealed how British jazz was acquiring its own identity. But most importantly, in terms of our discussion, it pulled together influences from American sources and others, such as those from India and the Middle East, that had become part of a London soundtrack that might include jazz, pop and classical music, but also British folk music, Jamaican bluebeat and ska, west African high-life, and Indian ragas and talas. And in this respect and in bringing together musicians from different educational backgrounds, the Rendell–Carr group, the "Five" as it was known to fans, was a microcosm of the changing face of British jazz and of British society.

Both the Labour and Tory post-war governments invested in higher education and opened it up to the bright and able of all classes. To do so made sound economic sense and reflected a concern that Britain should not lag behind its economic competitors, in particular in the areas of science and technology. But it did not quite happen as planned, and the picture that emerges requires careful examination in order for it to make sense. As is so often the reality with social change and social legislation, their effects are variable and inconsistent in their outcome. In some ways, that it did not go entirely according to plan may even have benefited British jazz.

Spending on higher education rose in real terms from £90 million in 1954/5 to £219 million in 1962/3. In that same period, the number of university places rose from 82,000 to 118,000. Between 1938 and 1962, the number of seventeen-year-olds in higher education had increased from 4 per cent of that age group to 15 per cent. On the other hand, education did not prove to be quite the great leveller in terms of social class or gender. The percentage of male undergraduates with fathers in manual occupations actually remained constant between 1947 and 1961, though the figures for females did show an improvement. Students from Social Classes I and II continued to be proportionately over-represented in higher education, as did those from direct grant and independent schools (Halsey 1972, chapter 7, in particular 193, 206, 219, 221). Additionally, while the percentage of students studying science and technology did increase between 1951 and 1961 by 22 per cent for men and 27 per cent for women and between 1961 and 1968 by 15 per cent and 3 per cent, respectively, the number of arts and social science places remained very steady during that same period (Halsey 1972, 223). The biggest decline in student numbers came in the area of medicine.

These figures do not take account of non-university colleges, such as polytechnics, teachers training and arts schools, who also offered degree and higher diploma courses. Polytechnics were set up in part with the intention that they should help bridge the technology gap and yet, in a consumer-oriented and demand-led educational economy, these institutions actually increased the number of arts and social science places to meet demand and were, of course, funded accordingly (Sandbrook 2006, 426–9). Increased educational spending might have increased the number of science and technology graduates, but it also increased opportunities to study at degree level in the arts and social sciences. To an extent, it was a case of two steps forward and one step back. Education was not really opened up to anything like the extent hoped – bright children continued to fail within the system and the chances of going on to higher education remained skewed in favour of those from direct grant and public schools (see Halsey *et al.* 1980). Nevertheless, it certainly did open up higher education to students from less well-off middle- and working-class backgrounds, who otherwise would not have gone to university. Some children from both the working and lower-middle classes clearly did benefit as individuals from access to grammar schools and many from all classes benefited from an expanding university and higher education system. Both Carr and Garrick were classic examples of this, as were composer–bandleader Mike Westbrook, saxophonists John Surman, Mike Osborne and many others. To these names we can add saxophonists Stan Sulzmann, Dick Heckstall-Smith, Evan Parker and Barbara Thompson, trumpeter Henry Lowther, bassists Dave Holland, Barry Guy, Gill Alexander, Rick Laird and Chris Laurence, vibes player/composer Frank Ricotti, bandleaders Neil Ardley, John Warren, John Williams and Alan Cohen, pianists Howard Riley, Pete Lemer, Roger Dean, Brian Priestley, Pete Jacobsen, Dudley Moore, Mike Ratledge, Karl Jenkins and John Horler, violinist Phil Wachsmann, trombonists Paul Nieman and drummer Nic France. In addition, several key players on the free jazz/ improvisation side of the music met and played together in Royal Air Force

(RAF) bands. These included John Stevens, Trevor Watts, Bob Downes, Paul Rutherford and Chris Pyne, while drummer Tony Oxley studied music in the Black Watch and both Jeff Clyne and Graham Collier were band-boys in the army. Collier went from there to study at Berklee School of Music in Boston. Additionally, vocalist Norma Winstone had studied in her teens at Trinity College of Music. This list is not exhaustive. Graduates, or at least those who had gone to university, were to play a larger and larger role within British jazz.

The entry into any workforce of a large number of more formally educated, more generally literate (and literary) workers must inevitably impact on what is produced whether this is in engineering, manufacturing or the arts. In terms of jazz, this is not about making value judgements about the quality or intellectual capacities of non-university educated musicians. Instead, it is a question of interpreting and understanding how education might have impacted upon those who were to become the most important figures in the music and how that might have resulted in the development of the music. And those developments can in turn be located in a broader range of cultural references and a more obviously "British" jazz, one that was infused by other ethnic musical identities coming from those countries with which Britain had strong ties.

Three records point us in that direction – Stan Tracey's *Jazz Suite – Under Milk Wood* (Columbia; Resteamed), John Surman's *How Many Clouds Can You See* (Deram) and Mike Osborne's *Outback* (Turtle; FMR). Tracey's quartet of that time comprised Scottish saxophonist Bobby Wellins, bassist Jeff Clyne and drummer Jackie Dougan. With Laurie Morgan in place of Dougan on drums, much the same group had recorded under the name of the New Departures Quartet the previous year. All were largely self-taught and schooled on the bandstand. New Departures, however, was a venture that had begun with poet Michael Horovitz at Oxford University; along with fellow poet Pete Brown, Horovitz had pioneered an approach to the arts linking poetry and jazz that was distinct from the endeavour that had been started by poet Jeremy Robson and Michael Garrick. By its very nature, New Departures drew on a broad artistic palette that brought together jazz, classical music and blues along with literature, theatre and even fine art. It was saxophonist Bobby Wellins who got Stan Tracey involved in the Horovitz/ Brown adventure, as the pianist recalled:

> I think it was through Bobby that I met Michael Horovitz. I can't be sure because it was in the late fifties and I don't have vivid recollections of things that were happening fifty years ago. But since I was working with Bobby at that time, I rather fancy that he knew Michael before I did, so that's how I got into it.
>
> (Interview with Stan Tracey, December 2009)

And he admits that he found it a positive experience, a slight reticence in his comments perhaps belying a genuine enthusiasm:

> Well, I enjoyed it back then, although I don't do much of it now, just the occasional foray with Michael Horovitz. I still enjoy doing it. I enjoy everything I do because anything that I don't fancy I don't do. I have to end up enjoying it. It's terrible.
>   (Interview with Stan Tracey, December 2009)

Bobby Wellins remembers that writer/producer Victor Schonfield initiated the New Departures Quartet record:

> Well, Victor encouraged a great deal of that and Stan and I were already performing with Michael Horovitz and Pete Brown doing background music to their librettos. So, we were quite involved and that's why Victor was involved because they were all friends. We had Laurie Morgan on drums and Jeff Clyne was on bass at the time. It was a sort of attempt at being more adventurous with things.   (Interview with Bobby Wellins, September 2009)

Though they did also perform numbers from their normal set, the set-up at New Departures gigs was that the musicians improvised to the poets' reading, as Wellins explains. Working in this way was a challenge, and Wellins's comments also reveal his questioning of his own abilities that the experience prompted:

> No, we just played. We didn't write anything. The venues that we played with Pete Brown and Michael Horovitz, they were places that we had never worked before. That was a different kind of thing than we had done. But we all got on quite well together. For my part it didn't last that long. I stopped doing it because I wasn't going anywhere. I stopped because I didn't feel that I had enough of the skills to improvise freely and make it interesting. I needed a lot more ability to achieve that. That was what I felt at the time.
>   (Interview with Bobby Wellins, September 2009)

The New Departures Quartet album (Transatlantic) is almost as good as *Under Milk Wood*. Wellins's folk-inflected melodies, in particular the gorgeous "Culloden Moor", which grew out of an improvisation between Wellins and drummer Morgan (Heining/Morgan), sit well with Tracey's Monk and Ellington influences and with a rhythm section that essays both with ease. But *Under Milk Wood* is just as much a calling card for British jazz as Joe Harriott's *Free Form*. *The Penguin Guide To Jazz On CD* describes it beautifully:

It remains one of the most distinctive records of its era, a setting of Dylan Thomas which uses spare, unadorned jazz materials to somehow evoke the eccentric light of the original play. A pioneering work which is a rare instance of jazz accommodating an outside inspiration in a way that honours the qualities of each side of the equation. (Cook and Morton 2000, 1476)

One might qualify their "rare" with the addition of "for the time" and note that this was not a "setting" as such, otherwise their comments cannot be faulted. As Tracey explains:

It came about through accident. I was supposed to record a quartet album for Lansdowne studios. We weren't happy with what we did. It was a run-of-the-mill type thing playing standards or whatever. We weren't happy with that and it was suggested that I should find a subject to write for and, at that time, I was just becoming familiar with *Under Milk Wood*. So, I chose *Under Milk Wood* as a vehicle and wrote the tunes, went in and recorded it and never expected much to happen.
(Interview with Stan Tracey, December 2009;
see also sleeve notes to Blue Note 789449)

Tracey expresses amazement at its success at the time and subsequently. It is, however, something he chooses not to analyse. "No, I don't. I wouldn't be able to work that one out. I wouldn't even go there," as he said in an interview in 2008 (Heining 2006d). Bobby Wellins, nevertheless, has a number of pertinent comments to make:

It wasn't till some time later as far as I was concerned when we were invited to a performance of *Under Milk Wood* and they used the track in the background. It was in this theatre at the back of Warren Street tube station. They then played "Penpals" in the interval and as it was playing Stan and I kind of looked at each other as if to say, "That's quite a nice record". I don't think at the time we were aware that it was a landmark of any description. I think the person who did was Jackie Tracey [Tracey's wife] because Jackie was at the absolute top of her profession as a P.R. lady for various top people. If it hadn't been for her, I don't think *Under Milk Wood* would have got the same exposure as it did, but it certainly put us on the map.
(Interview with Bobby Wellins, September 2009)

So, how is it "British"? First of all, there is its choice of subject matter. Second, there is its deliberate evocation of a world and terrain that is self-consciously

Welsh, but would apply equally to small town or village life anywhere in mainland Britain during the fifties or sixties. Thomas's characters and all their eccentricities are immediately familiar to any of us who have lived outside larger urban conurbations. It is not that cities do not have their share of eccentrics and oddballs or that such individuals no longer exist, but more that they are less noticeable among larger populations. At that time, distinctions between country and urban life were less blurred and far more differentiated. Third, and more than both the above, is the sense that Tracey is building upon all his previous experiences, which include non-American, British light entertainment and dance music as well as jazz, and that these have been distilled into this moment. Listening to the title track or "Starless and Bible Black" or even "A.M. Mayhems'" wake-up call, it simply does not sound American. And that is no longer a shortcoming but a virtue.

The author and critic, Alyn Shipton offers an additional insight with reference to both the earlier quartet recording and *Under Milk Wood*:

> I think the key to why it works is the way the New Departures group took standards apart. If you listen to "Love With Variations", which is Bobby's layering of an Italian song on top of a very loose interpretation of Fields and McHugh's "I Can't Give You Anything But Love", you'll hear that exactly the same principle is applied to "Cockle Row", which is largely a contrafact of "Sunny Side Of The Street" – also coincidentally by Fields and McHugh. The bravado of Stan's alternative melody matches Bobby's ice-cream van quote on "Love With Variations" and the piece takes on a new and individual life. I think this demonstrates the confidence with which the quartet was building on and departing from the American model. It had the sureness of touch to poke gentle fun at the standards tradition.
>
> (E-mail interview with Alyn Shipton, May 2011)

Would Tracey have come up with the idea without the poetry and jazz experience? The fact remains that, in the course of that involvement with Horovitz and Brown, Tracey and Wellins had somehow become part of an artistic landscape that was now contoured differently and which increasingly crossed divisions of education and, even, class. Even if it had happened without the poetry and jazz connection, its meaning has been altered through association with that context.

In a way, Mike Osborne's *Outback* offers a picture of a different but not unrelated world in microcosm. The choice of personnel for the quintet that perform on the record reflected Ossie's musical partnerships of the period, as well as the breadth of talent from Britain and overseas available to him. With regard to the group's trumpeter Harry Beckett, Osborne had worked in the Barbadian musician's quintet and sextet. The South African Chris McGregor, in whose Brotherhood of Breath Osborne also played, was on piano. The drummer Louis Moholo (now Moholo-Moholo) and bass player Harry Miller were both from South Africa and were Osborne's rhythm team of choice for much of the seventies. Interestingly, both Osborne and McGregor were both from middle-class backgrounds and Osborne had been educated at boarding school and music college, while the others had had very different and much more limited educational experiences. Again, earlier remarks about the Joe Harriott Quintet and Rendell–Carr Quintet apply here.

If we presume that these two long tracks, "So It Is" and "Outback", must therefore contain African, English and Barbadian elements, and possibly those from European art music, as well as American jazz, how do we determine which are which? Indeed, given what we now know of Osborne's underlying mental health problems (see Chapter 7) and the South Africans' experience of exile, where do we locate the emotions that these may have engendered? The answer is a simple one. If the artists have done their job properly, then these influences will have merged into a seamless, expressive whole that speaks firstly of itself. That is what we have here. It is true that listening to Moholo, it is hard to imagine that he came from anywhere other than Africa. But for the rest, what we hear is music in a constant state of flux, in a moment of becoming. It is at times, intensely moving, almost hymn-like and incantational but there is also often a lightness, in particular when Beckett is playing. It can be dark and wayward, when for example Osborne is at his most raw or when McGregor releases one of his wild, percussive, staccato runs. As for the rhythm section of Miller and Moholo, one is aware of the paradox that time is constantly implied without ever being rigorously adhered to. Compare it with whoever you wish from the States and their music of the time – Albert Ayler, Cecil Taylor or Jackie MacLean perhaps. However, this would be solely a listener's reference point rather than an indication of a direct influence on the music. This is mature music that brings together the diversity that underpinned British jazz at this time. And once again, we have that same combination of formally educated players performing alongside those whose education has taken a more personal and less structured course.

This is perhaps suggestive rather than conclusive. To a certain extent, we determine what we hear while we are hearing it. However, there are good reasons why British jazz of this period is now being discovered by a younger generation of American musicians and fans. Difficulty of access is a thing of the past with CDs and the internet, and it forms part of a global, rather than solely American, jazz history. If the comments above in respect of *Under Milk Wood* and *Outback* were accepted, then they would surely be even more true of John Surman's *How Many Clouds Can You See?*

Surman made three records for the Deram label with Peter Eden as producer. The first was the eponymous *John Surman* (Deram; Vocalion), which featured on its first side the jazz-calypso group Surman co-led with

Trinidadian pianist Russell Henderson, and on its second a larger group playing three of the saxophonist's more abstract compositions. The third was the big band/orchestral *Tales Of The Algonquin* (Deram; Vocalion), which was a collaboration with Canadian baritone saxophonist John Warren who composed the music for the album. The latter was as much Warren's record as Surman's. The sheer range of music on *How Many Clouds* makes it arguably more reflective of Surman's work and talent at that point in his career.

It features a mix of personnel over its five tracks. Side one of the original album opens with Surman's octet and the long "Galata Bridge", named after the bridge that links the Galata premonitory with the old citadel of Istanbul. Its inspiration is European but focuses on the point where Europe and Asia meet. The music does contain Middle Eastern elements and the sheer whirling ferocity of Surman's baritone solo hints at Islamic influences but its bedrock seems to lie both in jazz and European music. "Caractacus" follows and draws more on British, perhaps Celtic forms, and is a duet between Surman and drummer Alan Jackson. John Warren's "Premonition" is next. It is performed by a larger, twelve-piece ensemble and features some lovely, lyrical piano from John Taylor. While the rhythm section of Barre Phillips and Tony Oxley are allowed considerable freedom, the structure of the piece seems consciously classical in its form and shape.

The record closes with the title track, a delightful ballad with Surman on soprano, albeit one that also seems to contain folkish elements. But perhaps the most significant piece is the three-section "Event". It begins hauntingly with Surman playing bass clarinet over minimal percussion from Oxley. Baritone is then added via overdubs with both Phillips and Taylor adding oblique commentary. Gradually, the playing comes together, at first loosely so. Phillips' solo bowed bass bridges the first section, "Gathering", and he then leads the group into the powerful and repeating riff that becomes "Ritual" before Oxley's dramatic solo. Tension builds as we begin to move into the final section, "Circle Dance", only to fragment and fracture. It is a remarkable piece of music and a marvellous performance and yet it feels very different from anything in a similar vein that one might hear from the same period from any American artists. More than that, it has begun to explore a territory that owes at least as much to a British and European set of sensibilities as it does to those of African-American-based jazz.

Peter Eden, who also set up his own short-lived Turtle imprint in the early seventies, worked variously for Pye and Decca, as well as running Pye's progressive offshoot, Dawn. Eden had been a pop/rock producer with artists such as Lulu and Donovan, but between 1967 and 1972 he was also responsible for producing a series of very important British jazz albums.

By the mid- to late sixties, Surman was playing in the Mike Westbrook Concert Band, as well as running his own octet and playing with Mike Gibbs and John Warren. He was creating a lot of interest, but had not yet been signed by a record company. Then Eden heard him on a BBC broadcast.

I was producing pop and rock records, then I started to pick up on hearing John Surman. I heard a broadcast and I thought that this is somebody from Britain, who was really ahead of what you'd heard even from America at that time. A couple of weeks later, I picked up *Melody Maker* and there was this poll, and there was John Surman number one baritone in the world! I thought "this is silly". Here's this feller winning this poll and he hasn't got a recording contract. So I rang him up.

(Interview with Peter Eden, February 1996)

A colleague approached Decca and, once the door was open, one of the company's executives, Hugh Mendel, gave Eden carte blanche:

Hugh said, "Go ahead. Just book the studio and do what you want." He never queried anything. He was clever enough to let people get on with it rather than say "we want you to make an album of John Surman plays Bob Dylan".

(Interview with Peter Eden, February 1996)

Eden maintains that their first album together, *John Surman*, sold well, as did the one he made with tenor saxophonist Alan Skidmore, *Once Upon a Time* (Decca Nova; Vocalion). As a result, Eden says that Mendel asked him to produce the second Westbrook record, *Release* in 1968. Surman's role in the process clearly extended beyond that of recording artist, as Eden explains:

Then John said to me, "I'll tell you who else we should record." I said, "Who?" He said, "Mike Gibbs. He's great." So, I did the first Mike Gibbs album. Then we did *Tanglewood '63*. It was John who was saying, "This is good, this is great." They were all good. They were breaking new ground.

(Interview with Peter Eden, February 1996)

Also, according to Eden, when it came to the time to make Surman's third album, with relations with Decca having soured over disagreements regarding the cover and promotion of *How Many Clouds*, the saxophonist gave it over to a collaboration with his friend John Warren. John Surman's very real generosity towards his peers and Eden's modesty aside, it should be noted that the producer was responsible for some eighteen key British jazz recordings of the late sixties and early seventies. These included Mike Westbrook's *Release, Marching Song* and *Love Songs*, Mike Gibbs's *Tanglewood '63*, *Mike Gibbs* and *Just Ahead* (Polydor; BGO uncredited), Alan Skidmore's *Once Upon a Time*, John Taylor's *Pause, and Think Again* (Flight; FMR), Norma Winstone's *Edge of Time* (Argo), Howard Riley's *Flight* (Flight; FMR), Mike Osborne's *Outback*, John Surman's *John Surman, How Many Clouds,*

Westering Home and *Morning Glory* (Island; FMR), the Surman/Warren *Tales of The Algonquin* and the Surman–Barre Phillips–Stu Martin records *The Trio* and *Conflagration* (Dawn; Sanctuary). It is a remarkable track record.

These changes that were taking place in British jazz were midwifed in part by the education system, mirroring as they did the impact of improved educational access in wider British society. However, music schools remained set firm against the intrusion of jazz into their curricula. It was not just that jazz was unacceptable, but even Adolphe Sax's wonderful invention was proscribed. John Dankworth tells a lovely story of his experiences at the Royal Academy of Music:

> One day at rehearsal, the suite L'Arlésienne by Georges Bizet appeared in our folders. Flicking through the pages, I noticed that at one point my part had a cue on it marked "alto sax". I wondered what would happen when we got to that cue. By now I owned an alto sax, but rarely had the courage to bring it within a mile of the academy. When I did, and students enquired about the contents of the longish case, I used to tell them it held a bassoon.
>
> (Dankworth 1998, 36)

When they got to the saxophone section, the conductor asked if anyone owned a such an instrument. Prompted by a fellow student who knew his secret, Dankworth admitted that he did. He was asked to bring it to the next rehearsal. The following week, he played the piece on the saxophone. At the end of the piece, the lecturer said:

> The saxophone is a much maligned instrument. But this is because it is so often unpleasantly played by dance-band and jazz players, who give it a somewhat undeserved bad name. But you have just heard it used by someone who is quite untainted by such undesirable influences, and in consequence has produced the true beauty of which the saxophone is capable.
>
> (Dankworth 1998, 36)

That was in the mid-forties. But even by the mid-sixties things had changed little. As John Surman told me in 1998 recalling his days at the London College of Music studying clarinet, students could not admit to playing saxophone, let alone that they played in a jazz band. Barbara Thompson studied at the Royal College of Music (RCM) around the same time that Surman was at the London College. She says that it would have "horrified" her tutors to know that she played the saxophone.

> It would be have horrified them. Absolutely. I was the first person at the RCM who was a multi-instrumentalist. I went there,

I studied piano, clarinet and I took up flute while I was there. So, it was clarinet, flute and piano and then outside I learnt the saxophone. They'd never met anyone like me before. I don't know why but I was the first of the bunch. Now, of course, they've got saxophone tutors coming out of their ears.

(Interview with Barbara Thompson, March 2010)

As for improvisation, this had no place in any civilized musical form. Barry Guy was already something of a musical polymath by the time he went to the Guildhall School of Music and Drama. On the interview panel was Buxton Ore, one of the more open-minded British composers of the period. To his surprise, Guy was asked to embellish a piece of Mozart.

It might have been "Eine Kleine Nachtmusik" – the main theme – but I can't remember. It was a Mozartian-type piece, which they bashed out on the piano and they said, "That's the tune. Pick that up, play it, embellish it or develop it and come back and make a recapitulation." Well, I picked up the tune alright but I didn't know what to do with it. So, I just did the usual thing. I kind of deconstructed it and, at that point, two of the professors' jaws hit the desk and Buxton had a huge smile on his face. He thought it was a rather novel way of dealing with a bit of Mozart. Anyway, I came back to the theme again but it was a rather circuitous route, but it did the job. So I got in.

(Interview with Barry Guy, November 2010)

He is clear that it was due to Ore that he was admitted. However, improvisation was most definitely not included on the course. As Guy told me:

I think at the Guildhall, it was quietly ignored. It was never taken on board. I tried to get some kind of activity within the Guildhall School of Music itself but I suppose my concentration was primarily on chamber music and contemporary music. All of these activities in improvisation happened outside the institution and I just happened to find that some of the techniques of contemporary music I was involved in jumped ship onto the improvisation side of things.   (Interview with Barry Guy, November 2010)

He adds:

But in terms of the Guildhall, for the four years I was there improvisation was not even thought about with the exception of Buxton Ore, who eventually in the early seventies conducted the London Jazz Composers' Orchestra because we became really good buddies. He was the one amongst the professors who had a huge awareness of the potential of improvisation. Even though he wasn't an improviser himself, he was one of those really open-minded guys. He gave me all the encouragement I needed and filled in lots of bits in-between of the history and also to do with harmonic composition problems. He was the man, a surrogate father in a way. That period was very important for me, that Buxton Ore period.

(Interview with Barry Guy, November 2010)

I think that last point should also be noted. Jazz might have been frowned upon by these institutions and they might have been old-fashioned in their teaching methods; that, however, should not be taken to imply that the education that they offered was without value or that it had little or no impact upon those jazz musicians who studied at these establishments. In fairness, some further education rather than higher education establishments did embrace a broader canvas of styles. For example, mention has already been made of the Leeds College of Music course and Pat Evans, the baritone saxophonist and pianist who was instrumental in the formation of both the National Youth Jazz Orchestra and the Barry Summer School in Wales, taught at Morley College. The avant-garde composer Cornelius Cardew and founder member of the experimental ensemble AMM also taught at Morley in the late sixties. However, the broader educational picture was one that was neither supportive of nor friendly towards jazz.

Pat Evans and Bill Ashton, on the other hand, were two of the first people to recognize the possibility of and potential for teaching jazz. Ashton had studied modern languages at Oxford but worked as musician for several years after leaving university. In 1964, he was working as a supply teacher at Risinghill Comprehensive School in Islington. The school was run by Michael Duane, a man of vision or a naive and foolish individual, depending on one's point of view (see Berg 1969). Duane ran the school along the lines advocated by the controversial educationalist, A.S. Neil. Neil founded Summerhill School in Scotland in 1921 on progressive, non-authoritarian lines based on the ideas of Sigmund Freud, and it was an environment where corporal, or indeed any, punishment was banned and where attendance at lessons was voluntary. While this may sound like outright foolishness, Summerhill is eighty this year and, as recently as 2007, received a good report from Ofsted. It has also been acknowledged by the United Nations Children's Fund (UNICEF) for its treatment of children within its care. Risinghill and Michael Duane were not as fortunate. London County Council closed the school not long after Ashton arrived there.

One of the pupils at the school was Frank Ricotti, then just sixteen years old and a precocious talent on vibraphone, alto saxophone, percussion and piano. Ricotti was already interested in jazz but could find no-one to play with. Prior to this Ashton had had no interest in the idea of jazz education. In fact, even today, after forty-five years in the field, he still does not see himself in such a light.

> There is no magic way of becoming a jazz musician. Jazz educa-tion ... for a long time I never really recognized myself as being involved in jazz education. I've never stood in front of a class room and told people about 2-5-1s. All players prior to us had learnt by playing with people older and better than themselves. That's how it worked.
>
> (Interview with Bill Ashton, February 2009)

Ashton also notes that he felt that the music scene was being swamped by the beat groups, which left no place for someone like the talented young Ricotti. Ashton reasoned that if there were just one other like him in every London School, it ought to be possible to bring them together. Along with teacher and musician Pat Evans and with the support of several people on the London scene, Ashton began to put together what was initially called the London Schools Jazz Orchestra. With little help from the Local Education Authority and without any financial support, they managed to make a start. Two months later, they appeared on BBC2 on *Late Night Line-Up*. *The Times* and *The Times Educational Supplement* took an interest, as did *Morning Star* jazz writer Brian Blain. The National Jazz Federation provided administra-tive assistance, while a host of musicians from Graham Collier, saxophon-ist with the National Jazz Orchestra Dave Gelly, Tubby Hayes and baritone saxophonist and bandleader John Williams all gave their time generously. It was then that the Westminster Youth Service suggested that a change of name from "Schools" to "Youth" would enable the service to provide some financial aid. The London Youth Jazz Orchestra began to run courses across the city, played regularly at the Marquee Club in Wardour Street, and from that point on the venture acquired a remarkable life of its own.

The change from "London" to "National" came a little later, by which time its initiative had spread. By the time the band recorded their eponymous first LP in 1971 (Philips), the National Youth Jazz Orchestra (NYJO) was part of a network of youth bands. Writing the sleevenotes for their album, *Sunday Times* jazz critic Derek Jewell noted that youth jazz orchestras had by then been established in Essex, Birmingham, Stockport, Manchester, Bournemouth and Oxford (Jewell 1971).

The National Youth Jazz Orchestra is a very good record – a genuinely modern, of-its-time big band set. As Ashton acknowledges, the con-cern to make it a success meant that several alumni were brought back into the ranks for the session. Saxophonists Alan Wakeman, Chris Biscoe and Stan Sulzmann were already two years past the orchestra's upper age limit of twenty-one. All three deliver some fine performances on an album packed with some great tunes from Collier ("Gay Talk"), John Dankworth ("Clearway"), Harry South ("Six to One Bar"), Mike Gibbs ("And Upon This Rock") and others. One of the strongest tracks is Alan Downey's filmic "Eleven Years After" with its baroque brass and excellent organ from Geoff Castle. Castle was still only twenty when the record was made and he really seizes the opportunity. Castle would go on to work with Graham Collier and Ian Carr's Nucleus, while trumpeter and flugelhorn player Dick Pearce (just nineteen at the time) excels on Ken Gibson's lovely ballad "Negev". But the acid test for any big band lies in the ensembles and, here, the boys and girls in the engine room do Ashton proud. Its follow-up *NYJO* (Charisma CAS 1082) from 1973 is also well worth seeking out. Sadly, neither is available on CD at point of writing.

The list of NYJO alumni is now a long and venerable one. Several gifted and stalwart players have been mentioned already. To those names we have to add bassist Chris Laurence, trumpeters Guy Barker, Neil Yates and Gerard Presencer, saxophonists Mike Flood Page, Chris Hunter, Nigel Hitchcock, Dave O'Higgins, Julian Argüelles and Jamie Talbot, and singer Carol Kenyon. As Ashton notes with allowable exaggeration, "So, every jazz course, every band, every class, everything that there is in British jazz today stems directly from NYJO's start" (interview with Bill Ashton, February 2009).

It is an exaggeration nonetheless. There are some who feel that pianist and baritone saxophonist Pat Evans has rather been written out of the picture. Bassist and artist Gill Alexander knew Evans well and speaks very highly of him and his influence:

> Late on in the sixties I met Pat Evans. He started NYJO. In fact, he started virtually everything in this country but he couldn't handle the organization, you know. All the admin – he just couldn't handle that and so he started NYJO and then gave it over to Bill Ashton because he just couldn't handle organizing all the trips. He also started the jazz summer schools and the first one was in Barry. He started the jazz summer schools. He also started the jazz school in Leeds but he just couldn't handle trying to sort things out with managers and administrators – all that side of the business. So, he would always start something up and then leave and do something else somewhere else.
> (Interview with Gill Alexander, February 2009)

Alexander (also known as Levin) played in several of Evans's groups and found him inspirational. According to Alexander, Evans was one of the first to pioneer multimedia arts. He even combined live pottery and jazz! As she notes, Evans was responsible for the Barry Summer Schools and it was that which spawned a whole network of similar ventures. But the importance of the efforts of Ashton, and Evans, goes beyond NYJO and is in many ways responsible for promoting the very idea of formal jazz education in Britain. The notion that jazz, an improvisatory music, could be taught in schools and colleges took a leap of faith. Ashton still believes that what can actually be learnt in the classroom remains limited.

> All jazz classes and courses are if you like short cuts. They can help you because when you see this written then you can play that. They're not a waste of time but unless you are actually playing with other people, you might as well not bother. Playing in your bedroom will never make you into a jazz player.
> (Interview with Bill Ashton, February 2009)

NYJO in the sixties and early seventies represented and brought on the third generation of musiciansmentioned earlier. They were the ones who went through comprehensive and sometimes grammar schools. Some like Stan Sulzmann, Frank Ricotti, Chris Laurence and others went on to music college, while others like Chris Biscoe went straight into the music business. But they were all beneficiaries of the Butler Act and the opportunities it gave to young people.

Education had begun to create new possibilities in British society, not just in terms of access to it but in terms of what could be taught in schools and colleges. Through their new *entrée* to universities and other colleges of higher education, those from less privileged backgrounds were beginning to intrude into areas of work previously reserved for those from the upper classes. It was not a revolution but it would have an impact on wider society. A new generation of jazz musicians were emerging during the sixties, and their backgrounds reflected changes in education that had followed the Butler Act. They brought with them new and different concerns from the founders of British modern jazz but they would build upon the foundations already laid by Ronnie Scott, Joe Harriott, Tubby Hayes and Stan Tracey. We have already mentioned the importance of Britain's colonial heritage and this will prove a further element in the development of a British jazz. Education was not the only force that would shape British jazz in the period but it was, nevertheless, a very important one.

4 Coming of Age in Soho

Modern descriptions of primitive people give us a picture of their culture classified according to the varied aspects of human life. We learn about inventions, household economy, family and political organisation, and religious beliefs and practices. Through a comparative study of these data and through information that tells us of their growth and development, we endeavour to reconstruct, as well as may be, the history of each particular culture.

Margaret Mead, *Coming of Age in Samoa*, 1969, xiii

And yet, while the Samoans use these products of a more complex civilisation, they are not dependent on them.

Margaret Mead, *Coming of Age in Samoa*, 1969, 268

I love this club, it's just like home – filthy and full of strangers.   Ronnie Scott

We have touched already on the notion that the jazz – modern or traditional – produced in Britain from the forties through to the early sixties was little more than a copy of the African-American original. Hopefully, we have begun to see that from the outset it was much more than that. Whether at the Red Barn in Kent with George Webb's Dixielanders or at the Club Eleven with John Dankworth and Ronnie Scott, it was never less than a brave attempt by young musicians to grasp and apply forms that came from an external culture. They were hugely respectful of the originators of the music and its current purveyors. They and their fans concerned themselves with the situation of black people in America and discussed this music in clubs and bars and in university and school jazz societies with tremendous enthusiasm. But there was, for all the desire to know and understand just what Armstrong, King Oliver, Jelly Roll Morton, Dizzy or Bird did on their instruments and how they did it, a desire to produce jazz that was authentic in its own right.

It was clear that Joe Harriott was determined to make music that challenged American dominance in jazz, a desire echoed in the comments of both Chris Barber (page 19) and Michael Garrick (page 72). In later chapters, we will see that similar urges inspired the British free jazz and improvisation movements. Jazz may not be alone among musical styles in its emphasis on authenticity but – along with folk music – it certainly places a very high premium upon it. And detailed listening to the music produced from the late forties onwards reveals a growth and development that was rapid and progressive. Yet this is by no means a view accepted by all. It is not at all uncommon to hear fans of British modern jazz deride "trad" and even the efforts of the Club Eleven Bauhaus set. Nevertheless, British jazz had started to become a distinct entity in its own right before musicians and composers like Mike Westbrook, John Surman, Mike Osborne, Kenny Wheeler, Mike Gibbs and Graham Collier came along.

The argument that British jazz was, throughout the fifties and early sixties, a mere copy of American jazz, would seem to require a transformative event in order to explain developments after the mid-sixties. Indeed, certain commentators have been quite specific in locating the transformation of British jazz to a singular event – the arrival in Britain in 1964 of the South African group, the Blue Notes. For example, this assumption is raised in George McKay's *Circular Breathing – the Cultural Politics of Jazz in Britain* (2005). McKay quotes singer Maggie Nicols to the effect that there was resistance towards the group, and indeed a certain snobbish attitude to their technique. He then notes:

> As with some modernists' disparaging (and disappointing) responses to the experiments of Joe Harriott in London a few years earlier, here is confirmation, as if it were needed, that not only "trad" jazz was open to accusations of neoconservatism.
>
> (McKay 2005, 179)

He supports this point with a reference to similar comments from Joe Boyd, an American record producer based in London, who produced records by McGregor and the Brotherhood of Breath (McGregor 1995, 96; see also Boyd 2006, 215). McGregor's widow, Maxine, in her biography of McGregor and the band, points out that when asked later what the British jazz scene had been like before the arrival of the Blue Notes, her husband replied:

> There was the phenomenon of the Beatles and so on, but for many people – on the jazz scene at least it was we who were the happening thing during the late sixties and early seventies – it was we who gave the new breath. So, it is quite difficult to imagine how it would have been if we hadn't been there.
>
> (McGregor 1995, 115)

It is this view to which McKay is referring. We may note the anachronistic use of the term "neo-conservatism" here, but it is more sad that it is hard to find evidence in his book of a deep knowledge of or a wide listening to British jazz of the sixties or any other era. He gives the impression that, aside from Jamaican-born alto saxophonist Joe Harriott, there was nothing of interest on the British scene up to the arrival of the Blue Notes. There is no doubting the impact that the South African musicians had on British jazz but they came into a scene that had already been created and was already moving in new directions. Saxophonists Tubby Hayes and Don Rendell and pianists Stan Tracey and Michael Garrick are not mentioned at all in his book. And while trumpeter Ian Carr, John Dankworth and Ronnie Scott are referred to, their music is not discussed.

In fairness to McKay, there are those who have been involved in British jazz – drummer Laurie Morgan, producer Denis Preston (see Interview with Chris Barber, February 2008) and bassist Jack Bruce (see interview with Jack Bruce, October 2007) – who express doubts as to whether British jazz has ever achieved an authentic jazz expression of its own. Talking of the early days of British modernism, Laurie Morgan, for example, argues:

> [T]here wasn't behind it all anything other than the will to want to play as good as the Americans but jazz isn't about playing good. It's about expressing something very profound. In America of course the music grew out of an incredible social thing black and white and the church absolutely fundamental to it. You're never going to find – I have never found a black jazz musician who hadn't got his feet firmly planted in his spiritual background. It is always there. The inspiration was always there. You can hear it in Bessie Smith. You can hear it in Coleman Hawkins. You can hear it in every one of them. Ellington. You hear it all. We didn't have that. We bypassed that. It missed us. We didn't think that was part of it all.
>
> (Interview with Laurie Morgan, February 2012)

For Morgan, British jazz lacked a spiritual dimension. Yet, he also acknowledges the passion that his generation had for the music and how it represented the hopes for a new world to replace one that had seen two devastating world wars. Morgan places an emphasis on his peers' desire to achieve a musical competence in jazz rather than find their own forms of expression, something he calls "instrumentalism". At the same time, the mastery of a new form surely required precisely that attention to technical proficiency before it would be possible to advance a conception of one's own.

The suggestion that British modern jazz was, with the exception of Harriott and later the Blue Notes, essentially conservative, rather than reflecting different start points and levels of learning from those which prevailed in the

USA, must also be considered in relation to how jazz functioned within the recording industry in Britain. And it did so in ways that were not the same as those that applied to other musical styles, in particular to pop music.

Because of the nature of the recording industry in the fifties and sixties, access to it for musicians depended on promotion within the entertainment sector through the system of management and booking agents. In the main, records by jazz musicians came about through the patronage of various producers, people like Carlo Krahmer, Tony Hall, Denis Preston and, later, Peter Eden. This meant that any stylistic innovations might well pre-date an album release by several years. In other cases, a group might have an important impact on the live scene without ever getting to record. For example, one popular and innovative band of the sixties – Group Sounds Five, with trumpeter Henry Lowther, saxophonist Lyn Dobson, bassist Ron Rubin, drummer Jon Hiseman and various pianists including Tony Hymas – never recorded, though they did make two BBC broadcasts (Wickes 1999, 46–8). By most accounts, pianist Mike Taylor had already begun using a strikingly free and open approach to jazz composition by the early sixties, yet his first album *Pendulum* was not recorded (for Denis Preston's Lansdowne series) until October 1965. In contrast to Group Sounds Five, Taylor's group rehearsed a great deal but performed rarely in public. Had it not been for Ian Carr, who suggested recording Taylor to Preston, the pianist's music might well have gone undocumented. This gap between innovation and recording continued to be an issue for British jazz. In his review of pianist–composer Mike Westbrook's first album with his Concert Band, *Celebration* (Deram; Universal), critic Michael Shera referred to this problem:

> Mike Westbrook has had to wait far, far too long for his first chance to record. When I first heard the band some two-and-a-half years ago, it was worthy of the opportunity then. However, today the band has clearly established itself as one of the finest in Europe, and certainly the most original that I have heard in this country. (Shera 1967, 36)

In the same article, Shera quotes critic Steve Voce from a *Jazz Journal* review two years earlier, where Voce described the ensemble as, "one of the most remarkable British bands I have ever heard, whose work is fiercely original."

There are several records that one would point to whichshow how far British jazz had moved in a very short space of time. Once again, the gap between the development of a new idea or approach, its implementation and its recording could be several years. While the Beatles, Stones, Who and others documented their early careers with regular singles and LPs, this simply was not the case for any but the highest selling artists in the jazz sphere. This meant that Rendell–Carr, Stan Tracey, Joe Harriott and Chris Barber did quite well out of their relationship with Denis Preston and his

Lansdowne series, while Michael Garrick benefited from the support of Harley Usill and his eccentrically eclectic Argo imprint. And later in the decade, Westbrook, Surman, Mike Gibbs and others were assisted in their early recording endeavours by Peter Eden and the Deram label. At the same time, even several of these artists had to wait for their opportunity, while others not included in this list were not so fortunate.

Producer Denis Preston was a particularly foresighted individual and, as such, an important figure in British jazz. He was rewriting the rules about record production in a very big way. It was his idea that his company, Lansdowne, would own the means of production. It would create artistic packages and make records for a variety of distributors. Not all Lansdowne products were sold to Columbia (UK) or Parlophone. Some went to Decca and others to Pye or Nixa. The mix of Preston's vision, the engineering skills of Adrian Kerridge and a managed studio aesthetic was a wholly new approach. In fact, the sound that Preston and Kerridge created for the Don Rendell–Ian Carr Quintet, Stan Tracey and Joe Harriott was arguably as important for the success of the music as Rudy Van Gelder's engineering for Blue Note.

British jazz artists had made real progress in developing their art and they did so by practising hard and through increasing access to jazz recordings from the USA. Then, when the MU/Ministry of Labour ban was effectively lifted, they got to hear more and more of the best US musicians in the UK. In fact, looking closely at the history of British jazz in these years, it seems very much one of the overcoming of obstacles – by the musicians, by the promoters and club owners and by the fans. The MU ban was in itself a hugely important issue and, as we have seen, British jazzers and fans went to great lengths to hear their idols on the continent, in the Irish Republic or in the USA. Jim Godbolt (1989; see chapter 8), both the author of a two-volume history of British jazz and a booking agent for a number of artists (including George Melly and Mick Mulligan), notes that the ban had been almost total from its imposition in 1934 until 1956, though he adds that a number of American artists slipped through the restrictions under the guise of variety acts. Duke Ellington, with his trumpeter and violinist Ray Nance, appeared with British musicians at the Palladium in 1948, as did Benny Goodman in 1949. Norman Granz's Jazz at the Philharmonic played a charity performance in 1953 at the Kilburn Gaumont and, by the mid-fifties, the Ministry of Labour was beginning to be more relaxed in its issuing of permits, sometimes much to the anger of MU officers. Though as an agent not entirely impartial, Godbolt was one individual who was very active in campaigning against these restrictions with the support of the *Melody Maker* and at various times that of Steve Race, Humphrey Lyttelton and composer Bob Farnon. Perhaps the first major breakthrough came with the agreement between the American Federation of Musicians and the MU to allow a one-for-one exchange. In the first such exchange, Britain got the Stan Kenton Orchestra, while the Americans got Ted Heath. Vic Lewis's band also played the USA in 1956, and gradually the exchange system began to operate in a reasonably relaxed fashion. It must be acknowledged that the interchange this relaxation allowed was important for British jazz in various ways. However, the new arrangements were certainly not in any way an equal set-up.

Some British artists, it is true, did do quite well in America. John Dankworth and his orchestra played at Newport in 1958, as well as in New York and as support for Duke Ellington in New Jersey. Dankworth's music was available in America. *Bundle From Britain* (Top Rank) had been issued as *England's Ambassador of Jazz* on the US Roulette label, though the band leader's association with the company was not a happy one (see Dankworth 1995, 125–6). Over subsequent years, Dankworth would – with partner Cleo Laine – become a major attraction in the States, but even then Dankworth and Laine were hardly an overnight success, and it was not until the early seventies that their position in the USA was assured (Dankworth 1998, 124–36 and 181–4; interview with John Dankworth, February 2008). Chris Barber toured North America in 1959 and proved one of Britain's more successful exports, partly as a consequence of two hit singles – "Petite Fleur" and "Rock Island Line". His group received a fine write-up in the *New York Times* and also performed at President Kennedy's First International Jazz Festival in Washington, DC in the summer of 1963. Kenny Ball also did well in America (interview with Kenny Ball, May 2008), while Alex Welsh got a very warm response from the audience at the 1958 Newport Festival.

However, the harsh reality of the inequality between the perception of British jazz by North American promoters and fans, and the awe and respect in which British fans and musicians held the Americans, soon became apparent. In a *Melody Maker* interview following Barber's return from his US tour, Bob Dawbarn asked the trombonist for his opinion of the standard of the average American traditionalist musician. Barber replied curtly, "Cy Laurie and Mick Mulligan". He clearly had not been overly impressed. In October 1959, the *Melody Maker* reported that Ted Heath had turned down a tour of the "Frozen North". Veteran trumpeter Freddy Randall had fared far worse in 1956, when he found himself playing before segregated audiences on a package that included Bill Haley and his Comets. Meanwhile Ronnie Scott, in the States as an exchange for Eddie Condon in 1957, was placed on a rock & roll bill with Fats Domino, Chuck Berry and others. As he noted in *Some of My Best Friends Are Blues*, "We played our one number on each date to enormous and totally indifferent audiences and then got the hell off" (Scott 1979, 48).

John Fordham's description of the tour provides an elegant summary of the debacle:

> Six Englishmen careering their way through a handful of choruses
> of the single bebop tune that constituted their contribution to an

all-black package before escaping gratefully into the wings was a bizarre enough event in itself but the Scott band was made more uneasy by the fact that it had never performed before audiences of such size before – 20,000 or so was the average attendance on the gigs.   (Fordham 1986, 81)

No doubt Scott's well-honed sense of irony went down a storm with the teenyboppers.

Tubby Hayes fared somewhat better, playing several times in Greenwich Village and recording twice with American stars. However, the story of one British pianist's experiences takes some beating. Stan Tracey was involved in the early exchanges. As Dave Brubeck and Stan Kenton headlined concerts in the UK, Tracey got a week's residency in a New York jazz club. The idea that British jazz was given equal status in the land of the free is immediately dispelled when one notes that the British pianist was ordered to start his one-hour set at 8pm. The doors did not open till 9pm. As Tracey's son Clark told me: "No, it's quite true. He played to the waiters and waitresses who couldn't give a shit. It wasn't exactly a fair exchange" (interview with Clark Tracey, February 2011).

Tracey recently played at Dizzy's Club in Manhattan's famed Lincoln Center. As I noted in *Jazzwise*:

> One of our jazz icons appearing in a room named after one of theirs! Back in the fifties and sixties, when Stan was still learning the trade that might've been considered a case of coals to Newcastle. These days it's more a matter of Matthew Chapter 7, Verse 6!   (Heining 2010b, 33)

This did not ease the perception felt by some British musicians that they were seen as inferior by some at home. Interviewed by Geoffrey Smith for the BBC at Maida Vale Studios on 12 January 1994, Stan Tracey made this point very clearly:

> I was intensely patriotic at that time about British jazz. Mainly because I think the critics were always writing us off or the only mention you'd get would be, "... and ably supported by the British lads". Yeah, that was painting a different picture to the way it was in my eyes. Always making comparisons, always y'know semi-apologising to whoever or whichever instrumentalist was coming in. Semi-apologising in the review – "This wonderful man has to put up with this ... blah, blah, blah".   (Smith 1994)

Tracey certainly was not alone in feeling undervalued by the British public and the critics. His tenor saxophonist partner Bobby Wellins talks even five decades later with genuine hurt on the subject (interview with Bobby Wellins, September 2009). It was not that they felt inferior but rather that they resented being viewed as such. Talking about the early years at the club in Gerrard Street, Ronnie Scott recalled conversations with Stan Tracey, who led the house trio for more than a decade, about the American musicians that he played with. He quotes Tracey as follows, "I know British musicians were supposed to have an inferiority complex, but if I'd felt intimidated, I'd never have stuck it." Scott continues:

> Some British musicians in those days adopted attitudes of inferiority when they played with Americans – but they induced it in themselves. Stan says he never felt inferior – even when the visitors were giving him a hard time.   (Scott 1979, 63–4)

When the Jazz Couriers toured in support of Dave Brubeck's Quartet in 1958, the American had been impressed with Scott and Hayes's group. "They sound more like an American band than we do," he had said. Any irony was as much directed at himself and the style of conservatoire jazz that his quartet purveyed as at the Couriers. But it was a statement that spoke both positively of British jazz and acknowledging that while it copied the Americans – and it did so necessarily – it would remain essentially second-hand. For John Fordham, the big difference between the Americans and the Brits at the time lay in the availability of drummers of the standard of Art Blakey, Max Roach, Roy Haynes, Philly Joe Jones, Kenny Clarke and others whose approach allowed so much more space and freedom to the front line. It allowed a soloist to play less to make their point. Fordham notes in response to Brubeck's remark, "But American modernist outfits like those of Art Blakey and Hank Mobley in reality sounded quite different to the Couriers." He continues, though his comments are not directed as such at the Scott–Hayes group:

> Deep-rooted insecurities about their quality by comparison with the Americans also led British bebop bands to a kind of overcompensatory pyrotechnics as well, like teenagers driving cars to fast to prove that they were men.   (Fordham 1986, 90)

The reality, bearing in mind that we are concerned here with both affect and effect, was probably more complicated. Despite Scott's expressions of confidence in his abilities and that of his fellow British jazzers, Fordham notes in relation to a US exchange trip to play the Half Note in New York in 1963 that Scott "still felt like an interloper, bringing American music to its home soil" (Fordham 1986, 114). That there were, however, differences between the self-perceptions of the Scott/Tracey/Hayes generation and those of the fans was clearly evident in the struggles of Ronnie Scott and partner Pete King to provide a home for modern British jazz in Soho. The pair had opened their club in Gerrard Street in October 1959, in Scott's words, to provide a venue that would be "A well-appointed place which was licensed, and catered for people of all ages and not merely for youngsters" (Burman 1958, 5). It had had a degree of success in those respects, but the market for British modern jazz in London at the time was a limited one and, by 1961, it was becoming clear that the club would need more than a succession of local acts – though visiting Americans would also drop by and sit in – if it was to survive and grow into the kind of place that Scott and King had envisaged. This was, however, the reality within which British modern jazz and its musicians had to operate.

Even in 1961 with the embargo lifted, obtaining work permits for a visiting American musician presented enormous hurdles and involved negotiations with the Ministry of Labour, the MU and its American equivalent. By that point, American artists often promoted by Harold Davison's organization were touring fairly regularly in the UK, often supported by the same artists that could be heard in Gerrard Street. Fans could see these acts, American and British, in concert halls or in Britain's cinemas that put on musical events as well as films. Persuading the British jazz public to turn up regularly at Gerrard Street was not easy. Plus there was the problem that the club had no liquor licence. Talk about "the pub with no beer". Tackling Britain's arcane, Victorian licensing laws was, if anything, the easier difficulty to overcome. However, it was clear that they needed to get round the MU ban, which still applied to clubs like theirs. It was Pete King who succeeded in brokering a deal. In October 1961, Tubby Hayes went to New York's Half Note for a month's residency and American saxophonist Zoot Sims played at Ronnie Scott's. It was the first time an American jazz musician had played – officially – in a British jazz club for nearly 30 years. One has to wonder how this might have felt to British musicians. However confident they might sometimes have felt in their abilities, confidence is not a fixed state. It is subject to fluctuations and can be easily undermined. Britain had needed the Americans in 1917 and again in 1941. Ronnie Scott's club needed them once more in 1961!

Ronnie Scott's own story and that of the club that still carries his name has been beautifully told by John Fordham in his *Let's Join Hands and Contact the Living* (1986). After 1961, a succession of visiting American musicians would establish the venue as one of the world's great jazz clubs. In fact, by 1965, it had begun to outgrow its Gerrard Street home, and Scott and King were ready to move into larger and more salubrious premises in Frith Street, assisted financially by promoter Harold Davison. The new venue would still remain a home from home for many of Scott and King's musician friends. However, the move also changed the character of the club's audience. As it moved up-market, it became less the province of the die-hard fan and more reliant on out-of-towners, tourists and passing trade. Meanwhile, Gerrard

Street then entered a brief but remarkable new phase in its history. Its lease still had eighteen months to run, and Scott and King offered its use to the younger musicians who were just coming onto the scene. It re-opened in September 1966, becoming known for its short life and ever after as The Old Place. As John Fordham notes: "The impact on the British scene was as critical as the opportunity to hear American players of the calibre that Scott and King were presenting" (Fordham 1986, 148).

Along with the (marginally) more avant-garde Little Theatre Club established by drummer John Stevens, The Old Place provided a home for a new generation of British musicians keen to experiment and develop their ideas. In practice, many musicians frequented both venues creating the kind of vibrant scene that London had not really seen since the heady days of Club Eleven. We will hear more of the Little Theatre Club in Chapter 11. Here we will just note that among those able to make excellent use of The Old Place were musicians like John Surman, Mike Osborne, Harry Beckett and Alan Skidmore, and composer–bandleaders such as Mike Westbrook and Graham Collier. It also made an important space available to Chris McGregor and the Blue Notes, who came to Britain in the mid-sixties from apartheid South Africa. Indeed, several of the most significant ensembles to emerge in London in the late sixties owed their gestation to The Old Place.

The majority of Americans who played the club through the sixties and beyond were gracious and encouraging. But, as Ronnie Scott has noted, some of the tenor players gave Tracey and his rhythm partners a hard time. Don Byas was one such, Lucky Thompson another, while one of the worst-behaved of all was Stan Getz. At one point when Getz was at the club in 1964, he publicly criticized the rhythm section. Tracey responded with the tersest of replies – "Bollocks!" Getz backed off immediately. There was also a story that did the rounds that Dexter Gordon, who first played at Scott's in September 1962, got through eleven drummers during his month-long residency. There is a clear difference between Tracey and Scott over this. Tracey told Geoffrey Smith in 1994, "They [the drummers] were either destroyed by Dexter or he said he didn't want to play with them. Because those guys used to come on really heavy" (Smith 1994). Ronnie Scott acknowledges that first-class British drummers were rather thin on the ground in that period, but adds that there were at least a dozen more than capable of holding their own. The reality, he says, was simply that none of them was available for more than two or three nights at a time (Scott 1979, 66).

Stan Tracey describes Getz, Byas and Thompson with his usual succinctness: "Not very nice. Very dismissive." And he refuses to allow them the old excuse –that they were "strung out". According to Tracey, Dexter Gordon was the only one he played with who was using heroin during his residency: "Yeah, Dexter did. When he arrived he was sweet but by the end of the month, when he was all fucked up, he wasn't. To the best of my knowledge, Dexter was the only one."

Thompson, in particular, was very intimidating, not as a musician but physically. Tracey, however, devised his own way of getting back at grand-standing Americans:

> I used to fight back musically. What I used to do with Don Byas, in particular – he would finish on a phrase and I'd pick up the phrase and make a musical gargoyle out of it. I can't explain it, but it was that phrase but becoming more and more grotesque.
>
> (Interview with Stan Tracey, February 2010)

A musical raspberry, as it were, and one he also deployed with Lucky Thompson:

> Yeah, yeah. That was the only way I could get back at him because he used to do things like bending two bottle tops with two hands at the same time and inviting you to punch him as hard as you can in the chest because he wouldn't even feel it, so you wouldn't want to mess with him in that regard. Why would I mess up my chops punching him in the chest? I tried to do it musically. Whether or not he knew I was doing it, I don't know and I don't care! (Interview with Stan Tracey, December 2009)

Others, like Gerrard Street's first US visitors, Zoot Sims and Sonny Rollins, were warm and complimentary, with Rollins once making the famous remark about Tracey, "Does anyone here know how good he really is?" (Fordham 1986, 129). Sims cut two albums during his first trip to the Scott club, *Zoot at Ronnie Scott's* (Fontana) and *Solo for Zoot* (Fontana). Some of these tunes were later reissued as *Cookin'!* in 1965 (Fontana), with Ronnie Scott and Jimmy Deuchar on one track. The rest of the material, however, and the whole of *Solo for Zoot*, features Sims, Tracey on piano, Rick Laird (later with the Mahavishnu Orchestra) on bass and Jackie Dougan on drums. The significance of these records is that they were among the first modern jazz albums featuring an American musician backed by a British band. In due course, Prince Lasha, Ben Webster, Paul Gonsalves, Philly Joe Jones and others would follow suit. Tracey spoke with characteristic reserve on the subject with Geoffrey Smith:

> Y'know, we may not have been up to the standards they were used to but they could appreciate what we were trying to do and actually when I hear the album we did with Zoot, it's come out on CD again, it doesn't sound too bad – I mean the rhythm section. It had Kenny Napper, Jackie Dougan and I think we did OK.
>
> (Smith 1994)

Listen to "Stompin' at the Savoy" and "Autumn Leaves" from *Solo For Zoot*. They did a bit better than "OK".

This tension around the issue of British inferiority/American superiority continued, despite the often sincere compliments passed by the Americans on their British peers' playing. Godbolt notes at several points that British musicians were lauded by the Americans, often with an apparent degree of evident surprise on their part. In relation to the traditional jazz revival, he writes, "When, in the sixties, individual US jazz musicians visited Britain to be accompanied by British revivalists they were quite genuine in their praise of the home players" (Godbolt 1989, 144).

Later on he reports trumpeter Wild Bill Davison, a man noted for his brickbats as much as his bouquets, describing clarinettist Archie Semple as "the greatest since Ed Hall" (Godbolt 1989, 240). Even more intriguing is the story he quotes from another clarinet player, John Barnes, who toured with Earl Hines in the fifties. Hines was perfectly happy with the British musicians' skills but gave them a dressing down for their "unprofessionalism" in drinking and smoking on the stand. In Autumn 1953 in the *New Musical Express*, journalist and producer Tony Hall reviewed a Stan Kenton concert at a US Air Force airbase in Lincolnshire where Ronnie Scott's band played support. Kenton is quoted as saying, "I'm proud to have heard Ronnie's band. It's certainly the greatest we've heard since leaving the States" (cited by Godbolt 1989, 184).

When Woody Herman chose British drummer Tony Crombie to write arrangements and Ronnie Scott to join his "Herd" for dates in Dublin and at US Air Force bases, it evoked a real shared sense of pride in the jazz community in Britain. Herman finally toured the UK in 1959 with an Anglo-American Herd and included seven Britons and two Canadian ex-pats, including trumpeter Kenny Wheeler. British chests swelled accordingly. British musicians, pianists Victor Feldman and George Shearing, who had both emigrated to the States and experienced success there, would be treated like conquering heroes on return visits home. In a way, there was nothing unreasonable in this tendency among critics and fans, or indeed the musicians themselves, to compare the local guys with the Americans. It was in fact inevitable. They were the originators after all. However, with increasing contact, it became clear that even the very great might stumble and that one or two might well lose the shine on their haloes in the flesh. Chris Barber's comment about the standard of the average American traditional player noted above is just one such example.

The fifties saw tours and concerts by Earl Hines, Ellington, Kenton, Gerry Mulligan, Armstrong, Basie, Sarah Vaughan (with the Dankworth Orchestra), Dave Brubeck, the Modern Jazz Quartet, Eddie Condon, Jazz at the Philharmonic and others. Even the great Ellington's performances at the Royal Festival Hall in October 1958 had its naysayers as well as those who came to praise. John Dankworth was moved to yell, "What about playing some jazz?" at a Lionel Hampton performance at the same venue in November 1957. Hampton's tour had been greeted by mixed reviews at what many saw as an overemphasis on showmanship (Godbolt 1989, 204). Doubts were also expressed by some – bandleaders Vic Lewis and Eric Delaney, and drummer Allan Ganley – about the absence of any soloists of real calibre in the Kenton band that visited Britain in April 1956 (Godbolt 1989, 192–3). On the other hand, others (such as Count Basie's band, who came to Britain in spring 1957) were met by near-universal acclaim.

The flipside of admiration is envy and resentment. Ambivalence within a relationship that was in some degree unequal would be understandable. The arrival of a Coltrane or a Miles Davis was to the British jazz scene akin to a presidential or papal state visit. It was not that direct experience brought contempt or anything remotely like it. But bad behaviour or unpleasantness such as that noted by Stan Tracey and Ronnie Scott with regard to Don Byas and Lucky Thompson certainly diminished the visitors. Writer–photographer Val Wilmer worked harder than anyone to get close to the African-Americans who came here, as well as to the Caribbean and west African communities in London, and to understand a perspective that was born of centuries of oppression. She notes with some irony that she often got along "famously with some of those who sparked off dislike or resentment among the British musicians" (Wilmer 1991, 148). For example, she found Don Byas and Lucky Thompson quite charming and gentlemanly in a pleasantly old-fashioned way. She adds about Byas:

> Now I wonder what kind of racism he must have encountered during his visit to provoke him into the anger for which he was known. The local men always liked "their" Black visitors to be easygoing. Should any individual be bold enough to question the status quo or stand his ground, however, he was no longer seen as such an affable proposition. (Wilmer 1991, 148)

Is Wilmer too quick to excuse and accuse? These were very much first encounters. The African-Americans came from the more highly charged racial situation in the USA. Their British counterparts came from a position of some knowledge about that world but mixed with equal proportions of ignorance. It would be unsurprising if a degree of awkwardness on both sides did not accompany such contacts. Wilmer's comments are, nevertheless, a welcome reminder of the perspective of the "other". Elsewhere, she remarks in a particularly poignant passage:

> When the music ceased to be such a mystery and local musicians developed voices of their own, attitudes changed towards the people who gave them something to play in the first place. At some point, the relaxed personal style and apparently effortless elegance of the visitors began to inspire resentment, just as the affluence of American GIs in Britain during the war had done.

It is hard to pinpoint when this happened. What was noticeable was that local musicians gradually stopped turning out for the Americans, whom they had once crowded round, eager for a blow on a special mouthpiece or a tip about playing, taking delight in sharing a hip-flask or an "African Woodbine" and the sexual gossip that is a staple of male dressing-room bonhomie.

(Wilmer 1991, 45)

Wilmer compares this with changing attitudes to Caribbean migration among liberals in the face of increasing demands for equal treatment by black people in Britain. It is hard to criticize Wilmer's point of view or comments. She was very active around the scene and was a keen observer. Much that she witnessed in terms of racism and sexism, including in the latter respect her own experiences of sexual assault and harassment by white local and visiting African-American musicians, is appalling. However, some of her remarks are so general and unspecific, the link she makes between Commonwealth immigration and white attitudes to black musicians being just one, that they preclude further discussion. This approach also does not allow the accused, who are never named, to defend themselves. This tendency in her book is unfortunate because she has much to say that is very relevant indeed.

However, it is clear from what Wilmer writes that mixed feelings towards the Americans, black and white, existed among local players. Again, this is not perhaps quite so surprising. As their confidence grew the British musicians became more focused on what they could achieve in their own right. The sense that one has surpassed one's teacher is simultaneously exhilarating and frightening. One realizes that one is now responsible for what follows. Suggesting that this was what occurring does not exclude Wilmer's interpretation. Both trends may well have been present, after all. But British musicians could not stand still. They needed to find their own voices.

The suggestion that British jazz before the Blue Notes was, with the exception of Joe Harriott, of the original American model essentially conservative and imitative offers a one-dimensional perspective and is problematic on that level alone. Any indications of local innovation prior to that point would leave it untenable. There were certainly conservative strains in British jazz. But that was only part of the picture. By their very adoption of jazz as a creative practice, often, as we have suggested with limited reference points, British musicians were already innovating. They were forced to do so. And we can see that even in the early fifties, they were beginning to experiment with the form and content of jazz.

During a slightly later time period, Russian jazz would prove Trotsky's dictum of "combined and uneven development". It had passed from a state of swing to a state of free jazz without first passing through a state of bebop. The trajectory of British modern jazz was different but it too shows that notions of development and progress that are too linear in their account presume and ignore too much. In any art form, sometimes potentially fruitful paths remain inadequately explored, while blind alleys are relentlessly pursued until a wall is reached.

The story of Kenny Graham is a sorry one. A tenor saxophonist and, more importantly, a composer of unusual skill and potential, Graham and his Afro-Cubists cut some fifty plus sides for the Esquire label between 1951 and 1957, of which few have been available in recent decades. A further record was made for MGM in 1956, *Moondog and Suncat Suites* (MGM; Trunk Records), with a slightly different band under the name Kenny Graham and his Satellites. Graham's Afro-Cubists combined critical acclaim and financial failure with great aplomb and as a gigging entity the group only lasted two years, reforming from time to time to record or for occasional performances. By the late fifties, Graham was writing and arranging regularly for Ted Heath and Humphrey Lyttelton but was forced to give up the saxophone due to a serious illness. He wrote the charming and light-hearted *Beaulieu Festival Suite* for Heath in 1959 (Decca; Vocalion), a piece that suited the band perfectly, and, though he continued to compose, by the mid-sixties he had left the jazz scene entirely. He died in 1997, his last job being as a caretaker for a block of flats in London.

Graham's significance is that he was an original. Although his fusion of jazz and Afro-Cuban rhythms echoed the work of Parker and Gillespie with Machito and of George Russell and Chano Pozo in New York, his take was very much his own and his interest had been initiated by playing Latin-American music with British dance bands. Graham took Gillespie's experiments several stages further and his writing and arranging reveals a genuinely effective and successful fusion of the two forms. His ambitions as a composer could be seen both in his short pieces like "Skylon" and "Mango Walk", which transcend the three-minute limitations of the 78 rpm record, and in his desire to compose longer themes. "Skylon", in 12/4 time, is particularly unusual, and there is something about these tunes that recalls the otherness of Gillespie–Russell–Pozo's "Cubano Be, Cubano Bop". Even a piece of fluff like "Pina Colada" shows how successfully Graham and his percussion section, which included Dickie Devere and Nigerian Ginger Johnson, had absorbed the polyrhythms that underpinned bebop and Cuban music. Graham also recorded a beautiful and charming version of "Over the Rainbow". However, his ambitions went much further. His 1957 *Caribbean Suite* album (Esquire) featured "Haitian Ritual", an eight-movement suite that lasted over twenty minutes and took up one side of the record. It is quite magnificent, as is the whole album, and it sustains its mood, its colours and ambition throughout. The *Moondog* album was slightly less ambitious but no less successful artistically and was an intriguing British insight into the musical world of the strange, blind street musician and composer otherwise known as Louis Hardin (Harrison *et al.* 2000, 418–23).

And Graham was not alone in his ambitions. From the outset, John Dankworth seemed to epitomize several distinctive strands in British jazz. Coming from an Academy background he brought with him a broad knowledge of music beyond jazz. He discovered bebop very early in his career but, like many musicians, began working life playing Dixieland jazz and dance music. Compared with many of his peers, he was something of a musical polymath who loved jazz whether it was played by Bix Beiderbecke or Miles Davis, Charlie Parker or Barney Bigard. It was not surprising that he became the acceptable face of British modern jazz. He was articulate, serious and middling middle-class, but he was pragmatic too, all of these being qualities that were essential if British modern jazz were to prosper.

Dankworth's earlier description of Club Eleven as being "synonymous with progressive jazz thinking in Britain – a sort of jazz Bauhaus", may have the gloss of hindsight and nostalgia (Dankworth 1998, 63). However, it also conveys a sense that these musicians were creating jazz and not just concerned with recreating it. Dankworth had written at some length in the May 1950 issue of *Jazz Illustrated* (Dankworth 1950) on his strategy. He identified two schools in British modern jazz. The first he called the "raucous bebop school", while the second he dubbed the "self-styled progressives". The former, he argued, emphasized "physical excitement at the expense of musical value". The second, in emulating European impressionist composers, was moving ever further away from jazz. He argued for a course that stressed melody and musical content, in order that each piece could stand or fall on its own merits. Dankworth was quite clear in this. He saw jazz no longer as a folk music or a music essentially for dancers, but as one that had to claim its place in the concert hall. His early writing and arranging for the Dankworth Seven certainly indicated that he was actively exploring the forms of bebop, whether on a pastiche such as "Gone With the Windmill" (with Alan Dean's Beboppers) or on the fuller, richer more personal sounding "Seven Not Out". It is also obvious that he was trying to write music that had validity in its own right and not merely as a vehicle for soloists. The same could be said of "Leon Bismark" and "MYOB" and, while all of these Dankworth originals reveal the influence of Miles Davis' *Birth Of The Cool* sessions, the way the composer deploys the colours available from his instruments seems to reflect his own musical thinking (see Dankworth 1998, 71–2) Indeed, the original tunes the Seven recorded seem more convincing than their playing on bebop and swing warhorses such as "Cherokee" and "Stompin' at the Savoy". At the same time, Dankworth's ongoing concern with a rather European sense of colour and texture permeates his work throughout these early tracks.

He formed the Johnny Dankworth Orchestra in 1953 at the suggestion of agent and promoter Harold Davison and it ran pretty much continuously until 1965, playing as many as 250 gigs a year in Britain, Europe and beyond. In some ways, Dankworth's ambition and success seem to have led to him being seen as a popularizer or ambassador for British jazz and has de-emphasized his importance as a creative artist. Sometimes, his output could be quite twee and arch – the hit single "Experiments with Mice", for example, though even here Dankworth's unusual ability to parody the styles of other band leaders gave it some credibility. However, it was this populist attitude that allowed his film and TV writing to sit easily alongside the much more ambitious material featured on albums such as *Zodiac Variations* from 1965 (Fontana; Vocalion), *What the Dickens!* from 1964 (Fontana) and *$1,000,000 Collection* from 1968 (Fontana; Vocalion). In 1956, he produced *Journey into Jazz*, a fifteen-minute suite, with a dually didactic purpose. His spoken introduction describes it as "an excursion into the sounds of jazz", intended "to spotlight our friends the instruments in all their moods, sometimes noisy and boisterous or sometimes a little dreamy, sometimes gossiping about anything that occurs to them, sometimes uttering solemn words of wisdom." It parallels Benjamin Britten's *The Young Person's Guide to the Orchestra*, this being the first of its didactic intentions. Its second function is to show the tonal and timbral range that can be achieved by a jazz composer utilizing the brass, woodwind and rhythm section of a jazz, as opposed to a symphony or chamber orchestra. It does so successfully, and some of the writing, its slower second section in particular, is quite lovely. It says, "Take us seriously". But Dankworth did something more with his big band. The preferred big band line-up often consists of five saxophones, three trombones and four/five trumpets. The saxophones are used to provide softer tones in the ensembles and sometimes the solos. Instead, here and subsequently on albums such as *Jazz Routes* (Columbia) and *Bundle from Britain*, Dankworth uses just three saxes along with five trombones and five trumpets. Yet, instead of a heavily brass-laden sound, he uses the trombones and trumpets in a manner similar to that achieved by Gerry Mulligan and Gil Evans with Miles Davis and previously with Claude Thornhill. At the same time, he does so in his own way. The sound that he achieves is both fuller and, more surprisingly, more assertive than either of the Americans. It is no surprise that the Newport trip captured on *Bundle* was so well received because it is really fine jazz played with subtlety and control and no little fire. Drummer Kenny Clare is phenomenal, while Dankworth, trumpeter Dickie Hawdon, trombonist Laurie Monk and tenor player Danny Moss definitely, in the words of old Tammany hall boss George Washington Plunkitt, "seen their opportunities and took 'em!"

Dankworth had a second hit in 1961 with Galt MacDermot's "African Waltz", a record that even now can reduce grown men to cry into their beer at the fond memory of hearing this great tune and arrangement on the BBC's "Light Programme". By this point, he had returned to a more standard line-up of brass and reeds. Yet his writing for brass remained strong and convincing and the way he creates a dialogue between the woodwinds and brass continued to be a trademark. His next innovation came in the creation of a series of three suites for jazz orchestra – four, if one includes

Kenny Wheeler's marvellous *Windmill Tilter*. The first of these, *What the Dickens!*, was obviously inspired by Charles Dickens and is a picaresque series of portraits of Dickens's characters, using Dankworth's soloists such as baritonist Ronnie Ross on the good-humoured "Weller Never Did" and himself on the delightful "Little Nell" to fine effect. "Please Sir, I Want Some More/The Artful Dodger" is an even better piece of writing with excellent solos from trombonist Tony Russell, trumpeter Leon Calvert and Vic Ash on clarinet. The (for British jazz) success of *What the Dickens!* meant that his record company allowed him a bigger budget for the follow-up, *The Zodiac Variations*. For this, the composer went way off-piste elaborating an affair that included American and British soloists chosen according to their star signs and recording their parts entirely separately, as he explained in a 2008 interview along with contributions from his wife Cleo:

JD: But the thing I sold to the record company was exactly that, that I would do some in New York and some in London and that we'd splice the two together when I'd done it all. It was only one session that they paid for in New York plus my fare and hotel and I got Clark Terry to fix the band. I think it was only an eight piece band. Clark was the contractor which meant he got paid double for it and had to book all the players. I'd given him a list of the players I wanted but then he'd phone back and say, "I can't get Frank Wess but I've got Jerome Richardson instead." So I said, "That won't do." He would say, "What do you mean? Jerome's a wonderful player." I'd say, "Yes, I know he is but he's not a Capricorn!" Clark never got over this. But eventually we got all the right signs but then they couldn't understand that we'd be going along nicely swinging away and it all sounded nice and then Zoot Sims would say, "Hey John, my next page is missing." Then Phil Woods would say, "Yeah, John mine's missing too." So, I'd have to say, "That's as far as you go – the rest is to be finished in London", which perplexed them even further. It was very interesting to do.

CL: And wacky really, especially when he's not in the least bit interested in the subject matter. He doesn't believe in it at all. [laughing]

JD: It was like an exam paper really because I decided on two motifs and they had to go in each one. I decided to do everything ... there are twelve keys in music and I decided that there would be twelve tracks, so each one would be in the key that is next. I also did each track in a different mode, so the number of millstones I was putting round my neck and on top of that the people who were to solo could only be those of that sign. I thought afterwards, "Why did I do this?" but I must admit I'm not ashamed of the album. I can still listen to it, which I can't say about everything I've done.

(Interview with John Dankworth and Cleo Laine, February 2008)

This was not the first attempt to record in such a way. The Irving Townsend–Leonard Feather record *One World Jazz* from 1960 (Philips) did something similar with a band that included Americans such as Ben Webster and Clark Terry, British players Ronnie Ross and George Chisholm, as well as French musicians like Stéphane Grappelli and pianist Martial Solal. The music on *Zodiac Variations* was, however, much more ambitious. But it is not merely its quirky origins that ensure that these two records also give the lie to the notions regarding the alleged conservatism of British modern jazz before the mid- to late sixties. The longest track, "Sagittarius", is just four and a half minutes, while the majority last about two and a half minutes. It is the sheer quality of Dankworth's writing that – given the restrictions on length that the self-imposed structure dictated – is all the more astonishing. His strictures from 1950 which stressed melody and musical content are still in place and, although linked by two recurring motifs, each piece has a delicacy and completeness of its own. In addition, this album allowed listeners to hear and compare in aural if not geographical proximity American and British star players. *Zodiac Variations* speaks volumes about mutual respect.

Dankworth was never an out player or writer, but the third suite, *The $1,000,000 Collection*, was in many respects his most ambitious album and featured a new orchestra including several of the emerging younger players like trumpeter Henry Lowther, trombonists Mike Gibbs and Chris Pyne, and percussionist Tristan Fry. The pieces are each inspired by paintings, a kind of jazz *Pictures from an Exhibition*. For several of the compositions – "Winter Scene", "Sailor", "Composition with Colour", "La Clownesse" and "Madonna" – Dankworth uses the serial technique derived from Schönberg and Webern, which he had already experimented with in his film work, notably the Pinter/Losey films. Each piece is built upon a tone row but there is nothing remotely dry or academic about the music. "Winter Scene" one of the album's longer tracks, and "Composition with Colour" are those most obviously influenced by European art music. However, Dankworth again frames the solos with such care and the music has a lightness of touch that gives it a distinctively modern sound that is immediately approachable. The same is true of "Sailor", which features typically authoritative flugelhorn from Kenny Wheeler. Henry Lowther's violin is featured on "Two-Piece Flower", lending it an oddly modal feel, and Ray Swinfield provides some gorgeous flute on "Little Girl in Blue". As for his take on Hieronymus Bosch's "Garden of Delights", it simply surpasses expectation. This is one of the most successful big band records of the period, and perhaps one of the more under-rated. It stands comfortably alongside the orchestral work of Mike Westbrook, Mike Gibbs, Neil Ardley and others, and bears favourable comparison with the more feted Kenny Wheeler/Dankworth Orchestra album, *Windmill Tilter*.

If Kenny Graham represents innovation and experimentation that was brought to a premature close, Dankworth's music represents a continuity of these important qualities. Dankworth did not succeed because he was the acceptable face of British modernism but because he was an exceptionally gifted composer. And there are other examples that we can give that reveal how far British jazz had progressed, and that it was beginning to express an identity of its own. I have already talked about Stan Tracey in this chapter and about his quartet with Bobby Wellins in an earlier one. In later chapters, we will examine the important and innovative role played by British jazz musicians in the development of British R&B and subsequently jazz-rock, and will look at the music of several other musicians in Chapter 7. In particular, in that chapter, space is devoted to the important and enigmatic figure of pianist Mike Taylor. But there are other figures that George McKay's *Circular Breathing* (2005) neglects.

By 1960/1, British modern jazz might not have been in the best of financial health but artistically it was fit and well. In a short space of fifteen years the musicians gathering around Club Eleven had progressed. And what progress they made! It is well worth listening to Ronnie Scott's *The Night is Scott and You're So Swingable* (Fontana) to compare it with even the best of his work from the fifties. One hears a very mature and personal voice on tenor. A subtly emotional player, Scott could caress a ballad like few others. In a way, it's a curious record mixing quartet tracks with strings and another quartet that includes the brilliant Jamaican guitarist Ernest Ranglin. Yet it works largely due to the authority and integrity of Scott's playing. "What's New?", that beautiful song associated with singer Peggy Lee, is given the most assured of readings and, unlike some other jazz "with strings" albums, you never lose any sense that this is very much an idiomatic set of jazz performances. But then composer–pianist Richard Rodney Bennett did the arrangements. Nor was Scott ever afraid of up-tempo numbers, and "The Night Has a Thousand Eyes" and "Treat It Lightly" with Stan Tracey on piano, Rick Laird on bass and Bill Eyden on drums show that the tenor player could walk the bar with the best. In fact, on the former one can hear the influence of Coltrane upon Scott in his use of extended harmonies.

The Night is Scott ... was issued in 1966, and the tenor player had not recorded in his own right since 1960 and his last date with the Couriers. We are fortunate, therefore, in being able to refer to two club dates that were released in the 1990s on the Jazz House label. *When I Want Your Opinion I'll Give It to You* and *The Night Has a Thousand Eyes* include material from 1963 and 1964. The second of these features top-flight American saxophonist

Sonny Stitt, and it is Scott who pushes the pace rather than Stitt. Like Don Rendell, and like American tenor players such as Don Byas, Stan Getz and Paul Gonsalves, Scott never lost his love of swing and built new harmonic and melodic insights upon that edifice. And like them, his playing never sounds old fashioned or dated. From these two sets, one gleans both the continuities of Scott's playing and his development as a musician. Having begun his career playing bebop, he had absorbed a series of fresh influences since the days of Club Eleven. His melodicism clearly comes from Lester Young via musicians like Stan Getz and Zoot Sims. From Sonny Stitt, he had learned something else, namely a nimbleness and an ability to weave in and out of the music. There was also, perhaps courtesy of Dexter Gordon and Lucky Thompson, a masculine swagger about his style now, while the lessons from Coltrane were perhaps more about harmony, in particular in terms of the use of modes. This kind of learning process is the norm in jazz. The musician develops their own voice not in isolation but through assimilation, and the distinctive Scott voice can still melt hardened steel. He might never have made a truly great jazz record during his career but he made several very good ones, and none better than his next release.

A few years after *The Night is ...* and now in his forties, Scott formed an octet/nonet, which as well as featuring one or two older players like Scott and drummer Kenny Clare, brought in some of the more experimental musicians such as drummer Tony Oxley, John Surman, Kenny Wheeler, saxophonist Ray Warleigh and Chris Pyne. *Live at Ronnie Scott's* was made in 1969 (CBS; Sony/BMG) and is one of the most enjoyable records of the period (sadly, the equally excellent *Serious Gold* from 1977 falls outside our period and had not been issued on CD at the time of writing.) Some of the playing is quite astonishing. Surman is on blistering form on soprano on Laurie Holloway's "King Pete" and thunderous on baritone on Westbrook's "Too Late, Too Late", while Kenny Wheeler's flugelhorn is at its lyrical best on a lovely arrangement of Donovan's "Lord of the Reedy River". This is adventurous material, and Scott clearly relishes the challenge thrown down by these younger players. His solo on Joe Henderson's "Recorda Me" is superb, but the way he bustles his way out of the horns on the closing "Macumba" is mighty and magnificent.

In many ways, Scott's playing can feel more personal than that of the technically more gifted Tubby Hayes. It seems to sum up the man himself – tears and laughter co-existed not comfortably but almost dialectically. With regard to Hayes himself, I cannot improve on the following comment from Richard Cook and Brian Morton:

> He is a fascinating but problematic player. Having put together a big rambunctious tone and a delivery that features sixteenth notes spilling impetuously out of the horn, Hayes often left a solo full of brilliant loose ends and ingenious runs that led nowhere in particular. Most of his recordings, while highly entertaining

Tubby Hayes Big Band at the National Jazz Festival, Richmond 1964. Left to right: Tubby Hayes, Ronnie Scott, Peter King, Ronnie Ross. © Valerie Wilmer.

> as exhibitions of sustained energy, tend to wobble on the axis of Hayes's creative impasse: having got this facility together, he never seemed sure what to do with it in the studio.
>
> (Cook and Morton 2000, 689)

But they add that, "His live albums are nevertheless sometimes breathtaking in their impact and excitement" (Cook and Morton 2000, 689). Hayes was another who continued to grow as a musician between the fifties and sixties. Of his early sixties releases, *Down in the Village* (Fontana) comes highly rated and reveals the progress the "Little Giant" had made as a soloist. The music is played with verve and authority by a quintet that included both Jimmy Deuchar on trumpet and a young Gordon Beck on piano. However, it truly comes alive when Hayes comes to the mike. His tenor is hugely assertive on both "Johnny One Note" and gruffly emotive on "The Most Beautiful Girl in the World", while Hayes's vibraphone on his own tune "Down in the Village" confirms what a consummate musician he was on every instrument – tenor, soprano, flute and vibes – that he played. And listening to his soprano on "In the Night" (another Hayes original), his debt to Coltrane was becoming increasingly evident.

Hayes was the great white hope of British jazz in the early sixties. His success in New York was an achievement in which the British jazz community shared. It was an acknowledgement that had real worth. Hayes made two recordings there. The first, *Tubbs In New York* (Fontana), came about in 1961, and was with a trio featuring pianist Horace Parlan and a guest appearance by the wonderful trumpeter Clark Terry. It is a nice album, with a strong sense of intimacy about it. The second, *Return Visit* (Fontana), was recorded in 1962 but not released until 1964. It featured Cannonball Adderley's rhythm section of bassist Sam Jones and drummer Louis Hayes with Walter Bishop Jr on piano. Of even more interest was the presence of saxophonists James Moody (for contractual reasons credited as "Gloomy") and Roland Kirk, the latter yet to make his presence felt at Ronnie Scott's in Soho.

Return Visit has its moments but is never the summit meeting it promises. On Roland Kirk's "I See with My Third 'I'", all the soloists overplay their welcome. Kirk's "Lady 'E'" with Hayes on vibes, Moody and Kirk on flutes is better, with the winds and the two chordal instruments combining well. The old Couriers' staple, "Stitt's Tune", is even better but overall, and although Hayes acquits himself well in this company, there is a nagging feeling at the end of the record's long ballad feature of "so what?" The answer to that is simple. What mattered was that it happened at all. It indicated the growth in respect accorded to Hayes and by extension British jazz. As noted, a number of American artists recorded in London in the sixties often during residencies at the Scott club. The great Ellingtonian tenor, Paul Gonsalves, recorded two sets with Hayes in 1965 for Denis Preston, both now so sought-after that a few dozen pristine vinyl copies would buy a beach hut in Worthing. Around the same time, alto player and flautist, Prince Lasha cut an album with Stan Tracey and others for CBS. It has not aged well. Better by far is Ben Webster's *Webster's Dictionary*, although Stan Tracey remains unhappy with his own performance on the record. Yet, even more important than these Anglo-American outings was the appearance of Tubby Hayes in place of a drugged-out Paul Gonsalves with Ellington's band at the Festival Hall in 1964. As Godbolt reports, it was "a bolster for pride in British musicianship" (Godbolt 1989, 232).

As far as Hayes is concerned, as Cook and Morton suggest, he is best appreciated on live recordings. He was also a fine writer and arranger for big band and ran a student band for several years in the sixties, another example of how the jazz community sustained itself in the days before university jazz degree courses. Yet records featuring his orchestra like *Tubbs' Tours* (Fontana), *100% Proof* (Fontana) and *The Tubby Hayes Orchestra* (Fontana) might be at times highly charged affairs, while also seeming somewhat passé in light of the music that Dankworth – let alone Neil Ardley and the New Jazz Orchestra, Mike Westbrook, John Warren and Mike Gibbs – produced. A number of live recordings of his small groups such as *For Members Only* (Mastermix) have since become available. They reveal just how good he could be with the right musicians on the right occasion. His choice of pianists was always exemplary, whether it was Gordon Beck, Terry Shannon or, as here, the undersung Mike Pyne. Of his studio albums, *Mexican Green*

(Fontana) is arguably his finest and his most "out" official recording. By this point, he had definitely absorbed Coltrane. From the easy, loping swing of the autobiographical "Off the Wagon" through the full-on charge of "Dear Johnny B" to the heavily Coltrane-influenced title track, this is a marvellous example of Hayes's capacity, at his best, to shift moods and styles without losing integrity. *Mexican Green* featured a new group of younger musicians, though Hayes himself was just thirty-one at the time. With Tony Levin on drums, Ron Matthewson on bass and Mike Pyne on piano, these were players who were fully conversant with the new jazz and the result speaks for itself. Apart from a rather desultory big band record of pop tunes, it was his last official recording. Shortly before his death in 1973 (Hayes's personal and health problems are covered in Chapter 7), he began playing free bop in a band, Splinters, that included drummers Phil Seamen and John Stevens, Stan Tracey, bassist Jeff Clyne, altoist Trevor Watts and Kenny Wheeler. Who knows what might have been, but throughout his output Hayes was continually searching and growing as a musician and a composer.

It was not that the Americans no longer had any influence or that they were not valued. The Scott club continued its practice of featuring US performers, sometimes with the house rhythm section but sometimes, as the MU ban relaxed still further, with their own backing. The appearances of Roland Kirk were particular high points, and talking points, and his influence was felt by a lot of the younger musicians. Tours continued, often promoted by Harold Davison's organization, though as the jazz star waned and that of rock waxed, these became less frequent and were confined to main centres. Performances by both Miles Davis and Archie Shepp at the Jazz Expo in 1967 were particularly significant in their impact, while Tony Williams' Lifetime (with Jack Bruce on bass, Larry Young on organ, John McLaughlin on guitar and Williams on drums) had a similar impact at its London Marquee Club appearance in 1970. Such appearances had always tended to divide fans, critics and musicians. This phenomenon was seen most sharply by John Coltrane's only UK visit in 1961.

It seems astonishing to recall that Hayes was one of a number of musicians, critics and fans who struggled with the music that John Coltrane performed on his UK tour in 1961. When Hayes returned from his second trip stateside in July 1962, he spoke to *Melody Maker* about the experience and talked of seeing the Coltrane Quartet in New York.

> I did hear Coltrane with his Quartet – Eric Dolphy wasn't there. Compared with what he played on the British Tour I felt that he was, maybe, coming back to sanity. He played beautifully. Coltrane's rhythm section of Elvin Jones, Jimmy Garrison was the greatest I heard. Coltrane didn't play anything new – sticking to the things from his records. You know, when I first heard his "Village Vanguard" album I thought he was fluffing. But seeing

him in the flesh I knew he was meaning to do those things –
going for double notes.   (Dawbarn 1962a, 8)

Hayes was by no means alone in his reaction. The gigs split the British jazz
scene, perhaps indicating its innate conservatism or rather that new ideas
often take time to be absorbed. Bob Dawbarn writing in the *Melody Maker*
on 11 November 1961 (Dawbarn 1961a, 7) had predicted "Something's got to
happen ..." The following week after the gig, which featured a double bill of
Coltrane's group plus Eric Dolphy and Dizzy Gillespie's quintet with pianist
Lalo Schifrin, Dawbarn was eating his words: "I caught the second house at
Kilburn on Saturday and, frankly, the Coltrane Quintet was so far out it made
Gillespie sound as formal and easy to follow as Acker Bilk." He continued:

> Between them, Coltrane (on tenor and soprano) and Dolphy
> (alto, flute and bass clarinet produced the most extraordinary
> sounds I have ever heard. And the rhythm section! Pianist McCoy
> Tyner, bassist Reggie Workman and drummer Elvin Jones were all
> apparently playing in different tempos and frequently in different
> time signatures. Coltrane's soprano was used during a 25-minute
> "My Favourite Things" and sounded so Eastern, I kept looking
> into the wings for Wilson, Keppel and Betty. Dolphy's flute tone
> would have given Julius Baker a heart attack.
>   (Dawbarn 1961b, 15)

Dawbarn could see "no logical basis to any of it" and felt it "belonged more
to the realms of higher mathematics than music". As he begins to discuss
Gillespie's performance, one can sense his palpable relief. But, in all fairness,
Coltrane's 1961 tour caused wide consternation among some fans, musi-
cians and critics. Alan Skidmore, a devotee of Coltrane, saw the group at the
Walthamstow Granada:

> To be honest, I wasn't really sure what I was listening to but at
> the same time I knew I was listening to something special, some-
> thing very new, very unusual but I have it on good authority that
> the reason he never came back in 1962 or 1963 when he came to
> Europe and played in Paris and Stockholm with the classic quar-
> tet with Jimmy Garrison on bass was largely due to the press he
> got here in '61. In this country, they didn't quite grasp what he
> was doing and almost dismissed him. When he came back with
> that dynamite quartet, we never got to see them.
>   (Interview with Alan Skidmore, July 2009)

Guitarist and bassist, Goudie Charles also saw Coltrane on that tour:

You cannot possibly imagine the impact that had on us because the headliner was the Dizzy Gillespie Quintet with Mel Lewis. We went because of that. We knew Coltrane's name obviously but we didn't know about the quartet. He played this thing – we didn't know what it was but it was a half hour version of "My Favourite Things", but again that wasn't as well-known a tune as it subsequently became. "What the hell was that eastern waltz thing he did?" Unbelievable. I remember we were standing on the pavement outside the Gaumont discussing this mind-blowing gig and Elvin Jones.   (Interview with Goudie Charles, February 2008)

But as he also recalled:

Half the audience walked out. They hated it. I had the same experience when I saw Miles Davis when he came over with the band with Dave Holland and was into that Silent Way period. I mean he was playing free really. There were people booing and walking out and Archie Shepp had got rid of quite a lot because he was on the bill too. All these people who had come for Dizzy, they hated Coltrane. It was very hard for a while.
(Interview with Goudie Charles, February 2008)

But for those young musicians like Charles who got it, this was a life-changing experience. Nearly fifty years on, drummer Jon Hiseman still recalls the awe-inspiring nature of Coltrane's performances in Britain that year:

What I heard was the kind of integration that just takes your breath away. Just play "Tunji" from the *Coltrane* album. Just listen to the piano solo. This was extraordinary music by anybody's standard and it's not about technique. It's about something else entirely. The great tragedy to me is that the general public will never get that. They will never understand and, of course, the classical people haven't got a clue when it comes to touching something like that. It's a closed door unless you make the effort.
(Interview with Jon Hiseman, May 2009.)

New ideas, in whatever area of life or the arts, often do take time to be understood and, for my sins, when I saw the Mike Westbrook Concert Band in 1969 at the age of fifteen, my reaction was akin to Bob Dawbarn's response to Coltrane. That some reacted conservatively is obvious and actually unsurprising. The attitudes, encountered by Joe Harriott and referred to by Skidmore, Charles and Hiseman above, can be easily identified elsewhere. Reviewing Eric Dolphy's *Out There* in the *Melody Maker* (Dawbarn 1962b), Bob Dawbarn's comments indicate his struggles to understand where Dolphy is coming from. He concludes, "There ARE patches of fine jazz on this record, but much of it is, indeed, 'Out There'. I would be the first to welcome Dolphy back."

Even more telling are (the then-ubiquitous) Steve Race's comments in *Jazz Journal* on Charles Mingus's *East Coasting*. He describes the track "Memories of You" as "a fantastic bore"! He then proceeds to dismiss Mingus's "vertical" approach to composition, which suggests that he would not like George Russell or Oliver Nelson either. He concludes, "If we were giving marks, that record would receive a bored nil from me" (Race 1960, 7).

Here, the accusation of conservatism seems a fair one, but neither Race nor Dawbarn were completely representative of jazz opinion in Britain. As Mike Westbrook points out access to the more modern American jazz was still very patchy in the early sixties, certainly outside the main jazz centres of London, Manchester and Birmingham. One of the first records that he recalls opening that particular door for him was Art Blakey's *Jazz Messengers at the Paris Olympia*. This came out in 1958, but it was several years later that Westbrook actually heard it. While Georgie Fame did get access to US jazz albums in the early sixties, this was only through GIs visiting the Flamingo (interview with Georgie Fame, April 2009). Jon Hiseman played in Mike Taylor's quartet supporting Ornette Coleman on his first London performance at Croydon's Fairfield Halls in 1965, a concert that went ahead despite opposition from the Musicians' Union. Bearing in mind the fact that Mike Taylor's music was considered quite "out" at the time, Hiseman was genuinely shocked to hear that Coleman was doing something similar:

> Something else that must be mentioned about this – I remember being very surprised at what Ornette Coleman was doing for the simple reason that anybody was doing anything like we were doing anywhere else in the world. The reason for that was that there weren't any musicians coming into London playing that sort of music and as a young man who had just left school living in suburbia I didn't have access to the kinds of records that might be available in some famous shop in the centre of London. I had no idea that there was a movement in New York that was also playing free or improvisatory music.
>
> (Interview with Jon Hiseman, May 2009)

Hiseman notes that a lot of musicians who heard Coleman on that occasion "didn't get it at all" and that Taylor's music often met with the same reaction. There is a widespread presumption that echoes the ideas of philosopher Thomas Kuhn (Kuhn 1996). Kuhn meant his ideas to apply only to the hard sciences but they have percolated to other areas of thought and study. Through this process they have achieved a wider currency. This presumption suggests that a degree of progress is achievable within a certain paradigm or area, but when this becomes blocked a new paradigm is needed to achieve advance and change. In due course, the new replaces the old, leading to fresh developments in the form until the next disruptive force emerges. In this sense, both bebop and the new jazz of the late fifties represent paradigm shifts. One consequence of such an approach is that it leads to those who oppose or simply do not immediately embrace change becoming labelled as "conservative". In addition, this approach or understanding is overly deterministic. It reflects the belief that the "new" represents progress and its acceptance is unquestioning of the very notion of progress. It also over-simplifies and depoliticizes a far more complex process. Notions of progress involve value judgements that are often obscure and hidden and which them-selves reflect particular social, cultural and, in the arts, sometimes economic interests. What is needed is a more systemic and dynamic model that sees the process as one where equilibrium shifts continually due to the balance of such interests/forces within the system. Or to put it more prosaically, some got it like Hiseman and Goudie Charles, some got it later like Tubby Hayes and Alan Skidmore, and some like Steve Race never got it at all.

There was also a more widespread desire among British musicians to produce jazz that was not dependent on American models, and Joe Harriott was not alone in this regard. The development of a British approach to jazz was present from the outset, even though the shape it would take by the late sixties and early seventies or the process through which that would emerge could certainly not have been predicted. The dynamic for this lay in the proc-ess of assimilation, absorption, creation and recreation. It lay in practice, or rather in praxis, to use Marx's term for the dialectic of theory–practice.

The listeners must, however, be forgiven for failing to note such questions and instead immersing themselves in the sheer pleasure of British jazz of the early sixties. Some of it might have been twee at times. A record such as drummer Tony Kinsey's 1963 jazz version of the hit Frank Loesser musical, *How to Succeed in Business Without Really Trying* (Decca; Vocalion), may have looked good on paper, but the absence of any really strongly memo-rable tunes should have been a warning. Kinsey's output was patchy, but *An Evening With ...* from two years earlier (Ember; Fantastic Voyage) and featuring Tubby Hayes, Bill Le Sage, bassist Lennie Bush and trumpeter Jimmy Deuchar has some very good playing and several strong tunes. John Fordham identifies in British jazz of the period a tendency towards overly fussy arrangements with echoes of the dance bands. This could be heard in some of Kinsey's work and in fellow drummer Tony Crombie's as well. Much of Crombie's music is of its time, but *Atmosphere* (Columbia) certainly has its moments. That British jazz was a "mixed bag" is inevitable. But so too was a lot of American jazz of the time.

During this period so many musicians came through that it is impossible to discuss them all. Many fans still carry a torch for tenor saxophonist Dick Morrissey or for baritone saxophonist Ronnie Ross. For a time both were omnipresent on the scene. Morrissey went on to achieve some commercial success in the seventies, first with guitarist Terry Smith playing jazz-rock with If, and later with Scottish guitarist Jim Mullen in their eponymous jazz-fusion group. His *Here and Now and Sounding Good* and *Storm Warning* (both Mercury; Vocalion) were released in 1967 and marked major advances on his previous output. Ross produced a solid body of work of which *Cleopatra's Needle* from 1969 (Fontana) was probably the best example. Perhaps one of the most idiosyncratic players who emerged in the sixties was tenor saxophonist/clarinettist Tony Coe. Coe seemed as comfortable playing with Humphrey Lyttelton as he later did in improvising guitarist Derek Bailey's Company settings. His *Swinging Till the Girls Come Home* from 1961 (Philips) is disappointing, though highly sought-after. Recorded six years later for Denis Preston, *Tony's Basement* (Columbia) is, however, quite lovely. It features both jazz players and a string quartet in a setting, which suits his evenness of tone and highly personal sound perfectly and which recalls Stan Getz's beautiful *Focus* and its wonderful arrangements by Eddie Sauter. Unfortunately, Coe's 1977 Third Stream masterpiece *Zeitgeist* (Columbia), again recorded by Preston, falls outside our period.

From Crombie to Coe, from Kinsey to Ross these musicians illustrate some of the impulses that existed within British jazz at this point. Some of these were undoubtedly conservative, while others were more radical. But then the position of the music was an odd one. In its modernist guise it existed within the context of a burgeoning consumer society, which was at that time both consumer and market-driven. It sat awkwardly somewhere in the space between pop and light music/light entertainment, while being increasingly divorced from both. For a time, it coexisted alongside the enthusiasm among younger listeners for R&B, just as later it would overlap with progressive rock music. It was increasingly a music that hovered uneasily between the jazz club and the concert hall, while remaining prey to economic winds and cultural fashions outside its influence. All of this might have made life a constant struggle for the jazz musician or club owner but it would also prove liberating in a way. When there is no prospect of financial success whatever compromises are made, the pressure is off. The artist might then just as well make art without worrying about keeping a weather-eye on the look-out for prevailing fashions. And this is precisely what a new generation of jazz musicians did. In this respect, the Don Rendell–Ian Carr Quintet seem to exist somewhere between the old and the new.

I mentioned in the chapter on education that the Rendell–Carr Quintet seemed to represent in their membership and music a bridge between two generations of British jazz musicians and embodied some of the wider changes that were occurring in British society. The group boasted an incredibly empathic rhythm section in Dave Green and Trevor Tomkins, but also found in Don Rendell a fatherly presence and guiding hand, as well as a consummately gifted musician. It was, however, Michael Garrick and Ian Carr who were to have the bigger impact on British jazz.

The group's bassist Dave Green recalls that the identity of the early quintet was "very based on the Miles Davis thing":

> We were all trying to emulate these great players. I was trying to do a Paul Chambers and Trevor was trying to do a Jimmy Cobb. John (Burch) was very much influenced by Wynton Kelly. So, we had that sort of young inexperienced thing about it but as time went on with the band it really matured a lot.
>
> (Heining 2004b, 14)

Green again points out the importance of Michael Garrick's arrival in 1964. As he puts it, "His compositions were very strong and we started utilising a lot of Indian-type compositions Michael used to write and the whole band became really strong after Michael joined."

The Rendell–Carr Quintet would prove to be one of the most innovative, original and popular British jazz groups of the period. Interviewed in 2004, Ian Carr noted that there was something uniquely poetic about their music:

> I think that was one of the reasons people liked it so much. It wasn't hard-driving like a lot of American jazz was at the time. We had other influences, you see. I was at university living in digs with a whole lot of Indian students who played their music and we ate with our hands with them. We had different kind of focuses than the Americans. We were really into texture and, of course, we were into different rhythms as well and, of course, a lot of them were asymmetrical as well. And Michael Garrick was steeped in Indian music as well. That was a very interesting influence because we could do so many new things that we had never thought of before.   (Interview with Ian Carr, May 2004)

We have already discussed *Dusk Fire* (Columbia; BGO), their breakthrough second recording. However, the two albums that followed, 1968's *Phase III* (Columbia; BGO) and *Live* from 1969 (Columbia; BGO) were very nearly as good. *Phase III* was perhaps the Rendell–Carr Quintet's freest album, and it featured two tunes, "Crazy Jane" and "Les Neiges D'Antan", that Ian Carr had recorded in 1966 as part of a quartet with drummer John Stevens, saxophonist Trevor Watts and bassist Jeff Clyne for the album *Springboard*, released by Polydor three years later. These last three played together in Stevens's Spontaneous Music Ensemble (SME) and, although free improvisation was never his preferred mode of expression, Carr acquits himself well on *Springboard* and shows that he understands the idiom. *Live* was recorded in the studio before an audience of friends and fans, including a loudly appreciative Warren Mitchell (Alf Garnett's more urbane alter ego). The recent release in 2010 of a live recording of a performance in 1966 at University College London (Reel RR016) gives an even better picture of just how exciting this quintet was on the stand. Yet, *Live* remains a wonderful document as well, with Rendell's ballad "Vignette" contrasting beautifully with Carr/Tomkins's modal "rock & roll dance" piece "Pavanne" and Garrick's limpid, Indian-influenced "Voices" with its glorious flute from Rendell.

Their final record was *Change Is* (Columbia; BGO) and it introduced the percussionist Guy Warren of Ghana into the group. It had been Ian Carr's suggestion that Warren join the "Five" and for a number of reasons, musical as much as personal, his presence proved quite divisive. The album has some fine moments but Warren's contributions do not really gel with the group's sound or approach. One of the group's final performances was at the *Melody Maker*'s Pollwinners' Concert at the Festival Hall in May 1969. Warren had already been asked to leave and the packed hall heard a fine and majestic set from the quintet that had won the magazine's small group section three years in a row. Sadly, the rest really was silence.

Michael Garrick had continued to record with his own bands during his time with the Rendell–Carr quintet, often with Joe Harriott on alto and either Shake Keane or Ian Carr on trumpet or flugelhorn. To begin with he had used Coleridge Goode on bass and Colin Barnes (and later John Marshall) on drums, but towards the end of the decade, and certainly beyond, his rhythm section of choice was Dave Green and Trevor Tomkins. Garrick continued working with Green and Tomkins both as a trio and as part of a larger sextet-cum-septet featuring saxophonists Jim Philip, Art Themen and Don Rendell and trumpeter Henry Lowther and, later, in place of Philip, singer Norma Winstone. As well as playing with Garrick, Rendell led his own quintet, initially featuring Stan Robinson and later saxophonist–composer Barbara Thompson. Coincidentally, Rendell's lovely *Spacewalk* (Columbia) from 1972 used vibist Peter Shade, who had been a member of Michael Garrick's quartet in the late fifties. Ian Carr went on to great success with the jazz-rock ensemble Nucleus, as well as playing in the multinational United Jazz + Rock Ensemble and with composer–arranger Neil Ardley.

However, it is Michael Garrick who seems to have produced the most consistent body of work over the years. The recent release of *Silhouette* (Gearbox), an unissued live recording from 1958 with a quartet featuring Peter Shade, drummer Brian Barnes, Paul Hemmings on bass and vocalist Josephine Stahl, reveals what a confident and individualistic pianist he already was. Its two Garrick originals, "A Welter of Phenomena" and "Silhouette", show that he was also a precociously talented composer. Jump five years to Garrick's first album, *Moonscape* (Airborne; Trunk), and the progress is remarkable. This trio set with Dave Green and Colin Barnes offers a very free set of six Garrick originals. These performances sound exceptionally fresh and original. Even in their less successful moments, and at times the rhythm section does seem less than sure of itself, any clumsiness adds to the personal and individual qualities of the music. The sense is that the musicians are reaching for something, even if they are not quite sure what at this point. Garrick's first album in his own right, *October Woman* (Argo; Vocalion), featured a quintet of Harriott, Keane, Goode and Barnes, and was recorded in October 1964. His group had already made two poetry and jazz albums for Argo with poets Jeremy Robson, Adrian Mitchell, Dannie Abse and Laurie Lee, which will be discussed in more detail in Chapter 12. However, the strength and originality of Garrick's compositions on the poetry/jazz records, such as "Salvation March", "She's Like a Swallow" and "Wedding Hymn" – the latter with some lovely baroque trumpet choruses from Shake Keane – make it clear that this was no longer a jazz in thrall to its Stateside parentage.

October Woman and *Promises* (Argo; Vocalion) speak powerfully of Garrick's abilities and, I suspect, illustrate why he was asked to join Rendell–Carr. Both include three trio tracks, of which those on *Promises*, recorded in May 1965, hark back most to the more open format of *Moonscape*. However, it is the quintet tracks that provide the clearest statement of independence. Listen to the pedal points on "Anthem" from *October Woman* and the manic interplay between Keane and Harriott. "Sketches of Israel" revisits one of *Moonscape*'s strongest tunes but with much more emphasis on structure. Again, Garrick's deployment of the horns is fresh and imaginative, while the title track is a wonderful ballad full of tenderness but with an almost literary element to it. There is indeed something of a Shakespearean aspect – Keane's nickname comes from his love of poetry – in the trumpeter's delivery. It is as if he is speaking lines to a loved one. As for Harriott, Garrick's tunes seem to bring out a romantic, gentle side in the fiery Jamaican's playing. Unsurprisingly given its title, "Parting Is Such" from *Promises* continues in its duet and soliloquies the hint of the Bard. "Second Coming" is an amazing evocation of a train journey, with a delightful dialogue between Harriott and Keane, while "Merlin the Wizard" and "Leprechaun Leap" are examples of Garrick's sometimes playful, lighter-hearted approach to jazz. Both sound very English to me. However, it is "Requiem" with its gorgeous, heart-on-sleeve solo from Harriott that steals the show.

Along with bassist–composer Graham Collier and Stan Tracey, Garrick is one of the finest small-group composers this country has produced. The quality of his writing has been sustained in all of the contexts in which he has worked subsequently. Tunes that he contributed to the Rendell–Carr book included classics like "Dusk Fire", "Cold Mountain", "Black Marigolds", "Prayer", "Webster's Mood" and "Carolling". In the seventies and eighties, Garrick would continue to work with small groups but also composed a number of much larger scale works, some of which he has been able to record with his big band. All of his work reveals and continues to reveal that same care, attention to detail and literary bent that he brought to his own groups and to Rendell–Carr in the sixties. There were already many jewels in the British jazz crown and Michael Garrick was most certainly one. In fact, any notion that a distinctively British jazz only emerged later in the decade is easily dispelled with the simple injunction, "Go listen to Michael Garrick".

5 Can't Stop the Rock

Strange how potent cheap music is.   Noel Coward, *Private Lives*, Act 1

We're more popular than Jesus now; I don't know which will go first – rock 'n' roll
or Christianity.   John Lennon, *Evening Standard*, 4 March 1966

The quality of British modern (and mainstream) jazz and the advances being made by the musicians were never to be reflected in the kind of audience support or record sales that it might have deserved. We have noted the feeling among some such as Stan Tracey and Bobby Wellins that many fans within the modernist camp saw the local variety as being of lesser value compared with the North American original. We have seen that this had been an issue for Scott and King with their Gerrard Street club in attracting an audience for the British acts it promoted.

More importantly, beat music and then R&B had by the early/mid-sixties made huge inroads with the section of the record-buying public that jazz might have hoped to attract to its music. It is this that we need to concentrate upon now. Once again things are neither clear-cut nor straightforward. We find ourselves viewing a series of events that are connected to a greater or lesser extent.

These events, or rather trends, came together at a particular time in Britain and they did spell a change in fortunes for both "trad" and modern jazz. We can identify what these trends were reasonably easily. To begin with we have the rise of beat, then R&B and then rock music. We will, however, see shortly that this did not mean that jazz became entirely separated from these popular styles. Rather, a number of jazz musicians played crucial roles in the development of British R&B and, later, rock music. There was a considerable amount of cross-fertilization as well, though it may be argued that the departure of pioneering figures such as Graham Bond, Brian Auger, Jack Bruce and Ginger Baker to R&B may have impacted negatively on British jazz. In particular, their departure might have denied modern jazz in Britain the chance to find a different trajectory and one that might have chimed more loudly with the young. The drift of younger listeners to beat, R&B and rock in the sixties may not tell the whole story, but it takes up several important chapters.

There are, at the same time, other issues that need to be considered. First, there is the somewhat awkward relationship that both modern and "trad" jazz have with the mainstream media and with popular culture. We have touched on this, most directly perhaps with "trad", even if we have yet to offer a satisfactory answer as to where jazz should sit. Is it popular or folk music? Is it part of the world of light or popular entertainment or does it need to be considered more as an innovative, dynamic art form? Such questions were answered more effortlessly in the rest of Europe than in Britain due to the different trajectory of jazz in Germany, France, Italy and elsewhere. More obviously, the position of jazz in Britain was different again from that applying in the country of its birth. However, this general point has implications for another issue, which relates to the availability to jazz of the kinds of support networks – formal and informal, private and public, amateur and professional – that might sustain it. Though the sixties did see the beginnings of Arts Council funding for jazz, this came late in the day and, probably, in amounts insufficient to support it. Other possible sources of support from the media were at best inconsistent, while that from the major record companies and, in terms of access to certain types of venue, from major promoters, was similarly patchy. Jazz continued to rely as ever on the goodwill and hard work of the many fans who ran magazines, clubs, jazz societies and festivals throughout the country. Indeed, these have often been its main means of sustenance.

The other issue that needs to be addressed is one that runs throughout this book, though it is a central consideration in this and the next chapter. It is one thing to acknowledge the failure of jazz to maintain a sufficient level of audience support among younger fans in the face of the rise of rock music. But we also need to account for why this was so. That it failed is largely due to its difficult relationship with capitalism and, in particular, the capitalism of consumer culture that developed in the fifties and sixties. It will be suggested that the difficulties involved in that relationship are in fact inherent, and even arise from certain key elemental aspects of the music. This point is dealt with more fully in the concluding chapters but is at least implicit in the discussion that follows more immediately.

The story most often told of the fate of British jazz, traditional and modern, is that the beat and R&B groups swept all before them and jazz was cast into the wilderness. There is, however, a more interesting narrative that focuses on changes in public taste over time and a more complex set of links between jazz and popular forms. As we will see, the process of change was slower and less complete than is often assumed, and owed a great deal to the dynamic and fluctuating relationship between economics and culture.

The Beatles' story does not require recounting in detail. Like a lot of British groups of the time, they had developed their act in the clubs of Hamburg. They played a wide-ranging mixture of material drawn from rock & roll, R&B and the pop music of the day, and even included show tunes and music hall numbers in their act. Unlike those who followed after them their music owed less to the Chicago-style blues but owed a debt to other African-American musical styles, as well as to that very British folk-blues-derived form, skiffle. Their home town of Liverpool had for many years been a point of arrival and departure for those travelling to and from the States. This was one of the reasons that it provided unusually fertile soil for a burgeoning rock & roll scene. The Beatles were at the time one of a whole tranche of groups working the pubs and clubs of the city, most notably the Cavern Club, which had originally been a jazz venue. In a way, just as New Orleans around the turn of the twentieth century was just one of a number of American cities where a new, syncopated music was developing, Liverpool was not the only city where something of this sort was happening. At the time such trends could be identified in London, Newcastle, Manchester, Glasgow and elsewhere. Just as the form that came out of New Orleans determined the direction of jazz, so too, by virtue of the fact that it was the first to be noticed, Merseybeat provided the original template for "beat groups" in Britain. They were guitar-led, often using both lead and rhythm guitars, and with a strong emphasis on harmonized vocals.

Record-shop owner Brian Epstein heard the Beatles at the Cavern, was struck by them and their performance on a number of levels, but most importantly by their audience's reaction to them and in particular by the responses of the girls in the crowd. He became their manager, tried to sell them to several London-based labels and was famously turned down by Decca. He did, however, persuade George Martin at EMI to sign them to one of the company's less prestigious imprints, Parlophone. Parlophone was used by EMI primarily as a novelty and comedy outlet, though pop singer Adam Faith was also on the label. In fact, Martin had worked with traditional jazz bands and had recorded albums by The Goons, Peter Sellers's highly successful *Songs for Swinging Sellers* and Michael Bentine's *It's a Square World*. It was the Beatles' great fortune that their future producer was a man who was adept at using the studio and its still primitive technology to produce unusual results. It is worth stressing, however, that Parlophone was not a "pop" label, and, had expectations of the Beatles been higher, they would have been signed to the more prestigious Columbia outlet, along with Cliff Richard, The Shadows, Johnny Dankworth, Acker Bilk, Chris Barber, Humphrey Lyttelton, Helen Shapiro and Shirley Bassey, all of whom they would shortly eclipse.

The Beatles' success began when "Love Me Do" reached number 17 in the Top Twenty in December 1962. Twelve months later, the group had had four number one hits and had begun to force changes in the way the recording industry would develop over the next thirty or more years. In their wake, agents rushed to sign anyone with a Liverpool accent and a guitar. Then, when supplies from Scouseland started running low, anyone vaguely northern who could sing a bit would find a contract waved under the noses. The Beatles were followed by Gerry and the Pacemakers, Billy J. Kramer and the Dakotas, The Searchers (one of the best of these groups and a big influence on the development of American rock music post-1965), the Swinging Bluejeans, the Fourmost and the Merseybeats. From Manchester came the Hollies, Wayne Fontana and the Mindbenders, the execrable Freddie and the Dreamers and, a little later, Herman's Hermits. But it was not all "northern". Companies like Decca cast the net wide to make up for missing out on the Beatles and discovered both the Stones and Brian Poole and the Tremeloes around the same time.

Groups such as Ian and the Zodiacs, "Kingsize" Taylor and the Dominoes, the Kubas, Faron's Flamingos and the Big Three (whom many on Merseyside still hold in awe) were less successful due to a mixture of bad luck, bad management or just simply because they did not click with the public in some way. The fact these acts were discarded is intriguing. They did not fail because of lack of talent. Choices and decisions are made within the context of a marketplace. Those choices then cut off other possibilities and developments, rendering some choices obsolete or unlikely in the future. In this respect, and others, I am with Karl Popper rather than Thomas Kuhn.

The immediate effects of the rise of beat on traditional jazz were seen as catastrophic, as Chris Barber explains:

> What happened was that the people who were our followers for our sort of music, starting in the fifties, they had come to an age when there were younger teenagers in their families or even their own children. These younger people were suddenly only interested in the Beatles and the mopheads, that whole thing. And the press got solidly behind the pop explosion and the Beatles.
> (Interview with Chris Barber, February 2008)

Barber liked the Beatles both musically and personally, and was on the same bill as the group when they did their first BBC radio broadcast in 1962. In his view, later groups such as the Stones, Cream, John Mayall and others were continuing the same tradition of drawing on the blues that he and his peers had begun. However, he notes that the British press, and not just the music press, latched onto the Beatles and beat music in a way that had not happened with either traditional jazz or skiffle.

The thing was that older people had the impression that there were no jazz concerts any more. All there was was beat concerts. Inevitably, it was very tough for jazz, particularly when John Lennon said, "Our fans don't like jazz." That didn't help. Though John said to me in 1967, "I didn't mean you – your band's fine," he said. But the damage was done, not by John, but by the media taking hold of it. So, jazz was suddenly having a real hard time. We were playing a concert in the Royal Festival Hall one year, then two years later the best we could get was The George at Morden!
(Interview with Chris Barber, February 2008)

It is a point that Kenny Ball confirms. He remembers the Beatles supporting his band at the Cavern in 1962 and that shortly afterwards his band could not even get a booking at the club (interview with Kenny Ball, May 2008). He also recalls John Lennon's remarks on the subject of jazz with some horror. Acker Bilk, however, is more circumspect in his comments. Asked how the rise of the beat groups affected him and his peers, he remarks, "It wasn't bad. We still had our jazz clubs and there were still a lot of good jazz fans around. It didn't bother us that much. We just didn't listen to those groups" (interview with Acker Bilk, February 2008).

As we noted in an earlier chapter, by that time, Bilk, Barber and Ball had made some inroads into the American market. Bilk remembers doing the Ed Sullivan Show at the height of the Cuban Missile Crisis – his "Stranger on the Shore" topped the US charts. Barber had played President Kennedy's First International Jazz Festival in Washington, DC in summer 1963, while Ball tapped into the resurgence of enthusiasm for New Orleans and Chicago styles that took place in the States in the sixties. In a way, they were well-established enough to weather these changes in popular taste and all three survived successfully, as did some of the lesser lights such as Max Collie, Alex Welsh and Terry Lightfoot. Looking at the *Melody Maker* gig guide for the years from 1962–70, these and other similar bands continued to play regularly around what was admittedly a shrinking circuit. The larger concert venues were becoming less of a feature on tours and the contrast between the successes of the boom years must have been marked. Some, like Humphrey Lyttelton and the Fairweather–Brown Band, had already broadened their appeal anyway by increasing the stylistic range of their repertoire, and others, like trumpeter Mike Cotton and Alex Welsh, followed suit.

One suspects that Barber and Bilk are not actually at odds in their perceptions but are rather seeing the same picture in a slightly different way, which may have something to do with their personalities. Bilk's bluff, easy-going manner contrasts with Barber's more dynamic engagement with the worlds of music and commerce. It is clear, however, that a number of social and cultural processes began with the Beatles, some of which have taken a long time to unravel. These clearly have had implications for British jazz at the time and since.

Teenagers were, as we have noted, invented in the 1950s – in Britain, at least. They were a product of a period of growing prosperity and full employment. Their experiences of life contrasted greatly with that of their parents and grandparents both before and during the Second World War. They had money to spend and quickly became a market worth targeting. Unusually for members of the lower and middle orders of society, they achieved a degree of financial independence much younger than had previously been the case. What emerged was a strange, almost dialectical relationship between youth and the market, with most of the power inevitably lying with the former. However, these were not passive consumers. Rather, they had ideas, sometimes vaguely formed perhaps, that what they wanted from consumerism was that which would define them and offer an identity specific to their age group rather than their social position. The place where they found such images had previously lain across the Atlantic. At first, they were faced with the contrast between Presley, Dean and Brando on the one hand, and Cliff Richard, Mark Wynter, Adam Faith and Tommy Steele on the other. What the Beatles and their like offered was something quite magical – it offered them a glimpse into a world of possibilities much closer to home and more immediate. There was almost something narcissistic about it, though in neither a colloquial nor negative sense. It was possible to look at Paul, John, Ringo and George – and the girlfriends they were seen with – and somehow see oneself. The boys (and girls) in these groups came from Liverpool, Dartford and Newcastle, not from exotic Memphis or New York or Los Angeles, places that few even from the more affluent classes could ever hope to visit.

What is more, the music they played was home-grown. It often surprises quite how many different ingredients could be found in British pop and rock music of the sixties. How many teenagers of the period would have admitted to listening to music hall style songs, vaudeville, brass bands, baroque music, madrigals, folk, jazz, country or show tunes, or for that matter Indian music? Black styles of soul, R&B and white rock & roll might have been pre-eminent in terms of the rhythm and pulse of the music, but these other elements kept surfacing as well. The Kinks introduced a sitar-like drone on "See My Friends" in 1965, while their "Dedicated Follower of Fashion" offered a music hall setting for its acerbic, mocking satire. Herman's Hermits, however, went all the way with "I'm Henry VIII, I Am", a song from 1910. The Stones' "Lady Jane" played with images of courtly love and a pseudo-madrigal setting, while "As Tears Go By", written for Marianne Faithfull (and one of the first songs Jagger and Richards wrote together), was a fey, string-laden ballad. Its B-side was the Elizabethan tune, "Greensleeves". As for the Beatles, alongside the original tunes, rockers and soul ballads, they recorded the show tunes "Till There Was You" on *With the Beatles* and "A Taste of Honey" on *Please Please Me*.

To these one would add the country & western pastiche of "I'll Cry Instead" from *Hard Day's Night* and the cover of Buck Owens's "Act Naturally" from *Help!* George played sitar for the first time on *Rubber Soul's* "Norwegian Wood", while calypso and African drums surfaced on "Mr Moonlight" from *Beatles for Sale*. Then there was the "baroque" harpsichord-like solo on "In My Life". There are many other examples from The Who, The Move, Sandy Shaw, Cilla Black, Tom Jones and Dusty Springfield. The point is that sixties pop offered young people a music that was simultaneously exciting and exotic on the one hand but familiar on the other. What is more, it did so in a way that seemed immediately novel. Its sources were irrelevant and disregarded. It was new. It was theirs and nothing else mattered (see Laing 1972).

For reasons that should be obvious, jazz, in particular in its more modern guise, could not compete with that. It was not new; it was not based on youth; it was hard to play and hard to assimilate – you had to really listen – and it was hard to dance to. Jazz had a history and in that respect what might have been an advantage was instead to its detriment. Most of all, it was hard to market and sell.

The creation of a market with such a profound emphasis on youth would continue to reverberate to the detriment of jazz. What then began to happen was that those who experienced the bliss of life in that dawn proved remarkably reluctant to give it up. The irony of Herbert Asquith's often misattributed and misquoted words "Youth would be an ideal state if it came a little later in life" was lost on them, and was met with a resounding, "It has now!" Just as the young became older, so the old began to become younger. In the sixties, a man's thirtieth birthday would be greeted by a pipe and slippers, and a woman's by a bed-jacket and a warmer nightie. By the early eighties, the newly divorced, thirty-something male would be dancing to K.C. and the Sunshine Band and trying to pull, while his ex-wife would be out with her girlfriends at some Greek restaurant sipping retsina and being told that she had her whole life ahead of her. By the late nineties, dad with or without mum (both now in their forties) were up to their knees in mud at Glastonbury singing along with Oasis or Paul Weller, and ten years later they listen to pallid imitations of the music of their youth. They are no longer the older generation or "Generation X". They are the "Jools Holland Generation" dipping in and out of indie and world music and cheering along to a revived Tom Jones or Alison Moyet. If anything, the internet and availability of downloads have made their lives easier. Most such sites even have helpful hints that, if they enjoyed that particular track, then they would probably enjoy these too. There is no need to step outside their comfort zone. In *Peter Pan*, Wendy at least grew up.

Perhaps this sounds rather dyspeptic. However, as youth asserted itself and became a focus of market forces in the areas of clothes, music, make-up, transportation and other lifestyle trappings, this also led to far more wide-ranging changes. As each new generation carried key aspects of their young selves into adulthood and middle age, points of transition became increasingly blurred. This in turn allowed lifestyle industries greater flexibility, freedom and licence in marketing their products, as well as creating broader markets that no longer needed to be quite so age-specific. That which has continued to aid pop and rock musics, leaves other forms like jazz, classical and folk even more at the mercy of the vagaries of fashion.

It is a point that Chris Barber makes well, and he suggests a contrast with our continental neighbours that is also interesting:

> In other countries in Europe it wasn't the same, largely because in Germany, for example, youngsters never got into the idea that they were part of an adult universe without reference to what the adults thought. Of course, particularly in this country, people were selling them stuff, clothes that they told them they had to have. Here, they were encouraged to see themselves as a subculture and, of course, that meant that young people didn't hear jazz at all, whereas in the fifties young people did hear it because it was the only lively music around.
>
> (Interview with Chris Barber, February 2008)

Barber has a point, and there are differences in this respect and others between the UK and France, Germany and Italy and elsewhere in mainland Europe. These contrasts help explain how beat, R&B and rock did become so very dominant in the UK, while jazz seemed to survive more successfully in mainland Europe. To begin with, links between Britain and the USA are clearly stronger, not least in the area of language. Initially, Britain had remained outside the European Economic Community (EEC), which was formed following the Treaty of Rome 1957. Attempts to join the union failed in both 1963 and 1967. One of the issues for French President de Gaulle, who exercised his veto on both occasions, was Britain's ties with America. Britain had been one of the three leading Allied powers and with the establishment of two competing geopolitical power blocs post-1945, Britain inevitably tied its future to its North Atlantic ally. The influence of America on the UK and its culture during the fifties and sixties was huge and made more penetrable both by America's economic and military dominance. In a sense, British teenagers were not only subject to a set of powerful home-grown images targeted directly at them, but also to similarly youth-relevant images emanating from the USA. To a degree they defined themselves according to a hybrid of both sets. In contrast, historian, Arthur Marwick (1998) notes in relation to Italy in the early sixties, "What there was in the way of teenage subculture in Italy at this time was fractured and derivative." He draws a sharp contrast between the British scene, which had taken on board the influences of the more virile rock & roll performers, with the sentimentality of much Italian pop music. However, he points out that "Some sections of Italian youth were politicized as in France, and Communist party and Catholic youth organizations were even stronger." Otherwise, the picture he paints of Italian youth is a rather conservative one (Marwick 1998, 109–10).

In a way, Marwick is illustrating Barber's point about the less clearly defined separation of teenage and adult worlds in a Europe of which Britain was only a part. The Italian experience of jazz was also to prove quite different from that of the UK scene. While jazz in Britain struggled throughout the sixties, and even more so in the seventies, Italian jazz was able to secure a much stronger footing. Jazz musician Enrico Rava sees this as being in large measure due to support from the Italian left:

> Jazz became the big thing in Italy in the seventies because people identified jazz with revolution or leftist politics. During the Summer, there was thousands of festivals promoted by the Communist newspaper *l'Unitad* and all the time jazz musicians were exposed to a lot of people because the big festivals had fifteen to twenty thousand people there. We became known to a lot of people – not just to jazz hard-core fans. This faded away for a time but still we remain in everybody's minds much more than before. (Heining 2001c, 40)

The phenomenon of radical and socialist festivals featuring music and theatre alongside lectures and discussions is not just an Italian one. The French have a similar tradition, in fact one that goes back to the French revolution (Rudé 1964). Nor was it just a case of opportunism on the part of socialist and communist parties to include popular performers from jazz and rock music at these events. Rather, their inclusion was seen as a celebration of a radical tradition of culture and politics. In France too, jazz had made very significant inroads before the Second World War (see Jackson 2003). Both before and after 1939, a number of African-American musicians and artists had settled in Paris finding its open, cosmopolitan and tolerant atmosphere a major contrast to that of their own racially divided nation. Meanwhile, as Francis Newton notes, magazines dealing primarily with jazz had been established in Holland, Germany, France, Switzerland, Sweden and Belgium by 1933. He notes that jazz fitted easily in Europe into what he calls "the ordinary pattern of avant-garde intellectualism, among the dadaists and surrealists, the big city romantics, the idealisers of the machine age, the expressionists and their like" (Newton 1960, 244). Jean Cocteau and symbolist poet Max Jacob both patronized French magazine *Le Jazz Hot* and, after the war, it was in Sartre's *Temps Modernes* that theoreticians debated their ideas about jazz. While British and American pop and rock did penetrate France from 1963, jazz had established itself both during the inter-war period and in the period post-1945 to a sufficient degree to sustain its own niche. It should also be remembered that France had been occupied by the Reichswehr for five years and its own traditions, political and cultural, had been suppressed, including jazz. As Mike Zwerin has pointed out, jazz did survive in France and became a symbol of resistance. With France's liberation in 1944/5 by British, American and Free French forces, jazz became further associated with liberation and freedom.

Italy and Germany were in a rather different position. They were both defeated by the Allied powers and liberated by them. Germany, like France, had seen jazz survive the Nazis both in a corrupted, bastardized dance music form that passed the censor's pen and as an underground phenomenon (see Kater 2003; Heffley 2000). Michael Kater names four aspects of the music that made it unacceptable to the Nazis – first, improvisation; second, rhythm; third, its association with blacks, Jews and gypsies; and finally, its exaltation of individualism over collectivism.

He suggests:

> Jazz was one of those paradoxical quantities that could serve, from 1933 on, as a catalyst for those opposing the regime and those conforming to it, as undeniably, in the "ideological mix", it could also remain entirely neutral. The very existence of jazz, a music redolent of liberty, in the unfree society of Hitler's Germany raises questions about the efficacy of social and cultural controls commonly presumed in dictatorial, not to say totalitarian, systems. Finally, jazz possessed properties – as it possesses them today – that suits it for examination as an object of "popular culture", not of course in conventional history, but with the potential for enriching that history in a multi- or interdisciplinary vein.
>
> (Kater 2003, 13)

Michael Heffley (2000) is particularly instructive on the post-war period in Germany, while Rainer Lotz (1997) points out tellingly:

> Theoretically, this (the Nazi era) should have led to the complete erosion of the music in Europe. The opposite was the case: the intellectual and often physical threat from dictatorship, militarism, and fascism led to an astonishing phenomenon, that jazz overall took on an intensity that hasn't faded. Jazz became the emblem of freedom, democracy, individualism. Jazz became a symbol of rebellion against repression and conformity. While American musicians in Europe were only indirectly present through the media of radio and records, local musicians were free to develop their own seriously sincere interpretations.
>
> (Lotz 1997, 291–8; see also Heffley 2000)

After the war, the presence of American troops provided access to recordings, radio broadcasts and contact with white and black American musicians. In terms of West Germany, Heffley follows critic and producer Joachim Berendt in outlining how jazz developed in the Bundesrepublik, first in Berlin, then Munich and Frankfurt, and then Baden-Baden. Berendt, it should be added, also stresses the importance of television in pioneering jazz in Germany. However, in a very insightful and intriguing point, Heffley notes a further issue for German modernists. He suggests that they were unable to draw on the folk traditions of their country in seeking to develop a personalized language for jazz due to the discredited association of such traditions with the Third Reich. Instead, they turned more to European art music, which given the Nazis' banning of the music of Mendelssohn, Mahler and other Jewish composers, and of the radical music of Stravinsky, Bartok, Schönberg, Eisler and others, was not so tainted. Heffley is on more questionable ground in extending this notion to other European countries. The Scandinavians were, after all, able to draw on indigenous music to a large extent in their approach to jazz, as more recently have the French, Spanish and from the sixties onwards the British. However, his point about German jazz is instructive, and similar conclusions can be reached regarding Italy.

With regard to the attractions of jazz to West Germans, Heffley writes:

> Westerners had been educated to take full, informed responsibility for the sins of the Nazi past; they had a keen sense of guilt about and aversion to everything historically associated with it, from Wagner to Nietzsche to their own fathers and uncles. Their embrace of jazz as the antithesis of all that, as well as their extensions of it down German lines consciously eschewing it, in the tradition of both avant-garde and anti-art gestures, are directly traceable (most concretely, here, in my own interviews with them) to this deep discomfort with their own roots.   (Heffley, 2000)

The inclusion of Nietzsche is a case of guilt by misappropriation, perhaps. The philosopher was in fact an anti-anti-Semite and supported miscegenation. That aside, Heffley's point is well-made, as his quotation from the important and innovative German trombonist, Albert Mangelsdorf, makes clear:

> At that time jazz was for us youth in essence an American music that opposed the spirit of everything that came before us. The world of national socialism and its uptight stupidity, the march music and the entire crock of shit. Jazz was for us our outcry against the older generation that had lost all respect in our eyes, that moved from one day to the other after "Heil Hitler!" as though nothing had ever happened. We ourselves had been forced as school kids to raise the hand in a "Heil Hitler!" to our own teachers, to turn our heads to the right in sync and the devil

knows what all. This generation that raised us, at least in my eyes, had lost all right to respect. Then came the Americans with their jeeps and autos that we had never seen. That was magnificent then, because all our own cars were broken down. Simply to eat with the Americans was a royal treat. And then of course there was their music. That was for us. Our own music meant nothing.

(Heffley 2000)

Heffley does not ignore traditional jazz, which maintained a following in Hamburg, Berlin, Zurich and throughout German-speaking Europe. However, his concern is more to describe how modern jazz established itself in Germany after the Second World War almost as a cultural imperative. A similar point could be made in relation to Italy and France, though here as well it should be stressed that traditional jazz had its followers in both these countries, as well as in Holland and Belgium. But returning to comments above regarding the relationship between the left and jazz in continental Europe, it will be noted that in Britain, too, Communist Party members, such as Newton/Hobsbawm, Brian Blain and saxophonist Harry Gold, and other socialists were also active in the support and formation of jazz appreciation groups (see Newton 1960, 249–54). However, the connection between jazz and intellectual and left wing ideas on the continent was certainly stronger, as Francis Newton argues.

This does not as yet completely explain why jazz, and particularly modern jazz, became more securely established in Germany, France, Italy and Scandinavia than in the UK. For sheer quality and breadth of styles and approaches, British jazz was, after all, at least the equal of that of any of these countries or regions. Nevertheless, jazz's symbolic function as a demonstrably anti-fascist and pro-freedom art form in these countries did give it a touchstone-like quality that was not the case in Britain. We were never occupied by the Axis forces, however much we may have needed American military and economic aid to prevent this. Perhaps this difference helped to create different social, political and cultural priorities. The progressive, modernist, libertarian mould in which jazz was cast in mainland Europe allowed it to co-exist alongside the penetration by British, and later American beat groups. In Britain, with the arrival of the Beatles and the Rolling Stones, jazz merely seemed old-fashioned – the music of one's parents and older brothers.

There are, however, other reasons for this disparity between the UK and the rest of Europe. First, beat music, and later R&B and rock music, was essentially British. It owed a lot to American black and white popular forms but it was nurtured here and developed characteristics that owed much to our own cultural landscape. For the French, Germans, Swedes, Italians, Dutch *et al.*, it was – as was jazz – another cultural import. More importantly, its *lingua franca* was an English of a peculiarly mid-Atlantic form. It is significant that hardly any European acts achieved success in Britain and North America. Singer Francoise Hardy came close in the mid-sixties with exposure on the seminal TV show *Ready Steady Go!* Even the Swedish guitar group The Spotniks were over as far as Britain and the USA were concerned, come the arrival of the Beatles. By the end of the decade and in the early seventies, several German groups did break out of their linguistic confine. Dubbed in a non-politically correct era "Krautrock" by the *Melody Maker*, bands like Faust, Can, Amon Duul, Neu!, Cluster, Kraftwerk and Tangerine Dream developed a music that was successful across an international audience. However, this success owed a lot to the new British Virgin label, which was willing and canny enough to invest in these groups. And, of course, by that time the emphasis in progressive rock music had shifted from a vocal to a more instrumentally based music. The only other groups that registered from Europe in that later period were Gong, an Anglo/Australian/French group who sang in English; Magma, a French band who sang in a bizarre and invented language; the Italian group PFM; and the Danish jazz-rock outfit, Burnin' Red Ivanhoe. The success of the latter came despite the fact that they sang mainly in Danish, but in large measure due to the enthusiastic support of DJ John Peel. Slim pickings indeed. In fact, two of the most politically motivated and articulate groups and artists of the seventies, Udo Lindenberg and Ton Steine Scherben, remain essentially unknown outside German-speaking parts of Europe. In the case of the latter, that is the rest of the world's loss. Several years before punk rock, they provided a diverse musical tapestry driven by visceral energy alongside lyrics with a well-articulated and challenging political content that put them in a different league from later pretenders like the Clash, the Dead Kennedys, Billy Bragg and Paul Weller.

As a final point, we may note that the success of British groups in markets across the world effectively built the modern recording industry. The profits for EMI, Decca and others allowed a level of support in terms of promotion and advertising that simply was not available within indigenous mainland European pop scenes. The success of British and American acts singing in English was marked across Europe. Yet the very fact that it came in an alien tongue perhaps also allowed non-pop and instrumental musical styles like jazz a more acceptable slice of the market among young people and young adults.

The situation in the UK was also different from that in the USA. Rock & roll had been more important in terms of the charts in America. It had an authenticity and integrity, when played by Little Richard, Bo Diddley, Chuck Berry, the Coasters, Jerry Lee Lewis, Gene Vincent, Eddie Cochran and Dion and the Belmonts, that Cliff or Adam or Marty or Johnny could never match. Only those like Billy Fury, Johnny Kidd and Vince Eager could come close. But more importantly, both the trajectory and chronology of jazz in America and its relationship with popular music were quite unlike that which applied in Britain. What is more, social, cultural and economic circumstances were similarly distinct in many respects.

At the risk of oversimplification – and readers are advised to consult Alyn Shipton's *A New History of Jazz* (2001) for a much fuller account – jazz did not merely originate in North America. It also went through its major stages of development there, spreading gradually from New Orleans, in the form we came to know, first via the riverboats that worked the Mississippi and its tributaries and by touring groups of African-American musicians playing the new music. According to accounts cited by Shipton, jazz, or something approaching it, had spread to the West Coast, Chicago and elsewhere by the outbreak of the First World War. He adds that the music was already familiar to black artists on the vaudeville touring circuits several years before 1917, and the first recordings by the Original Dixieland Jazz Band and one of the music's most important figures, Jelly Roll Morton, had of course left New Orleans even earlier (Shipton 2001, 92–6; see also Collier 1978, 57–71 and 95–9). This process accelerated with the closing of New Orleans' Storyville district, through the resultant diaspora of musicians heading north to Chicago, New York and elsewhere (see Shipton 2001, 72–168; Collier 1978, 72–94).

Jazz, building on the earlier popularity of ragtime, went within a decade and a half from an underground music originating among the African-American and Creole players of New Orleans to become one of the most important popular musical styles of the twenties. Its relationship to the "pop" music of the day was complex. It drew simultaneously on non-jazz tunes that were well-known to its audience, but it also informed other styles, while also creating its own popular repertoire. This kind of connection continued between jazz and American "pop" music through the newer forms that developed in New York, Chicago and Kansas City, on through the big band and swing eras. This link did, nevertheless, begin to be severed with the emergence of bebop in the early forties, a style that in some ways expressed a growing consciousness of their identity and potential among African-Americans. Bebop was after all a deliberately difficult form, which was harmonically, rhythmically and melodically complex involving furious tempi and rapid chord changes that challenged both lesser musicians and audiences. All of these developments took place in a period of thirty years, give or take half a decade.

In turn, the fifties saw musicians like Horace Silver, Art Blakey, Lee Morgan and others working in a style that was dubbed hard bop and which drew on gospel and R&B, and was arguably more approachable for audiences. Blakey, Silver and Cannonball Adderley certainly became "popular" artists, as did "cool" jazz figures such as Dave Brubeck, Miles Davis, the Modern Jazz Quartet (MJQ) and Gerry Mulligan. In a sense, these musicians restored jazz to a place within more mainstream American culture, a position from which bebop had removed itself. At the same time, however, the separation of jazz from pop music was already becoming increasingly marked, as the process that had begun with bebop continued. With the arrival of free jazz – and its leading figures such as Ornette Coleman, Cecil Taylor, John Coltrane, Archie Shepp and Eric Dolphy – the decree nisi became absolute. Later, when the music moved into its jazz-rock phase, jazz again began to attract fans of pop and rock, obtaining airplay on AM radio stations and gaining access to rock venues and universities, but this reconciliation was short-lived.

America's jazz history is that of originator and, certainly into the sixties, the determining force behind the music's stylistic development not just in its homeland but elsewhere as well. To explain these processes adequately is impossible without reference to the socio-economic situation in America both in terms of new technologies, mass production and its huge domestic market and the impact of these on leisure and entertainment. Nor can the rapid changes that jazz underwent in that half century be considered without reference to the issue of race and the struggle for full civil rights across the whole of the country. If race is America's fault line, then jazz is both a commentary upon its fissures and a product or by-product of its shifting ground.

I acknowledged earlier that the history of jazz in Britain might go back to the arrival of the ODJB in 1919 or possibly earlier. In the pre-Second World War period, figures such as Spike Hughes, George Chisholm, Tommy McQuater and others stand out. We should also note Benny Carter's term with Henry Hall's BBC Dance Orchestra as a major landmark. However, I would suggest that the significance of jazz as an emergent music with firm roots in domestic social and cultural life goes back only to the formation of George Webb's Dixielanders. As we have noted, just five or so years later, jazz of a modern form began to stake its place in post-war Britain. For these reasons, our history in the music is more concentrated, and change and development within it, albeit influenced heavily by its North American originators and their progeny, were even more rapid. That this process took place against a background of austerity that was followed by unprecedented economic affluence is almost a given. The extent to which jazz – traditional, modern or mainstream – flourished would appear to have been affected, positively and negatively, by the social and cultural consequences of affluence. The processes involved here were not the same as those pertaining in the USA and in continental Europe. In particular, it will be seen from this that the processes of connection and disconnection between jazz and other musical forms and between jazz and the record-buying public was quite different in the British context compared to both other European countries and to the USA.

Turning now to the British entertainment industry as it stood between 1945 and 1960, there were other major differences compared with the North American situation. For example, television was in its infancy in the UK. Having begun broadcasting in 1936, transmission was suspended during the war and only recommenced in June 1947. A non-state-owned service began in 1955 but was only available nationwide from the following year. It was not until April 1964 that a third station, BBC 2, came on line, and this was only available to households with televisions and aerials capable of receiving the station, which broadcast on the ultra-high-frequency 625 line (see www.british-tv-history.co.uk). There were just three radio stations – the Home Service (later Radio 4), the Third Programme (later Radio 3) and the Light Programme (from 1967, with the launch of Radio 1 and Radio 2) – all run by the BBC.

The theatre circuit was dominated by a relatively small and influential number of companies. The Moss Empires Group, run from 1953 by impresario Val Parnell, also Managing Director of Associated Television from 1956–62, owned five theatres including the Palladium and the Colosseum in London (six until 1953) and a further eight in major British cities. Prince Littler, one of three siblings famous in theatre land as promoters and producers, ran the Stoll Theatres Corporation Ltd, a similarly powerful organization that later merged with Moss Empires. The Littlers were responsible for nearly every musical and pantomime on British stages through this period. Sidney, later Lord, Bernstein owned and led the Granada Group, which owned the Granada chain of cinemas. The Rank Organisation was the other major player in this world and from 1941 owned over 600 cinemas nationwide, including the Gaumont, Odeon and Paramount chains.

These chains were not just important for the plays they produced or films that they showed. They were also a major part of the variety and live music touring circuit in Britain. These tours mixed artists from different musical styles within pop music. In the early sixties, "trad" jazz bands might be included alongside pop artists like Helen Shapiro, Susan Maugham, Cliff Richard, Marty Wilde and Adam Faith. They always reflected what was in the charts and, with the rise of the beat groups, these began to top the bill. A fan could see six or seven acts for a few shillings, with newer or less successful acts performing a couple of numbers and the bill-toppers delivering a short round-up of their hits. Inevitably, such multiple bills produced some curious mixes. A friend of the author remembers seeing the Jimi Hendrix Experience, the Walker Brothers, Lulu and Engelbert Humperdinck at the Bedford Granada in 1967 (see Creasy 2007).

With the advent of independent television in 1954, those that shaped its direction came from these same theatrical backgrounds. Val Parnell was one and Lew Grade another. At the BBC, the Cotton family were also to prove influential. In effect, the entertainment, or rather light entertainment industry, was dominated by men whose own tastes and perspectives were formed in the music hall and variety theatres. They were open to what was new, but only if it proved popular. They were not in business to promote those areas that were on the fringes of their empire. It is not the case that British light entertainment was worse than its American, French, Italian, German or whatever equivalents but rather that its long-term and pernicious effect has been the creation of a shallow and narrow, consumerist monopoly within the entertainment industry in the UK. This has, in turn, affected television, radio, cinema, theatre and live performance for the worse. And there was within their realm, from the outset, almost an in-built expectation that young artists needed to broaden their appeal in order to survive in the business (see Melly 1970, 55–7).

Georgie Fame, one of the most significant talents to come out of Britain in this period, found himself trapped in that world when he left EMI for CBS:

> *Seventh Son* – that was the most adventurous. That was after three years at CBS doing a lot of MOR stuff. I had a difficult relationship with Mike Smith, who was a very good in-house producer at CBS but it wasn't where I was coming from. I was thrown into an alien regime. I did a strings album that wasn't bad. At least, it gave me the chance to sing some ballads but then again Mike Smith chose seventy per cent of the repertoire and a lot of those tunes like "A House Is Not A Home" and stuff like that were tunes I would never consider singing.
>
> (Interview with Georgie Fame, April 2009)

He recalls constant arguments over material. When he formed a partnership with Alan Price, the pair found themselves "hi-jacked by light entertainment".

> We put ourselves together because we were good solid friends and still are. We came from the same background. We loved the blues, rock n'roll. He was doing in Newcastle what I was doing in Lancashire. We did a guest spot on Lulu's TV show. We decided to sing "Back in The USSR" together at one piano dressed in tails. It was just a fun thing. It was rocking, really happening and we had the full orchestra doing this thing but we didn't know how to end it. So, on the rehearsal I suggested bring in the strings while it's all rocking and rolling and have them play the "Dr. Zhivago" theme over the top and we staged a mock fight – me and Alan – when the music goes all over the place. We ended up rolling on the floor fighting. And that was the end of the performance. It was very funny and I think Bill Cotton Junior was walking through the gantry at the time – or at least that's the rumour I heard – and said, "Give those boys a series." So, we got a series but then you're caught in the light entertainment trap at the BBC and this is the format that you have to work within and we also had this fantastic opportunity to play as guests on all these great shows – "The Two Ronnies", "Morecombe and Wise", "Tommy Cooper Show". And it's marvellous to be in these people's company. We were just the special guests for a whole series and we were allocated a little slot

and it had to be very light, quick and entertaining. So, we couldn't ... so the partnership never realised the artistic potential that was there because of that light entertainment element that dominated for two or three years and that's why we split in the end. We just said, this isn't going anywhere and we have remained great friends ever since.   (Interview with Georgie Fame, April 2009)

In many ways, the BBC's *Top of the Pops* reflected this same kind of thinking. In the sixties (and after) it would not be at all unusual to hear/see The Who miming on the show. They would then be followed by the granny-pop of Donald Pears or Ken Dodd. ITV did at least have *Ready Steady Go!*, which remains the best pop show the UK has ever produced. *The Tube* on Channel 4 ran it close in the eighties, as did Granada TV's *So It Goes* in the seventies. But only Tony Palmer's *How It Is* and *How Late It Is*, which ran from July 1968–March 1969 on the BBC, grasped the connection between the popular arts, fashion, cinema and music within an era to anything like the same degree. And while *How It Is* did feature jazz (on one programme Roland Kirk jammed with Colosseum), with the exception of Georgie Fame, *Ready Steady Go!*, had no interest in jazz (e-mail interview with Tony Palmer, July 2010; see Melly 1970, 170–2; Levy 2003, 127–9).

When beat music first emerged, it was like all other forms forced to interact with the world of Lew Grade, Bill Cotton and Val Parnell. However, what also began to happen, first with the Beatles but later with the Stones and other R&B bands, was that a divide began to become apparent within "popular" culture between what was "pop" and what was merely "popular". This is a distinction made by George Melly in *Revolt Into Style*. He argues convincingly that "pop" culture began in the UK with Tommy Steele, a point made also by Colin MacInnes, and that:

> The principal difference is that popular culture was unconscious, or perhaps unselfconscious would be more exact, whereas pop culture came about as the result of a deliberate search for objects, clothes, music, heroes and attitudes which could help define a stance.   (Melly 1970, 3)

From this it follows that what is "pop" is by nature ephemeral, transitory and, to a degree, ahistorical, that is unconcerned with antecedents. There was then, and is now, a lot of truth in Melly's argument. It is correct that it is no longer just teenagers that hanker after the excitement of pop music. Yet, for the teenager first hearing whatever might be flavour of the moment, it does not matter from whence it came but simply where it is and where it is going. The past is dad or mum's concern. Fashion is always "new". Melly is in essence describing "pop" in post-modernist terms, as bricolage:

Pop culture is for the most part non-reflective, non-didactic, dedicated only to pleasure. It changes constantly because it is sensitive to change, indeed it could be said that it is sensitive to nothing else. Its principal faculty is to catch the spirit of its time and translate this spirit into objects or music or fashion or behaviour. It could be said to offer a comic-strip which compresses and caricatures the social and economic forces at work within our society. It draws no conclusions. It makes no comments. It proposes no solutions. It admits to neither past nor future, not even its own. (Melly 1970, 7)

For Melly, it is this that separated "pop" culture from traditional culture and which defined its power and its limits. When it steps outside those limits or is co-opted into areas normally associated with traditional, high- or low- or middle-brow, culture, it ceases to be "pop". Although Melly does not make the point explicitly, it is clear that pop is dependent on mass communication as a means of transmitting coded information about itself to its audience and on mass production as a means of making its products available for consumption. Popular culture, by contrast, developed in the context of a slower, more lasting process of transmission and development.

Jazz, in its modern form at least, could not easily be part of the pop world. Traditional jazz, or rather Trad, could and did manage this briefly and had its "pop" moment but, almost by definition, it could not change, and therefore its supplanting was inevitable. In fact, its moment was due in part to its origins, as far as Britain was concerned, in an Edwardian era, one that was dominated by the music halls, just as the light entertainment industry would be dominated by those whose perceptions were formed in that period. This seems hardly coincidental. It could continue to fit into the world of variety, as was seen, for example, in George Chisholm's clowning on *The Black and White Minstrel Show*. Modern jazz was derived from a musical style that was designed for the aficionado not for the musical tourist. Some modern jazz musicians did, however, get to appear on *Sunday Night at the London Palladium*. Cleo Laine found herself both embarrassed and financially advantaged through appearing on the show:

I did London Palladium doing "You'll Answer to Me". A&R man Jack Baverstock for Fontana said, "It's creeping up the charts. All you have to do is the Palladium and there's a chance that we can get it for you." So I said, "Oh, sure!" and did the London Palladium. That was the power of the Palladium at the time. Everybody thought it was the place to be to plug anything. If you got on there, you got your record away. That's how "You'll Answer to Me" got away and I must admit [laughs] I have been forever embarrassed by it. (Interview with Cleo Laine, February 2008)

She and her husband, John Dankworth, apparently gravelled their drive from the profits – not exactly rock & roll! "You'll Answer to Me" was not actually a jazz tune at all, having been first covered by country & western singer Patti Page in the USA. But then Dave Brubeck also did the Palladium and landed a hit with "Take Five", and Oscar Peterson later played the show as well.

It would be unfair to suggest that jazz had no support within the British media. The *Melody Maker*, the main popular music paper still gave it decent coverage, as did a number of other specialist titles such as *Jazz Monthly* and *Jazz Journal*. The BBC gave it radio time with *Jazz Club* (1947–97), Humphrey Lyttelton's *Best of Jazz* (1967–2007) and Peter Clayton's *Jazz on One* (from 1968), *Jazz Notes* (from 1970) and *Sounds of Jazz* (from 1973). Other BBC radio programmes during the period included *Jazz Scene*, which ran for three years in a two-hour slot on Sunday nights for two years from 1966–8, *Just Jazz*, *Jazz Workshop* and *Jazz at Night*. In terms of television coverage, the start-up of BBC 2 also allowed the BBC to provide prime time slots for minority interest programming. Producer Terry Henebery had worked for four and a half years on *Jazz Club* and was given the opportunity, albeit on a miniscule budget, to produce a series for BBC 2. Interestingly, the request came not from Arts production under Humphrey Burton but from Bill Cotton, Head of Light Entertainment.

The first broadcast of *Jazz 625* went out on 21 April 1964 – planned to be the channel's second night, but which turned out to be the opening night after a fire at Battersea Power Station had blacked out Television Centre the previous evening. Compèred at various times by Steve Race, Humphrey Lyttelton and Peter Clayton, Henebery produced more than thirty shows featuring Art Blakey (including Sun Ra alumnus John Gilmore), the wonderful Henry "Red" Allen (with Alex Welsh's band), Ben Webster with Ronnie Scott, Cannonball Adderley with a group that included Charles Lloyd and Joe Zawinul, Bill Evans, Dave Brubeck Thelonious Monk, Tubby Hayes's Big Band, British trumpeter Kenny Baker, and Joe Harriott and John Mayer's Indo-Jazz Fusions.

Few copies of Henebery's later jazz series, such as *Jazz Goes to College* (1966), *Jazz at the Maltings* (1968) and *Jazz Scene* (1969), survive, having been made on videotape and subsequently wiped for reuse. *Jazz Goes to College* took Horace Silver, Thelonious Monk, Earl Hines, Bud Freeman, MJQ, Max Roach, Stan Getz and, in one remarkable never broadcast episode, Albert Ayler to Students' Unions around the UK. As an aside, several of Ayler's group had been subjected to humiliating customs searches coming in from France and were either rude and unpleasant to BBC staff, or reacted angrily to their offhand treatment by certain of the latter. According to George Foster, a student at University College who was present at the London School of Economics, Humphrey Lyttelton (overheard in a nearby pub after the show) was absolutely furious at the group's apparent unprofessionalism (interview with George Foster, March 2009). *Jazz at the Maltings* was recorded at the Benjamin Britten venue in East Anglia, while *Jazz Scene* was recorded at Ronnie Scott's Club and featured primarily US talent such as Gary Burton, Oscar Peterson, Brubeck, Monk and others. With these programmes, the BBC gave many jazz fans in the provinces the opportunity to see and hear these major artists, who might only have been in the UK to play London gigs as part of a European tour.

British jazz musicians and fans may justifiably argue that the BBC has as part of its charter the responsibility to cater for minority interests and tastes, and it seems that during the sixties the corporation went quite some way towards honouring that obligation. In fact, at the time of writing, the very thought of some fifty plus programmes on BBC 2 devoted to jazz over three or four years makes one salivate! Nevertheless, it is both justifiable and unfair to blame broadcasters for their failure to promote jazz satisfactorily. It is justifiable because of a much greater commitment to so-called "serious music" and because it is primarily through radio and television exposure that a minority art can access a wider audience. The BBC's later abandoning of regular jazz programming on TV can hardly have helped the music sustain an audience. At the same time, the failure of British jazz to reach and retain the younger music fan cannot in the main be blamed on the broadcasters. In fact up to 1964, pop music could hardly claim to have much more in the way of airtime.

The pop audience had *Juke Box Jury* (1959–67), *Top of the Pops* (from 1 January 1964), *Thank Your Lucky Stars* (1961–6) and *Ready Steady Go!* (August 1963–December 1966). However, until pirate radio stations like Radio Caroline and Radio London began illegal broadcasts in 1964, pop music on radio was limited to what was on the Light Programme with *Saturday Club*, *Easy Beat* and Alan Freeman's *Pick of the Pops* (on Sundays). Both *Saturday Club* and *Easy Beat* originally featured traditional and mainstream jazz but this was already being squeezed before the coming of the Beatles. In January 1960, the BBC axed its annual two-day *Jazz Saturday* concerts in favour of a single *Saturday Club (Jazz and Rock)* show. In the same issue, the paper announced a batch of new pop shows for the station and suggested that the BBC's annual festivals of dance music faced the axe (*Melody Maker* 2 January 1960). The following week, on its front page, *Melody Maker* announced "LYTTELTON BOYCOTTS BBC SHOW". His band were replaced by the John Barry Seven. Two years later, jazz drummer and vibist Lennie Best was quoted in the paper on the subject of radio coverage:

> I don't think things have ever been so bad for the modernists in Britain ... I can't see it getting much better in the near future either for the simple reason that you have got to bring people's tastes up to it and you can't do that overnight.
>
> (Dawbarn 1962b, 9)

Certainly, jazz was elbowed out of such prime slots on radio and television. It was, however, the pirate stations that gave Britain's teenagers and young adults unlimited access to pop. With the ubiquity of transistor radios – billions were sold worldwide in the 1960s – they could for the first time take their music with them to the beach, down the street, on the bus and to work. These often tiny pieces of equipment meant pop in the bedroom and, on Saturday, shopping trips for clothes, make-up and records would be accompanied by the sounds of pirate radio. In that kind of symbiosis that so often occurs between technology and culture, the pirate stations made these tiny radios essential bits of kit for every teenager, while the "tranny" made the pirates possible. Together they played a very significant role in the development of British pop music after 1964. We have to ask whether jazz could ever really have hoped to capture this mass youth audience. As George Melly suggested above, youth was focused on its search for those objects that might define it in the moment. Pop was its soundtrack and required just enough knowledge to know what or who was "in". History was for school and the older generation. Perhaps the best that British jazz might have hoped for was a place waiting at pop music's table.

Yet the impact that pop, as manifested by the Beatles *et al.*, had on modern jazz was, arguably, not of immediate significance in itself. Its effects on traditional jazz were more powerful and lay in the main in the loss of its fringe, less dedicated audience and, in turn, its access to certain venues and circuits. What did have more serious implications for the modernists was the rise of R&B.

The rise of pop and rock music in the sixties makes the most sense if one sees it as two parallel and occasionally intersecting streams rather than one rising tide. The first groups to hit the charts after the Beatles in 1963 included Gerry and the Pacemakers (Liverpool – March), Billy J. Kramer and the Dakotas (Liverpool – May), Freddie and the Dreamers (Manchester – June), the Searchers (Liverpool – July), the Hollies (Manchester – September) and the Fourmost (Liverpool – October). The Swinging Blue Jeans, also from Merseyside, and the Merseybeats made the charts early in 1964. As for the Stones, their first hit came in December 1963 and it was not until July 1964 that they had their first number one. Manfred Mann, originally the Mann–Hugg Blues Brothers and with strong jazz connections, also made the charts early in 1964 with the Pretty Things following suit later that year. The Animals arrived in July 1964 and the Kinks (then very much a R&B group) a month later, to be followed by the Who, Yardbirds and Them in 1965. These groups might have had hits and been on *Top of the Pops* and *Ready Steady Go!* but they, and their audience, were soon developing different aspirations.

Of the R&B bands that filled the clubs, quite a number of excellent bands experienced little or no chart success. The Graham Bond Organization was an obvious case in point, as was Alexis Korner's Blues Incorporated, yet both had substantial followings. Zoot Money's Big Roll Band played a mix of soul, jazz and R&B and were a major club draw, while the Paramounts might not have registered under that name but they would and did as Procul Harum. These groups often had strong jazz connections with ex-jazz players in their midst and their musical aims extended beyond the three-minute single. The list of musicians who began in jazz or around its fringes and who built careers in rock and blues is a lengthy one. It includes Jon Hiseman, Dick Heckstall-Smith, Tony Reeves, Jack Bruce, Ginger Baker, Graham Bond, Alexis Korner, Charlie Watts, Ian Stewart (pianist and then road manager with the Stones), John Entwhistle, Eric Burdon, Steve Winwood, Roger Daltrey, Brian Auger, Julie Driscoll (later Julie Tippetts), drummer Colin Allen, Ray Russell, John McLaughlin, John Marshall, Jim Mullen and Elton Dean. Manfred Mann himself had pretensions in that direction having been a jazz journalist in South Africa and Paul Pond (later Paul Jones) had been involved in poetry and jazz while at Oxford with Michael Horovitz. One could also include poet Pete Brown who, as well as writing many of Cream's lyrics, had his own fondly remembered Battered Ornaments and Piblokto. Few made the journey in the opposite direction. We might note here the members of Soft Machine and Robert Wyatt, guitarists Chris Spedding and Brian Godding (Blossom Toes), and, most notable of all, Steve Miller, one-time pianist with Carol Grimes and Delivery. Of even more consequence were the many who worked successfully (artistically at least) in both jazz and progressive rock, as we shall see.

R&B was also more able to move into the territory of jazz intellectually and culturally, as well as musically. Unlike pop, or at least its more ephemeral stylists, R&B had a history. It crossed over into jazz through figures like Ray Charles, Jimmy Smith and Cannonball Adderley. It might have grown into adulthood on the southside and westside of Chicago but it had been spawned in the delta of the Mississippi. In a way, it was the country cousin of the urban and urbane music that had come out of New Orleans. What is more, it attracted an audience who were knowledgeable about their music – the kind of fan who was previously drawn to "trad" or modern jazz. In fact, their heroes encouraged them to seek more widely and drew (as Barber and others had done) their attention to the originators of the music. These fans had been already prepared for improvisation in that music by the existence of traditional and, to a lesser extent, modern jazz. R&B was less cerebral than jazz and more immediate in its impact and, being a simpler form, it also allowed for flamboyance and improvisation in performance. In these respects, British R&B offered the young and curious some of the attributes of jazz, including the bestowing on its followers of a degree of intellectual cachet, but was easier to understand and far easier to dance to. To go back to Alexis Korner's remarks in the *Melody Maker*, R&B overtook modern rather than traditional jazz.

As John Wickes notes in his comprehensive study of British jazz (Wickes 1999), what really did the damage was not pressure on record sales or recording opportunities but the loss of venues that the accompanied the rise of R&B.

> For a while, stylistically overlapping boundaries provided a creative stimulus for a few, notably Alexis Korner and Graham Bond; but both media choosiness in matters of coverage, and resulting pressure from increasingly taste-conscious young consumers forced most groups' and clubs' musical policies along sectarian lines.
> (Wickes 1999, 30)

Wickes suggests that 1964 was the watershed year. After this, he argues, clubs started by jazz fans and musicians such as the Flamingo, the Marquee, Klook's Kleek and even the 100 Club had by and large deserted the jazz audience. In principle, Wickes is right. However, the process was slower and more incremental than he suggests. For example, Wickes notes that by the mid-sixties "even the 100 Club had gone over to rhythm & blues" and that clubs such as Klooks Kleek "split the week's gigs between jazz and rock" (Wickes 1999, 31).

For a period from spring 1964, the 100 Club was promoting almost entirely R&B, but by December of that year it was again offering three nights of traditional jazz and, by April 1965, it had returned to a traditional/mainstream policy. Wickes's comment does apply more directly to Klook's Kleek and the Flamingo. By August 1964, jazz at Klook's Kleek was down to just one night per week and by Christmas it had stopped functioning as a venue for jazz. The same happened with the Flamingo, which had even lost its Saturday night jazz set. By contrast, the Ken Colyer Club also started offering a night of R&B in 1964, but switched back to traditional jazz the following spring. The Marquee perhaps shows most clearly how events unfolded. In April 1964, it offered three nights of jazz with R&B filling the other slots. In twelve months this was down to two nights of jazz and, by 1966, to Saturday nights only. In 1967, the club had only become a very occasional venue for jazz (for example the newly formed London Youth Jazz Orchestra under Bill Ashton performed there on 23 July).

The same process can be seen with the National Jazz Festival. By 1964, it had become the National Jazz and Blues Festival, but in 1967 at Windsor it became the National Jazz Pop Ballads and Blues Festival with "blues" in large block capitals. It was at Richmond in 1964 that R&B was first given a toehold with the festival, and Memphis Slim, Graham Bond, Jimmy Witherspoon, the Stones, Yardbirds, Manfred Mann, Georgie Fame and Long John Baldry appeared alongside Kenny Ball, Chris Barber, Alex Welsh, Dick Morrissey, Ronnie Scott, Tubby Hayes and Mose Allison. By 1965, jazz was being squeezed out still further and, in 1966, only the Saturday and Sunday afternoon slots were devoted to jazz. In 1967, this had shrunk to just Saturday afternoon and, by 1970, while the bill featured a number of bands with some jazz influence in their music – Jon Hiseman's Colosseum, Burnin' Red Ivanhoe, Family, Patto and Audience – only Chris Barber flew the flag for jazz.

Yet, for Barber, these musicians were in a real sense continuing the music he and others had begun. As a director of the NJF he had been fully in favour of bringing their bands under the NJF umbrella and onto its festival stage. As Barber explains, "The idea was that it was the same music. The main difference between jazz and blues is that they are really just played on different instruments." Asked about his views of bands like Cream, he added:

> Yes, in general I liked them. I would have approved of the idea anyway. It was good music. I went to the Rolling Stones Hyde Park gig and Blind Faith. I knew all those people and it's very good music. They were lucky that their version of the music got an even bigger audience than we did in the fifties.
>
> (Interview with Chris Barber, February 2008)

What was happening in London was happening in the provinces as well. Jazz trumpeter and broadcaster Digby Fairweather had been a jazz fan since he was eight years old. But he too was captivated by the Beatles:

> So, when the Beatles came along you couldn't ignore them because they were so vital and they sent this kind of wind of fresh air down Tin Pan Alley, which up till then nobody took seriously. The jazz people didn't really have much time even for Elvis Presley, certainly not for Adam Faith or Eden Kane or Marty Wilde or the rockers because they were beneath our serious consideration. When the Beatles came along I remember questioning whether I ought to be liking the Beatles because you couldn't help but like them, because they were so virile and enchanting to watch and very exciting to hear. I got their first album *Please Please Me* on a reel-to-reel tape and I thought, "My God, this is wonderful!" and then I thought, "Wait a minute – there you are with these shelves of records by Louis Armstrong and Clark Terry and Ellington and Basie. How can you possibly like four young rock and rollers?" The big moment was when Georgie Fame produced his album *Fame At Last* and that had "Moody's Mood for Love" on it – a great version – and a lot of very jazz-inspired things like "I Live the Life I Love". It was very close to Mose Allison, who was one of his great influences. I remember thinking, "Great Scott, should I really be buying this?"
>
> (Interview with Digby Fairweather, July 2010)

Fairweather recalls the Studio Jazz Club in Southend-on-Sea with its regular Friday night sessions that featured many of the music's finest musicians. Yet this had begun, like the Marquee, Klook's Kleek and the Cavern in Liverpool, solely as a jazz venue. By 1964 most evenings were taken over by the R&B bands of the day:

> We had people like Art Themen, Don Rendell, Tubby Hayes. When Jimmy Skidmore came down with his son Alan, who was about fifteen and nearly as good as Jimmy back then, it was like having Paul McCartney. But a lot, nearly all I would say, of the emerging rock bands came down in the week. Certainly the Yardbirds with Eric Clapton, Geno Washington and his Ram Jam Band, Georgie Fame and the Blue Flames, The Alan Price Set and some of the lesser bands like Zoot Money's Big Roll Band.
> (Interview with Digby Fairweather, July 2010)

He adds, "Of course, in those days, we had no idea that they were going to be as big as they became. I mean Eric Clapton for 2/6 (13p)!" Fairweather's point is a useful one. The full impact of these groups and their individual members would actually be felt a few years later. Some like the Yardbirds, the Who and the Pretty Things (and, of course, The Rolling Stones) experienced chart success, but from 1967 onwards the foundations of the world of rock they had laid provided the ground upon which all manner of bands would build their careers. This process, with its greater emphasis on musical virtuosity and the album as opposed to the single format, did create both potentially positive opportunities for the development of British jazz, but it also put in train the forces that would eventually block its access to the pop/rock audience.

Even though the tide was turning towards R&B and rock around 1964/5, these young rockers still felt a degree of closeness to the jazz world whether as a means of attaching credibility to their work or out of a genuine enthusiasm for it. When recording sessions required well-honed musical skills it was most often the jazzers who got the call (see Renaud 1995; also MacDonald 1995). The Beatles provided a source of fairly regular employment, with Bill Le Sage, Les Condon, Ronnie Ross, Ian Hammer, Derek Watkins, Alan Branscombe, Harry Klein and, most famously (the tenor solo on "Lady Madonna"), Ronnie Scott making their way to Abbey Road. In fact, when Brian Epstein died in 1967, with the Beatles' permission, saxophonist Ronnie Ross gathered an orchestra together to record a set of Beatles' tunes in tribute to their manager. (*Beatle Music By the Session Men*, WRC T758, aka *In Tribute to Brian Epstein – 16 Great Beatles Hits*, WRC S-4415). Clearly, when those renegades from jazz like Bond, Korner, Mann and Bruce needed horns or drums or piano, they called their jazz mates to help out. The same was true for John Mayall, Georgie Fame and others.

Interviewed in the *Melody Maker*, the group Them were clear about their affection for jazz and their keenness to introduce the music as part of their set:

Van [Morrison] explained that on a club date they played every-thing from Charles Mingus to John Lee Hooker.

"We have tried some Mingus stuff, which we used to play in a club in Belfast. It used to go down a bomb."

Said Billy [Harrison], "I don't know if they understood it or not, but they seemed to enjoy it, and we felt good. If everyone goes away happy, and we feel happy when we play, we can't ask for much more." (*Melody Maker* 10 April 1965, 8)

They were far from alone. A very similar interview with Stevie Winwood and Spencer Davis can be found in the *Melody Maker* of 12 June 1965 (Welch 1965b, 8). They even mention Roland Kirk and Ornette Coleman. Now that is hip!

Georgie Fame discovered the music of Ray Charles through Eddie Cochran, with whom he toured in the early sixties as part of Billy Fury's back-ing band The Blue Flames, and whom he credits with introducing Charles to British musicians. Sacked by Fury's road manager for playing Ray Charles's numbers at a soundcheck in Paris, Fame spent some time in London living with a friend (Mike O'Neil of Nero and the Gladiators) in Soho and listen-ing to his record collection, which included singers like Mose Allison, Fame's second major influence.

It was through O'Neil that Fame landed the residency at the Flamingo that made him and his sound. Reforming the Blue Flames, the band consisted originally of Colin Green on guitar, Tex Makins on bass and jazz drummer Red Reece, with Speedy Aquaye on congas. John McLaughlin also played guitar at one time, as did Ray Russell, while other drummers included Tony Crombie, Bill Eyden and Mitch Mitchell. Mitchell went straight from Fame's band to play with Jimi Hendrix. Phil Seamen was also a Blue Flame at one point:

> Red Reece started to mess himself up after about a year down the Flamingo, where Phil became a feature. We all looked after Phil at one time and another in our lives. Red unfortunately took down the wrong path. If you look at the Blue Flames for the three-year period at the Flamingo, there were more drummers in and out of that band than any other band. I bump into friends of drummers who say, "My mate was in the Blue Flames." I can remember most of the drummers. (Interview with Georgie Fame, April 2009)

Fame recalls that as a "rock & roller", he was never allowed to play the club piano but was restricted to an upright.

> Rick Gunnell had to rent an upright piano for our sets at the Flamingo because the Kruger brothers who owned the club

wouldn't let me play the club piano because that was reserved for jazz musicians. There was Brian Dee, Johnny Burch, Brian Auger. They were all the frequent piano players at the All-Nighters and Bill Le Sage when he wasn't playing vibes. I've got photographs of me sittin' at the old upright facing the wall with John McLaughlin with a Gretsch guitar with my back to the band and I'm singing and playing. They wouldn't let me play the baby grand.

(Interview with Georgie Fame, April 2009)

By the end of 1962, Fame was playing organ to an appreciative audience of hipsters, black American GIs, West Indians, pimps and prostitutes, including Flamingo regular Christine Keeler. When his breakthrough came at the turn of 1964/5, he and his band were one of the finest and most accomplished live bands in the country. Their music was a rich hybrid that mixed jazz, blues, R&B, Motown and bluebeat to wonderful effect, and his break came with real style when he took a version of Mongo Santamaria's "Yeh, Yeh" (with words by Fame's mentor Jon Hendricks) to the top of the charts. Fame's ability to move between styles with ease was nearly his undoing, as we saw earlier with his disastrous move into light entertainment, but his commitment to the music he loves is unquestionable. In fact, his finest moment demonstrates how close jazz and rock were in this period. *Sound Venture*, the album he made with the Harry South Big Band, remains one of the best British jazz records of the period or ever. Jon Hendricks played a very important role in helping get the tunes together, as Fame explains:

He was my mentor really, Jon out of all of them. He did the first version of "Yeh, Yeh" and wrote the lyrics for "Yeh, Yeh" and did the first vocal recording. He was very influential in the material for the second session that completed the Sound Venture record. There are four Jon Hendricks tunes on that. Because by then Annie Ross had a club in Covent Garden called Annie's Room. After my version of "Yeh, Yeh" was a hit, Jon came over for a couple of weeks at Annie's Room and I used to go every night and he'd get me up to sing a bit and I was getting the material together to finish Sound Venture, so Jon went, "I've got all these tunes". So we were down at Harry's place in Streatham all the time sorting it all out. So, Jon and I got really friendly.

(Interview with Georgie Fame, April 2009)

Fame financed the project himself and it was a remarkably mature record from a twenty-three year old, beautifully sung, arranged and played by a band that included Tubby Hayes, Stan Tracey, Ronnie Scott, Phil Seamen, Kenny Wheeler and trumpeter Bert Courtley. Fame did throw in a few

R&B numbers – James Brown's "Papa's Got a Brand New Bag", The Clovers' "Lovey Dovey" – to keep fans happy, but it is his vocals on the gorgeous "It's For Love", "The Petals" and the Hefti-Hendricks's favourite "Lil' Darlin'", where Fame plays chase the tail with trumpeter Jimmy Deuchar, that stand out. Fame's own "I Am Missing You" is a fine piece of big band jazz with nice tenor from Hayes, while his version of country singer–songwriter Willie Nelson's "Funny How Time Slips Away" steals the show. Despite the success of *Sound Venture*, some from both jazz and rock were confused by Fame's move:

> *Sound Venture* was a great success because it went into the pop charts – not just the jazz charts. It went into the bloody pop charts. So, I was kind of accused by the old guard of the jazz scene of being a young whipper-snapper that didn't have a right to be on the same bandstand as Ronnie Scott and Tubby Hayes and the rest of them. But there was a certain element particularly amongst the younger journalists on the Melody Maker that saw the future and said, "This guy's one of us – give him all the encouragement you can." Then you had the traditional mod or rhythm & blues fans that saw me moving into this jazz thing that was beyond them and I was a bit of a traitor. I was deserting them. So, I was in the middle of this. I just followed my instincts. I didn't get any of that from the musicians. That only came from the media basically.
>
> (Interview with Georgie Fame, April 2009)

It would be comforting to see the success of *Sound Venture* as representing a blueprint for commercially successful jazz. Sad to say, it was more a one-off that suggested a false dawn that was achievable because of Fame's position as an already popular artist. What it did do was to show that attention to the presentation of the music as well as to its musical content could pay off. This has always been an area of weakness for jazz.

Fame was not alone in pursuing an interest in jazz. We have already mentioned Them and, by association with Steve Winwood, the Spencer Davis Group. By contrast, Manfred Mann, who had begun their career mixing originals with blues and occasional jazz standards, had drifted from their original strategy to become more or less a pop group. With no hint of irony, the *Melody Maker* of 30 October 1965 announced "Manfred Wants More Men". The article by Chris Welch that followed explained that the group had decided to add trumpet and sax to their line-up for their forthcoming tour with the Yardbirds. The process of recruitment was protracted and at first Dave Tomlin of the Mike Taylor Quartet was drafted in. He recruited trumpeter Henry Lowther but then Tomlin decided this was not for him. Lyn Dobson, who played with Lowther in Group Sounds Five, came in as a replacement. In Welch's article, Mann is quoted:

We want a really good modern jazz group within the group, and if we can get someone who doubles on drums then Mike Hugg can play vibes. We want somebody like Ray Warleigh on alto, who can play jazz but doesn't mind playing pop.   (Welch 1965d, 1)

Both Lowther and Jack Bruce, who was also with the group at the time, found it a largely unsatisfactory experience. John Wickes quotes Lowther on the subject as follows:

We didn't do solos in live situations. We never played that kind of music ever except perhaps once a month at the Marquee club. They always felt they could play more sophisticated music at the Marquee. Out on the road it was an out-and-out pop show, with no solos.   (Wickes 1999, 33)

Jack Bruce was even more blunt about the experience, when it was suggested that Manfred was dabbling in jazz at that point in the group's career:

I think that's stretching it a bit. What they really did was to incorporate horns into their set but it was still the same songs. I never thought of Manfred as a jazz musician. He was a nice guy and everything but he was more of a writer about jazz. That band was what it was. It certainly wasn't a rhythm and blues or jazz band by any stretch of the imagination.
                                (Interview with Jack Bruce, October 2007)

At the time, however, it clearly seemed a good idea to all concerned. In April 1966, the *Melody Maker* featured a short interview with a loyal Henry Lowther. Lowther acknowledged the financial imperative but also said he enjoyed working with the Manfreds and said, "I like the sort of thing we play." The author, Alan Walsh, concludes with an intriguingly ambiguous paragraph:

Lowther is one jazzman who's made the transgression [*sic!*] from jazz to pop without lowering standards. Perhaps there'll be others. Perhaps the two fields aren't as far apart as many people would like to think.   (Walsh 1966, 14)

It was all to no avail, and on 30 July 1966 the same paper announced "Manfred Prunes the Size of His Men". Later, in 1969 and when the musical climate had changed, Manfred Mann and Mike Hugg would form Chapter Three. Sadly, despite its jazz-rock orientation the group was not really taken that seriously by critics or fans.

As for the Animals, Eric Burdon was a fan of *all* African-American music, not just blues and R&B but jazz, gospel and worksongs. Coming of age in Newcastle, he used to hang out at the New Orleans Jazz Club, where he befriended a guy who played cornet in a local band:

> He was my way on to the stage with the first jazz band that I ever got involved with, Mighty Joe Young's jazz band. I would tug at the trombone players coat and say, "Please, may I get up and sing a song?" He would look at me and say, "Oh, okay." So, I would get up one week and sing one song, then the next week it would be two songs, and before I knew it, I had my own 20 minute set. That was my foot in the door with jazz folks.
>
> (E-mail interview with Eric Burdon, June 2010)

Burdon also knew Ian Carr and his pianist/organist brother Mike, and was a regular at the Downbeat Club, where the Carr brothers did an after-hours set after "the rockers went home". Apparently, he even did a recording session with them in his late teens, though no copies are known to exist. It was Burdon who introduced the Carr brothers to Ray Charles via the *At Newport* album. According to Burdon, he heard that Ian Carr was putting together a student orchestra in London for a small private affair in the West Country:

> At the time, I had already started working with The Animals and we were getting some national notoriety. It happened that day that The Animals were going to be on the same bill as the National Jazz Orchestra. I came up with the idea (which wasn't much of an idea) to fuse the two, Orchestra and Animals, together. Just like I'd convinced Ian and Mike Carr that it was okay to listen to blues music.

He continues:

> For a while, I had been thinking about the way that I'd heard John Lee Hooker on his early recordings and the riffs that he was playing and how exciting it would be if those riffs could be turned into orchestrations. I had this idea in my head and that idea became reality at this jazz festival. I got on stage and there I was in front of the band and everything was working fine when suddenly, the stage was invaded by this tall, lanky guy with blond hair. It turned out to be amongst others, Long John Baldry and Rod Stewart, who can be seen on a clip of film that exists, with the orchestra behind. They're hogging the microphone from behind and both of them are shoulders and head taller than me. I was fighting a losing battle, so I had to just go along with it, but it was a great jam.
>
> (E-mail interview with Eric Burdon, June 2010)

The experience was clearly an important one for Burdon, though as he explains rock took both him and the scene over in the years that followed.

> This did help me get my foot in the door with jazz as well as the rock crowd but unfortunately the rockers took over and jazz kind of dissipated and disappeared down to the back alley to the jazz club – cellars full of jazz musicians trying to get over the shock of just what was going on in the music world and trying to get across to people full of Newcastle Brown Ale at 1 o'clock in the morning. It became pretty tough for would-be jazz men at the time, only to be saved somewhere along the line by bands like Colosseum.   (E-mail interview with Eric Burdon, June 2010)

That was not quite the end of Burdon's and the Animals' connection with jazz, however. In August 1965, an augmented Animals stole the show at the National Jazz and Blues Festival at Richmond. Featuring arrangements by Ian Carr, Kenny Wheeler and Dick Morrissey, the Animals were joined by a seven-piece brass and reeds section. Chris Welch interviewed Eric Burdon and Hilton Valentine after the gig, and their comments suggest that the divide between jazz and rock might owe as much if not more to the prejudices of jazz fans than to those listening to rock and R&B. Welch's first sentence reads, "Jazz and Pop have collided head-on and produced a glorious explosion called the Animals' Big Band."

Burdon notes that the sheer expense makes the project untenable for more than the occasional gig but notes the possibility of a BBC Jazz Club broadcast. He continues, "Five years ago the pop and jazz scene were totally different. Jazzmen were more ethical about it all and were not prepared to change. And the bluesmen were all traddies like George Melly but that wasn't the real sound." Hilton Valentine adds, "Actually the musicians are okay, it's the modern jazz fans that are cut off from what's happening and they probably don't even know what's going on" (Welch 1965c, 3). Sadly, the concerts that Burdon hoped for never materialized. However, the band did get their BBC broadcast on 13 December that year. Somewhere, a recording awaits release.

6 The Brain Drain

In matters of style, swim with the current; in matters of principle, stand like a rock. Thomas Jefferson, *Notes on the State of Virginia*, 1787

The most brutal, ugly, desperate, vicious form of expression it has been my misfortune to hear. It is written and sung for the most part by cretinous goons and by means of its imbecilic reiterations and sly, lewd – in plain fact dirty – lyrics, it manages to be the martial music for every side-burned delinquent on the face of the earth. Frank Sinatra at 1958 Congressional hearings, *New York Times Magazine*, 12 January 1958, 19

In 1965, the *Melody Maker* ran a short piece by Chris Welch entitled "The Brain Drain! The Men Jazz Lost to Pop". Welch notes four musicians – Graham Bond, Dave Davani, Brian Auger and drummer Bobbie Graham – who had crossed the floor. He could, of course, have added quite a few more. Welch wrote:

> Like the expanding universe the world of pop and jazz are usually thought to be rushing away from each other at tremendous speeds. But a situation is developing in which modern jazz and pop seem to be merging, or at least coming closer than they have been for years. When rhythm & blues swept British Pop in 1964, it dealt a severe blow to jazz. Jazz clubs folded or changed to a rhythm & blues policy. But several jazzmen in the spirit of "If you can't beat 'em, join 'em", turned their talents to rhythm & blues. (Welch 1965a, 10)

He quotes Brian Auger:

> We play a brand of rhythm & blues and commercial jazz. I think we appeal to the more sophisticated rhythm & blues fans. I bought an organ and formed the Brian Auger Trinity. It was originally going to be a Jimmy Smith sort of thing, but we have evolved into our own style. (Welch 1965a, 10)

There were, however, differing levels of success. Whatever Bond, Auger, Zoot Money and others might have achieved in terms of success on the club scene did not translate itself into record sales. It was the guitar-driven bands like the Stones, Yardbirds, Pretty Things and John Mayall that led the charge. Georgie Fame was in this and other respects an exception.

Auger's group featured at one point John McLaughlin and bassist Rick Laird, who later joined the guitarist in the Mahavishnu Orchestra, and Glen Hughes, who died as a result of an addiction to heroin, on baritone. In 1964, he was joined by Long John Baldry and Rod Stewart on vocals and later that year by Julie Driscoll. Calling themselves Steampacket, the band was a self-contained review featuring Driscoll's fascination with soul, Baldry's love and knowledge of the blues, and Stewart's mixing of Motown and blues alongside Auger's jazzy instrumentals. As was so often the case with a lot of groups in this period, Steampacket were more important for what came after than what they achieved at the time. They were popular with audiences but just could not translate their live show into the kind of product that attracted record company interest. A bootleg live album plus fond memories mark their legacy. It was with a slimmed-down band going out as Julie Driscoll and the Brian Auger Trinity that Auger had his most significant success.

Auger's first record actually involved a British session with Sonny Boy Williamson, *Don't Send Me No Flowers*, which featured his group, saxophonists Joe Harriott and Alan Skidmore, and guitarist Jimmy Page, and which was not released until 1968. The quartet with Driscoll began in 1965 and recorded their first album, *Open*, in 1967 for manager Giorgio Gomelsky's Marmalade label. It was not until the release of the group's first single, a version of Bob Dylan's "This Wheel's on Fire", that things really took off with both the album and single making the charts. A second album, *Streetnoise*, followed in 1968, along with an American tour, though their second single, David Ackles's "Road to Cairo", had failed to chart. It is hard to know whether the group could have recovered from this setback because Driscoll left the group during their tour of the States. Press attention had focused on her to such an extent that she had become the face of 1968 and it became too much for her to handle.

As she explains, Gomelsky played a significant role in the selection of the group's material, including "This Wheel's on Fire":

Giorgio was amazing. He used to go off to America. He would suss things out. He was fantastic at sniffing people out and sniffing out … like Richie Havens, he went and saw him in a little club somewhere. He came back and said, "There's this amazing guy. He plays guitar with his thumbs." He brought these tapes and they were fantastic. I thought they were just wonderful and that's the period that I love the best of Richie Havens. So raw, and just him and the guitar. Just wow! We did "Indian Rope Man" and we got really pally with him. He's still alive. He's an amazing wonderful man, so lovely.

(Interview with Julie Tippetts, September 2008)

She continues:

He just turned up with this demo that Bob Dylan had done and "Wheels on Fire" happened to be on it and he just said, "Julie, Brian – you must record this!" I always hated that from Giorgio. It was always you must do this and you must do that. I got to the point where I objected. You go inside – "Haven't I got a mind of my own?" Anyway, he happened to play it and we went, "We can do that." So, it was brought out as a single.

(Interview with Julie Tippetts, September 2008)

Driscoll admits that the pressure on her was quite relentless and she was uncomfortable at how her fellow band members felt about being largely ignored by the media. The name of the group was supposed to be The Brian Auger Trinity featuring Julie Driscoll. Driscoll was, however, strikingly beautiful and photogenic, and management and media soon conspired to promote Driscoll as group spokesperson. As she explains, "It was never called or should never have been Julie Driscoll and the Brian Auger Trinity. It was much objected to by Brian, when they started twisting it around, and fair enough. He was the guy that got it all together."

Driscoll was just twenty-one when "This Wheel's on Fire" reached number five in the UK charts. However bright and streetwise she might have been, the attention of the press proved overwhelming, as she says:

I did get very, very stressed by being in the limelight. And I did get very, very stressed by the fact that I was always picked out from my bunch of mates, you know, which was what we were on the road. We worked together and I never thought of myself … I know girl singers were always thought of as out there, I know I was out front but for me it was never like that. It was us. And I used to try and draw everybody in for photo sessions and interviews and things. But it was awful. I just got hounded, really, really hounded. So, I had to pull out altogether.

(Interview with Julie Tippetts, September 2008)

Driscoll left the group during an American tour and for a time became somewhat reclusive:

> I really took a bit of time off altogether, virtually locked myself away almost. I used to go for 3 o'clock in the morning walks, so that nobody would see me, nobody would recognize me and I wouldn't be photographed. I really, really hated all that. I wanted anonymity. For me, it had nothing to do with the music. It was something that felt very, very uncomfortable to me.
>
> (Interview with Julie Tippetts, September 2008)

By that point, Driscoll had already developed into a powerful, soulful vocalist, and on tracks like "Czechoslovakia" and "Vauxhall to Lambeth Bridge" was developing as a songwriter in her own right. As well as Auger, the band also featured two fine musicians in guitarist Gary Boyle and drummer Clive Thacker. Certainly, there was more than enough music on *Streetnoise* to suggest that the band had potential and a future. Auger had some further success with his group Oblivion Express, while guitarist Gary Boyle has led various ensembles including Isotope, which at one time featured ex-Soft Machine bassist Hugh Hopper. Driscoll subsequently married pianist–composer Keith Tippett, taking his birth name "Tippetts" (he had dropped the "s"), and would go on to work both with her husband and on projects of her own. The stardom the media anticipated for the group never materialized, but it was this group that best illustrated the potential that Chris Welch had suggested several years earlier for a rapprochement between jazz and pop.

Of the others mentioned by Chris Welch, Graham Bond was probably thought to be the one "most likely to succeed". Instead, his career is littered with "might-have-beens" and "should-have-tried-harders". On the whole, Bond's failure is usually put down to his disastrous problems with heroin, bad career moves and to his numerous character flaws.

Bond began his career as a jazz musician playing with Brian Dee, Johnny Burch and Don Rendell, and played on Rendell's *Roarin'* album, which was released on the US Jazzland label. He left the saxophonist to join Alexis Korner's Blues Incorporated alongside (at various times) bassists Jack Bruce and Spike Heatley, pianist Johnny Parker, saxophonist Dick Heckstall-Smith and drummers Charlie Watts, Graham Burbidge and Ginger Baker. All of these, of course, came from jazz backgrounds. When Bond left Korner to form the Graham Bond Organization he took Baker and Bruce with him. Heckstall-Smith joined later and, for a while, John McLaughlin played guitar with the group. This band can be heard on the first two LP sides of *Solid Bond* (Warner Bros; Sunrise) playing live at Klooks Kleek in 1962, and their music clearly owes as much to jazz as to blues at this point. In fact, Jack Bruce compares them to the music of Ornette Coleman (interview with Jack Bruce, October 2007).

It is interesting to compare these sides with the Organization's set at the same club from 1964, *I Met the Blues at Klook's Kleek* (Music Avenue). The change is a dramatic one both in repertoire and approach. This is now most definitely an R&B group, albeit one that plays with jazz chops.

Listening to Bond's two Columbia/EMI albums, *The Sound Of '65* and *There's a Bond Between Us*, it is easy to identify the group's (and Bond's) strengths and weaknesses. The vocals from Bond, and Bruce, whom he encouraged to sing, were dynamic and exciting but it was the sound of the group in full flight that most defined them. Ramsey Lewis's "Wade in the Water", Muddy Waters' "I've Got My Mojo Working", Ray Charles's "What'd I Say?" and Bond's own "Walkin' in the Park" (on stage taken at a much faster pace than on the record) are great performances. But the group's original material, much of it by Bond himself, was pretty dire. Bond simply could not produce the material that might have translated real club success into chart positions. Yet they were a very busy band, as Ginger Baker recalls:

> We (Bond and Baker) were both sort of jazz musicians and we decided in 1962 that we were going to go commercial and the band was very popular, incredibly popular. We were working all the time, doing quite well. Seventy-five quid for universities but we were doing like three hundred and forty gigs a year.
> (Interview with Ginger Baker, August 2009)

Jack Bruce was eventually ousted from the Organization by Ginger Baker and when Baker left, having decided to form his own band, Jon Hiseman came in on drums. Hiseman is very clear on what he sees as Bond's problem with material:

> The central problem was that Graham Bond couldn't write. He could make up a blues as he went along and sing rubbish over the top but at the end of the day he never wrote anything that was ... "Walkin' in the Park" is about the strongest thing he ever wrote and, of course, we [Colosseum] played it to death. But there was very little else – a couple of other things maybe. Even the thing that most fans from those days remember, "Wade in the Water", was nothing to do with him at all.
> (Interview with Jon Hiseman, May 2009)

Hiseman notes that his band Colosseum and others had a similar problem to Bond's in this area and that it was this that stopped such groups hitting the big time:

> The other problem is that we were never able, as Graham was never able, to actually write iconic moments that would then

work at a three-minute length and get us the kind of publicity that could have made us a very big band. As a result of that, we are a small band and Graham, of course, never got close to any of that and he didn't have the vision to see that.

(Interview with Jon Hiseman, May 2009)

As Hiseman points out, Bond's potential and the sound he pioneered was realized not by him but by those he had fostered and encouraged:

Graham was a catalyst for a lot of other people who became much more successful and I've got to say that in a way this was Graham's demise because, while I was with him, he couldn't bear going into a club and hearing Cream being played. He couldn't bear it. And he couldn't bear their success because he couldn't understand why it wasn't happening to him but to them and his success was always just around the corner and it never came. And in the end it ate him away.

(Interview with Jon Hiseman, May 2009)

Solid Bond, the double set released on Warner Brothers, did reach number forty in the British album charts. In some ways it was the most satisfying of his releases. Two records followed – *Holy Magick* and *We Put Our Magick On You* – that were both made in America and were released by Philips. Both suggest the paradox that lay within the heart of Bond's talent. They revealed that both his vision and the musical ability were intact. At their best, his post-Organization releases suggested something akin to the music Dr John, The Night Tripper, was creating around that time. At the same time, the material lacked consistency and coherence, lyrically and musically. By the time poet/lyricist/bandleader Pete Brown put a group together with Bond it was all pretty much over for one of Britain's most mercurial jazz and rock talents. And Bond still had to watch Jack Bruce, Ginger Baker, Pete Brown, Jon Hiseman, Dick Heckstall-Smith, John McLaughlin and the many organ-led bands who followed in his wake achieving the critical and financial rewards that escaped him. The hoards of keyboard-dominated groups that featured so heavily in British progressive rock – bands such as the Nice, Procul Harum, ELP, Pink Floyd, Colosseum, Rare Bird, Egg, Caravan, Yes, Clouds and Soft Machine – are a kind of ironic tribute to the music he had pioneered.

Of all the groups who carried Bond's legacy forward, it was obviously Cream who were to prove the most successful. Their first three records – the first two in particular – covered a lot of ground from fashionable psychedelic pop and folky melodies to blues, as well as that strange and attractive hybrid that Jack Bruce fashioned from jazz, rock, blues and Celtic music. Ginger Baker emphasizes their commitment to improvisation and argues that describing them as a rock band is a misnomer:

Graham Bond with the Goudie Charles Quintet at Southend Rhythm Club, 6 March 1960. Left to right: Goudie Charles (guitar), Roy Surman (bass), Milton James (aka James Sampson – tenor sax), Graham Bond (alto sax), Art Terry (drums). Photograph courtesy of Goudie Charles, photographer unknown.

I mean, I don't think Cream was a rock & roll band in any sense of the word. When we got back together a couple of years ago, it was a very enjoyable experience. It wasn't rock and & roll at all. Eric's a blues player and the difference between blues and jazz is slim, if there's any difference at all. Eric, as far as I'm concerned, is a jazz player. He improvises. Eric never plays exactly the same two nights running. Neither do I. [Chuckling]

(Interview with Ginger Baker, August 2009))

Cream should most definitely be seen as heirs to Bond's legacy, though its members also transcended its limitations in terms of the quality of their material and performances. By contrast, Jon Hiseman and fellow Bond alumnus Dick Heckstall-Smith stayed closer to the Organization's template with their group Colosseum, but succeeded in refining Bond's vision. Formed in 1968, Colosseum's history illustrates both the popularity of jazz-infused rock and the complex and fickle nature of the music business. Each one of their four records made the album charts and yet, financially speaking, the band has been far more successful since they reformed in 1995. As Hiseman explains, "The advance from the record company went into the kitty to pay wages. Gigs often didn't cover their costs in those days. For example, we paid for all the posters and though we packed the Lyceum, we still made a loss on that gig."

He continues:

> We were on a wage, which we paid ourselves. It started out at twenty-five quid a week and after two years it went up to fifty quid a week. That was '71 and, when the band broke up that year, I gave each member of the band a thousand pounds, which was all there was in the kitty and we never received any record royalties or accounts until 1983. And then we got nearly thirty grand to split between us and all the various personnel and it wasn't basically until the records went to Sanctuary at Castle Communications and were released as CDs, that we started to seriously make money and then we got some very good royalties because they sold a lot of records.
>
> (Interview with Jon Hiseman, May 2009)

Though Colosseum never made the very big, "big time" they were a name band. From the release of their first album, *Those Who Are About to Die Salute You* in 1969 (Fontana; Sanctuary), their gigs were packed and they also put together a very successful tour in 1970 with the New Jazz Orchestra, with whom several of its members played. But what is still intriguing about Colosseum was that they achieved this as what was essentially an instrumental band, at least until vocalist Chris Farlowe joined for *Daughter of Time* in 1970. Their sound always gave the impression of a much bigger band and emphasized the guitar, first of James Litherland and then Dave Clempson, as well as the organ of Dave Greenslade. The way that these two instruments combined with Heckstall-Smith's blues-inflected tenor over the driving rhythm section of bassist Tony Reeves and Hiseman could be quite magnificent. *Those Who Are About to Die* ... provided the model, which *Valentyne Suite*, also from 1969 (Vertigo; Sanctuary), and *Daughter of Time* (Vertigo; Sanctuary) realized triumphantly. Both still stand up well today, with *Daughter of Time* benefitting enormously from additional horns and a string quintet on several tracks, and arrangements by Neil Ardley, leader of the New Jazz Orchestra.

However, perhaps the most original band to come out of this period fusing jazz and rock were Soft Machine. The group was originally a quartet featuring Robert Wyatt on drums and vocals, Kevin Ayers on bass and vocals, Australian beatnik Daevid Allen on guitar and Mike Ratledge on piano and organ. On attempting to return to the UK from France, Allen was refused re-entry and so the group continued as a trio. Listening to early recordings such as *Jet-Propelled Photographs* (BYG/Charley), made by Giorgio Gomelsky in London in April 1967, and the tracks issued under the title *Soft Machine Turns On Volume 1* and *Volume 2* (both Voiceprint) one hears a band similar to the many others plying their trade at the time. Blues, soul and pop influences exist alongside hints of jazz and contemporary classical music. However, their progress between those sides and the release of their first album, *Soft Machine Volume One* in 1968 (ABC; UMC), was astonishing. They might easily have collapsed under the combined weight of their inspirations but a vision was certainly coalescing.

Their second album, *Volume Two* (Probe; UMC), now with Hugh Hopper on bass in place of Kevin Ayers, was even better, and its quirky psychedelia sat intriguingly with its jazz enthusiasms. By the time their third record, *Third* (CBS; Sony BMG), hit the stores in 1970 the band had morphed into something much more focused and unique. They had poached several members of the Keith Tippett Group, and the double album featured saxophonist Elton Dean, who would remain with the group for the next two albums, flautist/saxophonist Lyn Dobson, Nick Evans on trombone, Jimmy Hastings on flute and bass clarinet and violinist Rob Spall.

Third could not have been made by an American band, though one could imagine something with a similar sense of itself being produced by Faust or Can perhaps. It drew sustenance from a wide range of sources, some of which were American. Minimalist composer Terry Riley and Mike Ratledge's experience of seeing Miles's new electric band in the States are both significant in this respect. But Soft Machine's music also seemed to reference European influences like Stockhausen and even suggested at times the *musique concrète* of Pierre Schaeffer and that of Delia Derbyshire of the BBC Radiophonic Workshop.

As Hugh Hopper recalled in 2003:

> Oh, we were all into that stuff. Robert was with me some of the time in Paris in '64 when I lived with Daevid Allen and Gilli Smyth. Daevid had studied a bit with Terry Riley and we were immersed in that pre-Psychedelia. Ratledge was open to all sorts of craziness too.
> (E-mail interview with Hugh Hopper, June 2003)

And interviewed for the same article, Robert Wyatt confirmed the eclectic series of inspirations that informed their music:

Absolutely. We used to listen to all that. Delia Derbyshire at BBC Radio Workshop was a wonderful woman and yes, we used to listen to all those things. I started out as a jazz fan as a teenager and am now, but in the intervening period I've been into all kinds of things and certainly the experimental music of the day – post-Stockhausen stuff and indeed my dad's record collection of pre-WWII conservatory music like Bartok and Hindemith. It just means that you know that there's all kinds of things you can do. It's not some lofty project. It's just trying to make things more fun and more interesting.   (Interview with Robert Wyatt, June 2003)

Other influences on the band as a whole and as individuals included Dada, the Pataphysics of Alfred Jarry and the gentle whimsy of British writers like Edward Lear and Lewis Carroll. Soft Machine's origins also lay in the bohemian home life of Robert Wyatt and his family, where sympathetic and like minds would congregate to listen to avant garde music and jazz, to talk about philosophy or just to listen to the BBC Third Programme or Home Service. In fact, the reason that this record, or indeed its predecessors or immediate successors could never have been made by an American band is because it seems suffused with the ethos that in a strange way underpinned the BBC or at least parts of it then. This was a place where "Woman's Hour", "Mrs Dale's Diary" and Wilfred Pickles might be followed by surreal radio comedy, electronic music, poetry reading, gardening or nature programmes or experimental theatre. It was not subject to the restrictions of commercial broadcasting or listener surveys, and odd things could happen. The first three Soft Machine albums most definitely have that something of that same English/British idiosyncrasy about them and, though internal conflicts would in due course destroy that shared sense of purpose, both *Fourth* and *Fifth* continued to reveal elements of that same sensibility.

Once again, Hugh Hopper's comments confirm that play and experimentation underpinned the group's ethos:

We were all into lots of different things – jazz, contemporary and ethnic. I always say that one of my major influences is the drone of Indian music and that slots very closely into the kind of modal ostinato basslines that Coltrane's bassists played. Ratledge was classically trained but I remember him coming back from a trip to the New York around '63–'64, raving about McCoy Tyner, having seen the Coltrane Quartet playing live. You can hear those Coltrane influences in both his and my playing on the Soft Machine records. And of course, Robert was a fan of Elvin Jones (who isn't?). But, yes, lots of influence from Riley, Stockhausen (and we actually did a piece at the BBC Radiophonic Workshop around 1970). And in my case, don't forget the influence of rhythm & blues and Motown. James Jamerson and James Brown's bass players are forever engraved in my subconscious.

(E-mail interview with Hugh Hopper, June 2003)

The first five Soft Machine albums represent their essential recordings, though much interesting material has surfaced later. Good though both *Fourth* and *Fifth* might have been, the group never again achieved the heights of "Facelift", "Out-Bloody-Rageous" "Moon in June" and "Slightly All the Time", the four tracks that comprised *Third*. Under the later leadership of Karl Jenkins (previously with Ian Carr's Nucleus and Graham Collier) the group changed dramatically and its vision and philosophy dissipated. The playing by musicians such as guitarists Alan Holdsworth and John Etheridge, drummer John Marshall (also at one point with Nucleus), saxophonist Alan Wakeman and bassist Roy Babbington could hardly be faulted, but it took place within a group that was markedly different from the original one. The sound that most fans associate with Soft Machine was really that first created by Wyatt, Ratledge and Ayers, developed subsequently with the addition of Hopper and nurtured and further extended with the arrival of Elton Dean and then John Marshall in the period 1967–72. *Fourth*, in the side-long "Virtuality" and "Kings and Queens", probably contained some of Hopper's and the band's best writing. However, *Third* does perhaps best define their music – Mike Ratledge's swirling Hammond organ, the oh-so-precise but melodic bass of Hugh Hopper, the spiralling, serpentine saxophone lines of Elton Dean and the wild but flowing pulse of Robert Wyatt's drums. It was a sound that would somehow cocoon you in its embrace and carry you through its labyrinthine time changes. Like the very best music, it transported you into its own world and time-frame and yet it was and remains vital and visceral music.

But Soft Machine also serve to illustrate several trends we have already observed. First, we see that an interest in jazz continued among a broad section of youth after the arrival of the Beatles and then the Stones. Second, Soft Machine exemplify the desire to produce a music that was not reliant on one style or format but rather drew on a range of musical ideas. This trend might not have been unique to Britain but it was still in every sense home-grown, reflecting the socio-cultural situation here and those source materials that made most sense in a British context. Finally, both in their approach and in *Third*'s set of four extended compositions, Soft Machine echo a commonly held sense that nearly anything was possible. In Soft Machine's case, and unlike many other groups of the time, they had the potential to realize their goals. Their impact is not only to be found in the subsequent and substantial solo work of Wyatt, Dean and Hopper but also in the interest that the group's music continues to attract.

The rise of beat, R&B and rock certainly did impact on jazz in Britain. Both "trad" and modern jazz struggled to sustain an audience in the face of the ubiquity of different popular forms. R&B and later rock, in particular, encroached on territory that had previously have belonged to jazz. However, we must stress again that the process of dominance and encroachment was neither as rapid nor as complete as is sometimes suggested. In a variety of ways jazz and pop music remained intertwined through the period. Indeed, the connections between modern (and traditional) jazz and the earlier of the two "blues booms" in sixties Britain were incredibly strong. In fact, the links went much further than Chris Welch's "Brain Drain" article. After all, many of those involved in playing rhythm and blues came from jazz, as Jack Bruce, describing the music scene in 1962, points out:

> There was no real rhythm and blues scene. There was Alexis's band and maybe a couple of other bands. It was really a very small scene and all of the people who were playing jazz and rock & roll at that time were jazz musicians. Famously, there were a lot of jazz musicians played on early American rock records. There were a lot of jazzers who were posing as whatever to get work but at the same time were very sneering about it.
>
> (Interview with Jack Bruce, October 2007)

Bruce is correct in what he says. From 1962 onwards, the presence of jazz or ex-jazz musicians in blues and rock bands was significant. In fact, the way in which British rock music developed owes a great deal to the jazz musicians who "crossed over" in the early to mid-sixties. We have mentioned Graham Bond, Brian Auger, Cream and Colosseum already. It will be remembered that the membership of Alexis Korner's Blues Incorporated reads like a "Who's Who" of British jazz, while Manfred Mann tried at various times to broaden his group's sound in a jazz direction. "Trad" jazz trumpeter Mike Cotton even changed his whole band in order to play R&B first as the Mike Cotton Sound and later as Satisfaction, a jazz-rock ensemble. As well as involvement with Graham Bond and later Colosseum, Jon Hiseman, Dick Heckstall-Smith and bassist Tony Reeves (Colosseum, New Jazz Orchestra, Mike Taylor) also played in John Mayall's short-lived Bare Wires group in 1968 (Decca; Decca), along with trumpeter Henry Lowther, guitarist Mick Taylor and saxophonist Chris Mercer. Saxophonist Alan Skidmore was another jazz musician who played with both Mayall and Korner and for him these were crucial learning experiences:

> That's like going to the "University of Jazz" because to learn to play the blues properly, you're set up for life. That's your honours degree. I've had various students over the years and I always say to them, "There's two things you need to be a jazz musician. You've

got to be hungry to play and perfect your art. But before that you've got to learn to play the blues. If you can't play the blues, you're stuffed!"   (Heining 2008b, 34)

In fact, one of the tracks on Mayall's *Bluesbreakers With Eric Clapton* (Decca; Decca) was actually to have a far wider significance and importance. When Skidmore met the American saxophonist Michael Brecker some years later, he learnt to his pleasant surprise that "Have You Heard?" influenced Brecker to take up the tenor saxophone:

> He said, "Wow man, I've got to tell you that you're responsible for me playing the saxophone." I tell you, Duncan, if the ground could've opened up, I would've jumped in. It came right out of the blue. To be honest I was embarrassed. He said, "No man, it was a solo you play with John Mayall and Eric Clapton on 'Have You Heard?' I heard that and I was blown away and it really made me want to play the sax." I mean, my jaw hit the ground. I was meeting this guy I really admired and for him to say that was jaw-dropping.   (Heining 2008b, 34)

Korner's band was very much a second home for a whole generation of young British jazzers. One of the finest drummers to emerge in the sixties, John Marshall, played with Korner for several years, and others who occupied the drum chair included Phil Seamen and Tony Carr. Danny Thompson, Carr's future colleague in folk-jazz group Pentangle, played bass in Blues Incorporated at the same time as Carr. Horn players who featured with Korner in the sixties and early seventies included trombonist Chris Pyne and saxophonists Ray Warleigh, Art Themen, Brian Smith (later of Nucleus) and John Surman. Somewhat naively, the author had expressed surprise at Surman's involvement with Korner in an interview in 1997. Surman's reply was very instructive:

> That's interesting because I played a lot and I feel it. I think it's understanding more than playing that stuff. If I do play blues I can really play it but the time is when you're playing that thing. Music is the language but there are these dialects that work and when you're in that context, that's the way to go for it. I haven't played blues for years. In fact, not since Alexis died. He used to come over to Oslo with Colin Hodgkinson and I'd be there with him all night!   (Heining 1997a, 5)

As for CCS, the big blues band Korner established in 1970, it featured a whole raft of British jazz musicians including trumpeters Kenny Wheeler, Harry Beckett and Henry Lowther and saxophonists Harold McNair, Tony

Coe and Peter King. The arrangements for the band, meanwhile, were by erstwhile jazz pianist-composer John Cameron. The personnel of CCS overlapped somewhat with Rock Workshop, the rock-jazz ensemble formed by Ray Russell and singer Alex Harvey. Of the two, CCS were the more successful, though both suffered from a deficit of good, well-crafted songs.

For jazz musicians playing rock, income was certainly an issue. However, when one speaks with people like Skidmore or Surman or Beckett, there is no sense that this was in any way lesser or demeaning work. Bassist Danny Thompson clearly loved all the music he got to play. Not only did he play with Blues Inc. and Pentangle, but he also worked extensively with singer–guitarist John Martyn. It was Thompson, who suggested bringing drummer John Stevens in when Martyn indicated a desire to add percussion. Together, Martyn, Thompson and Stevens recorded the excellent *Live in Leeds* LP in 1975 (Island; Recall), a record that still seems unique in its fusion of folk, blues, jazz and electronics.

Indeed, Thompson is a good example of another thread that runs through jazz in Britain, that which links it to folk music. Thompson has played and recorded with singer–songwriters Nick Drake and Donovan, as well as with folk-blues guitar virtuoso Davey Graham and guitarist–songwriter Ralph McTell, plus any number of other similar artists. These activities never stopped the bassist from working in a more straightforward jazz context either with Tubby Hayes or with Chris McGregor. Davey Graham is himself an interesting case in point. As well as featuring jazz players such as Thompson, Jon Hiseman, Dick Heckstall-Smith, Harold McNair and others, his albums invariably include a clutch of jazz instrumentals from the likes of Charles Mingus, Cannonball Adderley and Sonny Rollins. And if one looks at the lists of backing musicians on many of the folk-rock records released on Chris Blackwell's Island label, one will find names such as Chris McGregor, Dudu Pukwana, Harold McNair and Ray Warleigh.

Country-blues guitarist Mike Cooper was another innovator in this regard. Not only did he use a number of free jazz players on the albums he cut for Peter Eden's Pye/Dawn imprint but he even developed an approach that opened up the blues to create his own free jazz-blues hybrid. It is, however, Danny Thompson who seems most of all to embody the link between British sixties jazz and folk. Pentangle, the group he formed with singer Jacqui McShee, guitarists John Renbourn and Bert Jansch, and Tony Carr produced some quite lovely music that drew on both contemporary and traditional folk, jazz, blues and even baroque and early music. On record, perhaps their double album *Sweet Child* (Transatlantic) serves them best. And they were hugely successful, touring America and filling concert halls in the UK and Europe on many occasions. In fact, the contrast between Thompson's success with Pentangle and his experience on the jazz circuit could not have been greater. One night it was the Albert Hall, the next a pub room somewhere in London.

I did the Albert Hall with Pentangle which was completely sold out. I did that gig, sold out, big group blah, blah, but then the next night I was at the Kensington Court Hotel round the corner with Danny Moss, Alan Branscombe in the Phil Seamen Quartet, and my manager Jo Lustig phoned up and said, "Danny, what the hell you think you're doing? You do the Albert Hall sold out. The next night you're working in a pub round the corner for £40." To me it was an achievement to be able to play with Danny and Alan and Phil Seamen. I ended up playing with Red Rodney, Art Farmer and Freddie Hubbard and working with Pentangle and doing all that so-called folk stuff. Somebody said to me, "When you're doing all that folk stuff, don't you miss soloing?" I said, "That's all I do" [laughing] and it still applies. People have said, "When did you stop playing jazz and start playing folk?" I have only ever played me. Whether it's Ralph McTell or Red Rodney, I just serve the music.   (Interview with Danny Thompson, February 2009)

This open-minded attitude fuelled such collaborations and was just as important to these guys as the pay cheque. At the same time, no doubt, it was a refreshing change for hard-working jazzers to find their talents appropriately remunerated. As John Marshall notes, money was a factor in his decision to leave Nucleus to join Jack Bruce's group in 1971:

[Jack said] he could only pay £50 a gig, which doesn't sound a lot now, but I couldn't believe it. I'd never been paid so much in my life. With Nucleus at Ronnie Scott's, we said we wanted £10 a gig and they said we were money-mad! I left Nucleus to do this.
(Shapiro 2010, 145)

Yet Marshall enjoyed and valued his time with the bassist in more than monetary terms, just as he relished playing with Alexis Korner. As we have seen, Korner was the mirror image for Chris Barber. Korner is a bluesman who loves jazz – and the people who play it. Barber is a jazzman who loves the blues. By contrast, Jack Bruce refuses to describe himself as a jazz musician or as a blues musician either for that matter:

I tend to think of jazz not as a style of music. It's more the expression of certain individuals. I wouldn't really say that I was a jazz musician at all. You could say that are probably only a few jazz musicians in the world. If there are any now, I'd be surprised. There may be one or two. I think of jazz musicians starting way back in New Orleans and Louis Armstrong perfecting the solo and all of this kind of stuff. Tony Williams was a jazz musician, if you like. He was part of the tradition going back to Baby Dodds

and so on. I would say that there were a lot of people playing at jazz but I have never considered myself a jazz musician, at least not for a long time. I aspired to be one when I was very young, in a sort of romantic way. I was attracted by the romanticism of the music and the people who played it. But then I became more interested in trying to develop my own style of music, my own form of music, inventing my own scales, of tunings and obviously incorporating what my background is, Celtic music and so on.
(Interview with Jack Bruce, October 2007)

Bruce is yet another unusual character from an era that produced more than its share. Throughout his career, and like Thompson and others we have mentioned, he has worked in a wide range of idioms, some of which he feels have worked better than others. As a bassist, he worked with both John Mayall and (briefly and unhappily) with Manfred Mann.

I had just got married and I was very skint and thought this would be a way of paying the bills. It turned out not to be the case. I got to play "Do Wah Diddy" all night and still couldn't pay my bills. So, I learnt a lesson – don't try and be a commercial musician [pause] if you're me.   (Interview with Jack Bruce, October 2007)

At the same time, he played on pianist Mike Taylor's remarkable *Trio* LP – on several tunes alongside Ron Rubin. Both he and Rubin had worked in Group Sounds Five and Bruce played bass on the New Jazz Orchestra's *Déjeuener Sur L'herbe* 1969 release (Verve). In addition, in August 1968, he recorded his own "jazz" album, while still with Cream – *Things We Like* (Polydor; Polydor). Featuring Jon Hiseman on drums, Dick Heckstall-Smith on sax and, on some tracks, John McLaughlin on guitar, the record was quite an ear-opener for a lot of Cream fans. *Things We Like* was not released until 1970, not long after Bruce's first official solo release, *Songs for a Tailor* (Polydor; Polydor), which rather overshadowed it. Yet both are essential and rewarding records and important documents of the diversity of British jazz and rock music in the sixties and early seventies. *Things We Like* seemed to unite all Bruce's influences to date in a jazz context using compositions that had been built upon the shifting sands of various cyclical motifs and which allowed huge space for improvisation. *Songs for a Tailor*, on the other hand, utilized the complex song structure that Bruce had developed to match poet Pete Brown's words on Cream's three studio albums. In some respects, the music on Songs represents an advance in the collaboration of Bruce and Brown on a set that is often highly dramatic and rich in powerful, cinematic imagery. Some tracks utilize quite sparse instrumentation with just Chris Spedding on guitar and Jon Hiseman on drums (John Marshall also plays drums on two numbers). However, three tunes – "Never Tell Your Mother She's Out of Tune",

"Ministry of Bag" and "Boston Ball Game", 1967 – feature trumpeters Harry Beckett and Henry Lowther and on saxes Dick Heckstall-Smith and Art Themen (trombonist John Mumford also plays on the last of these tunes). It is neither jazz, nor funk, nor rock, nor blues but a marvellous amalgam of all of these. Bruce's explanation for using jazz musicians so extensively during this part of his career is intriguing coming from someone who in Cream had conquered the world of rock music:

> Well, that was simply that the only musicians that I knew were jazz musicians. I did a very failed attempt at doing a pop record and I had John Stevens on drums. [laughing] These were the only people I knew. I didn't know any rock players really. Also they were my friends, so any work I could put their way I would. I think I had Don Rendell on that. It was all a bit bizarre.
> (Interview with Jack Bruce, October 2007)

Bruce also played live with Mike Gibbs's orchestra on *Michael Gibbs* (Deram; Vocalion) soloing on "Some Echoes, Some Shadows" and also on Neil Ardley, Ian Carr and Don Rendell's *Greek Variations* (Columbia). In addition, he depped on three occasions with Ian Carr's Nucleus (see Shapiro 2010, 304–5). Bruce's openness to musical ideas that intrigue and inspire him has been a characteristic of his working life, even to the point where a change of direction might not be the most sensible career move. He had formed his first touring group early in 1970 to promote *Songs for a Tailor* in Britain and the USA, but changed course to join Tony Williams's Lifetime:

> I was playing with the first band that I had, which was called Jack Bruce and Friends. It had Larry Coryell on guitar, Mitch Mitchell on drums and Mike Mandel on organ. I was playing at the Fillmore East and John McLaughlin brought Tony along to hear the band and Jimi Hendrix was also there and Tony asked me, "Would you like to join my band?" I said, "Yes." That was the first date of the tour. I did finish the tour but my heart wasn't really in that band anymore. I was really excited about joining Tony.
> (Interview with Jack Bruce, October 2007)

Lifetime went from being a trio of McLaughlin, Williams and organist Larry Young to a quartet with the addition of Bruce on bass. Beset by management problems and technology that was never adequate to the group's distinctive approach, Lifetime lasted less than two years as a trio/quartet. The lucky few who saw it perform live still recall the shock that it left in its wake. Guitarist John Etheridge was one who saw the group on its only UK tour:

> That's another gig people still talk about in hushed tones. It was at the Marquee and everybody had the same reaction. It

was amazing. I couldn't figure out what was the tune, what was improvisation. The records that took me back into the jazz world were *In a Silent Way, Extrapolation, Bitches Brew,* not so much Lifetime's Emergency but when I saw the band live it blew me away. In Lifetime, McLaughlin was fabulous.

(Heining 2007c, 30)

Bruce remains disappointed that Lifetime's *Turn it Over* (Polydor; Polydor), on which he played, was so poorly recorded:

That whole band was just amazing – very ahead of its time and very difficult for people to know what to do with. It never got recorded properly, not the quartet. The trio record isn't bad recording-wise but when we tried to do it as a quartet, they couldn't get it onto tape. There was too much energy. It is without a doubt, the most amazing thing I was ever involved in. I don't know what it was either. There was something going on that none of us ever reproduced. The Mahavishnu Orchestra was a pale imitation of that but there was an energy and direction that was quite incredible. It just started, then it went on and then it stopped. The few people who managed to see that band live, I still get people coming up to see me and saying, "I saw you here or there and it changed my life." There was certainly something going on there but unfortunately it didn't really come to fruition, but a lot of things like that don't, I guess.

(Interview with Jack Bruce, October 2007)

Jazz and rock music continued to connect throughout the sixties and influence flowed in both directions. From its origins in the southern states of America, jazz has drawn on the popular music of the day to refresh itself and this was also true in Britain during the sixties and early seventies. Rock became an important musical element in the work of a number of major and lesser British jazz artists into the 1970s. Saxophonist Lol Coxhill had worked with pianist Steve Miller in the group Delivery. Together Coxhill and Miller produced the genre-bending albums, *Miller/Coxhill* (Caroline; Cuneiform) and *The Story So Far ... Oh Really!* (Caroline; Cuneiform) during the early seventies. Poet Pete Brown, encouraged by Graham Bond to sing and launch his own band, started Battered Ornaments, which included Mike Westbrook Concert Band alumni George Khan on saxes and guitarist Chris Spedding. Sacked rather embarrassingly from his own band the night before they were due to play at the Stones' Hyde Park concert, Brown formed Piblokto with jazzers Jim Mullen on guitar and Laurie Allen on drums. Allen had been involved in poetry and jazz with Brown and Michael Horovitz. Piblokto's first album, *Things May Come and Things May Go but the Arts School Dance*

Goes on Forever (Harvest; BGO), is a classic of the period. Trumpeter Henry Lowther and saxophonist Jimmy Jewell were to be found in the Keef Hartley Band – they actually played at Woodstock! – while trumpeter Harry Beckett, saxophonists Barbara Thompson, Lyn Dobson and trombonist Derek Wadsworth were among those added to create Hartley's Little Big Band. The band that saxist/flautist Bob Downes put together for *Electric City* (Vertigo; Eclectic) crossed both genres and the same must be said for the group pianist Keith Tippett assembled for *Dedicated to You but You Weren't Listening* (Vertigo; Repertoire). Other examples of this cross-pollination between jazz and rock would include Caravan, Hatfield and the North, Gary Boyle's Isotope, Soft Heap, Gilgamesh, Japanese percussionist Stomu Yamashta's ensembles, Daevid Allen's Gong and their numerous offshoots. This was in effect a thriving scene within a scene. Progressive rock (or to use its *Melody Maker*-invented title, Prog Rock) might have been dominated by ELP, Yes, Pink Floyd and others, but for a time it was a genuinely progressive and catholic musical style.

But the British jazz musician who most strongly embraced an alliance with rock music was trumpeter Ian Carr. In *The Music Outside* (Carr 2008), Carr wrote at length about the dissatisfactions he had in 1969 with the state of British jazz and his part in it. He talks eloquently about the conservatism that he felt underpinned the music that he was making with the Don Rendell–Ian Carr Quintet. Carr wanted to break free from the self-imposed and outdated image of jazz that he believed was based upon a set of misguided and defunct romantic notions that harked back to 1950s New York. For the trumpeter, this meant embracing a new professionalism and paying as much attention to the presentation of the music as to the music itself. Carr recognized that jazz had lost ground to the new rock groups and, as a devoted fan of Miles Davis, was keenly aware of the changes that Miles was making in his music. As a result, he began to look at new ways of working with jazz that might open up access to a new audience, that same audience that embraced Pink Floyd, Yes, Soft Machine and Colosseum. The group that he formed was Nucleus and, albeit with changing personnel, the band lasted a decade and a half. Its best records were those Carr made for Vertigo and later Capitol.

Nucleus's music broke, as did Miles Davis and that of Weather Report, with the notion of a series of head arrangements and solos or indeed with set lists built around tunes with fixed beginnings and ends. They presented the material as a constantly evolving stream derived from a set of themes where solos emerged before disappearing back into the fomenting waters. Carr had been keen to experiment within the Rendell–Carr Quintet – keener perhaps than his colleagues. As readers will recall, it was at his instigation that Ghanaian percussionist Guy Warren joined the group and he, at least, had gained a lot from that association, as well as from working on Amancio D'Silva's 1969 album *Integration* (Columbia; Universal). Carr had also recorded the excellent *Springboard* with John Stevens and Trevor

Watts from the SME and bassist Jeff Clyne. Nucleus' first record was called *Elastic Rock* (Vertigo; BGO), the title a description of the kind of elasticity and boundary-stretching that Carr was seeking. Its fold-out sleeve was black apart from a cut-out section that revealed the heart of a live volcano, which was exposed fully when the sleeve was opened out. Subsequent covers would share with those of Vertigo label mates that same sense that the music inside was important enough to warrant this expense, each in its own way conveying a kind of hip knowingness. And the music inside did justify the attention to such details.

Elastic Rock did break new ground and both the writing – all the group's members contribute – and the playing, collectively and individually is quite lovely. And yet its successor, *We'll Talk About it Later* (Vertigo; BGO), is even more successful in its grasping of the rhythms of rock music and the colours available with electronic instruments. Guitarist Chris Spedding is magnificent; Karl Jenkins on keyboards and reeds contributes most of the tunes; drummer John Marshall and Jeff Clyne provide a constant sense of movement while retaining that essential backbeat; and Carr and saxophonist Brian Smith move freely through the music. Smith, an undersung player originally from Australia, was arguably Carr's perfect foil and he constantly seems to inspire his front-line partner. The records that followed were as or nearly as good with *Labyrinth* from 1973 with its extended line-up (Vertigo; BGO) a remarkable achievement. But neophytes would do well to begin with *Elastic Rock* and *We'll Talk About it Later*.

It is clear that a number of British jazz musicians felt similarly to Carr and did not just look on the partnership with rock music as a way of accessing gigs, record deals and new fans. In his sleevenotes for *Our Point of View* by the Frank Ricotti Quartet with bassist Chris Laurence, drummer Bryan Spring and the ubiquitous Chris Spedding on guitar, Humphrey Lyttelton wrote with considerable insight:

> In 1969, the climate is much different. Today's young musicians have lived, in their formative years, through the "trad" boom of the early sixties, when it was impossible for anyone with his faculties in fair working shape not to glean some idea of the continuity of the jazz tradition from New Orleans onwards. And secondly, they have been surrounded by a "pop" culture, which has been increasingly involved with the very same blues and gospel music which lie at the foundations of jazz. Compared with the jazzmen of former days, hedged in by stylistic barriers on the one side and commercial barriers on the other, they are liberated beings.
> (Lyttelton 1969)

Lyttelton's open mind led him to draw attention to Spedding's wah-wah guitar on Stan Tracey's "Three Times Loser, Three Times Blueser", a markedly different version from the original, and he contrasts the group's take on Gary Burton's "Walter L" with that recorded by Burton's similar line-up. Here, Lyttelton notes that the country influences of the Burton original have been replaced with more of a R&B emphasis. This is fine, eclectic music, and Spedding's own "Late into the Night", written with Pete Brown and recorded by the Battered Ornaments, and Al Kooper's wildly flowing "House in the Country" add to the sadness that this group did not record more.

There is a lot in what Lyttelton has to say. It was not an issue of abandoning a tradition, more about updating it for a new generation and as Humph knew from experience when you did that you would invariably hear someone in the balcony yelling, "Judas!" Asked why he thought jazz lost out to rock music to such an extent, Jon Hiseman's reply is to the point: "All I can tell you is that I felt that jazz was second-hand. And I felt that rock was original" (interview with Jon Hiseman, May 2009).

This is not about abandoning one for the other but a matter of making your own music in your own way. One can hear strong echoes of this throughout Carr's *The Music Outside* (2008) in interviews with Mike Gibbs, Mike Westbrook and others, and in Carr's expression of his own musical aims. Jack Bruce's earlier comments also apply here. The desire to be as original as one could be in the music one created permeates this period in both jazz and rock. In fact, it is hard to escape the influence of rock and pop music upon jazz in these years. Listen to Henry Lowther's gorgeous *Child Song* (Deram; Vocalion) or Mike Westbrook's *Love Songs* (Deram; Vocalion), both from 1970, or Neil Ardley's sumptuous *Kaleidoscope of Rainbows* from 1975 (Gull; Dusk Fire). On the latter, Ardley uses an expanded Nucleus line-up to blend acoustic and electronic instruments to wonderful effect around the composer's beloved modes, here Balinese rather than Greek.

In fact, quite a few jazz musicians began turning up the volume and forming jazz-rock bands in the wake of Nucleus. Mike Westbrook had Solid Gold Cadillac, which featured Chris Spedding and, later, Brian Godding from rock band Blossom Toes on guitar. John Surman, one of the least technophobic of British jazz musicians, was quick to grasp the possibilities of synthesizers releasing the solo *Westering Home* in 1972 (Island; FMR), a foretaste of the solo records he would later make for ECM, as well as the sextet recording of *Morning Glory* through Chris Blackwell's Island label the following year. *Morning Glory* (Island; FMR) never seems to quite get its due. Yet this live recording is a beautifully executed and exciting addition to the genre, with some incredible guitar from Norwegian and George Russell alumnus Terje Rypdal.

Two other records need lengthy consideration here – trombonist and composer Mike Gibbs' *Just Ahead* (Polydor; BGO) and Keith Tippett's *September Energy* (RCA; BGO). Originally from Rhodesia, Gibbs studied at Berklee in Boston along with Britain's Graham Collier and a seventeen-year-old Gary Burton. In 1973, Gibbs's friendship with Burton led to *In the Public Interest* (Polydor), an album featuring the vibraphonist as principal soloist on a set of

Gibbs's compositions and arrangements for a crack US big band, including the Brecker Brothers and drummer Bob Moses. Gibbs came to Britain and played in Collier's Mingus-inspired groups, as well as in the orchestras of John Dankworth and Tubby Hayes. He released two fine albums for Deram produced by Peter Eden, *Michael Gibbs* (Deram; Vocalion) and *Tanglewood '63* (Deram; Vocalion), which drew on the talents of many of the top young musicians of the era and made extensive use of electronic instruments. Gibbs' records from this period and later are to be treasured but at times his work can feel unfinished. That certainly is not the case with *Just Ahead*, a live album where his band are given every opportunity to stretch out.

Gibbs knew the comedy actor Bill Oddie very well, at one time writing the music for *The Goodies* TV show, and it was Oddie who introduced him to some of the more interesting music coming out of rock music. By the time Gibbs began work on his eponymous LP, he was incredibly well-informed about jazz, classical and rock music, though he is typically modest about his efforts at bringing rock elements into jazz. "It was in the air at the time. My core is jazz. It's what excites me. I don't see myself as someone who fused jazz and rock. There are too many good rock people out there. I'm an amateur" (Heining 2001a, 37).

Just Ahead (Polydor; BGO) reveals how influences as diverse as Messiaen, Gil Evans, George Russell and Carla Bley had been absorbed by Gibbs. It remains one of the most exciting and authoritative British sets of the period. Gibbs is a notorious procrastinator and has never been the most industrious of composers, so it will not come as a surprise that the album features just a handful of originals alongside some bold arrangements of pieces by Carla Bley, Keith Jarrett and Gary Burton. Kenny Wheeler and Henry Lowther play with great solemnity and majesty on Bley's "Mother of the Dead Man", and saxophonist Alan Skidmore scorches his way through Gibbs's "Just a Head". Chris Spedding plays absolutely beautifully on Burton's shuffling "Country Roads" and Keith Jarrett's funky "Grow Your Own" and his comping, for want of a more appropriate term, behind Frank Ricotti's vibes on Bley's "Sing Me Softly of the Blues" is superb. Gibbs once remarked that some members of his big band felt that Spedding gave them too little to work with, seeing his role in terms of his place in the rhythm section. Gibbs would patiently explain that the guitarist was there to provide not just colour but a range of sounds that simply could not be obtained any other way. John Marshall is on great form throughout and vibraphonist Frank Ricotti confirms once again what a remarkable musician he really is. But it is Gibbs's own "So Long Gone" with solos from pianist Dave MacRae and trombonist Chris Pyne that seals this set. It remains one of the truly great performances to come out of British jazz in this or any other epoch.

We will discuss Keith Tippett further in Chapter 12, but his contribution to the jazz–rock debate goes far beyond his guest spots with Bob Fripp's King Crimson, which even included a *Top of the Pops* appearance. *Septober Energy*

(RCA Neon; BGO) was a conceit so vast it should have collapsed under its own weight. That a major record company would actually stump up money for it in the first place amazes, and that it even turned a goodly profit beggars belief. There has not really been anything like it before or since and yet its combination of voices – and Tippett is a phenomenally talented writer for the human voice – strings, electronic and acoustic instruments crosses genre boundaries with ease. The band Tippett put together was called Centipede because it involved fifty musicians (therefore 100 legs). A few years ago, Tippett was asked about the record and how well it sold and he replied with some pride, "It sold a lot, a helluva lot." He received a fairly sizeable, for the time, cheque from the record company. In fact, it was successful enough for RCA to pressurize him into making a follow-up. What began as a benefit for the Jazz Centre Society led to concerts in the Albert Hall and festival appearances in France and Holland. *Septober Energy* was, for jazz at least, a hugely successful work critically and financially. It marked Tippett out as a very particular kind of jazz musician, one who makes his own rules. As he says, "I didn't want to be involved in any school or somebody trying to create a dynasty. I didn't want to be part of that."

> We got a lot of publicity in the Daily Mirror and Melody Maker and RCA picked up on it. Suddenly, we were flying to Bordeaux and Holland in our own aeroplane. Centipede was at the Albert Hall when I was twenty-two. In the eighties, I wasn't even part of the furniture. Myself and others like me were forgotten, yet I was the Courtney Pine of '69.
>
> (Interview with Keith Tippett, March 2004)

Septober Energy demands to be heard and approached on its own terms. The uninitiated should not expect anything resembling a mainstream big band. Tippett uses both the full potential of the orchestra, as well as making the most of the opportunity to contrast this with settings involving smaller groupings of different players. It amounts to an epic journey through jazz, western classical music, British and other folk forms and rock. Yet it constantly reminds the listener that it is simultaneously all of these and none. It has its flaws, no doubt. Tom Callaghan, who wrote the sleevenotes for its BGO 2000 CD reissue, comments that it "gathered almost universally hostile reviews when it was released" and he refers to the "unwieldy" band's break-up as doing "nothing to improve sales". His remarks about the music itself also seem rather negative, which is really somewhat bizarre, given that BGO must have hoped they might sell a few copies. Callaghan damns with faint praise when he writes:

> Listening to *Septober Energy*, it's clear that the musical architec-
> ture that Centipede carved was part Gothic cathedral, part Lloyd

Wright palace, part ramshackle building. It may be something of
a curiosity now, but it's still standing, and it's still worthy of a tour.
(Callaghan 2000)

As Keith Tippett noted above, the record sold well enough that RCA hoped
for a follow-up, while Richard Williams (Williams 1971) certainly gave it a
very positive review in the *Melody Maker*. Contrary to Callaghan's views, the
balance that Tippett achieves between *Septober Energy*'s different stylistic
elements is due to the robustness of its architecture. For example, the composer uses contrast to great effect, allowing free improvisation to comment
upon the more formal building blocks derived from rock. This is music rich
in drama. There is one section in Part 2 where moments of unadulterated
jazz playing alternate with powerful voice-led anthemic rock, with the latter
functioning as a kind of Greek chorus within the structure. Tippett, himself
once a chorister, takes great care to integrate his vocal section into the whole.
This is particularly evident at the beginning of Part 3, a movement driven by
a strong martial pulse. Elsewhere, the inspiration that Tippett found in the
Blue Notes and Brotherhood of Breath is well to the fore, and both Dudu
Pukwana and Mongezi Feza play on the album along with other Brotherhood
of Breath alumni. There are some quite magnificent solos from the likes of
Ian Carr, Alan Skidmore, tenor player Larry Stabbins, Elton Dean and guitarist Brian Godding, but the strongest impression is left by the ensembles.
Towards the end of Part 3, there is an eerily beautiful combining of strings
and voices where the textures recall Ligeti and Penderecki. Yet this seems
in no way out of place on a recording where at other times rock rhythms or
brass-led big band jazz predominates. Perhaps the music is at its strongest
when jazz and rock combine as they do towards the middle of Part 4 as Elton
Dean's saxello weaves serpentine lines over a dense backing of electric and
acoustic instruments and voices. Yet it is the way that that the whole piece
hangs together that astonishes. That *Septober Energy* was written by someone just twenty-two years old at the time, makes one feel that nobody, but
nobody, should be quite that talented, but then just seven years later, Tippett
produced the even more remarkable *Frames* for Ogun Records. Tippett,
often working in tandem with his partner Julie, continues to make music that
remains within the context of jazz while pursuing his mission to expand its
boundaries.

If, as has been argued, jazz and rock continued to connect in various ways
to the benefit of both, we must still ask how, in the final analysis, jazz came
to lose out eventually to rock music and whether this situation was avoid-
able? The answer to the second part of the question has to be speculative,
but a suspicion persists that the potential for British jazz to build and sustain an audience of reasonable size did exist. To have done so would have
required a very different approach from that adopted by many of the key
players in jazz. After all, American-based groups like Miles's band, Weather

Report, Chick Corea's Return to Forever, Herbie Hancock's Headhunters and John McLaughlin's Mahavishnu Orchestra succeeded in maintaining very substantial audiences during the seventies. On that basis alone, one must assume that a market did exist for British musicians and bands to exploit.

One option that the majority of British musicians ignored to their cost was that provided by technology. While some like Mike Gibbs, Ian Carr and John Surman did explore the application of synthesizers, amplification and electronic instruments for more than texture and colour, they were a minority. In the main, British jazz remained determinedly an acoustic music and yet such technology could have enhanced rather than changed the nature of the music by offering it dynamic possibilities otherwise unavailable. As Ian MacDonald noted in *Revolution in the Head* (1995, 239), the development of heavy metal was inevitable given the "consequence of bigger and better amps and speakers designed for larger and more remunerative venues". One factor in rock's success has been its ability to exploit technological advances, though a corollary of this might well be a reduction in the diversity of the music promoted by major record companies due to the sheer costs involved. Miles, McLaughlin, Hancock and Weather Report had the backing of Columbia Records USA, and that is a hell of a machine to have pushing one forward. This helped them access the technological resources they need to exploit the music they were making. Resources at such a level were rarely, if at all, made available to British jazz musicians. One should not be too hard on British musicians. When struggling for survival one is just as likely to grab at a straw as at a passing life-raft. Nonetheless, I do think that more might have been made of technological advances in music by British jazzers.

Asked for his view on why jazz failed to compete with rock despite the market for improvised music that it had helped expose, Jon Hiseman offers a very succinct answer: "Jazz is hard. I think it was inevitable because it couldn't find a place in the modern world." He echoes a point made earlier by Chris Barber (see Chapter 5), that the key to the coffers for both rock and pop was that these were lifestyle accessories:

> We grew up thinking of music as music. We didn't – in the UK at least – we didn't concern ourselves with what John Coltrane was wearing or whether we had a beard one week or shaved it off the next, but if you read any articles about John Coltrane they weren't concerned with what his favourite television show was and what he liked for breakfast. Now what happened was that, spearheaded by the *New Musical Express*, music became a soundtrack for lifestyle and jazz had no place in that really. Its musicians were poor at presenting themselves generally. It began to lose any overt viewable connection with real life. It was an esoteric moment that was a tunnel that the guys themselves went down. A lot of developments in jazz, of course, spun off into the popular movement of

music. But when it lost its technological edge ... in other words, the technology of jazz didn't change at all. In fact, the drum kits stayed sixties' drum kits rather than new millennium drum kits. It did its very best not to acknowledge that the world was moving, that the world was changing.

(Interview with Jon Hiseman, May 2009)

Hiseman notes that even among younger musicians their efforts to adapt were half-hearted. He suggests that their attempts to incorporate what he calls "quasi-ethnic backgrounds" that appeared trendy were misguided. In his view, this disguised and avoided the need to revitalize the materials of the music itself and its presentation. Hiseman has a valid point in relation to the artificial adoption of ethnic forms. On the other hand, it could be argued that British jazz might actually have done more in utilizing the musics of the Commonwealth that could be heard in London streets at the time – music from India, Pakistan, the Caribbean and Africa. It could also have drawn more on indigenous folk forms from England, Scotland, Wales and Ireland and have done so authentically and with integrity. Had it done so, it might have reached out to audiences outside the predominately white, male jazz community.

In *Sixties Britain* (Donnelly 2005), Mark Donnelly describes the emergence of a new form of rock music around 1964–5 which fused together elements of modern jazz, folk protest songs and rock & roll in a way that "offered something for everybody". This he suggests opened up for a short time a shared space across class and stylistic boundaries for youth. But he also notes that despite the prominence of "Beat" groups, only seven of the top-selling singles artists in the UK between 1960 and 1969 could be described as such. In the charts, Cliff Richard, Elvis, Roy Orbison, Billy Fury, Adam Faith and Engelbert Humperdinck rode just as high as they did.

One suspects that Donnelly is correct but would want to add that the emergence of a style that "offered something for everybody" served to narrow the potential audience for modern jazz in Britain. As Jon Hiseman says, jazz is hard. British jazz musicians had helped introduce the British public to the idea of extemporization in music and, as we have seen, in some cases carried that into the rock music of the time. By its nature rock music is direct and, compared to jazz, simpler in its beats and rhythms, its harmonies and melodies. When it improvises it can be highly inventive but the materials it draws upon to do so are less complex. Consequently, improvisation in rock need not only focus on the music but is freer to attend to its presentation as well. It allows for spectacle, it relishes the show. Jazz could not compete in that regard.

But perhaps the remarks of Hiseman and Barber regarding the issue of "lifestyle" are of just as much significance in this respect. In earlier chapters, we noted that teenagers were not some artificial creation summoned fully formed from the minds of advertising executives. They arose out of a particular socio-cultural and economic situation. To an extent, they created themselves, but only within the limits of the times. They provided a new market for an increasingly consumer-oriented capitalism and created demands that could in turn be satisfied by a burgeoning leisure and entertainment industry. Market forces responded and in servicing this new clientele were able to shape and further foster demand. Given the ephemeral nature of "pop", its potential was enormous and insatiable. The canny entrepreneur need never be caught out with an overstock of last week's trends but would already be catching the next wave. Pop or rock was no longer "the thing" upon which all else was built but "a thing among other related things". Pop or rock could merely be something that played in the background on the radio or to which one danced to at the discotheque or youth club, a soundtrack essential to daily living. Or it could be something pursued by the collector with the zeal of a true fanatic. Even then it was still a prediction of other wants, desires and aspirations. Sadly or gladly, jazz could not lend itself to the ephemeral. It took too long, too much hard work, too much study to discover its laws, its rules, its values. It simply could not give these over wholesale to the world of commerce anymore than the mass market required by commerce could open its doors to it.

7 One Scotch, One Bourbon, One Beer

> I hate to advocate weird chemicals, alcohol, violence, or insanity to anyone, but in my case it's worked.
>
> Actor Bill Murray as writer Hunter S. Thompson in *Where the Buffalo Roam* (1980 film based on Thompson's stories)

Drugs and jazz go together like a horse and carriage – and probably far better than jazz and marriage. Arguably, British jazzers' main drug of choice has always been beer, followed closely by distilled alcohol of various kinds. In spot number three, we have the jazz woodbine, also known as grass, hash, Mary Jane and umpteen other corny nicknames. Coming up close on the rails, it is uppers – amphetamines, bennies, dexies, speed and what have you. Great for those long nights on the stand, especially when you are not feeling too good, or for those interminable trips up and down the highways of Britain. After that, there is coke, or cocaine – or as Ronnie Scott used to call it, "Peruvian marching powder". An anaesthetic and a more sophisticated high than speed, some say it is addictive, others that it can lead to psychological but not physical dependency. You pays your money, you takes your choice. Finally, there is heroin.

Heroin – smack, horse, gear, brown – is a painkiller and a very effective one. A young homeless addict once told the author when asked why she used, "When you're sleeping rough and it's cold and you're hungry and alone, smack makes you feel warm inside." That conversation took place seventeen years ago, not long after she had almost died from an overdose in a suicide pact that had killed her boyfriend. British drug laws were aimed precisely at denying her, an abused child in a grim reality, the means of feeling "warm inside". It was not always thus, as we will see.

Heroin kills people. They die from overdoses most often but also from things like septicaemia from dirty needles or simply from the long-term effect of abuse on the body. British jazz has seen a number of deaths related to heroin addiction, and other musicians have struggled to become and stay "clean". You can see drug addiction as a sickness, a vice, a personal failing or as a situational response to peer pressure or life's problems. Different individuals have different reasons for becoming involved in drug use. Generally, there is no one cause unless it is simply availability. Drug use can be understood socially, economically, politically and according to models of individual pathology. Perhaps by looking at the stories of musicians like Tubby Hayes, Bobby Wellins, Peter King, Alan Branscombe, Ginger Baker and others, we can tease out some of the common themes and hopefully provide a context for drug use in British jazz.

Let us start with the individual. Brian Dee was never a drug-user himself. He describes himself as a "beer man". However, he knew Tubby Hayes, Graham Bond, Alan Branscombe, Phil Seamen, Ginger Baker and many others who became addicted to heroin. I asked him whether he was surprised at the time at how many musicians took the drug:

> I'm amazed it still happens today but it's clear why it happened then, I think. Because of the great American black players, Parker *et al.* were on drugs, I think a lot of people in this country … the drug scene was in its infancy. I mean, outside of the modern jazz scene, I don't think you heard of drugs in the early days and I think there were people who thought that because, say, Paul Chambers was stoned out of his mind, if you did what he did, you might be able to play as good. I think there really was a lot of that. A lot of the great Americans were messed up with drugs and there was possibly an assumption that that was why they played that great.
> (Interview with Brian Dee, March 2008)

Dee turned professional around 1960 when he joined saxophonist Vic Ash's group. Ash had landed the support slot for the Miles Davis tour. Miles's bassist at that time was Paul Chambers, and Dee notes, "With Paul Chambers all you ever got was, 'Shit!', 'Yeah, man!', 'Shit!', 'Goddam!'. Then one night in a club in Manchester, he said to me, 'I'll be dead by the time I'm thirty, man!'" Anyone who finds it hard to find anything romantic in that may care to ponder the continuing veneration of Byron, Coleridge and de Quincy, plus any number of writers, musicians and artists who have been addicts of one substance or another. Check out Jim Morrison's grave, or should it be shrine, next time you are in Paris.

Like many ex-users, Ginger Baker sees no reason to be other than honest about his addiction. His early involvement with heroin is often blamed on fellow drummer Phil Seamen but Baker is keen to stress that this was never the case. "I was just using it for the music more than anything," he tells me. "I didn't go crazy on it." He laughs, and pauses, saying he does not want this to sound like an advert for heroin, then continues:

The first time I used it, I was working with the Johnny Scott Quintet. It was a gig in Brighton and all the band turned round to me afterwards, "You played fucking amazing tonight" and I thought I'd found the answer. I wasn't aware at that time that it was habit-forming. I thought it was just like smoking dope. That is how I got into it. It was nothing to do with Phil Seamen by the way. It was before I'd met Phil.

(Interview with Ginger Baker, August 2009)

As he explains, it took many years to get off drugs despite its impact on his personal and professional life:

I was a registered addict by 1961. That cost me a lot of work. It cost me the Dankworth job. I did the audition for the Dankworth band and all the band were raving about it and somebody told John I was using smack and Ronnie Stephenson got the gig and became a bigger junkie than me, which was really quite funny.

(Interview with Ginger Baker, August 2009)

Writer Harry Shapiro is more qualified than many to talk on this subject. Not only has he authored excellent biographies of Alexis Korner, Graham Bond and, recently, Jack Bruce, but he has worked in the drugs field for thirty years and (at point of writing) was director of communications and Information for the UK drugs charity DrugScope. His book, *Waiting for the Man – The Story of Drugs and Popular Music*, is authoritative and free of the usual voyeuristic, prurient content of such works (Shapiro 1999). His comments on British jazz musicians and drug use are instructive.

The thing about that was that they were trying to immerse themselves in a lifestyle. [Not] Art Pepper and Gerry Mulligan but the black guys, like Miles Davis and Charlie Parker – a lot of that was to do with the fact that they were black guys trying to operate in a white world. The likes of Phil Seamen and Red Reece certainly didn't have that excuse. But I think it was very much part of this sense of being an outsider in society. And, of course, they knew about Charlie Parker and people like that. Jack Bruce said to me that they called this the Charlie Parker death wish, that somehow in order to reach the heights of somebody like Parker you had to get into the depths of heroin to look for the inspiration, which was misguided clearly. But it had a certain sense to it in the way … not that heroin was an inspiration to great music but that somehow it let them insulate themselves from the world.

(Interview with Harry Shapiro, April 2009)

He, too, makes the link with the Romantic poets, noting that there was also an element of outsider cool involved, "It was like Byron and Keats. You were like some kind of Byronic damaged person. And few of them, of course, survived it. Phil Seamen, Tubby Hayes, Red Reece, Dickie Devere – they all got carried off prematurely."

Shapiro's description of the London jazz scene and its substance use seems pretty accurate.

> For the jazzers, cannabis was the main drug. There was some pretty strong dope around at that time, which makes me laugh nowadays when I read all this hoo-hah about how strong the cannabis is today. Because there was stuff that was coming in that these guys were buying from dealers in Notting Hill that would take the roof of your head off. Like kif or like a whole plant rolled up in newspaper. So, cannabis definitely. Cocaine – a bit as well because doctors could also prescribe cocaine as well as heroin. There was some of that about as well, and the purple hearts and all of that as well. But again it was small time then. Pills didn't really take off until '64/'65 I suppose. But there were also the drinkers. Dick Heckstall-Smith, in particular, was a pretty heavy drinker. Possession of amphetamines wasn't an offence until '64. Doctors continued to prescribe them for weight loss. It was still perfectly legitimate and continued through the seventies and later.
>
> (Interview with Harry Shapiro, April 2009)

Quite when Tubby Hayes began using heroin is unclear. In a Jazzwise article, Jack Massarik wrote:

> Towards the mid-60s, Tubby found life even harder. Flower-power and free-improv had arrived. He could ignore total radicals like Cecil Taylor and Albert Ayler, but when Coltrane sacked Elvin Jones and started playing totally free, Tubby's hey-day was over. Long hair and a moustache didn't suit him either, and in 1966 word spread that, having resisted the temptation for years, he had acquired a dope habit. Theories abounded. "Remember, Tubby started everything young," said Ronnie Scott. "He started drinking young. And he was always ready to experiment with anything."
>
> (Massarik 2005, 37)

John Fordham discussing Hayes and Scott's time together in the Jazz Couriers appears to suggest that the younger man's narcotic use had become a problem much earlier:

> Hayes was fitfully a cause for worry because he could not control either his drinking or his habits with narcotics. Unlike the

drummer Phil Seamen, who was sometimes incapable of performance, Hayes was rarely inhibited from playing at least acceptably, and often brilliantly, certainly in his early twenties. The effect of heroin use, when it finally took its toll of him, was to undermine his health before his willpower, in a manner that was first crippling and then fatal. But the Tubby Hayes of the late 1950s was a man at the height of his powers. (Fordham 1986, 85)

It is clear that Hayes's health had begun to decline by 1965 and the following year he was twice admitted to hospital, firstly with thrombosis and later with a blood clot that affected his lungs (Schwarz 1990). In 1967, he suffered a bout of jaundice and in 1968 he was busted by the drug squad for possession of diamorphine. It was in August of that year, and as a result of that court appearance, that he became a "registered addict". Saxophonist Simon Spillett is writing a biography of Hayes and suggests:

As for Tubby's drug addiction, well, I'm inclined to be careful. We know that he smoked a fair bit of pot and took the odd snort of cocaine during the early 1960s. Where things become somewhat clouded is the beginnings and development of his heroin habit. Jack M[assarik] is roughly correct. Hayes arrest on drugs charges came in August 1968, following a period of isolation and the quick decline of his career. As I understand it, Tubby drank heavily during 1965 into 1966, but following his collapse with thrombosis in autumn 1966, he was hospitalized and then ordered to lay off drink. This he found very difficult to do and in his own words he "stepped up the other scene".
(E-mail interview with Simon Spillett, April 2010)

Spillett draws on several documentary sources, as well as conversations with musicians who played with Hayes. In court in August 1968, Hayes's solicitor stated that his client has been using heroin for eight months and was glad that he had been arrested and could now seek treatment. His solicitor cited a number of factors behind Hayes's addiction, including the break-up of his marriage, the career pressure of a shrinking jazz scene and increased studio demands and ill-health. In one article, it was said that Hayes's income had dropped to £30 per week (see Guardian 1968). Hayes gave an extensive interview to Bob Dawbarn in the *Melody Maker*, which ran in its 21 September 1968 issue, and the *Daily Express* ran a surprisingly sympathetic interview on 12 September 1968. Reading these pieces, one is struck by Hayes's apparent honesty and directness. He makes no excuses for his actions but notes that he had "dabbled in this and that before then but it hadn't affected my work because I never let it." He also notes that his doctor had told him to quit drinking and that this too had been a struggle for him. He stresses again his gratitude for his arrest and his resultant access to treatment at the Hackney Hospital Addiction Unit.

Spillett has spoken with many of Hayes's former colleagues and he notes that they express "genuine shock that Tubby got into heroin – he was known to be indulgent but was very aware of the pitfalls of serious addiction, principally through exposure to Phil Seamen's titanic example" (e-mail interview with Simon Spillett, April 2010). Jack Massarik refers to Hayes's girlfriend, singer Joy Marshall, herself an addict, as perhaps the source of his involvement with heroin. However, Spillett is more circumspect on this point, noting that the saxophonist's first wife feels that Phil Seamen might have been the one who got him using the drug. Despite treatment for addiction, Hayes's drug use escalated after the death of Joy Marshall (from an overdose) and, for a time, he had two wardrobes – a thin one for when he was using heroin and a fat one for when he was drinking. Finally, Simon Spillett adds that when diagnosed in 1970 with a faulty heart valve, "he kicked the habit and never again used heroin".

One suspects that the early onset of severe illness in his case is more likely to have resulted from heavy alcohol consumption rather than narcotics. We can see, however, from the pattern of Hayes's life that he was a man of large appetites – for sex, alcohol and, most of all, for music. He is one of those musicians whose personality seems to burst through in his playing. He radiates simultaneously a hunger for life and a generosity of spirit that is immediately affecting. It is as if he wants to give one hundred per cent and nothing less will do. Pianist Brian Dee remembers Hayes's competitive spirit and how one time he had heard that Woody Herman tenorist Sal Nistico was in town. Hayes turned up determined to blow him off stage. In fact, Dee's recollections provide an excellent summation of the man:

> Tubby was an amazingly strong person in every way. Tubby was enormous in everything. In other words, he wasn't just some laying about jazz guy. He was a real "take-care-of-business" guy. He was shrewd with the money. He was into arranging and into sessions and everything he did was hyper-hyper. He was a hyper business man. Apparently when he was younger, he drank 32 Worthington White Shields [a strong bottle beer and about the equivalent of a litre and a quarter of scotch or vodka]. Everything about him ... when you hear him play, you hear the sheer exuberance of the guy. I mean that is the character of the man.
>
> (Interview with Brian Dee, March 2008)

Hayes's story reveals several things. First, it is a tale of personal frailties and vulnerabilities. Despite his remarkable gifts and the acclaim of his peers and of those Americans like Roland Kirk, James Moody and Paul Gonsalves with whom he played, Hayes was plagued by doubts about his inability to always meet his own exacting standards. Second, it tells how easy it was for those on the London scene to obtain access to cocaine and heroin and, therefore, how that scene also intersected with a criminal underworld. But it also reveals how it connected with the wider world around it.

It is no accident that the officer who obtained a search warrant for Hayes's flat was none other than Sgt Norman Pilcher. It was Pilcher, a notorious figure to many on the "underground scene" and a regular in the pages of *Oz*, *International Times* and *Frendz*, who busted John Lennon, Eric Clapton, George Harrison and Donovan. Lennon hated him and commented that, while some whom Pilcher arrested actually had the drugs when searched, others most certainly did not. Try singing "Sergeant Norman Pilcher" to the Beatles' "I Am the Walrus", in place of the words "semolina pilchards"; it is not an accidental fit. Pilcher and three of his colleagues were finally brought to book in 1973 for perjury in a case involving the smuggling of drugs. Pilcher got four years and received the following comment from Justice Melford Stevenson before sentence: "You poisoned the wells of criminal justice and set about it deliberately."

It is also worth pointing out that Pilcher's interest in Hayes continued after the bust (e-mail interview with Simon Spillett, April 2010) and that following his arrest Hayes was taken by Pilcher to a drug rehabilitation unit. This may seem unusually compassionate for an officer such as Pilcher. However, the problem with the Metropolitan Police drug squad that operated under Detective Chief Inspector (DCI) Kelaher in the West End of London was that it was very far from conventional. Kelaher was a big fan of the methods of the American Bureau of Narcotics and Dangerous Drugs (BNDD), the organization that took over in 1968 from the discredited Federal Bureau of Narcotics (FBN). In fact, the BNDD continued substantially the dubious practices of the FBN and was itself disbanded and merged with the newly formed Drug Enforcement Agency in 1973. Its methods included the cultivation of a network of informers, often themselves drug users and even dealers, who were repaid for their assistance with recycled drugs obtained by the Bureau through arrests and seizures or through the expedient practice of being allowed to continue their trade unmolested. It was standard FBN and BNDD practice to arrest and then try and turn small-time dealers and addicts into informants. I am not suggesting that Hayes became one of Pilcher's network of "stool pigeons". However, it seems very possible that this was Pilcher's intention for him (Cox *et al* 1977; Morton 2001).

In the example of Tubby Hayes, we can see the growing tension within British society over the issue of drug use. Enforcement and treatment make uneasy bedfellows and increasingly Britain was moving in its drug policies towards the former. What is more it was doing so under increasing pressure from the USA to comply with its perspectives on drug addiction, the drug trade and the methods required to combat these. However, as writers such as Andrew Cockburn and Jeffrey St. Clair (Cockburn and St. Clair 1991), Alfred

McCoy (McCoy 1991) and, more recently, Douglas Valentine (Valentine 2006) have shown, drug enforcement has taken second place in practice to broader issues of national security, the perceived threat of Communism and the need to maintain a strong American presence in the Middle East. These imperatives have seen the Central Intelligence Agency (CIA), and the FBN and BNDD, directly but covertly involved in the drug trade both as an active participant and in its willingness to turn a blind eye to the activities of drug smugglers, who worked for it in various capacities. The world of the individual drug addict is connected through a web of affiliations, small and great, to matters far beyond their experience and comprehension.

As Dee's experience shows, drug users mixed – on the stand at least – with drinkers. It was, after all, a small scene. He notes that he always found Hayes very approachable, though that was not the case with some of the lesser figures around.

> One thing about it I did find a bit of a downer was that as a young man you weren't perhaps as secure and you needed reassurance. They [musicians using drugs] would accept you on the stand but they wouldn't off it. They looked at you like through a glass wall and I found that a bit distressing really. So, I used to go down Archer Street where the more commercial players were, but they were like me. They liked a drink.
>
> (Interview with Brian Dee, March 2008)

One musician, who asked to remain anonymous told the author:

> The Downbeat Club – that was like the place where it was all emanating from. A lot of drugs were coming out of the Downbeat through Jackie Sharpe [altoist in Tubby Hayes's big band]. That was quite a source of the stuff. It was on the corner of Greek Street. He [Jackie Sharpe] went inside for it. It was a drinking club and if you were down there drinking – it was run by two musicians, Jackie Sharpe and Mike Sinn, an alto player who was as straight as a die – anyway, the phone would be going every two seconds – "Is Jack there? Is Jack there?"

Dee remembers Graham Bond from the late fifties as a besuited young man with a crew-cut, who looked for all the world like a white Cannonball Adderley. Describing him as being "as clean as a whistle in those days", Dee says that he was "the first guy ever to take Graham Bond into the West End" and had him play with his trio at the Flamingo. Dee points out that, "He played alto and he wasn't always on the chords as it were, so he was billed as 'The controversial alto player – Graham Bond'" (interview with Brian Dee, March 2008). Pianist John Burch remembers Bond being so clean, he would turn down the offer of a joint (Shapiro 2005, 39).

Bond played with various people, which included, as well as Dee's trio, a band with guitarist Goodie Charles and in a group with drummer Terry Graham. It was Graham, who recommended Bond to Don Rendell, who was looking for a front-line partner for his quintet that made *Roarin'* in 1961. This was actually the fourth British jazz LP to appear on Riverside's Jazzland label American label, the others being *The Jazz Couriers the Message From Britain* and Joe Harriott's *Southern Horizons* and *Free Form*. As we have already noted, Bond's ambitions lay wider than the field of jazz and he moved first to Alexis Korner's Blues Incorporated before forming his own group, the Graham Bond Organization, which featured first guitarist John McLaughlin, bassist Jack Bruce and drummer Ginger Baker before – in its most famous incarnation – Dick Heckstall-Smith replaced McLaughlin. Bond and Baker were both heavy heroin users, while Jack Bruce would later experience his own difficulties with the drug, but that was not the case then.

As Harry Shapiro points out, Heckstall-Smith was a drinker. He used alcohol as a means of coping with the stresses of a career in the music business, including stage nerves. Like heroin, alcohol is a depressant drug. This does not mean it makes you "depressed" or weepy. It can do both, of course, but here "depressant" refers to how it acts upon the central nervous system. It relaxes you, slows you down and makes you drowsy. Like heroin, alcohol is a drug that with habituation requires the user to take more of it to produce the same effect. The relaxed, convivial state that the drinker hopes to achieve becomes harder to sustain, and the line between that and slurred speech and dribbling out of the corner of the mouth is a fine one. For a time, Heckstall-Smith found his answer in "yellows" or amphetamines, the stimulant countering to an extent the depressant properties of the drink. When landlords advertise special offers on vodka and Red Bull, a caffeine-based "soft" drink, they are, of course, encouraging and enabling people to consume more alcohol at their bar. It is the same principle. Although he never used heroin, Heckstall-Smith remained curious. Knowing his father had been prescribed morphine during the First World War, he asked him about the experience, which Heckstall-Smith Snr had described in his autobiography as "even more profound bliss". His father's reply says something very important about heroin – taking it is extremely pleasurable. For that reason, we repeat his comment in full.

> Suppose you had a farm, which was just small enough for you to run on your own, and it was harvest time, so you had to work every daylight hour in the fields. Now, suppose it's the end of the day, and you've come home exhausted, eaten your dinner, and gone up to your bedroom longing for your bed. You undress and put on your pyjamas; you pull back the bedclothes and get in; then you pull up the bedclothes up to your chin. *That's* the moment. It's like that … 'Only it's all the time.
> (Heckstall-Smith 1989, 23; emphasis original)

The saxophonist also asked Ginger Baker that same question, though the drummer's response was less prosaic. "It's just like the moment you come. Except that it goes on. It doesn't stop" (Heckstall-Smith 1989, 24).

Both alcohol and amphetamines took their toll on Heckstall-Smith, as he was to realize, and the latter disappeared from his regime. But he remains a credible and articulate witness to the era and the lives of others whose problem drug use escalated and continued. He has a lot to tell us about the world in which musicians, whether addicts or dabblers or boozers or even teetotallers, moved together. It was a peer group of outsiders, to use Chicago sociologist Howard Becker's term (Becker 1963). Becker's research focused on examining how behaviour becomes "deviant" from social norms and how through a process of societal reaction and, in some cases, enforcement by state agencies a group subculture develops. Intriguingly, given earlier comments about class in this book, Becker also noted the middle-class origins of his Chicago-based group of jazz aficionados, who were the subjects of his study. British sociologist Jock Young subsequently applied Becker's ideas to marijuana smokers in Notting Hill, revealing how such groups establish their own norms and values (Young in Cohen 1972). The approach of Becker and Young actually has its shortcomings, most notably the absence of any kind of class perspective or clear identification of the basis of state/police power. Nor does it explain the relationship between how such definitions of self and group are internalized at either the individual and group levels. It does, however, serve to illuminate group processes within subcultures and shows that they do develop their own beliefs and practices in response to external pressures. They act as well as being acted upon.

The story Heckstall-Smith tells in his autobiography about Phil Seamen speaks volumes about this world. Seamen told him once about how he became addicted. The drummer had dabbled with cocaine and heroin for some time but had kept addiction at arm's length. He was exhausted physically but knew heroin would make him feel better and that, if he "shot up", he would be able to make and do justice to his gig that night. If he did not do so, he would perform badly. However, Seamen also knew that if he were to take the drug on this occasion, he faced a life of dependency on heroin. According to Heckstall-Smith, Seamen worried at his dilemma: "He had a really bad half-hour, and by the end of it he had decided. He was going to be as good a drummer as it was possible for him to be, for whatever time remained to him. He went off to the toilet with his works and shot up."

But it is Heckstall-Smith's next comment that is most telling, "The clarity of this story, and the clarity of the decision, increased my respect for Phil enormously" (Heckstall-Smith 1989, 27).

In an interview conducted by Victor Schonfield with drummer and free jazz pioneer John Stevens for the Oral History of Jazz in Britain series (British National Sound Archive, 29 December 1992), Stevens discusses Seamen's drug use in a very "matter-of-fact" fashion. Stevens makes it clear that he

John Stevens with the Brian Dee Trio circa 1960 at Ronnie Scott's, Gerrard Street. Left to right: John Stevens (drums), Brian Dee (piano), Freddy Logan (bass). Photograph courtesy of Brian Dee, photographer unknown.

made a decision to avoid the path taken by Seamen. However, his remarks indicate that he saw his mentor's heroin use as the means by which Seamen was able to concentrate his mind and his efforts on developing his art and that the state of being "stoned" allowed Seamen to exclude the extraneous and irrelevant in that pursuit. The alternative for Stevens was simple – he had to achieve this by hard work and mental discipline. Two points emerge from this narrative. First, Stevens admired Seamen for his single-mindedness and willingness to risk his health in this way. Second, for him, there was nothing reprehensible in Seamen's decision.

Seamen's behaviour was normal or at least not abnormal in this cultural and social milieu. In fact, within the albeit-changing context of British drug policy, this was not in any way an unreasonable position. The number of heroin and cocaine users registered with the Home Office may have grown during the 1960s – social historian Dominic Sandbrook notes that the number of teenagers registered as heroin, opium and cocaine users tripled between 1964 and 1965 (see Sandbrook 2008, 550). However, the actual numbers involved were very small, perhaps not even reaching four figures across all age groups by the end of the decade. And as Sandbrook points out (Sandrook 2008, 552), even allowing for the extensive popularity of cannabis and, to a much lesser extent LSD, the most popular British drugs of choice were then as now – alcohol, tobacco and caffeine. Addiction was widely seen as a sickness and was treated under the National Health Service (NHS) as such rather than as a criminal/legal problem. Why, then, should non-addicted jazz musicians look down on their drug-addicted peers?

This was a peer group of outsiders, which combined a relaxed tolerance of aberrant behaviour with cool detachment. Whether it was Bond, Baker, Hayes, Seamen or drummer Dickie Devere, who apparently first showed Bond the seamier side of London's demi-monde (see Shapiro 2005, 39–40), if that was your bag and you could still play, that was all that really mattered. Ultimately, however, the roll-call of heroin-related deaths among British jazz musicians would include all but one of the above, plus drummers Red Reece and Benny Goodman, singer Joy Marshall, baritone saxophonists Glenn Hughes and John Marshall and pianist/multi-instrumentalist Alan Branscombe.

Alan Branscombe deserves special mention here because he was one of the most talented musicians – he played alto and vibes as well as piano – to come out of Britain during this period. His solo record *The Day I Met the Blues* from 1977 (EMI) is another Dennis Preston production and well worth seeking out, though it falls outside our period. Branscombe did manage to get off heroin eventually but took to drinking, a similar story to that of Tubby Hayes's pianist, Terry Shannon. Shannon survived by removing himself from the London scene and its temptations. Branscombe did not. Brian Dee recalls seeing Branscombe at sessions where he was clearly far from well: "You'd see Alan at a session and Al Newman or someone would say to me, 'Hey, Brian – have you seen our Martian friend over there?' And there would be Alan and he'd be green. He was a shade of green!" (interview with Brian Dee, March 2008).

There is clearly no doubt that Phil Seamen was an enormously talented drummer, perhaps one of the very best anywhere, ever. Both Ginger Baker and John Stevens, formidable players themselves, revered him, and so did just about every other percussionist on the scene. Ginger Baker is still in awe of the man:

> He was just gifted, you know. He had that gift. It seems I've got it as well and not many people have. Especially white people – not many of them have it at all. Phil had the ability to bring tears to my eyes, in a similar way to Elvin Jones, Max Roach and Philly Joe and Art Blakey, you know. Phil was on that sort of level. This teacher–student thing – I never paid him for a lesson – he just took me under his wing. He was an evil bugger. When I was practising,

if I did something wrong, he'd whack me across the back of the hand with a stick. [laughing] He was just an amazing character.
(Interview with Ginger Baker, August 2009)

Seamen made a record shortly before he died, *The Phil Seamen Story*, for Decibel Records. As well as a number of tracks recorded with other musicians, it featured him playing drums and talking about his life and career. Here is what George McKay has to say about it:

> The slurred delivery, the semi-rambling structure, the inconsequentiality of most of the monologue, in combination with Seamen's percussive breaks, even the record's posthumous release, present a kind of masculine performance, a pathetic confirmation of what another British jazz musician claimed in his autobiography: that "to be a ruined man is itself a kind of vocation" (Heckstall-Smith 1989, 65). Just as interestingly, what was the hoped-for market for such a record? Who wanted to hear the ghoulish stripping away, the sad sound of a drummer without a band, who wanted to turn the flaunted failure of an extreme jazz masculinity into counter-cultural triumph or vicarious male fantasy?
> (McKay 2005, 258)

It is intriguing given McKay's use of the above quotation from Heckstall-Smith to consider that in relation to the material from that biography which we have already quoted. Sadly for McKay, one would answer his questions by referring him to Issue 2 of *The Wire* magazine (Winter 1982/3), whose writers, and presumably readers, delighted in the three pages of reminiscences about Seamen from Alexis Korner, bassist Danny Thompson, John Stevens and Ronnie Scott. The questions McKay raises above certainly do need to be addressed. It should be clear from Harry Shapiro's comments at least that some figures in the arts, or simply in life, are often admired in all their self-destructive, iconoclastic glory. We may find that tendency in others or ourselves alarming but understanding comes from being able to see such people in a way that is necessarily multi-faceted.

Clearly, not all of Seamen's peers were quite so willing to tolerate the impact of such self-abuse. Coleridge Goode recalls an incident when the Joe Harriott Quintet were opening for Dave Brubeck:

> Phil was not terribly reliable because he was under the influence of his habit. The worst incident that I can remember was we were playing in Hammersmith somewhere and Dave Brubeck was playing on that gig. It was his gig. We were the support band. Dave was standing in the wings when we were due to start. So, we go onto the stand but there's no Phil. He hadn't shown up.

So, what do we do? We have to start. So, we're playing away and suddenly there's a rush and Phil comes dashing in and on to the drum set and immediately was sick all over the drums. That to me was the worst experience I had ever had as a musician. Can you imagine that? In front of everybody. I wanted the stage to open up so I could just disappear. It was horrible, really horrible.

(Interview with Coleridge Goode, May 2008)

However, such embarrassments did not stop Harriott from hiring Seamen, nor did they stop Goode from being willing to play with him. It is in the nature of such subcultures to tolerate such behaviour and indeed to construct its own rules with regard to the acceptable and the unacceptable. The pursuit of musical excellence – and there is no doubt that Seamen was totally committed to his art – allowed for high degrees of tolerance.

Because a number of important British jazz musicians made use of it, it is worth considering how the system of registration and treatment worked, as well as how and why it was abandoned. The system was introduced in 1926 following the deliberations of the Rolleston Committee and did not end officially until the mid-nineties. Illicit drug use had not really been a major social issue in Britain, as Shapiro points out:

Those addicts notified to the Home Office were generally middle-class, middle-aged morphine users, often professionally employed, receiving maintenance prescriptions through GP's for pain. Their numbers were small and had been falling; from around 700 in 1935 to fewer than 300 in the early fifties. These figures began to rise sharply only in the early to mid-sixties, when the addict ranks were swelled by a younger group of largely working-class males using heroin rather than morphine "recreationally" rather than as a result of a dependence derived from pain relief.

(Shapiro 1999, 86)

In their original context, the recommendations of Rolleston made total sense and could be justified politically, legally, medically and morally. As Shapiro explains, once the context changed, the principle behind Rolleston began to be undermined:

This group of doctors decided that as a treatment of last resort, it was perfectly legitimate to prescribe heroin and, or more often then, morphine or cocaine for someone who had a habit. That carried on until 1968. It was changed then because of the activities of one or two doctors who were prescribing heroin like it was going out of fashion – Isobel Frankau, John Petro and one or two others. Therefore in '68 they introduced the licensing system.

You couldn't prescribe to addicts unless you had a Home Office licence, at which point most doctors ran a mile, saying, "Thank God, I don't have to prescribe heroin anymore. I can just say I haven't got a licence." But a few carried on, some of them within the NHS, some in private practice. You could apply to the Home Office for a licence and various doctors did, some of whom eventually got struck off because they fell out with the Home Office. The Home Office inspectors went in and checked their registers and things like that. They thought they were over-prescribing or being irresponsible. Sometimes, there were complaints from NHS psychiatrists about particular doctors because a patient could be being seen on the NHS and seeing somebody privately. There was a bit of a professional war going on and a belief that some of the NHS psychiatrists had it in for the private doctors and got investigations launched against them and the GMC invariably struck them off and all of this went on. But the registration was simply really a device by the Home Office (a) to keep track of the numbers and (b) so that a doctor could phone up the Home Office and check that somebody wasn't double-scripting.

(Interview with Harry Shapiro, April 2009)

Saxophonist Bobby Wellins describes how the system worked in practice:

I needed the drug to function, of course. From there on the resistance to the drug, I needed more and more and more. At the time, I wasn't using the barbiturates quite as much but certainly the cocaine because it was also being prescribed, you see. They go on today about cocaine, the pharmaceutical cocaine was the best in the world. [laughs] The coke was nothing like the rubbish they've got now. I was prescribed quite a heavy dose of cocaine. These clinics were prescribing. They weren't trying to get you off. They were just keeping you going and at the time they had been set up, it was in order that you wouldn't get yourself into trouble with the law because you were registered with the Home Office. If you were arrested by the police with a load of narcotics in your pocket, they immediately phoned a particular number and they would say, "Yes, he's on the list. He's a registered addict." And that was it. (Interview with Bobby Wellins, September 2009)

For a time, as Shapiro points out, there were two parallel systems in operation – one involving private practitioners, both psychiatrists and general practitioners, the other involving the Drug Dependence Units set up at a number of teaching hospitals at the behest of the Ministry of Health in 1968. This dual system amplified existing tensions within the political and medical establishments as to whether "addiction" was a medical disease, a social problem, a legal issue or some hybrid of these. More than that it raised questions about treatment – should this focus on "maintenance", thereby allowing the addict to function within society, or on "withdrawal" and "cure" (see Lart 1992; Smart 1984, 1985)? What is immediately clear from even a cursory reading of literature relating to UK drug policy is that issues of morality (perhaps inevitably) and the treatment preferences of medical practitioners (less inevitably) constantly intruded. Courtwright (2001) distinguishes between the "big three" of addictive substances – alcohol, caffeine, tobacco – and the "little three" – opium, coca, cannabis. He argues that the "big three" were essentially so integrated in all respects in diverse cultures across the world that it was all but impossible to prohibit them. However, this was not the case with the "little three" and, due to this factor, reformers have been able to make them subject to almost global restriction. Reformers' objections focused on a number of issues: first, users did direct harm to themselves or others; second, non-medical use inspired criminal violence; third, religious disapproval; fourth, the association of a drug with deviant or disliked groups; and finally, the perception that drug use endangered the future of society. It is facile to blame the rise between 1970 and today in opiate use on the abandonment of the model established by the Rolleston Committee. However, comparatively recent Home Office estimates suggest that there are now between 50,000 and 250,000 occasional to regular illegal users of opiates in the UK (Murphy and Roe 2007, 11). The author's previous professional experience leads him to see this as an underestimate. In any event, Home Office figures should be compared with the fact that only a few hundred such users existed in the 1960s.

Returning to the issue of why British jazz musicians turned to heroin use, the views of both Harry Shapiro and Brian Dee seem valid. There was a strong element of identification on the part of white British musicians with their black American heroes. More than that there was a belief, echoed above by Ginger Baker and Phil Seamen and reiterated by non-users Heckstall-Smith and John Stevens, that, if you were willing to make the sacrifice, heroin would make you play better. In addition, the social and cultural context of this small jazz community offered a benign tolerance of such behaviour. Extending that context further, we can see that tolerance also extended into the medical and even political establishments, though as enforcement came to dominate policy considerations, the degree of forbearance began to decline. While this change in opinion can easily be discerned, it was neither universally nor consistently applied. Nor were such shifts in views held consistently across the medical or political spectra. As a general thesis, however, an argument can be sustained to the effect that there was a shift from the identification of addiction as "disease" to one defining it as a "social problem". Alex Nicola Mold offers a similar account of the origins of the Rolleston system of drug treatment to that of Harry Shapiro in her Birmingham University PhD thesis,

"Dynamic Dualities: The British System of Heroin Addiction Treatment 1965–87" (Mold 2004). Many of those that were to be treated following the implementation of the Committee's recommendations had become addicted as a result of wartime experiences, injury or as a consequence of medical treatment. However, she adds, expanding on points made earlier by Shapiro:

> Addiction became a social problem as a result of a dramatic increase in drug use numerically and by new cohorts of the population, as older, middle class, therapeutic users were over-shadowed by young, working-class recreational users, but also because of wider changes in views of disease and public health. This brought a range of agencies into addiction, presenting a challenge to the authority of the clinic-based psychiatrist who had largely been responsible for the treatment of this condition since the late 1960s. (Mold 2004)

Mold's thesis counsels against simplistic understandings of drug treatment and enforcement but in teasing out further both the moral/moralistic and class dimensions she does us a great service. These are ideological questions that she raises and it is worth adding that there has existed and continues to exist within British society a tension between those sections that support and encourage licence and those that seek to curb it. In a very real way, the addict, be they a jazz musician or not, must function within that tension.

We must also acknowledge a certain naivety, as well as an ambivalence, among jazz musicians about heroin and other drugs. Ginger Baker thought heroin was just like smoking marijuana. Pianist Stan Tracey, who served a short prison sentence for the possession of cannabis with intent to supply, was a regular cocaine user in the fifties but had drifted into heroin use:

> Because before I started using heroin I was into cocaine and I got hooked on the mechanics of snorting, the chopping up and snort-ing. One night, the guy I used to get the coke from didn't have any but he had some heroin – I never did inject. He said, "You just crush it up the same as you do with coke and away you go." So, I did and I liked the effect. So, I used it for a few nights or maybe a week and then suddenly I discovered I was very pooped out and tired in the afternoon – I didn't realize I was having withdrawals.
> (Interview with Stan Tracey, December 2009)

The pattern Tracey describes is not unusual. Quite a lot of cocaine users slide into using heroin either out of curiosity or in the absence of their drug of choice or as a means of coming down from the high of cocaine. Bobby Wellins's addiction followed a similar pattern to Tracey's and for him, as with Tubby Hayes, one factor seems to have been a dissatisfaction with his art.

In Hayes's case, this focused on doubts about his own playing. In Wellins's case, as we noted earlier (see Chapter 4), his frustrations lay in a perceived sense that British musicians were seen as second-rate, even within their own country:

> I didn't even drink. I can only speak for myself when I say that I became disillusioned with the fact that British jazz musicians – as far as I was concerned – were third-class citizens and everyone else who came either from Europe or America were like the "bees' knees". The sudden shock of a young man, who at my age was very sensitive anyway and who was working hard to be a better and better musician but who didn't have a great deal of confidence, I suppose you could say I was disillusioned and I just found solace. It was nothing to do with playing better I can assure you of that. It didn't do anything to make one play better.
>
> (Interview with Bobby Wellins, September 2009)

He continues:

> Others from the community at the time suddenly get hooked and I think it was for the same reasons that I've been talking about. The American Federation of Musicians had made an agreement with the British Musicians' Union and, as soon as the Americans started coming in, the floodgates were open and we were in our little corner trying to get work. And as much as we were delighted that we were hearing all of our idols in the flesh, we suddenly realized that they were doing all the tours around the country, so our work suffered very badly.
>
> (Interview with Bobby Wellins, September 2009)

Ironically, it was Tubby Hayes who first gave Wellins some cocaine, as Wellins told me: "'Try a bit of this, old boy,' he said. 'That will cheer you up.' That was the start of it." He was then introduced to heroin by another musician, whom he declined to name, saying, "Yes, there was no cocaine available and the person in question said, 'I've got a bit of this, if you want to try it.' And so I did."

Wellins's account of his own addiction is both articulate and insightful. It took him years to come off drugs and, as he notes, his dependence on barbiturates was in some ways the hardest. These were prescribed to him almost routinely:

> And then in order to sleep properly and relax, they put me on Tuinal – of course, all these things are off the market now. The strange thing was – I don't know if it is just me – but when I look back, when I finally decided to stop everything after ten years, I

think the worst withdrawal was the barbiturates. In those days, they were so severe, they would just cut you off.

(Interview with Bobby Wellins, September 2009)

It is perhaps hard for some younger readers to appreciate just how widespread over-prescription by medical practitioners was in those days. Perhaps a personal anecdote will assist. The author's mother suffered from severe back pain from 1959/60 for which she was prescribed very strong painkillers. These made her drowsy during the day, and so she was prescribed some form of amphetamine. These kept her awake at night and, therefore, her GP prescribed her Tuinal Forte (i.e. 500 mg tablets). In addition, due to side-effects from the various drugs she was taking, such as panic attacks and anxiety, she was given medication to counter these. She carried her pills, some thirty or more different varieties, in a shopping bag and the names sodium amytal, physeptone, phenobarbitone, Tuinal and dexedrine were familiar to the author long before they began to appear in horror stories in the yellow press. When she became pregnant with her third child, she asked her doctor about the drugs she was taking and whether these put the foetus at risk. She was advised that they would not. The baby was born withdrawing from barbiturates and unable to suckle. He survived, but it was touch and go for months. "Mother's little helper", indeed!

Access to drugs for Wellins was in the main through other musicians and when that source dried up, one had to take other measures:

It was very easy to score cocaine, via other musicians. Then, of course, there was the registered doctor, who had been a police surgeon, Dr Wood. He was later convicted and, for £8, he'd write you out a prescription. He wasn't on the jazz scene. I just found out about him through someone else, who said, "Go and see him and he'll get you a prescription, if you need it." He was the very man, he knew that the clinics were coming up and he'd be prosecuted for writing out these prescriptions.

(Interview with Bobby Wellins, September 2009)

Registration was surely, then, the safest and most secure way of ensuring a supply and it was easy to register.

Have you uncovered the fact that during the clinic period you went along to whatever clinic you were going to register with? You had a blood test and a urine test and, as soon as that proved positive for heroin and cocaine, then you were admitted to the clinic and you had a weekly prescription. Now, because you didn't have to identify yourself because you were on their books, some people were going to three and four clinics and that was when it got completely and totally out of hand. I knew a bunch of people, who were living in the penthouse suite of the Hilton on the strength of that. Selling off prescriptions from three clinics and keeping the one for their own personal use. It was quite a dangerous time, actually. There was a lot of rather nasty people around. If you were short and you wanted to go black market, you had to be careful where you went because that could be quite dangerous. I don't think that that [organized crime] had taken an absolute hold as far as I know. But I only knew the people I dealt with.

(Interview with Bobby Wellins, September 2009)

Wellins remains one of the most personal and distinctive of the tenor players to come out of this country, and yet his best work during this period, due to his "problems", was limited to the two quartet records he made with Stan Tracey, both of which seem to date from before his drug involvement got out of hand. Still a magnificent and graceful musician, one can only wonder what he might have achieved. That said, we should be thankful he recovered and survived and continues to make beautiful music. One could add that alto saxophonist Peter King's late blossoming as a solo artist in the early eighties and since was in part the result of his recovery from his drug misuse.

Before leaving our involvement in heroin behind and considering one or two other artists whose careers were blighted by drugs of other kinds, we need to look at how the Rolleston system came into disrepute. Stan Tracey tells how he decided to quit using heroin due to the toll it took on his self-respect:

I was going to a doctor who helped with that. Just one day, I just got sick of the way I was living, what I was doing, lying, borrowing money, and I stopped from that day and never went back. I went to a doctor.

(Interview with Stan Tracey, December 2009)

Asked if the doctor was Lady Frankau or John Petro, his reply came with some force. "Oh, not that lot – they were supplying. No, this guy was curing. I can't remember his name but he put me on methadone and gradual reduction and that's how I came off" (interview with Stan Tracey, December 2009). Ginger Baker, on the other hand, did consult Lady Frankau and actually found her helpful, as he notes:

I was working very hard with Lady Frankau, the doctor, using less and less and less, cutting down over a six-month period. At the same time, Graham [Bond] was getting more into stuff. I was straight for the first nine months of Cream.

(Interview with Ginger Baker, August 2009)

Stan Tracey at the newly opened Ronnie Scott's Jazz Club at its new premises at 47 Frith Street, Soho, 1 May 1966. © Valerie Wilmer.

The general verdict, however, is that while some doctors were acting professionally, others were essentially dealing and profiting handsomely. Harry Shapiro points out that:

> During the course of one year, one particular doctor, Lady Isobel Frankau, wrote out prescriptions for heroin totalling six kilos. Some of the world's most famous jazzmen would land in London, for example en route to Paris, just to pick up heroin prescriptions from her ladyship.   (Shapiro 1999, 209)

And he adds by way of further explanation, "And in fact the black market in London was actually created by this overprescribing on the grand scale.

Invariably, the user would ask for (and get) prescriptions in excess of his personal requirements and then sell the surplus" (Shapiro 1999, 209). It was for this reason, among others, that the system was changed:

> After 1968 it became an offence for any doctor to prescribe heroin or cocaine to someone he knew would be using these drugs to support a habit. Only those with special licences could prescribe in the old way and these were granted only to doctors working in the drug clinics set up at the same time.   (Shapiro 1999, 209)

And with a "black market" now established and the door to medically prescribed heroin now closing, a new door opened to organized crime.

Cannabis was obviously the most popular illegal recreational drug among jazz musicians and others in the fifties and sixties. According to various sources, Bob Dylan introduced the Beatles to its pleasures on a visit to London in 1964, but prior to that its use among pop stars seems to have been limited. Georgie Fame, for example, notes that Billy Fury was one of the very few from that early sixties period who smoked and, as Fame notes, "he got it from the jazzers" (interview with Georgie Fame, April 2009). Cannabis, or more often marijuana, of considerable strength (see Shapiro above) was available through the West Indian and West African communities with little interference or overt concern from the authorities. When its use began to spread to young white people, some with middle class parents, a different approach was taken. In fact, DCI Kelaher and his drug squad led by Detective Sergeant (DS) "Nobby" Pilcher targeted the evil weed with great zeal (see Cox *et al.* 1977, chapter 2), again echoing the policy of the USA's FBN, which Kelaher so admired (see Valentine 2006). However, the smoking of marijuana on the jazz scene was really so ubiquitous that it barely deserves comment.

Saxophonist Dave Tomlin, who played in pianist Mike Taylor's groups, gives a rather amusing illustration of that aspect of the jazz life:

> We all used to get stoned. You could just go down the Nucleus or Sam Widges or anywhere. There used to be a guy called Jimmy Fox, a trumpet player, we mostly used to get it from. Grass mainly – in ten-bob deals. He didn't play the trumpet. No-one ever heard him play the trumpet. [laughing] He had a false bottom in his trumpet case, as he would look like a musician. It was a good cover. He would take his trumpet out and he'd have his deals in the false bottom. There were other people you could get it from. It was quite common.
> (Interview with Dave Tomlin, October 2007)

And he continues:

> Musicians in those days, it was like it was semi-criminal. A lot of
> these clubs were run by gangsters. They owned the places. But
> they never bothered the musicians. If you had an instrument you
> were safe anywhere. They wouldn't bother you.
> (Interview with Dave Tomlin, October 2007)

With one or two exceptions among the younger musicians of the period, the
use of LSD seems to have been very limited in jazz circles. The author once
asked John Surman if he were aware of any of his peers who used hallucino-
genics like LSD, Mescaline or Psilocybin.

> Not really. I don't think so. The drug of choice was pot and there
> weren't many who didn't have a crack at a joint from time to time
> in the best West Indian tradition. That and I think there was some
> cocaine recreational use, you know. LSD? No, not so much not
> with the jazz musicians, I knew. There was a sort of movement in
> San Francisco with Timothy Leary and I think one or two of the
> American guys might have been into acid but acid wasn't some-
> thing that was in my circle. Definitely a few joints from time to
> time. That was what it amounted to as far as I was aware in terms
> of drug use in the sixties. Everyone was doing that.
> (Interview with John Surman, November 2008)

He adds:

> In my experience, nobody I knew felt that acid did your playing
> much good. I think most people dropped a tab at one point or
> another and discovered that, "That will do very nicely, thank you."
> It's pretty weird stuff. That would be most unusual in my experi-
> ence which is no less limited than anybody else's I'll say. I shall not
> deny that I inhaled. That and a few pots of beer. That was then.
> Now sadder and wiser …
> (Interview with John Surman, November 2008)

Another musician, who knew a lot of the more experimental rock bands but
who prefers to remain anonymous, told the author:

> I took acid once and mescaline once and it was quite an incred-
> ible experience but I would never do it again or advocate that
> anyone else do it. I was young and it was around but if you were
> frail emotionally it can be very dangerous. There are and were a
> lot of casualties.

Asked if use was prevalent among the younger jazz musicians, they replied, "I don't think so. It was more amongst the hippy types. The main alternative drug – to alcohol that is – was cannabis."

As Harry Shapiro says succinctly – "I don't think you can hear LSD in British jazz, let's put it like that." There were, however, one or two jazz musicians who took to "acid". Dave Tomlin was one, as was Mike Taylor and, in many ways, the drug was the pianist's undoing. Tomlin was one of the first on or around the nascent British Underground to take LSD and he notes that, "A lot of the musicians [who] would smoke dope were quite straight in a way."

> Acid – that would be '64 or something. Acid came on the scene before '66. It was much more an elite thing. You didn't know about it. They had happenings in private flats and everyone would take acid. It was much later that it became a commoner thing about '65/'66. Round about '64, there were Americans coming over from America and bringing this new kind of energy, if you like. They were very fast people. The English thing was very polite and all that but they would cut through all that and so it was very attractive to musicians.
>
> (Interview with Dave Tomlin, October 2007)

The story of LSD is one of the twentieth century's most bizarre tales, representing in its history a peculiar tension between personal and spiritual liberation and mind control. It is a tale of Swiss chemists, mental health practitioners like Humphrey Osmond and later R.D. Laing, writers such as Aldous Huxley, Allen Ginsberg and Ken Kesey, academics such as Timothy Leary and Richard Alpert, and, of course, the CIA. The involvement of the latter is no "pot-head pixie" conspiracy fantasy but is well-documented in Valentine's The Strength of the Wolf (Valentine 2008; see also Green 1998b, 105–12). LSD began to take off in Britain around 1965 – or at least within the elite circles of the London Underground scene – with the return to the UK of Timothy Leary acolyte Michael Hollingshead and the establishment of the World Psychedelic Centre in Pont Street, Chelsea. It was all very serious and, frankly, like the underground scene itself, somewhat self-referential, as various bohemians, slumming debutantes and minor aristocrats, writers, film-makers, artists and pop stars gathered to experience nirvana (Green 1998b, 190–201).

For a brief period following its arrival around 1964 until 1966, LSD was not illegal. However, in the year of the Beatles' first acid-influenced masterpiece *Revolver*, the Labour Government under pressure from Fleet Street and the media added an amendment to the 1964 Dangerous Drugs Act and LSD was banned. Very soon the drug began to spread outside its inner circle to the further-flung, suburban shores of would-be bohemia.

The truth is that LSD was probably more talked about than consumed (Green 1998b, 105; Sandbrook 2008, 551–2). It was difficult and complicated to synthesize and the chemicals needed to make it were not easy to come by. Most of the initial sources of supply were legitimate and came from pharmaceutical labs in Czechoslovakia and Switzerland, or were brought back from the USA. What is more, LSD was stronger in those days than now and, while the effects of a joint would wear off in an hour or so, an LSD trip took eight hours out of one's day. LSD's importance culturally is perhaps more totemic, as a kind of touchstone of the times. Its message, even to those who did not take it, was that it was good to explore and experiment. Perhaps that atmosphere, of which acid was a part, did filter into the jazz of the time but jazz musicians young or old seem to have eschewed the drug for obvious reasons.

Mike Taylor was the notable exception. It is impossible to say whether the two records he made for Denis Preston – *Pendulum* from 1965 (Columbia; Sunbeam) and *Trio* from 1966 (Columbia; Universal) – betray the influence of the "heaven and hell" drug. They are, nevertheless, two of the most unusual records of the period and it seems clear that Taylor's approach to both composition and improvisation had already emerged at least a couple of years before the recording of his first record (Heining 2007e).

Ron Rubin was one of two bassists who play on *Trio*. The following extract from his diary reveals both his struggles with Taylor's approach and his desire to grasp why, given his doubts, the music works as it does. His comments focus on the standard, "The End of a Love Affair", which, like all of Taylor's takes on the Great American Songbook, are virtually recompositions:

> 1966 – Lansdowne studio recording of Mike Taylor Trio – Mike Taylor, Jon Hiseman, myself and Jack Bruce – basses singly or together. I've never liked the idea of two basses in tandem and Jack's sound is somewhat lumpy on the disc. Hiseman plays beautifully. For me, the best track is the hauntingly lovely "Abena". Mike told me it means "Tuesday" in some African dialect. When it was decided to play "The End of a Love Affair", I asked him to jot down the changes. I wasn't sure of them. Mike said, "I want you to play as far away from the standard chords as you can." Which I did – random notes and flying all over the instrument. Among the mostly glowing reviews, not one critic said anything about dodgy bass lines or harmonies. Is there no such thing as a mistake? I call this the "Jackson Bollocks Syndrome".
>
> (Extract from diary read during interview
> with Ron Rubin, October 2007)

He adds by way of further explanation:

I thought that if I'm playing a standard tune like "The End of a Love Affair" and playing as far away from the chords as I possibly can, there's something bloody wrong. You may disagree with me because this is what is at the root of the free thing and although I liked it at the time I thought it sounds quite good but there's something wrong about it and I still haven't resolved this in my mind to tell you the truth. I play that track sometimes and it sounds alright to me. So, how could it sound alright when I'm playing as wrong as possible. Can you explain that to me?

(Interview with Ron Rubin, October 2007)

Perhaps his use of LSD and cannabis had opened Taylor up to a different set of possibilities in the music. What does seem evident is that he thought and heard differently and there is something quite transcendent about his music. And he trusted his musicians to an unusual degree, as Jon Hiseman notes:

The most important thing for me about Mike was that he never asked me to play in any way at all. Now you've got to remember that when you start to play everybody around you is putting peer pressure on you to play in a certain style. So, if you were a trumpet player everybody would say to you, "Why don't you do what Miles Davis does?" If you were a saxophone player, "Why aren't you playing like Benny Golson" or if you're a drummer "Why don't you play like Philly Joe or Max Roach?"

(Interview with Jon Hiseman, May 2009)

He continues:

What happened with Mike was he would bring something along and I would often get a part which was very rudimentary and would simply show me what other people were doing. Which meant I wasn't reading drum music. I was reading fragments of what other people were doing at the important places. I then did entirely my own thing which he liked very much. And that was the first time I realized that simply by doing what came into my head being me in other words and not worrying about being something else could be successful.

(Interview with Jon Hiseman, May 2009)

In fact, Roland Kirk requested Hiseman for one of his residencies at the Scott club because of hearing the *Pendulum* album. Hiseman was more comfortable with Taylor's approach than Ron Rubin but his comments about Taylor's modus operandi are similarly instructive:

It was all about simplifying things, honing in on the centre of things with none of the normal convention going on around it. So, I developed this thing about playing without bar lines – playing pulse without worrying about where the offbeat was. Of course, this was an absolute and heinous crime when you are talking about traditional jazz drummers but Mike was very happy with this. He felt that this ebb and flow without there necessarily being an obvious or even an actual on or off beat was the way forward. (Interview with Jon Hiseman, May 2009)

Taylor was not a great pianist but it is clear that he led from the piano. The music was not "free" in the sense that the word would carry when applied to Evan Parker, Derek Bailey or the SME. However, it allowed a considerable degree of latitude to the individuals in the group, who became part of the compositional process itself. In this way, Taylor's two records are, like Joe Harriott's *Free Form* and *Abstract*, sui generis. Perhaps the closest parallel to Taylor's work can be found in the work of the two great Bill Evans trios – the one with Paul Motian and Scott LaFaro and the last one with Joe LaBarbara and Marc Johnson.

For a relative unknown Taylor certainly seemed able to pull some highly talented musicians into his orbit. Forty years on and Dave Tomlin marvels at the music they made together. For Tomlin:

He'd got his finger on something that was utterly unique and different. His compositions were just unlike anything else. It was so utterly beautiful but it was still jazz. It was an honour to play his music because nothing else was like it.
(Interview with Dave Tomlin, October 2007)

For Jack Bruce, however, Taylor was not alone on the scene in trying to find new ways of playing jazz:

I thought he was very forward-looking at the time and very open. I was originally in a trio with Ginger and Graham Bond but Graham was only playing alto sax at that time. So, it was very much along the lines of a sort of Ornette Coleman band really in the sense it was a trio without a piano. We were all trying to find our own music as it were.
(Interview with Jack Bruce, October 2007)

One might add that such searching was in practice a widespread feature of the decade. Musicians were not the only ones who were trying to find new answers to age old questions. And how often in the arts and in life has experimentation gone hand-in-hand with drug-taking? Think of the Romantic poets, or of Baudelaire and Rimbaud, or of the absinthe drinking in artistic circles in France and Britain at the end of the nineteenth century.

When Taylor's first album, *Pendulum*, came out some critics did not get it. For some, it simply didn't sound like anything else around. The group took standards like "A Night in Tunisia" and "But Not for Me" and fashioned wholly new compositions from them. On the Gillespie tune, only Tomlin ever quotes the theme in its entirety. The group play across bar lines and yet the music swings. As for the three Taylor originals, these work even better with the title track a classic of 1960s jazz and "To Segovia", a soulful, almost dolorous tune that would have sat well on a Coltrane album.

The follow up to *Pendulum* was a trio-cum-quartet affair called appropriately *Trio*, featuring as noted Hiseman and Ron Rubin on bass, with the addition of Jack Bruce on three of the eight tracks. "Abena" is quite magnificent and Taylor's "Guru" stands out as another dark, exotic masterpiece, while everything else – standards or originals – sounds fresh and beautifully weighted. *Trio* was Taylor's swan song, though Neil Ardley and the New Jazz Orchestra (NJO) would revive his work for the *Mike Taylor Remembered* album (Dusk Fire CD) and Jon Hiseman with Colosseum would keep his memory alive.

LSD use clearly affected Taylor psychologically and following the making of *Trio* he slept rough in Richmond Park for a time, communing with the deer, or otherwise living with Graham Bond, with whom he would consume acid in large quantities. It seems likely that he did have an underlying predisposition for psychosis, but given the volume of drugs he was using – LSD and cannabis – these alone would surely have done him no good. His death by drowning "under mysterious circumstances" near Southend-on-Sea in 1969 merely enhanced the myth. A tragic figure, dying romantically for his art? The evidence, what there is, suggests that it was misadventure, an accident but, no doubt, many will prefer the romanticized version (see Heining 2007e).

By contrast, alto saxophonist Mike Osborne's decline was slow and very painful for him, his wife and his friends. As with Taylor, his mental health problems were combined with drug use. In Osborne's case, he used cannabis, amphetamines, barbiturates and, later, cocaine. Excessive drug use of any kind can lead even the most stable individual into difficulty. With someone with a predisposition to psychosis, the combination is likely to prove disastrous. It is always hard, and often pointless, to separate the underlying illness from the drug use. Indeed, mental health professionals use the term "dual diagnosis" in such cases. Often, individuals, who experience emotional or behavioural issues, "self-medicate" with cannabis, amphetamines and/or alcohol for long periods of time before coming to attention of the psychiatric services. One suspects that with or without drugs Osborne would probably have become ill. Had he remained drug-free, perhaps his career might have extended beyond his early forties.

John Surman acknowledges that Mike's drug use was far from unusual:

> We're talking about the 60s, and smoking and drugs were every-
> where then. Everybody was into it. I think the problem there was
> that some of us got away with it and Ossie didn't. I think he was
> one of the unfortunate ones and it affected his mind. Eventually,
> it shut him down. He got twisted and couldn't find a way back.
> (Interview with John Surman, June 2008)

Like Mike Taylor, Ossie was special and no-one really has an unkind word
to say about him. He might have been taciturn, shy and awkward but he was
one of the most expressive and articulate musicians this country has produced and, while his flame burned, it burned very brightly. John Jack and
Hazel Miller, of Cadillac and Ogun Records, respectively, knew him probably as well as anybody. John Jack puts it beautifully: "You can't construct a
Mike Osborne school of jazz. It was about blowing, just playing. Bugger the
mathematics of it. Not that he wasn't a highly skilled and well-educated and
rounded musician" (interview with John Jack, June 2008).

And Hazel Miller adds, "There's hundreds of well-trained musicians but
there's only been one Mike Osborne." In 2009, Miller reissued Osborne's
classic album *All Night Long* (Ogun; Ogun), with South African bassist
Harry Miller, Hazel's late husband, and fellow South African Louis Moholo
on drums. It was a reminder for us all of the man's unusual talent, as Miller
explains:

> He was a true original. Because I've listened to lots of saxophon-
> ists and they're all different but he was one that really stood out.
> Nobody else played like him. He was prolific. The music was
> excellent. I really feel that he was a major voice of the era and still
> is. When we brought out *All Night Long* and listened to it again,
> we both went there's nobody like that anymore.
> (Interview with Hazel Miller, June 2008)

Osborne was by all accounts a highly sensitive individual, one of those people who seem to lack the protective layers of skin required to survive in a
social, and sometimes anti-social, world. Trumpeter Harry Beckett included
Ossie in his bands of the late sixties and early seventies and Beckett played
on Osborne's other great album of the period, *Outback*. Beckett remembers
travelling across Europe in minibuses to gigs with the saxophonist:

> With Mike, you had to start the conversation. You'd get him going
> and he'd talk, otherwise he'd just sit there. Like we'd be going in
> the van from London to Hamburg and different parts of Germany.
> He'd be sitting there and if you didn't say something, he wouldn't

speak the whole way. He wouldn't argue. He'd be just content to sit there and do the gig.

(Interview with Harry Beckett, June 2008)

Music was Osborne's life, which in the small world of British/London jazz did not make him unusual. Beckett continues:

Mike loved playing the saxophone and composing and doing gigs. He loved all of it. That was his life. He didn't want anything other than to be out there playing the saxophone. The financial aspect wasn't a big thing, so long as you got some money to live on. But playing and enjoying each other's playing, for Mike and myself as well and for a lot of musicians, that was what it was all about. He was a beautiful person. I mean I never saw Mike argue with anyone or have a heated discussion. He just enjoyed being there.

(Interview with Harry Beckett, June 2008)

The best way to explain Osborne's talent to the uninitiated is to play the section of *All Night Long* where the saxophonist somehow picks up the sparest of harmonic clues and launches into a double-time version of Monk's "'Round Midnight". It is a truly exciting moment. It just leaps out at you, emerging in the moment, as Louis Moholo-Moholo, drummer on the session, points out:

I had said to myself I would never play that song but, when it came, we just dove into it. It wasn't discussed. It just went straight ahead. Mike just went into it, as Mike would do things, and we just followed up. To be very sharp, was the name of the game. Those years were the times when you had to be really sharp and on your toes.

(Interview with Louis Moholo-Moholo, June 2008)

Osborne's skill lay in that almost instinctual grasp of harmony. From that he would build these long, extended melody lines that seemed to pour out of him and when it seemed he had exhausted all possibilities, he would then make his most eloquent statement. He was also a hugely adept rhythm player and, even when he appears to be disregarding conventional time, always knew exactly where the beat was. This made Moholo the perfect drummer for him.

We have already discussed Osborne's first album *Outback*. Given its unusual quality, the reader will hopefully forgive this reference back to it. Osborne modelled himself to a certain extent on Jackie McLean and his alto sound has that same sour lemons aspect that McLean took from Charlie Parker. On *Outback*, the themes are simple and open with a declamatory, Ayler-like quality. Their real purpose is to allow the maximum scope for improvisation, and both the title track and "So It Is" do precisely that. The contrast between Beckett's stately solo on *Outback* with the frantic outpouring that follows from Osborne could not be more marked. What is more, the differences between the quiet, shy individual and the force of nature that Osborne became once his horn was in his mouth are hard to equate. In a way, it is from this that his art derives its tension and its shock and awe.

If his other records under his own name do not quite achieve the heights attained by *Outback* and *All Night Long*, records like *Border Crossing* and *Marcel's Muse* run them close. His 1976 duo with Stan Tracey, *Tandem* (Ogun) is also an exceptional meeting of distinctive musical personalities, while the groundbreaking saxophone trio from 1975 with Alan Skidmore and John Surman, called appropriately *S.O.S* (Ogun; Ogun), is indispensible.

Osborne's life was a struggle. All of the descriptions of him by friends and peers, and those glimpses of his childhood and upbringing afforded by stories he told to those closest to him, suggest possible incipient mental health problems, albeit with hindsight. Osborne suffered his first psychotic episode in 1972. He had been in Germany on tour and came back home in a highly paranoid state. His then wife, Louise, recalled how frightening the experience was for the saxophonist and for herself:

> It was winter time, and he was in an absolute panic. He said, "Have the police been around?" I said: "No. Why would the police come round?" He said the police in Germany were looking for him. He couldn't relax at all and said he'd done some terrible things. Of course, I had no experience of mental illness and he had never shown any sign of it until then but he was in a terrible, terrible state. I was really frantic but I persuaded him to see our GP and to cut a long story short Mike was persuaded to go along to the psychiatric hospital the next day. He was in there for about seven weeks. He was diagnosed then as "paranoid schizophrenic".
> (Interview with Louis Palmer, June 2008)

For those with no experience, personally or professionally, with this debilitating illness, it is worth reading Silvano Arieti's *Understanding and Helping the Schizophrenic* (Arieti 1981). Few books on the subject convey as well both the bizarre thought patterns and fantasies that characterize schizophrenia and the stress that results for the sufferer and those close to them. In many respects, Osborne fits the picture described by Arieti very closely. Its comparatively early onset – he was thirty-one – would also have indicated a poor long-term prognosis. There can be little doubt that his use of stimulants like cocaine and amphetamine made his condition far worse and the management of it far more difficult.

As is often the case, Osborne could not accept his illness at first and would not take his medication. Inevitably, he became ill again and was readmitted to hospital. Following his first illness, John Surman came to the rescue. Their mutual friend Alan Skidmore had suffered a serious car accident and had been hospitalized for several months. For several years, Surman had been working very intensively with Barre Phillips and Stu Martin in The Trio and was feeling burnt out. It was then that he came up with the idea of a saxophone trio. Surprisingly, given the still rather conservative character of the British jazz audience, the group worked extensively both in the UK and Europe for about three years. The group's eponymously titled album utilized Surman's growing interest in the possibilities of synthesizers and Skidmore's love of the drums and, like Surman's previous group The Trio, the sound these three produced is both powerful and exhilarating. Listening to this record, and indeed others made by Osborne over the next few years, it seems hard to believe that by the early eighties, he was pretty much incapable of surviving in the community, let alone appearing on stage.

Recent releases of live material by Reel Recordings – *Force of Nature* – and by Ayler Records – *Live At The Plough* – reveal that Osborne was by no means a depleted force even as late as 1979–81. However, the light was surely becoming dimmer. One always hoped he would recover enough to resume his career but he died of cancer in 2008, his last years spent in a "half-way" house.

"Speed", the working-class pick-me-up of choice, was at one time Mike Osborne's preferred stimulant. It is a particularly nasty drug. Taken in moderate amounts, it boosts energy, makes the user feel convivial and confident. It feels as if one is truly alive and the brain seems fit to burst with brilliant ideas. The comedown is invariably unpleasant and leaves the user feeling restless, jittery and, often, nauseous. Protracted and heavy use can lead to drug-induced psychosis or, at the very least, dramatic mood swings, risk-taking behaviour and aggression. In the latter respect, "speed" reduces sensitivity to pain.

Surprisingly, possession of both amphetamines and barbiturates without prescription remained legal in the UK until 1964. Their use, or misuse, by young people became a moral issue for the gutter press, and pressure on government resulted in the Drugs Prevention of Misuse Act 1964. However, their prescription by GPs for weight loss and other diseases of affluence continued, as did the provision of all manner of tranquilizers. Prior to that, these and other pills could be easily obtained at any nightclub, discotheque or street corner in or around Soho. And before that, beatniks and traditional jazz fans could remove the benzedrine strip from the inhaler they bought at the chemist, dump it in a cup of coffee and rave the night away to Barber, Bilk, Melly or whoever. Being a bronchodilator, this had the additional and medically intended function of easing nasal congestion.

Certainly, some of the illicitly used pre- and post-1964 amphetamines and their far more dangerous cousin the barbiturates, came out of mum and dad's bathroom cabinet but as Harry Shapiro explains, lax security at the manufacturers' factories was probably the main source of supply:

I think the main routes of it were pharmacy thefts and actual thefts from the factories, like Smith-Kline and French, who was the main manufacturer and I've got a strong feeling that people were walking out of the factory with pockets full of speed and then just selling them on. I think that explains best the quantity that was around. It wasn't like organized crime or being imported, though I think that people like the Krays took a percentage for the drugs that were sold in the clubs in the West End. You wouldn't dare try to sell any of that stuff in their manor but in the clubs like the Marquee and The Scene clubs that were for the younger kids it was different. Some of the clubs in the West End were quite notorious for it.   (Interview with Harry Shapiro, April 2009)

When Osborne came to London in the mid-fifties to study music, he got into that scene and he was to be one of its casualties. Stan Tracey, though he had overcome his addiction to heroin, also developed problems with Dexedrine later in the decade. His big band album *Seven Ages of Man* (Columbia) was, in his view at least, affected negatively by his use of "speed":

Yeah, I'm not entirely happy with that one. I was treating myself to certain substances during *Seven Ages* and some of the stuff I wrote came out of a place it shouldn't have done. It was bloody Dexedrine. I got into it the same way I got to taking everything else. I got so that I wouldn't write unless I had some. You know that album with Ben Webster – *Webster's Dictionary* – that was entirely Dexedrine. It just used to spark me off but *Seven Ages* I was trying too hard.
(Interview with Stan Tracey, December 2009)

Such drugs continued to be widely available. While parliament might have made amphetamines and barbiturates illegal without prescription, and LSD simply illegal, this did not stop their use. In fact, with regard to LSD and other drugs including heroin and cocaine, changes in the law and medical practices, have not led to reductions in consumption. Whether there is a causal link or not is an open question but, either way, the irony seems obvious.

And prohibition and more stringent enforcement might have been one thing, but there is further irony in the fact that the means of getting high could still be found at the pharmacy and be bought over the counter. One of the saddest and strangest tales of addiction and demise is that of trumpeter Bert Courtley, the husband of saxophonist Kathy Stobart. Courtley's case is worth recounting for several reasons. His addiction was not to cocaine or heroin or alcohol but to a proprietary brand dating back to Victorian times, called Dr Collis Browne's Chlorodyne. It could be bought at pharmacists and even corner stores as a remedy for all manner of complaints and was certainly still available well into the seventies. The fact that one could be busted for possession of cannabis but take a perfectly legal but extraordinarily dangerous medicine like this perhaps says something about the morally determined character of British drug laws. However, the cause of Courtley's addiction also reveals links with other musicians we have discussed.

Kathy Stobart is a fine saxophone player and has had a remarkable career while also bringing up her children. We will talk more about her later. Her husband Bert Courtley died in 1969. He had played with Ted Heath, with Don Rendell in the Jazz Committee and the Jazz Six and had done sessions for pop groups like the Beatles. As Stobart tells me, her husband's problems began when he was asked to share lead trumpet duties in the Heath band. Courtley was very talented but he lacked confidence in his abilities. What began as a "stiff one" before a gig to calm his nerves became something else all together.

As Stobart says:

> I was really proud of him. Well, bless his heart, he was on his way to ruination because he risked all to play with it and it only lasted two or three years. He just became so hooked on this terrible stuff. It was chlorodyne. It was a very old-fashioned remedy, you're not allowed to mention the name, but when my mum was a little girl this chlorodyne was in a very small bottle. It couldn't have been more than four inches high and you'd have two or three drops in warm water and it was very beneficial for people with chest trouble and that sort of thing and a very regular remedy. But he became ... he was putting bottles away every day. God, it was dreadful, dreadful. I remember the time I found out what he was doing and why he was so ill. I called the doctor and he used to come up and shout at Bert, "You bloody fool. You're ruining everything." The doctor said, "You'll have to do something, Bert, because I'll give you two years and if you get your hands on any money you'll do it far quicker." By then he wasn't on sessions anymore because nobody would cover up for him. That's brutally frank but that's the way it would be in any position like that. Their mates would cover for them but they can't do it for more than a time. Dr Collis Browne's Chlorodyne, that was it. I remember opening a cupboard and a whole load of them falling out. I couldn't believe my eyes. When the doctor found out what he'd been taking, he said that the medical profession had been trying for years to get it taken off the market. Eventually, it was taken off the market, but not until it had finished Bert's liver.
> (Interview with Kathy Stobart, March 2009)

Dr Collis Browne's potion was advertised in the late nineteenth century as "a liquid medicine which assuages pain of every kind, affords a calm refreshing sleep without headache and invigorates the nervous system when exhausted." Given that it was a mixture of hydrochloride of morphine, chloroform, ether and prussic acid, with treacle, liquorice and peppermint to make it palatable, it would surely meet current advertising standards! It did exactly what it said on the tin – and more.

In this chapter, we have seen that users of drugs among the British jazz community may have had their individual reasons for turning to heroin and other substances. But there are also underlying patterns that users have in common, as well as broader social–psychological factors that were involved. Use of heroin among British jazz musicians in the 1950s and 1960s certainly owed a great deal to their desire to identify at a deeper emotional level with their African-American heroes. Clearly, they could not change the colour of their skin to be like Bird, Fats, Philly Joe or Miles and the social, cultural, racial and political context was totally different, but maybe they could share some of their highs and lows through imitating their use of narcotics. Before condemning such British jazz musicians, perhaps we should wonder how our some of our own assumptions will look to observers fifty years from now. But we do have to admit that there certainly was a significant degree of naivety among users. At one level their desire to identify across cultural and racial boundaries involved a strange kind of deracination. At another level, we can see this as an admittedly extreme manifestation of a very positive desire among musicians and fans for cultural engagement across racial boundaries.

There was also a high degree of ignorance among musicians about drugs, their effects and the potential for addiction. Those working currently with drug users would no doubt confirm that this continues to be the case. Nevertheless, Ginger Baker's assumption that heroin was just another drug like cannabis, or the drift from use of cocaine to use of heroin seen among several of these we have discussed, has to be noted. In this respect, and in terms of more general drug use among jazz musicians, there is a strong sense that any such risk was worth it for membership of this club of bohemians and outsiders. And this was a club and it supported, if not encouraged, aberrant and extreme actions and behaviour. We can also see in several cases we have discussed a pattern that, for some, any sacrifice the jazz muse demanded had to be paid, with one's life or soul if necessary. Ginger Baker and Phil Seamen might exemplify this but so in their way do Mike Taylor and Dick Heckstall-Smith and others. And then, of course, there were those such as Bobby Wellins and Tubby Hayes, whose failing confidence or self-belief led them to use amphetamines, cocaine and heroin.

Drug-taking among jazz musicians took place in a context – moral and political, as well as medical and legal. Jazz musicians, like their younger siblings in rock & roll, ran the risk of attention from the authorities – police, courts and prisons on the one hand and doctors, mental health professionals and hospitals on the other. This wider social–political environment was being shaped by debates that ranged from the professional, medico-legal level through the levels of pressure group politics and on to parliament. And above that, drug policy was caught in a maze of patterns of trade, economic and geopolitical interests and intrigue. While in the fifties and sixties, in Britain at least, heroin users could get their heroin from legitimate sources, this was not the case elsewhere in the world. British drug policy would soon fall into line with that operating in the USA and, slowly but surely, Britain would be opened up to the international drugs trade through organized crime and its allies within the American intelligence community.

By the end of the decade, rock musicians were abandoning LSD, dope and pretensions of peace and love for darker pleasures that would include heroin and cocaine. In a way this was part of the process that had begun more innocently in the early sixties with the Beatles and their peers. Public adulation brought levels of wealth undreamt of before and an almost necessary distancing from their fans. The more insular and isolated these artists became, the more feted they were by those who wanted to kiss the hem of their cloaks. Meanwhile, their managers would work harder and harder to keep their drug and sexual activities a secret and ensure their charges were protected from undue attention from the authorities. This world of drug use was quite different from that of musicians like Phil Seamen, Stan Tracey and Tubby Hayes and its wellspring was not the same. In many respects, it was a disease of wealth and ennui – a kind of anomie perhaps, if specific to that hermetically sealed milieu. This retreat from the public gaze was paralleled by an ever-increasing emphasis on spectacle in public performance. What is more, these highly successful rock musicians would fashion a separation between rock and the wider pop and musical worlds, and even splinter the audience for rock music itself. And we have seen the impact on jazz of that process in this chapter and the previous one.

8 Rivers of Babylon, Rivers of Blood

> Bigotry is the disease of ignorance, of morbid minds; enthusiasm of the free and buoyant. Education & free discussion are the antidotes of both.
>
> Thomas Jefferson, letter to John Adams, 1 August 1816

Before the late forties, small pockets of people from non-British minorities were living in dockland areas, such as London, Cardiff and Liverpool. There are no hard figures for the for the year 1951; however, statistician Ceri Peach has estimated that there were approximately 28,000 West Indians, 31,000 Indians, 10,000 Pakistanis and 2000 Bangladeshis resident in the UK at that time. The growth in numbers since then has been remarkable, as is the degree to which our society and culture have been enriched by immigration. By 1971, the figures were 548,000, 375,000, 119,000 and 22,000, respectively. In subsequent years, while the numbers of West Indians declined, the numbers arriving from the Indian subcontinent continued to increase (Rosen 2003, 89–90).

The background to immigration of different populations into Britain can be found in the post-war period. After the Second World War, Britain found itself with severe labour shortages, primarily in unskilled and low-paid jobs but also in the NHS and other public services. Though substantial numbers of those filling these jobs were from countries such as Eire, Poland and Italy, it was those from the Caribbean and Indian subcontinent who caught media and public attention (Glyn and Booth 1996, 175).

The British jazz scene, with notable exceptions, could justifiably be described as "sexist" in its attitude and behaviour towards women performers. In this respect, it was probably behind the times when compared with other areas of life in the kingdom. However, when it comes to racism and British jazz, the verdict has to be more generous. Wider British society in the fifties and sixties was most certainly racist; racism was often tolerated, and racist comments would frequently pass unquestioned. Hopefully, there have been changes for the better since then and what we understand now by the word "racism" is arguably not the same as it was forty, fifty or sixty years ago. The "best" standard of those times was one of "racial tolerance", inadequate though this might have been. Going back to the fifties and sixties, it is highly probable that non-white jazz musicians were not always treated equally and did suffer offence from remarks and comments by their white comrades. Nevertheless, by the standards of the time the UK jazz scene appears to have been more egalitarian in this respect than much of wider society.

The word "immigrant" is still used today as a term of abuse. It was during the fifties and sixties that immigration became heavily associated with race and colour. In practice, the immigrants who came to Britain after the Second World War came from Italy, the Caribbean, west and southern Africa, from Australia, New Zealand and Canada, as well as from the Indian subcontinent. Their contributions to our world have changed it for the better and we will see that the world of British jazz benefited from immigration to a significant extent. Musicians came to Britain from the Caribbean, Australasia, India, Rhodesia (now Zimbabwe), South Africa and Canada. They did so, as did many other individuals from these countries and regions, because of ties with Britain through Empire and later through Commonwealth. Other options for migration would have been less easy to many such individuals both white and black due to immigration restrictions that applied elsewhere, for example, to the USA or to parts of mainland Europe. For example, the Canadian trumpeter Kenny Wheeler came to Britain in the fifties because at that time Canadians found it virtually impossible to get working visas in the USA (Shipton 2010). We must not ignore, as commentators and politicians did at the time and since, that immigration was not just a matter of "coloured" immigration. In terms of jazz, we will consider the contributions of a number of immigrants to the music, both white and black. Yet, we must at the same time remember that the experiences of such white immigrant musicians and those of their black colleagues will not have been the same. Our aim is to understand how immigration contributed to British jazz, and a part of that process lies in our understanding the different experiences of white and black musicians coming to Britain to work.

As a music that draws extensively on the heritage of African-Americans, in terms of its performance, its practice and reception in this country, British jazz must necessarily be seen through the prism of race. This would be the case even if it were not for the presence of numbers of black musicians in Britain who have contributed significantly to jazz and popular music. At the same time, it is clear that the social, economic and political position of people of colour in Britain was quite different from that of African-Americans in North America. Historically, Britain profited enormously from slavery but did so from its export. Slavery never provided a significant element of the UK's domestic workforce. Nor was it ever institutionalized in Britain. In contrast, America was never an imperial power in the sense of owning colonies. At the same time, the presence of large numbers of African-Americans post-1865 has left an inheritance that has inevitably resulted in continuous tensions and often bitter struggles between blacks and whites for full civil and economic rights. This was frequently a class issue as well as one of race.

The work of Swedish economist, socialist and reformer Gunnar Myrdal played a major role in the integration of American schools in the 1950s. In his seminal work, *An American Dilemma* (1944), Myrdal describes this situation eloquently and succinctly:

> To the great majority of white Americans the Negro problem has distinctly negative connotations. It suggests something difficult to settle and equally difficult to leave alone. It is embarrassing. It makes for moral uneasiness. The very presence of the Negro in America; his fate in this country through slavery, the Civil War, and Reconstruction; his recent career and his present status; his accommodation; his protest and his aspiration; in fact his entire biological, historical, and social existence as a participant American represent to the ordinary white man in the North as well as in the South an anomaly in the very structure of American society. To many, this takes on the proportion of a menace – biological, economic, social cultural, and, at times, political. This anxiety may be mingled with a feeling of individual and collective guilt. A few see the problem as a challenge to statesmanship. To all it is trouble.　　　　　　　　　　　　　　(Myrdal 1944, 122)

In Britain, post-1945, race was refracted through a different history and legacy – that of Empire and the belief in its civilizing mission and the myth of white superiority. But black people came to the UK in the fifties to fill job shortages, often in settings where white, indigenous Britons were unwilling to work. Others came from Africa, Pakistan, India and elsewhere as a matter of right due to the granting of British passports. These people were not abducted from their homeland, transported in slave ships and then subjected to enforced labour. They were, in one sense or another, invited.

Whether this extended to a "welcome" is another matter entirely. These people were greeted differentially by the British according to the degree of their proximity to the newcomers. Many of the immigrants were forced by circumstance, and the failure of the government to offer any form of resettlement in the host country, into areas of poor housing and pre-existing poverty. Their presence brought fear and resentment by a lower, white working class who saw them as a threat to their own meagre resources. Empire had left white Britons with a sense that they were racially superior to those Britain had colonized, yet when the conquered came to the UK to work or study they came as unwanted guests. Intolerance of foreigners runs deep in Britain and readily attaches itself to people of colour, just as it has in the past focused on the Irish and the Jews, and more recently on white people from eastern Europe. For those further removed from the environment within which the incomers settled, immigration could be seen as almost a matter of pride in our civilizing mission, that Empire had now been replaced by the multinational, multiracial Commonwealth. There were others who were driven by political or Christian ideals, who saw a common humanity or brotherhood first rather than race, or, to use Arthur Marwick's excellent phrase, were simply inculcated with that peculiar "secular Anglicanism", that combination of social values that call for consensus rather than conflict, tolerance and fair play, as opposed to mistrust and injustice (Marwick 1996, 10). But there were also those of a more vicious political coloration, whose hatred was ideological in nature. Their forces would become more organized and their voices louder and more hostile from the late 1960s onwards.

The position of people of colour in post-war Britain was not that of equals. That is as true of those who worked as jazz musicians within the wider context of their position in society, as it is of those who worked as nurses, bus conductors or in factories. Prejudice can often be "institutionalized" but is more regularly informal in nature, if no less systemically rooted. Legislation was passed in the UK parliament in the sixties to protect or enhance the rights of black people without the often violent struggles of the campaign for civil rights in the USA. However, those who had come from the Caribbean or Asia were still left in a constant position of uncertainty, of never knowing when the next insult, blow or act of unfairness would come or from where. But broadly speaking, and in comparison with the situation in the USA, race as an issue was negotiated in Britain, albeit from a position of gross disparity as far as the new immigrants were concerned.

Black musicians had already played an important role in the British entertainment industry before the Second World War. Jim Godbolt, speaking of the pre-war and war years, might have noted that, "The black contribution to British jazz was slight" (Godbolt 1986, 185). The numbers of black people in Britain, as well as those involved in jazz, were small. Yet Godbolt's comment is far too sweeping. What was and was not jazz in Britain before 1945 was less clearly defined than in the years following the defeat of fascism. A number of bands and artists, as in fairness Godbolt later goes on to note, did ply their trade in the UK. Though not strictly a jazz singer or pianist, Grenadian-born Leslie "Hutch" Hutchinson, was one of the biggest cabaret stars in the world during the 1920s and 1930s. Val Wilmer is one writer who is keen to point out the disparity between the way black people were generally portrayed – she refers to her experiences of Sunday School education in this respect – with the way "Hutch" was seen.

> At the same time, we would often hear pianist-entertainer "Hutch"
> on the radio, singing songs such as These Foolish Things and Begin

The Beguine with effortless charm and the merest "hint" of his colour. Hutch (Leslie Hutchinson) was a longtime British resident, a Black man beloved by the public; he'd win nods of approval whenever his light baritone boomed over the airwaves.

(Wilmer 1991, 19)

Hutch rose high and fell far. He had affairs with Cole Porter and Ivor Novello, and more significantly with Edwina, Countess of Mountbatten. This was his undoing, and eventually led to his ostracism (though not Mrs M's) from the upper class world he had courted, and which had courted him. And there were other artists who were both more important in jazz terms and more modest in their social aspirations.

Jamaican trumpeter and later bandleader, Leslie "Jiver" Hutchinson played with Cyril "Happy" Blake's Cuba Club Band. After that, he joined fellow Jamaican trumpeter Leslie Thompson's Emperors of Jazz and was then with dancer–bandleader Ken "Snakehips" Johnson, until joining Geraldo's band in 1939. Hutchinson led his own band from 1944 to 1950, featuring many of the musicians from Thompson's band, and toured the UK and Europe and even played concerts in India in 1945. The band made several recordings, as did "Snakehips" Johnson's West Indian Dance Band and Rhythm Section. "Jiver's" daughter, incidentally, is the singer Elaine Delmar (see Simons 2010, 2001; Thompson 2009).

In fact, there were quite a few musicians from different parts of the empire working in London and who featured with many of the white and black swing/dance bands of the era. There was Barbadian trumpeter Dave Wilkins, later a regular at Club Eleven, who also worked with Sandy Brown, Wally Fawkes and Bruce Turner. And there was Trinidadian guitarist Lauderic Caton, who played with singer/percussionist Ray Ellington (of "Goons" fame) and who was, with Coleridge Goode, a member of the Caribbean Club Trio. Guitarists Joe and Frank Deniz were brothers and born in Cardiff, and both played with saxophonist Jimmy Skidmore among others. Then there was the fine pianist York de Souza and saxophonist Bertie King, who worked with Kenny Baker's Jazz Today Unit and Kenny Graham's Afro-Cubists, as well as leading his own groups. Mention must also be made of Trinidadian clarinettist Carl Barriteau, who at one time led a ten-piece band, which came fourth in both the *Melody Maker* and *New Musical Express* Swing Polls of 1954. Pete King, co-owner of Ronnie Scott's Jazz Club, was a member of his band. As a soloist, Barriteau won the *Melody Maker* Clarinet Poll seven years in a row (I am indebted here to David Taylor's excellent jazz site "British Modern Jazz – From The 1940s Onwards").

Many of these players, and their white peers, along with a coterie of white suburban fans would gravitate afterhours to Jig's Club in Wardour Street. Godbolt, who visited the club himself in 1941, describes it thus:

During its long run – strangely perhaps – in view of police interest in these shady establishments – many Archer Street jazzmen visited the club (and others like it) "after hours", escaping from the gilded fleshpots of their normal employment. In these less acceptable, socially speaking, environs where the air was undoubtedly fouler they, musically speaking, could breathe more freely.

(Godbolt 1986, 187)

Sadly, as Godbolt points out, with the exception of Topic Records' now-deleted *Black British Swing*, very little of this music was ever documented.

In fact, Godbolt recanted somewhat upon his previous comments in his later volume on British jazz, *A History of Jazz in Britain 1950–70* (Godbolt 1989):

During the mid-thirties jazz in Britain was enriched by the presence of West Indian musicians like trumpeters Dave Wilkins and Leslie Hutchinson; saxophonists Bertie King, George Roberts, George Tyndale, Louis Stephenson and Freddy Grant; pianist Errol Barrow; bassist Coleridge Goode; drummer Clinton Maxwell and guitarist Lauderic Caton. They were often joined, in various combinations, by the Cardiff-born blacks, Joe and Frank Deniz, on guitar. (Godbolt 1989, 119)

Yet on the next page, he seems to contradict both this and his earlier remarks, when he suggests:

The post-war West Indian contribution to the popular music scene was mainly in the fields of calypso and Latin American music. Expatriate South Africans Louis Moholo, Mongezi Feza and Johnny Dyani aside, the black contribution to jazz was minimal, Harriott, alto saxophonist and flautist Harold McNair, trumpeters Dizzy Reece, Harry Beckett and Shake Keane being the exceptions that proved the rule. (Godbolt 1989, 120)

Even allowing that these were the only names to be considered in this context – Dudu Pukwana, Ernest Ranglin, Amancio D'Silva, Wilton "Bogey" Gaynair, pianist Russell Henderson and singer-percussionist Frank Holder are missing for a start – that does seem a hell of a list of exceptional exceptions. The contribution of these players – and of white immigrants like Kenny Wheeler, Mike Gibbs, Dave MacRae, Brian Smith and Ray Warleigh – was most certainly out of all proportion to their numbers.

However, Godbolt's focus on musicians from the Caribbean and South Africa – and black musicians at that – does raise a further and important point that we need to pursue. In a way, he is echoing the response of the indigenous population to immigration, which saw this not as a general issue that involved "white" immigration as well but as one that was solely concerned with and by "black" and Asian immigration. We need to think more broadly on the subject and understand it more systemically and try to appreciate how such attitudes may have affected white and black musicians differently in the UK. Clearly, racism must feature largely in our deliberations.

The most extreme aspects of white British reaction to immigration were seen in the Notting Hill and Nottingham riots of August 1958, and in the related propagandizing by fascist and racist organizations in these areas. At the far more liberal end of the spectrum, we may note the campaign by John Dankworth, Cleo Laine, Humphrey Lyttelton and others to those same events and the formation of the Stars' Campaign For Inter-Racial Friendship. We might also see the response by magistrates and judges to the riots in a similarly generous light. As Val Wilmer noted, "In 1958 the liberal conscience among the judiciary was still alive and white youths were imprisoned for their part in the racist attacks" (Wilmer 1991, 51). Yet, for black and Asian immigrants, their experiences of life in the mother country fell somewhere between these poles. They had, in the main, been invited here. Yet, their lives would increasingly be framed and formalized by legislation.

In 1961, for example, following growing opposition to immigration from a variety of political groupings, the Macmillan government responded with the Commonwealth Immigrants Act 1962. This restricted the rights of Commonwealth citizens to come to Britain unless they held government-issued employment vouchers allowing them to settle. It was a blatantly racist piece of legislation directed at the Caribbean and Asian subcontinent countries in particular, and reflected the strength of such sentiments inside the Conservative Party, notably among its Monday Club members. Had such restrictions applied earlier, then several important musicians from the Caribbean might not have made their homes here. Those wishing to come here from the "white dominions", on the other hand, would not have been affected. Labour leader, Hugh Gaitskell called the act "cruel and brutal anti-colour legislation" and rightly so. However, six years later, the Wilson government would choke on these fine words.

If we turn to the experiences of black musicians coming to the UK, a picture begins to emerge. They might have been equals on the bandstand but they also had to exist outside that environment in a world that could be very hostile indeed. Coleridge Goode came to Britain before the war to study electrical engineering at Glasgow University, where he led the second violins in the university's symphony orchestra. He started to play jazz bass and decided to move to London around 1940, where he played with Johnny Claes and his Clae Pigeons, alongside Kenny Graham, Lauderic Caton and drummer and (later) Tempo Records' boss Carlo Krahmer. During the war, Goode made several BBC broadcasts with Stéphane Grappelli in a band that included George Shearing. To a degree, his position as a musician, and an unusually adept reader, allowed him to function within a milieu distinct from that of other black people in Britain. Asked whether he ever experienced racism from other white players, he replied with a certain hesitation:

> I can't say ... the people that I worked with were all okay and fine. I never had any problems with musicians that I worked with because in the first place I think proper musicians have a certain other feeling to other good musicians – people who can play their instruments and behave themselves – and that's one thing I could always play my instrument better than a lot of them. So, they couldn't put that down to me at all. So, I got on with the musicians alright. It was other people who were horrible. I think things are a bit better but they could be a whole lot better. So long as one is respected for what one is and one does in life that's all you can expect.   (Interview with Coleridge Goode, May 2008)

Coleridge Goode's distinction between being with fellow musicians and dealing with other sections of white society is echoed by Harry Beckett, "I've never had any problems with musicians. To me, it's just one huge family, the world of musicians" (interview with Harry Beckett, June 2008). Trumpeter/ bandleader Leslie Thompson first came to Britain from Jamaica in the 1930s. Interviewed by Val Wilmer in 1986, he makes a similar remark: "We were not mitigated against because we were artists. All the theatrical people, the musicians accepted us." Nevertheless, asked by Wilmer whether he felt he had to ingratiate himself, when he arrived in the UK, Thompson replied, "Oh yes, oh yes. You were more or less conscious, particularly because of colour, that everybody's eyes were on you" (Wilmer 1986, 52).

Certainly, in the early fifties, there was a degree of separation between white and black musicians in terms of the work they undertook or could undertake or in the terms of the clubs where both could play. We would also have to note that, while some black musicians – Joe Harriott, John Mayer, Dizzy Reece, Harold McNair, Wilton Gaynair and Ernest Ranglin among them – did get opportunities to record their music, others of talent did not. Shake Keane, for whatever reason, went under-recorded and Russell Henderson was another whose abilities warranted a wider audience. Henderson, in fact, does feel that this was the result of a neglect in his case that had something to do with, if not prejudice, a discrimination arising from the invisibility of black musicians on a predominantly white scene (interview with Russell Henderson, March 2012).

In terms of the clubs, in the early to mid-fifties there were clubs that were essentially for black musicians and others that were for whites. And there were white bands and black bands. Russell Henderson came to Britain from Trinidad, having worked as musician in his homeland and elsewhere in the Caribbean, to study to become a piano tuner at the North London

Polytechnic. His skills as pianist soon came to the notice of other black players.

> When I got here, I started at the Polytechnic doing piano tuning but the guys realized there was another piano player in town, a black piano player because in those days there were black bands and white bands. They weren't mixing much. "Jiver" Hutchinson played with Geraldo and some others played with different people but usually it was black bands and white bands. There were quite a lot of bands playing different functions and things.
> (Interview with Russell Henderson, March 2012)

Asked what he thought caused this separation, his response is a cautious one:

> I don't know why but everybody was keeping their thing to themselves. I don't think there was any threat at all. It was different music entirely. We played more Caribbean jazz and there was a lot of ... strictly, they were more trying to copy the Americans. Everybody was trying to play [Charlie] Parker and we were doing the same. (Interview with Russell Henderson, March 2012)

This is a point that singer–percussionist Frank Holder echoes. He notes that the Feldman Club in Oxford Street (to be followed later in this by the Flamingo in Wardour Street) was most definitely an exception:

> They were ones who gave a lot of opportunity to young musicians and jazz musicians etc. Then it began to spread because people began to realize that "jazz" wasn't a dirty word. That was the good thing about the Feldman club. It was the only club in those days that offered an opportunity for black people to come in and play because the other people were in a way afraid of doing so because of what people might say and because of not having the opportunity to see and see and be around musicians of a black nature. They were a bit, how can I say, unsure and wary of doing so.
> (Interview with Frank Holder March 2012)

And he adds that other clubs would eventually follow this example as barriers, often invisible, came down, "The Flamingo, that became more or less ... it took over from the Feldman Club. From there the other clubs began to do so too" (interview with Frank Holder, March 2012).

It is important, however, to understand that these were early days. Understandings of race, racism and discrimination have developed since then and necessarily so. Yet the application of modern standards and expectations to an historical situation is unhelpful. People were learning and adapting to a new situation and, in some respects, the pace of learning among some within the worlds of jazz and entertainment was fast indeed. Musicians, white like John Dankworth, Tony Crombie and Kenny Graham or black like Joe Harriott, Dizzy Reece, Frank Holder or Russell Henderson, did much to change understandings and cross any divide that might exist. Russell Henderson talks particularly positively, for example, of another club in central London.

> The Sunset Club in Carnaby Street was run by a Jamaican and you'd get a chance to jam. Everybody would come in but that was a mixed club because the resident pianist was at one time Eddie Thompson, and Joe Harriott would play saxophone. So, you had things like that. You'd get a little situation going and then it would be whoever was up next.
> (Interview with Russell Henderson, March 2012)

As Henderson explains, in the sixties, saxophonist John Surman became his next door neighbour. They became friends and formed a band together and the pianist elaborates a picture of shifting positions and of an opening up of boundaries, both musical and interpersonal:

> When, later on, John Surman came to live next door to me, he would introduce me to his crowd. There was no one way it developed really. I can't really say how it happened but you get this kind of segregation and it moves from that to like everybody being together. It just gradually happened and the musicians began to rub off on each other too. I gained something from them and they gained something too. That formed the sort of nucleus of the English scene of black and white jazz players. Because in all those big bands, like Tony Crombie's, they all had black musicians such as Dizzy Reece playing with them too.
> (Interview with Russell Henderson, March 2012)

In fact, Henderson played regularly with Surman and others at the Old Place, as well as making his own significant contribution to inter-jazz harmony with the jam sessions he organized at the Coleherne Pub in Earls Court.

> People used to come and sit in like John Surman, Joe Harriott. Everyone came down there. American artists when they came into town would say where can we find a jam and they would come down when I had my Sunday session there. Graham Bond come down one time. Philly Joe Jones when he was living in London. Joe was a regular. He came down most Sundays. Shake Keane. (Interview with Russell Henderson, March 2012)

Apparently, one night the entire Basie band were in town and found their way to the venue. Sometimes talking in monochromatic language even about issues as important as this over-simplifies and creates its own set of barriers. It also disempowers the people who most need to act and whoever the greatest potential to do so. We should acknowledge instead how significant were the efforts of musicians during this period – both black and white – in creating a scene that was becoming and became increasingly inclusive.

Val Wilmer has done more than any other writer to stress the black contribution to British jazz. Her articles on Wilton "Bogey" Gaynair in the magazine *Jazz FM* (Wilmer 1992) and on Shake Keane in *The Wire* magazine (Wilmer 1989) are timely reminders that British jazz was first shown in black and white. Her comment in the piece on Keane on why the studious, intellectual teacher and poet who came as a student to the UK chose to return to the bandstand speaks volumes about British attitudes to black people in those years:

> A teacher in his native St. Vincent, he arrived in 1952 intent on studying English. He was already an acknowledged poet – "Shake" derives from Shakespeare – and only returned to playing in London when he found that as an immigrant his qualifications counted for nothing. It was either manual labour and with "spade" bands in demand to play Latin/American music, survival dictated a return to maracas and shirts with frilled sleeves.
>
> (Wilmer 1989, 45)

Keane is not well-served on record. His best playing is to be found on the sides he cut with both Joe Harriott and Michael Garrick, and those records are, as we have seen, rightly celebrated. Keane's exceptional abilities as a sightreader and his highly developed melodic sense made him much in demand in the session world, and in due course led to his joining the Kurt Edelhagen Orchestra in Germany. Work of this kind was very lucrative but it did take the trumpeter away from more creative endeavours within jazz. Releases under his own name were limited to three EPs, a single and two "easy listening" albums. In terms of the latter, *Dig It!* (with the Ivor Raymonde Orchestra) and *Shake Keane with the Keating Sound* (Decca; Vocalion) offer sophisticated mood music, good of its type but of little real substance. Even so, Keane's performances transcend the soft focus background reasonably successfully. The remaining material on record includes an incredibly rare EP, *In My Condition*, with what was essentially Harriott's group and a single made in 1955 for export only, "Akinla/Fire, Fire". A further eight tracks taken from three different sessions from the period 1959–64 were released by Trunk Records in 2011 under the title *Rising Stars*. The first of these involved the Hastings Girls Choir and the second the Gordon Langford Orchestra. These, it must be said, are rather bizarre, though, as ever, Keane rises above

Thirty-nine jazz musicians, Trafalgar Square, 1962. Top row, left to right: Bruce Turner (alto sax), Tony Milliner (trombone), Al Fairweather (trumpet), Johnny Burch (piano), Don Rendell (tenor sax), Tony Archer (bass), Tony Russell (trombone), Les Condon, Gus Galbraith (trumpets). Second row, left to right: Sandy Brown (clarinet), Dick Heckstall-Smith (tenor sax), Coleridge Goode (bass), Wally Fawkes (clarinet), Wally Wright (bass), Peter King (alto sax). Third row, left to right: Brian Lemon (piano), Brian Prudence (bass); Bottom row, left to right, Dave Davies (Dobell's jazz shop), Laurie Morgan (drums),

Herman Wilson (trombone), George Melly (vocals), Chris Staunton (bass), Buzz Green, Tony Kinsey (drums), Peter McGurk (bass), Dudley Moore, Michael Garrick (piano), Maurice Gaurensky (bass), Vic Ash (tenor sax), Gordon Beck, Brian Dee (piano), Graham Bond (alto sax), Jimmy Deuchar (trumpet), Allan Ganley (drums), Tubby Hayes (tenor sax), Benny Green (baritone sax), Stan Robinson (tenor sax), Bill Eyden (drums), Colin Purbrook (piano). Photograph by Terence Donovan, © Terence Donovan Archive – courtesy of Diana Donovan.

the setting. The other set was released on the tiny Airborne label as *A Case of Jazz* and featured the Shake Keane and Michael Garrick Quartette. This is music worth hearing, with a strong rhythm section of Coleridge Goode and Bobby Orr on drums. It might not startle but it is all beautifully played, and it is always a joy to hear the gorgeous tones of Keane's trumpet and flugelhorn.

Shake Keane also features on three tracks on Wilton Gaynair's *Africa Calling* (Candid), a set produced by Tony Hall in 1960 for Tempo, but apparently unreleased until 2006. The music is of a very high standard and it is unfortunate that the Gaynair/Keane partnership did not continue. Gaynair left for Germany not long after the session, also as it happens to find work with Kurt Edelhagen. He had one of those huge tenor sounds that recalls Hank Mobley, Dexter Gordon and Stanley Turrentine, but with just a hint of Coltrane in there as well. However, it is his accuracy and the quality of his articulation that really impresses. Gaynair also writes well and the three tracks with Keane – "Blue Ghana", "Just for Jan" and, best of all, "Africa Calling" – are as good as anything in British jazz of the period. It is no surprise that Joe Harriott made it apparent that London was not big enough for both of them (Wilmer 1992, 42). Keane is every bit a match for Gaynair, his speed and bright tone razor sharp against Gaynair's broadsword tenor, while on the title track, Keane plays flugelhorn with all of that rich, mellifluous lyricism that was his trademark. This date ranks alongside Keane's work with Harriott and suggests that he was one of the very finest foils that any saxophonist might wish for.

Wilton Gaynair's previous album *Blue Bogey* (Tempo; Jasmine) was even better. It featured ex-Jazz Couriers Terry Shannon on piano (also Tubby Hayes's first choice for his quartet in subsequent years), bassist Kenny Napper and Bill Eyden on drums. The production by Tony Hall is excellent, with Gaynair's powerful tenor right up front in the mix. The rhythm section play with the contained strength that might more often be heard on American Blue Note or Riverside albums than on those made in Europe at the time. It is this that lends the music its emotional weight. Once again, Gaynair's compositional skills are also to the fore on the flowing, upbeat opener, "Wilton's Mood", and the tender ballad, "Deborah". Both have the authority of standards, while two spontaneous takes – "Rhythm" and "Blues for Tony" – suggest a more uninhibited and down-home side to Gaynair's muse. This is exceptional jazz that ranks with the best of the period. Sadly, there was little more of this to come from the tenor player.

The contributions of two other musicians should also be acknowledged here. The first of these is Goan guitarist Amancio D'Silva. Patronized by the Maharani of Jaipur, an ardent jazz lover, D'Silva came to London with his family in 1967. He was introduced to Denis Preston by comedian/writer/broadcaster/theatrical producer Jonathan Miller, who saw him playing in the West End. Preston put him in the studio with what was the Rendell–Carr Quintet without Michael Garrick, and *Integration* (Columbia; Universal) was born. It is a fine set of raga-based tunes but with a strong blues feel throughout that is utterly captivating. The rhythm section of Dave Green on bass and drummer Trevor Tomkins play superbly, while Ian Carr and Don are both supremely elegant and eloquent. As for D'Silva, if one imagines a sitar player inspired by Wes Montgomery and Charlie Christian, that is just what he sounds like. *Hum Dono* with Joe Harriott made a few months later was just as good. D'Silva made the disappointing *Reflections* (Columbia) the following year in an orchestral setting arranged by Stan Tracey, and the somewhat strange *Dream Sequence* (Regal Zonophone), with the group Cosmic Eye, which included Alan Branscombe, percussionist Keshav Sathe and John Mayer. He also worked with Guy Warren of Ghana. D'Silva did not record again but continued until a series of strokes sadly took first his ability to play and then his life. On the evidence of *Integration* and *Hum Dono*, one is left wishing that there was more to be heard.

The second figure who must be mentioned is another guitarist – Ernest Ranglin. Ranglin was born in Jamaica and has made for himself a career spanning jazz and reggae. He has worked with legendary producers Coxone Dodd and Lee "Scratch" Perry and played with the Skatalites, the Wailers and Prince Buster. He visited the UK in 1963 to play at the Scott Club and returned intermittently throughout the period. His two jazz records *Wranglin* from (Island) and *Reflections* from 1965 (Island) are very hard to find but suggest a style, which, like D'Silva, drew on Charlie Christian and Wes Montgomery, though in Ranglin's case it was more of the former and less of the latter. Ranglin's importance is more in terms of his influence on a younger generation of British black musicians, including his nephew bassist Gary Crosby. Ranglin remains a beautiful player, however, whose style has developed over the years to draw on both reggae and jazz in equal measure. But to hear how he sounded in the sixties, *Soul D'Ern* (Jazz House) reveals an artist rich in ideas and with strong rhythmic skills. One just needs to ignore the pedestrian rhythm section who dog him at every turn.

One thing that continues to strike home about all these musicians is the innate decency and dignity with which the likes of Keane, Goode, Thompson, Beckett and Gaynair dealt with their situation. Alan Robertson in his *Joe Harriott – Fire in His Soul* (Robertson 2003, 214) quotes Harriott's lover, Sharon Atkin, who recalled Harriott walking out of a recording studio because a technician called him "nigger". And Harry Beckett has similar stories:

> Even today you still get this. When I go to a gig at a venue I just go and do the gig. I'm not a party animal, so I don't go to parties. I just go along and perform. I enjoy hearing myself playing the trumpet and listening to the other musicians. But one time I was walking along the street after a gig in Soho. I was with this colleague, George, and we were going to catch the tube. George was white and this white guy was walking towards us and he started

saying, "Why don't you go and jump in the trees and swing in the trees, gorilla." I turned to George and he just said, "Ignore him. He's just a stupid person." It happened to me in Holland as well, this white Dutchman called me "nigger". But you hear these things and what can you do about it?

(Interview with Harry Beckett, June 2008)

Perhaps it is a generational thing. One would anticipate that younger Afro-Caribbean musicians would respond differently and with justification. But as Coleridge Goode puts it:

If you've got any kind of decent upbringing you learn how to deal with these sort of things. Although you feel personally at times hurt, you know what you ought to do and how you ought to deal with things like that. So, I was able to come through it but I knew very well that it existed and personally there were various incidents. But as I said, one has to deal with it and get on with your life. I wanted to play music and I could only do it here. It was suggested many times that I should go to America and I said no way would I go to that country under the circumstances that existed. I would probably get killed or something because I couldn't put up with what those guys had to put up with. That was unbelievable what happened to people there. Certain places you couldn't go in and other places you had to go through the back door. That wasn't for me. (Interview with Coleridge Goode, May 2008)

The Irresistible Rise of Multi-Racial Britain (Phillips and Phillips 1999) paints a grim picture of life for black people in fifties and sixties Britain. Sir Herman Ouseley, the ex-Chairman of the Commission for Racial Equality, told author Trevor Phillips:

I think perhaps the biggest problem that I faced was knowing very quickly where to go and where not to go; where you weren't welcome, where your face wasn't welcome. Where hostility could be violence, for instance. Teddy boys were rife in south London – Walworth Road and the Elephant and Castle. It was getting connected very quickly to be certain that you weren't stepping down the wrong alley, going in the wrong street, being in the wrong place in the wrong time because I felt very often instinctively that there were places where you had to avoid, and I think that was proved to be right by people who would get their heads beaten in and had very difficult experiences. And for me that was new, but at the same time I think it was very much part of growing up – growing up very quickly. (Phillips and Phillips 1999, 143)

Another interviewee, Sam King, remembered with sadness how hard it was to find accommodation. It would often mean paying more than a white person and often meant sharing. "They always put on the board, 'Black – Niggers not wanted here', on the board, you know, these boards out there, 'No Niggers' or 'No Colour', things like that. So, it's very hard to get a room" (Phillips and Phillips 1999, 89).

In the same book, Jessica Huntley talked of the employment difficulties facing black people, however well-qualified:

> Then I went to Haringey, an office of the Ministry of Pensions of National Insurance, and I went temping, and the manager interviewed me, he gave me tests and whatever, and I did that, he was happy. And he said, it was just a temporary job, and I said, "Fine". And I left and I came back home. And we lived by that time on Whiteman Road itself. And ten minutes after I got there, the door knock, and the landlady said to me, she was a Greek lady, she called out, she said, "A white man here for you." And I said, "Oh, my God. Which white man ... to see me?" And it was the man who interviewed me, you see. And he said, "I'm terribly sorry, Mrs Huntley, but the job is really very temporary, it's only for a week." And I said, "I don't mind, even if it's a week, I will take it." He said, "But it might be less than a week." And I said, "It doesn't matter if it's less." I said, "I'll work for two days. If there's no work, for a day." And I spent five days there. And what happened was that when the staff heard I was taken on, as a nigger – by that time, "nigger" was even going out, between "nigger" and "coloured", you know, they were floating between those two terms – and they really didn't want me to be there at all.
>
> (Phillips and Phillips 1999, 150–1)

Nor should we forget that discrimination in terms of accommodation was the reality for black musicians on the jazz scene. Frank Holder talks for example of touring with Leslie "Jiver" Hutchinson in the early fifties and of the difficulties in obtaining accommodation due to their "colour". Often, the promoter would ask from the stage, if members of the audience could put a musician or two up for the night. As he explains, more often than not to their credit people would raise their hands and beds would be found for the night. Touring with the Dankworth Seven, as the band's then only black member presented another slightly different set of difficulties, as Holder notes:

> We never went for expensive hotels. We went for digs. Imagine, I used to pick up the rear with the guys and the landlady or landlord would say, "Oh, we can't have him," when I came up the back. So the boys would say, "Right, everybody out." Nobody

stayed at these digs because of that because I was not accepted fully at that time. They were well behind me. Well, one thing in music, in those days, they didn't see colour. So long as you could put it down and do something well we just played for each other and enjoyed our music, hopefully the public would enjoy it too.
(Interview with Frank Holder, March 2012)

Such daily, routine slurs and slights and worse were the reality for black – and Asian – people living in Britain in those years, whatever their trade or line of work. In the previous chapter we discussed how far barriers existed between white and black musicians on the British scene. But there is another question relating to race in this context that one cannot escape when considering the careers of black musicians on the British jazz scene of the fifties and sixties. Were their opportunities in any way restricted by issues around their race? It is a far from easy question to address. "Racism", "racial discrimination" and "prejudice" are highly loaded and emotive terms and our understanding and application of such terminology has shifted over the decades. In the fifties and sixties, the issues were understood in terms of very specific attitudes and explicit behaviours, expressed often by individuals and groups who saw nothing wrong in their beliefs or actions. Now, we would tend to see the problem of race discrimination as something that has become fixed in processes and practices, both formal and informal, that are rarely made explicit and of which we may remain unaware. Contrary to the saying, opposites do not attract. We identify most easily with others who are most like us. This is not a problem in many situations. However, when decisions about resources such as employment are made upon such a basis, the effect can lead to bias and disadvantage to people from groups that are least like us. The process and what underpins it may not be "racist" but its consequences may be, and it may justifiably be experienced by those affected as "racist". Was this the case in British jazz?

Joe Harriott has become a kind of touchstone for discussion around this issue. As the trombonist Paul Rutherford, a Communist and anti-racist, told Mark Wastell in 1998:

> I understand that one of this countries [sic] leading black musicians is on record as saying that Joe Harriott drunk himself to death because of racism, now that is bullshit – they never even saw or heard Joe Harriott. I did, I knew and loved Joe Harriott's music and he was perfect, a true gentleman. He ran a mixed race band, he had no such problems with the music. (Wastell 1998, 17)

Alan Robertson does not shy away from this matter in his biography of Harriott, and his conclusions must be read as balanced rather than equivocal. He quotes Harriott's producer Denis Preston, Jamaican saxophonist Andy

Hamilton, Indian violinist and composer John Mayer and, perhaps most significantly, Coleridge Goode – all of whom felt that, had Harriott been white, his music would have been more widely acknowledged. Goode's comments to Robertson clearly indicate that he held those "who had the power to present, broadcast, explain and publicise his music" responsible for this and felt they had instead "often ignored or neglected it" (Robertson 2003, 216). Goode had told me with sadness of his last session with Harriott on Swings High (Melodisc; Cadillac):

> That was in '67, my last record with Joe. After that, no contact. He just disappeared off the scene. What a tragedy! I'm sure he was very disappointed but we never really discussed anything. We weren't really friends outside the group. We never met outside the job.
> (Interview with Coleridge Goode, May 2008)

Shake Keane takes a slightly different view and expressed this originally in an interview with writer and broadcaster Peter Clayton. He clearly saw the saxophonist as a deeply troubled and even flawed individual. For Keane, it seemed almost inevitable that Harriott would never end his days in anything approaching domestic bliss (Robertson 2003, 216–17). While John Mayer clearly took the view that Joe would have received wider recognition had he been white. However, his comments to writer Kevin Le Gendre in 1998 indicate how frustrating he found working with Harriott, and Alan Robertson cites other comments from members of Indo-Jazz Fusions to similar effect (Le Gendre 1998; Robertson 2003).

There is something quite discomforting about discussing an individual in the context of ideas and opinions that he never claimed for himself. Yet it is a door that has already been opened and forces us to consider the evidence in some detail. In doing so, a picture emerges that is at odds with that of "Harriott as victim".

To begin with, we must note the recording opportunities made available to Joe Harriott. Up to 1967/8, Harriott certainly did not go unrecorded and he made several of the finest albums of the period. He had recorded three EPs for Denis Preston and Southern Horizons (Columbia) for Lansdowne in the 1950s, prior to making Free Form and Abstract. Those two groundbreaking albums were followed by Movement in 1963, High Spirits in 1964 and Personal Portrait in 1968. The last of these featured Harriott with both a nonet and a string quartet. As well as three releases with Joe Harriott–John Mayer's Indo-Jazz Fusions, he made the intriguing and unusual Hum Dono in 1969 with Goan guitarist Amancio D'Silva, Ian Carr, Dave Green, drummer Bryan Spring and Norma Winstone on wordless vocals. All of these were for Denis Preston's 'Lansdowne Series' of Columbia-issued releases. That is a total of ten releases in as many years. Harriott also held the Saturday (and at one time Sunday) night residency at the Marquee for several years. This was one of the most prestigious gigs in town. Chris Barber was an active supporter and recorded Joe's "Revival" and has kept it in the band's book. Barber's support meant that the Harriott Quintet would feature at most of the NJF Festivals. Harriott also guested on the Modern Jazz Quartet's tour of 1959, and his quintet supported Dave Brubeck in 1961.

Despite this backing from certain sections of the jazz community, Hilary Moore, *pace* Goode's comments, notes:

> The release of *Movement* in 1964, only half of its tracks in the free genre, heralded the end of Harriott's free form concept. The quintet had performed the music widely, but to principally negative reviews, and it seemed there was little sustainable appetite for it within the mainstream jazz scene or critical establishment. This pallid reception was despite *Abstract* being awarded a five-star rating by *Down Beat* in 1963. As an achievement unequalled by any other group, one would expect nationalistic outbursts of enthusiasm and support but instead it was virtually ignored.
>
> (Moore 2007, 93)

She continues, "Harriott's music seemed least acknowledged and celebrated in his adopted homeland. Subsequent free jazz musicians in Britain showed distinct reluctance to acknowledge his significance and seem far more indebted to American models" (Moore 2007, 94).

It is indeed surprising that Harriott's *Down Beat* success was not apparently more widely celebrated. Brian Dee suggests that Harriott's way of mixing free form and straightahead numbers in his sets left audiences puzzled and unsure, though going by Harriott's comments regarding positive audience response (particularly among university students) noted in Alan Robertson's *Fire in His Soul*, such a feeling was not universal (interview with Brian Dee, March 2008; Robertson 2003). As Harriott told *Melody Maker*'s Bob Houston at the time of *Abstract*'s release, this was a deliberate policy on his part. The same article tells a story of Dizzy Gillespie visiting Ronnie's during a Harriott set and being invited to sit in. Apparently, the trumpeter responded, "I don't want to play any of your damn weird music!" Harriott took this as an indirect compliment. He also noted that the response of audiences to his free form pieces had begun to change, saying, "It is getting across now and people are asking for individual numbers by name." The new album is reviewed within the article and Houston comments that, while many might want to dismiss Harriott's experiments, *Abstract* "contains too much good music to be summarily dismissed." He adds that the music has an "almost Mingus-like drive and intensity" and describes Harriott and Keane as "nakedly emotional players" and as "two of the most musically articulate jazzmen in Britain" (Houston 1963, 15).

When it came to reviewing *Movement* in August, Bob Dawbarn – never perhaps the best choice to review a "new wave" album – found himself torn between admiration for Harriott and his group and his own struggle to grasp the value and meaning of the altoist's free form pieces. Yet, even so, he stated that he found the music "more coherent" than Ornette Coleman and that there was "greater effort" made to achieve "some sort of group improvisation than one hears in John Coltrane's records". He concludes, "Joe Harriott's many admirers will no doubt enjoy every groove of this LP. Those who can't take Free Form [here Dawbarn is referring to the approach, not to Harriott's previous album of that name] will still find enough good jazz to justify the expense" (Dawbarn 1964, 10).

Dawbarn struggled with the new music and his review reveals an honest and fair-minded attempt to get to grips with Harriott's approach. In the issue of 22 February 1965, Bob Houston gave *High Spirits* a favourable review, even if he felt that the musical score, by Hugh Martin and Timothy Gray and based on Noel Coward's *Blithe Spirit*, "did not deserve the undivided attention of Harriott's Quintet, probably the finest group on the British scene at the moment" (Houston 1965, 14). In 1966, veteran jazz critic Max Jones wrote a favourable piece on Harriott's new venture with Indian composer John Mayer under the title "Harriott Yielding Ground to the East" (Jones 1966, 4), while Bob Houston gave his approval to the album in his review later that month (Houston 1966, 12). The following year saw a similar review of the double quintet's second album, *Indo-Jazz Fusions* (Houston 1967, 14). *Jazz Monthly* also provided an extremely in-depth and supportive survey of Harriott's approach in one of its 1965 issues (Martin 1965, 2–4). So the *Melody Maker* was not alone in lending encouragement to Harriott's efforts.

More than that, Harriott featured in the *Melody Maker* polls every year without fail up to 1970. In several years he came top in the British "alto" category – 1960, 1961, 1962, 1964, 1965, 1967, 1968, 1969. His quintet came fifth in the "small combo/small group" category in 1960, fourth in 1961, third in 1962, second in 1963, sixth in 1964, second in 1965, sixth in 1966 and seventh in 1968. He came fifth in the "musician of the year category" in 1960, fifth in 1961, third in 1962, fourth in 1963, seventh in 1964, fourth in 1965, seventh in 1966, fourth in 1967 and third in 1968. Readers picked *Indo-Jazz Suite* as their album of the year in 1967, the first year the magazine had had this category, and in 1968 *Indo-Jazz Fusions* came second. Shake Keane also featured regularly in the *Melody Maker* polls during these years, as did Coleridge Goode in 1960, 1962, 1963, 1964 and 1965.

Joe Harriott may have received less recognition than he deserved, but it does appear that this was more the case in the later stages of his life and career. Michael Garrick, for one, did much to keep his flame alive long before Courtney Pine and other members of the Jazz Warriors were in a position to remind British fans of his contribution. The evidence, in fact, suggests that Harriott was far from ignored, by either fans or critics, between 1960 and 1969. The issue regarding his supposed neglect invariably focuses on the free form work. But it has to be remembered that there was no context in Britain for this approach. It was literally ahead of its time. We have seen that, in 1961, Coltrane met with an astonishingly negative response to music that was far from "free form" and never played the UK again. The British press and music fans did not really latch on to the American new wave of Archie Shepp, Cecil Taylor, Charles Lloyd and Ornette Coleman until the mid-sixties. Coleman did not appear in the UK until 1965, when he played the Fairfield Halls, Croydon with the Mike Taylor Quartet as support, and records released stateside often did not find a British release until much later. When Archie Shepp and others began to be heard and later seen in the UK, they met with a very upbeat response from fans and writers. The *Melody Maker* was quite vociferous in its support for the new music.

By that time, however, Harriott had moved on. A prophet definitely but surely not one entirely without honour in his own country and among his own kin. Given the period when Harriott made his free form jazz, he was alone in this and there are no other players – black or white – with whom he can be compared. British free jazz did not begin to be heard until several years later and, while Hilary Moore is correct that the new wave of free players did not perhaps acknowledge him as an influence, she is incorrect in ascribing this to their being "far more indebted to American models". The sources of inspiration and motivations for musicians such as John Stevens, Tony Oxley, Evan Parker, Derek Bailey, Barry Guy, Howard Riley, Eddie Prévost, Keith Rowe and others lay neither in America nor in Harriott's experiments. We will examine this further in later chapters, though I would suggest that the freeing up of the drummer's role (in particular in Phil Seamen's work with the Harriott quintet) was an important development upon which John Stevens certainly built. We should, nevertheless, share Moore's regret it has taken us so long but now at least, albeit too late for Harriott, we recognize his vision.

Harriott's work with Indian composer and violinist John Mayer remains another important part of his legacy. At the same time, there is a nagging feeling that here the credit that he is given for the *Indo-Jazz Fusions* project might more rightly belong to Mayer. For example, the first record in their partnership, *Indo-Jazz Suite* from 1966 (Columbia; Rhino), is credited to "The Joe Harriott Double Quintet under the direction of John Mayer". It is worth telling the whole story about how this pairing came about, as it tells us a lot about the workings of the record business.

John Mayer had come to the UK to study and hopefully pursue his compositional ambitions. He had to cut short his studies at the Royal Academy of Music due to finance problems but, through a friend, secured an audition with the London Philharmonic Orchestra and landed the position of first violin, later moving to the Royal Philharmonic. Despite the fact that he had not completed his degree, the desire to compose still consumed him and even then he had this idea of fusing the musical techniques of India and the West.

In fact, long before he and Joe Harriott crossed paths, Mayer had achieved real success in this area. He wrote pieces for two of the most famous classical clarinettists of the day, Jack Bramwell and John McCaw. Of more significance, however, was the support of the composer/conductor Malcolm Arnold, who provided an introduction to Yehudi Menuhin. Menuhin performed but sadly never recorded John's unaccompanied Violin Sonata, but the patronage certainly helped. Adrian Boult, then conductor of the London Philharmonic Orchestra, included his *Raga Jai Javanti*, while two subsequent compositions – *Nine Raga Pieces* and *Dances of India* were also performed by leading UK orchestras. Denis Preston also produced Mayer's *Shanta Quintet Sitar and Strings* between the recording of the second and third Indo-Jazz albums with the Lansdowne String Quartet, which also featured on the Harriott *Personal Portrait* sessions (interview with John Mayer, June 2001; see also Hunt 2004).

By the early sixties, he had been chasing Dennis Preston for a while to record some of his music but with little success. Finally, a letter came. Preston was doing a record for Atlantic's Ahmet Ertegun and they needed a three-minute track to complete the album. The session featured Humphrey Lyttelton, Don Lusher and Kenny Baker, among others, and Preston needed a piece scored for trombones, flutes, trumpet and percussion. Asked if he had anything suitable, John told the author, "I sat up all night and wrote this piece "Nine for Bacon". I got £20, which was a hell of a lot of money in those days." A short while later, another letter arrived saying that Preston wanted to see him. Initially, Mayer says that he thought that they wanted their money back. However, Ertegun had liked the track and he and Preston were now suggesting a collaboration between John and Jamaican saxophonist, Joe Harriott. As Mayer points out, "I'd been telling him all the time, I wanted to make a fusion of Indian and Western techniques but Denis Preston had always dismissed it. Now he was saying, 'We have had this idea.' I said, 'What a marvellous idea!'" (interview with John Mayer, June 2001).

With no knowledge of jazz, Mayer was forced to learn as much as he could about the music before the project commenced. While Indian music has its own improvising tradition, it is as Mayer described it, "a disciplined improvisation". Musicians improvise on scales or ragas but the improvisation must begin and end on the first note of the scale. There is also no harmony or counterpoint as such in Indian music and this added to the challenge of bringing together these radically different traditions. Mayer dealt with this by scoring everything and then providing the jazz musicians in the band with the notes on which they would build their solos.

The group gave its first public performance at the Chichester Festival in 1965 and were an instant success. Asked why he thought this unique fusion struck such a chord with audiences, Mayer noted simply, "I think God smiled on us," he replied. "Forgive me if I sound boastful but this was the first attempt to bring these two musics together in a coherent manner." At the same time, it is clear that the sixties had ushered in a greater openness and the Beatles and others had also helped to make a younger generation aware of the musics of the East. That combined with the uniqueness of this musical project is perhaps explanation enough for its success.

Alan Robertson is correct in his assertion that *Abstract* and *Free Form* were Harriott's great achievements. To these, I would add *Hum Dono* and *Movement*. But all three Indo-Jazz albums remain filled with some wonderful music. To some, and Robertson quotes from a Graham Collier piece in Crescendo and from a Michael James' review in *Jazz Monthly*, the affair was less than the sum of its parts (Robertson 2003, 165 and 168). Harriott plays himself throughout, changing his usual approach little if at all for the context. Mayer puts this rather neatly when he recalls, "Joe was a stalwart jazz musician who played in his own jazz tradition. He'd say, 'I don't know anything about Indian music. I just play what you write.' Like a tree, you couldn't budge him" (interview with John Mayer, June 2001).

Perhaps, the music might have first struck a chord due to its exotic nature. Yet, it is these strange juxtapositions between Occident and Orient, between the rhythms of jazz and those of Indian music and between two very different improvisational traditions that give it both its sense of movement and tension. The expectation that these should somehow resolve themselves into a kind of synthesis seems a peculiarly dull notion. Indeed, the work of Japanese composer Toru Takemitsu is another example of music gaining its dynamic from the tension between Eastern and Western influences. In fact, music can unfold like a journey, flow like a river or grow ever upwards like a tree.

Shake Keane does not play on *Indo-Jazz Suite* and nor does Coleridge Goode. Rick Laird (later with Mahavishnu) plays bass, while Eddie Blair is on trumpet. Both play extremely well and Blair is quite magnificent on "Raga Megha" and "Raga Gaud-Saranga". "Overture", which opens side 1, was entirely scored and is perhaps one of Mayer's finest compositions with some fine rhythm playing from Laird and drummer Alan Ganley. Indian music might be lacking in harmony but Mayer makes intriguing use of counterpoint and counter rhythm. It is swing alright, just not as we previously knew it.

Hilary Moore makes a fine point in relating this project to Harriott's involvement with poetry and jazz and his work with John Mayer:

> Although Harriott participated in, rather than pioneered, *Indo-Jazz Fusions* and the jazz-poetry initiative, it is striking that both projects involved blending jazz with marginalised discourses from beyond US borders. In different ways, they both redefined the assumed parameters of jazz performance and challenged its established aesthetic underpinnings. (Moore 2007, 93)

The music still sounds uncanny and one cannot imagine this collaboration coming about except in the sixties, with "Contrasts" perhaps the most completely satisfying piece on the record in its mix of scored and improvised sections. Jazz and its fans have a tendency to prize long solos by its players but here each musician is pithy and apposite in their statements. Pianist Pat Smythe draws out a delightful and even eccentric solo on this piece, while Harriott plays as if its structure were not there. It is well-titled – contrast is what it is all about.

"Partita", the long opening piece on the second *Indo-Jazz Fusions* released in 1967 (Columbia), is not perhaps quite as satisfying compositionally. Mayer seems to have tried to put too much into the number. The playing, however, is magnificent. Harriott seems re-awakened with the return of Shake Keane and there's a wonderful sense of the "old firm" reunited. The difference is that where Eddie Blair played his part beautifully, Keane knows exactly where Harriott is heading and picks up at the end of his solos as if there is no separation between them. The Indian musicians, sitarist Diwan Motihar especially so, play as if they are on fire, while Mayer's violin is equally incandescent. Over-complicated perhaps, but truly exciting as well. The other long track, "Multani", is stronger compositionally, and its use of texture and rhythm is fascinating, not least in the duet between Ganley and tabla player Keshav Sathe. Both "Gana" and "Acka Raga" succeed in packing a great deal of music into their two minutes plus, while the latter with some gorgeous flute from Chris Taylor will be familiar to anyone who remembers the British TV quiz show, "Ask The Family". Joe Harriott's "Subject" from the *Abstract* LP closes the record in a wonderfully structured arrangement from Mayer, yet remains unmistakeably Harriott's original tune. Coleridge Goode's bass playing is quite amazing here, as ever, in its authority, while Pat Smythe takes one of his finest solos in any context. This is probably the place to start for anyone wanting to discover what the fuss was about.

Indo-Jazz Fusions II from the following year (Columbia) is just as good. In fact, there is an even greater sense of integration in the music, even though one senses that Harriott misses his sparring partner in Shake Keane. Kenny Wheeler is an admirable replacement, however, and Pat Smythe again succeeds in making his instrument sound like something far more esoteric than a well-tempered clavier. Chris Taylor, a classical flautist and colleague of Mayer's from the Royal Philharmonic Orchestra, is the real revelation here. He is clearly not a jazz improviser but the way he attacks his solos is astonishing and enchanting. One has to listen carefully to hear Coleridge Goode's bass but the lines that he contributes seem to bridge the east–west divide perfectly. There is so much to enjoy here, whether it is Mayer's forays on violin, the drama that both Wheeler and Harriott bring to proceedings or the sense that something quite unworldly is happening before one's ears. The record also includes "'Song' Before 'Sunrise'", another highly successful and ethereal Mayer composition and the darkly hued, easy-swinging "Mishra Blues".

Mayer continued the group after Harriott's departure, though he later said that his heart was no longer really in it. That comment aside, readers may wish to listen to *Indo Jazz Etudes* recorded in 1969 for the Swedish Sonet label. It is a beautiful record with Tony Coe on tenor sax and clarinet in place of Harriott and playing quite magnificently. John Marshall is on drums, Ian Hamer on trumpet with Viram Jasani replacing Chandrahas Paigankar on tambura and providing additional sitar and tabla. Otherwise, the group is unchanged. The music is quite exquisite, with the long "Serenade" with its gorgeous violin from Mayer a stand-out performance in all respects.

Some years ago, the author interviewed John Mayer and asked him about Joe Harriott. Comparing his response to comments expressed to Kevin Le Gendre and those contained in Alan Robertson's biography, time had clearly mellowed the violinist's views. "He was a marvellous saxophonist and a marvellous character," he explained. "People say he was difficult but I didn't find that at all. It might have helped that there was no competition. I was a composer and I wasn't trying to show what a fine fiddle player I was. And I always gave full credit to him for the band" (interview with John Mayer, June 2001). Yet, as Robertson notes, drummer John Marshall, tabla player Keshav Sathe and Coleridge Goode all recall Mayer losing his temper with Harriott on a number of occasions. It is clear that Harriott was a difficult personality. He drank heavily, chain-smoked, was not good with money and was a serial womanizer. He fathered four children by different women, two of whom never met their father.

Harriott did deserve better than a death in a Southampton hospital from lung cancer. It was true he had been scuffling for the last few years of his life, homeless and not far off destitute. If Shake Keane's assessment of Harriott as a troubled, flawed individual is right, it is hard to believe it could have been different. But the saddest tale of Harriott's end took place in St Ives on 24 January 1971 – two years before he died.

Goudie Charles, a bass player and one-time guitarist, is a man whose own life has intersected with a number of legends – he gave pianist-composer Mike Taylor his first gig and played gigs himself with Graham Bond as well as with Alexis Korner's Blues Incorporated when Charlie Watts was on drums. Charles got to know Harriott in the late fifties and kept in touch until the bassist quit London for a coastal retreat. Charles told the author how he met the altoist one last time.

> At the end of his life he couldn't buy a gig in London. He was reduced to trolling round the country. I think by then he was ill and he obviously had a lot of personality problems by then. He ended up in Cornwall eventually and he was playing with a local dance band just playing waltzes and foxtrots and I bumped into him and said, "Let's organize a jazz gig." So, we organized one in Penzance. It was guitar, bass, drums and Joe on alto and he was absolutely magnificent.

Sadly, attempts to tape the session were unsuccessful. Charles continued:

> I think that was the last jazz performance he ever gave. He played
> absolutely beautifully. It was all standards. A lot of the numbers we
> were doing were from Kris's [Charles' singer wife] book because
> the bass player was from her first group. And, of course, being
> a singer everything was in a different key but Joe just whizzed
> through them as if they were in the usual key. He was brilliant.
>   (Interview with Goudie Charles, February 2008)

According to Charles, prior to the gig, there had been an altercation between
Harriott and the session's drummer over who was the greatest alto player.
The drummer had said, "Charlie Parker" and, in Charles's words, "Joe
grabbed him by the coat and slammed him against the bar wall and said, 'I
am and don't you fucking forget it.'" Harriott was staying at the time with a
local artist and his wife. The couple were quite well-off and had a nanny. As
Goudie told me:

> Alan and his wife went out to do some shopping one afternoon
> and Joe made advances on the Swedish au pair and it actually
> ended up front page in the local paper. He got fined. He was very
> lucky actually – a black guy in Cornwall at that time who'd gone
> for a white lady? He got fined £20, I think, and bound over or
> whatever they call it. Funny thing they printed his name through-
> out the thing as "Joe Herriott – the well-known jazz musician".
>   (Interview with Goudie Charles, February 2008)

Actually, the young woman's name was Linda Rumbold and Harriott was
fined £25 for "maliciously wounding" her. It was stated in court that Harriott
had punched and kicked her, and that photos shown to the bench revealed
cuts and bruises on the inside of her mouth, lips and face, and bruises and
abrasions on her arms and one of her legs. Harriott is quoted as telling the
magistrates, "I can only repeat how sorry I am. I think I was goaded on in this
matter" (*St Ives Times and Echo* 1971, 1).

This story seems to reveal a sorry picture of a troubled and bitter man.
It was not an isolated example and, in the second edition of his biography,
Alan Robertson gives others involving the saxophonist's abusiveness towards
women (Robertson 2011). There can be no doubt that Joe Harriott experienced the racist behaviour that was sadly commonplace in Britain at the
time. It may well have been the case that the attitudes of some on the jazz
scene may have been unacceptable and even tainted by racism. It might be
that such experiences affected his behaviour in ways that, in turn, led him to
be seen as "difficult". However, in relation to his misogyny, we see Harriott as
a man and not as a "black man". Why then should we imply that responses

towards him resulted from his being a black musician in a predominantly white scene? The implications behind such assumptions are very clear, indeed.

It remains hard to square the impression of Harriott as a victim of discrimination, or of anything at all, with what we know about him as a person. On balance, one would have to share Shake Keane's assessment of him as a man: that his life would not end well. Attempts to turn him into a martyr do not just do British jazz a disservice; they do the man and his art a grave injustice as well by denying him the right to be seen as what he was – a remarkable musician but also a flawed human being. Harriott did get plenty of opportunities to pursue his musical aims and to fulfil them. His records stand as his monument and they are now being recognized for the significant works that they are, just as he is, once again, being acknowledged as one of the most, if not the most, talented artists to emerge from the British scene. That is how he should be remembered.

9 A Race Apart

Let us all hope that the dark clouds of racial prejudice will soon pass away, and that in some not too distant tomorrow the radiant stars of love and brotherhood will shine over our great nation with all their scintillating beauty.

Martin Luther King, "Letter from a Birmingham Jail", 16 April 1963

Lukewarm acceptance is more bewildering than outright rejection. *Ibid.*

Before continuing to look at the careers of a number of other important musicians, including Harry Beckett, Kenny Wheeler, the Blue Notes and others who came to Britain to work in the fifties and sixties, we need to examine the context of immigration in Britain. We need to know how and why these patterns emerge and how they have arisen in a British context. Most importantly, we need to acknowledge that immigration from the Caribbean, African and Asian parts of the Commonwealth was viewed very differently by those in government and by sections of the indigenous population to immigration from the "white dominions". These themes have all been touched upon in the previous chapter. We now need to understand what this meant in practice and how it might have impacted on British jazz.

Individuals are generally motivated to migrate, often leaving behind family and all that is familiar to take a leap into the dark, by a number of factors. They may want to escape poverty, hoping for a materially more satisfactory and secure existence. They may be escaping persecution or oppression or, in some cases, they may be forced to move as happened in the case of the Ugandan Asians in 1972. But the process requires additional factors to result in significant population migrations. In general, when migrants migrate in large numbers they do so to countries with which they are in some important way connected. Often, that connection comes through imperialism.

The establishment by the major seafaring nations of Europe – Britain, France, Spain, Germany, Portugal and Holland – of colonies in Asia, Africa,

Australasia and the Americas from the sixteenth century onwards created a series of migrations from the northern hemisphere. These empires needed administrators, commercial enterprises needed managers and colonial rule needed to be maintained by military force, if necessary. J.A. Tannahill notes that "Britain is not by tradition a country of immigration." One might dispute that point. However, the following points are important:

> Between 1815 and 1914, she not only quadrupled her population without resorting to large-scale foreign immigration, but also despatched over 20 million people to destinations beyond Europe, at first largely to the USA and later in ever increasing proportion to the developing countries of the Commonwealth.
>
> (Tannahill 1958, 1)

The drive behind these ambitions was clearly economic and geo-political in nature, both in terms of extending the nation's power base, securing raw materials and new markets. Like many of the nations of Europe and the North Atlantic, the level of prosperity Britain experiences today still owes much to those centuries of colonial expansion. It was through Britain's colonies that political and economic ties were forged with people across four continents. In the case of the Caribbean islands, Britain forced the migration from Africa of populations to work on sugar and tobacco plantations. With the abolition of slavery, those people remained and were linked to Britain first through Empire and later through Commonwealth. These were not the only people Britain caused to uproot and leave their homes. Many of the Asians in East Africa (Uganda, Tanzania and Kenya) and South Africa were brought to these areas as indentured labourers from British India to undertake clerical or manual labour, such as the Indians who worked on the Kenya–Uganda railway.

During the Second World War, many people came from the white, black and Asian colonies to serve in the forces or fill labour vacancies. Alongside these individuals came the Free French, Irish, Dutch and Poles, while Jews escaping the Nazis also came in significant numbers. Some would return home after the war but for others, Poles and German Jews for example, their countries had been occupied by the Soviet Union and many had no wish to go back under such circumstances (see Conway 2007, 62). Tannahill gives the following figures:

> Whereas in 1939 there had been only about 239,000 aliens over the age of 16 in the United Kingdom (of whom ... about 80,000 were refugees) this figure had, by December 1950, been increased to 424,329. The increase of roughly 200,000 was the net gain from the admittance in these years of approximately 250,000 aliens.
>
> (Tannahill 1958, 5)

David Conway states in *A Nation of Immigrants? – A Brief Demographic History of Britain* (2007) that some 100,000 Poles had served in the Polish Air Force and were offered permanent residence after the Second World War and were joined by 30,000 dependants. There was a further group of 17,000 nationals of countries against which Britain had fought in the war who were only temporarily admitted. They comprised 10,000 Sudeten German women, 2,000 Austrian women, and 5,000 Italians of both sexes. Most of this group subsequently returned home. A number of prisoners of war were also to be found in Britain in the final years of the conflict. Initially, the majority of these were Italians. By 1944, there were 150,000 Italian prisoners of war in camps throughout the UK. With the Normandy landings and military success in north Africa, increasing numbers of German soldiers needed to be removed from the theatre of war. By 1945, there were over 400,000 Axis prisoners housed in over 500 prisoner of war camps throughout the British Isles (see Thomas 2003; Moore 2005; Overmans 2005).

Many of these prisoners were put to work in agriculture and Bob Moore (2005) suggests that one reason for the slow progress of repatriation after the cessation of hostilities was the ongoing need for labour in the industry. The last Axis soldiers to be returned left the UK around 1948/9. Some, however, had met British women and chose to stay and build lives here. Other Europeans – Ukrainians, Latvians and Poles, for example – had fought for the Nazis. Facing the prospect of death if they went home, some of these individuals were allowed to remain. In itself, war creates migrations, whether through the mobilization of armies or through the creation of refugees. No precise figures exist for the numbers of displaced persons at the end of the Second World War but estimates vary from 11 million to as many as 20 million. For many people, including returning soldiers, life would never be quite the same again. According to Conway some 85,000 plus displaced eastern Europeans were in Britain at the end of the war and were to remain here (Conway 2007, 69).

In addition, the war itself was also a cause of future migration. As Conway points out, "However, unknowingly at the time, those whom the war brought to Britain from overseas were preparing the ground for a large wave of immigration from many of Britain's former colonies who began to arrive there not long after hostilities ceased in 1945" (Conway 2007, 63). He then quotes James Walvin: "It was of course impossible to realize it at the time, but the war was ultimately responsible for many of the demographic changes which took place in Britain in the post-war years" (Walvin 1984, 27).

Conway might be writing within the "classical liberal" political perspective of the Civitas think-tank for whom he works, a perspective that is far from value-free on this or other issues, but the figures he uses are derived from several sources. He notes in relation to the next waves of immigration – first from the Caribbean and later from India and Bangladesh – that not only did these people face "unpropitious economic conditions in their countries of origin" but there was in addition "an acute labour shortage in Britain during the latter part of the 1950s which prompted public and private sector employers to recruit directly from these two regions" (Conway 2007, 70). Asians, for example, were recruited to work in the mill towns of Yorkshire and Lancashire.

During and after the Second World War, the causes of immigration lay in the requirement, for humanitarian and strategic reasons, of housing the displaced, whether those in this situation were moving voluntarily or out of necessity. After the war, the driving force became economic. Rebuilding Europe's shattered economies and meeting the repayment of debts acquired due to the hostilities was the major task for the northern hemisphere. This in itself created a demand for labour outside existing sources. While the deaths of British citizens and soldiers were small, when compared to the Soviets or to Germany, nearly half a million Britons had died between 1939 and 1945.

Immigration in the post-war period was a fit, therefore, between the economic needs of Britain and the desire of the migrants to improve their circumstances. We can add to the numbers of those that came some 50,000 Chinese, 50,000 Greek Cypriots and 11,000 Turkish Cypriots fleeing the conflict at home (they too were linked to Britain through its annexation of Cyprus in 1914), 100,000 Italians and 40,000 Maltese (a British colony since 1814; Conway 2007, 78). However, if one tries to discover how many Australians, white South Africans, Rhodesians (Zimbabweans), Canadians and New Zealanders or, for that matter, white Americans came to live and work in Britain during these years, it is extremely hard to find figures. The National Archives hold all manner of government documents, including Cabinet papers and others relating to the Foreign Office and the Commonwealth Relations Office. Without exception these focus on "coloured immigration", which is frequently referred to as a "problem" or a "social problem". There is, for example, a paper headed "Colonial immigrants" (C. (57) 162; Kilmuir 1957), which was a secret document prepared to brief ministers on the desirability and potential for legislation restricting the right of Commonwealth citizens, or rather certain Commonwealth citizens, to enter the UK and be treated as British subjects. This principle based on common law had been enshrined in the British Nationality and Status of Aliens Act 1914.

The paper notes that "the coloured community" in Britain had increased by more than 40,000. It even provides an ethnic breakdown of these figures. Nowhere are the numbers of white Commonwealth immigrants noted or recorded. Would that the comments in the document spoke only of a bygone age but these quotations clearly illustrate its tone.

> There has been a steady influx of Indians and Pakistanis, amounting in total to some 9,000 in 1956, though many of these are students who will ultimately return home. However, many others are illiterate and of low social standing.

Taking an optimistic view of the situation, the rate of coloured immigration has fallen considerably compared with last year and although the number of new arrivals has lately tended to rise slightly there is at present no cause for alarm. For the most part the coloured immigrants are law-abiding, tend to keep to themselves, and form a useful addition to the country's labour force, particularly as most of them are young people.

On a more pessimistic assessment, a continuing increase in the coloured population of some 2,000 a month, including more than 1,000 West Indians, is still substantial enough to give rise to problems and to justify misgivings. The present reasonably amicable relations between the white and the coloured population might not long survive the onset of an industrial recession leading to competition for employment. But perhaps the most disturbing element in the situation is the transformation, in some areas, of whole streets into completely "black" streets.   (Kilmuir 1957)

Following the implementation of the Commonwealth Immigrants Act 1962, legislation that distinguished between the "white Dominions" and the coloured Commonwealth countries, the Cabinet was briefed on the workings of the legislation. "Operation of the Immigration Control under the Commonwealth immigrants Act – Memorandum by the Secretary of State for the Home Department" (CP. (64) 89; Brooke 1964) states:

In the period just before the control started, net immigration from the Commonwealth (excluding the "white Dominions") was running at a rate of 100,000 to 150,000 a year. Between 1st July, 1962, and 29th February, 1964, net immigration from the whole Commonwealth was 78,000, and net immigration from the predominantly coloured parts of the Commonwealth (excluding the "white Dominions") was 72,000: this is the equivalent of a net rate of coloured immigration of about 44,000 a year. The average figure conceals a wide fluctuation from one period to another, quite apart from the seasonal movement of people from the "white Dominions".

It continues:

The control is only at the port of entry, and is designed to avoid inconvenience to genuine visitors and students from the Commonwealth. The arrangements made for them, including the "working holidaymakers" from the "white Dominions", have worked well.   (Brooke 1964)

The figures included with this memorandum are too complex for analysis here. They do show, however, that people from the "white Dominions" were less likely to stay in the UK, but that some certainly did do so. For example, in 1963 of the 190,000 people arriving in the UK from Canada, Australia and New Zealand some 8,500 remained in the UK as opposed to returning home. However, whether or not there was a net immigration from the white Commonwealth was not a major concern for the British government. White immigration, at least until very recently, has been invisible and it is hard to find figures for American, white or black, immigration. Readers will note that there were a number of US Air Force bases in Britain at that time as well as a large number of companies that were American-owned. The figures in CP. (64) 89 (Brooke 1964) also reveal that a much higher percentage of applications for the voucher scheme introduced by the 1962 Act from the "coloured Commonwealth" were refused than was the case with the "white Dominions". It probably was the case that young Anzacs and Canucks would return home in due course but then they had much more materially awaiting them there.

It is a fact that Australian immigrants, in particular, contributed a great deal to British culture and to the "counter-culture" in the sixties immigrants. They came in part to study but also because Australia was, if anything, even more culturally conservative than Britain at that time. The list includes actor–comedian Barry Humphries; writers Richard Neville, Jim Anderson, Jill Neville, Germaine Greer and Clive James; artists Martin Sharp, Arthur Boyd, Brett Whitely and Philippe Mora; art critic Robert Hughes; writer, and later co-founder of *Spare Rib*, Marsha Rowe; and film director Bruce Beresford. It was, however, comparatively easy for these individuals to move into influential circles such as the media because they were white, educated and drew on the same Anglo-Saxon cultural framework as their British (and American) peers.

The experience for people coming from Asia, the Caribbean and Africa was, as we have seen very different. They were a "social problem". Their employment was a "problem", their housing was a "problem", their education was a "problem" and so forth. The huge contribution to British culture of these groups has, therefore, to be seen not in the welcoming, accommodating context experienced by those from the white Dominions but against a climate that saw their presence here as "problematic" and which had to be addressed by ever more restrictive legislation. Again, it is worth bearing in mind that many of those who made great contributions to British jazz might not have been allowed to come to Britain or remain in the country. The same would probably have been true of the parents and grandparents of musicians like Courtney Pine, Gary Crosby, Denys Baptiste, Dennis Rollins and the Mondesir brothers.

It is perhaps worth contrasting the careers of two of the finest trumpeters to grace our music – Barbadian Harry Beckett and Canadian Kenny Wheeler – if only to remind ourselves that a number of immigrants from the white

Dominions also contributed to British jazz. Indeed, of all the fine trumpeters to play and record here in the sixties – Jimmy Deuchar, Mongezi Feza, Henry Lowther, Dave Holdsworth, Eddie Blair, Shake Keane and many others – the three who have made the most substantial contributions and built major bodies of work are Ian Carr, Harry Beckett and Kenny Wheeler. That two of the three were immigrants seems significant in this context.

Harry Beckett came to Britain in 1954. Reference books give his date of birth as 30 May 1935, but the order of service for his funeral in July 2010 gives the date as 24 April 1924. His wife Veronica told Steve Voce, "He was really 86, but he always knocked the years off. He told me it was because he thought if they knew his age nobody would want to hire him because he was too old." Voce adds that "Beckett occasionally had difficulty when asked to show his passport because the date of birth on it had been defaced" (Voce 2010). Beckett had studied music informally in Barbados but as he told the author a few years before his death, "I came over here to study. I got private studies from here and there from other players. I kept studying with different people. So, I became a studious person eventually [laughing] and it just became a habit. I'm still studying" (interview with Harry Beckett, June 2008).

Kenny Wheeler, on the other hand, was a music student at Toronto Conservatory before moving to the UK in 1952. In Britain, he also had lessons in composition with Richard Rodney Bennett and in counterpoint with American composer–arranger Bill Russo, who lived in London in the early sixties. Wheeler worked in the dance band of Roy Fox, then in Vic Lewis's big band before joining the Dankworth orchestra in 1959. It was with Dankworth that Wheeler began writing and arranging. For a few months in 1967, Wheeler was unable to work due to a problem with a wisdom tooth. Dankworth suggested he write an album for the band and the trumpeter jumped at the chance. As Dankworth told John Robert Brown:

> So once, when he was at his lowest, I said, "Kenny, when you get better, make an album, do all the arrangements. Feature yourself only in it, and we'll do it." So, we did it. There were such a lot of people in it; I've forgotten who they all were. John McLaughlin was on guitar. Mike Gibbs was playing in the trombone section. Dave Holland, who played with Miles Davis, was the bass player. I insisted that Ken did all the soloing, because he was very retiring, but I forced him to, and there was only one place where he insisted on me taking a solo. The tenor player Tony Roberts did the only other solo.   (Brown 2007, 13–17)

Windmill Tilter (Fontana; BGO) is one of the finest British jazz albums of all time and a great big band record. It is incredible how wonderfully mature and distinctive the trumpeter's compositional voice was even then. There's a richness and concern with texture that has remained Wheeler's hallmark ever since. Two tracks – "Sweet Dulcinea Blue" and "Propheticape" – feature a quintet of Wheeler, Tony Coe, John McLaughlin, Dave Holland and John Spooner, a source of contrast the trumpeter would repeat later with *Music For Large & Small Ensembles* (ECM). The other seven pieces contain some truly remarkable orchestral writing. Dankworth's memory is slightly at fault above; it was Tony Coe who was the other main soloist in the orchestral settings, with a brief and gorgeous solo from Dankworth on "Bachelor Sam" and a trombone solo from Chris Pyne on the Gil Evans-like "Don the Dreamer". The arrangements carry the soloist, whether it is Wheeler himself, Coe, Dankworth or Pyne and it is that which makes this so very special. Intriguingly, Wheeler was thirty-eight by this time and this is his first release under his own name. He was once asked what had held him back. His reply speaks volumes about his shyness and social awkwardness.

> So, I was a late starter. I suppose nerves – being afraid, that kind of thing which I've never completely got rid of. They went away but they seem to be coming back. I'm not sure what to do about that. I think that some of the older guys took drugs to get rid of that but I don't want to go down that road. I'll just have to hope they go away again.   (Interview with Kenny Wheeler, October 2005)

Harry Beckett's progress was even slower but was aided by his playing on the soundtrack of the 1961 film *All Night Long* with an ensemble led by Charles Mingus (Beckett also has a cameo role in the film.) As he told me:

> I had originally planned to go to the States. But when I got here I met so many beautiful musicians who were willing to help me that I stayed. I listened to people like Joe Harriott, these great players on the radio, and Geoffrey Hutchinson – I met him eventually. He was a beautiful trumpet player. I listened to all these people like Kenny Wheeler. I was just a nobody then.
> (Interview with Harry Beckett, June 2008)

Like most jazz musicians, throughout his career Beckett took whatever work came his way. He did bluebeat and rock sessions, played with Guyanese singer Frank Holder's sextet in a Mayfair night club and depped regularly with Ken McIntosh's dance orchestra at the Hammersmith Palais. It was, however, his association with Mingus and Mingus's admiration of Beckett's playing that made other British musicians take notice. As he told the author:

> I wasn't really a jazz trumpeter in Britain, I was a trumpeter learning to play jazz. It was one of those lucky things that happen. At the time, nobody really took any notice but these other musicians

saw me doing this thing with Mingus. Harold McNair and Jackie Dougan were involved. Mingus played piano and bass. So, these people got to know about me.

(Interview with Harry Beckett, June 2008)

It was not surprising that it was Mingus fan and bassist–composer Graham Collier who was the first to hire Beckett. In fact, Beckett played on just about every Collier album or tour since. The trumpeter was soon a regular at The Old Place playing with Mike Osborne, John Surman and Chris McGregor. He played in Surman's octet and in Osborne's quintet, and worked on the remarkable series of records made by guitarist Ray Russell between 1969 and 1973.

Beckett made his first LP, *Flare Up* (Philips; Jazzprint) in 1970 by which time he was "officially" thirty-five but in truth forty-seven. It featured an octet that included saxophonists John Surman, Mike Osborne and Alan Skidmore, pianist John Taylor, bassist Chris Laurence, drummer John Webb and vibraphonist Frank Ricotti. With Taylor on Fender Rhodes for much of the album it has a strong feel of the period but this is vibrant, propulsive music with four tunes contributed by Graham Collier, Surman's "Where Fortune Smiles" – in perhaps its finest incarnation – and with the other four tunes coming from Beckett. "Third Road" offers one of those lovely, loping blues that almost typified Collier's small groups of the time with marvellous vibes from Ricotti, sinuous soprano from Surman and some glorious playing from Beckett. Beckett's "Flow Stream Flow" has a strong Caribbean lilt to it and Osborne's gritty alto contrasts well with Beckett's supremely assured flugelhorn. The range of tones that Beckett could draw from his horn can be heard on Collier's "The Other Side" and there's a tenderness to his flugelhorn here that reflects the man. Beckett's "Fool's Play" may be the best piece of writing and arranging on the album and it closes the set perfectly. If the record has any shortcoming, it lies in its rather muddy sound. That reservation aside, it is an astonishing debut.

Warm Smiles (RCA; Vocalion) came out in 1971 with the same team as *Flare Up* but with Skidmore and Surman, the latter now working extensively with The Trio with bassist Barre Phillips and drummer Stu Martin, absent. It is even better. The tunes, all by Beckett, lend themselves to a continuity of form and style, while the smaller group seems to allow more space for solo contributions. John Taylor is particularly strong on the lovely ballad "Tender is the Sky", but the rhythm section of John Webb and Chris Laurence also comes into its own. The opening track "Harambee" is a lively, yet loose and flowing piece graced by a long Beckett solo that pours with invention. "To Me, for Me", a jazz waltz that allows both Beckett and Taylor full rein, featuring a highly musical drum solo from Webb, closes side one of the record before the quartet becomes a sextet with the addition of Osborne and Ricotti. The title track is a very open, modal piece with some strange ambient voices in the background and has some fabulously lyrical playing from the altoist followed by a duet with Beckett's understated flugelhorn. *Warm Smiles* finishes with the Caribbean lilt of "Tomorrow Morning Early", nine minutes of unadulterated joy and great jazz. This record is close to flawless, and one just wonders what a truly great producer like Teo Macero or Manfred Eicher might have made out of it.

Themes for Fega from 1972 (RCA; Vocalion) completes a trio of exceptional recordings with a live performance at London's Institute Of Contemporary Arts, where Beckett had made *Live at the ICA* with Ray Russell's quintet a few months earlier. It reflects that same freer, more abstract approach. In the Spanish-sounding "Cry of Triumph" it includes Beckett's finest composition, a piece that would resurface on his later album with Kathy Stobart, *Arbela* (Spotlite). Featuring a septet with the return of Skidmore, this is an excellent and typically strong British jazz album of the period. Two more excellent albums, *Joy Unlimited* for John Jack's Cadillac label and *Memories of Bacares* made for Hazel and Harry Miller's Ogun imprint, followed both featuring Ray Russell.

Beckett's standing among other musicians was such that he was almost ubiquitous during these years and he played on some of the finest British jazz records of the time. These included John Surman's *How Many Clouds Can You See?* and (with John Warren) *Tales of the Algonquin*, Graham Collier's *Songs for my Father* and *Mosaics*, Mike Gibbs's *Just Ahead* and the first three Brotherhood of Breath releases, including their finest hour *Live at Willisau* (Ogun; Ogun). He also played on both Rock Workshop releases, on Jack Bruce's seminal *Songs for a Tailor* and with Keef Hartley, as well as cropping up on any number of sessions by pop and rock artists. It is no surprise that he became a father figure for a new generation of British–Caribbean musicians in the eighties and an essential member of the Jazz Warriors.

Kenny Wheeler's second LP was *Song for Someone* (Incus; psi) and was recorded for the independent label Incus set up and owned by saxophonist Evan Parker, guitarist Derek Bailey and drummer Tony Oxley. The record is an unusual one in a catalogue that is essentially devoted to free improvisation. It was made over two days, early in 1973 and quite consciously featured an orchestra that drew on both mainstream and *avant garde* musicians including the three directors of Incus. Once again, the approach was repeated later by Wheeler later in his career on the ECM double album, *Music for Large and Small Ensembles*. But *Song For Someone* also reflected the diversity of Wheeler's activities since the mid-sixties. He had become involved in the free jazz scene quite early on, playing with the SME on both *Challenge* (Eyemark; EMANEM) and *Karyobin* (Island), and perhaps even more significantly on Tony Oxley's *Baptised Traveller* (CBS; Columbia Sony) along with Parker and Bailey and bassist Jeff Clyne. As he recalled in 2005:

> I suppose the time when it first happened I was a bit frustrated
> musically. I wasn't getting many jazz gigs because bebop was very

prevalent in London and there were such fantastic bebop players – Tubby Hayes, Jimmy Deuchar and all them. I couldn't seem to find a niche for myself. I wasn't depressed. I just wanted to play. Then, I heard about these young guys who were playing at the Little Theatre Club. So, I went up there and listened. I didn't like it all what I heard but I went back a couple of nights and then they eventually said, "Do you want to sit in?" So, I did sit in and I just went quite berserk on the trumpet for about ten minutes and that's how they started to ask me to play with them. I've always sort of liked doing it but I could never say whether it was good or bad. I just found it very therapeutic to play with them.

(Interview with Kenny Wheeler, October 2005)

For Wheeler, melody and lyricism remained paramount and yet he found ways of playing and writing that incorporated elements from free music. On *Song for Someone*, both "Causes Are Events" and "The Good Doctor" have extended free passages, and the latter also features a trio improvisation from Bailey, Parker and Oxley. In the context of the more "traditional" big band arrangements of "Nothing Changes" with its delightful vocal from Norma Winstone or "Ballad Two" with its fine trombone solo from Chris Pyne, this juxtaposition comes as quite a shock.

From 1971–6, Wheeler also worked extensively with saxophonist Anthony Braxton in a quartet with Dave Holland and drummer Barry Altschul, as well as with pianist Alex von Schlippenbach's pan-European Globe Unity. Both involvements helped raise his profile internationally and may have drawn the intention of ECM owner–producer Manfred Eicher. Asked how his contract with that label came about, he noted first that Parker and Bailey were the first British musicians to record for the label:

I'm not actually certain but in the early days of ECM he was recording a lot of free improvisation with people like Derek Bailey and things like that that he was interested in. I've got a feeling that Evan and some of those people told him about me and said that he should record me. So that's why – I don't know for sure but I think that's why he asked me.

(Interview with Kenny Wheeler, October 2005)

That association led to a body of work that has grown over the years and includes albums like *Gnu High* with Keith Jarrett, *Deer Wan* with Jan Garbarek and the gorgeous *Angel Song* with Lee Konitz. Wheeler also played in several of Dave Holland's groups which recorded for ECM and was part of the much-loved Azimuth trio with Norma Winstone and John Taylor.

Beckett and Wheeler are perhaps the two most important trumpeters to emerge from the British sixties scene. Of the two, given his vast body of work for that major independent label ECM, Wheeler is understandably the more feted of the two. Yet the parallels between them remain very intriguing. They were both immigrants coming to Britain in the early fifties in search of work, and both were latecomers to band-leading and recording. Both played on many of the most important and highly regarded records of the late sixties and early seventies. They played both free and more straightahead modern jazz and both eschewed in their playing the more frantic, aggressive styles in favour of an approach that drew on lyricism and melody. Booker Little was an important influence on Wheeler, while Clifford Brown was a key figure for Beckett. As John Wickes points out in respect of both, "the influence of saxophonists, rather than trumpeters, predominates, resulting in an acute sense of timing that operates from moment to moment" (Wickes 1999, 75).

Leading on from this comment, we can hear that both men adapted to freer contexts more by breaking up or fragmenting their melodic lines and by bringing together apparently disconnected phrases than by resorting to the squeals and squawks sometimes associated with such music. They both played in jazz-rock contexts – Wheeler with Mike Gibbs, Nucleus and the United Rock & Jazz Ensemble, Beckett with Ray Russell, Nucleus, Gibbs and Keef Hartley. And finally, both were in considerable demand as session musicians, as well as in continental Europe.

Wheeler deserves every success that has come his way. If he and Beckett were equals as trumpeters, then the Canadian is the finer composer. We still have to note that studies in Toronto and with Bill Russo and Richard Rodney Bennett, working with Dankworth and the opportunities provided by ECM gave him considerable advantages in this regard. It is also worth noting that, as Wheeler has suggested, his reticence in pushing himself forward was also in some degree compensated for by friends who pressed his cause such as Dave Holland and Evan Parker. Given that by 1973, Beckett had released three albums as a leader and Wheeler two, one might have assumed that the two men might have had almost parallel careers. This did not prove the case – though neither grew wealthy from jazz! One is forced to ask if there has been any disparity between their careers and, if so, why this might be.

It would be wrong to use heavyweight words like "racism" or "discrimination" but we may question whether unconscious processes might have affected the careers of both musicians. John Wickes (1999) gives a full and detailed account of both musicians in *Innovations in British Jazz*. He is the exception, however. While few books have to date been written on British jazz, a survey of those that have and of guides to and encyclopaedias of jazz, does suggest a pattern. Look, for example, in the indices of the fourth and fifth editions of Cook and Morton's *Penguin Guide to Jazz on CD* (2000). Beckett has less than half as many mentions as Wheeler. The authors may well defend this on the basis of what records were commercially available. But Beckett did, in fact, have several CDs that are not referenced at the time that both issues went to print. *The Illustrated Encyclopedia of Jazz* (Case *et al.* 1986) has a long entry on Wheeler, but none on Beckett. *The Essential Jazz Records Volume 2: Modernism to Postmodernism* (Harrison *et al.* 2000) features a lengthy and beautifully written review of Wheeler's *Windmill Tilter* by Eric Thacker. Beckett is mentioned solely in the personnel of the Brotherhood of Breath's first album, which Thacker also reviews. But most tellingly, in Ian Carr's *The Music Outside* Wheeler is mentioned thirteen times, including detailed reference to his skills as an improviser and writer (see Carr 2008, 12–13), while Beckett appears just three times in the index. Yet, in the detailed discography of key albums of the period that Carr includes, Beckett played on twenty-nine of these including his own albums, while Wheeler appeared on twenty-three.

Ian Carr was an honourable man, who was utterly opposed to racism. None of the writers above has ever deserved any such accusation and this is not the intention here. However, there does seem to be both a certain irony and a discrepancy that cannot be ignored. Black immigration to Britain in these years might have been highly visible, while white immigration has been quite the opposite. However, black people can still, even now, be overlooked within the most progressive, liberal circles no matter how great their talent. We have noted earlier that pianist Russell Henderson rarely recorded in a jazz context despite his undoubted abilities. There are others we can name – clarinettist Carl Barriteau, saxophonist Bertie King, trumpeter Dave Wilkins and guitarist Lauderic Caton among them – who went similarly unrepresented. Comparison of Harry Beckett's career trajectory with that of Kenny Wheeler also gives us something to ponder.

British jazz also saw quite an influx of white jazz musicians from the Commonwealth in the sixties. Saxophonist Ray Warleigh came to London in 1960 from Australia and has maintained a presence on the scene since then. His one release from this period, *Ray Warleigh's First Album* (Philips; Sunbeam), produced by singer Scott Walker, for whom he was musical director at the time, does not come close to doing him justice. The tracks arranged by Harry South on the record stand up best but it is very much an easy listening affair. *Reverie* (Vinyl) is far more representative of his talents but made in 1977 falls outside our period. The often overlooked and undersung saxophonist Brian Smith came here from New Zealand in 1964 and played with Tubby Hayes, Mike Westbrook, Alexis Korner and Ian Carr's Nucleus. He proved the perfect foil for Carr and each man seemed to lift the playing of the other. In fact, Ian Carr seemed to employ quite a number of antipodeans in Nucleus in the seventies – saxophonist Bob Bertles was from Sydney, drummer Roger Sellers was from Melbourne, while bassist Billy Kristian came from New Zealand. Pianist Dave MacRae was another Nucleus member. He came here from New Zealand in 1971 via the States where he had worked with Buddy Rich. As well as with Carr, MacRae worked with Robert Wyatt in Matching Mole and with Mike Gibbs. His solos on Gibbs's arrangement of

Gary Burton-Steve Swallow's "Country Roads" and on Gibbs's own "So Long Gone" from *Just Ahead* are high points on a very fine album.

Two other musicians who made their homes in Britain in the sixties need to be mentioned in more detail. The first of these is Rhodesian-born composer–trombonist Mike Gibbs. I have already discussed Gibbs in relation to the influence of rock music on jazz and specifically in relation to what, for me, remains his magnum opus, *Just Ahead*. Gibbs returned to the States in 1974 to take up the post of composer-in-residence at Berklee. As noted earlier, Gibbs made two albums with Peter Eden for Deram and *Just Ahead* for Polydor. These were followed by *In the Public Interest* made with Gary Burton. Gibbs later returned to Britain in 1975 to record *The Only Chrome-Waterfall Orchestra* for the Bronze label with a mainly British orchestra featuring a number of soloists including saxophonist Tony Coe, trombonist Chris Pyne, Belgian guitarist Philip Catherine and two American musicians, bassist Steve Swallow and sax player Charlie Mariano.

The second of these was the Jamaican saxophonist and flautist Harold McNair, a light-skinned black man. McNair studied at the famous Alpha Boys School in Jamaica alongside Joe Harriott and Wilton Gaynair but arrived in Britain somewhat later than they in 1960. He acquired a formidable reputation as a sax player very quickly and worked regularly at Ronnie Scott's. Readers may recall the impression he made on the young Andrew Loog Oldham (see Chapter 2). Before arriving in London, he had toured Europe with Quincy Jones's orchestra and, like Harry Beckett, played on the score for *All Night Long*. Two factors kept McNair from fulfilling his huge promise. The most obvious of these was his premature death from lung cancer in 1971. The other was the demand for his talents, and in particular his unique flute playing, by musicians across the spectrum. For example, he worked extensively with composer–arranger John Cameron, and toured and recorded with folk-blues singer Donovan. All this hard work should have laid the ground for a long and glorious career in the seventies and onwards. It was not to be and none of the few albums he made is completely satisfying in representing his gifts. *Affectionate Fink* (Island) was cut in 1965 with Ornette Coleman's rhythm section, bassist David Izenzon and drummer Charles Moffett, and with British pianist Alan Branscombe. It is a fine set of standards played with great confidence with the self-penned title track one of two standout performances on the album. The other, "Angel Eyes" features some absolutely stunning flute from the leader and some nice piano from Branscombe.

In 1969, McNair recorded *Off Centre* (Deram; Vocalion) as part of John Cameron's quartet, which also included Pentangle's rhythm section of Danny Thompson and Tony Carr. While this is clearly Cameron's record, McNair is on startling form with his flute featured beautifully on "Go Away, Come Back Another Day", and he essays the complex, polytonal "Omah Cheyenne" with ease. "Flute & Nut", made with John Cameron as arranger can, however, be quickly dispensed with. His second and eponymous album as a leader was made for RCA in 1970, and was a rather unsatisfactory mix of standards and newer, more interesting material such as a highly affecting version of Donovan's "Lord of the Reedy River". The same arrangement was later used by Ronnie Scott on *Live At Ronnie Scott's* with Kenny Wheeler taking the flute part on flugelhorn. "Mento" is an all too rare entry into British jazz of a Caribbean music style, while "Indecision" also nods in a homewards direction. Perhaps the best, and, certainly, most well-known piece McNair recorded is "The Hipster". Understandably a hit with the jazz dance crowd, it is a telling slice of jazz-funk. The record was bowdlerized by B&C on reissue as *The Fence* in 1972 (B&C; Hux), with its three standards taken out and their replacement with a lengthy jazz-rock workout, "Spacecraft", recorded two years later. However, it actually makes for a more satisfying set. The only McNair record available at time of writing is *The Fence*. Fortunately, it is his best and reveals his ability for taking unpromising material such as the Beatles' "Here, There and Everywhere" and "Scarborough Fair" and turning these into little gems, as well as his skill with down-home tunes like the title track and the traditional "Early in the Morning". As is also the case with Amancio D'Silva, it will take a properly annotated reissue of all available material to allow an adequate evaluation of his unusual talents.

Perhaps the most important and influential group of immigrants to impact upon British jazz was the Blue Notes, who came here came here from South Africa in the mid-sixties. They began as a sextet comprising Mongezi Feza on trumpet, Dudu Pukwana on alto, Nick Moyake on tenor, Chris McGregor on piano, Johnny Dyani on bass and one of the greatest drummers of all time, Louis Moholo. Five black musicians and one white in post-Sharpeville South Africa, it became impossible for them to play together and, with great difficulty, they obtained passports to play at the Antibes Jazz Festival in France. Following short engagements at the Blue Note in Geneva and Afrikaner Café in Zurich, they made their way to London (see McGregor 1995; Heining 2009a, 40–43). They played the Scott Club to an incredible response before undertaking what proved to be a transformative residency at the Montmartre Club in Copenhagen. It was there they first came across the music of Albert Ayler, Cecil Taylor, Don Cherry and Archie Shepp. This experience, coupled with the relief and freedom of being able to make music without the fear of criminal sanctions or worse, truly liberated the music these musicians made. At first, it began to take on the abstract shapes and forms they had discovered in Denmark. However, once these influences began to merge with preexisting ones such as Ellington, hard bop and, most significantly, township and kwela musics from back home, the Blue Notes and later the monumental Brotherhood of Breath big band became something quite unique. They were perhaps the first world music orchestra.

Their first year in London was particularly hard. Despite their unusual situation, the MU was not prepared to bend its twelve-month qualification

The South African Blue Notes make their London debut at the Institute of Contemporary Arts, Dover Street, London, 26 April 1965. Left to right: Dudu Pukwana (alto sax), Mongezi Feza (trumpet, Johnny Dyani (bass), Chris McGregor (piano), Louis Moholo-Moholo (drums, not visible). © Valerie Wilmer.

rule. Without membership, the Blue Notes could not take work that would otherwise have gone to British musicians. They could, however, organize their own gigs. This and questions over their reception by certain sections of the British scene continue to be contentious issues. There are several quotes in Maxine McGregor's biography of her husband both from the pianist and from others such as Joe Boyd, who was briefly their manager and who produced their first records, that suggest a dissatisfaction with the response to their music that they met in Britain. For example, Christopher Bird of the *Melody Maker* did a piece on McGregor's new big band (the precursor of the Brotherhood of Breath) noting the rather swift demise of the Blue Notes and that "there just was not the scene to sustain it". McGregor told him:

> Somehow we got tagged "far out", although we looked upon ourselves as a fairly conventional unit; certainly we weren't considered avant garde or anything like that at home. I suppose we tended to overestimate the jazz scene here. From South Africa, it looked pretty good and, of course, the liberal attitudes were an attraction so that we could go on playing together. We just naturally assumed that there would be the same sort of open-mindedness to music here that there is to colour.   (Bird 1967, 6)

Joe Boyd, speaking with Maxine McGregor, contrasts the Blue Notes' initial reception at Ronnie Scott's with what he believes followed:

> When that happened they were welcome because they were exotic and interesting and they were going to go home. And when they didn't go home they became a threat. I felt there was a certain amount of racism involved. Visiting black musicians are O.K. because they're going to go home, but when they stay and they nick your girlfriends, that's a different thing.
>
> (McGregor 1995, 96)

This is the version recorded by Maxine McGregor. The story of the ecstatic welcome followed by rejection is repeated by veteran writer Richard Williams in his notes for the CD reissue of *Very Urgent* (Polydor; Fledg'ling) and in Marcello Carlin's notes for the Cuneiform 2007 release of *Eclipse at Dawn* (Cuneiform) featuring the Brotherhood of Breath recorded at the Berlin Jazztage in 1971. Boyd talks of meeting McGregor, having heard them at The Old Place:

> I invited them to play at U.F.O. (my psychedelic club), and then I started asking Chris about his professional life and was horrified to hear that nothing was happening and there were no records out or much work. I took it upon myself to get them a deal with Polygram [*sic*] and did so, and the budget for one record.
>
> (McGregor 1995, 114)

In Boyd's *White Bicycles – Making Music in the 1960s* (Boyd 2006) the producer similarly presents himself as the knight coming to the rescue of the South Africans.

> I got them a deal with Polydor ... and my agency took on the task of booking them. It seemed clear to me that they were playing music more vital than anything else on the British scene, but that turned out to be part of the problem.   (Boyd 2006, 215)

Yet the group were certainly not alone in scuffling for work on the London scene. As Mike Westbrook had told Michael Shera late in 1966:

> We would like to play at clubs in London, but it's very hard to break in... Generally speaking, though, we get a better reception out of London. London audiences tend to be rather blasé and indifferent. This is even true about students. There used to be a big following for jazz among students, but nowadays all they want is pop. It can be very disheartening.   (Shera 1966, 10)

The problem with remarks like Boyd's is that they are vague and general enough to apply in some degree in some situation at some point around such a time in some set of circumstances or other. The bigger problem, however, is that such comments are non-specific and become applied to both "innocent" and "guilty". It is hard for anyone to defend themselves against such vague accusations. More than that, such statements, when picked up and repeated, acquire a veracity they do not deserve.

Nevertheless, due to the shortage of regular work, the Blue Notes began to fall apart. Tenor player Nick Moyake had left the group in Zurich to return to South Africa, where he died shortly afterwards from a brain haemorrhage. Louis Moholo was soon playing in Europe, first with Roswell Rudd and John Tchicai, and then with Steve Lacy, Enrico Rava and Johnny Dyani. A disastrous tour of Argentina with Lacy left them stranded there for a time in 1966. The one fortunate outcome of that experience was the excellent record they made in Buenos Aires, *The Forest and the Zoo*. Mongezi Feza, barely out of his teens, had split to Copenhagen with his new Danish bride. Only Pukwana and McGregor remained in London. With the return of Dyani and Moholo, the musicians regrouped under the name of the Chris McGregor Sextet with the addition of white South African tenor saxophonist Ronnie Beer (he and McGregor had played together in South Africa) and made *Very Urgent*. It was quite probably the most "out" recording made in Britain to date.

Released in May 1968, Bob Houston gave it a definite thumbs up in the *Melody Maker* (Houston 1968, 14). With the exception of Pukwana's "Marie My Dear" (aka "'B' My Dear") and "Don't Stir the Beehive", a traditional arranged by McGregor, the tunes were penned by the pianist. It remains an important album of the period, if also a transitional one. The Pukwana track represents the Blue Notes of old, while "The Heart's Vibrations" emphasizes the influence of Cecil Taylor and would not be out of place on *Unit Structures* or *Conquistador*. The same might be said of "The Sound's Begin Again", whereas "Don't Stir the Beehive" suggests Archie Shepp. A second album, *Up to Earth*, was recorded for Polydor with Evan Parker in for Ronnie Beer, either Barre Philips or Danny Thompson replacing Dyani, and the addition of John Surman. Dyani and Moholo had presented McGregor with a "him or me" dilemma and it had been resolved in Moholo's favour. Dyani returned to Denmark, where he became a hugely important contributor to that scene and to the bands of various American ex-pats. In due course, Harry Miller, a South African Jew who had arrived in the UK in 1961, would become a permanent fixture in the circle though never a "Blue Note". It is a great shame that *Up to Earth* was not issued until 2008 (Fledg'ling) because it reveals how quickly McGregor, Pukwana, Feza and Moholo had absorbed the influences of the "new music" but were now incorporating these alongside their African and bebop inspirations. A trio set with McGregor, Phillips and Moholo also went unissued at the time.

As producer Peter Eden told the author in 1996, it was hearing John Surman on the radio that made him want to record the artist. What struck Eden was how advanced the music sounded. It was through Eden, and in some instances also Surman, that other artists such as John Warren, Mike Gibbs, Mike Osborne, John Taylor and Norma Winstone got to record in their own right. It was publicist/promoter/journalist Victor Schonfield, whose efforts led to the earliest recordings of the SME and Mike Westbrook's first album, *Celebration*, while Eden produced the other releases made by Westbrook for Deram. We have also seen the role played by Denis Preston in recording a wide range of British jazz artists and, in Chapter 11, will note the assistance given by David Howells at CBS to a number of the more *avant garde* British jazz musicians. Boyd's enthusiasm for McGregor and the Blue Notes and his help in recording them is to his credit, but what he achieved is hardly unique in the world of jazz.

Certainly, one might view the MU's position towards the Blue Notes as unduly rigid. However, the union also faced a situation where there was (as is still the case) too little work for too few of the many musicians wanting to make a living playing jazz in London and the UK. Many of the clubs and venues in London and beyond began as musician- or fan-run gigs. Consider Scott's, the Bull's Head in Barnes, the 100 Club and many others. One could offer an alternative account of the situation of McGregor *et al.*, namely that just three years after arriving in London McGregor had an album out on a major label. Graham Collier's first album came out in 1967, as did Westbrook's, both several years after leading their own bands. As we have seen, Kenny Wheeler and Beckett were both middle-aged before releasing their debuts. Mike Gibbs's first record came out in 1970. He came here in 1965. Quite a number of jazz musicians made their debut records on tiny labels or even released them as limited editions of ninety-nine copies to avoid purchase tax. This was the case with Howard Riley, who released *Discussions* on Opportunity (it was a one-off!), and Michael Garrick, whose *Moonscape* came out on Airborne. McGregor's experience seems far from untypical of the scene at the time.

It would also be helpful to know which British jazz musicians were so opposed to the Blue Notes and their music, and what their view might have been of the new jazz being made by Westbrook, the SME, John Surman and Mike Osborne. A lot of the younger musicians on the scene – Keith Tippett, Nick Evans, Elton Dean, Evan Parker, John Surman, Alan Skidmore, Mike Osborne, Malcolm Griffiths and Gary Windo all gravitated to the band, and many featured in Brotherhood of Breath line-ups. Interviewed in 2008, Hazel Miller offers what seems to be a more balanced assessment of attitudes to the South Africans:

> Initially, the guys were wary but it's like Keith Tippett says, it changed his life the first time he heard them. The people who

used to turn up to try to get into the Brotherhood! I mean I chased Gary Windo away like nobody's business. He got in. Elton [Dean] got in that way. The only thing I would say – and that applied to John Surman as well – is that the session musicians blocked all that out. But then they didn't want to become session musicians. Stan [Tracey] would say that as well. He was blocked out from that scene. Those guys sold their souls but then when Stan put a big band together those guys loved it because they're frustrated musicians. I can understand being a bit wary of Mongs when he was pissed or Dudu but anybody would be wary of them like that but Chris was a gentleman. You couldn't not like Chris.

(Interview with Hazel Miller, June 2008)

It sometimes seems as if the story of the Blue Notes is actually too hard to let it stand on its own. Their struggles in South Africa, their escape from apartheid, the disasters and false starts they had to overcome and then their brief moment in the sun before one by one first Mongezi Feza, then Johnny Dyani, then Chris McGregor and finally Dudu Pukwana were to die prematurely – it is almost too painful to bear. Yet, a twist here, an innuendo there, an unsubstantiated allegation or two, and suddenly you stop feeling the sadness and the pain. Anger takes its place and as soon as a ready target is identified, the pain goes away. This is "mythification" and it is necessary to expose it as such, for it does not allow us to experience reality in all its glorious light and, at times, under its heavy pall.

The remaining Blue Notes truly began to fulfil their potential with *Chris McGregor's Brotherhood of Breath* from 1971 (RCA Neon; Fledg'ling) and *Brotherhood* from 1972 (RCA; Fledg'ling), both produced by Joe Boyd. In 1969, McGregor's then unnamed orchestra had worked on the soundtrack of *Kongi's Harvest*, a film of a play by Nigerian poet, playwright and activist Wole Soyinka. Then, in June 1970, the Arts Council had given McGregor a grant of £400 towards reconstituting the big band. Evan Parker played with the band then, although he left before they recorded their first two albums, only to return later. By the time, they got into the studio, other musical commitments in Europe had pulled Parker away. However, as he says, the gestation period was crucial and really set the seal on what this band was to become.

> Chris started to do this ten-piece band with me and John Surman added in. We did two weeks at the new Ronnie's when they were trying to run the room upstairs as a separate venture for slightly more adventurous music. Everybody was following what was going on at The Old Place and Little Theatre Club and I think they wanted to see if they could start something there with a similar kind of policy. That was effectively the band that did

Evan Parker at Company Week, ICA, London, October 1977. © Valerie Wilmer.

that thing that has just come out called *Up to Earth*, although quite how representative it is of what we were doing in the club I can't remember. Then, in due course, Chris established the Brotherhood of Breath and I was in the first version of that. After a few rehearsals, we did the initial concert at the Notre Dame Hall and Jon Hendricks sat in. I don't know if anybody has ever written that down anywhere but he wrote some words for a tune of Dudu's called "The Bride" and sang that. Everybody was very keen to be supportive because that was in effect a fund-raiser for the ANC. Then I remember a gig on Haverstock bill and a few others after that.   (Interview with Evan Parker, September 2008)

Parker was to return later in what turned out to be one of the band's most active periods. As he notes, the band which (with one or two changes) lasted from 1969/70 to 1977 was an amazing collection of larger-than-life musical personalities:

They were pretty strong individuals. You had to somehow learn what you were in order to be among them. It was not a place for shrinking violets. Everybody knew what they stood for and what they wanted and they got on with it and you could stand there watching in amazement or you could try and make sense and join in. It was pretty clear that they had come through an ordeal to play together. They came from a police state where it was illegal for them to play together and they had managed to survive all that. All the little issues that came up in travelling around Europe were nothing to them. They weren't scared of anything. They were living life very full. It was exciting to be with them.

(Interview with Evan Parker, September 2008)

And as John Surman (who played on the Neon release) comments, rehearsals were certainly not for the faint-hearted:

I remember distinctly that Chris was forming this big band and he got together a lot of the guys from Westy's band but he also phoned around a lot of the top session guys. You know – get a bit of a buzz going and get everyone down to The Old Place. They're milling around for a while, then Chris sits down at the piano and hammers out a riff and then shouts, "Trumpets!" These guys are looking at each other and there's no music. He was going to teach these big band arrangements by ear. That came as a rather a nasty shock to some people, who all of a sudden were saying, "Hang on. What's all this?" It sorted out the men from the boys, that did. It all changed radically after that.

(Interview with John Surman, November 2008)

Their debut release was like nothing one had ever heard before. Quite how it did not collapse under the weight of its apparent musical contradictions is a source of amazement. Who would have believed that a music born of Ellington, free jazz, church music, South African choral music, Kwela and bop could be transformed into something as life-affirming and communally and individually validating as this? Yet that is what jazz at its highest level achieves, whether it comes from Ellington, Coltrane, Westbrook, Parker (Charlie or Evan), John Surman or Ornette. The first record is the better of the two for all its rawness and ramshackle, shanty-town brilliance. Pukwana is one of the most heartfelt altoists since "Bird", and his interactions with Feza on "Davashe's Dream" and "Andromeda" are uncanny. Nick Evans and Surman are the other main soloists. Evans seems to rise above even his own high standards on both these pieces, but Surman's soprano on Pukwana's tune "The Bride" is just coruscating. The twenty-minute "Andromeda" is the album's centre and its loosest in structure. If anything, it reminds one of the Art Ensemble of Chicago with its eerie flutes and fabulous percussion from Moholo and collective improvisation. *Brotherhood* is perhaps its more sophisticated twin, with Pukwana's "Do It", here as on *Live at Willisau*, a stand-out. McGregor's "Joyful Noises" is perhaps the most interesting tune here, combining, as it does, choral brass against an open and free rhythm section with chording that succeeds in suggesting Rachmaninoff, as well as Cecil Taylor, at times. Yet it is *Live at Willisau*, with its fabulous Niklaus Troxler cover, that is perhaps the best representation of the brilliant, syncretic music that the Brotherhood could produce. Not that they were an easy band to record; as Evan Parker recalls, "Nobody played on mike or anything. There was a lot of excitement on stage, so it was very difficult to capture that by a recording engineer" (interview with Evan Parker, September 2008).

Hazel Miller's CD reissue of the album adds another five tracks and is one of those examples where more actually adds rather than detracts from the performance. The solos from Parker on "Do It", Pukwana on "Restless" and "Davashe's Dream", Harry Beckett on "Camel Dance" and Mongezi Feza on "Tunji's Song" are magnificent. As for the rhythm section of Harry Miller and Louis Moholo, they are every bit as responsive and original in this setting, as they were working in trios and small groups with Mike Osborne. But the key with this band was that the individual is not just supported by the collective, the individual is affirmed by the ensemble and in turn validates it. The notion of jazz as a democratic art form has rarely achieved a higher expression. Since the band's demise, and since the deaths of all the Blue Notes apart from the now-septuagenarian Louis Moholo-Moholo, several recordings have surfaced on the Cuneiform label. Evan Parker, Hazel Miller and John Jack (Cadillac Records) have all expressed doubts to the author about these. All three question whether McGregor, a perfectionist when it came to the representation of his music, would have wanted them to see the light of day. To the listener, however, even the weakest of these still succeeds in celebrating McGregor, Moholo, Pukwana, Feza, Miller, Dyani and their impact on British jazz.

Mongezi Feza was the first of the Blue Notes to die before his time. Perhaps of all of them, his death was the most tragic. Hospitalized late in 1975 following a psychotic episode, somehow he got out into the grounds of the hospital in the depths of winter, caught pneumonia and died. If ever there were a case to answer of medical negligence, and possibly of racism, this was surely it (see McGregor 1995, 162–6; also interview with Hazel Miller, June 2008). Johnny Dyani was next in 1986. His death has been attributed by Richard Williams to an overdose of heroin in the sleevenotes for *Up to Earth*, while Joe Boyd also states that the bassist had been addicted to the drug. According to three sources closer to "Mongs" – Hazel Miller, Louis Moholo-Moholo and Maxine McGregor (McGregor 1995, 205; interview with Hazel Miller, June 2008; interview with Louis Moholo-Moholo, September 2008) – Dyani died from hepatitis, a condition he had had since childhood. Chris

McGregor's death from lung cancer in 1990 was followed just a month later by that of Dudu Pukwana from chronic liver disease. A heavy drinker for many years, his death remains a great loss (Schonfield 1992).

It is worth suggesting that the Blue Notes, like John Mayer, Harry Beckett, Joe Harriott, Amancio D'Silva, Ernest Ranglin, Harold McNair and others from the "black dominions", contributed something that fine musicians and composers such as Kenny Wheeler and Mike Gibbs did not, and, indeed, could not. Perhaps the intimations of the different musical styles of the Caribbean are not always easy to gauge in the work of those who came here from the islands. But it is there in Harriott's "Calypso" and "Revival" and in all of Beckett's albums. It is worth speculating what might have happened had British jazz embraced some of those styles more readily – ska, bluebeat, mento, calypso and reggae. John Surman's first album featured a whole side of calypso tunes with Trinidadian pianist Russell Henderson, and it worked astonishingly well. Instead, we had to wait at least another twenty-five years for Courtney Pine, Ernest Ranglin and his nephew Gary Crosby to open our ears to that possibility. The influence of Mayer and of Indian music has come through more strongly but the African sounds of the Blue Notes have proven the most lasting legacy. These sounds can be heard in the music of Harry Miller's Isipingo, in Elton Dean's groups and Loose Tubes, as well as in the work of Andy Sheppard, Annie Whitehead and Alan Skidmore's Ubizo. They were celebrated by the Dedication Orchestra, by Louis Moholo-Moholo in Viva La Black and other groups, as well as by Keith Tippett and Julie Tippetts. And that is not to forget the bands of Italian saxophonist Carlo Actis Dato and Danish guitarist Pierre Dørge.

In a sense, musicians like Wheeler and Gibbs brought new ideas to British jazz, but these largely fell within our Anglo-Saxon and European musical frames of reference. Those from the Caribbean, Asia and Africa brought forms that enriched and broadened the range of styles that British players could draw upon to create music that remained within a jazz framework. That was their genius. We must also acknowledge that they expressed this against a backcloth that reflected hostility to immigration in some sections of British society and, at the very least ambivalence, towards it in some more traditionally liberal areas of British social and political life.

The Labour Party in opposition opposed the Tory Commonwealth Immigration Act of 1962. In 1968, facing the prospect of an influx of Asians from East Africa and the implications of white working class opposition to that and the potential consequences for its electoral chances, the Wilson government introduced its own Commonwealth Immigration Act. This restricted the right of residence and settlement still further. Worse than that, it rendered thousands of former British subjects potentially stateless. Labour's reluctance to confront white racism among its own supporters was an act of cowardice recognized by left-winger Richard Crossman. He wrote in his diary that the White Paper would "probably have a deeper undermining effect on the moral strength of Harold Wilson's leadership than any other thing we have done". Later he wrote:

> This has been one of the most difficult and unpleasant jobs the Government has had to do. We have become illiberal and lowered quotas at a time when we have an acute shortage of labour. No wonder all the weekend liberal papers have been bitterly attacking us. Nevertheless, I am convinced that if we hadn't done all this we would have been faced with certain electoral defeat in the Midlands and the South-East. Politically, fear of immigration is the most powerful undertow today.
>
> (Crossman 1979, quoted in Donnelly 2005, 114)

To assuage liberal opinion, and its own conscience, the Labour government introduced a new Race Relations Act that same year. This went further in terms of outlawing discrimination, and gave the Race Relations Board additional powers to investigate abuses and was passed in the face of Monday Club opposition and Tory back and front bench opposition – and Enoch Powell's notorious and deceitful "Rivers of Blood" speech (see Donnelly 2005, 168–9) Its weaknesses notwithstanding, such legislation has contributed to changing both attitudes and practices in Britain. However, if the Labour Party were ever anything other than an electoral machine with the sole purpose of creating a parliament less antipathetic to working class and trades union interests, or to use Lenin's telling phrase "Minimising insecurity in a situation of scarcity", then this surely revealed that its flag was not red but deepest puce. As the Right Reverend Wood told Trevor Phillips:

> I think what happened was that Labour took fright, and there became a kind of Dutch auction between the two parties, each one showing that they're likely to be less friendly to immigrants and immigration and black people, and so on. And the Wilson government hit upon the idea of saying, in order to safeguard good race relations in this country, we will introduce a limit on the number of black people coming into the country. And despite the fact that, frankly, the number of black people had already begun to decline. But what the press and the racists had managed to do was to associate the word immigrant with black people.
>
> (Phillips and Phillips 1999, 287–8)

The contribution of immigrants to Britain, to its way of life and culture, has been predominantly positive. Looking at those who came to play jazz here, they did not just enrich the music. They expressed an implicit belief that great art could be created by all regardless of colour or place of origin and that culture was a shared and even collective endeavour. They found in their music a mechanism for expressing their own dignity, all too often degraded during the ignominies of empire, as well as the worth of all peoples and all individuals. They were expressing the very ideals of Commonwealth. The irony was that they did so while those holding the reins of power were busily dismantling those same values.

10 Sisters of Swing, Brothers in Arms

Real excellence and humility are not incompatible one with the other, on the contrary they are twin sisters.

Jean Baptiste Lacordaire (French cleric and political activist, 1802–1861)

There is really very little to say on the subject of British jazz and "the permissive society" or "the sexual revolution" that the sixties heralded. Clearly, jazz musicians had sex. They had it in the fifties and even earlier. Anyone wishing to know how British jazz musicians performed the act can consult George Melly's amusing biography, *Owning Up* (1974). Though we cannot be entirely sure, we can safely assume, that their sixties and seventies counterparts continued to have and enjoy sex. Possibly, like their pop and rock counterparts, they had sex more often than the majority of the British population. But they were the exception rather than the rule. Whether something similar was true of the jazz audience in Britain is hard to tell. Certainly, jazz clubs – those "smokey dives" – provided meeting points for young men and women far removed from grown-up supervision. Beyond that there is nothing really to add.

It is actually worth questioning how far sexual behaviour really changed in this period. According to some commentators, the sixties signalled in an era of free love and challenge to authority and traditional values. For those on the right, the sixties and this aspect of it are the source of much that went wrong later. In *The Young Meteors*, Jonathan Aitken (later a guest of Her Majesty) wrote, "London is now widely alleged to be the sexiest city in the world, the mecca of permissiveness, promiscuity and perversion. These are strong words, but they are well-earned" (Aitken 1967, quoted in Sandbrook 2008, 477). While Aitken viewed this from a more puritanical position, Brian Masters (1985) concurred with the perception but defended the changes in behaviour on the grounds that these signalled a new honesty and openness in relationships within society. If one were to believe some of the figures interviewed by Jonathon Green some twenty-five years after the event (see Green 1998a), the period saw an explosion of sexual activity among the young and unattached. In fact, Green himself is much more circumspect and insightful in his comments on the issue in his *All Dressed Up: The Sixties and the Counterculture* (Green 1998b, 51–86). Other commentators are similarly cautious in their analysis. As Donnelly notes:

> People may have had more freedom to do all kinds of things in the sixties and indeed they may have welcomed it but they did not necessarily exercise that freedom. Individuals often expressed liberal attitudes on issues of personal morality but behaved in ways that were little different from their morally buttoned-up predecessors.
>
> (Donnelly 2005, 116; see also Sandbrook 2008, chapter 23)

Donnelly refers to a *New Society* survey published in November 1969, which suggested widespread unease among the public with regard to liberal law reforms stewarded by Labour's Home Secretary, Roy Jenkins. And both Sandbrook and Arthur Marwick (1996) refer to research by Geoffrey Gorer published in 1971 under the title *Sex and Marriage in England Today*. Sandbrook notes:

> Gorer concluded that only 11 per cent of the unmarried population, usually young men, were even relatively promiscuous, having had three or more sexual partners. He estimated that of the English population aged between sixteen and forty-five, about a tenth could be called "licentious", in other words extremely permissive, and about twice as many could be termed "censorious". The rest, "who do not get over-excited about the idea of sex in either direction", were floating somewhere in between, their values uncertain or ambiguous. "England", he concluded, "still appears to be a very chaste society..."   (Sandbrook 2008, 494)

The belief still exists that the sixties "sexual revolution" was sparked by the availability of the pill. Marwick, however, notes that 92 per cent of respondents in Gorer's research sample answered the question, "Now that the pill provides absolute safety, do you think faithfulness is or is not as important as ever in marriage?" in the affirmative (Marwick 1996, 170). Intriguingly, Marwick adds, "Use of contraceptives, or perhaps one should say effective use of them, had not kept pace with sixties' changes in moral attitudes. Gorer found that the majority of the sexually active unmarried were not regularly using any form of birth control" (Marwick 1996, 171).

At the same time, it is evident that sex began to be spoken about more openly. Perhaps even more significantly, as people became more able to speak about sexual matters, they also began to acknowledge difference – differences between men and women, differences between gay men and lesbians and heterosexuals. This was far from being the immediate outcome of changing attitudes but once difference is accepted, it becomes possible to distinguish between social and cultural myths and biological and economic realities. If the "sexual revolution" did have an impact on the British jazz scene, it came in the form of a slow but growing acceptance of the place of women in jazz – and to a lesser degree of gay men and lesbians.

In terms of wider society, of which British jazz was a part, "speaking openly" about sex and sexual preference was in the sixties accompanied by legislation in a whole number of areas which began to open up the situation of women and gay men. In the longer term, legislative changes did affect attitudes and behaviour but this process was really just beginning to take place in the sixties and there was an inevitable time lag before these unravelled and their full impact could be seen.

In what follows, we will examine the position of women in British jazz during the sixties, noting that their contribution was more significant than their numbers. This discussion may also allow us to see how changes at a cultural level are made possible by economic changes and how these, in turn, affect the lives and opportunities of groups of people in British society.

There were many reasons why it became more possible to talk about sex. Changes in post-war capitalism and, in particular, major technological developments required a more educated workforce. Those growing up with the benefit of free access to secondary schooling and even higher education were inevitably more and better informed. They had access to a wider range of information sources – television, radio and magazines that were targeted at niche groups. Workers had become consumers and that process itself generated information and access to it. As we have seen, there was also an increase in the extent of social mobility, though this was probably less significant than sometimes suggested. These were all important factors in the creation of a growing consensus that the Victorian/Edwardian "Little England" attitudes that had survived the war were unnecessary in a modern society and constrained rather than enabled social, cultural and commercial life.

The key events of the sixties are easily identified. The first of these, the *Regina v. Penguin Books Ltd* (*Lady Chatterley*) trial, for some marks the beginning of the decade. Its significance lay in Penguin's successful testing of the Obscene Publications Act 1959 (introduced as a private members' bill by Roy Jenkins MP) and its clause that allowed the publishing of such material, if it could be shown that a work was of literary merit. Even then, the floodgates did not exactly open. For example, theatrical censorship under the offices of the Lord Chamberlain's office was not abolished until 1968 and the coming into law of the Theatres Act 1968. In fact, the opening of *Hair* was postponed until the act came into effect. Playwright Edward Bond's *Saved* was actually prosecuted in 1965 and it was this that actually led to the change in legislation. However, the Penguin trial did signal a change and presaged a relaxation in what could and could not be talked about or written about. It is worth noting here that Harold Wilson, fearing that playwrights "might say rude things about the royals", was actually opposed to George Russell Strong's 1968 Theatre Bill. According to Patricia Hollis, biographer of Labour Arts Minister Jennie Lee, the bill only passed through Cabinet because Wilson was away on that occasion (Hollis 1997, 274).

The key legislation and social provision often cited as evidence for sixties permissiveness was not in fact enacted until the second half of the decade. The Sexual Offences Act that allowed men to have sexual relationships with each other, granting them the same rights as women, did not come in until 1967. The pill might have been available on prescription as early as 1961 but access was only possible through the family GP. Family Planning Association (FPA) clinics only catered for married couples and, though the first Brook clinic was set up by a wealthy birth control campaigner in 1964 to fill this gap, by 1966 only four such clinics existed and then only in major cities. It was only in 1970 that the FPA changed its own rules about seeing unmarried women (Sandbrook 2008, 489–90). The Abortion Act of 1967, championed by David Steel MP was another important milestone but again came later in the decade, and perhaps the two most important pieces of legislation for women and women's rights were not enacted until very late in the Wilson government's term in office. They were the Divorce Reform Act of 1969 and the even more crucial Matrimonial Property Act of 1970 (Marwick 1996, 147–8).

The reputation of the Wilson government may have been sullied over the years by revelations in the memoirs of Cabinet members and by its economic failures. It did, however, enact a number of key reforms and it is upon these that its status as a liberal reforming administration rests. As well as the above, it introduced the first Race Relations Act in 1966, the Equal Pay Act of 1970, lowered the legal age of majority and the voting age to 18 from 21 and introduced redundancy payments for workers "laid off" by employers. True, the shortcomings of these acts were evident at the time, but taken together they did amount to a shift in social practices that eighteen years of Thatcherism and thirteen of Tony Blair have not quite eradicated. This achievement should not be underestimated. The problem with the Labour Party runs much deeper than its conservative and liberal critics or even its own supporters will allow. Nevertheless, its successes and failures between 1964 and 1970 do in various ways frame the context in which jazz struggles to survive (see Chapter 12) and continue to affect positively the position of women and gay men working within the jazz community, as well as others in society.

Through these years, British society was in a state of becoming; that is of one moving towards a position of greater equality and diversity. It will be noted that, in what follows, my sources of information are limited in respect of the experiences of gay men in British jazz. They are fuller in respect of women working on the scene.

In the fifties and sixties, women wishing to become involved in jazz as musicians, writers, promoters or fans faced a number of obstacles. In the main, these were probably little different from those experienced by women in other walks of life. However, in relation to jazz as a part of the world of show business where women worked as actors, singers, dancers and performers, as well as backstage, one might have expected perhaps a greater degree of appreciation of women as fellow artists. In comparison, it seems that British jazz presented women wanting to be singers and musicians with an environment that was exceptionally bloke-ish.

The reasons for this can be easily identified. First, earning a living as a jazz musician was (and is) hard. Many jazz musicians, even those who have quite settled family lives, often seem to have one child and stop there, as if the financial pressure of two or more would overwhelm and force a change of vocation! The nature of the jazz life in the fifties and sixties involved long hours and late nights, considerable amounts of travelling by car or van on single carriageways, staying in less than salubrious accommodation and living on a diet rich in saturated fats and carbohydrates. And all that to play for a handful of punters in some smoky dive. It is not that women are not equipped to cope with such privations. Rather that such a life would surely only attract the most determined or insane.

Second, jazz was not alone in presenting itself to the outside world as a closed shop. Indeed, many working class occupations were effectively closed to women, as were areas of professional employment such as banking, the law, accountancy and the higher echelons of business and social administration. The world of the fifties and sixties as far as women and work was concerned was not that of a glass ceiling but one made of reinforced concrete. The gains made by women since then in these respects are significant but one cannot judge the sixties in terms of those gains. It was what it was to a large extent.

Third, and this applies to jazz as much if not more than other areas of labour, maleness reinforces maleness. Without role models, it is harder for members of oppressed groups to envisage a role or career for themselves in such a world. At the same time, the perception in the dominant group becomes one of "like us" versus "not like us". The expectation among male jazz musicians, unconscious or conscious, becomes one where the role of women on the stand is restricted to that of guest vocalist, for example. Where women, as singers or instrumentalists, did break through this bloke-ishness of the jazz world, they did so as exceptions. They were both exceptionally talented and exceptions to the rule. How men in jazz responded to those allowed exceptions is itself intriguing and telling.

Back in 1950, saxophonist Kathy Stobart had formed a nonet, ground-breaking in its instrumentation and approach. Her group rehearsed, attended and passed an audition for the BBC. A meeting with the BBC's Head of Light Music followed and it was there that things went awry:

> As soon as she walked into the office, Kathy realised she was in the presence of a man who not only disliked women but, being a frustrated musician himself, had less than no time for women players. His first question was, "What do you want to see me about?" And this he followed with, "Why do you do what you do?"
>
> (Wilmer 1982, 43)

Stobart had been a professional musician since she was fourteen, had been on the road with Vic Lewis's orchestra and guested with Ted Heath's band at the Palladium. As Wilmer notes:

> To her amazement, he went on to ask, "What real purpose is there in letting the public hear your band?" When she pointed out that the music had been favourably received, he told Kathy that her expectations were "very naive". That was it. A temper that she seldom unleashes, exploded. "You ask me why I do it? What sort of question is that, for God's sake? I do it because I must do it. I do it because it's there. I do it. You're sitting like a judge, talking to me

Kathy Stobart at home in Norbury, January 1977. © Valerie Wilmer.

– you're the person dishing out the broadcasts. I want a broadcast because I'd like people to hear the band." (Wilmer 1982, 44)

Forced to take another audition over a technicality, Stobart subsequently received her rejection slip. The result was that Stobart has never to this day done a BBC broadcast with her own band. She told Wilmer that this proved a "turning point" in her career and had "a huge effect on my ultimate success as a bandleader and a public figure."

Stobart had been turned on to bebop through her association with pianist and trumpeter Dennis Rose, in whose band she had played at the Jamboree Club. As she recalled, "There were really two up-and-coming young small jazz bands in the late 'forties – that was Johnny Dankworth and myself. We ran concurrently. I just didn't have the money to carry on; we were really losing quite a bit" (Tomkins 1974, 14–15). The group included altoist Derek Humble, Pete King on tenor, Bert Courtley on trumpet and Dill Jones on piano. Stobart describes the music as "pretty advanced", drawing especially on the ideas of blind American pianist Lennie Tristano. As she notes, it was the wrong material for the ballroom gigs they were playing and, without broadcasts on the BBC, the group had little chance of success.

Stobart's experience at the BBC was nothing new, of course. With many male musicians called up during the Second World War, Ivy Benson had formed her all-women swing band and met with considerable success. For a time, the orchestra served as the BBC's resident dance band, despite opposition from several bandleaders, notably Billy Ternent (see www.ivybenson-online.co.uk/Biographies/Ivy_Benson.htm; also Tracy 1997, 29). Lucy O'Brien in her excellent and authoritative *She-Bop II* (2002) quotes Benson trombonist and broadcaster Sheila Tracy on the issue:

> When the BBC made Ivy their resident house band all hell broke loose, because it was the plum job in the country. The male band leaders didn't want to know her, they loathed her guts. And the reviews for the first broadcast were vitriolic.
>
> (O'Brien 2002, 37)

After the war, Tracy told O'Brien, that Benson found many doors closed to her both at the BBC and on the theatre circuit due to an alliance of male bandleaders. Although booked for broadcasts after the war, Benson was forced to pull out by the Stoll Theatres Group, which threatened to cancel her contracts because of the competition posed by the medium. On the same page, O'Brien notes this comment by trombonist Don Lusher: "We had nothing against girls in a band … but you've got to remember it was a pretty high standard in those days. And maybe it wasn't as fashionable for girls then."

Once Stobart had married Bert Courtley and the couple had children, her husband became the main breadwinner and her playing was limited to one-night stands. Though she did do three months in Humphrey Lyttelton's band depping for Jimmy Skidmore, the needs of the family meant that she had to turn down a tour with Woody Herman's Anglo-American band. Stobart had also played in Tony Kinsey's group, as well as with Dizzy Reece and pianist Eddie Thompson. However, it was for her various stints with Humphrey Lyttelton that most jazz fans of the time remember her. Readers can hear just how good she is on *Buck Clayton with Humphrey Lyttelton and His Band* (Lake) from 1966. The big sound of her tenor graces the easy-swinging blues "Talkback" and there's a delightful swagger to her playing on "An Evening in Soho". But it is her feature duet with Buck Clayton on "Poor Butterfly" that really hits home. However, Stobart is not well represented on record. While family commitments were obviously a factor in this, it was not the only reason.

It was not until 1976 and *Saxploitation* (Spotlite) with baritone saxist Joe Temperley that she recorded in her own right. Though it comes outside even our elastic temporal definition of the period, the best example of Stobart on record has to be *Arbela* (Spotlite). The title track was co-written by Stobart, as was "2HS", and is a Latin-inflected ballad with some lovely flute and tenor from the leader and typically fiery trumpet from Harry Beckett. "2HS" is a fine piece of hard bop and opens with some exceptional unison work from Stobart and Beckett and bluesy piano from Martin Blackwell. Stobart's own solo is strong and articulate and all too brief. Her playing on Beckett's fast-paced "As Is" is even better and on Beckett's long suite "Enchanted/Cry of Triumph" her soprano solo is quite astonishing. "Arbela" allows the listener both to hear Stobart's talent in a setting that she determined herself but it also offers a glimpse of what she might have achieved – had the playing field been more level, that is.

Unlike other areas of show business, which in other ways were no less sexist, there were fewer opportunities for women in jazz. A woman might progress as a singer but this was generally seen as a lesser role to that of a trumpeter, drummer, saxophonist or pianist. There was certainly a strong element of prejudice around. It is striking that even Cleo Laine – though rightly confident in her abilities – seems to have seen her role as a singer as being less important than those of the instrumentalists. Her comments, from an article that appeared in *Jazz UK* magazine in 2008, are intriguing:

> The pair will bicker good-humouredly about the minutiae of their biographies. When I suggest that their role in British jazz goes way beyond that of their contemporaries, Cleo immediately says: "John more than me really. Anybody that plays an instrument, and writes music, is much more historically important." "On the contrary," John interrupts, "vocalists draw bigger crowds." "That's got nothing to do with the evolution of a music," Cleo responds, "unless they're iconic figures." "So, strike off Ella Fitzgerald and

Billie Holiday and the rest from American jazz history," John replies. "You can't win like that." "All right, dear, I concede," Cleo responds unconvincingly. "You're more important than you think, that's what it amounts to, darling," says John, now turned peacemaker.   (Heining 2008e, 27)

One might argue that Laine is herself an iconic figure. However, this is not the point. The reality was that, in the fifties and sixties, the door to this male-dominated world would open more easily to the singers, who were in turn seen to be of secondary status. At the same time, they were tolerated to an extent that did not apply to instrumentalists. As bassist and artist Gill Alexander explains:

It was a men's club and, unfortunately, it still is a men's club. And it was very difficult but I was so in love with the instrument, I would have just done anything to keep playing and I just had to ignore all the ... I mean, people divided into two. They either patted me on the head and said I was a clever little thing. "Have a little dabble then off you go." And there were the other guys who hated having women on the stand and didn't like it at all and, in particular, I have to say these men's wives hated me. They would put up with a singer but a musician? No, no! Because singers weren't supposed to have a bean in the head but somebody who knew about music and could read and could actually learn and play an instrument – they didn't like that at all. I made a lot of enemies.   (Interview with Gill Alexander, February 2009)

Alexander (at that time going by her married name of Lyons) had played banjo in an early version of the Temperance Seven and worked in modern, Dixieland and mainstream settings. Walking into a club carrying an instrument and asking to sit in requires chutzpah and there's many a male ego that ended night in shreds when the competition got too fierce. Cutting contests have long been commonplace in jazz and unwelcome intruders can easily be shown up by unusual chord changes or keys. Gill Alexander's determination was exemplary, even if it meant biting her tongue sometimes and tolerating the comments of male musicians. Alexander knew it was the only way to learn how to improvise. As she says:

Nobody in those days taught improvisation at all ... I found that the only way I could actually learn the business was to go round the clubs and ask to sit in, which would be just for one number and that's how I really learned the craft. That's what I did and gradually people asked me to dep for them and so I did.
(Interview with Gill Alexander, February 2009).

Some men were very supportive of women singers and instrumentalists, as we will see. However, the issue is far less one of individual attitudes but rather concerns a situation and setting that was constructed on a number of masculine images, two of the most potent of which were that of the male hipster and the suffering and misunderstood artist. Others have covered this in more than adequate detail (see Horrocks 1995; Reynolds and Press 1995). Here it suffices to note that the uses that the "hipster" had for women in his life were for sex and unquestioning, long-suffering devotion, while the "artist" required a woman as muse and solace from a cruelly misunderstanding world. We will leave it to readers to decide which, if any, British jazz artists might have fallen into which category. Again, it was not that similar images could not be found in other areas of the entertainment industry or that these were not dominated by men. It was more the case that pop music or light entertainment generated much greater revenue. Therefore, with a larger share of the market, a wider set of female images was possible, albeit often constructed on male fantasies such as "the girl next door", "the vamp" or "the goddess". A number of female singers emerged in the sixties and seventies in pop and rock who were allowed a certain latitude. One notes here Sandie Shaw, Elkie Brooks, Lulu, Maggie Bell and, the most talented of them all, Dusty Springfield. But again, they were singers rather than instrumentalists. It was not until the rise of the singer–songwriter in the early seventies that women artists would find a much broader, self-defining role.

In one sense, Cleo Laine's view of jazz singers being popularizers of the music rather than innovators is a fair one. Jazz has always been first and foremost an instrumental music, and singers such as Ella Fitzgerald and Billie Holiday have drawn on a source material shared with instrumentalists in the "Great American Songbook". In the past, the voice in jazz has often been an optional extra or a means of broadening appeal and audience. Ironically, it was the move away from the AABA 32-bar song form by post-bop, male instrumentalists and the use of modal forms that began to create a distinctive place within improvisation for the human voice, and this, as we will see, was an opportunity exploited by several British women singers. However, within her own terms, Laine must be seen as an important popularier of jazz and in certain respects as an innovator.

Although the image of Dankworth and Laine commonly held is that of a husband and wife team, both worked separately for substantial periods. As noted previously, Laine had a hit in her own right in 1961 with "You'll Answer to Me", a cover of a Patti Page song.

Laine had joined the Johnny Dankworth Seven in 1951 and continued to play with Dankworth until the couple married, at which point she began to branch out on her own. Given that this was in the late fifties, this was a bold and assertive move. She demonstrated that it was possible for a woman to be successful in her own right, even when married to an equally famous partner and being a mother. One could with justification suggest that Cleo

The John Dankworth Seven with Cleo Laine. From the front, left to right: Eddie Harvey (trombone – sitting), Don Rendell (tenor – crouching); middle row, left to right, Eddie Blair (trumpet), Frank Holder (percussion), Cleo Laine (vocals), Bill Le Sage (piano, vibes). Back row, left to right: Eddie Taylor (drums), Eric Dawson (bass). Other figures not known. Photograph courtesy of Cleo Laine.

Laine provides the first female role model in British jazz. She branched into both straight and musical theatre performing at the Royal Court in a play by Jamaican playwright Barry Rekord, *Flesh for a Tiger*. Further theatre roles followed and included the musical *Valmouth*, but even more significant were her performances at the Edinburgh International Festival in Kurt Weill's *Seven Deadly Sins* in 1961 and in *Showboat* ten years later. Laine actually took over at the last minute from Weill's ex-wife Lotte Lenya in the opera, as Lenya had refused the director's request that she dance. It was a huge step and change of direction, but as Laine says, "I just said 'Yes' before I really knew what I had let myself in for, which is basically what I do all the time."

Laine shared with Dankworth an entirely open-minded approach when it came to music and the arts. Both saw no reason why these should be separate, and put this into practice in their work and in the creation with like-minded friends such as André Previn, Dudley Moore, John Williams, John Ogdon and Richard Rodney Bennett of the Wavendon Allmusic Plan (WAP). A recording of William Walton's jazz-influenced *Façade* in 1967 featuring Laine, singer Annie Ross and an ensemble directed by Dankworth provides a further signpost for the direction both were taking, as the following interview extract reveals:

> J: It's always nice to find a piece like that because it enabled us to get to know William Walton a bit.
> C: But we were very eclectic in our tastes, I think that was the whole thing.
> J: Walton was someone who was very interested in jazz.
> C: And everybody surrounding us at the time felt very much the same as we did.

And Laine adds:

> There was John Williams, Richard Rodney Bennett – he was someone who had a foot in each camp. He was a highly regarded classical composer and he was writing for films and loved to play the piano jazz-wise and sing, which is what he does now, of course. Who else was it? John Ogdon, who was another of the directors of the Wavendon Allmusic Plan. They all felt the same and most of the artists who came down also felt as we did that there was only one kind of music – good music. It didn't matter what style it was it had to be good and people went along with that. There was Dudley Moore, who was a trained classical organist and an amazing composer, and then there was André [Previn] – he came down.
>
> (Interview with Cleo Laine and John Dankworth, February 2008)

Not all of Laine and Dankworth's genre-hopping would prove so successful. Later Laine recordings with flautist James Galway and guitarist John Williams are bland and disappointing. But the point for both was the creation of an audience for "good" music across a wide range of styles as opposed to allowing these categories to remain ghettoized according to their respective groups of listener. It might be added, here, that Dankworth had always understood the advantage to be gained in the market place by a product that could be attached to multiple identifications. Several of his own big band albums over the years have carried semi-programmatic themes. As for Laine herself, she could essay the "Great American Songbook" in her sleep and there is plenty of evidence to demonstrate her strengths as a standards singer. However, perhaps Laine's finest and most groundbreaking record of the period is *Shakespeare and All That Jazz* (Fontana).

In his arrangements of The Bard, John Dankworth does not ignore earlier efforts by Arthur Young and Ellington and Strayhorn to "jazz up the swan of Avon"! Rather, he incorporates them within a suite that works magnificently as jazz and successfully as a concept. A project like this could so easily have proved pretentious but then it is hard to imagine which other jazz singer of the time could have negotiated Shakespeare's sixteenth-century poetry with such ease or have pulled this off with such aplomb. Arthur Young's swinging "Blow, Blow Thou Winter Wind" is taken at a furious pace, while the Strayhorn–Ellington setting of "My Love Is as a Fever" becomes a torch song of the deepest passion. But Dankworth's own arrangement for "Shall I Compare Thee" is just as gorgeous and "Witches Fair and Foul" pairs Titania with Macbeth's "three weird sisters" to eerie, after-hours effect. The richness of Laine's voice and phrasing are perfect and each song is given exactly the right weight. "Fear No More" is just as good and Laine even makes sense of "The Compleat Works", which sets the titles of all the bard's plays to Dankworth's score without sounding arch. "Dunsinane Blues", for a sextet including Kenny Wheeler on trumpet, is perhaps the highlight, linking jazz and Shakespeare as though the intervening centuries were but a moment. It is worth suggesting that Laine showed the way forward for other singers with this album and that others, like Mike and Kate Westbrook or Norma Winstone, who followed had this signpost to guide them.

Laine's career from the late sixties and early seventies was an even greater commercial success, as she established a fan base in the States, Australia and in Europe. At the same time, her work became more mainstream in approach, though her voice lost none of its range or quality. The rise, slow perhaps, of several other female singers would eclipse Laine in terms of adventure, as they took on the challenge thrown down by the young musicians hanging out at the Little Theatre Club and Ronnie's Old Place. Such options were not open to Laine, even if she might have found them attractive.

Of the female singers who emerged in British jazz in the late sixties, three deserve in-depth analysis. They are Norma Winstone, Maggie Nicols and Julie Tippetts. All three share a similar history and began singing the "Great American Songbook" before moving into more experimental territory. Since her arrival on the scene, Winstone, however, has followed more than one path and has continued to develop a song-based repertoire that includes standards and contemporary material, as well as writing her own lyrics.

She attended Trinity College in her teens studying piano and organ, as she explains:

Norma Winstone and Michael Garrick recording for Argo, West Hampstead, London, 21 January 1970. © Valerie Wilmer.

> Nobody suggested I take singing and I didn't even think of it because it wasn't the kind of singing I wanted to do. From ever since I can remember, my parents loved Sinatra and Lena Horne, people that played that kind of music and big bands. My dad loved Fats Waller. That's the music I was interested in and that I wanted to sing. It didn't occur to me to sing classical music, so I just took piano and did organ as a second study.
>
> (Interview with Norma Winstone, May 2006)

That love of jazz grew and, on hearing Miles's *Kind of Blue*, Winstone began to think of a career in the music. She had lessons with a local singing teacher and started gigging but soon became unhappy with a repertoire that offered no scope for improvising. "I was getting really dissatisfied, because I kept thinking, 'These people don't sound a bit like Oscar Peterson or Ella and Louis. If I've got to do this, I'd rather not sing'" (interview with Norma Winstone, May 2006). After a hiatus of a couple of years, she began working with a local trio and even ran sessions at the notorious Regency Club in Amhurst Road, an after-hours hangout for the Krays and other East End villains. It was when Ian Carr guested at the club that things began to move for Winstone. "One week we had Ian Carr and he came and I was singing and he sat in and he said, 'You should sing with the New Jazz Orchestra,' and he introduced me to Neil Ardley and through Neil I met Michael Garrick" (interview with Norma Winstone, May 2006)

It was around that time that she was introduced to pianist John Taylor, later to become her husband, and also trumpeter Kenny Wheeler. In 1977, Winstone formed the trio Azimuth with Taylor and Wheeler, one of the most enduring and successful chamber jazz ensembles of all time.

> Kenny I met at the Little Theatre Club because there was this free music explosion around '68 and '69. It all seemed to happen around that time because I'd met John Stevens through another pianist who was playing with him and John went and told Ronnie Scott about me and to cut a long story short I got an audition and got some work there. John had discovered free music and had stopped playing anything conventional anymore but he asked me to sing with the Spontaneous Music Ensemble and I met Kenny through my involvement with that because he was also in that group. And he said, "Would you like to do something with my big band?" Then he began to write me in as part of the band. It's strange how these things happened.
>
> (Interview with Norma Winstone, May 2006)

Interviewed by Victor Schonfield late in 1992 for the National Sound Archive's Oral History of Jazz in Britain, John Stevens told Schonfield how he first came to hear of Winstone:

> I was working at the Charlie Chester Club with Chris (Goode) on piano and some really weird singer guy – might have been Italian – with really greasy hair and long sideburns, and most of the gigs like that were "jazzy" at least – I mean you played jazz and [Amarell] would come in there and sing with the band some-times. Also, that's where I first met Norma Winstone, 'cos Chris (Goode) said to me, "I know you like singers ... there's this friend of mine who sings brilliantly ...", and I said "well get her down here". He brought her down and I said "Well what do you want to do?", and she said "I Don't Want to Cry Anymore". Normally that song, if somebody was singing it, it would be [sings] "Last night, just about sunset, I saw you passing my door ..." I loved that song. She went "one, two" and she took it like that! She sang it at half the tempo against this fast thing and I've gone, "Wow! What a fantastic singer!" It was a revelation, I thought she was brilliant. So, I went down to Ronnie Scott's and said, "Look, you've gotta hear this singer," and raved on and they said, "Well ask her to come down and we'll give her an audition" – and I can't remem-ber whether I did the audition with her or not but there's always been this friction between myself and the Ronnie Scott establish-ment, so I probably wasn't invited, and already I'd started pulling away anyway by then.   (Schonfield 1992)

Winstone first sang with Stevens and the SME in January 1968 at an unissued recording session at Olympic studios that took place a few weeks before an entirely instrumental grouping recorded the amazing *Karyobin*. She then performed in July at a BBC gig at the Playhouse Theatre, which was broadcast in September. The group on that occasion was Kenny Wheeler on flugelhorn, Paul Rutherford on trombone, Trevor Watts on bass clarinet and, of course, John Stevens. Even more importantly, she played at the Baden-Baden Free Jazz Meeting organized by Joachim E. Berendt in December 1970 under the auspices of Süddeutsche Rundfunk as part of an orchestra that included the legendary American improvisers Don Cherry and Steve Lacy, and a host of major European players such as saxophonists Trevor Watts and Peter Brötzmann, trombonists Paul Rutherford and Albert Mangelsdorff, bassists Johnny Dyani and Dave Holland and percussionists Stevens and Han Bennink. Of special interest here was the presence of Norwegian vocalist Karin Krog, a singer with a similar history and pedigree. Winstone also sang in various small groups at the festival including one that featured just her, Krog, Dave Holland and John Stevens. Recordings were made of all of these sessions and details can be found in Paul Wilson's comprehensive and thorough John Stevens discography (Wilson 2002). Other gigs went unrecorded. By the end of 1970, Winstone was working regularly with Mike Westbrook's Concert Band and Michael Garrick and her involvement with Stevens and free improvisation seems to have declined.

Some musicians struggle to articulate the processes through which their work has developed. Winstone is as unusually articulate in this respect, as she is in her lyrics:

> I think that when I started I was singing standards and didn't sing wordlessly at all. If I improvised I kept the words but created a new melody or added a few words or would leave some out. It was only when I joined Michael Garrick's band – I took over from Jim Philip who was leaving and the line-up was two saxophones and trumpet but it became saxophone, voice and trumpet. I sang his lines, the saxophone lines, and I'd improvise on those. I never really thought of it as scat singing because it was a different kind of music from the type I'd heard people like Ella scatting on. So, I didn't use any of those syllables that scat singers used. I tended to think of myself as just trying to sing this musical line without anything getting in the way like a sound which might seem alien to me anyway. I could never really sing those bebop sounds.
>
> (Interview with Norma Winstone, May 2006)

The experience of singing with Garrick enabled Winstone to begin to find her own voice. No mean lyricist himself, Garrick's songs were perfect for her:

It was liberating to sing songs that I'd never heard anybody else sing because I felt that there was nothing I had to come up to. I sang these songs with my own voice – no American accent because there was none of that influence. When I next sang a standard, I stopped and thought, "What do I sing?" I thought, "This is me." So, I then became more myself as a singer.

(Interview with Norma Winstone, May 2006)

The result of all this was one of the finest, if also more neglected of jazz records, a total synthesis of everything that Winstone had been developing up to this point. *Edge of Time* (Argo) included her distinctive wordless singing, as she wove gorgeously evocative lines around Kenny Wheeler's blistering trumpet solo on "Enjoy This Day", as well as beautiful open-ended experiments with the song form on the title track and the delicate "Songs for a Child". The majority of compositions and arrangements are by her then-partner John Taylor, and the sense is very much of a collaborative effort from all involved. Mike Taylor's "Song of Love" features in an arrangement for a drum-less, chamber jazz group foreshadowing both Winstone's later work with Azimuth and involvement in the Mike Taylor Remembered project in 1973. Sadly, the latter – a Denis Preston/Lansdowne production – was only officially released in 2007.

Looking back at *Edge of Time*, Winstone expresses her dissatisfaction at the sound of her voice, a comment she also makes about her singing on Mike Westbrook's *Love Songs*:

I can only think that I don't like the way I sound. [laughs] I didn't like the way I sounded at the time and I still don't like it. It's been a whole process over the years of getting a sound that I can bear to listen to really. Perhaps most singers go through that. Also, the recording didn't really do a lot for the voice. Recording techniques back then aren't what they are now. I was singing in different way but I do think the music's interesting.

(Interview with Norma Winstone, May 2006)

That might be Winstone's view. However, the sheer, majestic force that she brings to John Surman's tempestuous "Erebus (Son of Chaos)" and "Shadows" astounds. Others might have been overwhelmed in such a context but she easily holds her own with Alan Skidmore's tenor on the former and Henry Lowther's trumpet on the latter. Few singers were willing then, or since, to work in such "out" territory, and her only possible peer in jazz would be Karin Krog (one thinks perhaps of Cathy Berberian in the field of contemporary music). *Edge of Time* was Winstone's first solo album, and it was not really until the eighties that further solo projects were recorded. Yet, if Winstone's reputation were to rest on this album, Westbrook's *Love Songs* and Michael Garrick's *Heart is a Lotus* (Argo; Vocalion), *Troppo* (Argo; Vocalion) and the genre-busting oratorio *Mr Smith's Apocalypse* (Argo; Vocalion), she would still be one of the most important jazz singers, and one of the most significant figures to emerge from British jazz.

It was clearly hard for women to establish themselves on the British jazz scene. There was a reluctance to take female singers and instrumentalists seriously. Yet, as we will see with Maggie Nicols, Julie Tippetts/Driscoll, Norma Winstone, Kathy Stobart, Gill Alexander and later with Barbara Thompson, some women were able to achieve both status and respect within a male-dominated scene. They did so by dint of their own talent and, again it must be acknowledged, with some support from some male musicians on the scene. This no doubt aided the process of their assimilation, which came nevertheless at a price and took place within a context where male dominance was not really being challenged or threatened by these women. Had there, perhaps, been larger numbers of female artists emerging at this time, a more hostile response from some quarters might have been evident.

Maggie Nicols began singing with John Stevens and the SME around the point when Norma Winstone had moved on. Like Winstone, and Tippetts, her career began in a more mainstream musical context. Along with Tippetts, Nicols has done a great deal to create new possibilities for the human voice in jazz and free improvisation both by a commitment to teaching and by example. Listening to her voice can mirror the human condition. She can cause confusion in listeners through her willingness to experiment but, far more often, a Nicols performance can be a transcendent and cathartic experience. She can also be side-splittingly funny. In terms of her work in this period, there are few recorded examples available – readers should check out her more recent work with Les Diaboliques, featuring bassist Joelle Léandre and pianist Irène Schweizer, the Glasgow Improvisers' Orchestra and The Gathering. After all, the journey she is now on began in the late sixties.

Nicols's approach and ideas will be discussed in Chapters 11 and 14, on free improvisation and on jazz and politics, respectively. What follows relates more immediately to women in British jazz in the sixties. Nicols is justifiably keen to emphasize that she came to free music having already learnt her trade in the clubs singing jazz:

> I was 16 or 17. I was a Windmill girl and I left the Windmill in 1964. Gradually, from then on, I started singing with Denis [Rose] when I was about 17 and in the pubs, clubs and so on. I would really like this stated because people just know me from free improvisation and they have no idea that I paid my dues on the circuit singing jazz standards. I really got a very strong grounding in that. Just as not many people know that Derek Bailey played in dance-halls. They think we just started making so-called weird noises. It evolved as a musical history.
>
> (Interview with Maggie Nicols, October 2010)

It is important to note that Nicols found the active encouragement of several male musicians extremely helpful. At risk of over-emphasizing this point, valuable though this was, it has to be seen in the context of an environment that generally discouraged the participation of women. In a way, the best a female singer or instrumentalist could hope for was to be seen as an exception and/or as "one of the boys". "People can go, 'Oh well, you're different,'" she notes, "and that then is a way of dividing you off from other women." And it can be a seductive process, as Nicols explains:

> Because for a while I basked in that. Because from feeling this very low, really low status when I first came on the jazz scene because I was just seen as some sort of ... well, I won't go into that but it was very painful. If it hadn't been for Denis, that would have continued. For Denis to actually mentor me, because that's what he did, he mentored me, he developed me as a singer and then to go from that to suddenly having this status of "Oh, but you're different from the others. You're not like the other chick singers." It was very, very flattering and thinking to myself "Oh, I'm not like the other chick singers. I've left them behind."
> (Interview with Maggie Nichols, October 2010)

In Julie Tippetts's case, with Brian Auger she had suffered a great deal of press intrusion and had left the group in the middle of an American tour. She is clear, however, that she sees the music she made with Auger as a significant aspect of her career, and one that she carries with her. It is therefore important to consider here her contribution to the music of that group and how this informed her subsequent work. She had been introduced to the music of pianist–composer Keith Tippett through her manager, Giorgio Gomelsky:

> He played me this music and Keith's group were playing a gig, at the Marquee I think, and Giorgio said you must come down and hear him. It was almost like it was something I wanted to hear but didn't know what it was. It was really quite odd. And Giorgio introduced me to him and we were just ... Keith remembers it that it wasn't a very good gig, and I said, "Oh that was amazing!" And he just did a strop. It was kind of like that. I was impressed and he wasn't having it. It was that kind of situation but we just became pals. (Interview with Julie Tippetts, September 2008)

At Driscoll's suggestion, Gomelsky hired Tippett to work with the singer on her first solo album, *1969*. As noted earlier (see page 158), they became more than friends and married not long afterwards, and Julie Driscoll became Julie Tippetts. Given the direction that her music would take in later years, it may surprise some readers that she began her career singing standards with her father's band. But the experience left her with a love for the craft of a good song, and this has informed her first songwriting efforts with Brian Auger, as well as her subsequent solo work.

The first Trinity album, *Open* (Marmalade; Made in Germany), had been an album of covers, with the exception of the Auger–Driscoll track, "Why Am I Treated So Bad?". The double follow-up, *Streetnoise* (Marmalade; Made in Germany), featured three songs by Driscoll alone – "Czechoslovakia" (a protest song about the Soviet invasion), the folky "Vauxhall to the Lambeth Bridge" and "A Word About Colour". Lyrically, "A Word About Colour" is the strongest and most interesting. *1969* (Polydor) was something of a leap forward, if not a complete change of direction:

> I suppose then, I had a lot to get off my chest really. "Czecho-slovakia" was with Brian Auger – "Word About Colour" for *Streetnoise*. I did stuff on there. I started writing before 1969 because I bought a beautiful guitar in California, a beautiful Martin guitar, and I'd been learning since I was 11 but I hadn't kept playing because being on the road I never had much chance. But when I bought this guitar, I really knuckled down to teaching myself and rediscovering – which is all forgotten now – which is tragic, and I can't play any of that stuff anymore. Really tragic, but it's gone. I just fell into writing stuff.
>
> (Interview with Julie Tippetts, September 2008)

1969 featured four band tracks with various members of the Keith Tippett Group on horns, as well as members of prog-rock band Blossom Toes and several other jazz players of note, as well as several more acoustic numbers. What strikes most, however, is her growing confidence in her songwriting and the ease with which Driscoll moves between the group setting of numbers like "A New Awakening" and gentler pieces like "Those That We Love" and "The Choice". "Walk Down" is the most interesting cut, both in terms of its structure, its lyric and in the way Driscoll uses her voice to declaim against the dense musical backcloth. At the same time, both positively and less so, *1969* is of its time.

By *Sunset Glow* (Utopia; Voiceprint), Driscoll (now Tippetts) had sung on husband Keith's epic *Septober Energy* and written its libretto. She had also sung on Carla Bley's *Tropic Appetites* from 1974 and was working with the improvising quartet Ovary Lodge, with Tippett, bassist Roy Babbington and percussionist Frank Perry. Sunset Glow was both better and more consistent than its predecessor. In the six intervening years Tippetts had grown as a songwriter and her voice had acquired a gorgeous timbre that recalls Sandy Denny of Fairport Convention. Some have compared *Sunset Glow* to Robert Wyatt's work, and in particular his album *Rock Bottom* (Virgin; Domino). They have a similar feel and both albums explore a musical terrain between jazz, folk and rock with equal skill. Yet Tippetts's record is also a remarkable summation of her career to date, as well as a glorious synthesis of all the places that she had been musically in that time. There is the jazz-rock that she had sung with Auger and with husband Keith in "Mind of a Child" and "Oceans and Sky", complete with a horn section of Elton Dean, Nick Evans and Marc Charig, while "Sunset Glow" and the overdubbed "Lilies" echo the quiet intimacy of Ovary Lodge. The album has a strange, somnambulistic quality to it, as if one is hearing it through the drowsiness of a long, warm summer afternoon, which lingers long after it has ended. It is all over far too quickly.

The issue of role models is crucial. Wherever possible, from a developmental perspective, it helps where role models are in some degree as "like oneself" as possible. The capacity to project imaginatively that human beings possess is aided when we can see ourselves reflected in some way in the person and behaviour of a potential model. The situation in which Nicols, Tippetts and other women artists found themselves was one with a distinct paucity of such figures. Fortunately, these women had both talent and their own personal resources to draw upon and were able to find sympathetic male artists, who were able to help create a space within which that talent could flourish. Nicols is a committed feminist and leftist activist. When asked her how far she had been affected by the developing women's movement, her answer illustrates reflects the fact that the kind of feminism described by the term "Women's Liberation" was slower to take root in Britain than in North America or continental Europe:

> I wasn't until … it wasn't until … I didn't really come across feminism until the late seventies. In fact, it was a huge … that was another liberation. There are landmarks in my musical development. There was definitely Denis Rose. He really took me under his wing when I'd been really badly used and dismissed and made to feel worse than unimportant by some musicians and then Denis took me under his wing and developed me as a singer of standards. And then, of course, John Stevens who woke me up to free improvisation and then the women's liberation movement that gave me a lot of self-respect and self-worth because up to then I had felt that, if a man didn't approve of me, I didn't exist. It was huge for me. The women's movement had a huge impact on me in every way. Probably in the mid-seventies really.
> (Interview with Maggie Nichols, October 2010)

In one sense, the women we are discussing are heirs to an earlier, less vociferous wave of campaigning for women's rights rather than that which emerged in the late sixties and early seventies. The issues around feminism in Britain and its impact on British society in the post-war period are complex.

It certainly seems that the kind of activism associated with it that was seen in the USA was slow to arrive in the UK. Germaine Greer's seminal *The Female Eunuch* was not published until 1970, Sheila Rowbotham's *Women's Consciousness, Men's World* came out in 1973, while *Spare Rib*, the UK feminist magazine, only began publishing in 1972. Arthur Marwick and others have gone so far as to argue that the legislation that was passed in the fifties and sixties to enable women to achieve equality and maximize their role as citizens was the result not so much of the "exertions of active Feminists" as of "deeper social and economic forces favourable to a general liberalisation" (Marwick 1996, 149). However, in some ways this misses the point.

In fact, feminism as an influential force in British social life did exist prior to this point in the UK. As Samantha Clements (2008) argues, the question is one of nomenclature. Women were very active in the UK following the Second World War in a range of campaigns for equal pay, women's property rights and reproductive rights, as well as in a variety of more general campaigns such as the peace and anti-nuclear movements. Clements cites several other writers in support of her argument, including Joyce Freeguard and Olive Banks (Banks 1981; Freeguard 2004). All three stress that many of the legislative changes such as the Equal Pay Act 1970, the Sex Discrimination Act 1975, as well as the Life Peerages Act 1958, the Abortion Act 1967, the Divorce Reform Act 1969 and the Matrimonial Property Act 1970, stemmed from feminist agitation in a range of women's organizations, in trade unions and in the Labour Party. By the time Winstone, Nicols and Tippetts began to build their careers, the trends and currents that Clements identifies had already begun to impact on British social life. Whether or not such artists were aware at the time is not strictly relevant to our deliberations. The movement towards greater flexibility in gender roles and expectations underpinning these was already beginning to change its shape and focus. This was one aspect of the situation within which Winstone, Nicols *et al.* were working. At the same time, male dominance of the world of work, including in the music business and jazz, was slow to reflect these important social developments.. The next phase of feminism, the one most often identified with the sixties, in fact came into being later.

This point is echoed by Mark Donnelly, who writes:

> The "third phase" feminisms (deliberately plural) that developed in the late sixties shared some of the objectives of earlier feminist campaigns, but ultimately they were more ambitious and profound than their forerunners: what they aimed at was a radical shift in male–female relations. (Donnelly 2005, 158)

Donnelly's point is well made. What Marwick is describing is a later and distinct phase in the women's movement. The first key event in the history of a new, radicalized feminism Movement was the women's history conference and women's liberation workshop held at Ruskin College, Oxford in February 1970. Jonathan Green notes that the first National Women's Conference was initiated by "various American ex-pats, somewhat further down the feminist path than their British sisters". He adds that almost 600 delegates from various trades union, socialist groupings and from both middle class and working class organizations attended, and that the conference led to the formation of new women's groups throughout the UK (Green 1998b, 405–6). Samantha Clements writes that the conference resulted in four key demands – equal pay, equal education and opportunities, twenty-four-hour nurseries, and free contraception and abortion on demand. She continues, "These were not new demands, but into the 1970s feminism became a stronger, more vocal, if even more fractured ideological movement" (Clements 2008, 256). The difference between the new and the old feminism stemmed both from the movement's links with the new left, and dissatisfactions with it, while it also drew support from activists who had grown disillusioned with the old left and worker's organizations. It was both more militant and visible, as Clements suggests. Perhaps the most important example of this militancy occurred in 1970. The Miss World Contest of 1969 had seen women protesting against the event. In 1970, however, 30 activists disrupted the contest held at the Albert Hall. Compère Bob Hope was pelted with flour following a remark about Vietnam and television transmission was temporarily blacked out. Five of the women were put on trial in February 1972 and fined for their involvement (Green 1998b, 407–8). The new Miss World, from Granada, declared, "I do not think women should ever achieve equal rights. I do not want to. I still like a gentleman to hold a chair back for me" (quoted in Sandbrook 2008, 704). Prince Charles, just to show that the apple never falls far from the tree, said of the protesters, "Basically, I think it is because they want to be men" (Sandbrook 2008, 704).

Issues such as equal pay were not ignored by this new wave of feminist agitation. However, as Donnelly suggests, the campaign now focused as much on "women's bodies and the sexual act as important sites of struggle" (Donnelly 2005, 162–3). Women's health, the abuse of women (and children) by men, rights of access to public areas without fear of violence or threat, the right to organize independently of men and male dominance in the area of cultural production became as significant as more obviously material demands. As the quotations from Miss World and Prince Charles seem to indicate, it was not hard to marginalize radical feminism, and yet, through the network of women's groups that were established in the wake of the National Women's Conference and after, these ideas began percolate. Women students formed their own university women's groups and women academics provided a powerful role model for many such young people. Socialist groups also had their women's sections. The International Socialists, for example, had Women's Voice. The process of dissemination was, nevertheless, a gradual one.

It is not surprising, therefore, that female jazz artists were not touched directly by the new feminism. As Norma Winstone comments (interview with Norma Winstone, December 2010), the male dominance of British jazz seemed almost a given reality:

> I think the situation in jazz was the same as the situation for women everywhere really. It was no different but I always felt that jazz music seemed to attract more men than women, as listeners even. You would see people and it was the wives who were generally not so interested in the music as the husbands were – in the audiences. And the people I knew, it always seemed to be the men who were really interested. I don't know … jazz has changed. I mean the word has stretched to incorporate all different sorts of music, so maybe we have a bigger female audience now. I don't know. As far as the impact on me is concerned, I didn't really notice anything.

And she offers an insight into how the situation of women in jazz might have been perceived:

> Being a singer in jazz – that affected me. If I had ever felt any negativity, which actually I didn't very much, I would have put it down to the fact that I was a singer not a woman. Most of the jazz singers were women anyway. I'm not sure why that was, though I suppose it was for decoration at some point in the history of jazz. But I think that there was an anti-singer thing.

Winstone mentions again John Stevens's support and encouragement, and adds:

> I have always just found the male musicians I've worked with to be helpful and I can't make up something. I've talked about this with Nikki Iles, who obviously came up much later, but she said the same. She's never felt any hostility from any musicians she worked with.
> (Interview with Norma Winstone, December 2010)

Feminists, or "Women's Libbers" as they were pigeon-holed, were readily associated in the media and in the public mind with lesbianism, man-haters, bra-burners and so on. And there was often a strident tone to the new feminism that, at the time at least, alienated some women musicians. Asked whether she was aware or affected by the movement for women's liberation, Kathy Stobart replied, "I had nothing to do with it. No, once I had something to do with it. It was a very … I regretted it very much." The situation she was referring to concerned being asked to do some "jazz" for a lesbian art film. Her immediate association for the term "feminist" was with "butch" women. Clearly, she had no problem with the sexuality of the director or cast, but found the project and her involvement artistically frustrating.

Barbara Thompson's reaction was similar to Stobart's,

> I was not popular with the feminists, I'm afraid. I kept well away from them. I actually went to Vienna and taught and spent a week coaching and teaching women musicians and they were a weird lot. I was quite frightened of them actually. They looked terrifying. I'm not into segregating sexes. I'm not a feminist. I'm for anyone who's a good person or a good artist. I don't care what sex they are. Actually, I didn't realize it but when I work abroad a lot of my audience are gay. I didn't know that. I get fifty per cent of my audience are women when I work abroad because they trust me because they know it's not going to be loud and leery. And, say in places like Austria, a lot of people, who are gay couples come.
> (Interview with Barbara Thompson, March 2010)

Thompson had studied at the RCM and began playing jazz in the student bands of Alan Cohen, Gordon Rose and Graham Collier. She joined the NJO led by Neil Ardley in 1964, while still at college.

> They were looking for a saxophone player who could read. They had lots of players, jazzers who could blow but none of them could read. I went in there as an audition and, because I could read and play in tune, they invited me to join the band.
> (Interview with Barbara Thompson, March 2010)

Thompson admits that she experienced a degree of chauvinistic behaviour on the scene. "Those were the days when the brass players would get very drunk and leery," she told me:

> and they'd say things to me like, "Oh, you're alright! You haven't got a family to support." [laughs] They'd always hold up some other saxophone player, like always raving about someone like Skid or these other people and I used to think, "Why don't they encourage me? I can hold my own with him." On the whole, I got away with it because I was alright, because they did respect me because I was very innocent and naive, and if they told dirty jokes I didn't get them. I did not get them and they could see that so they didn't persevere. They left me alone because of [my] being quite middle class, which was a bit unusual in those days, let alone female.   (Interview with Barbara Thompson, March 2010)

By the early seventies, Thompson already had an impressive discography. She had played on both NJO albums, and her skills as a reader are used on flute on the title track of their second release, *Le Déjeuner Sur L'herbe* (Verve) and on soprano on Michael Garrick's *Dusk Fire*. However, her performance both solo and in duet with trumpeter Henry Lowther on Mike Taylor's setting of Segovia, "Study", reveals her highly developed sense of dynamics and what a fine musician she already was. This is even more evident on the live album, *Neil Ardley's New Jazz Orchestra – Camden '70* (Dusk Fire). Thompson played on all Neil Ardley's recordings in the seventies, as well as on records by Keef Hartley, Colosseum and Howard Riley. However, it was only after 1976/7 with the formation of Jubiaba and Paraphernalia that she began leading her own bands. Her first records under her own name came out in 1978, since which time she has built up a remarkably loyal audience, particularly in continental Europe, and has established an impressive body of work.

Prior to that, from the early seventies onwards, Thompson co-led a group with Don Rendell and played regularly at the Bull's Head in Barnes:

> In 1969, Bill Le Sage really took me under his wing at the Bull's Head. I was there every fortnight for 15 years and built up a really strong following there. I played there with Art a lot, as well. Art Themen was great. I learned a lot from him.
> (Interview with Barbara Thompson, March 2010)

Confidence in her musical abilities was one thing but the impression remains that Thompson still felt she had to learn the business, as well as the craft. She took her time and this strategy stood her and her husband and musical partner, Jon Hiseman, in very good stead. In a way, her career seems what one might describe as "old school". She paid her dues with bands led by others, serving her apprenticeship before branching out on her own.

As we have seen, women in British jazz in the sixties and seventies seem to have dealt with their situation pragmatically and were able to negotiate their place in the music by virtue of their abilities and by avoiding those who were unreceptive of their talents or unaccepting of their presence. Fortunately, there were those like John Stevens, Trevor Watts, Kenny Wheeler, Michael Garrick, Denis Rose and others who were supportive of women musicians. Unsurprisingly, for a gay male jazz musician, the strategy was much the same, as Graham Collier notes:

> I don't think it was ever a problem – possibly because I was more of a loner composer/bandleader than a regular gigging musician. The musicians I worked with never bothered if I brought a boyfriend to a gig, probably never noticed until it was someone regular. Although when John [Gill] and I met in 1976, he came on an

Arts Council Great Britain tour with me and they certainly knew then, but there were never any problems. I even got my band to play at a Campaign for Homosexual Equality conference for free in Sheffield.

I think there's a certain kind of man who mouths off against women and gays, etc. when they're together because of that social milieu. When the dynamic changes, they don't talk so much publicly. And I was always surrounded by nice people – kind of a vicious circle but if I had suspected any strong anti-feminist or gay vibe, they wouldn't have been there in the first place. Actually it's a bit deeper than that, I think that as a bandleader you choose musicians because of their overall vibe, because you want to be around them, be close to them. "Know how they play poker", as Duke said, and one senses in some people that you just won't get on. And that comes across in their music as well sometimes. There are many musicians I admire musically, who I wouldn't hire because of their vibe.

(E-mail interview with Graham Collier, December 2008)

The gap in skill between a student or a semi-pro musician can be cruelly revealed by a competent professional in most forms of music. In jazz, the difference can be even more sharply highlighted due to two things – one is the ability to swing, the other is the ability to improvise. Acceptance by fellow professionals can be hard-won, whether you are male or female, straight or gay. Stobart, Laine, Winstone and others survived because they were very, very good and won their peers' respect, as Stobart recalls:

To put it in a nutshell, when I first entered the business ... you see people often say they've no time for women. No, they won't have them in the band. The real reason is – I'm not blowing my own trumpet – if you're good enough, they'll have you. That's the way it was. Those coming out with the old sour grapes bit, it was because they weren't good enough, that's all. When I came down and discovered I could play jazz and I played in one or two well-known ones in the West End, the lads actually they really took me to their heart. They treated me like a little sister. I came down to London and I worked at playing jazz in London – I was only 17 you see. They did. They just treated me like a sister and, if anybody said any swearing or any hint of a bad joke somebody got a dig in the ribs and "Now, now. Don't you..." That's the way they were with me. They treated me with respect. I could play in a competitive manner with a lot of men and that was good enough for them – I was accepted. No question.

(Interview with Kathy Stobart, March 2009)

Stobart clearly has a point, but we must also acknowledge that the strain of coping with intolerant and intolerable behaviour did take its toll on some very talented women musicians. Trumpeter Gracie Cole had played in Ivy Benson's band and had led her own all-female band. She joined the Squadronaires in 1951 and experienced male prejudice – and not for the first time (see Tracy 1997, 341–2). One male trumpeter, Ron Simmonds, was particularly obnoxious:

> He criticized my playing, would chat to others and ignore me, as if I didn't exist. I had to really control myself and my playing because I knew he'd have a ball if I cracked a note. It got to a point where I gave up rather than play in those conditions. He said later he was envious because I was a famous player while he was up-and-coming at the time, and that made him mad. He was prejudiced pure and simple.   (Cole quoted in O'Brien 1995, 34)

Ivy Benson's band was not the only all-female ensemble. When one remembers that the big bands of Ted Heath, Geraldo, Ambrose and so on were feeder schools for both modern and mainstream British jazz, one might have expected that more women instrumentalists might have made that same transition from Benson or whoever to the British scene of the fifties and sixties. Trombonist Sheila Tracy and fellow Benson alumnus Phyl Brown had some success as a vocal and trombone duo under the name of the Tracy Sisters. Gracie Cole also had some success up to the sixties, when she retired to look after her two daughters. After those names, it becomes hard to find any others. Other names we have not mentioned would include saxophonist Betty Smith, who began her career with the Freddy Randall Band in the fifties and co-led a quintet with pianist Brian Lemon. Smith continued to play into the eighties most often as a member of "The Best of British Jazz" with Don Lusher and Kenny Baker, and Kathy Stobart recalls her as "a good player, she was and a fine big sound she had". The other names that spring to mind are those of Dixieland pianist Ramona Swale and, of course, those two "trad"/blues vocalists Beryl Bryden and Ottilie Patterson. Given all the women musicians we have discussed or mentioned, we would barely have enough for a big band.

What is more, even if we see these artists as pioneers and role models, there was still a substantial gap between this earlier generation and the emergence of a larger female presence on the British scene. For that, we have to wait for the late seventies and the emergence of musicians like Annie Whitehead, Deidre Cartwright, the Guest Stars and others. We can note that social developments can be uneven in their emergence but that seems insufficient as an explanation in itself. It seems that we can only assume that the social and economic conditions were not as yet right for the surfacing of significant numbers of women musicians, just as by the end of the seventies women were only just beginning to claim their place in a range of occupations. If anything, British jazz was a late developer in this both compared with the USA and continental Europe and compared with rock music.

One is tempted to suggest that the arrival of a number of all-female groups around 1976–80 in punk rock was much more important in creating the necessary space for women musicians in jazz, than were our sixties pioneers. Groups like the Runaways and the Go-Gos (USA), the Slits, the Raincoats, Girlschool and the Dolly Mixtures (UK), Kleenex and the Mo-Dettes (Switzerland) and the confrontational front-person roles taken by Siouxsie (the Banshees), Pauline Murray (Penetration), Poly Styrene (X-Ray Spex) and, of course, Patti Smith, did a great deal to change the image of women in music. In fact, several women jazz players of note – for example, Deidre Cartwright and Alison Rayner – came from rock music in the first instance. Prior to this, the role of a women in rock tended to be confined to certain proscribed roles – there was the fey, ethereal goddess or nymph-like figure (Jacqui McShee, Celia Humphris of Trees, Maddy Prior), the raunchy rock chick (Maggie Bell, Elkie Brooks, Janis Joplin) or the older sister, confessional singer–songwriter (Bridget St John, Sandy Denny, Carly Simon, Carole King) plus the occasional earth-mother type. There were exceptions such as all-women bands Fanny and Bertha and the explicitly feminist Joy of Cooking, who were led by pianist Toni Brown and guitarist Terry Garthwaite. But that was about it.

Ideas from radical feminism had become more accepted, or at least more widely disseminated by the end of the seventies. Legislation outlawing (overt) discrimination had been in place for several years and one of the effects of legislative change is that it can change attitudes, as well as behaviour. But there were also examples of women coming together in different situations to aid, encourage and support each other. Behind this we can identify certain shifts ideologically in relation to how women were seen that were beginning to be coupled with a growing possibilities for women of personal and financial independence in British society. Jam Today, featuring several later members of the Guest Stars, formed in 1976. By the late seventies, Maggie Nicols had become an active feminist and had co-founded the group OVA. Not long after this, she started the Feminist Improvising Group, with bassoonist–composer Lindsay Cooper (ex-Comus, ex-Henry Cow). In 1980, she began organizing Contradictions, a women's workshop performance group that dealt with improvisation and other modes of performance in a variety of mediums including music and dance. Prior to that, the Feminist Improvising Group (FIG) was established in 1977 in London by Nicols and Cooper along with cellist–bassist Georgie Born, also from Henry Cow, vocalist–pianist Cathy Williams and trumpeter Corinne Liensol.

With notable exceptions, attitudes towards women in jazz have been slow to move within what was throughout the fifties, sixties and seventies very much a male-dominated British scene. Those artists who came out of that period were in all senses exceptional and survived due to their determination and talent. How far was jazz behind the rest of the entertainment industry or society as a whole in this regard? Certainly, there were more opportunities in the theatre and in popular music for women. Quite a number of women artists sold records in significant numbers in the sixties, from Petula Clark to Sandie Shaw. Yet in terms of overall total sales, as Donnelly (2005, 44–5) points out, only three female acts made the list of top-selling singles artists in the UK during the sixties – the Supremes, Cilla Black and Dusty Springfield. Of these, only Springfield could be said to have established herself as a "serious" artist, who determined the direction of her own career.

If we were to sit in judgement, then we would have to view the British scene at the time as being highly unfriendly to women. In this instance, we must look at the significant changes that were happening elsewhere in society for women and at the male jazz musicians, who did encourage female participation. I think we must also recognize that female artists from the mid-seventies onwards took a very active role in changing the scene in these respects, and the impetus for later change came primarily from women themselves. That takes nothing away from pioneers like Laine, Winstone, Stobart, Nicols, Tippetts and others. To an extent they helped by paving the way.

11 The Best Things in Life Are Free

Improvisation is too good to be left to chance.
Paul Simon, *International Herald Tribune*, 12 October 1990

Liberty is precious – so precious it must be rationed.
V.I. Lenin (quoted in J.L. Hill, *The Political Centrist*, 2009)

Upon the other hand, Socialism itself will be of value simply because it will lead to Individualism.   Oscar Wilde, *The Soul of Man under Socialism*, 1891)

The emergence of free jazz in the USA in the late 1950s with Ornette Coleman and later Cecil Taylor, Archie Shepp, Albert Ayler, Coltrane, Sun Ra and others was to prove almost as important politically and socially as it was musically. In Britain, Joe Harriott's experiments occurred simultaneously and, to an extent, independently of what was happening across the Atlantic. Subsequent developments in free playing in the UK were certainly influenced by the American *nouvelle vague* but took place in a very different cultural context far removed from the imperatives of racial politics that confronted white America. Perhaps what linked these two essentially separate movements was something in the spirit of the times, which identified "freedom" as a desirable state to be sought in life and in music. It is surely no coincidence that the birth of these "new" approaches to making music should occur during an epoch when issues of personal freedom and liberation had begun to occupy such a central place for debate. What separated British from American free jazz would prove more important than what still linked the two approaches. And that was a desire to produce a music influenced by but no longer dependent upon African-American forms.

Barry Miles in *Hippie* (Miles 2004) sees the birth of the counter-culture in Britain as a reaction to post-war austerity. In the sixties, he suggests, young people at last had some money in their pockets and were for the first time able to make their own economic, social and cultural choices. "They looked around and saw that everything was controlled by old people – those hypocrites intent on maintaining the status quo as if World War II had never happened."

Why were the hippy and, by inference, the counter-culture so significant? Miles answers his own rhetorical question, "Because it was only by stepping outside society that people were able to look at it objectively – to see what was wrong with society, to see how they'd like to change it" (Miles 2004, 9).

Barry Miles was there at the inception of the British counter-culture, involved in many of its defining moments and was one of the founders of *International Times*. If the war had changed the political landscape and agenda, in Miles's view, this was now being obstructed by the older generation and there is some truth in his argument. The Second World War was, after all, a political and ideological struggle as well as a military one. In waging war against totalitarianism, it was inevitable that questions of freedom and the nature of democracy should arise. The demand for independence by subject nations became louder and more vociferous after 1945, ironically at the same time that the capacity for self-determination of some states in the northern hemisphere was becoming compromised by the Cold War.

The question of freedom had also been at the heart of Roosevelt's commitment to American involvement in the fight against fascism. The USA declared war, first against Japan and then a few days later against Germany in December 1941. However, Roosevelt had already used his State of the Union address on 6 January 1941 to articulate "The Four Freedoms" – fundamental rights that humans everywhere had a right to expect. In hindsight, Roosevelt was preparing the ideological ground for US involvement in the war. His words, often satirized since, remain worth reading and reflecting upon:

> In the future days, which we seek to make secure, we look forward to a world founded upon four essential human freedoms. The first is freedom of speech and expression – everywhere in the world. The second is freedom of every person to worship God in his own way – everywhere in the world. The third is freedom from want – which, translated into world terms, means economic understandings which will secure to every nation a healthy peacetime life for its inhabitants – everywhere in the world. The fourth is freedom from fear – which, translated into world terms, means a world-wide reduction of armaments to such a point and in such a thorough fashion that no nation will be in a position to commit an act of physical aggression against any neighbor – anywhere in the world. That is no vision of a distant millennium. It is a definite basis for a kind of world attainable in our own time and generation. That kind of world is the very antithesis of the so-called new

order of tyranny which the dictators seek to create with the crash of a bomb.

Not only did the last two "freedoms" go far beyond the US Constitution and Bill of Rights but the president's wife, Eleanor, fought to ensure their inclusion in the United Nations Universal Declaration of Human Rights (General Assembly Resolution 217A, 1948). It was not, therefore, just affluent, well-educated, post-war youth who were taxed by such matters.

The Cold War did far worse than push such concerns into the political wasteland. It created a situation in which these could only be legitimately expressed through the preference for one of two artificially constructed opposites. It was left to philosophers, academics and artists to find new ways of confronting the dilemmas facing humankind that allowed for a broader range of possibilities and potential choices. Brief consideration of the ideas of three such individuals will help set the context to allow us to explore the impetus for "freedom" in areas of musical and artistic expression.

The first theorist we must consider is American academic psychologist, Abraham Maslow. Credited as the founder of humanistic psychology, a third way between psychoanalysis and behaviourism, Maslow developed his ideas through considering those that he identified as being "self-actualizing" individuals. Arguably, his choices seem to indicate his underlying preferences and values, as he chose to examine people such as Albert Einstein, Eleanor Roosevelt, Nobel Peace Prize winner and suffrage campaigner Jane Addams and Frederick Douglass, the escaped slave who came to epitomize the struggle to abolish slavery. The latter, incidentally, was one of the signatories of the Declaration of Sentiments prepared at the first convention of women's suffrage held in 1848 in Seneca Falls, New York. Douglass was a firm believer in the equality of all people, whether black, female, Native American, or recent immigrant and was fond of saying, "I would unite with anybody to do right and with nobody to do wrong." Maslow recognized that few people reached this level but, nevertheless, saw this as an intrinsically human potential. Though he first proposed his "hierarchy of needs" in a 1943 paper, it was not until 1954 that these were fully articulated in his book *Motivation and Personality* (Maslow 1954). In this, he identified five levels of human need – physiological, safety, love/belonging, self-esteem, self-actualization. As a humanist, it was axiomatic for Maslow that it was impossible for human beings to achieve higher psychological and emotional needs when basic physiological and security needs were thwarted.

A number of criticisms can be levelled at Maslow's schema, most obviously that it derives from a white, essentially middle-class, liberal, eurocentric perspective. That said, his ideas were important because it was explicit within his schema that poverty, oppression and social and economic injustice could be seen to obstruct essential human needs that were located within each individual. In defining these as needs established within a coherent framework of human development, Maslow was, in one sense at least, suggesting that these might even be rights and that society might be ordered to meet these needs rather than obstruct them. One student for whom Maslow proved a major influence was Abbie Hoffman, later to become a major American counter-culture activist. Another important influence was upon writer Colin Wilson, author of another key text for sixties bohemia, *The Outsider* (Wilson 1956). Wilson's book focused on the psyche of the outsider, his effect on society and society's effect on him, and did so, not unlike Maslow's *Motivation and Personality*, by examining the lives and works of a diverse group of writers, artists and thinkers.

By contrast, Isaiah Berlin could hardly be described as a counter-cultural figure. However, his inaugural lecture, "Two Concepts of Liberty", as Chichele Professor of Social and Political Theory at All Souls College in 1958, saw him, both a Russian and a Jew, grappling with the same kind of questions that would tax the young and rebellious. The twenties and thirties had seen the rise of totalitarianism and anti-Semitism in Germany, Italy and Spain. The Russian revolution had been followed by the Stalinist purges and terror and, after the Second World War, similar regimes had been installed in eastern Europe. Add to this the very real possibility of Cold War turning hot and the task of the philosopher had achieved a new urgency.

Berlin's arguments were far more cautious than those of Herbert Marcuse, from whom we will hear in a moment, and would appeal less to the young and angry. Yet there is a resonance within them as well. Berlin was a liberal rather than a libertarian and yet in distinguishing between "positive" and "negative" freedom or liberty, he was asking just how far the extension of the state into the private lives of its citizens could be justified. As Berlin put it:

> The first of these political senses of freedom or liberty (I shall use both words to mean the same), which (following much precedent) I shall call the "negative" sense, is involved in the answer to the question "What is the area within which the subject – a person or group of persons – is or should be left to do or be, what he is able to do or be, without interference by other persons?" The second, which I shall call the "positive" sense, is involved in the answer to the question "What, or who, is the source of control or interference that can determine someone to do, or be, this rather than that?" The two questions are clearly different, even though the answers to them may overlap. (Berlin 1969, 2)

Berlin recognized that the extent to which one might be free to exercise free will depended on a variety of factors and he was under no illusions that all were not equally free within any kind of stratified society with major disparities of wealth or power. Nor was he anti-state. He understood and accepted the state's role as a provider and as the preserver of rights and liberties. On balance, however, if asked to choose between negative liberty as "non-interference" and positive liberty as being able – or being enabled – to do or be, Berlin was clear that he would choose the former.

Roberto Toscano, the Italian diplomat and former ambassador to India and Iran, put this distinction rather neatly in a lecture in Tehran in 2005. He addresses the issue of negative liberty first and then its positive sibling. "The former is the realm of individual self-determination, the latter addresses the area of institutions and rules which can supply (or deny) the means through which individual goals are attained" (Toscano 2005). As Toscano notes, Berlin recognized that both were essential aspects of any democratic society. His fear remained, nevertheless, that the greater risk to liberty and freedom came from advocates of positive freedom. As he wrote in his introduction to Two Concepts of Liberty:

> whereas liberal ultra-individualism could scarcely be said to be a rising force at present, the rhetoric of "positive" liberty, at least in its distorted form, is in far greater evidence, and continues to play its historic role (in both capitalist and anti-capitalist societies) as a cloak for despotism in the name of wider freedom.
>
> (Berlin 1969, xlvi–xlvii)

Berlin was essentially asking his audience to think about and even to take responsibility for answering these crucial questions. His thinking goes to the heart of what Plato's "Good Life" might mean in a fractured, fearful world. The young and the radical, free as perhaps never before, might not share Berlin's conclusions but they were demanding answers to the same questions.

When Herbert Marcuse spoke at the Roundhouse in London in 1967 at The Congress of the Dialectics of Liberation, it was as if he were speaking to a generation who had been awaiting his arrival. David Widgery, a writer and medical student who would edit Oz while its editors were indisposed in 1971, remarked to author Ronald Fraser, "We felt very isolated, marginal crazy, an embarrassment to our parents and the authorities – and then we'd see old Marcuse beaming out at his audience as though we were his spiritual children" (Fraser 1988, 144).

It is ironic that the young rebelling against parental authority still felt the need for such parental validation. Yet, it was that which Marcuse, and others such as psychiatrist Ronald Laing, and anarchist and writer Paul Goodman, bestowed on their willing listeners. In a sense, they took the subjective anger of the young radicals, located it in a political context and recast it as a rational, objective response to a mad, bad world. And one did not have to look far to see how bad and mad this world could be in the late sixties. America, in its war in southeast Asia, and Britain and Germany in their support for US foreign policy, had long ago forfeited the moral high ground when Warsaw Pact tanks brought an end to the Prague Spring in 1968. And if that were not enough, one had only to look at Nigeria and the Biafran War or the Greek Colonels' Coup D'état in 1967 to see a world where that which should have been unthinkable was now the reality.

Marcuse was a member of the Frankfurt School of writers and social theorists based at the Institute for Social Research at Frankfurt University. This group also included Theodor Adorno, Erich Fromm, Max Horkheimer and Walter Benjamin. Like Adorno, Horkheimer and Fromm, Marcuse emigrated to the USA in the 1930s. The concerns of the Frankfurt School arose from the failure of Social Democratic parties in Europe to stop the First World War in accordance with commitments made to the Second International, the revolutionary failures of 1919, the rise of fascist parties and their influence among sections of the working class and the rise of the Stalinist dictatorship in the Soviet Union. Their aim was to revisit Marxist theory in light of other philosophical approaches such as Kant, Hegel, Weber and, perhaps most distinctively, Sigmund Freud, and to establish which conditions might allow for social change and the establishment of rational institutions. Marcuse's development of a Marxism that also drew on a critical reading of Freud began in the 1940s, and his ideas reflected the social, political and economic changes that he witnessed following his emigration to North America. It is not necessary to examine his ideas in depth and for our purposes reference to key aspects of his thinking and their appeal to the young will suffice.

First, for Marcuse and his colleagues of the Frankfurt School, Freud's libido theory provided the bridge between Marxism and Psychoanalysis. The id was not just the repository for the sexual drives of the individual, it was the source of creativity and was the unsocialized and unsocializable part of the personality. As John Rickert has noted:

> Marxism originally turned to psychoanalysis in an attempt to understand the role of psychological factors in social phenomena. Specifically, it sought an account of the origin and power of ideology, the subjective conditions for social change, and the processes by which society enters the individual psyche.   (Rickert 1986)

The reason the unconscious and the id were so crucial for Marcuse, Adorno and others of the Frankfurt school is simple. Unless some part of the personality remained uncontaminated by bourgeois values and beliefs, the individual and the mass could never break free and establish a society based on freedom from capitalist exploitation and social alienation. In *Eros and Civilisation*, Marcuse goes beyond Freud and identifies Eros (or Id) as a liberating and creative drive that can be harnessed by progressive forces in creating a non-repressive society, one based upon "a fundamentally different experience of being, a fundamentally different relation between man and nature, and fundamentally different existential relations" (Marcuse 1973, 24).

Where Freud saw psychological repression as necessary for the maintenance of civil society – the accommodation of the pleasure principle to the reality principle – Marcuse argues that capitalist society, and that of all authoritarian regimes, is characterized by surplus repression. The psychic conflict experienced in the individual between desire and the demand that she/he adjust to the reality of work is not, for Marcuse, inevitable but a specific consequence of an exploitative economic mode of production. The individual's adjustment is not to Freud's reality principle but to what, Marcuse calls "the performance principle". The conflict is between Eros (the pleasure principle, the sex instinct) and alienated labour (the performance principle, economic stratification). Marcuse's emphasis on sex as a liberating force inevitably chimed with young people drawn into conflict with parents and authority that all too frequently sought to justify itself according to social mores that increasingly appeared hypocritical and irrelevant.

Yet Marcuse went further still in championing issues so close to the hearts and minds of radical youth. In *An Essay on Liberation* from 1969, Marcuse departs from orthodox Marxism in identifying youth culture, radical students and the New Left as the force and agency for social and economic change and not the economically compromised and politically accommodated organized working class. As Marcuse writes:

> The "trip" involves the dissolution of the ego shaped by the established society – an artificial and short-lived dissolution. But the artificial and "private" liberation anticipates in a distorted manner an exigency of the social liberation: the revolution must be at the same time a revolution in perception which will accompany the material and intellectual reconstruction of society, creating the new aesthetic environment. Awareness of the need for such a revolution in perception, for a new sensorium, is perhaps the kernel of truth in the psychedelic search.   (Marcuse 1969, 37)

The essay built on Marcuse's 1964 critique of capitalist and Soviet societies, contained in *One Dimensional Man* (1970). Here Marcuse identifies consumerism as a major form of social control and one which has effectively emasculated organized labour as a revolutionary force within society. Marcuse's thinking seems quite consistent with Barry Miles's comment at the start of this chapter. He seems to be saying that, to change society, one must first stand outside it. This was clearly music to the ears of many, who heard or read him.

It was within this context of ideas, that notions of freedom began to influence the social practices of certain, radicalized sectors of society. Ideas such as communitarianism, de-schooling society, sexual libertarianism and the replacement of "work" with "play" came to the fore. Was it an accident then that like-minded musicians, mainly but not entirely from the world of jazz, began to explore a music without predetermined form or structure, in which spontaneity and responsiveness were its crucial elements?

As both John Wickes and Hilary Moore have suggested, different imperatives lay behind the evolution of free jazz and free improvisation in the USA in comparison with Britain. Moore's concern lies in contrasting the differing socio-cultural setting within which Ornette Coleman's free form experiments emerged with that within which Joe Harriott was working. In her analysis, she draws on writings by African-American poet Amiri Baraka, Val Wilmer, the American Marxist writer Frank Kofsky and others, and she makes several very cogent points. First, she notes that Harriott, Coleridge Goode and Shake Keane shared the desire of other white British musicians for greater independence from America. In fact, as she and Harriott's biographer Alan Robertson stress, this was a very significant question for the Jamaican saxophonist (Moore 2007, 81; see Robertson 2003, 80 on Harriott's reaction to Dizzy Gillespie's dismissive response to his music). A little later, Moore comments that the black members of the Harriott quintet were hardly unaware of racism in the UK and were "unlikely to have identified themselves as 'activists' for black empowerment" but adds:

> This is reflective of the general racial climate in 1960s Britain. Although racism and racial disputes were relatively commonplace, Britain's black population lacked the politicized, coordinated and self-motivated mass movement that personified the civil rights and black power movements of 1950s and 1960s America.
> (Moore 2007, 82)

Moore is alive to the issues facing African-American musicians, what one might describe as conflicting pressures, the desire and indeed demand that they speak out on the one hand fighting the powerful pressure of a white establishment insisting on circumspection and circumlocution. She quotes Frank Kofsky's remark that the "avant-garde movement in jazz" was "a musical representation of the ghetto's vote of 'no confidence' in Western civilization and the American Dream" (Moore 2007, 84). Furthermore, she identifies the radical developments of Ayler, Coltrane, Taylor and Coleman within a broader expressive range that would include Shepp, Roach, Mingus, Marion Brown, as well as members of Chicago's Association for the Advancement of Creative Musicians.

John Wickes also expresses this point rather well, albeit with a slightly different emphasis:

> For black Americans free jazz asserted, in the strongest musical terms they could muster, a long overdue response to issues of pride and identity which no decent, truly civilised society should ever have posed. For them, free jazz amounted to the

jettisoning of decades of accumulated aesthetic debris; but not for non-American exponents. For others, as Val Wilmer (1990) and others have pointed out, the issue was one of a backlog of received wisdoms blocking the liberative spirit jazz has to offer any musical culture. This fact runs like a thread through the experiences British free jazz musicians relate.   (Wickes 1999, 40)

Those involved in the new music in Britain came from jazz backgrounds and drew inspiration from African-American – and white American – musicians. But, however much they might identify with that aspect of American culture, there was at other levels a rejection of much that the USA stood for – not least, its foreign policy and rampant consumerism. Hilary Moore locates some of this in Britain's drastically changed position as a global power and its increased reliance and even subservience to the USA. Clearly, this is not a case of cause and effect. Moore is talking about the ideological or superstructural context in which ideas emerge and are discussed. And in this respect, she is right. One can most certainly see evidence of a profound ambivalence towards America that can be traced from the colloquial description of US forces in Britain in the Second World War – "overpaid, oversexed and over here" – through the writings of George Orwell, Raymond Williams and Richard Hoggart, the folk music revival, books such as E.P. Thompson's seminal *The Making of the English Working Classes* (2002) and A.L. Morton's *The English Utopia* (1969), to the Campaign for Nuclear Disarmament. There was much about America that was attractive to both British youth and intellectuals – the poetry and writings of the Beats, jazz, blues, rock & roll, the crime novels of Hammett and Chandler, and even some aspects of its consumer culture. But there was also an underlying resentment that allowed for a kind of unconscious, cultural bricollage that grasped some elements greedily while rejecting others with a vehemence.

As with the Beatles and the Stones, African-American music was a starting not an end point for these players. Guitarist Keith Rowe played initially with Mike Westbrook before moving into the ever more abstract areas of AMM Music with Lou Gare, Eddie Prévost and Cornelius Cardew. As he explained to John Wickes:

We weren't reacting against black American musicians themselves – we were inspired by them – we were reacting against the idea that we had to do it their way. What they had achieved fundamentally, was to look at their own conditions and create, and that was what we were inspired to do.   (Wickes 1999, 52)

A remarkable piece of happenstance occurred when several (later) leading lights in British free jazz – drummer John Stevens, saxophonist Trevor Watts, trombonist Paul Rutherford and flautist and saxophonist Bob Downes

– met in the RAF in Germany. Germany had no equivalent of the MU ban on American artists and there were plenty of opportunities to hear and see the best American players live and to obtain American jazz LPs. As John Stevens told Victor Schonfield:

> The initial influences were, apart from the music that was inspiring us – and that's Trevor & Paul and myself in particular – in Germany – which was ... Paul had a real passion for John Coltrane. I could say I loved John Coltrane but what I really had a passion for was the bit between Elvin and Coltrane. That was a very significant thing for me though I'd loved earlier stuff that John Coltrane had played. So there's that and then the Ornette Coleman Quartet from "Shape of Jazz to Come", because I heard "Shape of Jazz to Come" before I heard "Tomorrow is the Question" and "Something Else". I think what happened was it was on the radio and Paul, Trevor and I were in the same billet and I think that's where we first heard it. I think maybe Trevor had a tape recorder and recorded it, so we could listen to it. So there's Ornette, of course Eric Dolphy, of course Charlie Mingus, Bill Evans Trio... There was all this taste for "the new", if you like, which that was at that time.   (Schonfield 1992)

Saxophonist Albert Ayler would also prove to be a significant figure for Stevens, and also for saxophonist Evan Parker. On a brief sojourn in Copenhagen, Stevens and Parker saw Ayler live and got to meet him. As Keith Rowe suggests, the influence of these African-American musicians was crucial not least in providing the inspiration to create authentic music that draws on one's own background and experience.

Two aspects of African-American free jazz strike one immediately. The first we have already noted lies in its relationship with the black struggle for social, cultural and economic emancipation. The second is that it was saxophonists who led the way in the USA. This does not take anything away from Mingus or Cecil Taylor or Max Roach. But if we think of those musicians who most quickly spring to mind in this context it is John Coltrane, Ornette Coleman, Albert Ayler, Archie Shepp, Anthony Braxton and Marion Brown. Although not strictly free players, one might also want to add the names of Roland Kirk, Eric Dolphy, Charles Lloyd and Sonny Rollins. Amiri Baraka noted comparatively early (in 1967) that most *avant garde* reed players "are intrigued by the sound of the human voice" (Baraka 1998, 77) The saxophone became a means of expressing anger, frustration, pain, suffering and pride while departing from the "white" timbres and tonal qualities for which Adolphe Sax had created the instrument.

And yet, in the British sphere, it was drummers who seemed to take the lead. Again, this takes nothing away from musicians such as Evan Parker,

Derek Bailey, Paul Rutherford, Trevor Watts or Barry Guy. Nevertheless, the names of Eddie Prévost, John Stevens and Tony Oxley stand out. To these three, I would add Jon Hiseman and Phil Seamen. If saxophonists led the way in America for the reasons that Baraka suggests, one may ask why percussionists played a more central role here. Perhaps the difference lies in what Wickes says about the two situations above. But if the imperative for African-American musicians was to speak out in their own voice and the British imperative was liberation from "received wisdoms", we still need to ask why the latter might focus on percussion. A possible explanation might lie in the centrality of rhythm in African-American music. It certainly was not the case that Stevens, Oxley and co. could not play time. All were or are very fine time players. However, perhaps in the British jazz context it was necessary first to liberate the beat or find a different way of expressing it, if the music were to become free to develop in its own, British or European approach.

This notion does have some support. John Stevens, for example, drew inspiration from the pleasure he took from art and painting, something he had begun doing as a child. For him, it allowed him to express himself freely and openly and even at the RAF music school in Uxbridge he had begun to explore that same potential in his music. Stevens would in due course even abandon the conventional kit for a quieter, smaller set of his own invention that allowed the strings to be better heard within the ensemble. And perhaps the greatest single influence on Stevens was the British drummer, Phil Seamen, as he explained to Victor Schonfield.

> I saw playing music in terms of a free expression, if you like. Now because the music at that time was bop, or post-bop, that wasn't in any way free music, obviously, but having seen Phil (Seamen) interact freely with the soloist, that encouraged that – this interaction bit. Because I'd be invited to play in standard jazz settings, I remember trying to get my brain around what it would be if we were exchanging fours, how should I approach this ... and I thought the most natural way to approach these spaces that one is given within the music, was to try to approach it like speaking. So, for a time that's what I did. (Schonfield 1992)

And he added, "Phil was an enormous inspiration, enormous, and I'd say now that he's one of the freest drummers that I've ever seen."

Although, the first intimations of free playing could be found in Joe Harriott's work with both Bobby Orr and Phil Seamen (but particularly the latter) and shortly afterwards in the music of Mike Taylor, these were very much first steps and it is hard to discern any significant relationship between these two musicians and what followed. Stevens had certainly been impressed by the free form records Harriott had made and once sat in with the quintet but found the experience less than satisfactory.

I'd been listening to the free things that they'd been doing with Phil and I felt "Wow! This is gonna be it, I can contribute freely!", but as it turned out it was a lot more conservative than I had imagined because they were saying, "We just want you to play straight behind our solos". (Schonfield 1992)

As for Mike Taylor, the connection between his music and what followed, is a slender one but is there nevertheless. Evan Parker recalls meeting Taylor and his saxophonist Dave Tomlin when they were in their late teens and he was just fifteen or so years old:

I knew him briefly at several stages of my life and his life. The first period was before he had made any records because we had friends in common, who came from Eltham, whereas I was living over in Stanwell, Middlesex and in Staines was where a lot of my jazz friends lived. There was a guy whose parents had a big house and who let us use one of the rooms as a music room and they came over to play with him and the saxophone player Dave Tomlin and they were so much better than we were. In a way, we were sort of wasting their time but it did allow them to show off their clothes and their skills, which is very important at that stage. We were all teenagers but they were maybe 18 or 19 we were 15 or 16. (Interview with Evan Parker, April 2009)

Their paths crossed again a few years later, as Parker explained:

Meanwhile, the records had come out and they seemed to have done well. And Mike used to come to The Little Theatre Club and used to sit in a chair on the stage. He didn't play but he used to talk or play a little clay drum and used to interject remarks. John [Stevens] always welcomed him and that special chair was his if he wanted it. He came a few times and the next thing I knew he had died. (Interview with Evan Parker, April 2009)

But this question of the beat and how to play it more freely was clearly present for both Harriott and Taylor. Jon Hiseman found that he needed to develop a new approach to play Taylor's tunes but this coincided with his own recognition that he did not want to copy Max or Blakey or Elvin and certainly had no desire to develop a career doing so, as he explains:

If you think about Mike's uncanny ability to reduce everything to its simplest and most quintessential form, in a way that's what he was about. It was all about simplifying things, honing in on the centre of things with none of the normal convention going on around it. So, I developed this thing about playing without bar lines, playing pulse without worrying about where the offbeat was. Of course, this was an absolute and heinous crime when you are talking about traditional jazz drummers but Mike was very happy with this. He felt that this ebb and flow without there necessarily being an obvious or even an actual on or off beat was the way forward. So, we always had rhythm. So, of course, when John Stevens and co got in on the act, they destroyed even that and they basically didn't bother with rhythm for much of the time. It was known as texture playing but I always played rhythm with Mike, maybe not the whole time but it would not be for very long before I would break into time but it wasn't necessarily on or off beat time. (Interview with Jon Hiseman, April 2010)

Such considerations were also there for Paul Rutherford when he launched the drum-less trio Iskra 1903 (Incus), as Barry Guy suggests:

Paul was intent on putting a group together without drums and maybe that was to counteract the John Stevens or percussion-centred music. So, he was interested in finding a music that had no percussion. So, that's where Iskra started. It was kind of interesting for me because Rutherford was one of my really good mates. Derek [Bailey] – I didn't know so well but obviously knew him from The Little Theatre Club but it was an interesting sound-world in a sense that it would be two string players and a horn player. We found ways of compensating or at least at times providing a percussive element that wouldn't have been there otherwise. We would find ways of delivering on that front as well. (Interview with Barry Guy, November 2010)

The importance of establishing a rhythmic approach that was relevant to a British context and was not reliant on the African-American model was certainly one issue. However, it is also apparent that in seeking to establish their own musical identity, British free jazz or improvising musicians looked increasingly to European Art Music for inspiration. For example, John Stevens was interested in Webern, while Paul Rutherford loved Shostakovich – one can hear echoes of the Russian in the trombonist's work, not least on the first Iskra 1903 recordings. Others such as Barry Guy, Henry Lowther, Howard Riley and, later, violinist Phil Wachsmann brought an incredibly wide knowledge of twentieth-century composition to the music in which they immersed themselves. It was not so much that they were deliberately attempting to explore the sound world of European abstraction but rather that their explorations took them into similar territory, one where an appreciation of Stockhausen, Ligeti, Penderecki, Messiaen and Schönberg was an advantage.

Perhaps then, returning to our earlier discussion of the lack of influence of Joe Harriott upon this new generation of experimenters, we can see why this might have been. First, the Little Theatre Club crowd were looking to make their own break with the past; and, second, to do this meant going into musical areas where Harriott's music had not ventured. In his Postscript to Ian Carr's *The Music Outside* (2008), Roger Cotterrell writes:

> Joe Harriott is mentioned briefly as the totally neglected figure he then was. Now, three decades on, he has widespread recognition in Britain and abroad as a great pioneer of contemporary jazz and many of his records are available again. But his "abstract music" at the beginning of the 1960s – a free form jazz that was free enough to include free improvisation, modal improvisation and bop as required – clearly was a false start in historical terms. It took another half decade before the kinds of musical freedom he used so successfully in his quintet began to filter into the jazz of the "music outside" generation. Why Harriott had so little influence on a development that occurred so soon after his classic *Free Form* and *Abstract* albums were issued is not discussed in this book, and the question still remains unanswered.
>
> (Cotterrell in Carr 2008, 168–9)

A different reading of Carr's book tells us that Carr excluded Harriott from his account for much the same reasons that he did not include Phil Seamen and Tubby Hayes, whom he mentions in the same sentence early in *The Music Outside*. The book is concerned with those musicians who were working on the scene at the time Carr was writing. They are his focus, rather than those who have gone before. As we suggested earlier, Harriott's experiments lacked a broader context. He was not alone in attempting to broaden the palette of British jazz but alone – with the possible exception of the yet-to-record Mike Taylor – in attempting abstract music of that particular kind. By the time a community of British musicians had come into existence whose concern was with abstraction, the imperatives and the goals had shifted and by that time Harriott had abandoned his free form music. There is no mystery here but rather the unfolding of history in a particular set of cultural, social and political-ideological circumstances.

Differences would also in due course emerge between what we might describe as "free improvisation" and what we should more correctly call "free jazz". The distinction would become more sharply defined during the seventies and eighties. However, in the period that concerns us, from the mid-sixties to mid-seventies, there was considerable overlap among practitioners from each of these camps on the concert stage and in the studio.

While I intend to concentrate on recordings located more towards the "free improvisation" end of the continuum, in this context, there is little point in being too rigid in our definitions. Free jazz and free improvisation are better understood as emergent practices where individuals would choose to play together due to shared concerns rather than (at this point at least) what might constitute a kind of ideological positioning. And as noted there was a considerable degree of cross-fertilization.

We might define the Mike Osborne Trio with Louis Moholo and Harry Miller as "free jazz" because the music was clearly freely improvised, but at the same time maintained a strong relationship with African-American jazz. Howard Riley's early trio records owed much to Monk, Ellington, Bill Evans and, less surprisingly than one might think, Art Tatum. Yet his solo work in the eighties, fine though it was, seemed to owe more to European contemporary music than to jazz. On the other hand, Evan Parker played with Riley's quartet in the mid-sixties, with the SME and with Tony Oxley's quintet/sextet before embarking, around 1969–70 on a more severe and ascetically pure approach to improvisation. However, that did not stop him playing with the Brotherhood of Breath. And many more obviously "jazz" players such as Kenny Wheeler, Henry Lowther and bassist Jeff Clyne were very happy to explore abstraction with their more experimental colleagues.

In this respect, I think we can identify three distinct early groupings. The first of these is the collection of musicians gathering around John Stevens. The second was the Joseph Holbrooke Trio (or simply Joseph Holbrook) in Sheffield. And finally, there is the less easily defined AMM Music. In a way, looking at them in this order, places them on a continuum in terms of their proximity to what we might understand as "jazz".

John Stevens is a hugely important figure in jazz and free improvisation. By the time he died in 1996 aged just fifty-four, his career had encompassed jazz, free improvisation, folk music, the Great American Songbook, dance music and rock – albeit always with Stevens's own distinctive imprimatur. He was a wonderful proselytiser and a man of total conviction, who drew others in to what he was doing and who was quick and generous with encouragement. He was the first person to persuade a reluctant Kenny Wheeler that he could and should try this new approach (see Davidson 2001). He helped, as we have seen, Norma Winstone and Maggie Nicols in their careers and introduced them to free playing. Trombonist Annie Whitehead is another who has particularly fond memories of working with Stevens. In an interview for *Avant Magazine*, she stressed how Stevens had given her a sense of her own value as a musician, as well as a complete education in the music business. At a gig at the Bracknell Festival with Stevens's Fast Colour, she recalled, "John said, 'I don't know about anybody else but I want to play a solo with Annie.' I thought that was so validating because Bobby Bradford and Courtney Pine were there and he was saying he wanted to play with me" (Heining 2000, 10).

Maggie Nicols is another musician who also acknowledges how much she learned from Stevens, in particular in her case, about how to run workshops for amateur and even non-musicians.

By 1964, Stevens was working regularly at Ronnie Scott's Club and had formed a septet that included some of the other young jazz musicians on the scene. Around 1965, he met up again with his only RAF buddies Paul Rutherford and Trevor Watts who were then co-leading a quintet and joined the group on drums soon after wards. It was towards the end of that year that Stevens began looking for a regular venue where they could play. With the help of singer Amorel Weston, they located premises in a tiny theatre behind St Martin's in the Fields church near Trafalgar Square (Wickes 1999, 55). The deal was the musicians could use the place after the actors had finished. Inevitably, there was an overlap between performers who worked at The Old Place and The Little Theatre Club. However, a clearly discernible group of musicians could be identified, who hung out in the upstairs room. It included Stevens, Watts, Rutherford, Evan Parker, Barry Guy and Amorel Weston. Derek Bailey, Tony Oxley, Maggie Nicols, percussionist Jamie Muir, organist and electronics pioneer Hugh Davies and the musicians grouped within AMM Music would later be added to that list, while other visitors of greater or lesser frequency might include trumpeters Mongezi Feza, Kenny Wheeler and Henry Lowther, saxophonists Bob Downes and Dudu Pukwana, Louis Moholo and bassists Jeff Clyne and Dave Holland.

Around this time, the Watts–Rutherford Quintet became the Spontaneous Music Ensemble, as Stevens told Victor Schonfield:

> I remember sitting there thinking I'd like to name the group –
> name what we were doing. And I thought and thought and came
> up with The Spontaneous Music Ensemble and the reason I
> thought that was it would be something to live up to, something
> to work towards. So, the "Spontaneous" is the thing that's most
> difficult to achieve, and "Ensemble" means it can be any size. And
> there were times when I thought, "Well, I'll carry on playing this
> music – even if it's just me on my own" – which would have been
> a bit crazy! [laughs] But, you know, it just felt that "Ensemble"
> would be a flexible thing and, as it turns out, it has gone from
> duos to large ensembles. So, I think a key factor there was find-
> ing this space, an open workshop space where you were free to
> negotiate the music.   (Schonfield 1992)

Stevens continued to draw other musicians into his orbit, including (as noted) a reluctant Kenny Wheeler. Like Derek Bailey, Stevens often heard things in the playing of other musicians from outside his preferred modus operandi which would convince him that he wanted to make their sound part of his musical world. It was an ethos that Bailey would also follow, in particular, in relation to his Company series of concerts which ran from 1977 to 1994 (Watson 2004). Stevens acknowledged to Victor Schonfield that Wheeler was considered by some an odd choice for the SME:

> but we always loved Kenny's playing though his ... Kenny's involvement with free music was very much me, not forcing him, but saying, "Come on Ken, you've gotta come and do this..." So, it wasn't his choice, but, more and more as he did it, I suppose it has become more of his general language of music-making now.
> (Schonfield 1992)

Within weeks of opening The Little Theatre Club, the SME went into the studio to record *Challenge* (Eyemark; EMANEM) with a quintet that featured Rutherford, Watts, Wheeler and Stevens with either Jeff Clyne or Bruce Cale on bass. It is a transitional album, and the additional quartet piece on the CD reissue recorded just over a year later with Parker, Watts, Stevens and bassist Chris Cambridge shows how quickly things were developing. And yet it is a remarkable record in its own right. Despite still being in thrall to Ornette and Ayler and with hints of Mingus in the ensembles, this is unusually original music. Stevens, Rutherford and Watts all contribute tunes to the record and in this sense the music is composition-led with melodic themes, chord sequences or motifs used as points of departure. It is worth contrasting the two versions of "End to a Beginning" that appear on the CD reissue. The first version is shorter by ninety seconds and features a quartet of Rutherford, Watts, Bruce Cale and Stevens. Though the two horns interact quite freely, there is a constantly flowing, if loose, pulse throughout. The second version, which appeared on the original release, adds Wheeler and Clyne replaces Cale. The melody, though recognizable at the outset becomes fractured quite quickly and the rhythm section pushes the three horns continually with constantly shifting rhythms devoid of anything resembling a set pulse. At times bass and drums seems to play against each other both in their duo section and in the group improvisation. Stevens does not play on his "Little Red Head" and the impression here is that a simple motif was used as a basic idea to inform a collective improvisation. This is how Stevens described these two numbers to Victor Schonfield:

> The SME started with us playing compositions, so from my point of view, and there's an example on "Challenge" – more than one actually – the strong feelings I had were towards complete free group improvisation – the possibility of that – so the means I was using through the compositional side of things, one of which was that on "Little Red Head" the line goes [sings] ... those little clicks, instead of having a linear melody, it was dotted, and also the fact that there was an arco bass – [sings] which was all trying

to get it to hone right in – so, it was hard for these clipped notes not to synchronise with where the bass was – and yet there was this little gap between the two elements and I chose not to play the drums on that. So it was like, what's going to happen after going through this very concentrated process? And it turned out to be like a completely free group improvisation, though of parallel lines and linear kind because this is the way the people were playing at that time. "End to a Beginning" was getting closer to a way of finding out how to get this pure interaction bit, but in the end that turned out to be quite linear. But the way that worked was – the line went … [sings] and would then gradually fragment – I actually wrote it out so the lines fragmented – again, so that as it breaks into a fragment we're into this detailed sort of area, though at the time people were playing in quite a linear way. The way I'm playing on that track is trying to get into the delicacy of what Sunny Murray was doing on Spiritual Unity. I was very influenced by Spiritual Unity, particularly the relationship between Gary Peacock and Sunny Murray. Now I wasn't attracted to be a nerve-pulse player, but I wanted to get that delicacy and try to get it so that I could play in that detailed way, but in the same way that I would normally play – which would be to interact [underlined in original] – say something specific if you like.

(Schonfield 1992)

Other tracks use more conventional heads or chord sequences. Rutherford's "After Listening" opens with a definite but simple melody before leaving the space for Cale to solo. A series of trios follow between the horns and rhythm section before all return to the head. Here, the compositional ideas involve both the original melody and the overall architecture of the piece which breaks the number into five parts, that is "head – trio with trombone – trio with flugelhorn – trio with alto – head". The difference between this and more straightahead bop-influenced jazz of the time lies both in the absence of any chordal instrument and obvious reference to any harmonic sequence, and the extent to which soloist and rhythm section depart from the original theme or melody in their improvisation. A similar approach and structure is evident on other tracks such as Watts's "Club 66" and "E.D.'s Message" and on Rutherford's "2.B. Ornette". The playing is outstanding throughout with Wheeler fitting in quite perfectly. If Rutherford sounds the most unorthodox in the conception and content of his solos, this takes nothing away from Watts, whose performance is beautifully balanced and creative. It is an essential album in all respects.

In 1997, EMANEM issued music from three different sessions that had been recorded between September 1966 and March 1967 but which previously been unreleased. The first session was made for a short experimental film under the title *Withdrawal* and the group Stevens put together on this occasion included Kenny Wheeler, Paul Rutherford, Trevor Watts, Evan Parker, Barry Guy and Stevens himself. Six months later, Stevens took the opportunity to rework this material adding Derek Bailey on guitar. The final session used the same septet personnel on a four-part suite entitled *Seeing Sounds and Hearing Colours*. Each session revealed both a growing confidence in grasping this new idiom and an expanding sense of the possibilities it offered. The ensemble's progress could be clearly heard in the second of the two *Withdrawal* recordings, where the music is now much freer and more open. Describing the interim period between the SME's first release, *Challenge*, and their second, *Karyobin*, Stevens told Victor Schonfield:

> I got very personally involved in that very concise type of improvisation which was placing controlled sounds alongside of each other, or whatever, though where the people did those things and what they did was up to them, but it would be within the realms of a composition. (Schonfield 1992)

Composition was seen as a process not so much of notation but one that began with the selection of personnel, involved their growth together as a collective and developed in the context of performance or recording within certain parameters often set by Stevens himself. Again in conversation with Schonfield, Stevens notes that, "So much of the influence of the compositional side of things was to do with, I suppose, in a sense, getting from 'A' to 'B' according to who the people were who were involved with it." In the case of the earlier recording of the film soundtrack, composition is informed both by the content of the film, by the reading of the original book by David Chapman on which it is based and certain ideas or motifs brought by Stevens. The main differences between this and, say, Miles Davis' improvised soundtrack for Louis Malle's "L'ascenseur pour l'éschafaud" lie in the fact that *Withdrawal* was intended to accompany the entire thirty-five minutes of the film and the absence within it of any notion of time or chord changes.

On the soundtrack version Parker is heard only in the ensembles and even then only incidentally. He admits that initially he felt overawed in this company, though he would of course increasingly make his presence felt. On the second date, he plays glockenspiel only on the first two long segments and picks up his saxophone just on the short third sequence. Where the soundtrack is dark and slow-moving, almost funereal in mood and pace, the second recording reveals that pointillist aspect so associated with the group from *Karyobin* onwards. The music seems to flutter, quiver and tremble but there's a much stronger impression both of movement and of a collective working together. Barry Guy's role has shifted away from the restricted drone role he performed on the soundtrack and he is allowed much greater scope within the music. Given his apparent initial reluctance to be involved,

Kenny Wheeler's playing is quite magnificent, while Derek Bailey's stylistic approach is already discernible – fragmentary and angular but at the same time empathic in the way he contributes to the group's soundscape. Trevor Watts plays oboe, flute, alto and even vibes here with astonishing proficiency, though it was around this point that he would decide to concentrate primarily on alto and soprano. Two things are immediately evident. First, Stevens was already pursuing his notion of an ensemble as a flexible rather than fixed entity in terms of personnel. Second, the "spontaneous" aspect of the music could increasingly be understood as something that would unfold perpetually with recordings merely representing stages upon a journey.

Seeing Sounds and Hearing Colours is more important still, as its suite represents the first flowering of the next phase of the SME. As Martin Davidson has noted, "At the start of 1967, there was an additional move towards creating a wide variety of colours using multi-instrumentation – something the AACM was doing in Chicago at the same time, although neither group was then aware of each other" (Davidson 1997b).

Stevens told Schonfield that the idea first came to him while he was in Amsterdam on his way home from an attempt to emigrate to Denmark. The very title of the piece links Stevens' dual interests in music and art and he actually drew the score he could see in his mind. Even twenty-five years later, Stevens's excitement can be heard in his voice, as he retells the story:

> And I drew it, just drew it out and it was like shapes, lines, and when I got back to England that was the first thing that I suggested that we did. So, we did this piece called *Seeing Sounds and Hearing Colours*, which actually made, in a sense ... it brought about something else. The *Seeing Sounds and Hearing Colours* – there was lots of specific colouration in a sense, because I got a lot of people, as well as actually playing their instruments, to be playing glockenspiels, marimbas – little ones, like children's ones – because we had a lot of children's stuff. (Schonfield 1992)

As he remarked, the piece revealed a move into the contemporary music arena of Pierre Boulez, as opposed to jazz. Not that Stevens was using the kind of notation favoured by Boulez at that time but rather that it was occupying a similar sonic universe. The music becomes again quieter and more introspective. Its players retain their identity rather than submerging this entirely into the group sound – the word, "ego-less", often used in this connection is perhaps less than helpful. Yet listening, interacting and a heightened awareness became the core virtues of this approach. By no means a quiet drummer, Stevens even built himself a much smaller, quieter kit that would not drown out the string players. Again, the issue of finding new ways of expressing rhythm seems to have been the key. Perhaps, the term, "non-hierarchical", goes some way to conveying what Stevens was trying to create, even if he could at times be quite dictatorial in his demands. It is now a music of small sounds, textures, gestures and silences. Is it jazz or has it now abandoned any such linkages? We might prefer to say simply, "This music came from jazz and this is where it went."

The SME was then briefly a duo with just Stevens and Evan Parker. Though no recordings appeared at the time, EMANEM have subsequently released material, *Summer 1967*, that reveals the link to what may the finest SME record of this period – *Karyobin: Are the Imaginary Birds That Live in Paradise* (Island; Chronoscope). Its title reflects Stevens's then-recent interest in Japanese court music. *Karyobin* is quite one of the most lovely pieces of atonal music in any style. The group here comprises Stevens, Parker, Wheeler and Bailey with Dave Holland – shortly to take up Miles Davis's invitation to join his band – on bass. Apparently, Holland played *Karyobin* to Davis, who listened attentively and replied, "Just don't expect my band to sound like that." According to Holland, it was not a dismissive comment and more a statement of fact. Holland clearly enjoyed his period playing this music. Indeed, he subsequently left Miles along with Chick Corea and spent the early seventies playing with the pianist, saxophonist Anthony Braxton and drummer Barry Altschul in Circle. Later he joined Braxton's quartet along with Kenny Wheeler and also played with saxophonist Sam Rivers. Braxton, Rivers and Altschul feature on Holland's debut ECM LP *Conference of the Birds*, an album that contains its own echoes of *Karyobin*. The association with Stevens, Bailey and Parker clearly made a lasting impression on Holland, as he explained in 2009:

> After being with Miles, I wanted to go back to the more open form improvisation things that I was involved with before joining Miles and with certain approaches that were happening. I felt that was unfinished business. I think through most of the seventies up through the eighties I was working with Braxton and with Sam.
> (Interview with Dave Holland, January 2009)

And he added,

> In the end, free playing is a state of mind. It's not just about not having anything written on paper. It's about how you integrate material into the music. The greatest free players for me are the ones that have a great sense of form to their playing. Evan Parker, Derek Bailey have a great vocabulary that they have explored and developed that creates form for their work. It's all a matter of different perspectives.
> (Interview with Dave Holland, January 2009)

On *Karyobin*, no one player ever dominates. With *Seeing Sounds and Hearing Colours*, certain compositional devices are evident – Movement 1 takes a long oboe note as the starting point for collective improvisation, Movement 2 takes "C" as its lead noteand Movement 3 begins with three clearly articulated chords – even these slight musical cues and devices appear absent. For the first time on record, Stevens seems to have realized his aim to create a "group music" where each musician is part of the whole rather than a distinct and separate identity in their own right. It is evident that Stevens, going by his remarks to Schonfield subsequently, is very much the group leader and almost in himself provides a frame of reference for the improvisation, but the listener can certainly sense that a new agenda is being set for jazz and improvised music (Schonfield 1992). Instead of formal structures sounds form patterns only to diverge and reform in fresh shapes and hues. The feeling is akin to watching clouds driven by breezes passing across the sky. At times, the music is hurried, busy – like birds in flight – but it is always purposeful. It is almost without beginning or end and it is always as if it is a scene passing across one's vision.

Oliv followed in 1969 for Giorgio Gomelsky's Marmalade label, but sadly remains unreleased on CD at the time of writing. The album further extends Stevens's approach, which he would later dub "Search and Reflect", and introduces vocals for the first time on an SME recording. The second side features a fine early performance from Maggie Nicols alongside a trio of Stevens, Watts and Johnny Dyani, while the first uses a slightly larger ensemble with three voices including Nicols. Both *The Source – From and Towards* (Tangent) and *"LIVE" – Big Band and Quartet* (Vinyl) also await reissue. The absence of *"LIVE"* is a particular shame as it includes a first recorded foray into the possibilities offered by an orchestra and has one of Julie Tippetts's earliest recordings using this approach.

Stevens's importance cannot be underestimated. There is no question that he pioneered community music-making or that he was relentless in pursuit of every opportunity to make music across a huge variety of styles. While musicians are understandably keen to protect and ensure acknowledgement of their own contributions and innovations, few who worked with him would dispute his effect on them and their development. What may be slightly more controversial is how far he influenced the development of a distinctly British approach to free improvisation that can be seen in the work of Iskra 1903, Evan Parker, Derek Bailey and others. For Martin Davidson (Davidson 1997b) this was "his greatest achievement and legacy" and the author would feel obliged to agree with him.

Stevens was certainly no saint and he liked a drink. Photographer Jak Kilby remembers accompanying Howard Riley, Trevor Watts, Stevens and Barry Guy to an ECM recording session in Germany:

> It happened when we travelled to Germany for the recording of *Endgame* and had a series of delays and mishaps, not least of all problems caused by John on the road. This resulted in

us arriving at our hotel in Ludwigsburg around 6am instead of about 12 hours before. We were quite shattered from the journey and, when booking in, the hotel gave us a note from Manfred announcing that he'd meet us for breakfast at 8am sharp and that we would go to the studio for 9am. This did not go down well and we went to our rooms in states of collapse. What we did not realize was that John did not go to sleep but stayed in the hotel restaurant drinking beer, just as he had done on the 4-hour boat trip to Belgium. I came for breakfast at 9am to find John at a table full of empty beer bottles ranting on about "The War". The ashen-faced Manfred Eicher was sat opposite and obviously not used to John's style of cultural intercourse.

(E-mail interview with Jak Kilby, January 2011)

According to Kilby:

Manfred was kind of put off by this incident. The music was recorded quite quickly in one take on the first day. As soon as that happened, Manfred excused himself and left all the balancing and production work to the musicians and Steve Lake, the producer. He did not show his face again and never invited John again.

(E-mail interview with Jak Kilby, January 2011)

Brian Dee, one of Stevens's first employers, talked of an unpleasant incident at a gig some years after, where Stevens made a very dismissive comment about him and his music while Dee was on stage. Stevens was a complex, larger-than-life character but one who pioneered an unusually gentle, quiet approach to music-making. Though an advocate of communal and community music, this often had to be on his terms and in turn caused musicians like Trevor Watts and Paul Rutherford to leave the SME and start their own groups. He was also very single-minded about what he wanted or expected from those who played with him, as bassist Barry Guy explains:

Within the group of people, who were active at the Little Theatre Club, there were different moments where – say within the SME – John had some idea or other that one or more of us weren't playing the right way for that particular time. So, it was by invitation that you played with the SME and if you didn't cut it you had to find something else to do.

(Interview with Barry Guy, November 2010)

And Martin Davidson, owner of the EMANEM label and who has documented much of Stevens's work on CD, notes in an appreciation from 1997:

He was a man of extreme contradictions. He gave an enormous amount, but he also took a lot too. He could be one of the nicest, most intelligent, most interesting and most inventive people around, but could also (particularly after imbibing) be one of the most obnoxious and foolhardy. This dichotomy, combined with his apparently inexhaustible energy alienated many people.

(Davidson 1997b)

Yet what people emphasize about Stevens most of all is his energy, enthusiasm, commitment and inclusive and open approach to music-making. For many years, he ran community music workshops for amateur and even non-musicians – in fact, this was often his main source of income. He is far more often spoken of with fondness than with frustration and he remains rightly respected for his unique contribution to British music.

Derek Bailey, drummer Tony Oxley and bassist Gavin Bryars came together in Sheffield in the early 1960s. They began working as a unit in 1963 during Bryars's second year at Sheffield University. They took the name Joseph Holbrooke from a rather obscure twentieth-century English composer – "The English Wagner" – at the bassist's suggestion. Bryars was studying philosophy at the time and had a trio that included guitarist Ed Speight, who later worked extensively with Graham Collier and others. Bryars had heard about a group playing in a Sheffield pub and he hoped that his trio might be able play the interval slot. Bailey and the other musicians agreed and liked what they heard of the young bassist. Their group did not have a regular bass player and they invited Briars to a rehearsal at Bailey's house. It was a testing audition, as Bryars recalls:

They were kind of throwing pieces at me to see if I could cut the changes. One I remember doing was Coltrane's "Moment's Notice", where there are lots of really fast changes. It changes almost every beat and I just wanted to make sure the right notes went with them.

(Interview with Gavin Bryars, November 2010)

As Oxley explains, at that time, it was highly unusual to find three musicians who shared such diverse musical interests, let alone for them to find each other:

You see, we were all in Sheffield and it was absolutely unique to have three musicians in Sheffield who were into everything but jazz and we all had the same desire – how we achieved it was up to us and we got a desire to play music without relying on the next record coming from America to tell us how.

(Interview with Tony Oxley, April 2010)

Derek Bailey, Baden-Baden, Germany, December 1970. © Valerie Wilmer.

If Bryars's background was fairly middle class, with a highly developed interest in contemporary music as well as jazz, Bailey and Oxley were most definitely from working-class backgrounds. Oxley had received his musical education in the Black Watch. Bailey, on the other hand, was essentially self-taught but had been playing professionally since the late forties and early fifties. In fact, by the sixties, Bailey was an extremely successful "straight" guitarist playing in jazz and dance bands and doing sessions for the BBC and a variety of recording artists. If all three came from jazz, something about playing it, or playing it as one was expected to play it, made them uncomfortable and dissatisfied. For Bailey, this seems to have been about authenticity and there is a very telling remark that he makes in Ben Watson's biography, *Derek Bailey and the Story of Free Improvisation* (2004). Talking about playing jazz in London in the early sixties, Bailey told Watson:

I still worked in mainly in clubs. Did a certain amount of jazz clubs playing in that time too. By this time, I'd realised I didn't really understand what jazz was. What, since childhood almost, I'd taken to be some sort of exploratory process – a continuing development - turned out in practice more of a ritualistic thing.

(Watson 2004, 48)

He continued:

My disenchantment with jazz stemmed from the realisation that I couldn't do what the people I admired had done. I'd started in the wrong place at the wrong time, possibly in the wrong race, a conclusion I'd reached much earlier. I wasn't going to be Charlie Christian. After that, it was about playing every fucking thing I could lay my hands to and looking to get rid of my musical ignorance.

(Watson 2004, 48)

Joseph Holbrook's pianist Gerry Rawlinson left not long after Bryars joined and it continued as a trio with the occasional addition of another piano player called Bunny Thompson. It was at a pub called The Grapes in Trippett Lane, still a popular music venue in Sheffield, that their experimentation really began. It was a gradual process, and one that drew primarily upon the abilities, ideas and interpersonal dynamics of the three musicians. They had no idea what else might have been happening in London, or indeed anywhere else. There was no internet. Most people did not have phones. There were two TV channels and three radio stations in the UK, none of which was likely to promote avant-garde music. Initially, the focus was on the newer approaches that were emerging from American players like Bill Evans, Coltrane and Dolphy. Bryars recalls that Sonny Rollins's *The Bridge* with guitarist Jim Hall was also influential. Their main sources of inspiration were, however, Bill Evans and Coltrane with Bailey stretching to achieve Evans's voicings on his guitar. As Bryars explains:

We tried various little devices as ways of breaking up the tune. Instead of just playing it as a kind of song form, I suggested various ways of experimenting with harmonies – playing essentially on the wrong chord, as it were – and other devices like freezing the sound at one point and just improvising on one particular harmony and then moving out of it back into the song.

(Interview with Gavin Bryars, November 2010)

Evans's influence is to the fore on the one rehearsal tape of the trio released on Bailey's Incus label. It reveals a group still playing within what can best be described as a jazz idiom. According to Bryars this was recorded early in 1965:

By Easter '65, we started trying to play without any kind of changes at all and I did some kind of graphic scores as a way of codifying what we did – these sort of charts with loads of colours and stuff. But eventually, we just abandoned that completely and just played completely freely without any sense of a jazz pulse at all.

(Interview with Gavin Bryars, November 2010)

The three continued with other work, playing in cabaret clubs like the Carlton Club in Chesterfield and the Greasborough Working Men's Club – "The Palladium of the North". Bailey and Bryars even did a summer season in Jersey together. They backed Lee Konitz on a short tour of the north of England and Bryars and Oxley, with pianist Tony Bowden, even backed tapper and rapper Will Gaines on *Sunday Night at the London Palladium*. Bryars remembers they did "Summertime" – the Bill Evans arrangement – and that Tom Jones topped the bill, while the Oscar Peterson Trio also appeared. The thought of the curmudgeonly Oxley waving from the Palladium's revolving stage at the end of the show is a fine one indeed! Maybe there is a tape of the show somewhere.

But for three years, their Saturday lunchtime gig at The Grapes was sacrosanct. The audience was never huge – around thirty or forty – but it was very loyal with most people coming every week. Sometimes musicians would drop in to see what was happening. Bryars remembers that Dave Holland, who was touring with Johnny "Cry Boy" Ray, came on one occasion. The general response from musicians was of bafflement, though some enjoyed it, even though they did not quite know what to make of it. It ended almost immediately after they played in London for the first time. One Saturday afternoon in November 1966, they played at the opening of an art gallery in Northampton. From there, they drove down to London and played that night at the Little Theatre Club. After the gig, Bryars says, "I put my bass in its case and never played it again. I stopped that night" (interview with Gavin Bryars, November 2010). In fact, Bryars did play the instrument again albeit years later, including with a reformed Joseph Holbrook.

By that time, Bryars had taking a teaching job and had started studying composition. He is now, of course, one of the leading and most eclectic composers in contemporary music. Works like "Jesus' Blood Never Failed Me Yet" and "The Sinking of the Titanic" have almost taken on a life of their own. As he told the author:

I started studying composition and I was getting more into that. Eventually, the nightly bass playing got a bit too much. I got fed up with it and decided I would teach and psychologically, mentally I was probably moving away from the ethos of that kind of work. Just generally playing all the time, I wanted to be more reflective.

(Interview with Gavin Bryars, November 2010)

The fact that Joseph Holbrooke did not record during their short life and hardly played outside The Grapes as a unit let alone outside Sheffield, obviously severely limited their influence. They reunited briefly in 1998 and a CD, *Joseph Holbrooke '98* (Incus), was issued as a result. One cannot know how close this performance might be to their original sound. After all, they each brought with them to that gig more than thirty years of music-making, in Bryars' case within a completely different approach. A reprise perhaps, rather than a valediction but it is nevertheless a magnificent one. Their significance as a trio lies rather in the practice they developed together, that particular way of making music, and which Oxley and Bailey then took into the rest of their work as improvisers and gave to the development of others. Not only that, with Evan Parker and business man, Michael Walters, they established Incus, the first musician-owned British independent label, and provided an outlet for many of the musicians from that first wave of home-grown free improvisation.

Tony Oxley was the first of the three members of Joseph Holbrooke to record when he got a deal with CBS, who had been quick to pick up on the new wave of British jazz. Its enthusiasm did not last, of course, and died once the sales figures failed to match expectations. However, between 1969 and 1971, the label released a clutch of fine albums by British artists. There were three from guitarist Ray Russell, including the marvellous and "out" *Rites and Rituals*, two from Howard Riley, *Angle* and *The Day Will Come*, as well as Ronnie Scott and the Band *Live at Ronnie Scott's* and vibraphonist Frank Ricotti's *Our Point of View*. Before the door slammed shut, Tony Oxley was able to release *Baptised Traveller* and *Four Compositions for Sextet*. *Four Compositions* is the more challenging of the two with its harsh, often dissonant compositions, and adds Paul Rutherford to the quintet of Evan Parker, Kenny Wheeler, Derek Bailey, Jeff Clyne and Oxley featured on *Baptised Traveller*. The latter remains one of the classic records of the period. Oxley was everywhere in this period. He was the house drummer at the Scott club, played on John McLaughlin's justly feted *Extrapolation* (Marmalade; Decca) and Alan Skidmore's fine debut *Once Upon a Time*. In fact, he won the critics' poll at Montreux when Skidmore's group played there in 1969. He also recorded *Gyroscope* (Morgan; Art Of Life) and *Experiments With Pops* (Major Minor; Art Of Life) with pianist Gordon Beck and *Live at Ronnie Scott's* with Scott's nonet, which also included drummer and Dankworth alumnus, Kenny Clare. Each of these is a fine testament to his talents and, yet, *Baptised Traveller* reveals his ability to create something more personal and elegiac.

By this point the SME, Joseph Holbrooke and, as we shall see, AMM had already moved some distance away from a jazz directly derived from African-American models. Of the quintet used on *Baptised Traveller* all four members apart from Oxley himself played regularly in the SME. With such an overlap of personnel, one might have expected something not dissimilar from *Karyobin* but we are most definitely in free jazz territory here. The music is arranged as a suite opening with Oxley's compositions "Crossing" and "Arrival", continuing with "Stone Garden" by American altoist Charlie Mariano and concluding with the drummer's "Preparation". The feel or mood is not unlike that on the *Springboard* LP, which paired trumpeter Ian Carr with Clyne, Trevor Watts and John Stevens, or that of Skidmore's *Once Upon a Time*, which featured Oxley's composition "Majaera". As additional reference points, we might also include John Surman's *How Many Clouds Can You See?* on which Oxley also played, most notably on the long, three-section "Event", and McLaughlin's "Extrapolation". There is no reason to suppose that Oxley was influenced by any of these. It is rather that they all seem to share a certain sensibility that defined certain areas of British jazz and improvised music at that time.

Oxley had got the record deal with CBS through producer David Howells, who had seen him at the Scott club. According to the drummer, he had written and arranged the music that became *Baptised Traveller* not long after Joseph Holbrooke had started. By that point, his music had moved on and he had just written his first serial composition. He recognized, however, that the form and structure, loose and abstract though these might be, of the music he had shelved would be more appropriate for his first release. Oxley says that Howells was somewhat surprised by the session:

> Remember he'd heard me at Ronnie's. When he heard I was going to do *Baptised Traveller*, he put up with it and then when we did *Four Compositions* for Sextet, which was nearer the mark, he put up with that. But they weren't happy. They wanted something that was more approaching what was going on in Ronnie's, you see, and I disappointed them and I didn't get the third record. I should have had three records for CBS and I only did two. The third one was really the one. That was *Ichnos*, which I did in the end for RCA. (Interview with Tony Oxley, April 2010)

The inspiration for the album lay in the idea of a spiritual journey but there is nothing ambient or meditative about this project. Both "Crossing" and "Arrival" are powerful tunes delivered to startling effect by the musicians. Parker and Wheeler are on ferocious form, one moment gently coaxing and persuasive, the next releasing furious bursts of stuttering, argumentative, broken lines. The rhythm section is quite astonishing with Oxley railing wildly against Clyne's powerful bass. It is on Charlie Mariano's "Stone Garden" that Bailey really comes into his own. His guitar almost seems to weep at times and drips with haunting echo effects. It is Bailey, who seems primarily responsible for the soundworld of this track, although both Parker and Wheeler play with remarkable introspection given what has gone before. The short, hymnal "Preparation" closes the record to fine, if sombre and bathetic effect. *Baptised Traveller* may well be a transitional record for Oxley but it remains an extraordinarily beautiful one.

Another venture from this period from within this group of Little Theatre Club habitués was the Music Improvisation Company. Derek Bailey and Evan Parker had begun to work together with percussionist Jamie Muir, electronics pioneer Hugh Davies and, occasionally, vocalist Christine Jeffrey. MIC formed in 1968 and, along with AMM and American group Musica Electronica Viva, was one of the first to make extensive use of electronics as a core element in its group sound. The combination of Davies's organ and electronic, sound-generating equipment and Bailey's use of foot pedals marked a leap forward in British free improvisation. It might share some of the pointillist characteristics of the SME but there was also a shocking, iconoclastic quality to the music. Percussionist Jamie Muir was also a painter and his artwork decorated the sleeve of *The Music Improvisation Company 1968– 1971* (Incus; Incus). Muir later played with King Crimson in a group that also included ex-Yes drummer Bill Bruford before retiring first to a Buddhist retreat and then to painting as a vocation. According to John Wickes, the first edition of MIC involved Parker, Bailey, Muir, Gavin Bryars on makeshift electronics and pianist John Tilbury, and began by playing the music of Cage and Cornelius Cardew (Wickes 1999, 90). It was the arrival of Davies, at one point assistant to Karlheinz Stockhausen, that marked the departure into new musical territory.

MIC were the first British ensemble to record for ECM, and their eponymous debut (ECM; Japo) was a stark, even apocalyptic manifesto. Christine Jeffrey sings only on "Third Stream Boogaloo" and "Untitled No. II". Otherwise, the group that gathered in London in August 1970 was a quartet. It is difficult to say how far the music contained on the ECM release differs from what the group played in other contexts. However, the material on the Incus release both echoes the ECM date while also reaching beyond it. The mono recordings from 1968 have a home-made, almost folkish ambience, while those from 1971, and, in particular, "Its Tongue Trapped to the Rock By a Limpet", "The Water Rat Succumbed to the Incoming Tide", have the advantage of stereo and have a fullness and intensity that goes even further than the ECM album. However, "Dragon's Path", "Packaged Eel" and "Tuck" are as powerful and confrontational as anything from the period, while "Wolfgang Van Gangbang" (guess you had to be there!) builds from pointillist beginnings to a dense, claustrophobic conclusion.

The album *The Topography of the Lungs*, the first release on Incus, is different again. Here, Parker and Bailey are joined by Dutch percussionist Han Bennink and it is his performance and the absence of electronics that offers perhaps the greatest contrast with the MIC recordings. Space and silence seem more important here, though the music derives much of its force from the intensity of the interaction between the players. With MIC, Jamie Muir seemed to be everywhere in the sound – sometimes surrounding it with waves of percussion, sometimes providing its beating heart and at others just offering a backdrop to better reflect his colleagues' efforts. Bennink is even busier but always at the centre of the music. Not that he is in anyway insensitive to the contributions of Parker and Bailey, rather he is determined to drive them on and to throw down a constant series of challenges.

Parker had played with Bennink on Peter Brötzmann's stunning assault on the senses, *Machine Gun* (FMP), while all three (including Bailey) had performed in Brötzmann's sextet on several occasions and in a septet that also included Paul Rutherford. Bailey had also played in a duo with Bennink and in a quartet involving Danish altoist John Tchicai and Dutch pianist Misha Mengelberg. Contacts between the older, more straightahead British jazz musicians and their European counterparts had been somewhat slower to develop. But the newer players had very quickly developed a European focus. Both Parker and Bailey would build on these early contacts over the years and soon became leading figures on the European scene. Perhaps unsurprisingly, the USA was more parochial in its attitudes at this time. In the last fifteen years, American artists such as saxophonists Ken Vandermark, John Zorn and Tim Berne have come to recognize and value the vibrancy and excitement of the European scene. In that, now global, context both Parker and Bailey are recognized as two of the most important jazz and improvising musicians to come out of the UK. Parker, in particular, has established a body of work as a solo performer, with his trio involving Barry Guy and drummer Paul Lytton, with his Electro-Acoustic Ensemble and in any number of other settings that is *sans pareil*.

The story of Eddie Prévost and AMM Music is more problematic in terms of our subject matter. The original grouping of Prévost, saxophonist Lou Gare and guitarist Keith Rowe had formed in 1965 and had soon begun to move beyond the confines that might be suggested by the word "jazz". Rowe had been at art school in Plymouth with Mike Westbrook (Warburton 2001). In the late fifties, Westbrook formed a rehearsal band and Rowe was one of its first members. Westbrook was a little older than the other students having worked in accountancy and completed his national service by the time he started in Plymouth. According to John Surman then aged 15, it was Rowe who invited him to join the Westbrook band, while Westbrook recalls him arriving at the first rehearsal wearing his school cap (Shera 1966).

By 1962, Westbrook had decided to pursue a career in jazz and moved to London with both Surman, who was now a student in the capital, and Rowe joining him (Shera 1966, 10; Lock 1985a, b). Lou Gare joined Westbrook around 1963/4, by which time he was already playing with Eddie Prévost in a hard bop quintet. The other important figure in relation to AMM's early history was Lawrence Sheaff, who as it happened was also the bassist in Westbrook's band. While Westbrook's music has always contained elements of surprise and spontaneity and even though at that time he was viewed by some as the *enfant terrible* of British jazz, structure and form have been equally important elements in his conception of jazz. Rowe, Gare and Sheaff were, however, beginning to chafe at such constraints. In a *Jazz Journal* article on Westbrook and his musicians from 1966, Michael Shera noted, "Guitarist Keith Rowe is the first avant-garde guitarist I have heard, and he is an entirely convincing and exciting exponent of the genre." He was less taken with Gare, however, writing, "Tenorist Lou Gare can be an intensely moving and passionate soloist, though occasionally he lapses into a jerky and unswinging way of phrasing" (Shera 1966, 11).

Before the article had actually appeared, Gare and Rowe had left Westbrook to work with Prévost, and Sheaff joined them shortly afterwards. Jac Holzman's Elektra Records gave the group their first opportunity to record, which given the label's forays into avant-garde classical music and the use of synthesizers (for example, Milton Sobotnik, Beaver & Krause) is less surprising than it might first seem. If the group sat somewhat uneasily with the London jazz scene, they found some affinity with the new free jazz that was represented by the SME, and played several times at the Little Theatre Club. By this point, avant-garde composer Cornelius Cardew was also part of AMM and, for a brief moment, the group found some common ground with the burgeoning underground rock music that was making its presence felt. To be sure, any such interest (with the notable exception of members of the Soft Machine) was brief and ephemeral, but AMM did have some degree of influence on both Pink Floyd (through guitarist Syd Barrett) and on John Lennon, who recorded *Unfinished Music No. 1: Two Virgins*, *Unfinished Music No. 2: Life with the Lions* and *Wedding Album* with Yoko Ono after exposure to AMM. Barrett was particularly taken by Keith Rowe's guitar playing, as Barry Miles notes:

> This was free-form music at its cutting edge and to reinforce the sense of serious scientific investigation AMM played in white lab coats. The idea that all sound could have a musical value was absorbed by Pink Floyd who later took up the idea and spent hours using non-conventional sources to try and make an album. Some of the sounds AMM made were impossible to identify. Watching from the side of the stage Syd Barrett was intrigued to see that Keith Rowe achieved some of his special effects on electric guitar by rolling steel ball bearings up and down the strings to produce peculiar sounds. (Miles 2006, 56)

Miles adds, "Syd borrowed this procedure and later used it himself on stage." Miles cites Peter Whitehead's film of the group as an example of this, in which Barrett can be seen with the guitar laid flat in what Rowe called the "table top position" (Miles 2006, 56). Robert Chapman in an excellent biography of Pink Floyd's Syd Barrett (Chapman 2010) locates AMM clearly within the UK/London underground and quotes John "Hoppy" Hopkins:

My impression was that many people were open to lots of different influences ... There was a great deal of crossover. Musicians of
one sort listening to what musicians of another sort were doing;
black soul music, white rock and pop music, classical and serious avant-garde stuff, the Cornelius Cardew end of things. There
were American jazz musicians visiting like Ornette Coleman and
Steve Lacy. There was also the British jazz of course and there was
AMM. Their music was so far out it was on the border between
music and noise and street sound. Of all the music and groups
and ideas from that era, the ones that have stayed closest to the
original concept are AMM, who are still around today.

(Chapman 2010, 96)

Chapman notes:

AMM played several significant gigs with Pink Floyd between
March 1966 and February 1967 including the Spontaneous
Underground events at the Marquee Club that took place
between March and June 1966, gigs at All Saints Hall in Notting
Hill, and the *International Times* launch party at the Roundhouse
in October of that year. Syd also attended the recording session
for AMM's debut album in June 1966.   (Chapman 2010, 99)

And as Chapman also points out, the producers of *AMMMusic* (Elektra;
RéR) were Hopkins, Peter Jenner, Ronald Atkins and Alan Beckett – each of
whom were associated with the Floyd. Chapman also quotes guitarist Fred
Frith of Henry Cow on the issue of AMM's influence and originality.

Prévost's essay "AMM and the Practice of Self-Invention" in *No Sound
is Innocent* (Prévost 1995) provides a detailed outline of the group's history, its working methods and its unravelling in the face of ideological
pressures stemming from the adoption of Maoism by two of its member's
(Rowe and Cardew). It will come as no surprise that the group engaged in
intense, internal discussions about methodology and philosophy. Their practice was informed by ideas as seemingly diverse as Taoism, Buddhism and
Confucianism and Marxism, but was never, until the conversion of Rowe
and Cardew, driven by any one or combination of these. The spiritual and
idealistic frameworks of Eastern belief systems might seem at odds with the
rigorously materialistic ideas of Marx and Engels. However, those systems
are also practices involving study, meditation, question and answer, paradox,
contemplation and reflection. In a meditative or contemplative state, with
or without artificial stimulant, thoughts and ideas are allowed to flow unrestricted without the kinds of self-censorship or imposition of structure or
meaning that might apply in a more actively conscious state. This can present
new possibilities and ideas and/or new configurations of more familiar

ones. It may be true that these practices are essentially introspective ones. However, in their focus on meaning, purpose and, to use the Buddhist terms from the "Noble Eighthfold Path", on "right intention, right conduct and right effort", they also concern themselves with actions and consequences. In these respects, their function, alongside Marxism, in the context of AMM should be more obviously apparent.

Prévost reveals that the members sought to understand and appreciate the contexts – social, political, cultural, aesthetic and environmental – in which they and their music functioned. It is worth pointing out here that both ethics and aesthetics are located within the broader field of philosophical study of value known as axiology. Put simply, while ethics weighs actions, statements and ideas in terms of what is deemed "good" or "bad", aesthetics weighs art and its products in terms of what is considered "beautiful" or "harmonious". As the philosopher Don Ritter suggests:

> By understanding the ethical consequences of compositional decisions and aesthetic judgements, artists and audiences can have increased responsibility for the propagation of ethical values, the concepts that dictate which behaviours we deem appropriate and which we do not. Without this awareness, a person might promote any value whatsoever through aesthetic judgements. Having an awareness of the influences and consequences of aesthetic judgements is desirable because it enables a person to promote specific values with intention. (Ritter 2008, 14)

Indeed, considered in such terms, the stance of AMM was most definitely an ethical one, though not in any formulaic sense. In practice, Ritter's comments convey very well the close relationship between these two philosophical disciplines and also the kinds of questioning that AMM, and others, were engaged in during the sixties. AMM, however, raised and tried to answer questions of value and practice with a degree of articulacy that grew from their own internal dialogue. In his sleevenotes to *The Crypt* on CD, Prévost is not just expressing the group's understanding with hindsight. His words state unequivocally how they saw the music they were making:

> *AMMMusic* served no demand and it supplied no market. Neither did it swerve into the slip-stream of any cultural correctness. And although the experience of AMM informed the more jazz-like playing of my duets with both Gare and (later) Rowe, and also my work with other musicians, AMM could not, would not it seems, be made to serve the objectives of any reality other than its own. AMM was, and "is", both a medium for discovery and a mirror by which it could meditate upon things, but its concern was itself. (Prévost 1995, 10)

And while on an American lecture tour in November 1967, Cornelius Cardew addressed the key issues that – for him, for AMM and others – were raised by improvised music-making:

> Written compositions are fired off into the future; even if never performed, the writing remains as a point of reference. Improvisation is in the present, its effect live on in the souls of the participants, both active and passive (i.e. audience) but in its concrete form it is gone forever from the moment that it occurs, nor did it have any previous existence before the moment that it occurred, so neither is there any historical reference available.
>
> (Quoted in Prévost 1992)

Cardew even argues, as others continued to suggest, that recordings of improvised music were pale reflections of the real event:

> Documents such as tape recordings of improvisation are essentially empty, as they preserve chiefly the form that something took and give at best an indistinct hint as to the feeling and cannot convey any sense of time and place.
>
> (Quoted in Prévost 1992)

He continues by describing AMM's approach and its rationale:

> Informal "sound" has a power over our emotional responses that formal "music" does not, in that it acts subliminally rather than on a cultural level. This is a possible definition of the area in which AMM is experimental. We are searching for sounds and for responses that attach to them, rather than thinking them up, preparing them and producing them. The search is conducted in the medium of sound and the musician himself is at the heart of the experiment.
>
> (Quoted in Prévost 1992)

AMMMusic certainly broke entirely new ground, and yet other material recorded at the same sessions suggest that the focus was softened to a degree for the Elektra album that was finally released. It is interesting to note that Cardew, somewhat ignorant of jazz, had thought that he was joining a "jazz group" with AMM. At this juncture, some jazz inflections remained and the origin of the sounds made are pretty clearly discernible. It is a remarkable debut, but *The Crypt – 12th June 1968* (Matchless; Matchless) is like nothing else. One gets used to hearing music described as "dark", "disturbing" or "disorienting". The Crypt session, though finally released way outside our period, stretches such words to snapping point. It is one of the most extreme examples of music-making. There are times when one can make out a sound and attribute it to a piano or saxophone but mostly it is a collage of sounds. It is, as Prévost describes it, music without beginning or end and one can still hear its presence, rather than influence, in much that came later – in Paul Rutherford's *Iskra 1903*, perhaps, and in the growth of electro-acoustic music, perhaps, in the 1990s and the early part of this century. One is forced into analogy, as opposed to description, in discussing music like this. It disturbs in a way similar to the cut-up writing techniques of William Burroughs and Brion Gysin or the art of Max Ernst. It does not so much shock or force one to flinch or withdraw. Instead, like William Burroughs's *Naked Lunch* or Max Ernst's *The Robing of the Bride*, it holds you suspended in a kind of state of severe foreboding and remains with you, whether you wish it or not, when it is over.

The articulacy with which Cardew and Prévost sought to express their musical ideas was not unique to AMM. More than any other area outside classical music, free jazz/improvisation has sought to express itself in words on both its theory and practice. Derek Bailey's *On Improvisation* explores improvisational activity across a wide range of genres, as if to force the conclusion that improvisation is more than just an important part of music but possibly also its centre. John Stevens in countless interviews has been no less articulate. In 1992, Stevens gave Victor Schonfield just such an example:

> I used to imagine a hundred-piece orchestra, if you like, and there's no possibility within that, that you could hear all those elements in detail. But the way it would work, if it did work, is that within the vicinity of you as an individual, you might be able to clearly hear four other people in your particular unit. So, if everybody's functioning in relationship to being as aware as they could be, in relationship to how far their aural sight can take them, then the whole unit would be like an organism, which made sense, because everybody was interacting in the same way and the music would be the manifestation of this activity.   (Schonfield 1992)

Stevens did work through his life with larger groups, even if he never quite achieved this goal. But what he alludes to here is an inherent series of problems for improvisation, which also to a degree apply to jazz. However, chaotic free improvisation may sound to some people it is not a "free-for-all". It requires many of the qualities that all musicians need and, in some cases, free improvisers must develop these skills at an even higher level. The improvising musician must listen with incredible intensity to those performing with them. They must be aware of time, both musical and real. They must hear every sound and, in hearing it, identify its value and its potential. They must know when to play and when not to play and where and when silence is an important component of the music. Whereas the musician working from written material has the score to assist them or where the jazz musician has a chord sequence or harmonic structure to guide them, the free improviser has the responsibility for determining form, structure and content in the moment.

"Responsibility" is a key word here. It is a point that Julie Tippetts makes in her work with students, as she explains:

> That thing of responsibility – this is a word that comes up a lot in my sharing with people, if you like. It's not teaching. It's a sharing with people for me and trying to portray to somebody or a group of people what you've discovered, what you've learned and sharing it with them. But responsibility always comes into it with me. It's a word I use a lot because we have huge responsibilities as musicians, absolutely huge and not just in our discipline of what we do and how we do it. It's the intent behind things because of the fact that music affects people so much we have to ... as musicians, I think we have to have this responsibility of knowing that it's going to affect people. So, it makes what you put to people, what you perform to them, it puts an angle on it that is not just about you going on and entertaining people to give them a rest after work or give them a good time. It's like you're really trying to touch something in people because it will touch them.
>
> (Interview with Julie Tippetts, September 2008)

Tippetts's comments seem to echo those of Don Ritter. That same question of responsibility or, to be more even more specific, that same ethical sense is present in the comments of Eddie Prévost and John Stevens and runs through this field of musical endeavour. For Maggie Nicols, this clearly moves into a broader political dimension. She stresses repeatedly that improvising is a skill and one that necessitates the learning of a difficult and remarkably creative language.

> It's a skill. It really is! It's extraordinary, isn't it, how ... I think it's because in some ways it's subversive, it's got to be almost disempowered by making it ... by dismissing it as something weird and, in that way, it will keep people away from it and they won't get the opportunity to experience the liberation and the autonomy that comes both individually and collectively.
>
> (Interview with Maggie Nicols, October 2010)

The notion of music as a problem-solving process is more familiar to musicians than to those whose listen to their efforts. Again, that notion is perhaps most accentuated in the areas of composition and improvisation, both separately and where these two meet, and correspondingly less so in the interpretation of through-composed material. The idea that ethical choices are involved in this activity may not be specific to the area that concerns us – both Schönberg and Bernstein have something to say on the subject – but are more generally associated with it.

Barry Guy's *Ode* (Incus; Intakt), written and conceived for the London Jazz Composers' Orchestra (LCJO), illustrates these questions particularly well. It might not have involved John Stevens's 100-piece orchestra, but it stands as a major document, an astonishing work of art and one that reveals its composer's struggles to address the relationships between composition and improvisation in bold and exciting ways.

Contrary to Cook and Morton's suggestion, neither *Ode* nor the formation of the LCJO were initially inspired by the example of Michael Mantler and the Jazz Composers' Orchestra (JCO; Cook and Morton 2000, 927), as Guy explains:

> It was intriguing because I had decided to put on this big piece Ode mainly as a gesture to all the musicians I had been working with. Basically, it covered quite a large area of the scene from players at the most experimental end to those more involved in jazz. Mike Osborne was an example of the much more Afro-American jazz-oriented approach, whereas somebody like Evan would be on the other side of the division.
> (Interview with Barry Guy, November 2010)

He had already commenced the project and then heard of Mantler and his orchestra:

> When I had begun writing the score I came across the Mike Mantler record – the Jazz Composers' Orchestra. I don't think I had even decided the name of my band, let alone that it would be the London Jazz Composers Orchestra. When I first started sketching it, it was just a piece I wanted to get out of my system. So, it seemed appropriate that I should come across that record at the right time. So, as kind of a homage to Mike Mantler and the JCO, I called it the LCJO.
> (Interview with Barry Guy, November 2010)

Both *Ode* and Mantler's first release with the JCO were written using a complex system known as "time-space notation", an approach associated with Polish composers such as Penderecki and Lutosławski. Guy had studied at the Guildhall, concentrating primarily upon contemporary and baroque musics, but the sheer breadth of his work before, during and after his studies is astounding. It has included playing free jazz with Howard Riley, Mike Osborne and the SME, as well as work with a number of chamber ensembles such as the Orchestra of St. John's Smith Square, John Elliott Gardiner's

Monteverdi Orchestra and The Academy of Ancient Music with Christopher Hogwood. To these he has added sessions for films and pop music – Guy played on the Rolling Stone's "Angie" and, on top of that, with Bob Downes Open Music, he worked with the seminal London Contemporary Dance Theatre.

The making of *Ode* was fraught with difficulties. Not only was time-space notation quite alien to some of the musicians, not all were strong readers. Because of its complexity – Guy describes it as being akin to a Wagner score – he had decided to use his college professor and mentor, Buxton Ore, to conduct the ensemble. For some, like Derek Bailey, the very thought of composition was bad enough, but to be asked to work with a conductor was anathema! When Butch Morris first brought his conduction approach to improvisation to London, Bailey was one of the musicians chosen to perform in the ensemble. Early in rehearsals, Bailey became so enraged by Morris' commands and direction that he put his guitar in its case and left. Fortunately for Guy and *Ode*, he stayed the course in 1972.

At times, the musicians become sorely irritated and frustrated by the demands being put upon them, their anger often turning on a very patient and understanding Buxton Ore. As Guy noted:

> They [conductors and free improvisers] just don't go together but Buxton, as well as being a great musician and great composer, was also a Doctor of Psychology, so I think he had to bring out everything that he'd learnt over the years to keep the band together and under control. I just let him get on with it. I just thought "I'm going to keep my head down here and play the notes." [laughs]
> (Interview with Barry Guy, November 2010)

After two years of writing and preparation, it was finally performed in its entirety at Oxford Town Hall at the English Bach Festival in April 1972. With hindsight, it was a triumph, but, as Guy says, getting there was hard: "It was a process of building up the piece incrementally but it was thrilling to finally do the whole thing in one hit and it was extremely hard on everybody. I know that. The poor trumpeters' lips were hanging off after the performance" (interview with Barry Guy, November 2010).

In conceiving the piece, Guy had drawn on the notion of Greek Choric Theatre, on the work of Olivier Messiaen and had taken inspiration from works by several surrealist painters. He took as his structure the same pattern of strophe–antistrophe–épôde found in Greek poetry used by Messiaen in his 1962 work, *Chronochromie*. Like Messiaen, Guy extends these with the addition of a second strophe and antistrophe, together with an introduction and coda. In the Greek poetic form, traditionally the strophe and antistrophe share form and metre, while the épôde provides a crowning conclusion. These elements feature extensively in both *Chronochromie* and in *Ode*.

Messiaen was a keen ornithologist and used transcriptions, often his own, of birdsong in his works, and Guy utilizes woodwinds and strings to achieve similar effects with great success. In his programme notes for a Philharmonia Orchestra performance of Messiaen's work, Peter Hill comments upon its negative reception at its premiere in Paris in 1962 and quotes the composer's spirited defence of *Chronochromie*. His words would surely ring bells for improvisers everywhere:

> My permutations of durations are rigorous, my birdsongs are entirely free. Rigour is implacable, but so too is freedom. Mingling them together shocks audiences of all persuasions. And when in the Épôde a vast counterpoint of birds in eighteen real voices unfolds simultaneously, with all the freedoms tangled, the apparent disorder of inextricable sounds is the last straw for the audience, and provokes shouts and tumult.   (Hill 1992)

Messiaen continued defiantly, "Freedom! Doubtless we're afraid of this word. In the end it is freedom that triumphs in my music. And if I had given a title to this modest defence, perhaps I would have called it: 'A Plea for Freedom'" (quoted in Hill 1992).

Messiaen, a medical auxiliary during the Second World War, was captured by the Reichswehr in 1941 and spent the rest of the war in Stalag VIII-A, a Nazi prisoner of war camp. It was there that he wrote *Quatuor pour la fin du temps* and this remarkable quartet was first performed for an audience of prisoners and guards in the camp. When it came to discussion of "freedom" Messiaen clearly knew of what he spoke.

Guy needed no such defence. Just ten years after *Chronochromie's* first performance, *Ode* could be heard both as a tribute and as a piece in its own right. It is an album that is as much a Third Stream masterwork as Miles Davis and Gil Evans's *Porgy and Bess*. Cook and Morton, comparing *Ode* to Michael Mantler's record, suggest:

> Whereas Mantler's group still remains audibly rooted in blues-based jazz, however subtly mediated by 12-tone music and other avant-garde inflexions, the LCJO is much closer in spirit to a European strain of collective improvisation.
> (Cook and Morton 2000, 927)

The link to emerging European approaches to collective improvisational practice is justifiable. However, there is also a great deal of jazz to be found in *Ode*. Listen for example to Trevor Watts's alto solo in "Part VII" of the complete concert issued on Intakt. Charlie Parker and Eric Dolphy would surely have smiled on Watts's bravura performance. And Harry Beckett is in masterful form later in the same section, while the orchestra revels in its opportunity to swing. One can certainly hear Messiaen, and perhaps also Penderecki and Xenakis as well, but the enormously important (indeed central) section of the composition, "Part III – Antistrophe I", calls upon the ghost of Ellington and Johnny Hodges in Mike Osborne's solo. The brass choruses in this section are astonishingly beautiful and lush before the band launch into some fine big band flourishes that presage events in "Part III – Coda". "Part IV – Strophe II" is the most difficult and challenging section of this 100-minute piece, and it is this section that best fits Cook and Morton's description. Derek Bailey and pianist Howard Riley are quite remarkable here, not least in Bailey's case when, according to Guy, he "appeared to hate every minute of it!" The word "pointillist" might well apply once again but there is jazz too in some of the brooding brass choruses used here to comment upon the actions central to the "play". *Ode* is one of those rare works that offers new insights each time it is heard. Guy's acknowledgement that he has learnt other ways of resolving the composition-improvisation dichotomy since 1972 in no way detract from the glory that is *Ode*.

> I had the feeling that some of the musicians felt they were looking at this wall of notation and here was I expecting that they play a bit here, then start improvising there. It was difficult enough to get the first bar in place, let alone go off and improvise, then follow the conductor twenty minutes later and come in at the right place again. So, there were a lot of logistic problems but we didn't fail. Something came out of it that was extraordinary. It isn't that I'd written extraordinary music but that the players dealt with it and gave an incredible creative push to the music and I'm acutely aware that all this stuff that goes down on paper doesn't mean a thing unless the musicians can actually negotiate a way through it and the improvisers can make their sense of it and people can feel happy with it.   (Interview with Barry Guy, November 2010)

That such a spirit of adventure and the pursuit, to a greater or lesser extent, of "freedom" and spontaneity infused the music scene in the late sixties and early seventies is obvious. The free improvising saxophonist Lol Coxhill might be found in any number of places – busking Rollins-like on Hungerford Bridge, near London's Festival Hall; performing in Kevin Ayers's Whole World or with Carol Grimes and Delivery; gigging at the Little Theatre Club or any of the clubs around the metropolis; or turning up on John Peel's BBC show "Top Gear". Coxhill's partnership with ex-Delivery pianist Steve Miller would lead to several fine recordings, including *Coxhill–Miller* and *Story So Far … Oh Really?* (Caroline; Cuneiform), while Soft Machine drummer Robert Wyatt could be heard performing freely with the Amazing Band with illustrator and trumpeter Mal Dean, saxophonist Mick Brannan and violinist Veleroy Spall (FMR).

The massive and shifting collective that was the Continuous Music Ensemble and later the People Band embodied an even more anarchic spirit. Their personnel included Westbrook saxophonist George Khan, sax and flute player Lyn Dobson, drummer Terry Day and multi-instrumentalist (and later film director) Mike Figgis. Their one recording released during the sixties was *People Band 1968* (Transatlantic; EMANEM), which was produced and financed by Rolling Stones drummer Charlie Watts. It is a ragged affair, if not without a certain charm, while later recordings issued on EMANEM are even wilder. The People Band "believed in the liberating and creative value of music and delivered the liberating power of musical freedom". They eschewed the need for musical training and redefined notions of musical competence accordingly, much as John Stevens would do within his workshops and even recordings. They played anywhere they could and had a fondness for playing in woodland environments! As they wrote, their approach inferred "political/social stance: a music of the people by the people – 'equality'" (see sleeve-notes to EMANEM 4102, 2004).

Such notions might be idealistic but they drew sustenance from a well-spring that informed thought, action and musical practice at the time to an unusual extent. The same ethos could be found equally in the music of Mike Westbrook, John Surman, Mike Osborne, Alan Skidmore and pianist Gordon Beck or in the rock music of King Crimson, Soft Machine, Kevin Ayers, Gong, Pink Floyd and Henry Cow. Some musicians like guitarist Ray Russell, arguably the most innovative guitar player to emerge during the sixties, crossed boundaries with remarkable ease, producing two exceptional "out" recordings *Rites and Rituals* and *Live at the ICA* (RCA; Moikai). Even some more obviously "jazz" players proved keen to test the waters of free playing. The short-lived group Splinters featured John Stevens, Trevor Watts, Jeff Clyne and Kenny Wheeler but also included Stan Tracey, Tubby Hayes and Phil Seamen. Tracey, of course, would go on to record in some very free settings with John Surman, Keith Tippett and Mike Osborne. In fact, although a divide would emerge between free improvisation and jazz even in its more avant-garde manifestations, this began later in the seventies and, anyway, still allowed for fraternization between these forms.

Pianist Howard Riley, as well as being one of the finest pianists to emerge in the sixties, and not just in Britain either, perhaps provides a good illustration of this process. By the last years of the sixties, Riley had completely absorbed the influences of Monk, Ellington, Tatum and Bill Evans. In the eighties, his approach would change becoming more austere, angular and abstract, as he seemed to move towards a music that owed a debt to European art music. Again, when he returned to a more definably jazz-oriented improvisational practice, he brought with him those ideas he had explored and developed in the eighties. A graduate of Bangor University, Riley studied with the great jazz educator, and ex-student of George Russell, David N. Baker at Indiana University writing his MA thesis on Russell's Lydian Chromatic Concept.

He made his first record, *Discussions* (Opportunity; Jazzprint), for the tiny Opportunity label in 1967 with Barry Guy and Jon Hiseman. While several of the original pieces become fairly "out" performances, on the standard tunes Riley sounds the more conventional player of the three. Hiseman is given considerable latitude, while Guy's role is perhaps akin to that of Jimmy Garrison in the classic Coltrane quartet. In this context, he seems quite unrestricted by the chord or harmonic sequence.

Angle followed in 1969 for CBS. By that time, Hiseman was already involved with Colosseum and his place was taken by Alan Jackson. Jackson's name crops up far too rarely in discussions about British jazz drummers and he is not even included in Carr, Fairweather and Priestley's *Jazz: The Essential Companion* (1987). However, the drummer has played with many of the bandleaders we have already mentioned including Keith Tippett, John Surman, Mike Westbrook, Michael Garrick and Harry Beckett, and his contribution to modern British jazz drumming in this period (and later) seems unfairly overlooked. His style is not flashy or scene-stealing. Rather his ability to play time and yet allow for a certain freedom and looseness within an ensemble truly suited the modern into free jazz that characterised much of the music on the scene. The music on *Angle* still sounds somewhat reserved and even a little self-conscious. However, with Barry Guy continuing on bass, this was very much a working trio and one that was very active, not just in London but outside as well. Recently checking through old diaries, Guy had been pleasantly surprised at how steadily the trio had worked.

> I was really surprised to see that Howard was taking us all over the country. So, there was obviously some kind of useful network going on either in clubs or Arts Council tours. So, it was a good period. It was important because it was a solid working group with a real forward direction rather than being an ad hoc meeting of musicians. (Interview with Barry Guy, November 2010)

Today, it seems amazing that a major label would consider putting out music that was at the cutting edge of jazz. However, back then, musical categories had not become quite so ossified and record companies did have a commitment to maintaining a catalogue in depth. Sales were obviously a major consideration but they were not, as we saw in an earlier chapter, all-important. The prestige of a label stood as well on the quality of the music that they released. Riley sent a copy of *Discussions* to CBS and was rewarded with a contract for two albums and an option for a third. As he suggests, the music business in the fifties and sixties relied on the intelligence and intuition of its producers, and allowed such figures considerable latitude.

> At that particular time large record companies – this is me being a sociological analyst [laughing] – at that particular time it was

the height of the rock thing and you often got a syndrome in major record companies where there would be one person who was a jazz fan who was in a position of some power and there was a guy at CBS called David Howells.

(Interview with Howard Riley, May 2006)

Howells's brief tenure at CBS, as noted, produced a couple of handfuls of exceptional British jazz albums in the late sixties, and Riley was just one musician who benefited from this. His second record, *The Day Will Come*, was to be the last album the pianist would make for CBS and his last for a major British label. One can only suggest that, if ability and excellence were the primary determinants of record contracts, then company executives would still be beating a path to Riley's door. He has continued to make music of astonishing beauty and, if *The Day Will Come* marks a pinnacle, it would be because all of the right circumstances came together with perfect symmetry and synchronicity. Over several years as a working band, the trio had developed a very high degree of empathy and shared understanding of its musical values. An already precocious talent of nineteen when *Discussions* was made, Guy had become a musician of consummate taste and imagination. In Alan Jackson, Riley had a drummer capable of great control and precision, but one who also had great time and an ability to swing. Both Guy and Riley had grown as writers and their approaches complement each other magnificently. One could also hear a new lyricism in Riley's own playing as well as a gloriously, almost classical pianistic touch. Given the chance to work in a good studio, with a fine piano and a sympathetic producer – a set of coincidences unusual in jazz then and through the seventies – the winds were set fair.

One of the reasons the music works so well lies in its use of contrast. Freer, more abstract tracks like Riley's "Eclipse" and the brief opener "Sphere" are tense, edgy affairs, while Guy's slow, autumnal "Sad Was the Song" and Riley's dark-hued, ghostly "Winter" provide a sombre counterpoint. Guy's "Dawn Vision" and "Games" are marked by their epic sense of poise and grandeur, while the former features some of Riley's best playing and shows what an exceptional rhythm section this was. The record's finest moment comes with Riley's long "Funeral Song", which builds from its quiet, stuttering beginnings into something of sad, elegiac beauty.

Riley's next two albums used Tony Oxley in place of Alan Jackson. *Flight* (Turtle; FMR) was made for Peter Eden's Turtle label, while *Synopsis* (Incus; EMANEM) appeared on Incus. Both extended the potential of the piano trio with effective use of electronics and amplification. Riley's reputation does not rest on this sequence of four/five albums but is most definitely enhanced by their sheer quality.

Few musicians seem comfortable with the terms "free jazz" or "free improvisation". Riley talks about "so-called free jazz" and adds that the music he plays, "gets labelled as free jazz but I'm talking about people like Barry Guy, Evan Parker, Tony Oxley – people I've played with over the years – people who are definitely coming out of jazz music." For Tony Oxley, the words are just a lazy journalistic shorthand. "'Free improvisation' was just an invention of journalists. It's nothing to do with 'free'. There's no such thing as 'free' music. It's music that is free from regular time and from regular changes" (interview with Tony Oxley, April 2010). And he continues by pointing out that he and others were moving in directions that had been suggested anyway in contemporary classical music, "The harmonies had already been negated by Anton Webern, who was a classical composer, and by Cage and Stockhausen and whoever else was relevant at the time. We were playing music that was now free from bebop time and changes" (interview with Tony Oxley, April 2010).

We can surely forgive these musicians if their tone becomes occasionally frustrated, tetchy and even defensive. They and their music have operated on the margins and with little support in Britain for years, in contrast to their experience and reception in mainland Europe. Criticisms have come from the informed and ill-informed alike, when similar efforts in other musical areas and artistic fields have been applauded for their boldness and iconoclasm. Vocalists perhaps suffer even more from this than their instrumentalist colleagues. And yet, these musicians came from strong backgrounds in conventional music, something that they are quick to emphasize and as Maggie Nicols stressed in an earlier quote emphasizing that their evolution had "a musical history".

For Howard Riley, this process – the one he and his peers were engaged upon – was a natural, almost organic one, as he explains:

> But the thing with everybody I played with in the sixties was that they all had a very good grounding in, for want of a better word, conventional music. What I'm saying is that what they eventually called "free jazz", that came out of a quite disciplined approach using conventional music and, in fact, a lot of people ... the developments they made were what you would do when you get dissatisfied with playing in a certain way.
>
> (Interview with Howard Riley, May 2006)

And he continues:

> My theory about this is that in jazz everybody is aiming for greater freedom in their playing whether they know they are or not. Because once you've started playing the tendency is to free things up rather than to make them more rigid and hide-bound and really so called freer playing was a very logical development

in the sixties from playing conventional jazz because to begin with there wasn't any free improvisation.

(Interview with Howard Riley, May 2006)

In fact, Riley is echoing a common theme. The desire of all jazz musicians is to find their own voice. It is after all a highly personal music within which those most admired are those who achieve that elusive goal. It is a process of discovery and, even if the grail is never actually found and held, the journey remains essential. Riley gives Ellington as perhaps the primary example of this:

> I listen for individuals and that was probably what attracted me to Ellington – that he was an individual. You can't say he was a bebopper or a mainstream player. He was just Ellington. That was the thing that interested me and is what I have tried to pursue in my own music to get something together that is your own individual statement. Obviously, you are influenced by what we hear around us. And I do think that was in the air in the sixties.
>
> (Interview with Howard Riley, May 2006)

Individuality is as important in jazz as in any area of life. In jazz, as elsewhere some will pursue that search ruthlessly to the detriment of others. However, in jazz and even more so in free improvisation success is not dependant on egocentricity. These are musical approaches within which the collective and the individual are of equal importance and the relationship between them is essentially a dialectical one. For some it might be a paradox but for many working in the field, musical freedom and individuality are to be discovered in the collective experience of music-making. And it can be a powerful, liberating and political experience, as Maggie Nicols suggested earlier.

Even a strong, intelligent individual such as Julie Tippetts found in this music a sense of herself that was even more distinct and very real. Immersing herself in jazz and free improvisation perhaps even allowed her to recover those aspects of her personality that had been threatened by the show business world she had been caught up in during the late sixties. She certainly found it personally affirming as she points out:

> Yeah, absolutely because free music – in inverted commas again – was something that took you away from the emulating and copying. You can't emulate and copy in that world. If it's free, you have nobody to pull from but yourself. And, okay, you're responding to other people but you're responding as yourself and not as anybody else because you haven't heard it before. Until that moment it doesn't exist. (Interview with Julie Tippetts, September 2008)

And, as we have seen, freedom was very much in the air during those years. Our understanding of it might have been confused and confusing. Its exercise might sometimes have been selfish and self-regarding but it was not intended to be so. If that sounds contradictory, then that surely arose from the reality that those who argued for it and pursued it did so within a social, economic and cultural context that was riven with contradictions. To paraphrase Angela Carter's remark about de Sade's heroine, Juliette, in her study of the Marquis' novellas (Carter 1978), a free individual in an unfree world would always be a monster.

None of these caveats negate the search for freedom in art as in life in any way. Rather, that search resonates with comments from several of the musicians we have discussed about responsibility and ethics in relation to the exercise of personal and artistic freedom. This and the notion that freedom might be found within the collective experience may be paradoxes but they are not contradictions. They reveal an understanding that life is at its heart a dialectical process. This fact is something that Eddie Prévost clearly understood when he wrote:

> Far from being a negation of individuality, the group (as perhaps The Crypt illustrates more vividly than any other of our albums) allows each to express himself without fear of being subordinated or exploited. The players could, at times, share a timeless immersion in a world of sound, while simultaneously being free to pursue their individual paths. It was not uncommon for the musician to wonder who or what was producing a particular sound, stop playing, and discover that it was he himself who had been responsible. (Prévost 1992)

It is an ideal of music-making, whether one calls it "free improvisation", "jazz" or "free jazz", that finds resonances elsewhere and not just in the area of music and the arts. The contemporary French philosopher of politics and aesthetics, Jacques Rancière, offers a definition of politics based on actions and activities that disrupt or transgress the given social order of hierarchies, fixed statuses, positions and occupations. By contrast, he describes what is most commonly spoken of as "politics" – political parties, elections, governance – as the "police order", meaning by this that these are systems that seek to determine and impose place, status and order within society. In a very real sense, Prévost's views seem to find a fit within Rancière's schema. Peter Hallward, in an intriguing analysis of Rancière's work, suggests that for the Frenchman, "Politics is the contingent demonstration of a disruptive equality, the unauthorized and impromptu improvisation of a democratic voice" (Hallward 2006, 113). Surely, and certainly for Prévost, free improvisation, free jazz and other experimental approaches to jazz would appear to be engaged in just such a demonstration.

In fact, in Rancière's discussion of what he sees as the virtual programme of "politics", we find a quotation that echoes that of Eddie Prévost quite remarkably. In *The Distribution of the Sensible*, he talks favourably of certain "regimes of the arts" linked to a certain "regime of politics" that is characterized by "the indetermination of identities, the delegitimation of speaking positions, the deregulation of divisions of space and time" (Rancière 2011, 13–14). This is precisely what jazz or improvisation of this kind seeks to achieve. The right or opportunity to speak or to play or perform are not dependent on status that is externally imposed. The identity of who is speaking or producing which sound or set of sounds is often unclear and has no need of such clarity. And lastly, the space or spaces used for performance or speaking are frequently not those where such performance is usually found and, within those arenas, time is to some extent suspended.

12 The Artsman Cometh

or: Things May Come and Things May Go But the Arts Council Grant Goes on Forever

I would I had bestowed that time in the tongues that I have in fencing, dancing, and bear-baiting. O! had I but followed the arts!

William Shakespeare, *Twelfth Night*

As jazz advances technically, as it assimilates harmonies more and more complex, as it absorbs rhythmic variations that would have whitened the hair of the primitives of New Orleans, as it takes Chromaticism in its stride without strangling itself, it also advances socially, from the brothel to the ginmill to the dance hall to the concert stage and the cultural festivals of the world. Of course the music itself lost its innocence a long time ago, perhaps in the ballrooms of the Roosevelt era. But its practitioners still wrestle manfully with the terrifying problem of keeping alive the earthy spark of its beginnings. And every time somebody introduces a new harmony into the jazz context, then the task becomes more difficult.

Benny Green, *The Reluctant Art*, 1962, 16

For jazz, traditional and modern, much of the sixties had been taken up with the negotiation of a space within a number of potentially related areas of the music industry. Was it part of the pop or light entertainment worlds? Was it a folk form more related to the blues or traditional folk music? Alternatively, was it an art music able to claim a cultural authority equal to that of classical music? These were not arcane or abstract discussion points – they had huge financial implications as well.

In practice, the answers that British jazz discovered to these questions were partial and confused. Certain jazz styles, such as traditional and mainstream jazz, maintained a link with a hardcore jazz audience while holding on to a more peripheral one that serviced light entertainment. Dixieland bands could frequently be found on variety-type shows on TV. For example, George Chisholm was a regular guest on the dreadful *The Black and White Minstrel Show*, dressed in bowler hat and striped waistcoat. Those who had followed the movement of jazz into rock maintained links with more a more experimental jazz audience, often pursuing almost parallel careers. Keith Tippett, Jamie Muir, Elton Dean, Henry Lowther, Ian Carr and Barbara Thompson offer good examples of this, crossing as they did musical boundaries with ease. This worked well so long as a section of the rock audience, in particular that based around colleges and universities, remained supportive of improvisation within what was broadly termed "progressive rock". However, a sense had begun to emerge that jazz as a developing practice, one as reliant on composition as upon improvisation, was becoming a separate musical sphere, similar to that of contemporary art music.

The sixties had created a wealth of possibilities in the arts, allowing new forms to emerge in dance, music, theatre, literature and, to a lesser extent, film that had been peripheral to what was understood as "high culture". In arenas like the Royal Court Theatre, playwrights such as Arnold Wesker, Edward Bond, John Arden, Ann Jellicoe and N.F. Simpson challenged audiences' expectations of the medium, just as film directors Karel Reisz, Lindsay Anderson, Joseph Losey and Tony Richardson offered audiences a more European auteur-driven approach to the cinema. Television and radio, independent and state-owned, offered new opportunities to young writers of the calibre of Alan Plater, Dennis Potter, Alun Owen and Harold Pinter, and photography and modern dance began to take their places alongside, rather than in the shadows, of fine art and classical ballet, respectively.

The process was perhaps more diffident in the area of music. However, the response to the arrival of the Beatles by "serious" critics and authorities such as Wilfred Mellers and Leonard Bernstein provoked both respect and hilarity in equal measure. There was a questioning of what constituted "art", as people wondered whether the music being made by young musicians might one day be held in the same awe as that of Mozart and Beethoven. Even comedy, tragedy's poor relation, became the focus for serious analysis, not least with the arrival of the "satire boom" led by *Beyond the Fringe*, *That Was the Week That Was*, *Private Eye* and later *The Frost Report*. And when Peter Cook and Nick Luard opened The Establishment in Greek Street, Soho, its soundtrack was jazz played by the Dudley Moore and Brian Dee trios.

If in the end, all this promise could not ultimately be delivered, the commitment to an ecumenical world of the arts was very genuine and very real. The message was enshrined as early as 1959 in a Labour Party Statement, "Leisure for Living".

> "Culture" does not exist in a vacuum. It is difficult for a child to grow into a whole man in a disintegrated society such as ours has been for the last two centuries; but it takes a whole man to enjoy the art of Henri Matisse and the art of Stanley Matthews, or the music of Gerry Mulligan as well as the music of Wolfgang Mozart – and better still, perhaps, to play guitar in a local jazz group as

well as being a research chemist by day and a trade union branch secretary, too.

Leisure, in short, is enjoyed most deeply and creatively by those who have a sense of direction in their everyday life and work. Good as it would be, therefore, to increase the Government grant to the Arts Council (and this we certainly intend to do), it would be even better that this should be done as part of the more purposeful replanning of the economic and social structure of society. (Labour Party 1959)

The Labour Party and MU also sponsored a concert at the Royal Festival Hall in 1963 featuring Terry Lightfoot, Dorita y Pepe (!) and the Johnny Dankworth Orchestra. Its programme contains this message from the Rt Hon. Harold Wilson, OBE, MP, Leader of the Labour Party. It reads:

Why is the Labour Party associating itself with this event? We do so, with pleasure and in full co-operation with the Musicians' Union, because our objectives are not limited to such things as decent homes, better education and Britain's economic recovery, vital though they be.

Our sights are set wider and higher. We want a society where, amongst other things, everybody has the opportunity for the widest choice and the fullest enjoyment in their leisure time.

Like much of the best art, jazz appeals not merely to a select few. It has deep roots, and its rich varieties appeal to greater and greater numbers today.

Mighty words indeed, and Labour in government was ultimately unable to live up to the intention expressed in the final sub-clause of "Leisure for Living". It did, however, take some steps that did have positive implications for jazz, as well as for the arts in a broader sense. First and foremost was the decision to appoint as a full member of the cabinet, a Minister for the Arts. The post's first incumbent was Jennie Lee.

Lee is an interesting figure and one less acknowledged today than she deserves. The daughter of a Scottish miner, she had joined the Independent Labour Party and was elected as MP for North Lanarkshire in 1929. She had been active in support of the miners during the General Strike of 1926 and had opposed Ramsey MacDonald's formation of a national government in 1931. She also campaigned on behalf of the Spanish Republican government in its fight against fascism. She married left-wing Labour MP Aneurin Bevan and, while the couple agreed on many issues, Lee opposed her husband's support for Britain's independent nuclear deterrent. As Arts Minister, she played a key role in the formation of the Open University and renewed the charter of the Arts Council of Great Britain in 1967, which saw an expansion of its work in the regions as well of the creation of the new arts institutions at London's South Bank Centre. She also introduced the only UK White Paper for the Arts in 1965. This set out a strategy which even though it was not to be fully realized remains one well worth aspiring towards. In it, Lee recognized that the traditional hierarchy of culture was breaking down. Paragraph 71 reads:

> Appreciation of this kind of good design is not the end of the matter. Indeed, diffusion of culture is now so much a part of life that there is no precise point at which it stops. Advertisements, buildings, books, motor cars, radio and television, magazines, records, all can carry a cultural aspect and affect our lives for good or ill as a species of "amenity". No democratic government would seek to impose controls on all the things that contribute to our environment and affect our senses. But abuses can be spotted and tackled, high standards encouraged, and opportunities given for wider enjoyment. It is partly a question of bridging the gap between what have come to be called the "higher" forms of entertainment and the traditional sources, the brass band, the amateur concert party, the entertainer, the music hall and pop group—and to challenge the fact that a gap exists. *In the world of jazz the process has already happened; highbrow and lowbrow have met.*
> (White Paper Cmnd. 2601 1965, emphasis added)

That the paper had prime ministerial approval was made clear by Harold Wilson's memorandum accompanying the paper:

> I have considered as a separate matter whether the government's administrative arrangements for dealing with the arts should be modified. My conclusions, which I have discussed with the Ministers immediately involved, are embodied in paragraph 78 of the draft. I invite my colleagues to agree that the White Paper should be published at an early date.   (H. W. 10)

Paragraph 78 basically reaffirmed existing funding through the Exchequer. However, later paragraphs stress the need for "new values, new ideas", funding for regional arts and arts centres, community involvement in culture and improved access for all. The aim was nothing less than to make the best of the arts available to all regardless of class, income or social position. It concluded with a clarion call:

> Today a searching reappraisal of the whole situation in relation to cultural standards and opportunities is in progress. More and more people begin to appreciate that the exclusion of so many for

so long from the best of our cultural heritage can become as damaging to the privileged minority as to the under-privileged majority. We walk the same streets, breathe the same air, are exposed to the same sights and sounds.

Nor can we ignore the growing revolt, especially among the young, against the drabness, uniformity and joylessness of much of the social furniture we have inherited from the industrial revolution. This can be directed, if we so wish, into making Britain a gayer and more cultivated country. It is fitting that the present Government should seek to encourage all who are furthering these aims. The proposals outlined in this White Paper, though no more than the first steps in the direction of a fully comprehensive policy for the Arts, demonstrate the Government's concern that immediate progress should be made towards the new objectives.   (Paras 96–97, White Paper Cmnd. 2601 1965)

Static in the fifties, between 1960 and 1964, Arts Council funding more than doubled and it increased further with Labour in power. The Arts Council's annual grant increased from £3.2 million in 1964–5 to £9.3 million in 1970–1. This was mainly spent on the "higher" forms of the arts, but funding did begin to go outside the metropolitan centres of elite culture as well. As Donnelly notes:

Regional arts associations benefited, so too did art forms which had previously been ineligible for grants – jazz, for example, was supported in 1967 when Graham Collier was given a small award – and a fraction was spent on encouraging "experimental" projects.   (Donnelly 2005, 99)

Nor was Labour alone in proposing improved state funding for the arts. The Conservative Bow Group published a paper in 1959 that subsequently influenced Tory policy, which argued that "the state should compensate for shortfalls in private patronage and encouraged greater business generosity towards the Arts Council of Great Britain (ACGB)" (Black 2006, 120)

The origins of the Arts Council lay in the Second World War. While the Entertainments National Service Association (ENSA) was revived to entertain the troops, the Council for the Encouragement of Music and the Arts (CEMA) was established as a means of boosting public morale among a populace facing heavy bombing, blackouts, rationing and the evacuation of children to safer areas. Under John Maynard Keynes, the CEMA carried out its task "to carry music, drama and pictures to places, which otherwise would be cut off from all contact with the masterpieces of happier days and times; to air-raid shelters, to war-time hostels, to factories, to mining villages" (quoted in Hollis 1997, 247). And it was remarkably successful. The

Council discovered that it was actually taking the arts to people who had never experienced their touch in peacetime. However, in just two years, their art exhibitions had been seen by half a million people, the concerts they staged under the watchful eye of Vaughan Williams heard by thousands and their plays enjoyed by one and a half million. As Patricia Hollis notes in her biography of Jennie Lee:

> They played in factory canteens, in munitions hostels, in Underground stations, in internment camps, in the basements of department stores, in air raid shelters, and in church halls. "People felt that music, the ballet, poetry and painting were concerned with a seriousness of living and dying with which they themselves had suddenly been confronted," wrote Stephen Spender. "A little island of civilisation surrounded by burning churches – that was how the arts seemed in England during the War." During the blitz, performers worried that they were singing and playing while England was burning; their audience arrived 'looking grey and anxious, with newspapers tucked under their arms, and an hour later they were every one of them looking radiant and transformed. (Hollis 1997, 247)

For those like Lee, her husband Nye Bevan, writer J.B. Priestley (whose The Arts Under Socialism was a major influence on Lee), Arnold Goodman and J.M. Keynes, the experience of wartime was catalytic. The arts in society, whether under a state of war or peace, were not merely a desirable or dispensable luxury, they were a necessity. After 1945, during the Attlee government, the Arts Council focused its attention on sustaining excellence. In practice, and despite a Commons Select Committee report in 1949, it resisted attempts to make the arts more accessible and concentrated its energies on a few institutions based entirely within metropolitan centres, primarily London. This emphasis continued under the Tories in the years that followed.

It was not the case that Lee, and Goodman, broke with traditional notions of culture. In a sense, they were unashamed elitists, who saw classical music, ballet, drama and art as pinnacles of creative endeavour. They were, however, determined that all citizens could and should have access to the best. To use Nye Bevan's phrase, "Only the best is good enough for the workers." More than that, she and Goodman sought to bring new activities such as children's theatre, film and photography, jazz, folk-song and literature – "all those fields where critical judgement was harder and peer review less clear cut, where performance could be controversial" – within the remit of the Arts Council (Hollis 1997, 249).

These changes in government policy did not in any sense cause the shift within British jazz from a place in light entertainment or popular music to one closer to the arts. As the White Paper notes, the highbrow and lowbrow had already met within the music. In terms of the amount of funding that was given to jazz after 1967 and Graham Collier's first commission – Mike Westbrook, Chris McGregor, Mike Gibbs, Keith Tippett, Neil Ardley and others all applied for and were given grants from the Arts Council – this was certainly not large enough to alter the position of jazz within the arts. As Lawrence Black points out, the cultural elite was too well placed to lose its grip on government funding and the government's appointee as head of the Arts Council, Lord Goodman, resisted successfully all attempts to move the offices of the council out of London (Black 2006, 123–30). To an extent, this was an consequence of Labour's attitude to culture. For all it might proclaim the desirability of an open-minded outlook to what constituted culture, it was really quite traditional in what it defined and funded in practice. Indeed, Richard Hoggart writing in the arts magazine *Focus* in March 1965 was critical of what he saw as Labour's watering down of genuine culture (Hoggart 1965, 33–4). As Black argues:

> Labour was a convinced advocate of traditional elite culture, liberal and inclusive in purpose. It regarded it as civilizing, uplifting and a barrier to commercial mass culture. Lee's efforts in the 1960s involved a belief in the moral value and uses of culture and a desire to infuse Britons with it; a populist awareness of its commercial potential; focus on its consumers and audience besides producers and artists; the state as enabler rather than deliverer.
>
> (Black 2006, 135)

We should not be blind to Lee and Goodman's failures, several of which still haunt jazz and theatre. They ducked certain key issues. For example, London had then two national opera companies both based in Covent Garden, the English National Opera and the Royal Opera House. By 1970–71, these two were taking a quarter of the much-expanded budget of the Arts Council under Goodman (see Hollis 1997, 265). London also had five major orchestras – the London Symphony Orchestra, Royal Philharmonic Orchestra, the London Philharmonic Orchestra, the New Philharmonia Orchestra and the BBC Symphony Orchestra – each one playing a remarkably similar repertoire. Any suggestion that this was in excess of either cultural or market need was met with total resistance. As Arnold Goodman noted with irony, surely no-one wanted to hear Beethoven's Ninth Symphony more than once a week. Instead of meeting the issue head on, the Arts Council and the Great London Council (GLC) established the London Concerts Orchestral Board to resolve such programming problems at a substantial cost then of £250,000 per year, roughly one-third of the Council's total grant to orchestral music. It failed to do so quite miserably (Hollis 1997, 266–7). The problems facing jazz and other minority arts in terms of funding compared to that granted to classical music are not new now and were not new then. Under Jennie Lee, a marvellous opportunity to rationalize such funding of orchestral music in London – without sabotaging quality – was lost. Not only was this to the detriment of British jazz but also to regional funding of classical music.

At the same time, Lee's successes far outweighed her failures. In some degree, British theatregoers have her (and later Labour Arts Minister Hugh Jenkins) to thank that the National Theatre was actually built, and film buffs have her to thank that a National Film School was created. Lee more than trebled the budget for the arts. She, and Goodman, restored the philosophy that had determined arts policy during the war of "the best for the most", which under the Conservatives had become "the best for the few, who might appreciate it" (Hollis 1997, 288). But perhaps most important of all her achievements, as far as jazz was concerned, was the start of devolution of arts funding to regional arts authorities, which were established across Britain apart from the south-east. In time, these would fund arts festivals, theatres, arts centres and the like which, in turn, would provide both venues and work opportunities for jazz musicians. In fact, much of the "new money" that Lee obtained from the treasury went to the regions.

In terms of British jazz and the arts, the desire to create a music of lasting cultural value predates these events and could already be seen as early as the fifties. It is present in remarks made by musicians such as Dankworth, Barber, Garrick and others we have quoted and in their work. That desire can also be found in the efforts of mavericks like Kenny Graham and Tony Kinsey. Labour's support for a broader-based arts policy was clearly welcome and, perhaps, even a source of encouragement but, in a sense, it represented a shift which British jazz had contributed to and of which it was itself a part. What was more important in terms of Labour's arts policy were its long-term effects in establishing the principle of funding minority arts such as jazz and the confirmation it gave to the notion of jazz as an art music worthy of public support.

As the beneficiary of the first grant to a jazz musician, Graham Collier wrote a four-part suite, *Workpoints* and was able to tour the work with a twelve-piece band comprising some of the finest new players. The orchestra was built around Collier's current group, who had recorded *Deep Dark Blue Centre* for Deram (Deram; BGO). Karl Jenkins (later of Nucleus and Soft Machine) was on baritone and soprano saxes, oboe and piano, both Kenny Wheeler and Harry Beckett played trumpet, while Dave Aaron was on alto and flute with Collier's fellow Berklee graduate Mike Gibbs on trombone. John Marshall was on drums and Collier himself played bass. Only guitarist Phil Lee was absent. The big band brought in Henry Lowther on trumpet, John Surman on baritone, soprano, bass clarinet and piano, Frank Ricotti on vibes and Chris Smith and John Mumford on trombones. *Workpoints* was very successful critically, achieving reviews in the broadsheets as well as in the music press and it also played to reasonable audiences.

Graham Collier at a school lecture in Dagenham, 7 July 1966. © Valerie Wilmer.

Collier did not, however, get the opportunity to record the piece at the time, though a recording of a concert in Southampton was finally released in 2005 on the US Cuneiform label. Much of Collier's work in the sixties, seventies and eighties concentrated on smaller ensembles and between 1967 and 1974, he issued six LPs of exceptional quality. Collier deserved his Arts Council grant, grasping the opportunity brilliantly, and the availability of *Workpoints* gives present-day audiences the chance to hear his earliest work with a larger ensemble. Of the small group recordings, the reissue of *Deep Dark Blue Centre* on Beat Goes On records gave the world a stereo version – most vinyl copies had been in monaural – and allowed its beautiful colours and textures to be appreciated afresh. *Down Another Road* (Fontana; BGO), with saxophonist Stan Sulzmann in place of Dave Aaron and Nick Evans replacing Mike Gibbs, was a beautifully flowing and often funky record, while *Songs for My Father* (Fontana; BGO) featured a new group now called the Graham Collier Music along with various guests. Harry Beckett was singled out on the sleeve as a personal "thank you" from Collier. Dedicated to Collier's own father, *Songs* contains some of the bassist's most personal writing and fine performances from Beckett, Alan Skidmore, John Taylor and Phil Lee in particular. These are wonderful examples of British jazz of the period but Collier was already moving beyond notions of jazz composition as a fixed and determining structure. His motto, "Jazz happens in real time, once", reflected a determination to allow the music to breathe. His strategy as a leader and latterly as a conductor is to use the written material more as a guide for the musicians. New ideas are allowed to emerge and develop, as he explained in the liner notes for *Songs*:

> In the separate pieces there are various options for continuation or not and only when there is an absolute need of it is the choice of soloist dictated before we start a piece. These freedoms within the overall design can, of course, lead to embarrassing moments but when they work well they provide my present solution for the jazz composer's problem – that of retaining overall control while still allowing the musicians their own freedom and to allow the occasion to dictate some of the content. (Collier 1970)

It is intriguing and important to note that as early as the mid-sixties Collier was devising his own approach to writing for jazz ensembles as well as deriving from this a performance philosophy. More than that, he was doing so within a British context of advances and experimentation in the music. This praxis or practice-theory is essentially inductive in origin, as he explains:

> There are too many writers who want to write too much and impress with their techniques. To be brutally honest, you listen to great orchestrators like Stravinsky and Bartok. Most jazz composers can't write that well, they're trying to do something that's almost doomed to failure. They simply cannot create the kinds of textures that classical people do when they have orchestras with twenty-five different flutes and all kinds of instruments. For me, the path to go down is to say, "the jazz small group does this" and, like the Miles' group, can be very flexible in the way they approach a tune. They can stretch things out. The rhythm section drops out occasionally. So, there's all that textural flow, that changing flow that the classical people can't do because of the nature of their beast. They've got to write it in order to play it. (Interview with Graham Collier, November 2004)

Collier does draw inspiration from Mingus, Miles and Ornette, who he says "opened up the music so much that it enabled us to do many, many more things within a big band." Yet, his method has developed primarily in a British and European context. If one looks at his source materials these are both Anglo-European and African-American. If one listens closely to the music he made during this period, one hears Mingus and Miles but also the European impressionists, notably Ravel, elements of a nascent, local jazz-rock music and even elements of the English pastoral tradition in music. While this last aspect is most evident on "The Barley Mow" from *Down Another Road*, it is also present on *Songs* and continues to surface in Collier's music. As Shipton notes in his excellent and insightful sleevenotes:

> And being British meant not only that he could draw on the language of contemporary English composers such as Finzi and Britten, but that he could identify with the sweeping changes being made in popular music by the likes of the Beatles and the Rolling Stones. (Shipton 2007)

The reissues of these records on BGO with original notes, reviews and detailed sleevenotes, if anything, enhances their reputation by allowing them to be heard sequentially. Alyn Shipton's notes to the *Down Another Road/ Songs for My Father/Mosaics* quote Stan Sulzmann tellingly on where this music came from: "(It was) very much our music – rock, contemporary classical, Olivier Messiaen, who has nothing to do with American jazz – nobody else was doing it. You didn't feel you were making a bad copy of an American record" (Shipton 2007).

But it is *Mosaics* (Philips; BGO) that best demonstrates Collier's approach to jazz in real time, though the less well-recorded *Darius* (Mosaic; BGO) is also significant in this respect. The BGO reissue of *Deep Dark Blue Centre* and *Mosaics* also includes a further, very different version – from the same evening – of the latter, which allows the listener to hear clearly how Collier's approach to material works in practice. The original album again featured Harry Beckett, the most loyal of Collier's musical servants. Collier's own bass playing reveals a much underrated talent and his performance on the alternate take is even better. As for the rest of the band, with the exception of drummer John Webb, these are all comparatively inexperienced musicians, several of whom had played with NYJO. This takes nothing away from the quality of the playing. The first thing that strikes about *Mosaics* is the quite dramatic tension it exudes. There is a palpable sense that each player is totally committed and determined and the recording bristles with electricity. As the music unfolds, it is by turns edgy, exciting, stately and elegiac. There are hints of Ravel and Rodrigo in there and Beckett's brass cadenzas echo Miles at times, in their controlled passion. It is once more music strong in both texture and colour and it is one of those rare records where one returns to specific passages just to hear again how they take shape.

It is worth considering *Workpoints* in further detail in this context, even though Collier's ideas had yet to develop fully. It remains an exemplary piece of British jazz of the period. As Val Wilmer noted in her *Down Beat* review of 16 May 1968:

> In spite of the impressive show of manuscript paper on hand, I gather that the chart for Workpoints was limited to a loose framework, allowing freedom of movement for the soloists and limiting the occasional bursts of collective improvisation to manageable lengths. (Wilmer 1968, 36)

Collier, as was also the case with his peers such as Westbrook and Surman, is weaving together different elements in the music. Mingus' influence is strong but where Mingus taunts and provokes, Collier organizes and leads his ensemble. The performances that he gets from his musicians, in their very consistency at least, suggests that he might even have the edge on his muse here. There are moments of unusual and unexpected beauty such as the three trombone section in the third movement and in the fine duet between Surman and Jenkins on baritones. The musicians who most stand out on this performance, however, are Frank Ricotti, whose vibes playing is a constant source of delight, and John Marshall, whose powerful, muscular drumming creates a state of constant, fluid momentum. Yet it is ultimately Collier who deserves the bulk of any plaudits with this work, as with his other recordings of the period.

He was, after all, a very literate and articulate composer, whose methodology, or at least his description of it, perhaps belies the extent to which he shapes these musical works. Collier's pieces often refer to his interests in art and literature and *Workpoints* takes its title from Lawrence Durrell's "use of the word to sum up his starting points in *Justine*, the first volume of his Alexandria Quartet" (Collier 2004). The French word, "auteur", used in film criticism to describe a particular directorial style, seems highly appropriate here and conveys well the composer's ongoing presence in the work long after the manuscript has been completed.

The notion that jazz could be about something more than chords, charts, rhythms and melodies was certainly not new within jazz or within the music in Britain. We have talked about Dankworth, Kenny Graham, Joe Harriott, John Mayer, Michael Garrick and Stan Tracey already. Such notions were central to the differing strands of poetry and jazz that began with the Christopher Logue–Tony Kinsey collaboration, *Red Bird: Jazz and Poetry* in 1959 (Parlophone EP) and continued through Michael Horovitz and Pete Brown's work with Tracey and Wellins, and Michael Garrick's partnership with Jeremy Robson and John Smith. Though these were separate enterprises, there was inevitably some overlap of personnel. Their importance, however, lay in their pioneering of multi-media approaches to the arts – the very same practices that Jennie Lee was speaking of in her White Paper – and these concerts were quite astonishingly popular. This was no fad or passing fancy. Garrick's involvement with Jeremy Robson and John Smith continued from around 1962 to the early seventies, while Michael Horovitz has sustained *New Departures* for fifty years and still gigs with pianist Stan Tracey from time to time, and Pete Brown's foray into blues and rock has continued alongside his writing.

As a figure, Horovitz embodies many of the qualities and enthusiasms that seemed to coalesce in the sixties. To begin with, he knew many of the people who were to play a key role in several aspects of British cultural life in the sixties. He had been at Oxford and, partly through Cambridge student and musician Dick Heckstall-Smith, had also got to know a lot of British musicians. As a poet and arts activist, he also knew numerous important British writers including playwright John McGrath, and poets Adrian Mitchell and Stevie Smith, as well as American Beat writers such as Allen Ginsberg, William Burroughs and Gregory Corso. The original *New Departures* (see Chapter 3) was an anarchic blend of poetry, music and theatre. Anything could happen, and frequently did, as Horovitz describes in his strangely elliptical style:

> It seemed a good time to put together the young contemporaries who were either at university or whom I met whilst I was finishing – Pete Brown who was at a journalism school, Adrian Mitchell left Oxford the year I came up. So, we created a kind of fraternity and the minute *New Departures* number one was out, which included Burroughs and Beckett and Adrian Mitchell, Stevie Smith *et al.*, I was doing my jazz poetry also with Dudley Moore. We thought we don't just want a printed magazine and immediately started Live New Departures and performed the poems with and without music and [Cornelius] Cardew who had his indeterminate music and that of John Cage and others played by John Tilbury and him and John McGrath got various actors together there was a great troupe of actors that travelled with us initially round universities and places like the ICA and at Ronnie's. We gradually were doing things on Sundays and we were doing little club sessions and bigger gigs. We hired St Pancras Town Hall twice in 1960 and 1962 and gradually evolved what we called the New Departures Quartet and Sextet. There was one Transatlantic LP of the New Departures Quartet with Stan and Bobby Wellins.
> (Interview with Michael Horovitz, February 2009)

He continues:

> Then we had a New Departures Ball with Dudley and Dick Heckstall-Smith and others jammed. There were lots of different

musicians around Oxford who tended to come together at our gigs. Somebody who was then called Paul Pond who became Paul Jones of the Mann–Hugg Blues Band. Miles Kington was playing bass. So, most of those people jammed at these balls and parties and every time there was a new issue we'd have a New Departures ball and as well as the music we'd start off early with plays by Beckett and Eugene Ionesco and John McGrath and his troupe. That included very good actors like Donal Donnelly and Kate Binchy. Donal did the Joyce *Finnegan's Wake*. It's become commonplace but I think we were catalysts for the mixed media idea. Our whole purpose in starting *New Departures* was to break down these barriers which kept poetry as a game reserve only for people who were well-educated with degrees in Greek mythology and so on.   (Interview with Michael Horovitz, February 2009)

And:

We had folk singers and pop singers and rock & rollers. It became an art circus quite quickly. First, it was Live New Departures and when we featured mainly jazz poetry, we'd call it Jazz Poetry Super-Jam or even the World's Best Jam. There were so many different artists who slowly came on board like Lol Coxhill and Ron Geesin. I did poetry with Joe Harriott and Bruce Turner. Each one was responsive in different ways. Bruce was quite sceptical. He said, "I don't know about all this, Horoscope." He was always very witty. Then, when we got going, I said, "Come on, Bruce. You've defined jazz as a musical conversation. So, this is just another form of conversation but you're actually having words back at you instead of sounds and gradually they'll come together." And they did.
     (Interview with Michael Horovitz, February 2009)

It is essential (if somewhat problematic) to quote Michael Horovitz extensively here. In a page of dialogue, those he has mentioned, spin out into a web of connections. Adrian Mitchell connects with Mike Westbrook, who himself also worked a couple of times with Horovitz. Pete Brown connects with Jack Bruce, Cream, Graham Bond and Jon Hiseman, while his first group Battered Ornaments included saxophonist George Khan and guitarist Chris Spedding. Both Khan, who has continued to work in theatre, and Spedding are connected to Mike Westbrook. Spedding also connects with Mike Gibbs and Jack Bruce. Dick Heckstall-Smith played with Bond, Jack Bruce and Jon Hiseman, as well as in the New Jazz Orchestra. Paul Pond/Jones toured Bulgaria with NYJO, worked in mainstream and experimental theatre as well as singing with Manfred Mann, who had included Henry Lowther and Lyn Dobson in his first attempt at introducing jazz into his group's set. Dudley Moore connects with Peter Cook, *Beyond the Fringe*, *Private Eye* and The Establishment club, while Cornelius Cardew and John Tilbury were both part of AMMMusic. Ron Geesin links Horovitz to Pink Floyd and Lol Coxhill to Kevin Ayers. And that, of course, is not all. In a lot of ways, it was a remarkably small scene but also a very fertile one.

There were marked differences between the poetry and jazz pioneered by Jeremy Robson and Michael Garrick and New Departures, though some poets such as Christopher Logue and Adrian Mitchell performed with both. Michael Horovitz notes:

> We were sort of rivals as impresarios. I was more concerned with bringing musicians and poets together in live performance, whereas he tended to have people alternating a bit of solo poetry with jazz. He included, as we did, people like Spike Milligan, but his poets were more or less conventional English verse-makers – Vernon Scannell, Danny Abse, fine poets but not particularly jazz-cadenced. Michael did a few things with a poet called John Smith who died – *Jazz Praises*, which I thought was very good. Michael Garrick was always very adventurous.
>
> (Interview with Michael Horovitz, February 2009)

And he adds, "You know how young people were. We were competitive. We were a bit scornful. Brown and I would say, 'Oh, that's the square lot. Oh they're so dull.' They weren't really. They were good poets. Adrian Mitchell did both" (interview with Michael Horovitz, February 2009).

While the Argo recordings of *Poetry & Jazz*, some of which have been reissued by Dutton-Vocalion, convey very well the authoritative and perhaps formal setting that Robson and Garrick provided, no such documents have been issued of the Horovitz–Brown set-up. Tapes do exist, though whether these will ever see the light of day depends on a lot of factors, not least whether they are of a sufficient sound quality worthy of release. They reveal a pretty wild and open-ended approach, most notably on the Brown–Horovitz epic *Blues for the Hitch-hiking Dead*. It is a difference that Jeremy Robson acknowledges:

> Their Poetry & Jazz concerts were very different I think. Ours were much more organized and I think the poets who took part were more perhaps established figures. I think they looked on us as a bit square. [laughing] I think they were a lot wilder and a lot more "beat". We included Ted Hughes, Stevie Smith and Laurie Lee. They read unaccompanied but they loved it as a setting in which to read. Stevie Smith did quite a few. And Adrian Mitchell who appeared both with us and New Departures. And we both included Christopher Logue as well. It wasn't like we were

enemies. There was a bit of a crossover but I think they more ... it was a different kind of poetry.

(Interview with Jeremy Robson, April 2009)

The key point is that both ventures attracted a lot of interest and support. It was clear that the audience for this kind of genre-bending, to use John Wickes' term, was quite substantial and larger than for either jazz or poetry alone. The boundaries between the arts were becoming less restrictive. For Michael Garrick the bringing together of his love for jazz and his love of literature was obvious:

> We were all very aware of the difficulties but because we felt we were speaking with one voice that drew us together. What the poets were saying and what the jazz musicians were saying were in two different mediums but they were saying essentially the same kinds of things. They had the political unease. They had the satire but they also had the love of what was human. When you look at satire what it's really saying is that human life and human beings can be superb and we're blocking it. We want to allow that love to come through.
>
> (Interview with Michael Garrick, March 2003)

Garrick had also begun to explore the possibilities of liturgical works involving jazz in the early sixties. "It occurred to me that jazz music should be able to have a place in what was aspirational and devotional because we were all devoted and aspiring and we weren't doing it for a commercial motive," he explains. "It uplifts us and the two things didn't seem poles apart after all." *Jazz Praises at St Paul's* (Airborne; Jazz Academy), recorded with the Chorale de St Michael and a jazz sextet, came out in 1969, but it was with *Mr Smith's Apocalypse* that the pianist achieved a most remarkable synthesis that brought together poetry, jazz and choral music. It featured a powerful, witty and agnostic libretto from poet John Smith, an unusually committed vocal chorus and some quite delightful singing by a junior school choir from Hampshire. Yet it is the way these elements combine in Garrick's hands that turn this into something quite remarkable. Somehow the sextet with Garrick on organ sounds louder and more potent than its size might suggest and its interaction with the choir is completely assured throughout this hour-long work. Henry Lowther on trumpet and flugelhorn is excellent, as are both wind players Don Rendell and Art Themen. But plaudits must go to the rhythm section of Coleridge Goode and Trevor Tomkins, who succeed in powering this potentially unstable machine. The music is quite magnificent taking in moments of Ellingtonia, blues, Latin and even rock. There is simply nothing quite like it anywhere else in the jazz canon.

Garrick's point about those things which jazz and religion might have in common is an intriguing one. It is underpinned by notions of value as much as it is of belief. Indeed, it is traceable to a stronger tradition in British social and cultural life. It is not unrelated to Arthur Marwick's "secular Anglicanism" but goes beyond that. Much has understandably been made of the role of the church and church leaders and the struggle for African-American emancipation and full civil rights. Less is made of the role of religion in British traditions of dissent. The role played by Quakers, Methodists, Baptists and Anglicans in seventeenth-century British politics continued in the eighteenth and nineteenth centuries, and members of these same religious groups have continued to be active in the peace movement and the movement against apartheid, as well as in support of social reform and social justice. The 1985 report authored by the Archbishop of Canterbury's Commission on Urban Priority Areas, "Faith in the City" (O'Brien *et al.* 1985), came from that same tradition and was an expression of those same values and concerns.

One can also trace a lineage from these beginnings through the work of Mike Westbrook with John Fox and Sue Gill of the Welfare State International, an experimental theatre group, in Cosmic Circus to Westbrook's projects with Adrian Mitchell (who also wrote for Welfare State) and partner Kate Westbrook. Here we would also note the subsequent involvement of Lol Coxhill and then guitarist G.P. Hall as musical directors of Welfare State. We would draw attention to poet Adrian Henri and the Liverpool Scene and that group of performing poets and musicians, the Barrow Poets. We might then mention Michael Garrick's other thematic, programmatic works such as *Judas Kiss*, *Bovingdon Poppies* and *Zodiac of Angels* and the establishment in 1982 by Tony Haynes of the multi-racial Grand Union Orchestra. Finally, we might consider certain projects by composer–bandleader Colin Towns in such a vein. The combination of drama, poetry, dance and film with jazz can and has produced a heady mix and one which can open up new audiences for jazz. Sadly, the cost of mounting such projects on any regular basis is all too often prohibitive.

Although it comes from 1999, Welfare State's statement of philosophy of values reflects much that we have discussed so far in this chapter. It underlines what for many of these artists is the close bond found in art between aesthetics and ethics:

> Welfare State International is a company of artists who pioneer new approaches to the arts of celebration and ceremony in the U.K. and internationally.
>
> We are seeking a culture which may well be less materially based but where more people will actively participate and gain power to celebrate moments that are wonderful and significant in their lives.
>
> We advocate a role for art that weaves it more fully into the fabric of our lives; that allows us to be collaborators rather than spectators:

Building our own houses, naming our children, burying our dead, announcing partnerships, marking anniversaries, creating new sacred spaces and producing whatever drama, stories, songs, ceremonies, pageants and jokes that are relevant to these new values and iconography.

We design and construct performances that are specific to place, people and occasion.

Special festivals of celebration that reach a wide audience, collaborative exhibitions and installations, original songs and soundscapes, and ceremonies for important occasions in people's lives.

WSI's artists are deeply concerned for the survival of the imagination and the individual within a media-dominated consumer society, in which art too has become a commodity. All our work – especially our generation of primary artwork – takes a holistic and educational perspective.

Our long-term aim is to establish creative communities on our doorstep: to work in partnerships to develop a creative society where the full potential of each individual may be realised in a supportive environment, through active participation and imaginative play.

We offer full access and opportunities for the dispossessed and seek a multi-generational and multi-ethnic congregation.

Art has a central and radical role in our lives. In the everyday, it's about what we value, how and why we celebrate.

(www.welfare-state.org)

It was in the main, the two groups of musicians – one based at the Little Theatre Club, the other based at The Old Place – who were responsible for new developments in British jazz that moved it closer to the art music camp and further from the world of popular entertainment. Whether this was conscious or not is open to question. Certainly, some such as Eddie Prévost and John Stevens derived a practice theory from their work as improvisers that took it far away from the mainstream. Others such as Mike Westbrook, Michael Garrick, Graham Collier and, to a lesser extent, Keith Tippett had already begun to pursue an authorial approach to bandleading and composing that was clearly conceptual in nature. To an extent, the trend within jazz generally was towards greater freedom. This was no less the case with British jazz, in particular among the younger musicians. The paradox is that this movement was led both by the composers, who looked to Ellington and Mingus for inspiration but also to twentieth-century art music, and by the improvisers, who in their pursuit of greater and greater abstraction brought their music closer in its aural landscape to that pioneered by Schönberg and Webern and further extended by those of the Darmstadt school.

The key words here are "aspiration" and "ambition", and much of the impetus for the changes that were taking place in the music came from the musicians themselves. It was this combination of writer/bandleaders and improvising musicians occupying that square mile in central London around Soho that gave British jazz of the late sixties its particular character. Those who led their own bands – Surman, McGregor, Westbrook, Tippett, Garrick, Beckett, Collier, Prévost, Stevens, Oxley and, later, Harry Miller, Dudu Pukwana, Skidmore, Osborne and Elton Dean – were able to develop their music, their group sound, their art due to the breadth of like-minded musicians available to them. They did so in circumstances that were largely without commercial pressures from agents, club owners or record companies. Their music was in those terms strictly uncommercial. There could be no hope of million-selling singles or top twenty albums. The major concert halls would not be throwing wide their doors. There was no need for and no point in compromise. So, what does one do when there is no real hope of wider commercial success? Well, you might as well make art, which is the option that many of these musicians chose. The result, however, was that these emergent approaches to composing and playing jazz shifted it further away from popular music and closer to art music.

As we have seen, quite a few musicians moved between the Little Theatre Club and The Old Place. However, an additional meeting point for musicians across the jazz-improvisation spectrum was provided by Neil Ardley's New Jazz Orchestra. The orchestra had formed originally as a rehearsal band but it was when Ian Carr introduced Ardley to the other members that it began to become important on the British scene. Ardley's academic background was in the sciences, an interest he continued to further as an author. In the seventies, he began to use synthesisers for coloration to marvellous effect on records such as *Kaleidoscope of Rainbows* and *Harmony of the Spheres*, and in the eighties he formed an electronic jazz group, Zyklus, with Ian Carr, Walter Greveson and composer–critic Jon L. Walters. Throughout his career, he continued to utilize many of the early players of the NJO on his recordings. In a sense, the orchestra ended its career proper in 1970 after the release of *Déjeuner Sur L'herbe* (Verve) and a successful UK tour with Jon Hiseman's Colosseum. However, it reunited in 1973 to record a tribute to pianist Mike Taylor, who had contributed several pieces to the band's book. Though unreleased at the time, *Mike Taylor Remembered* was finally issued on Dusk Fire in 2007. In another sense, the NJO continued in all but name playing on both *Greek Variations & Other Aegean Exercises* (Columbia; Universal) and *Symphony of Amaranths* (Regal Zonophone).

The band's importance lay in part in the way it brought musicians from different backgrounds together and also in the opportunity it provided to writers and arrangers. *Western Reunion* (Decca; Vocalion) included *avant gardists* Trevor Watts and Paul Rutherford, alongside other newcomers such as Jon Hiseman, Tony Reeves and Barbara Thompson, and already established talents like Ian Carr, trombonist John Mumford and saxophonist Dave Gelly. *Western Reunion* is a good album with Ardley's own Gil Evans-inflected

"Shades of Blue" the standout track. It was, however, a record that sounds today deeply in thrall to American jazz and, compared to other music being made by British musicians at the time and earlier, slightly dated. It was with their second release, *Le Déjeuner Sur L'herbe* in 1969, that the sheer beauty and majesty this orchestra had achieved under Ardley was fully revealed. By this point, the band also included Frank Ricotti, Mike Gibbs, Dick Heckstall-Smith, Jack Bruce, Harry Beckett and Henry Lowther.

For several years, the NJO had had a regular gig at University College London through George Foster, who ran the college's jazz society, and would often rehearse there as well. In addition, according to Ardley (Priestley 1971), the NJO had had averaged a gig a week for two years from 1965–7, quite an achievement in the economic climate of the time. This had certainly helped the orchestra develop its identity. *Déjeuner* is one of the finest British jazz records of any period. If the textural writing of Gil Evans still holds some sway, all but two of the tunes – Coltrane's "Naima" and Miles Davis's "Nardis", in a gorgeous arrangement by Ardley – are by young writers associated with the orchestra. Howard Riley's edgy "Angle", better known in its piano trio version expands perfectly in this setting, while Mike Taylor's simple sketches, "Ballad" and "Study" (after Segovia), glisten in the orchestra's hands. The arrangement of "Study" is credited to Taylor himself but is more likely to have come from the pen of Neil Ardley. It was this piece with its duet between Henry Lowther and Barbara Thompson, here on soprano, that was often the high spot of an NJO performance. The record also offers one of Mike Gibbs's strong, theme-led pieces in "Rebirth" and Michael Garrick's evergreen "Dusk Fire" but it is Ardley's title track that steals the show. It is a minor masterpiece of form, deceptively easy on the ear but utilizing a number of different scales. Ardley's harmonic sense allows this exercise in polytonality to develop and, while it sounds exotic in its use of modes, it never seems odd or discordant. Throughout, the playing is magnificent and it is great to hear musicians like Ian Carr, Barbara Thompson and Dick Heckstall-Smith in a big band setting.

Ardley told Brian Priestley in August 1971, *Le Déjeuner Sur L'herbe* was for him a breakthrough composition:

> *Le Déjeuner Sur L'herbe* was the first time I tried to compose a piece from beginning to end, with no repeating chord sequence. The tune actually comes from a secondary part in a Debussy prelude, and I used the notes in it as motifs from which the rest of the piece came.   (Priestley 1971, 12)

Ardley was actually talking to Priestley about both the album *Greek Variations* and his forthcoming release *Symphony of Amaranths* and it is very apparent from the interview that Ardley is looking outside African-American inspirations – the title of course comes from Manet's impressionist painting. Ardley explains how he is looking to develop a compositional approach that is essentially thematic and the use of a sequence of notes as the foundation for both composition and improvisation was one that he continued to pursue with his next three records, including both the above and *Kaleidoscope of Rainbows*. With *Greek Variations*, Ardley also made extensive use of a string section. On *Symphony of Amaranths*, he added harps, additional tuned percussion, celeste, electric piano, harpsichord, bassoon and oboe to more traditional jazz instrumentation. With *Kaleidoscope*, on the other hand, Ardley utilized synthesizers and other electronic instruments. Not only was he extending the scope of the jazz composer and the range of instrumentation available to achieve his aims, he was constantly drawing on modal ideas from European folk music, specifically that of the Balkans and Greece in particular, as well as on Balinese modes on *Kaleidoscope*. *Greek Variations* also featured a number of pieces for jazz quartet by Don Rendell and an early recording by a proto-Nucleus. However, its main interest lies in Ardley's title track, a long, six-part suite which uses Rendell and Carr as its primary solo voices and which was the first time the Arts Council had subsidized a jazz recording. It is not surprising, given the use of Greek modes, that there are similarities between this work and the music of George Russell. However, this seems to have been less of a direct influence and more the consequence of exploration of similar musical territory. This and the four-part *Symphony of Amaranths* are stunningly beautiful pieces of music, sensuous and delightful and bold in both conception and execution. The rest of *Symphony of Amaranths* is devoted to a setting of Lewis Carroll's "Dong with the Luminous Nose" recited by Ivor Cutler, an acquired taste perhaps, and three other poems by Joyce, Yeats and Carroll sung inimitably by Norma Winstone. Falling just outside our period, *Kaleidoscope of Rainbows* is arguably Ardley's masterpiece, but these earlier records reveal an important and unique compositional voice.

Neil Ardley was one of a number of graduates coming into British jazz in this period. Between eight and ten of the NJO's members at any one time had degrees of one sort or another. Throughout this book, we have emphasized the impact that education, and higher education in particular, had on the scope and direction taken by the music in this decade. However, it has to be stressed as well that there were many others, who had risen up the ranks but who were bringing their own vision and abilities to bear. There were those such as Keith Tippett, who had moved to London before his twentieth birthday from Bristol and others like Elton Dean, trumpeter Marc Charig, Alan Skidmore, Roy Babbington and drummer John Marshall who had begun their careers playing R&B. Tippett had formed his first London-based sextet around Charig, Dean and trombonist Nick Evans whom he had met at the Barry Summer School in 1968. Other musicians like pianist John Taylor, bassist Jeff Clyne, tenor saxophonist Gary Windo, Ray Russell, Harry Beckett, pianist Mick Pyne and his trombonist brother Chris were also indispensable members of the British scene, none of whom were university scholars. They still brought well-developed musical personalities and ideas about the music they wanted to make into an already rich and diverse musical scene. It was this combination of the musically gifted and the artistically visionary that fashioned the next and most distinctive phase in British jazz. Records by Harry Beckett and Ray Russell bear comparison with any released anywhere in the late sixties and early seventies. Artistic vision is never the sole province of the formally educated alone. John Taylor's first release under his own name, *Pause, and Think Again* (Turtle; FMR), came out in 1971 on Turtle and provides another perfect example of this.

Though largely self-taught, John Taylor is one of the finest pianists to emerge in the sixties. Although he has recorded under his own name over the years, he is better known for his work with friends like John Surman, Norma Winstone and Kenny Wheeler and for his role as one third of Azimuth. *Pause, and Think Again* is one of the essential records of the era. It justifies inclusion for Taylor's piano playing alone but there are tremendous performances on it from Kenny Wheeler, John Surman on soprano, Stan Sulzmann on alto, Chris Pyne, Norma Winstone, Chris Laurence and drummer Tony Levin. Its sound is quite unmistakeably British and it occupies a similar sound space to records by Harry Beckett, John Surman, Henry

Alan Skidmore at the Jazz & Folk Cellar, Penzance, Summer 1970. Left to right: Alan Skidmore (tenor sax), Goudie Charles (bass), John Cox (soprano sax), Jim King (drums – not shown). Photograph courtesy of Goudie Charles, photographer unknown.

Lowther, Kenny Wheeler and others. It also has a similar ambience to many of the albums that have appeared over the years on ECM. But there is as well a confidence and ambition in the writing that is quite refreshing. The horns are elegantly voiced, the rhythms muscular and assured and it moves easily between form and freedom.

Taylor also appeared on Alan Skidmore's *Once Upon a Time* – another favourite of the period – contributing the fast and tricky "The Yolk" to the set. It is no surprise that Skidmore's quintet with Kenny Wheeler, Harry Miller and Tony Oxley won a clutch of awards at the Montreux Jazz Festival in 1969 taking the gongs for "Best Group", "Best Musician" (Skidmore) and "Best Drummer" for Oxley. As with *Pause, and Think Again*, it is the ease with which these musicians move between freer, open-ended numbers like Skidmore's "Free for Al" and Oxley's strange, abstract "Majaera" and the lush harmonies of John Surman's waltz "Once Upon a Time" and John Warren's "Old San Juan". Skidmore's follow-up, *TCB*, (Philips; Vocalion) was very nearly as good, and his contribution to the hugely original trio S.O.S. with Mike Osborne and John Surman was further evidence of his ambition and openness to challenge.

By this point British jazz was no longer just a poor relationship of its American originator. It functioned increasingly within a context where it was understood as a music capable of serious analysis not just historically or sociologically but aesthetically, culturally and musically. A whole series of changes cultural, economic, political and contextual had affected British jazz in ways that had fostered the creative ambitions of a remarkable body of musicians. It retained some links with the rock scene, with a lot of younger players spending part of their working week in rock bands and its fanbase had begun to overlap with an audience that listened to Pink Floyd, Soft Machine, Yes, as well as Gong, Stomu Yamashta, Hatfield and the North, Caravan and others. Ian Carr writing in the *Melody Maker* in the autumn of 1971 struck a positive note:

> The Progressive Rock scene with its increasing musical sophis-
> tication and its use of improvisation has certainly helped make
> audiences more sympathetic to jazz. In recent years, the whole
> pop scene has split down the middle and now it's clear that there
> is a fundamental difference between pop music pure and simple,
> and what is happening in rock music.   (Carr 1971, 24)

With hindsight his optimism was misplaced. The audience for pop/rock music actually fractured in the early seventies between the teenyboppers, the mums and dads, the glam rockers, hard rock fans and those looking to an increasingly bombastic "prog rock" for stimulation. What is more, the distance between the fans and their rock/pop heroes grew ever wider as the money poured in. Over the next few years, even the student audience which had remained relatively steadfast would desert jazz.

Whether British jazz had sealed its own fate by becoming more and more cerebral is really irrelevant. The world of music had shifted on its axis and the space occupied by jazz had altered accordingly. It had become a serious music, an art music. It had progressed while the younger audience it might have hoped for sought simpler musical pleasures.

* * *

Jazz fans living in London in the late sixties could most weeks catch one of several composer-led big bands playing in a club or hall somewhere nearby. There was Westbrook, Mike Gibbs, Canadian saxophonist John Warren and the Brotherhood of Breath, while the transatlantic orchestra of Kenny Clarke and Francy Boland might well be playing at Ronnie's. And as we have noted, smaller bands such as those of Collier, Tippett, Garrick and Surman or Ian Carr's Nucleus were just as concerned with form and composition, as they were with improvisation.

Kenny Clarke/Francy Boland Big Band with Chris Pyne (trombone), Kenny Wheeler (trumpet) and Ronnie Scott (tenor sax), Hammersmith Gaumont, Jazz Expo' 1969. © Valerie Wilmer.

We have already looked at the work of many of those mentioned above. Three remain to be considered in appropriate depth. They are Keith Tippett, John Surman and Mike Westbrook. Though the music they have created is quite different and personal, these three share certain key aspects of the Britishness of British jazz – the influence of Anglican church music and its close cousins – the English folk and pastoral traditions.

Keith Tippett experienced considerable success, artistically and even commercially, as a young musician with his vast Centipede project. He had, however, attracted quite an unusual amount of attention prior to that work with a musical approach that drew quite unambiguously on a huge range of stylistic influences. As Richard Williams noted in a *Melody Maker* review of the album *September Energy*:

> It's hard to discuss the band's music within a conventional frame of reference because what it is seems almost as important as what it does. Were the music less than spectacular Centipede would still have a function, would still be a symbol of all the very best developments in music over the past five years.
>
> (Williams 1971, 37)

Williams echoes a point made by Christopher Bird in the sleevenotes to Tippett's first album, *You Are Here ... I Am There* (Polydor; Discinforme). Commenting on Tippett's early influences, Bird noted:

> Those early years have marked his conceptions to this day with a curiously lyrical, pastoral, English quality. As well as the raw, violent excitement of the band's music, a subconscious feel which hints at Walton, Elgar, Britten is never too far away. These were the sounds that floated round the Tippett household as a young man. Unfashionable ones today, perhaps, when many young musicians are dropping names like Stockhausen and Penderecki – but they were good ones to grow up with.

Those pastoral, lyrical concerns were most obviously present on "This Evening Was Like Last Year (to Sarah)" from *You Are Here ... I Am There* and on "Green and Orange Night Park" from Tippett's second album, *Dedicated to You But You Weren't Listening*. On both records, the sense of constant forward momentum seemed to owe much to rock music, though Tippett never saw his music as "jazz-rock", noting instead, "We might've been doing a couple of pieces with eight fills but the sextet was never really part of the English jazz-rock scene like Back Door or Nucleus" (interview with Keith Tippett, March 2004). Tippett is, in fact, very precise about the different musical styles that have affected him, as he explains:

Coming to the folk and choral thing, a potted history from me is when I was four my grandfather lived with us and he used to play the piano beautifully – Liszt and Chopin – and I asked if I could do what granddad does. My parents said, "Yes, if you practice regularly." My father was a policeman then and it wasn't a well-paid job particularly after the war. I'd have to practice because it was going to cost two and six (13 pence) for a half-hour's lesson. I started that and at the age of five I joined the choir and was a chorister till I was thirteen in a fantastic choir.

(Interview with Keith Tippett, March 2004)

Tippett retains a real pride for this aspect of his musical education:

St Thomas the Martyr Beckett in Bristol – at its best equal to the Cathedral choir. Everybody who knows would say that. Doing two anthems on Sunday – that was incredible. Then when my voice broke, I studied Church organ for three years. All the time I was studying piano and when I went to secondary school I learnt the cornet, then moved to the tenor horn and became first horn with the Bristol Youth Brass Band.

(interview with Keith Tippett, March 2004)

It is not hard to hear these elements in Tippett's music, then and now. It is perhaps there in the pedal points that he likes to use and even more in the often baroque horn choruses and simple, but highly effective way, he uses counterpoint. At the same time, he is one of the world's finest improvising pianists and very strong rhythmically. Given his musical background in church and brass band musics, it is not surprising that Tippett writes extremely well for voice and for brass. These aspects of his approach to composition and improvisation can be identified as essentially British in origin.

Tippett's later work has included solo and small groups, big bands, piano and string quintets, music for chamber ensembles and choirs, much of it in association with his partner Julie. If anything, these characteristics of his music derived from a British cultural context have become more pronounced. After the success of Centipede, Tippett felt the need for something on a more manageable scale, as he explains:

Centipede was a broad brushstroke, a young man's work but after that I wanted to experience something more intimate after a fifty-piece circus. Ovary Lodge was formed with Frank Perry and Roy Babbington was the first bass player. Then Harry Miller came in and then Julie came in. I'd always been interested in spontaneous composition – sometimes I prefer to use those words instead of free improvisation, which can really put people off.

(interview with Keith Tippett, March 2004)

In fact, the group's first release, *Blueprint* (RCA; BGO), came out under Tippett's name. If anything, it proved beyond a doubt how diverse music in this idiom could be. It featured Roy Babbington on bass, either Frank Perry or Keith Bailey on percussion, and Julie Tippetts on vocals, acoustic guitar and recorder. RCA had pressed Tippett for a follow-up to *September Energy* but, despite the fact that he saw himself first and foremost as a composer rather than improviser, the pianist could not face the prospect, as he told John Wickes:

> That messed RCA up something wicked. Centipede was a big deal and extrovert but with *Blueprint* I wanted an opposite thing. With hindsight I must admit, although I wasn't aware of it at the time, it was an artistic reaction to all the hullabaloo of Centipede."
>
> (Wickes 1999, 198)

According to Tippett (interview with Keith Tippett, March 2004; Wickes 1999), RCA did little to promote the record, allowed the group (now Ovary Lodge) to make Tippett's last contracted album for the label and cut him loose. In fact, it was their third album for Ogun, which falls just outside our period, that would prove to be the group's most completely effective recording. However, all three have their merits and define a particular artistic side to Tippett, and to his partner Julie, in their musical approach. This music has the capacity to express itself quite explosively, with Tippett launching Tayloresque/Tyneresque flurries of notes as the rhythm section keeps pace in a remarkable release of passion. Its main characteristic, however, is one of intimacy, closeness and delicacy. It derives its moral and aesthetic weight from a different kind of communion to that achieved by Centipede, Ark or Tapestry – Tippett's three big bands – or for that matter by improvising quartet Mujician or Tippett's occasional octets. It concerns itself with improvisation rather than composition and subtle intercommunication within the group. Where a riff emerges as on "Dance" or "Glimpse" from *Blueprint*, it can develop a similar dramatic dynamic that is often apparent in Tippett's larger group compositions, but in the main this is more music of brooks and streams than rivers and waterfalls. It ambience seems both pastoral and folk-inflected, where *September Energy* and Tippett's early small group records owed part at least of their energy to rock music.

Tippett's contribution to British and European jazz, improvised and composed, is immeasurable. Its sheer breadth has expanded the language and possibilities of the music without ever losing sight of its origins, in terms of both the music itself and his own discovery of it. For a time in the seventies, Tippett functioned almost as the house-pianist for the Ogun label and his connections with the South African musicians who came to Britain in the sixties remain strong both in his work with drummer Louis Moholo-Moholo and as pianist with the Dedication Orchestra formed to celebrate the music of McGregor, Pukwana *et al.* His very openness to African and European folk forms, rock and classical music in no way detracts from his own distinctive voice as a pianist and composer.

Much the same could be, and indeed has been, said about Mike Westbrook. Westbrook's experience of major record labels was less unsatisfactory than that of Keith Tippett. Between 1967 and 1975, Westbrook released a succession of ten astonishing and varied albums on Decca, RCA and Transatlantic. He had also issued a live quartet performance on John Jack's Cadillac Records, which presaged his rock-jazz recordings with Solid Gold Cadillac. The music encompassed jazz in all its forms, as well as influences from rock and classical music but it added one crucial element that has informed Westbrook's work throughout his career – drama. In fact, he and his partner Kate have almost single-handedly created a genre of musical theatre that is unique in Britain, if not in mainland Europe.

Westbrook deserves his own biographer, but here we will concentrate on his first two Deram albums, *Celebration* and *Release*, the two-volume *Marching Song* (Deram; PSALM), and the two large ensemble records made for RCA, *Metropolis* (RCA Neon; BGO) and *Citadel/Room 315* (RCA; BGO).

Mike Westbrook Concert Band, *Marching Song* live. Left to right: Mike Westbrook (piano); front row, John Surman (baritone sax), Mike Osborne (alto sax), George Khan (tenor sax), Bernie Living (alto sax); second row, Paul Rutherford (trombone), Dave Holdsworth, Mick Collins (trumpets); Harry Miller, Dave Holland (basses). Not visible, Denis Smith and Alan Jackson (drums), George Smith (tuba) and Malcolm Griffiths (trombone). Photograph from the Mike Westbrook Archive, photographer unknown.

Broadly speaking, the Concert Band's second album *Release* was more favourably received than *Celebration*. The *Melody Maker* brief comment on the latter read, "Mixed offering from one of Britain's finest young bands. Emphasis on rather monotonous scoring, but worth hearing for soloists like baritonist John Surman" (*Melody Maker* 1968, 14).

The writer and composer Patrick Gowers also commented:

> Whether you like this heavy and rather unvaried sound or not is a matter of taste. What is undisputable is that it provides a fitting support to some fiery and occasionally brilliant solos, and that the band is an important feature of contemporary British jazz.
>   (Quoted in Hennessey 1999).

Others like Ronald Atkins and Michael Shera were more favourably disposed to Westbrook's debut, but critic Barry McRae saw *Release* as being far superior to its predecessor, which had also garnered strong reviews from Derek Jewell in the *Sunday Times* and from Miles Kingston in the *Times*. In his *Melody Maker* review of *Release* and John Surman's eponymous first album, Bob Houston remarked that *Celebration* had failed to capture "the band's extraordinary vigour and power". In terms of the new record, Houston described Westbrook as an "astute arranger" but one who "obviously sees his band's function as a launching pad for the solo voices, with little orchestrated winks, nudges and cues which link the whole album quite ingeniously". He continued:

> His awareness of that vital ingredient excitement runs through the music and the use of big band perennials such as Flying Home (with Surman's clever cadenza leading into the theme), Opus One and Sugar emphasises that far from having fresh tricks up his sleeve, his great skill lies in the use and deployment of traditional resources.   (Houston 1969, 21)

For all Houston's positive response to *Release*, he missed the point quite dramatically, but then he was looking at a career at its very outset and lacked the benefit of hindsight. The reference to "traditional resources" is, however, insightful. What Houston could hardly have anticipated here was that this would prove to be a key aspect of Westbrook's art, namely, that it maintains a discourse between tradition and history on the one hand, and modernity and the present on the other. This was particularly evident in his next album *Marching Song*, which looked at a past unnecessary, destructive imperialist war (the First World War) to reflect upon war in general. This juxtaposition in Westbrook's work serves to create an internal dialogue that allows historical or traditional elements to reflect upon those from the present and vice versa. This aspect of his art is also, for example, found in *Mama Chicago*

(1979), *Westbrook Blake* (1980), *London Bridge is Broken Down* (1988), *The Cortège* (1982) and *Art Wolf* (2005). In the first three, the issues raised might be in the broadest sense political. With regard to *Art Wolf*, however, the questions appear to be aesthetic in nature contrasting past and present artistic values and their relevant social contexts, while the concerns of *The Cortège* were perhaps more spiritual–philosophical in nature in their focus on life and death.

Form and structure has always been important to Westbrook, as he explained in an article in *Avant Magazine* in 1997:

> In my band I had a combination of free improvisers and straightahead players, as well as people from the rock world. As a composer, I've always been interested in structuring music in some way. That can mean a formal arrangement or chord sequence or just a concept or even a poem. There were a lot of people around – still are thankfully – like Kenny Wheeler and Paul Rutherford who enjoyed playing in a range of settings. The ideal world is one where all these things can come together.   (Heining 1997a, 22)

It is surprising, therefore, that he was seen by some fans as the enfant terrible of British jazz at that time. At the *Melody Maker* Pollwinners' Concert at the Royal Festival Hall in May 1969, a provocative Concert Band set closed the night, summoning as many catcalls and jeers as applause and cheers (see Carr 2007, 30–1). As it happened, Archie Shepp's group had opened for Miles Davis at Jazz Expo in Summer 1967 in Hammersmith to a similar response. It is correct that, from *Celebration* onwards, Westbrook had embraced atonality and abstraction. Yet, where others saw this as an end in itself or at least the means to a specific performance aesthetic, for Westbrook this was a compositional tool among many others. Both *Celebration* and *Release* make used of extemporized passages, sometimes solo and sometimes collective. These are often used to bring closure to a particular "movement" or idea or lead into another section, while at certain points they allow for an explosion of energy or catharsis. It is no accident that Westbrook later became involved in musical theatre – drama and dramatic intent have always informed his approach.

These two early works contain some quite beautiful writing, some under the influence of Duke Ellington. The closing "Portrait" on *Celebration* illustrates this well and shows how far John Surman had drawn on Harry Carney in developing his baritone sound. In fact, listening to Surman two years later on *Release* one can clearly hear his development as a musician and how far he has established an unusually distinctive sound on both baritone and soprano saxes. Surman proved a crucial element in early Concert Band and it is fair to say that he was an important figure in the leader's own growth as a composer and arranger, with Surman also contributing both "Awakening" and "Image" to *Celebration*. As Westbrook noted in 1997, Surman's arrival in the early sixties was significant in several respects:

> It's very much developing one's compositional ideas and about having a band to write for. It really was a great day when John Surman joined the band and I then had four horns. That unleashed a whole range of possibilities and I was able to move from straight-ahead arrangements to writing suites.   (Heining 1997a)

Saxophonist Gary Bayley – currently working for a doctorate on Westbrook's music – also notes parallels with Charles Mingus's *Black Saint and the Sinner Lady*, in particular in relation to the accelerandi on "Echoes and Heroics". Bayley suggests that "this must have been an influence as it is a rare device" (e-mail interview with Gary Bayley, April 2011). *Celebration* was originally a fifteen-part, two-hour suite (Schonfield 1967). Perhaps that it is why some sections seem somewhat truncated, for example, the opening "Pastoral" and the introduction to the Debussy-like "Image" with its gorgeous flute from Bernie Living. One suspects, that the lack of enthusiasm of Barry McRae and the *Melody Maker* for *Celebration* lay in its sense that it contains itself emotionally, while the band in concert was frequently a far more explosive prospect. Actually, that feeling of contained emotion is part of its beauty and makes for a remarkably mature work from what was in 1967 one of the most intelligent and articulate big band albums to come out of Britain or mainland Europe. If Westbrook had used this as a calling card intended to showcase the talents of his band and his own as a composer, he could hardly have done a better job.

Release, on the other hand was much closer to the live Westbrook experience. With producer Peter Eden's background in pop and rock music, the sound was much better than that on *Celebration* and one hears a band truly reaching out to its audience. The whole set, which includes several non-original tunes such as the Goodman–Hampton "Flying Home", the Charlie Parker/Billie Holiday vehicle "Lover Man" and Jobim's "The Girl from Ipanema", is again organized as a suite. If there is an ironic aspect to the inclusion of these pieces, it is an affectionate one, as Westbrook suggested to Mike Hennessey. Noting Duke Ellington as his primary influence, he continued, "I also drew inspiration from blues and boogie as a youngster, from Jimmy Yancey and Louis Armstrong. I still love New Orleans jazz and often listen to it" (Hennessey 1999). Indeed, Westbrook is happy to throw in a burlesque contribution or two of his own, most notably with "A Life of Its Own". Once again, the notion of theatricality is relevant, here delivered with a good deal of humour.

Several themes recur throughout the recording – "The Few", "Folk Song" and "Take Me Back" – and sections are linked by the simple device of a cadenza played at the end of one tune before the band leads into the next.

Bob Houston's comment about *Celebration* that Westbrook used his arrangements, Ellington-like, as a means of framing the distinctive solo voices of his band, is if anything more applicable here. Indeed, players like Mike Osborne, Surman, tenor saxist George Khan, trumpeter Dave Holdsworth and Malcolm Griffiths on trombone do leave as strong an impression as the tunes themselves. Surman's significance notwithstanding, the Concert Band was quite astonishing in terms of its talents. George Khan's solo on the Jobim tune is one of the album's most unrestrained moments and a real highlight, while Dave Holdsworth's flugelhorn solo on "Rosie" is a thing of beauty. As for Griffiths, the service he gave to the music of both Westbrook and Surman really should be acknowledged. He played on every Westbrook release up to and including *The Cortège*, with the exception of the Westbrook Brass Band series, and was an important part of the jazz-rock Solid Cadillac group. The more one listens to these records the more important his contribution seems. He added to an approach derived from J.J. Johnson, the more bizarre sounds of the avant-garde and some of that New Orleans–Chicago tailgate trombone. His strengths are even more evident on Westbrook's "pop-soul-jazz" *Love Songs*, his elegance and poise matching an accuracy of articulation and a strong dramatic sensibility. One must also note the support of Harry Miller on bass and Alan Jackson on drums. Both gave so very much to the band's unique sound, that the word "gravitas" is no overstatement here.

Marching Song was Westbrook's first masterpiece. Originally intended as a double album, Decca executives blocked this with the result that it was released as two separate volumes (interview with Peter Eden, February 1996). The fire power of the Concert Band was expanded for *Marching Song* and for much of the record two bass players and two drummers provide a profound sense of drama at the music's heart. This does more than create a feeling of martial momentum. It imitates the sounds of battle and the physical shock of gun, mortar and canon. In fact, the playing of Alan Jackson and John Marshall is one of the great joys here. Most of the musicians who had performed on *Celebration* and *Release* are present, including Malcolm Griffiths, Dave Holdsworth, Bernie Living, George Khan and Mike Osborne, with the addition of others of the calibre of Kenny Wheeler and Alan Skidmore. However, of all the talented musicians that Westbrook drew upon in these years, saxophonist John Surman was without doubt the most important.

Westbrook used several of the younger man's compositions on *Celebration* and *Marching Song*, and Surman is the featured soloist on the long work from 1975, *Citadel/Room 315*. So inseparable were the two men in the imagination of the jazz public in Britain that it was hard to read a review or interview on either without reference to the other. John Dankworth and Cleo Laine even called two of their cats Westbrook and Surman.

It would not be unfair to suggest that Surman was for Westbrook his Johnny Hodges, his Harry Carney and his Ben Webster. Just as these three musicians gave voice to particular aspects of Ellington's melodic and harmonic

Mike Westbrook and John Surman, the *Citadel* sessions, 1975. © Kate Westbrook.

gifts, John Surman's rare abilities allowed Westbrook to reach further as a composer. This was particularly evident on *Marching Song*, which features three of Surman's compositions, while the saxophonist solos on four of the seventeen tracks. This record is not the first "programmatic" work by a British jazz composer but it remains the most successful and articulate example of an attempt in British jazz to convey meanings through its musical content. Its subject is war. While it can be read in terms of a narrative, it can perhaps be better understood as a series of pictures of a changing landscape. One thinks immediately of Paul Nash's First World War paintings with their horrific, scarred landscapes but also, in relation to the title track itself, of a painting by Nash's Slade School peer Richard Nevinson, "Column on the March". In its dark blues and greys, it portrays an infantry column, packed tightly together and completely occupying the landscape. Its technique owes something to Futurism but it offers a horrifying rather than uplifting spectacle of the degradation of the individual subject. The citizen has become simply part of a great fighting machine.

Westbrook's programme notes describe graphically this surrender to the machine:

> When the soldier moves into the landscape, he is a being from another world. To him the landscape is a strange and disturbing place, full of sights and sounds he cannot understand, of unseen forces and unknown dangers ... The landscape is an arena ... the soldiers march in tightly closed ranks ... Individually, they count

for nothing ... Individuals are subordinated to the plan. Some struggle free, only to lose themselves in the crowd as the reality of war becomes apparent.

When *Marching Song* was reissued on CD in the USA, the sleeve referred to the work thus:

Here is an anti-Vietnam [*sic*] big band symphony, from this progressive big band leader from the UK whose influences include Ellington, Weill and Brecht. This was multi-faceted music and performance art at its most politically charged.

(Searle 2008, 168)

Coming close on the heels of Charlie Haden's first Liberation Orchestra LP, it was perhaps understandable that it was seen as a reaction to events in southeast Asia. Yet, on another level, *Marching Song* challenges such a reading. Chris Searle notes that its first performance was at the Camden Jazz Festival close on the heels of the fiftieth anniversary of another conflict – the First World War. Searle may be allowed a little licence in his comment:

The military disasters and mass murder from the Somme in 1917 to Songmy in 1968 were shown not to be so far apart in Westbrook's epic musical vision, and close to the conception of three of his heroes, Blake, Weill and Ellington.

(Searle 2008, 168)

Its origins and gestation, in fact, owe nothing to the Vietnam War as such, as Westbrook explains:

It wasn't conceived as a statement on Vietnam, but war in general, inspired by a dream, as I recall. My references were European. A US LP version was issued at the time of the original release in the 60s. They'd done their own cover, which I think related it more to Vietnam. I remember a Coke bottle buried in the sand. Needless to say I wasn't consulted, and never had a copy.

(E-mail interview with Mike Westbrook, July 2011).

On one level, the composer's original notes detail the events underpinning its musical episodes – cheering crowds on "Hooray!", the theatre of war on "Landscape II", scorched earth on "Tarnished" – suggesting a programmatic work which can be read in such terms. However, look closely at Westbrook's notes and it is more about the reaction of human beings, collectively or as individuals, to events than about the events themselves. As suggested, it is also a work that is concerned with landscape. Indeed, not only are two movements titled "Landscape" and "Landscape II" but the picture that appeared on the back of the original Volume I of the LP is of mangled and broken war wagons foregrounding the explosions of shells and bombs. The picture on the back of Volume II is of patriotic German crowds in front of the Brandenburg Gate. By contrast, the sleeve artwork is taken from a crayon drawing by David Desire, the child of a neighbour of Westbrook's. It has that graphic intensity of childhood – a childish grasping for the sounds, colours and violence of events. These images complement the music and the project perfectly.

The performances are astonishing throughout, whether one is listening to the two tenors of George Khan and Alan Skidmore on the title track, Paul Rutherford's trombone growls and slurs on "Other World" over the drums of Alan Jackson and John Marshall, or Dave Holdsworth's gloriously romantic trumpet on "Rosie". In lesser hands, *Marching Song* might merely have echoed the *Sturm und Drang* of much free jazz of the period. Here it is the contrasts that Westbrook creates – between the trusting, unaware world of hearth and family at home and the horror of life at the front, between the hours of terror and days of uneasy calm, between the beauty of the natural world and its violation – that gives the music its authority and majesty.

This is illustrated perfectly on Volume II. The first three pieces here are "Transition" (a beautiful, Ellingtonian theme), "Home" (with some fine trombone from Malcolm Griffiths and a further bass duet, this time by Miller and Chris Laurence) and "Rosie" (which also featured in a very different context on *Release*). These are moments of calm and reminiscence before John Surman's "Prelude" arrives with its unusual and slightly unsettling modal scale. Using the intertwining woodwinds of Bernie Living, Mike Osborne and Alan Skidmore, it once again introduces a sense of otherness. Surman's "Tension" follows, perhaps one of his finest early tunes, beautifully arranged and it sets the scene powerfully for a further saxophone tussle with the composer on baritone and Skidmore on tenor. As it leads into Griffiths's muscular trombone solo, this is music to stiffen the sinews and summon up the blood before Westbrook's "Introduction" returns us once again to the idea of landscape, as we watch the soldiers "unready, helpless and ridiculous" looking out into the field of battle that awaits. Westbrook's notes tell us, "And death is not the heroic gesture, but a protracted, ignoble struggle to hold onto life. The hands clutch, bodies twitch and go limp. How can anything grow again, here?" The syntax is crucial with its emphasis on the word "here", which once more positions us. The notes continue, "How can men forget? Tidy it up with a slab of stone, a flower wreath, a row of ribbons on a cripple's chest."

In a way, both the work itself and Westbrook's commentary find an echo in Paul Fussell's *The Great War and Modern Memory* when he writes:

> If the opposite of war is peace, the opposite of experiencing moments of war is proposing moments of pastoral. Since war

takes place outdoors and always within nature, its symbolic status
is that of the ultimate anti-pastoral.   (Fussell 2000, 231)

Again, the crucial use of contrast is present as the music comes to a close. The terror that is to come is preceded once again by a beautifully Ellingtonian and pastoral moment on "Ballad", with its achingly lovely alto solo from Mike Osborne, before "Conflict" envelopes the listener. Chris Searle describes this section as a "monstrous artillery passage" of "nearly eleven minutes of agonising ensemble sound, unremitting sonic violence and pain that is unique in the canon of jazz". Paradoxically, the piece is lent its unusual human essence by George Smith's tuba and its strange, pitiful and mammalian cries. In fact, Smith's performance is the most bold and exciting on a record filled with bravura playing. It is left to John Surman's "Tarnished" to bring home the wounded and bury the dead. There is a beauty in the sadness found here in Westbrook's all too brief piano interlude before a raucous and bitterly ironic "Memorial" brings a dramatic and abrupt end to the album.

Westbrook would go on to write even greater compositions, but *Marching Song* was in many respects his first completely satisfying work and proved beyond doubt his talent. It combines emotion with intellect, and gut feeling with a musical language that is articulate and imaginative. It succeeds in making its point without being didactic or doctrinaire. It is angry but compassionate and never abdicates its sense of responsibility to its subject or its audience. It offers a union of aesthetics and ethics, and as such it is possible to engage with it on a variety of levels. It asks us to look into that landscape and see it for what it was, what we have made it and what it could be. For these reasons, it is the quintessential British jazz recording of the 1960s.

Surprisingly or not, Westbrook followed *Marching Song* with the charming, if lighter weighted *Love Songs*, a record noteworthy for some excellent bass guitar from Miller, fine alto from Mike Osborne, lustrous trombone and trumpet from Griffiths and Holdsworth, respectively, and most of all the voice of Norma Winstone. *Love Songs* marked the end of Westbrook's association with Decca and Peter Eden. The real successor to *Marching Song* was, however, *Metropolis*, which came out on RCA in 1971. This could be the hidden gem in Westbrook's career. At the time, Richard Williams saw it as one of the pianist's strongest pieces to date being both "more unified than *Release*" and "more compact than *Marching Song*". He continued, "It may lack some of the fun of the former and a little of the starkly programmatic quality of the latter, but the subject matter is different and, of the three, it is almost certainly the most effective and enjoyable" (Williams 1972, 32).

After noting Westbrook's successful deployment of certain rock techniques, he added, "Westbrook's writing for a large ensemble has never sounded more confident than it does here" (Williams 1972, 32). In fact, it was a very large ensemble indeed using five trumpets, five trombones and five saxes. Westbrook played piano within a rhythm section that included

Harry Miller on bass and cello, as well as Chris Laurence on acoustic and electric basses, Gary Boyle on guitar, John Taylor on electric piano, both Alan Jackson and John Marshall on drums and Norma Winstone. It deserves to be heard not for the sheer range of styles the composer explores but for the bravura manner in which these are used. Williams was spot on in his reference to "rock techniques" and the comparisons, here, would need to be with George Russell, Mike Gibbs and Don Ellis. Much of the music is in fact quite funky with an almost danceable pulse, though Westbrook also uses a series of effective collective improvisations to link different sections. The standard of soloing is if anything higher than on either *Celebration* or *Release* and just as strong as on *Marching Song*. Surman is absent, though he would return as featured soloist for *Citadel/Room 315*. If his own unique voice were still missed, the performances of Gary Boyle, Alan Skidmore, Kenny Wheeler, Malcolm Griffiths, Henry Lowther and, in the wonderfully compelling final statement, Harry Beckett are compensation aplenty. *Metropolis* is a very special achievement.

Citadel/Room 315 began life with a commission to write an extended work for the Swedish Radio Jazz Group with John Surman as main soloist. The concert was recorded but several of the Swedes were unhappy with their performance and plans to issue it were shelved. As Westbrook explained to Alyn Shipton, the opportunity to write for a full jazz orchestra came during a time when the scale of his activities had shrunk in size:

> In 1971 the Concert Band had come to an end. Our last album with that band was Metropolis, but that was actually recorded shortly after our final live gigs, and, so, in a sense, that LP marked the completion of a period of work that was already largely over. As a result, the early 70s became something of a period of diaspora, both for me and the musicians, who had been part of the Concert Band in the late 1960s.
>
> In my own case, this first drew me into theatre music, and also briefly into the rock world, with Solid Gold Cadillac. However, the main – and lasting – thing that came out of this period was the Brass Band, which was in essence, a new way of exploring very simple ideas. It was a time when, after a number of years of continuous development, everything suddenly changed. It was also a moment when we all had to find new ways of making a living after all the excitement and drama of that early period was over.
>
> (Shipton 2006)

With Arts Council support, Westbrook was able to form and tour for the first time under the rubric of the Mike Westbrook Orchestra. On this outing, it was an eighteen-piece orchestra, once again using electric instruments alongside more common jazz big band instruments. The original commission from Swedish Radio had given Westbrook the time to refine his approach and produce a composition that was both coherent and challenging. In the interim, Surman had grown further still as a musician. Several years on the road with The Trio and then with S.O.S. with Osborne and Skidmore had not just established him as a major presence in Britain and Europe. He had developed a voice as distinctive and special as those African-American musicians such as Coltrane, Carney and Rollins who had inspired him. For this new composition, Westbrook had realized that he could not direct the band and play piano and had made the inspired choice of hiring Dave MacRae who had played with Mike Gibbs, Nucleus and Robert Wyatt's Matching Mole.

Citadel essentially explores similar territory to *Metropolis* and, if anything, does so to greater effect. The pacing of the set seems just right. The soloists are all deployed for maximum impact and there is a concern for timbre that goes beyond all of Westbrook's previous efforts. Listen, for example, to the way Surman's soprano combines with Brian Godding's electric guitar on "Construction" and the extensive use of echo on the piece or the use of *sotto voce* brass behind Surman's bass clarinet on "View from the Drawbridge". This is one of Westbrook's loveliest tunes and the arrangement shines and shimmers. There is also a very strong emphasis on rhythm on *Citadel* and the addition of percussionist John Mitchell creates a powerful feeling of movement on sections like "Love and Understanding" and "Bebop De Rigeur". The suite is also beautifully balanced – up-tempo pieces such as the latter are bracketed and separated by gentle, pastoral tunes, while the delicate "Pastorale" with excellent flugelhorn from Henry Lowther is followed by "Sleepwalker Awakening in Sunlight's" three clarinet improvisation, which in turn leads into a swinging and forthright big band setting. It closes with great majesty with Surman's baritone leading the orchestra through "Outgoing Song" and the manic outpouring of "Finale".

Westbrook's achievements mark him as one of the truly great ambassadors of British jazz. His work represents a high water mark in this music that belies (periodic) levels of public and critical neglect that are quite shameful. His career has fortunately been characterized by an inspiring level of commitment and determination. As he once remarked to the author during the course of an interview a few years ago, "People don't realize. This is how we earn our living. There aren't any pension plans in jazz."

We can see in the work of Westbrook, Garrick, Collier, Tippett, Barry Guy and others a readiness to grasp new opportunities in the arts. They were keen to broaden the range of influences and reference points available to the jazz composer, while at the same time expanding the language upon which he/she might draw. They posed new challenges for their musicians and demanded new responses from them. The environment in which they worked had begun to change, not just in terms of the space occupied by British jazz but in terms of the musical skills that were available. Increasingly players were able to draw on formal schooling, as well as a wide knowledge of musical forms from rock, folk and classical music.

For all the sixties' expansion of notions of art, the distinctions remained between high brow, middle brow and low brow. For the first, we mean basically fine art and literature, music, opera, ballet and theatre usually preceded by the word "classical", As far as "middling" taste is concerned, this would be anything that might want to call itself "art" most often preceded by the word "modern". Finally, "low brow" would be defined as anything preceded by the word "popular". In a sense, British jazz – or at least a significant section of it – might have moved closer to the art music of the concert hall but was still at some distance from the kinds of public funding available to opera and classical music.

Nor did it have the support of the record industry to the extent that would have allowed it to secure a market position for itself. It is true that for a brief period, some musicians did have the opportunity to record for major labels. However, company executives had little understanding of how to market this music and were unrealistic in their expectations of quick returns on their investments. In the days before computers, record companies did not have ready access to sales figures and data was compiled manually. Even the accuracy of the pop charts upon which the industry relied was frighteningly impressionistic. Some companies did employ consultants but it is interesting to note that the earliest breakdown of sales figures that the author has been able to locate is from 1977 and was compiled for the British Phonographic Industry. It provides four categories for sales – popular, classical, MOR and others. Nationally, popular accounted for 62 per cent, classical for 12 per cent, MOR 25 per cent and others 1 per cent. There is no indication under which category jazz sales might have been located! It is a sad fact that jazz, whether it should be called "art" or, like other minority musics, must function in the market place.

With or without precise figures, it was clear that, by the beginning of the seventies, British modern jazz found itself in a shrinking market, with even the colleges – once a regular source of work – turning more and more to progressive rock music. Keith Tippett is far from alone in noting the significance of this change:

> Of course you had a university and college circuit then. There used to be a circuit going right down to Plymouth and right up to Stirling. If you were industrious the bandleader or agent could work a tour through England but you can't do that now. In the eighties politics changed anyway and students became apolitical. The majority in the sixties and seventies … there was a strong socialist, left-wing movement and I think that permeated everything and when the eighties comes in there's Capitalism with a big "C" and they'd much rather put on the Who than Don Rendell. It dissipated that college circuit and it's never come back.
>
> (Interview with Keith Tippett, March 2004)

If anything, this trend had become more and more marked from the early seventies onwards. In terms of recording, the replacement of 25 per cent purchase tax by 10 per cent VAT on 1 April 1973 did at least create scope for a number of fledgling independent record companies. Incus, Hazel and Harry Miller's Ogun Records, John Jack's Cadillac and Stan Tracey's Steam imprint were all set up around this point and benefited from the change. At this time, although the market was dominated in overall sales by large retail chains such as Woolworths, W.H. Smith and Boots, record stores such as Harlequin, HMV and Our Price became increasingly powerful. At that time, a lot of discretion was allowed to store managers as to what records they were allowed to stock. There were also a large number of independent stores around, many of whom specialized in different areas of music. But even more important as far as jazz musicians were concerned were direct sales, that is sales at gigs and on tour, as Hazel Miller explains: "We did really well. Our house was full of LPs and the bands were working quite a lot in those days and they were never allowed to go off to a gig or on tour without boxes of LPs under their arms. We sold a lot and so it was gathering momentum" (interview with Hazel Miller, June 2008). This practice had significant advantages. With many musicians looking increasingly to mainland Europe for work, LPs could be taken abroad without going through the requirements of export licences and the like. Income could go directly to the company and the musicians. It worked for a time at least but the combination of an increase in VAT from 8 per cent to 15 per cent during the first Thatcher administration and intensified attention from Customs and Excise made life more difficult. Miller remembers this only too well:

> Then the VAT went up and there were all these problems with exporting. The government ... I couldn't give LPs to people to take abroad because the customs had got hip to it. Derek Bailey was the one that got caught with stuff in his car originally and that put the kybosh on it. They took umbrage and after that all the regulations started coming in. So, we couldn't do it as easily. It still went on but we couldn't do it in the way we used to.
> (Interview with Hazel Miller, June 2008)

It is ironic that while jazz was gaining critical and cultural acceptance, it was increasingly losing out to rock music, which was itself placing increasing emphasis on improvisation and instrumental virtuosity. Jazz musicians, promoters and fans did try to find solutions to the difficulties facing the music at this time. The Jazz Centre Society was established with Brian Blain as chair in 1968 to expand and promote performance opportunities and, eventually, fund a concert and rehearsal space in London. The London Musicians' Co-operative was also set up by several free improvisers and was followed by the more successful and longer-lived London Musicians' Collective (see Wickes 1999, 97; interview with Evan Parker, April 2009).

Despite such efforts, the seventies proved to be years of famine rather than plenty for most British jazz musicians. As doors closed at home, new ones began to open abroad. The more avant-garde players had already established links with counterparts in Germany, Denmark and Holland and jazz had not suffered the same audience decline in Continental Europe. Increasingly, British musicians looked to France, Italy, Germany, Holland, Scandinavia and even eastern Europe. The career of John Surman illustrates this particularly well. An article by Charles Fox from 1972 described Surman as the "Common Market Jazzman". The piece focused on the saxophonist's then ongoing work with bassist Barre Phillips and drummer Stu Martin. Phillips and Martin were both Americans and, though they and Surman had played together in London, the ongoing MU restrictions stopped this becoming a permanent arrangement. As a result, they decamped to a farmhouse outside Brussels and, following several months of rehearsal in autumn 1969, The Trio was born. It lasted just a couple of years, though the three musicians came together several further times up to Martin's untimely death in 1980. Surman was not alone among British musicians in looking to Europe's wider horizons. Nor was he the only one to benefit in the longer term from the associations, musical and otherwise that he established then. Harry Beckett, Harry Miller, Alan Skidmore, Kenny Wheeler, Evan Parker, Derek Bailey, Tony Oxley, Chris McGregor and many others found themselves better able to make a decent living across the Channel than up the M1. For all the efforts of Jenny Lee, Lord Goodman and later Hugh Jenkins, for all the acceptance in certain quarters and for all the attempts at self-help from within the jazz community, jazz could not survive on its own in the context of a market-driven entertainment business. British jazz needed Europe. As Surman told Charles Fox:

> There's no reason why your musical associates shouldn't live hundreds of miles away. European jazz is like a large, spread-out family. Because of the spaciousness nobody need worry that someone is pinching his special gig – which isn't true of a small static scene like London. Continental radio and TV producers have more money to put on shows by artists they like. And more people read what the jazz critics write – they're actually influenced by it, too.
>
> (Fox 1972, 88)

Surman's comments about "Continental radio and TV" are important. Surman did several broadcasts, for example, for Norddeutscher Rundfunk. One of these, from April 1969, has just been released on Cuneiform Records and it reveals Surman leading an Anglo-German ensemble including from Britain Mike Osborne, Alan Skidmore, Malcolm Griffiths, Kenny Wheeler and Ronnie Scott. Another broadcast from 1971, as yet unreleased, saw Surman, Skidmore and Swedish trombonist Eje Thelin playing with Weather Report. As Alan Skidmore recalls:

> That was weird. John [Surman] and I had done some things for North German TV called Jazzwerkstadt. Anyway, they had booked Weather Report, who had only been going a couple of years, for a programme. But the man in charge wasn't sure if they would be any good [laughs], so he decided to invite three European guys he knew very well. That was John, the Swedish trombonist Eje Thelin and me. We ended up being with them for two weeks and played a concert in Berlin at the Philharmonic Hall. The audience was amazing. Talk about roaring for Britain.
>
> (Heining 2008b, 37)

That they were asked to do this was indicative of the respect with which they were held in mainland Europe, as well as the fact that such opportunities existed there. This contrasted with a situation at home where rock was all-conquering, while there simply was not – as yet – an infrastructure that could adequately support the scene.

John Surman's recorded output prior to 1970 had been three albums for Deram. The first, *John Surman* featured one side of jazz-calypsos *à la* Sonny Rollins featuring a band co-led with Trinidadian pianist Russell Henderson, while the second was taken up by a long suite played by an expanded version of Surman's octet. Both sets worked on their own terms but with hindsight the contrast between them is too great. Surman's second album, *How Many Clouds Can You See?*, was much more consistent and reflected the saxophonist's confidence in his own music. Much is rightly made of Surman's abilities as an improviser but *How Many Clouds* revealed what a fine composer he had already become. A clear understanding is evident in his writing of the potential of jazz to grow and develop as an art form. For his third and final Decca release, *Tales of the Algonquin* he shared the project with fellow baritonist and composer John Warren, though Surman's voice on soprano and baritone saxes is well to the fore.

Over the next five years, the array of projects in which Surman was involved was quite staggering. Of these, two – *Shapes*, a recording from 1972 with Mike Osborne, Alan Skidmore, Louis Moholo, Harry Miller and bassist Earl Foreman, and *Way Back When*, a jazz-rock album with Osborne, John Taylor, John Marshall and bass player Brian Odgers – have only become available much later. However, between 1970 and 1975, he recorded *The Trio* (1970; Dawn; Sanctuary) with Barre Phillips and Stu Martin; the "big band" *Conflagration* (1971; Dawn; Sanctuary) with Phillips, Martin, John Taylor, Chick Corea, Kenny Wheeler, Mike Osborne, Harry Beckett and a cast of thousands; *Where Fortune Smiles*, with a quintet including Dave Holland

John Surman at NDR, Hamburg, April 1969. Left to right: Fritz Pauer (piano), Alan Jackson (drums), Harry Miller (bass), John Surman (soprano sax), Alan Skidmore (flute), Ronnie Scott (tenor sax), Mike Osborne (alto sax), Kenny Wheeler (trumpet), Erich Kleinschuster and Malcolm Griffiths (trombones). Photograph courtesy of John Surman, photographer Hans Ernst Müller.

and John McLaughlin (1971; Dawn; Sanctuary); *Live at Woodstock Town Hall* (1975; Dawn; Sanctuary) in a duo with Stu Martin; the solo *Westering Home* (1972); the marvellous jazz-rock *Morning Glory* (1973) with John Taylor, Norwegian guitarist Terje Rypdal, Chris Laurence, Malcolm Griffiths and John Marshall; and *S.O.S.* (1975) with Osborne and Skidmore. In addition, there were semi-official releases of The Trio performing at the Altena Jazz Festival in Germany and Jazz Jamboree in Poland in 1970 and *Alors!!!* a French studio recording of the group playing with French saxophonist Michel Portal and percussionist Jean-Pierre Drouet. There is even a recording of The Trio playing with mainstream trombonist Slide Hampton in Prague in 1971. And this list does not include the other projects where Surman appeared as guest soloist or sideman. The Trio did manage one tour of the UK in 1970. Because Martin and Phillips were Americans, they were part of what Charles Fox calls "a complicated swap, which sent a pop group, the Pink Floyd to the United States" (Fox 1972, 88). The rest of their work was pretty much constant and in Europe, this being prior to Britain entering the Common Market (as it was then) in 1973. No wonder Surman found their two years on the road exhausting.

The majority of these projects were innovative in different ways. Surman was one of the first to explore the use of synthesizers and overdubbing, and *Westering Home* represents a foretaste of the format of solo performance he would later develop with ECM. *S.O.S.* also made effective use of technology, as well as Skidmore's abilities as a drummer, and was one of the first sax-only groupings. The Trio was one of the most forward-thinking groups of the time and together these three musicians established an approach that many a larger ensemble would envy. Indeed, few could match the onslaught and *force majeure* of The Trio in full flight. If anything, their double album was actually less "out" than their live recordings from Altena or Warsaw. Only *Conflagration* disappoints. It is not that it does not contain some strong performances from this expanded unit or that the writing is unsatisfactory. The idea of pairing players, so that there are two basses, two drummers, two saxes and so forth was a good one. It is more the case that too many compositional ideas are presented without being fulfilled. This was never the case with The Trio, and their eponymous album for Dawn is one of the most remarkable to come out of the UK. The empathy between the musicians still amazes but more than that their distinctive backgrounds and interests – Surman's love of folk melodies, Phillips's reputation as one of the finest free jazz bassists and Martin's still more varied musical history with the big bands of Quincy Jones, Duke Ellington, Slide Hampton, Maynard Ferguson as well as small group work with Dexter Gordon, Donald Byrd, Art Farmer and others – somehow produces something unique that transcends and surpasses its elements.

Each of these records has a value of their own, some like *Live at Woodstock* exceed expectation. They include in *Morning Glory* perhaps the finest example of British jazz-rock from the period and in *S.O.S.* one of the most dynamic and exciting recordings of the seventies. Surman's commitment to music-making and developing his art has even extended to the instruments themselves and he has created for himself a whole upper register for the baritone sax. As Ian Carr has said of him:

> John Surman is that rare phenomenon in jazz, a musician who was brilliant and innovative at the beginning of his career and has gone on slowly evolving and maturing, so that in mid-career his music has great technical and emotional breadth and depth. Like Albert Mangelsdorff, he is a major figure who chose to remain in Europe. His compositions, and the evocative moods and atmospheres he creates with electronics, derive in part from his European heritage: his experience of church music as a choirboy, his awareness of folk and ethnic music such as Irish jigs, Scottish reels and laments, his knowledge of European classical music and brass bands. (Carr *et al*. 1987, 480)

So, it remains to be asked, would the interests of British jazz have been served had it remained closer to the world of popular and rock music rather than pursuing a path that led it ever closer to classical and art music? The simple answer is that such a path was never really open to it. Many British rock musicians valued the technical abilities of British jazzers, indeed relied on these at times. Keith Tippett played extensively with Robert Fripp's King Crimson, Henry Lowther worked with Keef Hartley's various bands and Lol Coxhill with Kevin Ayers. However great the applause from the rock audience, such players were always essentially peripheral to the main event. Though some groups – for example, Yes, Manfred Mann, the Nice, Gentle Giant, Hatfield and the North – included jazz elements (or at least extended solos) in their acts, most of these did far better when they dropped such pretensions. Just think of Pink Floyd, Yes and Emerson Lake & Palmer. Nor did British jazz-rock achieve anything like the success of American acts like Herbie Hancock, Chick Corea or Mahavishnu. Jazz, like any musical form, is vulnerable to fads and shifting fashions. However, it is quite a different beast from rock or pop music in this regard. It develops much more slowly and adapts uneasily to the fickleness of the market.

There were two articles in the February 1974 issue of *Into Jazz* that concerned themselves with just these questions. The first was an interview with Ian Carr (Brown 1974, 7–11) in which Carr bemoans the frustrations of working within what he describes as a highly conservative cultural context. For Carr, many of the difficulties facing British jazz lie within the particular development of culture in the UK, in a context dominated by class and the cash nexus. He identifies London's role as the determiner of aesthetic responses as a peculiarly British phenomenon that has blocked the prospects of a more devolved intellectual and cultural life. His analysis, though at times unfocused, seems a pretty fair summation of some of the problems. His solutions range from the realistic (improved public funding) to the utopian (the cultivation of personal relationships with record company executives). Perhaps Carr's comments about the naivety and unprofessionalism of some British jazz musicians are justified. In fairness, Carr did sustain, through a lot of hard work on his part, a very good working relationship with his record company Polygram. By the time that Carr was talking, the record industry was increasingly able to identify from sales figures what sold and what did not, or at least what turned a quick and profitable return and what sold slowly at best.

Carr was one of a group of musicians who formed the Musicians' Action Group around that point. Others included Stan Tracey, Mike Westbrook, Evan Parker, Michael Garrick and Sandy Brown. Simply, their aim was to lobby for improved conditions, notably within the broadcasting and recording industries, and more consistent and generous arts funding. The group and its aims are discussed in Richard M. Sudhalter's article "Patient Healthy; Prognosis Uncertain" (Sudhalter 1974, 34–5). Sudhalter offers a potted history of jazz in Britain from its brief period as popular music, through its passing onto the edges of the entertainment industry to the point where more experimental elements at least had reached out to the fringes of art music. The author's arguments and solutions are far from simple, but they share two things with Carr. First, he concurs regarding the need for a body better able to promote and negotiate terms with the music business than the MU. Second, he believes that jazz musicians have to create a different relationship with their audience – not the one of artist on a pedestal of classical music, nor the rock hero/god or pop idol, but one that is more responsive and democratic. Perhaps British jazz has at last begun to find such a third way, but it has taken a long time and a lot of frustrations to get there, and its present and future still feel far from secure.

13 Lutte Ouvrière

Have nothing in your houses that you do not know to be useful or believe to be beautiful. William Morris, 1880

The ideas of the ruling class are in every epoch the ruling ideas, i.e. the class which is the ruling *material* force of society is at the same time its ruling *intellectual* force. Karl Marx and Friedrich Engels, *The German Ideology*, 1846

In the next two chapters, we will examine the connections between British jazz in the sixties and wider political events and concerns. In this chapter, the emphasis will be on what can broadly be described as "issue-based politics", while in the next the focus will shift to consider the nature of the music itself, its aesthetic and ethical underpinnings and its position within the context of a capitalist market economy. It will be argued that analysis based upon the former actually tells us very little about British jazz of the period, or indeed about politics. By contrast, we will seek to show how an approach based upon an understanding of class and history allows us to explore the interaction between cultural processes and economics in ways that can deepen our awareness of jazz as a social practice. In our examination of links between jazz and politics we will ponder the differences between the situation in Britain and that which applied in the USA and elsewhere in Europe. It will also be necessary to reflect upon key elements in the contrasting origins and histories of jazz and African-American soul music and how these reflect upon the differing fortunes of these forms. This will in turn throw certain core qualities of jazz, here in its British dialect, into sharper relief.

It will be obvious that the sixties was a period of political ferment. Of all of the images one associates with the times, some of the most visually striking focus on protesting youth. From France, Germany, Italy, the USA or Britain, the documentary film-maker or chronicler can summon up pictures of young people throwing stones, confronting riot police or soldiers, carrying placards and marching with arms linked or clenched fists raised. From this perspective, the sixties was a time of protest – against nuclear weapons, for civil rights (in Northern Ireland as in the USA), against war or simply against an authority that was perceived as arbitrary and outdated. Students occupied their campuses and took to the streets, while trades union activists closed factories or staged sit-ins.

As George McKay (2005) notes, British jazz of the period certainly did intersect with wider political and social events. On occasions, such as the CND Aldermaston marches of the early sixties, it did so quite directly. Yet, at others, the relationships between jazz and politics are far less obvious and harder to define. What emerges from close examination of those links that can be identified is that the situation in Britain was different in several important respects from that in the USA or in mainland Europe. It is, in fact, much easier to determine how jazz in the USA or in Germany or Italy connected with radical politics, whether issue-focused or more challenging of the status quo. More than that the form that political protest took in those, and other countries within the North Atlantic Treaty Organization (NATO) alliance, was both more far-reaching and broader in nature than was the case in Britain.

For example, if we look at the way American, and in particular African-American, jazz musicians responded to civil rights issues or to the Vietnam War, we can immediately find many illustrations of this process at work. Max Roach's *We Insist! The Freedom Now Suite*, Sonny Rollins's *The Freedom Suite*, Mingus's *Fables of Faubus*, Archie Shepp's *Fire Music* and *Attica Blues* and Charlie Haden's *Liberation Music Orchestra* provide a testament to struggle. In his intriguing study *Forward Groove* (Searle 2008), Chris Searle explores these and many other records that document black and white political concerns and activity. More than that, Searle succeeds in locating this within a longer tradition of activism within black music and jazz. However, when he turns to the UK, and in particular the sixties and early seventies, the musical examples he gives of British jazz being used as a vehicle for radical political expression are essentially limited to Ken Colyer and CND, Mike Westbrook's *Marching Song*, and the work of the South African Blue Notes and the various bands they formed and led.

In the USA, the issues of African-American civil rights and economic emancipation run through the music, while opposition to the war in South-East Asia seemed at times close to tearing the union apart. Both these struggles and, in particular, that concerning race, contained the potential to become broader campaigns. The civil rights movement in the USA always contained a threat, indeed made explicit by Dr King's "Poor People's Campaign" begun in 1967, that the nature of US capitalism itself might become the subject of challenge (see Fairclough 1983). Meanwhile, the students, hippies, yippies and leftists protesting against the war raised issues about the broader underpinnings of American foreign policy, from its origins in Manifest Destiny and the Monroe Doctrine to the Domino Theory. Archie Shepp, Charlie Haden and George Russell were just three US jazz musicians who made these connections quite explicit (see Heining 2010d).

Further distinctions between Britain and other European countries emerged earlier when we considered the way that jazz, as an American music, was received in the immediate post-war period in Britain as opposed to countries in continental Europe. In France, following the defeat of the Nazis, jazz was seen as the music of liberation. Italy and Germany might have been in a different position, having been both defeated by the Allied powers and liberated by them. However, in these countries too, and elsewhere in those parts of continental Europe occupied by the Nazis, jazz emerged as a powerful force representing freedom from tyranny and a more democratic way of life.

The enthusiasm for jazz was just as great in Britain but its associations with freedom and liberation, and therefore politics, seemed to resonate more immediately on the continent than in the UK. In addition, the connections between jazz and left-wing politics have remained much clearer in mainland Europe. As Mike Westbrook notes:

> The Left in France has always allied itself with progressive ideas in the arts and the same is true in Italy, which we saw a lot of. Some of the major avant-garde music festivals were promoted by Communist councils. These huge festivals, we used to tour with Henry Cow and with the Brass Band and used to play these enormous popular events that were mounted by the left. Here, we never had that alliance between the left and progressive ideas in the Arts. That never really happened, possibly in the immediate post-war period in the Jennie Lee era when the Arts Council was more or less founded in its present form. Then there was more of an awareness of the social importance of the Arts but on the whole we haven't had this thing and, of course, it's not as you say with the current [New Labour] government. They're a total bunch of philistines.
>
> (Interview with Mike Westbrook, January 2006)

As we have seen, Enrico Rava made a similar point in a *Jazzwise* article in 2001, when he noted the connection between the left in Italy and jazz through the political festivals organized by the Communist and Socialist parties in the sixties and seventies (Heining 2001c, 40).

Interviewed recently for the Italian All About Jazz website, Westbrook expands on his previous comments and offers a pretty comprehensive survey of the period and of the differences between the socio-political context of jazz in Britain and that applying in mainland Europe:

It seems to me that the revolutionary student activities of '68 which had a major effect in Italy, France and Germany had little long term impact in the UK. I am no expert, but I don't think there was a rapport between the student movement and the British working class, on one hand, or the cultural avant garde on the other. Our experience was different in France and Italy particularly, when we played in the Orckestra with Henry Cow in the mid '70s at left wing rallies and student-promoted concerts and festivals. There were two concerts in The Round House, organised by the Communist Party, and the Morning Star, but on the whole the attempt to bring jazz and contemporary music into the cause of political change was not as successful as in other countries.

From the early '60s modern jazz had a following in the universities and for a time the new music seemed to accord with student cultural and political aspirations. My band did many college gigs. Jazz, because of its history, its internationalism, commitment to individual freedom within the community, perhaps should be the art of social and political change. However, true jazz demands creative freedom, and is opposed to orthodoxies of all kinds. It is a sophisticated and demanding art in its own right. Rock music, with its simplicity and truisms became the preferred musical expression of the '60s generation in this country. However, there was a general opening up, culturally and socially, that persisted into the '70s on the fringes with which jazz was involved. Performances with the multi media group The Cosmic Circus in colleges and elsewhere continued into the early '70s. With the Brass Band we took part in political rallies, community arts, alternative arts festivals (as in Bath), a Tribune Rally, and at one point the *Rote Leider* Festival in East Berlin. It seemed there was desire in left wing circles in Europe to embrace the *avant garde* in the building of a new society. We still find traces of that idealism, of the Alternative Culture the Underground, existing around Europe. We find very little of it in Britain. And we did notice that throughout Europe when big cities swung to the right, sponsorship of jazz festivals and contemporary Art in general abruptly ceased. (Santosuosso and Casanova 2011)

Kate, Westbrook's partner and musical collaborator, taught in Leeds in the late sixties. In the same article, she echoes these points, recalling both the increase in student activism in the late sixties but also the differences that she saw between the European situation and that in Britain:

There were pockets of radicalism in the UK in 1968, and Leeds University was one of them. I was teaching part-time then at

Leeds College of Art, just before I joined Mike Westbrook's Brass Band. In the immediate aftermath of the '68 unrest, it seems to me that in general it was the musicians involved in "Free Jazz" who laid claim to the radical crown in music. The dilemma for those musicians, was that their music didn't appeal to the mass audience with whom they wished to be connected. Those musical sophisticates, (among them Cornelius Cardew and his circle), whilst enjoying recognition from the cultural elite, wanted to reach a larger audience and so went for simpler music, but had only limited success in touching a popular pulse. The UK Musicians' Union supported the important Grunwick strikes of the mid-'70s. The Brass Band marched in solidarity with workers from the Grunwick factory, as did Cornelius and his band. But as far as we were concerned, these efforts had little long term impact on the comfortable '80s and in England we saw the end of that attempt to bring together jazz with political change.

(Santosuosso and Casanova 2011)

We can see further differences in the levels of anger and ferocity that accompanied political events during the sixties when we compare the USA, France, Italy and Germany with Britain. The USA saw ghetto riots and demonstrations which threatened to disrupt political and economic life, while middle America watched the beating and shooting of its children in Chicago, in San Francisco and at Kent State, Ohio. France saw student occupations of universities and worker occupations of factories mushroom into a general strike in May 1968. Germany experienced riots in many of its major cities, while Italy experienced strikes and sit-ins. But young Britons did not face the draft like their American peers. They did not burn the Union Jack the way their counterparts in the USA burned the Stars and Stripes, and Grosvenor Square's two demonstrations – 17 March and 27 October – had nothing on Paris 1968.

In London in March 1968, 6,000 of the 25,000 anti-war demonstrators broke away from the main march intending to storm and immobilize the US Embassy in the West End of London. They encountered "flailing truncheons and a charge by mounted police – but no tear gas". Some 246 people were charged with public order offences, while 117 police and 45 demonstrators received medical attention (see Caute 1988, 72). Despite the *Times*' prediction of 5 September, the "Militant plot feared in London" planned by a "small army of militant extremists" to seize control of "highly sensitive installations and buildings in Central London" did not materialize at the next demonstration in October that year. Three thousand activists did again try to storm the citadel but were rebuffed. This time, there were just eleven arrests and twenty-five police officers, and twenty-two protestors were given medical attention (see Caute 1988, 313). Unlike the May events in Paris, spring protests in Italy, demonstrations throughout Germany from spring into summer or the police riot in Mayor Daley's Chicago in August, the actions of both police and marchers seemed proscribed by an unspoken code of conduct (see Marwick 1998, particularly chapters 11 and 12; Caute 1988, particularly chapters 5, 6, 11, 12 and 16; Mailer 1968). There were no water cannons, riot sticks or tear gas. Cars were not turned into street barricades or set on fire. Paving stones were not ripped from the ground and thrown at police. And no-one got shot.

In some ways, the limits here were not just self-imposed but existed within the very politics themselves. As noted, the civil rights movement in the USA threatened to become an economic campaign aimed at the very nature of US capitalism itself, while anti-Vietnam protests were questioning the legitimacy of American foreign policy. With regard to France, David Caute suggests that in May 1968, "France had come out on general strike by national reflex." Adding that, "The strikers of May 1968 were playing 'Republicans' against 'Kings' on a historical board-game which is not available for example in the British or German cultures, still less the American" (Caute 1988, 226).

While Caute's observations carry some weight, events in France did go further than in any of the countries of the North Atlantic area, with the possible exception of Italy. Theirs was, however choreographed, a genuine challenge to the state. In Germany as well, protests expanded beyond their immediate causes and frustrations. As the philosopher Jürgen Habermas argued in 1967, the students were no longer pursuing university reform but instead were seeking "the immediate overthrow of social structures" (quoted in Caute 1988, 81). In West Germany, unlike in France and (to a degree) in Italy, the gap between students and workers was far wider. However, the establishment of a coalition government of the Christian and Social Democrats, which effectively created a parliament without a real opposition and which many saw as an unholy alliance, did lend a greater legitimacy to the SDS (the German Student Socialist League led by Rudi Dutschke) and to the broader Außer Parliamentarische Opposition (APO). The issue for these young Germans was, like their French comrades, the very legitimacy of the state (Mager 1967).

There were other differences between the British situation and that elsewhere. While the Vietnam Solidarity Campaign provided coordination in respect of that issue, the left in Britain was fragmented into quite small and specific organizations. There were the three main Trotskyist groups – the International Socialists (later the Socialist Workers' Party), the Socialist Labour League (later the Workers' Revolutionary Party) and the International Marxist Group. Of less significance in this context were the Militant Tendency, which functioned within the Labour Party, and the Communist Party of Great Britain. In terms of the coordination of student protests, such as the occupations of the London School Of Economics, Hornsey College of Art, Essex University and elsewhere, this took place through local students' unions and was often driven by college Socialist Society members (see Crouch 1970; Cockburn and Blackburn 1970; Hornsey College of Art Students and Staff 1969). However, in Britain protest remained focused in the main on educational reform or on Vietnam. Such concerns might have been common across Britain, North America and continental Europe, and, in Britain, Vietnam had replaced CND as the main focus of leftist activity. Nevertheless, in the USA and in Germany, France and Italy, very early on, activism was reaching beyond single issues. More than that, in Europe and in the USA, the "movement" was not just broader but drew sustenance from a surprising alliance drawn from the counter-culture (hippies, yippies, diggers *et al.*), anarchists (in France and Italy, the Situationists were very influential), student organizations and the new left. In the UK, the gaze looked no wider than southeast Asia and university reform.

If anything, as Kate Westbrook seems to suggest, the period 1970–4 and after in Britain saw a much stronger and broader political engagement than was the case in the 1960s. Ireland became a major issue for the left, while industrial militancy – political in terms of the Heath Government's Industrial Relations Bill and economic in the form of two national mineworkers' strikes and another by building workers – intensified. There were also a number of worker occupations, most notably of Upper Clyde Shipworkers (UCS) in Glasgow, and there were rent strikes in deprived areas of the north of England, as several Labour councils refused to implement council house rent increases. In respect of foreign affairs, Vietnam continued to be an issue, as did apartheid in South Africa and Rhodesia and, following the US-sponsored coup d'état, Chile. Two Conservative government ministers were implicated in questionable property deals, while the Angry Brigade attempted to promote armed insurrection. At the same time, the role of the police became more obviously politicized in their action against striking workers, surveillance of Irish and Black British militants, and in prosecutions of *Oz* magazine and *Gay News*.

These distinctions between Britain and mainland Europe, and between Britain and the USA, define the broader political context with which British jazz might have engaged in the period under study. Where Searle's *Forward Groove* (2008) examines the relationship between politics and jazz in a Northern Atlantic context, George McKay's *Circular Breathing* (2005) seeks more specifically to elaborate "The Cultural Politics of Jazz in Britain". Towards the end of his book McKay reflects upon the territory he has mapped out:

> I have sought to trace jazzy inflections on, and direct incursions into, British communist organizations, the New Left, the anti-nuclear and peace movements, anti-apartheid and postcolonial identities and campaigns, anti-racist mobilizations, gay liberation, and the women's movement, among others. The foundational fluidity

of the form, so confirmatory for its participants of a political openness, has granted me a definitional openness: where relevant I have been comfortable with using as well as looking at "jazz" in relation to other practices of dance band music, folk, calypso, avant-garde, rock, pop. This is not to say that the liberationist rhetoric of "political" jazz should be accepted from any source, nor that my construction of such a social culture is all-inclusive or complete. Of course, there are persistent and important obstacles and problems in any such reading, and I have identified and explored the limit points – jazz as American propaganda, exoticism and racism from its white British enthusiasts, anti-jazzisms in music organizations and cultural establishments, jazz as a consensual heteropatriarchal culture. But I have tried to alter the scape of British jazz understanding to include its compelling engagement with social activisms. (McKay 2005, 302)

He adds, "My purpose has not at all been to claim jazz as some sort of purely ideological culture: *it has rather been to refigure British jazz history to more comprehensively include its ideological assumptions and actions*" (McKay 2005, 302–3; emphasis original).

The clearest examples of social/political engagement by British jazz musicians and fans, as McKay notes, can be found in the CND Aldermaston marches between 1958 and 1962, in the response of jazz musicians and others to the Notting Hill and Nottingham race riots and later support for the movement against apartheid in South Africa. However, even in these examples, the problem for McKay and Searle in examining the British jazz/political context lies in the fact that one is faced by contradictory evidence. On the one hand, it is clear that there were strong ties between the left and British traditional jazz in the 1940s and 1950s. Jim Godbolt notes that it was the Young Communist League that promoted concerts by George Webb's Dixielanders and that the executive committee of the National Federation of Jazz Organisations included "two hard-line Communists" (Godbolt 1989, 22 and 24). As he later points out the MU executive in the fifties was dominated by members of the Communist Party (Godbolt 1989, 170). One or two musicians – notably saxophonist Harry Gold and trombonist Paul Rutherford – were Communist Party members, as were writers Brian Blain, Francis Newton and Max Jones. One might add that Ken Colyer's Omega Brass Band "frequently appeared at left-wing demonstrations" (McKay 2005, 51). However, these seem very fine, fragile threads upon which to hang an argument about the political orientation of British jazz, its musicians and fans.

McKay does succeed in showing that the ideas he refers to and music he discusses function within a dynamic system that is never overly deterministic. Yet the dilemma he faces in providing a coherent analysis of the links, if any, between British jazz and politics and between youth subcultures and political activism lies both in the material itself and the way he interrogates it. He appears to be attempting to sew together what seem to be vastly different strands into a coherent tapestry and it is as if the material will not stand the weight he wants to bestow upon it. This is most obvious in his discussion of traditional jazz and CND. In his own terms, McKay sets out to present the "New Orleans parade band in Britain" as *a leftist marching music of the streets*" (original italics), explaining this as follows:

> I seek to shift the balance slightly in the study of a social movement organization (the Campaign For Nuclear Disarmament, or CND, founded in 1958) from considering it in terms of its "official" history toward its cultural contribution and innovation. CND's early subcultural politics mainly happened during the annual three-day Aldermaston protest marches, to a soundtrack of jazz and folk. (McKay 2005, 47)

The links between jazz, its fans and at least some of its musicians, and CND in its early days is well-established (see Green 1998a, b; Melly 1970; Nuttall 1970; Minnion and Bolsover 1983). CND grew amazingly quickly from its beginnings in 1957 and at its height had 1,000 local branches throughout the UK. Folk singer Ian Campbell recalled in the 1980s those heady, early days of the campaign:

> It is significant that 1958, the year that saw the climatic boom in jazz popularity, also produced the first Aldermaston march. The jazz revival and the rise of CND were more than coincidental; they were almost two sides of the same coin. Similar social attitudes and positive human values informed them both. At any jazz event a liberal sprinkling of CND badges, and perhaps even leaflets and posters, would be in evidence; conversely, at every CND demonstration live jazz music set the tempo for the march. (Minnion and Bolsover 1983, 115)

According to Jeff Nuttall, numbers marching from Aldermaston rose from 10,000 initially to 100,000 by the final major event. Nuttall may be forgiven some poetic licence in describing its carnival atmosphere: "Furthermore, although teenagers made up by no means the bulk of the marchers, as the square press consistently claimed they did, they nevertheless made each march into a carnival of optimism" (Nuttall 1970, 47). And he continued:

> It was this wild public festival spirit that spread the CND symbol through all the jazz clubs and secondary schools in an incredibly short time. Protest was associated with festivity. There was a new feeling of licence granted by the obvious humanitarian attitude of the ravers themselves. (Nuttall 1970, 47)

And yet, it has to be noted that, despite this activity and the participation of British traditional and revivalist musicians (amateur and professional), it is hard to identify a single piece of recorded British jazz from the period that sought to express either the genuine fear of the Aldermaston marchers or the festival-like atmosphere that Nuttall describes. Perhaps the fear was all too real and immediate for such expression. The same is, of course, not the case when one looks at the other musical strand that connected with the campaign – folk music. John Brunner's song "The H-bomb's Thunder" became the unofficial anthem of CND and Collector Records released an EP, *Songs from Aldermaston* (JEP 3005), while Topic Records put out an LP, *Songs Against the Bomb* (Topic 12001), featuring Ewan McColl, Peggy Seeger, Leon Rosselson, Fred Dallas and the London Youth Choir.

In one sense, McKay is seeking to understand British jazz in this context in terms of "subcultural politics" and in terms of his notion of "carnival", something that one suspects would have appealed to Nuttall. This, for McKay, seems to function as a kind of "refusal", in its sociological sense, among its participants. However, with regard to the issue of subcultural politics, it is unclear whether the author has established successfully that the jazz fans, and musicians who came together on these marches can really be described as a genuine "subculture" at all. The British sociologist Dick Hebdige certainly sees it as such (Hebdige 1980, 51), and McKay's designation of the jazz-loving protesters in such terms would seem to be supported by definitions offered by both Sarah Thornton (1995) and Ken Gelder (Gelder and Thornton 2007). There is also some suggestion that certain traditional jazz fans and CND supporters would go on to play a part in the formation of the underground/counter-culture (see Green 1998a, b; Denselow 1990, 93; Nuttall 1970). Nevertheless, it is easier to trace through specific figures who would shape the London underground scene – Michael Horovitz, Barry Miles, Pete Brown, Adrian Mitchell, John Dunbar, John Hopkins, Peter Jenner, Alan Beckett – a shared interest in modern and avant-garde jazz. As we have argued earlier, the same could be said of many of the musicians who helped shape the late sixties rock scene.

More than that, the group that McKay describes seems to have been a very transitory one both in respect of its interest in the anti-nuclear campaign and traditional jazz. Whereas other subcultures of the period – teddy boys, mods, hippies, skinheads and, later, punks – left behind a legacy associated with particular identifiable styles of dress, behaviour and attitudes, this was not the case with these young people. We are talking about at most of a period of four years, a period that also covers the lifespan of the Beaulieu festivals. Trad's popularity was already on the wane by the time the Beatles arrived. The allegiance of students and young people had already begun to lean more towards R&B or modern jazz, and CND's membership decline was not caused by such ephemeral shifts in taste but rather by the Cuban Missile Crisis and its aftermath. In this sense, the group that McKay describes might constitute a "proto-subculture" but beyond that it seems that he is stretching the definition.

The late Frank Allaun, Labour MP and peace activist, considered the Partial Test Ban Treaty of 1963, which followed the Cuban crisis, to be the main factor in the waning support for CND at that time (Minnion and Bolsover 1983, 56–9). Other factors were also involved, not least the splitting of the movement between those supporting and those opposing direct action. This was perhaps both consequence and cause. Nigel Young has noted that CND actually experienced a temporary renewal in its growth in early 1963 but acknowledges that this was short-lived (Minnion and Bolsover 1983, 61–3). For some, there seemed to be a noticeable change in atmosphere within British society following the "resolution" of the Cuban Missile Crisis. For Michael Garrick, it represented almost a cultural watershed, as he explained in an interview for *Jazz UK*:

> It was part political, part social. After the Cuban Missile Crisis, America seemed to have got things under control. People were no longer absolutely scared stiff of the Russians. I was involved in Poetry & Jazz and the poets were writing about it in very bitter terms. That passed and the sixties then emerged and people relaxed. (Heining 2003a)

Growing concern over America's involvement in southeast Asia also impacted on CND, as many activists switched their attention to that cause over the next few years. That CND declined in this period is evident: by 1970 it had just over 2,000 members. While the period 1958–62 is seen as CND's heyday, if anything the campaign became even more politically significant in the late seventies and early eighties in the face of Margaret Thatcher's decision to provide a home for US Air Force Cruise Missiles, a first-strike weapon of mass destruction. Between 1980 and 1984, CND's membership increased from 9,000 to 100,000 (Byrne 1997, 91).

The fan base for traditional jazz also seems to have been much wider than just these "beatniks", as the attendance at the Beaulieu and other festivals would seem to suggest. Looking at that aspect, and the musicians looked to by such fans, we see a somewhat heterogeneous group. If, as McKay suggests, the likes of Lyttelton, Melly, Colyer and Nuttall and certain of their fans supported CND, then what of the rest? What indeed do we know of the views of Barber, Bilk, Ball, Lightfoot, Dick Charlesworth or The Temperance Seven or those of their fans on CND?

McKay is talking only of a section of the jazz community of fans and musicians. That a section of that community intersected with CND seems clear but, unless we know how widespread such perceptions were, we must struggle to judge its significance. Here, and elsewhere, McKay relies on an understanding of political activism and politics that is quite limited and limiting in its scope. CND was a single issue campaign, for all the anti-American sentiment that might have underpinned it. As such it was a movement that drew extensively on middle class support (see Marwick 1998, 65–6; Masters 1985, 195–216). As Arthur Marwick notes:

> It was not a youth movement. It was not really a part of youth subculture. It does provide a link between the New Left revival of the mid-1950s, and the radical student movements of the middle and late sixties; it also provided a symbol, the upturned "Y", and a badge, which many young protesters sported for the rest of the decade, even if not directly associated with CND. But on the whole it highlights the fact that political radicalism at this stage was a general feature neither of working-class nor of middle-class youth. (Marwick 1998, 66)

The potential ramifications of the campaign in terms of Britain's wider world role, its "special relationship" with the USA, its NATO commitments and its arms exports were certainly not lost on British politicians. The right-wing Labour leader Hugh Gaitskell fought to overturn the party's 1960 conference decision committing Labour in government to abolishing Britain's nuclear deterrent, and succeeded in doing so in 1961. Even the crown prince of the Labour left, Aneurin Bevan, had spoken against unilateral disarmament at the 1957 conference citing as the reason for his opposition the effect this would have upon Britain's relationship with its allies. According to one source (Parkin 1968, 39), some 75 per cent of CND supporters were Labour voters. Some, at least, may well have understood the implications of the action they proposed and considered these positives rather than negatives. And yet CND was at that time essentially a moral campaign, supported as well by liberals and many whose views on the matter derived first from religious rather than political beliefs. Its primary focus was on disarmament and upon the moral lead that this might give Britain in global politics.

The connections between CND and British jazz of the period do need highlighting. However, McKay leaves two key questions unanswered. What do these links tell us about British politics and what do they say about British jazz? We do know that such connections seem to have been short-lived. British jazz musicians and fans may well have opposed US involvement in Vietnam but we have no evidence of this on any scale let alone on the kind of level that seems to have applied to CND. We do know that CND's support within the general populace at the time of the Aldermaston marches was between 25 and 33% of the electorate. This might not have been a majority but it would indicate a significant level of concern among the population. Perhaps the strongest conclusion we can draw from the relationship between sections of the jazz community in Britain and CND is that it reflected those same concerns. This would hardly be surprising. To argue for a greater significance would suggest an understanding of politics defined in essentially liberal terms; that is in terms of issue-based political activity, of interest and pressure groups seeking to influence government policy. There is certainly no evidence here of a more far-reaching political understanding seeking to achieve system change. Should the "New Orleans parade band in Britain" be seen as "*a leftist marching music of the streets*", as McKay claims? At most, we might allow "leftish" but not "leftist".

Questions of race and opposition to racism also provided a link between British jazz and wider social issues. Given the origins of jazz, this is not too surprising. Indeed, it would be very sad were it otherwise. British jazz magazines featured articles on the subject (see for example Capel 1961; Postgate 1963), while many of the titles published by the Jazz Book Club revealed a similar understanding of the impact of slavery and racism upon African-Americans. This might be explicit in a volume such as Jewish-American clarinettist Mezz Mezzrow's autobiography, *Really the Blues* (Mezzrow and Wolfe 1959), or acknowledged in passing as in Francis Newton's *The Jazz Scene* (1959) or in Rex Harris's *Enjoying Jazz* (1961, 19–20). *Melody Maker* also featured news items on the MU boycott of South Africa. While it gave space to those pop artists, like Cliff Richard and Clyde and Jeremy who defied the ban, it was more generally supportive of those – John Dankworth, Dusty Springfield, The Rolling Stones and others – who supported it.

As George McKay again points out, the nascent London jazz community responded promptly to the Notting Hill and Nottingham Riots and were instrumental in the formation of the Stars' Campaign for Inter-Racial Friendship. Those involved included not only musicians like John Dankworth, Cleo Laine, Humphrey Lyttelton, Ottilie Patterson, Tubby Hayes, Ronnie Scott, Mick Mulligan, Chris Barber, Ted Heath and Ken Colyer, but critics Max Jones and Francis Newton and author Colin MacInnes as well (McKay 2005, 124). Lonnie Donegan and folk singer and critic Karl Dallas were also actively involved in the campaign, while other signatories included Tommy Steele, Marty Wilde, Peter Sellers, Harry Secombe, Dickie Valentine, Matt Monro and Frankie Vaughan. The signed statement read:

> At a time when reason has given way to violence in parts of Britain, we, people of all races in the world of entertainment, appeal to the public to reject racial discrimination in any shape or form. Violence will settle nothing; it will only cause suffering to innocent people and create fresh grievances. We appeal to our audiences everywhere to join us in opposing any and every aspect of colour prejudice wherever it may appear.
>
> (*Melody Maker* 1958, 1)

It should also be noted that *Melody Maker* announced the campaign on its front page and stated its own position categorically:

At the time of the MELODY MAKER going to press it was apparent that the P.1 statement of attitude would find support throughout the profession which, itself, practices no discrimination as to the class, colour, race or creed of the audience before which it appears. It is perhaps superfluous to state that the MELODY MAKER wholeheartedly supports the viewpoint expressed and urges its serious attention upon its readers.

(*Melody Maker* 1958, 16)

To a modern readership, the language may sound dated and reflective of earlier times. Yet, it is unequivocal and suggests that, after years during which Britain's two main political parties have sought to appease racism and racists, in some respects, we may have lost more as a society than we have gained since then. Given the prevalence of racist views across British society at that time, several of those signatories – Tommy Steele, Ted Heath, Marty Wilde and others – took a risk with their popularity and their audience to take a stand. That surely matters more than the actual words used.

These two areas of Britain were already in severe decline when the riots took place, and white residents living there did so at standards lower than most working class Londoners or Midlanders (Sandbrook 2006). The white attacks on black immigrants in August 1958 in Notting Hill, and Nottingham, followed a long build-up of ongoing assaults on black people by white gangs. As in so many dilapidated and desperate areas, the law was barely enforced and, when it was, it was done so arbitrarily. Mosley's fascist Union Movement was active in Notting Hill and according to Val Wilmer had taken part in the disturbances (Wilmer 1991, 51). This is confirmed by a *Kensington News* report of the time (Sandbrook 2006, 337). The Nazi Colin Jordan and his White Defence League (sound familiar?) were also quick to try to capitalize on this outbreak of white racist thuggery. Jordan had even attempted to storm the stage of a Labour election rally in Notting Hill but had been prevented from doing so by a swift right hook from later Defence Secretary and Chancellor of the Exchequer, Denis Healey. In a BBC news item following the setting up of the Stars' Campaign, John Dankworth and Lonnie Donegan were both interviewed. Like Denis Healey, neither Dankworth nor Donegan pulled their punches.

South Africa was another issue of ongoing concern to British jazz musicians. Although John Dankworth had visited and played in the country in 1954, as he notes in *Jazz – In Revolution* (Dankworth 1998), this was prior to apartheid. He spent time there with British-born pianist Dave Lee (Lee was later one of the founders of Jazz FM). Lee left Dankworth with no illusions about the nature of South Africa, and its racism, injustice and corruption. In fact, Dankworth describes him as "the first dissident I had met in my life" (Dankworth 1998, 107). On his return, Dankworth was offered a substantial sum to tour South Africa with his orchestra. In fact, the bandleader was one of the first to register his support for Bishop Trevor Huddleston's call for a cultural boycott of South Africa. In 1957, the Dankworth band played a benefit concert for Christian Aid's South Africa Treason Trial Fund in support of Mandela, Oliver Tambo, Joe Slavo and 153 other opponents of the racist state. Dankworth notes that Humphrey Lyttelton, American bandleader Lionel Hampton and others were quick to support Christian Aid's work in this respect (Dankworth 1998, 108).

However, Dankworth's stand was based on personal principle rather than political allegiance, as he explains:

> My refusal to go to South Africa had other repercussions on my life apart from being considered a sort of "safe house" for escapees from the regime. I had hitherto been totally non-political, in common with the majority of people in arts and entertainment – it was then the British tradition for such people to be seen as unaligned. (Dankworth 1998, 110)

He found himself being asked to support all manner of causes from opposition to blood sports and the campaign to abolish capital punishment:

> I did in fact espouse some of these causes (I spoke at the Royal Albert Hall against capital punishment), but I was somewhat irritated to find that in the eyes of some, all issues proposing change to existing law or practice were the responsibility of the left. Some of the crusades I was asked to join I considered should be treated as cross-party matters, and felt strongly that racialism was one of them. To make it a party issue would alienate lots of would-be sympathisers. (Dankworth 1998, 110)

With regard to the Stars' Campaign, Dankworth sums up its aim in terms of giving "prominence via the media to the fact that most celebrities had liberal views on race" (Dankworth 1998, 111). Dankworth is far from alone in taking such a line. CND's campaign both in the late fifties and early sixties and in the eighties also brought together some strange political bedfellows. Indeed, many later campaigns such as the Anti-Nazi League have also relied on such broad-based support.

Further support for the struggle against apartheid came from a new generation of British jazz musicians in the late sixties and early seventies. Given the involvement of players like John Surman, Mike Osborne and Evan Parker with Chris McGregor, Louis Moholo, Dudu Pukwana, Harry Miller and other South Africans, this was an issue that was personal and moral at the same time. As Evan Parker notes, the very first Brotherhood of Breath concert at London's Notre Dame Hall was a benefit for the anti-apartheid movement.

We can also see attempts by musicians to organize themselves in campaigning or at least promotional organizations. In 1966, bassist Danny Thompson created the Fellowship of British Jazz Musicians to bypass the booking agencies that many musicians felt were exploiting them (interview with Danny Thompson, February 2009). Then in 1968, a number of musicians, fans, writers and others based in London set up the Jazz Centre Society. Those involved included a number of key individuals on the scene, including Brian Blain (MU activist, writer and promoter) Charles Alexander (later proprietor of *Jazzwise Magazine*), John Jack (Cadillac Records) and writer/broadcaster Charles Fox. From the outset, there seem to have been differences of opinion within the committee about quite what was required – whether this should be some kind of promotion/booking agency or whether it should seek to establish a permanent base in the capital and, if so, what exactly this might require. In the end a great deal of money was raised, premises were found in Covent Garden, architects employed and builders engaged. The project was due to open in spring 1985 with a performance by Mike Westbrook's band. It never happened. The money simply ran out (interviews with Mike Westbrook, March 1996; John Jack, June 2008; George Foster, March 2009).

Other attempts at self-organization were more successful. A year after the formation of the Jazz Centre Society, a number of free improvisers, feeling that their music was not being adequately represented, separated from the society and formed the Musicians' Co-operative. The Co-op involved Evan Parker, Derek Bailey, Barry Guy, Howard Riley, Paul Rutherford, drummer Paul Lytton, John Stevens and Trevor Watts, though Watts and Stevens later rejoined the Jazz Centre Society. After some initial success, the Co-operative began to struggle to sustain itself. Ironically, several of its members had been successful in developing links with other musicians in Europe and as a consequence found it increasingly hard to sustain commitments to the Co-operative (Wickes 1999, 97). In 1975, the London Musicians' Collective was set up by a slightly younger generation of improvisers and continues to this day (Bell 1999).

One of the problems facing working musicians when it comes to any form of collectivism is the matter of time. They work as individuals, to an extent isolated from each other, and much of their lives are taken up by the need to earn a living. Alan Skidmore described his working schedule in the late sixties in a *Jazzwise* article in 2008:

> I was with the BBC Radio Orchestra during the day time and I'd go home to get something to eat, get changed and get to The Talk Of The Town. I'd get back about one or two in the morning, maybe later if I went to The Old Place in Gerrard Street. Then, I'd get up very early to get back to Bond Street to work at the BBC.
> (Heining 2008b, 34)

This kind of regimen was not untypical for many British jazz musicians and militated against the kind of self-organization that can be seen in other areas of the arts. In some ways, it also makes it harder for individual musicians to engage in political activity or indeed any activity outside of music.

So far, we have examined a number of examples of political engagement by the British jazz community. However, it is hard to see how these could be construed to present a consistent, coherent and representative picture of the cultural politics of the scene at that time. What does perhaps emerge is the willingness on the part of some fans and musicians to take a moral stand. We simply do not know how widespread such stances might have been. In fairness to George McKay, he does not solely rely upon activism or personal statement in building his case. He also looks at race, gender, anti-commercialism and anti-Americanism as well. An example of this broader approach can be seen in his attempt to construct a new understanding of "whiteness" as opposed to the word's racist associations with the American South, apartheid South Africa and Nazi Germany. This would clearly act as one manifestation of the "politics" of jazz, namely as an expression of "whiteness" that is opposed to racism. However, McKay notes:

> The simple facts are that there are questions about whiteness in jazz in Britain that need to be explored, that have not been explored in the past, and that there are also striking black contributions to the development of the music in Britain which themselves warrant – demand – serious critical appraisal.
>
> (McKay 2005, 90–1)

One might agree that this is problematic and accept that without such a definition white anti-racists cannot counterpose a radical, white identity against the reactionary, right-wing "patriotism" of the BNP. McKay may well be right that whiteness in British jazz has not been explored adequately in the past and that this needs to be rectified, however, even generalist books on British jazz would barely fill a library shelf let alone a whole section. It is perhaps less the result of a racial lacuna, as much as one of lack of opportunity and of the non-commercial nature of books on British jazz. It is unfair, however, to argue as he does that the contribution of black musicians to British jazz have been ignored. Alyn Shipton makes reference to it in his *A New History of Jazz*; John Wickes (in a book from which McKay quotes several large sections) clearly addresses this and he devotes a whole chapter to the Blue Notes; Val Wilmer and Dick Heckstall-Smith have both considered the issue; Northway Books have published books on/or by black British jazz musicians such as Coleridge Goode, Leslie Thompson and Joe Harriott; while Roger Cotterrell in his postscript to Ian Carr's *The Music Outside* (Carr 2008, 168–9) addresses succinctly the issue of Joe Harriott's later neglect and lack of influence. McKay's remarks are even more curious given his reference to the

CD compilation *Black British Swing* (Topic TSCD781), which is subtitled *The African Diaspora's Contribution to England's Own Jazz of the 1930s & 1940s.* McKay draws on Andrew Simons's excellent notes in telling a story which, at the same time, he also claims has been ignored. The larger question that surely needs to be raised here is that of the marginalization of jazz within wider cultural discourses and practices.

In a recent article, Alan Stanbridge (2008) attempts to do just this by exploring the relationship between jazz and mainstream culture, and by raising questions about the reasons why jazz functions at the periphery of the world of music and culture. His essay has quite a broad sweep covering the use of jazz to convey marginal lifestyles of characters in films and the creation – by Wynton Marsalis, Stanley Crouch, Albert Murray and others – of a narrow and limited jazz history that can be sold to (predominantly) white commercial and political interests. Further to this, Stanbridge is critical of the effectiveness of arguments in support of public arts funding made by supporters of jazz and other minority arts based upon the assumed social or economic benefits that culture can offer society, and he also decries what he sees as the elitism often associated with avant-garde cultural activity. He is particularly critical of claims made by some practitioners and critics for the communitarian potential of, for example, improvised music. He notes:

> Various forms of contemporary jazz and improvised music continued to develop, independent of these mainstream pressures and often self-consciously – and proudly – aware of their cultural marginality. The roots of this perspective can be traced back to the bebop revolution of the 1940s, in which primarily black musicians adopted a specifically non-commercial stance in the face of the commercial success of a predominantly white swing music. Since, that time, the marginal status of particular forms of jazz and improvised music has often been linked to an oppositional politics, most notably in the Black Nationalist agenda of 1960s free jazz. Claims for the socio-political potential of artistic practice are not peculiar to jazz, however, and the discourse of social and political relevance has been a common trope in various arts disciplines. (Stanbridge 2008)

Going further still, Stanbridge questions claims for the marginality of such approaches, in particular in the USA, where noted avant garde figures such as Anthony Braxton and George Lewis hold professorships at major music schools. Far from weakening their political positions, he argues that – in parallel with the success of abstract art and even antagonistic forms such as Dada in invading the institutions of fine art – this mainstreaming might actually increase the influence of jazz and improvised music politically and culturally. Stanbridge is aware that such a position is one of both opportunity and danger – the opportunity for influence and a wider audience on the one hand, the danger of a limiting of artistic possibility on the other.

Like McKay, Stanbridge offers a liberal, essentially idealist account of his subject. His arguments are both cautious and measured, though dismissive of those with whom he disagrees, such as Frankfurt School philosopher and music critic T.W. Adorno, and French economist Jacques Attali, author of the influential *Noise: The Political Economy of Music*. He shares what he sees as George McKay's scepticism of "broader utopian claims" made, for example, by Eddie Prévost "in favour of a focus on 'micropolitics'". And he quotes McKay, "micropolitics matter, and are rarely as small as appearance suggests". Stanbridge's reference to "Frankfurt School orthodoxies" is telling, as is his remark about "'ideologically correct' paternalism" (the phrase appears in inverted commas in the original article). He then quotes writer and critic David Chaney on "Marxist attitudes toward popular culture":

> Even within Marxism, despite beginning with a self-avowed philosophical attack on established beliefs, there had in practice been a successful evasion of discovering or articulating an indigenous aesthetic in popular culture. Instead of confronting real issues, cultural theorists had too often been hijacked by the intellectual hubris of formulating an "appropriate" culture for the masses. (Chaney 1994, quoted in Stanbridge 2008)

Both Chaney and Stanbridge, and to a lesser extent McKay, seem to take the wider social, political and economic situation within which different areas of the arts functions, as a given. The view they seem to espouse or at least accept is that the music business is determined by market principles and forces like any other and that jazz functions within this business world. The size of its audience may vary according to fashions or according to whether the imagery or symbolism associated with it becomes attached to other media, such as film, or is picked up by other commercial interests or public funding bodies. Popular culture, on the other hand, is seen as another given, perhaps driven to an extent by market forces or advertising but essentially that which appeals to the broadest segment of the music-listening public. Jazz's marginality or proximity to mainstream culture is subject to these variables. One must presume, though this is not Stanbridge's argument, that the closer it accords with mainstream expectations, the more popular it may become. The question as to how far popular taste is driven or even determined by forces beyond the consumer is not examined.

As a counter to this position, we might respond that capitalism is a competitive economic system that supposedly operates within a demand economy. It is assumed that that which sells meets a demand. Clearly not all consumers are passive in their consumption. However, it follows that more products that sell will be produced and promoted than those which are harder to sell. Often record companies are caught on the hop by new phe-nomena that emerge within popular culture. This was certainly the case with the rise of the beat groups in Britain in the sixties and later in the decade with psychedelic and progressive rock music styles. Market forces are nei-ther swift in reacting to change nor remotely scientific in predicting demand. Many of the groups signed by record companies in these periods were both very good at what they did and even popular but failed to sell records. British examples of this might be The Graham Bond Organization, Zoot Money's Big Roll Band, the Action, The Creation and The Big Three. It is understand-ably rare that a record company will persevere with an artist or group that does not sell records, though in this respect Island Records in the sixties and seventies was perhaps an exception. The process of determining what is available and in what quantities was, even if this is not quite the case today, within the music business decidedly inefficient. In fact, a lot of the music that did sell in substantial amounts did so, as Dave Harker points out, despite not having access to the charts because it was excluded from them. For example, this included budget labels, certain compilations and even some easy listen-ing records (Harker 1980, 94–100).

Jazz did compete successfully with other styles of popular music in America for periods of time. Yet its relationship with mainstream popular culture has never been as consistently successful in terms of sales as other forms, with the possible exception of the swing period and the big bands. In Britain, it achieved a certain level of popularity in the thirties and forties, rivalled the dance bands in its traditional form in the fifties and even took on more teenage-oriented pop music around the late fifties and early sixties. Such moments have nevertheless been brief.

Mike Westbrook has suggested earlier that the history of jazz, along with its internationalism and commitment to individual freedom within the com-munity, perhaps gives it a particularly special function as an "art of social and political change". Clearly, an important element in that history is its origins as a music in which African-Americans as an oppressed people played a major role. This is an important consideration and one we will shortly return to. However, at the same time, attempts to use race as a kind of touchstone explanation for the "marginality" of jazz encounters an immediate difficulty – namely that other black music forms have attained consistently higher sales and levels of popularity both in the USA and in Britain. One need only refer to the soul music released by Motown, Stax and Atlantic record com-panies and artists such as The Supremes, Temptations, Four Tops, Smokey Robinson, Marvin Gaye, Aretha Franklin, James Brown and later groups such as the O'Jays, Harold Melvin and the Blue Notes and Billy Paul. Even quite explicitly socially and racially conscious artists like Gaye, Brown, Curtis Mayfield, Gil Scott Heron and from reggae Bob Marley and Winston "Burnin' Spear" Rodney have sold their music successfully to white and black listeners. The history of slavery, racism and exploitation surely runs through this music just as it does through jazz, though the rewards may have been less for black as opposed to white popular music artists (see Gillett 1975). As the Staples Singers sang, "When will we be paid for the work we've done?"

We have to ask – "Why one but not the other?" At the outset, it seems reasonable to suggest that other factors than the race origins of jazz or soul are involved, most notably musical accessibility. Song forms, whether from folk music, the blues or the standard 32-bar AABA and verse–chorus forms, are clearly common to black and white pop music and were for several decades common in jazz. Even bebop, while subverting many of the rules associated with the form, drew extensively on the Great American Songbook. However, the further that jazz moved away from such familiar structures, indeed departing at times from recognizable structures entirely, the fewer reference points it shared with pop or soul musics and as a predominantly instrumental music it rarely had a lyric that allowed neophytes to follow its trajectory. This, too, is part of its development as a music and therefore also a part of its history.

By contrast, soul music in the USA crossed over, maintaining its popularity in the African-American community and also establishing itself with young white fans. Motown Records had only been established in the late fifties by Berry Gordy Jnr. Yet, by 1963, not only had it broken out of the Detroit area where the company was based but it came third in the year's single record sales after RCA and CBS (Frith 1975, 37). James Brown, on the other hand, had considerable success among black audiences in the southern states but it was not until the release of his 1963 LP *Live at the Apollo* that he made the national charts. The record peaked at No. two, stayed in the top 100 for fourteen months and was followed by a string of single chart successes. The progress of the "deep soul music" of the American South – of Otis Redding, Carla Thomas, Aretha Franklin, Sam & Dave and others – was somewhat slower. Redding had just begun this process with his performance at the Monterey Pop Festival in 1967. Sadly, he died in a plane crash shortly after "Sittin' on the Dock of the Bay", his most successful single, was released. Aretha Franklin also began to experience major chart success around 1967 and was one of the first soul artists to appear at the hippy venue The Fillmore West, along with fellow Atlantic Records artist, tenor saxophonist King Curtis. Both issued live albums from the concert. Sam & Dave, like Otis Redding, Stax recording artists, had their first national chart hit in the States with "Hold On, I'm Comin'" in 1966 but really broke through to wider appeal the following year. In one sense, all these artists were capitalizing on the national and international reputation already achieved by Ray Charles and Sam Cooke.

The cultural position of soul music in Britain clearly cannot be read in quite the same way. The second generation mods had picked up on Motown and other highly danceable soul records very early on. Many of the beat groups drew heavily on this same material, particularly in their live acts, and, in practice, the audience for soul was quite a broad one in the UK, reaching both aficionados and more mainstream fans. Towards the end of the decade a separation did emerge, however. As early as 1967, with the rise of psychedelic rock, the music began to fall out of favour with middle and lower middle-class youth (see Copasetic in Gillett 1972). By 1969, it had become heavily associated with skinheads and violence and was even further out of favour with the hippy/progressive audience. In Britain, there was seen to be a distinction between "authentic" black music – blues and jazz – and "inauthentic" black pop music – soul.

Nevertheless, it remains the case that the success of soul music in America, and in Britain, lay in its capacity to cross over. After all, the links between rock music and soul music through R&B were very strong and both relied heavily on the song form, even though progressive rock bands would by the late sixties and early seventies begin to move away from this format. While jazz and soul music may share similar roots and experiences of racism, their respective fortunes in the market place have proved very different. It is worth suggesting that the rise of soul music in America began in the late fifties/early sixties and accompanied the ultimately successful struggle for civil rights. It perhaps became a music of optimism, even when it drew attention to the poverty and discrimination that continued to plague black American lives.

The rise of jazz during the twenties and thirties told a different story. It achieved popularity while segregation of the races, not only in the south but also in the north, persisted. It was exotic and even forbidden. In *Jammin' at the Margins – Jazz and the American Cinema*, Krin Gabbard points out that black people and jazz in early Hollywood films "were invariably confined to stories of alcoholism, drug abuse, and self-destructive behaviour" (Gabbard 1996, 42). In an analysis that draws heavily on Eric Lott's study of "Blackface Minstrelsy" – *Love and Theft: Blackface Minstrelsy and the American Working Class* – Gabbard suggests that the black male was ever-present in American cultural life. Following Lott, Gabbard suggests that styles of dress, mannerisms, talk and musical styles were often borrowed by white American youth even if this was at times unconscious.

Both Lott and Gabbard relate this process of identification to myths about black male sexuality. The minstrel in blackface could explore behaviours otherwise taboo for white – and in particular respectable white – society. One can, of course, see similar processes at work today in the adoption by white youth around the world of the patois of the New York and Los Angeles ghettoes and the musical styles of hip-hop and rap. The difference between the epochs, however, lies in the fact that such taboos have diminished greatly in the intervening seven or eight decades. As Lott suggests, the source of this identification may have its roots in white male fears of sexual inadequacy and of black male potency but had moved beyond such repressed material to become so imbedded in the white male's "equipment for living" as to be invisible (Lott 1993, 53).

One might suggest that jazz had done the hard yards for soul music from the twenties through to the fifties. As for so many African-Americans of those generations, it did not reap the rewards of that struggle as fully. In surveying the use of jazz as soundtrack music in Hollywood films and American TV series in the 1950s and early 1960s, Alan Stanbridge echoes Gabbard when he points out:

> It is interesting to note the manner in which jazz is called upon to signify in these movies, inevitably connoting the seamy underbelly of contemporary life and serving to instil a remarkably persistent image of the music in mass consciousness.
>
> (Stanbridge 2008, 2)

However far jazz may have transcended such images, it has still had to fight continually to create and sustain a cultural position for itself in America and elsewhere against other less complex forms from popular music and against the exalted, socially and culturally preferred forms of Western art music. Its marginality is a part of its history and perhaps also part of its attraction for those who love and value it, though its position within the market remains fragile. To suggest as Stanbridge does, on the other hand, that this is due to its practitioners places horse and cart in quite the wrong order.

In an article from 2007, Simon Frith notes that sales of jazz records on both sides of the Atlantic amounted to only 3 per cent of the total, and these sales included highly successful artists such as Jamie Cullum, Norah Jones and Kenny G. (Frith 2007). Historically, both in this country and in North America, the cultural and economic position of jazz has fluctuated. At times, it has received major label support but often it has relied on entrepreneurs who were themselves fans. In Britain and Europe by the early seventies support from the majors had all but dried up and musicians relied increasingly on small labels or their own imprints as a means of producing and marketing their music.

Certainly, within the time frame that concerns us, several of the record companies involved in promoting black music were also established by entrepreneurial-fans of the music. These included the Ertegun brothers (Atlantic), Berry Gordy (Motown), Jim Stewart and his sister Estelle Axton (Stax) and, in Britain, Chris Blackwell (Island). The success of these companies in marketing these particular genres of black music allowed them to achieve the same market penetration and product distribution as the larger corporations that would eventually gobble them up due to saleability and marketability of their product. As a slight contrast to this, jazz in America during the fifties and sixties survived both due to the existence of strong independent imprints, such as Blue Note and Prestige, and relatively stable relationships with certain of the majors, such as Decca and Columbia. The establishment in 1960 by producer Creed Taylor of Impulse Records, as a subsidiary of the larger entertainment conglomerate ABC-Paramount, was particularly important for the new music being made by John Coltrane, Charles Mingus, Archie Shepp, Albert Ayler, Pharaoh Sanders and others.

The situation within the market place in Britain during these years was different. Initially, in terms of modern jazz, Tempo was the most important outlet, followed by Esquire and Doug Dobell's 77 Records. Tempo's last recording was made in 1960, while both Esquire and 77 continued into the seventies. Denis Preston's Lansdowne series was initially leased to Pye before he switched to Columbia, then part of the EMI group. Fontana, which issued albums by Ronnie Ross, John Dankworth, Tubby Hayes and Ronnie Scott, was the other important company. Towards the end of the decade, we have noted that with the rise of progressive rock music and a British jazz avant-garde in the late sixties, companies like Decca, Philips, Pye, RCA and CBS issued a number of albums by a range of artists of note including Mike Westbrook, Chris McGregor, Keith Tippett, Graham Collier, John Surman and others. This enthusiasm was, nevertheless, short-lived and by the early seventies only Westbrook and Ian Carr's Nucleus continued to record for major labels. The emergence of small independents in the seventies such as Ogun, Incus, Black Lion, Spotlite, the Scottish label Hep, as well as Humphrey Lyttelton's Calligraph, Graham Collier's Mosaic and Stan Tracey's Steam proved increasingly significant in maintaining a British jazz presence in the market place. In addition, burgeoning relationships across the channel with, for example, MPS, FMP and ECM in Germany, JMS and Owl in France and, later, Hat Hut in Switzerland provided additional recording opportunities. Essentially, British jazz has been more heavily reliant on small labels than has been the case in the USA and, arguably, in Europe (see Priestley 1988).

The economic position for many American jazz artists – excluding the big earners like Miles Davis, Dave Brubeck and Herbie Hancock – was also fragile, as jazz struggled to compete in a market driven by the combined forces of pop music and rock. However, in Britain, the situation was even more precarious and, while jazz musicians sold their records and performances within the same capitalist cultural market place as other musical styles, they existed increasingly in the margins of that world.

The success of the Beatles, Stones, the Who, the Kinks and even one or two far lesser groups like Herman's Hermits and the Dave Clark Five in exporting British pop music to the States was an important factor in the development and expansion of the music industry. With the rise of rock music, other British bands – Cream, Led Zeppelin, Pink Floyd, Yes – capitalized on this success and continued to compete successfully with American acts both in Europe, in North America and in the developing Japanese markets. The irony that this was music that was supposedly connected to the underground/ hippy/alternative society was lost among record company executives, who did what their companies required of them – that is, they produced profits.

One company, Columbia Records (USA), even marketed their rock catalogue on what was termed their "revolutionaries program". Slogans included:

The Man can't bust our music.

Know who your friends are. And look and see and touch and be together. Then listen. We do.

Don't compromise because the music doesn't.
(See Lydon 1969, 61; also Harker 1980, 104)

These same rock stars might have been surprised to discover that the record company they recorded for also made guidance systems for US Air Force bombers (Decca) or guided weapons, radar and predictors (EMI) or owned defence-related subsidiaries (CBS) (see Harker 1980, 87–90 and 103). However, the marketing of protest or revolutionary sloganeering was well within the capacity of these multinational corporations. More than that, the very presence of such alternative figures on these labels creates a kind of cognitive dissonance between content and process on the one hand and context on the other. In allowing, indeed publicizing, the grievances of the young and disaffected, the democratic and liberal qualifications of "the system" were reinforced, at the same time that they are questioned. And with increased sales comes increased wealth and the gap between the artist and her or his audience grows ever wider. It truly is a Faustian pact.

In turn, it becomes harder to bridge that gap, while content and context exist, not in opposition, but in a false, deluding unity. Songs such as Dylan's "Blowin' in the Wind" or "The Times They Are a-Changin'" rely on a generally confirmatory message that is carried to his audience. We are on the same side, they say, while "Oxford Town" – the story of two racist murders – contains the line "Somebody better investigate soon". Far from being revolutionary or radical, these songs reaffirm a certain faith in the system, that it will listen to reason or passion and change course. Columbia, one may recall, baulked at the more direct lyric of "Talkin' John Birch Society Blues" and refused to allow it on Dylan's *Freewheelin'* LP. There is an argument to be made that "Hard Rain's a-Gonna Fall" from that album and later Dylan songs such as "Desolation Row" from *Highway 61 Revisited* and "Subterranean Homesick Blues" from *Bringing It All Back Home* are actually far more effective as "protest songs". First, they neither offer nor suggest possible solutions. Second, the world they depict is bleak, repetitive and grim. In the case of "Hard Rain" the sense of loss and destruction following a nuclear war is palpable. With the two later songs, they depict the American Dream stripped bare.

Ironically, the tendency of many protest songs to offer solutions depoliticises their message. A good example of this is Jackson Browne's "Lives in the Balance". It offers a devastating critique of American foreign policy and how the US electoral system is manipulated by powerful interests to ensure that the majority never call its legitimacy into question. Browne's song was written in 1985 and appeared on a major record label that is itself part of a much larger media conglomerate. It did not stop America invading Afghanistan or Iraq and, no matter how many times it might be played on the radio, it is unlikely to change America's continuing attempts to shape the world according to its own economic and geopolitical interests. Art can be critical of aspects of society. However, it can easily be accommodated within that framework so long as it operates within the core economic relationships of that society and where its critique implies that change within the system is sufficient to remedy its shortcomings. There is little, however critical of or distasteful to bourgeois values, that capitalism cannot market and sell. Even Herbert Marcuse was forced to acknowledge in his 1966 preface to *Eros and Civilisation* that his belief that the development of a "polymorphous sexuality" within society would undermine capitalism had underestimated the pliability of bourgeois hegemony.

We share with McKay an agreement that gender, race, anti-Americanism and anti-commercialism are important areas for examination and consideration in the field of jazz studies. Indeed, we have touched on certain of these same questions albeit in a rather different way, perhaps. We would also agree with him that the concern shown by British jazz musicians and fans regarding a number of social issues from the late fifties onwards helps to sketch those areas where the music and politics overlapped. However, a fundamental question remains to be addressed. Once again, what exactly does all this tell us about the nature of British jazz or, for that matter, about British politics in the sixties? In order to discover a satisfactory answer to this question we need to adopt a very different approach.

We have, with the help of McKay and Stanbridge, sketched the contexts in which any art form must function. Art does not function in a pure environment and "art for art's sake" was always a highly utopian autotelic slogan. It operates in a complex environment but one dominated by economics. It is not ideas or ideology or beliefs or values that shape lives, but the material world and our engagement and interaction with it. In terms of jazz, soul, pop, rock and classical music, these all function within a market-driven economy that is driven by the pursuit of profit. It is this understanding that is missing from the analyses of McKay, Stanbridge, Cheney and, to a far lesser extent, Chris Searle. It is not that ideas and values are completely determined by economic forces but that they are in some significant measure dependent upon them. In trying to understand the relationship between British jazz in the sixties and its broader political, social and cultural potential, we have to move beyond issue-based, liberal idealist politics and examine instead the relationship of jazz to capitalism and its ideological underpinnings.

14 Lotta Continua

Its essence is in improvisation. I often say it, and at the risk of repeating myself, the one thing the state cannot do is improvise. They can busk badly but they can't improvise.   Maggie Nicols, interview with author, October 2010

Taste for *any* pictures or statues is not a moral quality, but taste for good ones is.
John Ruskin, *The Crown of Wild Olive*, 1866

We face several hurdles in attempting to establish the nature of the cultural politics of British jazz, in the sixties or later. No matter how many statements or actions by jazz musicians or fans one examines on issues such as racism, nuclear weapons or apartheid, one can never be sure how far these are representative of the wider community of artists and listeners. More than that, even if we could conduct a comprehensive survey of attitudes, beliefs and political affiliations of that community, it would not actually tell us anything about the nature of jazz itself, only that those of a particular ideological persuasion found in some way their own preferences reflected within it. One suspects that such a survey might reveal a preponderance of left-of-centre views, which might be useful for marketing purposes but little else.

In order to understand this aspect of the politics of consumption we need a sharper perspective than that offered by Stanbridge, Chaney or McKay. Looking at this in respect of British jazz, there are few completely satisfactory theoretical perspectives to direct us. The work of Antonio Gramsci, Herbert Marcuse, Theodor Adorno, Walter Benjamin and others have proved important in the development of cultural studies as a discipline. Confronting the failure of the proletariat to oppose the victory of reactionary politics in Germany, Italy, Hungary and Spain and the need to explain the emergence of Stalinism in Russia, the focus of these theorists on ideology was critical, if the potential for revolutionary political action was to be understood and grasped. It was this imperative that led to Marcuse's theorizing of the Id or, in his terms, Eros, as the part of the personality that remained impermeable or at least resistant to bourgeois ideology. Gramsci, independently, developed the conceptualization of "ideology" not as a fixed and permanent state but as a "shifting equilibrium" that reflected the balance of class forces or antagonisms.

These analyses offer some guidance, particularly in their acknowledgement that superstructural phenomena such as culture and ideology are not to be seen as being entirely determined by the economic infrastructure. It will be clear that without such a conclusion, a Marxist or materialist analysis of any cultural phenomenon would fall into exactly the opposite problem to that which faces a liberal, idealist viewpoint. The former would be over-determined, while the latter would be under-determined! At the same time, the risk that arises with an over-reliance on, for example, the Frankfurt School, is that one emphasizes the independence of the artist or philosopher to the point of romanticizing and over-estimating the value and revolutionary promise of their vision. Paternalism and elitism follow not far behind.

If we are to avoid such philosophical sink-holes, we need to locate our analysis, as far as possible, in the material of class, economics and history. This can then allow us to reflect on both the practice and content of British jazz in the sixties and seventies, while at the same time weighing the views of leading practitioners. Far more speculatively, we can then perhaps begin to identify political strands in British jazz and locate these historically. Maggie Nicols expresses these points both articulately and concisely, when asked whether jazz can be read as a "political art form":

> Yes. I think so, if you think of its roots in the blues and the whole struggle against slavery and against racism and the survival of black people with dignity against all odds and the creative expression and transformation of that through the music. Jazz has sometimes been treated as a poor relation of classical music but it has shown its creativity and how advanced and what an advanced black music it is. I think it is and I think improvisation is revolutionary. I really do. Not all jazz musicians are political but the music itself is.   (Interview with Maggie Nicols, October 2010)

It must be stressed that Nicols is not suggesting that jazz is political because of its origins, though she makes clear that this is a dynamic aspect of its past and present. Its history is inescapable. To this point she adds two others – first, its marginalization against Western art music and, second, the essential element of jazz practice that is improvisation. Seen from this perspective, jazz is an already politicized musical form. Leading on from Nicols's comment, we can begin to sketch those elements that might be the key to an understanding of the politics of jazz and, therefore, of British jazz in the sixties, some of which have in fairness been recognized by McKay, Stanbridge and others.

First, there is its history as a music born in a situation of racism and oppression, coupled with its historical development initially into a popular musical form but later into one that became marginal in its relationship to mainstream popular and more elitist cultures. A further part of that history is its emergence as an articulate and distinctive art form in its own right. Second, there is the cultural, social and economic position that it occupies within the broader social life of society. Third, there is the persistence of a series of associated images around jazz in the public consciousness that signify an exoticism, an outsider status and even a dark sexuality. Fourth, there is the issue of race and oppression that continues to inform and intrude upon discussions about the nature of jazz. Finally, there is the issue of the class position of jazz musicians. In terms of this last point, readers will recall that we earlier defined this in terms of their relationship to the means of production both of the music *per se* and of cultural production. According to this reading, the class position of jazz musicians in Britain in the sixties is an ambiguous one or, to use Wright's term, they occupy "contradictory class locations" (Wright 1978). It will be seen that it is their position as creative artists functioning simultaneously within and outside a market economy that has enabled musicians such as Mike Westbrook, Barry Guy, Evan Parker, John Stevens, Maggie Nicols and others to reflect in their work on wider social and political issues.

The socially conscious or politically aware artist must still tread a careful path in order to balance political involvement and the commitment to artistic integrity. This is not always easy. Mike Westbrook suggests that it was really with hindsight that he can see the continuity in his own work between artistic and political engagement. Over time, he began to realize that the struggle to develop a means of personal, artistic expression had parallels with political activity and concerns. While, as he says, this "kind of coincides with the broader political situation" at times, this is not always the case. As he implies, the position of the artist in society is an unusual, and even privileged, one after all. "Because I think as an artist you also have to kind of be outside and be independent of orthodoxies of all kinds really. You've got to retain a certain freedom in yourself that questions everything" (interview with Mike Westbrook, November 2008). Westbrook is also quite specific in locating the changes that he himself experienced in terms of his own understanding of the relationship between art and politics within a broader post-war Zeitgeist, as he explains:

> I would say that broadly one was engaged in political change post-war and then going on into the sixties and so on and in my case all those kinds of experiences led into and contributed to this

thing, including the study of Art that I was engaged in. A view was evidently forming at that time and so a lot of the work that one did in that period sometimes overtly did coincide, for example with the Campaign for Nuclear Disarmament. There were a lot of events, there were Jazz & Poetry events and things like that one participated in. There were the beginnings of street theatre or alternative theatre that were going on.

(Interview with Mike Westbrook, November 2008)

For Westbrook, and for many of the artists who we have discussed, there is a pattern to this process that locates their worldview and ethical/aesthetic response in the post-war period. The victory over fascism was bought at a very high cost and, despite the optimism that carried the Attlee government to power in 1945, the continuation of rationing was part of the formative experience of the majority of musicians who came through in the mid to late sixties. They saw, and even participated in, the anti-nuclear protests. They observed the invasions of Suez and Hungary and the nightmare of the Cuban Missile Crisis. They watched the relaxation of social taboos and benefited from access to education, health care and increasing living standards. Both the achievements and the disappointments of the post-war period were part of their youth. Perhaps this generation of which they were part was an unusual one but they carried these experiences with them into the sixties and beyond. If anything, the coming together of political activity and artistic endeavour did not stop as the clock crept past midnight on 31 December 1969. Rather, the next decade saw an increasing closeness between art and politics.

The "cultural politics" of British jazz are not just about ideas. They are grounded in social, historical, economic and class realities. And more than that, they are materially grounded in practice. What concerns us here is not just the compositional or performance processes of British jazz but the dialectic of theory-practice that informed it. The only word we can really use to describe this is "praxis": that is the synthesis of theory and practice. As Maggie Nicols once again suggests:

Its essence is in improvisation. I often say it, and at the risk of repeating myself, the one thing the state cannot do is improvise. They can busk badly but they can't improvise because to improvise you have to have a certain kind of flexibility and openness, a willingness to surrender, a willingness to reflect, to negotiate. Capitalism is all about obeying orders – giving and obeying orders. You can't improvise if you are doing either. The improvising impulse has completely had it! [laughs]

(Interview with Maggie Nicols, October 2010)

Ironically, improvisation is so essential to jazz practice that several British composers have developed their own methodologies to allow compositional forms that allow high levels of freedom to soloists and performers. They are not alone in this, of course. A number of American composers including George Russell, Gil Evans, Lawrence "Butch" Morris and John Zorn have done this too. The point is that composer–musicians as distinctive as Mike Westbrook, Kenny Wheeler, Eddie Prévost, Keith Tippett, Graham Collier, Barry Guy and, more recently, even that master free improviser Evan Parker have each addressed this problem in their own way. The sheer diversity of their approaches to this problem has resulted in works as different in tone and mode of expression as Graham Collier's *Mosaics*, Mike Westbrook's *Metropolis*, Barry Guy's *Ode* and Keith Tippett's *Septober Energy*. One thing that these approaches have in common is a shared relationship between form and content that is dialectical. The excitement and vitality of the music is created by the unresolved tension between the compositional elements and the improvisational content. Here, we must stress that what is happening is not a synthesis but that composition and improvisation exist in a state of tension. Neither element is resolved into the other.

This does not mean that the compositional forms developed by British jazz composers of the sixties arose solely in the situation that these artists found themselves. They continued to owe a great deal to the history of the music, to that potent and ongoing dialogue between past and present. One can see this in Mike Westbrook's continuing engagement with the work of Duke Ellington or Graham Collier's acknowledgement of the importance of Charles Mingus in his work. At the same time, these represented new compositional solutions to the problems of the present. They were neither prescribed nor determined by the past. We might also note that the form of the composition neither determined the improvisations that resulted in response to it, nor was the form determined in any way by the improvisations. This seems to involve a set of priorities that do not exist for Western art music, or in folk or rock musics, even where improvisation is an important component in these styles. This is, therefore, a core part of the aesthetic praxis of jazz.

This in turn has implications for hierarchy within the music. In free jazz or improvisation, the musicians actively seek to create something that is non-hierarchical, as Maggie Nicols explains:

> We are groomed through generations to be part of that hierarchy [of Western capitalism]. To be a part of that army of unemployed to keep wages down, to be a wage slave or to administer somewhere in the middle or to rule. That hierarchy goes against improvisation. That's what is so wonderful about this music and why it is so subversive and revolutionary, whether people are aware of it or not – and especially free improvisation because it is amazing. You've seen it yourself, whether it's you or you're watching

a group. Sometimes somebody is leading, sometimes nobody is leading. Sometimes someone will initiate something and maybe no-one will follow. There's just so much choice. Sometimes there will be genuine consensus, you know when a piece suddenly ends and you all feel that together.

(Interview with Maggie Nicols, October 2010)

And she adds:

That's the phenomenal thing because you realize you don't actually need leaders. It doesn't mean that it makes composers redundant or leadership redundant in a flowing sense but it takes you away from dependence on leaders and that's threatening.

(Interview with Maggie Nicols, October 2010)

While this may not be the case to the same extent with jazz where the role of the composer is more central, the desire to embrace both the collective and the individual continue to be present. For Barry Guy, this involves finding ways of composing music that are sensitive to the needs of the musicians he chooses to work with:

I was always aware that there was another way of expressing the creative impulse. If I can deliver some of my ideas to a group of people, a group of musicians then great but it's a changeable situation. It's like reinventing the wheel every time. One also has to think about the characters of each player, how they fit in with the structure, what their desires are musically.

(Interview with Barry Guy, November 2010)

For Guy, such considerations go back to involvement with CND in his teens. If anything, his understanding of the relationship between art and creativity on the one hand and politics and how society is organized has crystallized over the years. Working extensively with Paul Rutherford during the early years of the Thatcher government has brought an even sharper focus to his reflections:

I suppose in my early days with Rutherford, we talked a lot about politics. We were, of course, active when Thatcher was destroying the country and I suppose we thought that in terms of music and improvisation this was one of the last bastions of freedom or apparent freedom. Where the individual could express themselves but importantly that expression could be channelled into a kind of communion or communication with other musicians. Where politics is a divisive action, what we were doing was something completely different. We were trying to channel music and ideas into a singular creative process and at the same time we had humility and we had support from each other. If anything it was a kind of socialism. For me, that has been the overriding principle throughout the whole of my life.

(Interview with Barry Guy, November 2010)

As a child living through the rationing of food that continued in Britain after the Second World War, Guy had an experience that proved pivotal. Responding to his demand that he be given more food at the dinner table, his mother pointed out that he could have hers as well but then she would have nothing:

The penny dropped right there. It was just a small thing but it's been with me all my life – the act of taking without thought. Now before doing anything I like to think of the consequences in humanitarian terms of the action and it's the same with music. My greatest ambition is to make music in very, very humanitarian ways, in organic ways so that it grows naturally without tension and to be honest I think that is the best way to get through life.

(Interview with Barry Guy, November 2010)

Mike Westbrook offers a similarly reflective conclusion, "I think my root to political awareness has come through the music. It has come through the activity of being a band leader and composer and the jazz group in a sense being a sort of model of socialist society" (interview with Mike Westbrook, May 2011). For Westbrook, jazz remains a music that reveals its potential through communication and interaction, between the musicians, and between the musicians and their audience:

It's also an area of the world where there's quite a lot of idealism and quite a lot of honesty in the jazz world. You can't just pretend or pose. You've got to mean it and you've got to be good because among musicians there's a great equality. It's not stars and groundlings. We're all in it together. And there's a huge love of the music and a desire for a world in which this was a really powerful force for good in the world. People are motivated by that and not, by and large, so much by commercial interest.

(Interview with Mike Westbrook, November 2008))

These are themes that recur in discussion with British jazz musicians of this era. There is a deeply held belief that music and the arts can be a force for "good in the world" and that the effective communication between performer and audience is essential to that process. But this is neither utopian nor idealistic. Rather it is rooted in practice and in the relationship between artist and audience. On the whole in jazz, and this was very evident in British jazz in the period under discussion, the gap between the audience and the musicians is slight. Most performances take place in small venues, often without a formal stage and audience and artists mix together easily. Often the players know members of the audience and the occasion frequently allows for social interaction. Given that many clubs and festivals are organized and run by volunteers, high levels of mutual respect exist between artists and the wider jazz community. If anything, the relationship between performer and audience in the world of free improvisation is even closer and one often has the sense that the audience even affects the performance itself.

This notion of community is sometimes misunderstood. George McKay quotes Eddie Prévost as follows, "Our music *is* outside the mainstream, but over the years we have developed an audience, a community, a group of people all around the world now, who believe in it" (McKay 2005, 231; emphasis original). McKay then comments:

> The notion of constructing what Prévost calls a "community" through the music is an important claim, though this may equally be no more substantive than the carving out of a specialist audience or a niche market. It is of course possible to view much of the preceding activity as a petit bourgeois practice, a minor cultural entrepreneurship, low capitalism for high cult music – so that mutual aid becomes self-help, in effect.
>
> (McKay 2005, 231)

Alan Stanbridge notes this remark favourably, adding that "his recognition of the socio-political limits identified above" are evident in "his attitude toward the wilful marginality of the free improvisation scene in Britain and toward Eddie Prévost's claims of community-building" (Stanbridge 2008, 10). These comments raise questions regarding both writers' understanding of capitalism and class. The description of Prévost's efforts to make a living from his desire to work in a particular area of music as "low capitalism" seems to ignore issues of extraction of surplus value or profit, let alone wealth accumulation that are prerequisites of "high" capitalism, or as we might prefer simply capitalism. There is also something discomfiting in the implicit suggestion of elitism that pervades both McKay's and Stanbridge's analysis. There seems to be an assumption that Prévost, like John Stevens, Keith Tippett, Evan Parker, Derek Bailey, Maggie Nicols and others are being "wilful" in their "marginality". Surely these musicians are simply responding according to their own aesthetic and ethical imperatives within a society that is dominated by very different modes of production. They do so frequently foregoing other rewards that might be available should they be prepared to prostrate themselves before mammon. As for the charge of elitism, Chambers gives the following definition:

elitism n. 1a The belief that society should be governed by an
elite, 1b such government, 2 pride in or awareness of being one of
an elite group.   (Chambers 2009, 379)

Its thesaurus provides several synonyms for the noun "elite". These include
"upper class", "aristocracy", "high society" and so forth. None of these definitions apply to Prévost or any of the other musicians we have considered.
Prévost's music is marginal as a result of particular social, economic and
cultural processes over which he cannot exercise control. To blame him,
and others like him, for the "wilfully marginality" of his music while ignoring
the wider context seems a poor excuse for critical analysis indeed. In fact,
Prévost describes that wider context extremely well:

> Bourgeois art is negative because it reduces all men and their
> works and their aspirations to commodity exchange. Sounds
> which resist this tendency are therefore perceived as ugly and
> repulsive to the possessive individualist. If it's true that ugly
> music repels the cash nexus, the music of the Sex Pistols becomes
> beautiful to bourgeois culture the moment it becomes market-
> able. If atonal atrocities begin to communicate the technocratic
> ethos – i.e. experts manipulating ideas and materials – bourgeois
> life senses not threat but renewal. Such musics in their difficulty
> become finger-breaking fetishes: they appeal because they now
> celebrate neo-capitalist mastery.   (Prévost 1995, 181–2)

Indeed, Prévost's commitment to music-making as a collective enterprise
and symbolic reflection of notions of community can be clearly seen in the
music of *Silver Pyramid* (Matchless MRCD40). The recording remained
unreleased until 2001 but is taken from the four-day Music Now festival
held at the Roundhouse in north London in May 1969. The performance is
of Prévost's Music Now Ensemble with additional performers from Morley
College and Maidstone College of Art. Prévost is unsure today who of those
present actually contributed, and yet it is a testament to the times and to the
desire to produce music that expressed something other than what could be
written down or predicated solely on its composer's intent. And it is remarkable – strange, at times confusing and yet at others it shines with a wonderful
luminescence that has to be heard to be comprehended. It presages a radically different set of notions about composition, improvisation or performance and about the relationship between the artist and their audience. It is
music that is capable of answering any question that the liberal critic can
put to it.

Understanding of context is absolutely crucial. Works that were in some
measure critical of existing society or by artists who took oppositional
stances can see their meaning changed dramatically through their placement

in another environment, for example as Alan Stanbridge suggests the presence of the works of Dadaist Marcel Duchamp in major galleries. Robbie Burns's song of brotherhood, "Auld Lang Syne", when sung at the closing of the annual Conservative Party conference, becomes a statement of confidence in the party's right to govern. Blake's "Jerusalem" in Parry's musical setting becomes a patriotic anthem. But relocated by Mike Westbrook in the album *The Cortège*, taken at a slower and more elegiac pace and sung by Phil Minton in a rich West Country burr, its original meaning is reaffirmed. Music, perhaps more than any of the arts, is multivalent. It is capable of carrying a broad range of meanings, from its surface or manifest content, to its latent content through other possible meanings that may stem from the performance context or the manner through which it is delivered. Lou Reed's "Perfect Day" and The Stranglers' "Golden Brown", both hymns to heroin, retain their original coded message played by a fan on a turntable or CD deck. Played on BBC Radio 2 or Capital Radio they are pleasant, summery anthems for mass consumption.

Given both this mutability of meaning, which is probably greater still with instrumental music, the artist's intention and willingness to be open about that intent becomes an issue for the quality of the relationship between artist and their audience. It is therefore an ethical matter, as well as one of communication. This emerges repeatedly in discussion with British jazz musicians of the sixties and seventies. Michael Garrick spent many years working with local education authorities to bring jazz into schools. Mike Westbrook and his partner Kate place great emphasis on this and Westbrook's determination to make this a central aspect of his art can be traced to the very beginnings of his career.

> I can only really speak for myself and I and Kate in the work that we have been doing for over thirty years have always been concerned with communication as part of the Art. We work very hard on that aspect and I don't think everybody has or takes it that seriously. I think we've been proved right over the years. The music follows its own course and it's not geared to commercial success. Unfortunately, it just has to be whatever it is that we come up with and some things are more immediately accessible than others. Some of the stuff is difficult – for us and everybody else as well. We just have to do it.
>
> (Interview with Mike Westbrook, November 2008)

These examples from both Prévost and Westbrook emphasize a concern for an ethical, as well as aesthetic, engagement both with their music and their audience. In fact, Mike and Kate Westbrook along with the other members of their brass band went to considerable lengths to do so:

We were all left and very committed to taking music to the people. Getting out of the jazz clubs and the elitist situations and much more to where people were and the Brass Band were deeply committed to that and we made a point of playing in factories and hospitals, for old people or children, wherever anybody asked us. Stuff that had nothing to do with the jazz world at all but really playing good music and improvised music in whatever situation.

(Interview with Mike Westbrook, August 2011)

This goes far beyond playing the occasional CND benefit. The Westbrooks have also always been keen supporters of community music-making and they are far from alone in this. Obviously, the building of the next generation of musicians and fans is important. So too is the desire to bring the music to new audiences. But it is also a question of a social practice. Not only do such activities break down barriers between performer and audience, they also enable participants to experience a sense of liberation in the release of personal creativity that is involved. John Stevens, Maggie Nicols, the Tippetts, Eddie Prévost, Michael Garrick, Ian Carr and others have all actively supported this approach and it continues today in their work and in that of younger musicians like bassist Gary Crosby and Nikki Yeoh. For John Stevens, his role as tutor was at odds with what constitutes for most people a mainstream learning experience, "What I have to keep in touch with at the workshops is a feeling of freedom about playing music, and coupled with that, the feeling of wanting other people to have that freedom" (Bailey 1992, 121).

Maggie Nicols learned a lot from Stevens about how to develop the workshop techniques that allow people to find their own voice. Nicols accepts that professionalism and skills may be essential to jazz and classical music but stresses that these are not the only ways of making music:

John Stevens really championed social diversity in music and was really a pioneer of mixed ability, and the virtuosity of mixed ability, which stayed with me forever, thanks to John, because with John you could do John's pieces whether you had been playing an instrument for sixty years or had never played one in your life and yet the overall effect would be one of stunning musicality and complexity. It wasn't ever just, "we'll be kind to them". He understood the power of community music and mixed ability and obviously you can't really do that in jazz because it's so much based on knowing your scales and your chords.

(Interview with Maggie Nicols, October 2010)

Thirty or more years on, there is a passion in her voice as recalls her first foray into the area on her own:

Then when I did my very first workshop after John and I had this thrilling experience of hearing all these amazing voices, many of whom weren't singers and were mainly women and I remember thinking "Alright, okay there are a lot of beautiful singers".
(Interview with Maggie Nicols, October 2010)

The need to keep the process open to all possibilities is also central to Julie Tippetts's way of teaching. For her, this requires a shared rather than didactic approach: "I don't look on it as teaching. I look on it as everybody is discovering together. Of course you give people tips and stuff and give them the chance to fly." In an earlier chapter, Julie Tippetts raised the issue of the responsibility that musicians owe to their audience. She is clear that this is an essential part of the relationship between performer and audience. The capacity to affect people emotionally through one's art also conveys a duty of care. As she noted during our discussion, "It's such a privilege and such an amazing thing that we have to be careful with it" (interview with Julie Tippetts, September 2008). And Tippetts is far from elitist in her attitude to other musical forms. Asked how she responded to music that was merely another market commodity, she responded quite passionately:

But I do understand that everything also has a place – has its reason for being there. Like the music that you listen to as a teenager, it has its role. It has its place. So, I don't dismiss any music at all. Yes, some music can make you feel "yuck!" For me, my only reason for listening to music is if it makes me breath differently, then it has moved me.
(Interview with Julie Tippetts, September 2008)

Her partner, Keith, shares her performance philosophy:

I go into each area of the music that I'm deeply involved in with the same heart with the same brain and with the same techniques really. I have a philosophy as a performer that I want to be a servant to the people and to move them and leave them with an afterglow. And I achieve it as well, quite often.
(Interview with Keith Tippett, March 2004)

Once again, this is hardly the attitude of the elitist. It is rather that of an artist with an intense desire to communicate with his audience. As Barry Guy also notes, "It humbles me to think that if we deliver the music in the right way with the right intentions with the right rhetoric that we will communicate with somebody. But we can't do it across the whole Earth" (interview with Barry Guy, November 2010). One could almost suggest that the function of improvisation lies in the possibility of completeness in the act of communication. Or as Evan Parker explains, "Well, for me to improvise freely is to engage with the other person as fully as you can and to be as open to wherever that leads. That's the joy of it for me" (interview with Evan Parker, April 2009).

Parker, in fact, offers a good response to McKay's comment about "specialist audiences", "niche markets" and "petit bourgeois practice", and Stanbridge and Chaney's charges of elitism. In the liner notes for *Topography of the Lungs*, he quotes Aldous Huxley from the foreword to *Brave New World* (1946 edition) – "Only a large scale popular movement toward decentralisation and self-help can arrest the present tendency towards statism." Parker is clear that his motivation stems in part from such an impetus. A little later, he quotes the socialist writer G.D.H. Cole to even more telling effect:

> The revolt that will change the world will spring, not from the benevolence that breeds "reform", but from the will to be free. Men will act together in the full consciousness of their mutual dependence: but they will act for themselves. Their liberty will not be given them from above: they will take it on their own behalf.
> (Cole and Mellow 1918, 4)

Mike Westbrook sees the discovery of William Blake and the process of reflection on the social place of art as the beginning of an opening up of a political dimension to his work. In 1971, the composer had worked with Adrian Mitchell on *Tyger*, a musical based on the life of poet William Blake that was premiered by the National Theatre Company at the Old Vic, London. Westbrook would continue to use Mitchell's settings of Blake's poems on albums such as *The Westbrook Blake* and *Glad Day*. The context of Blake's work was simultaneously artistic, religious and political. Jerusalem was an important image for the poet and a recurring vision. It was perfection, justice, the absence of poverty and inhumanity and ugliness – those aspects of eighteenth- and nineteenth-century Britain that so tormented Blake. Jerusalem was also a vision of Albion, both the oldest known name for Britain and a powerful myth of loss and the theft of birthrights stolen from the people of this island by successive invaders (see Thompson 2002). Jerusalem is also linked in Blake's poem to an early Christian myth that has Christ coming to Britain, possibly with Joseph of Arimathea, as a boy. This is the meaning of the lines:

> And did those feet in ancient time
> Walk upon England's mountains green?
> And was the holy Lamb of God
> On England's pleasant pastures seen?
>
> And did the Countenance Divine
> Shine forth upon our clouded hills?

> And was Jerusalem builded here
> Among these dark Satanic Mills?
> (Blake 1804)

The Westbrook Blake did not appear until 1980 and falls well outside our period but it derives from the earlier *Tyger* and its thrust and artistic intent are evidence in Westbrook's work of the continuity of concern. The full implications of the songs chosen by Mike and Kate Westbrook are not always immediately apparent. However, Adrian Mitchell provides a commentary on the album's inner sleeve. What emerges is a dialogue between composer and poet. "London Song's" use of the word "charter'd" – "charter'd streets" and "charter'd Thames" – are references that these were owned by men of commerce, while "The Fields" echoes the themes of "Jerusalem", as does "I See Thy Form", both being taken from the same larger work. "Holy Thursday" refers to Ascension Day's service for orphans at St Paul's Cathedral. As Mitchell notes, "This moved many philanthropists to sentimental tears. Blake wept too, but tears of rage." The music Westbrook composed to accompany Blake's prophetic and raging words is elegiac and powerful. It is played primarily by the Brass Band, with additional musicians and a children's choir on "The Fields/I See Thy Form", while "Holy Thursday" adds cello, bass and piano. The record derives much of its effectiveness from understatement and apparent simplicity, though on "Holy Thursday" the "tears of rage" are expressed by Alan Wakeman's powerfully aggressive tenor saxophone.

Its finest moment, however, has to be the final track "Let the Slave", which incorporates "The Price of Experience" read/spoken by Westbrook himself. The composer's achievement throughout the record is twofold. First, his approach allows the poet to speak and be heard. One might argue that, by contrast, Hubert Parry's setting of "Jerusalem", stirring though it is, obscures Blake's lyric. Second, Westbrook frames these poems so successfully that music and words seem almost indivisible.

As with Westbrook's reference to Blake, Parker's choice of Huxley and Cole is highly significant. It refers to a tradition in British literature, art and philosophy that supports the practice ethos and aesthetics of these musicians and composers. That tradition can also be found for example in Ford Madox Brown's painting "Work". Madox Brown was a close friend of William Morris and was interested in socialist and anarchist ideas. In fact, the painting makes reference directly to the Reverend F.D. Maurice, a pioneer of working class education and Christian socialist, and Thomas Carlyle, the writer–historian and philosopher, who appear in the painting. As Madox Brown wrote in the catalogue that accompanied the painting's first exhibition:

> At that time extensive excavations, connected with the supply of water, were going on in the neighbourhood, and, seeing and studying daily as I did the British excavator, or navvy in the full swing

of his activity (with his manly and picturesque costume, and with the rich glow of colour which exercise under a hot sun will impart), it appeared to me that he was at least as worthy of the powers of an English painter as the fisherman of the Adriatic, the peasant of the Campagna, or the Neapolitan lazzarone. Gradually this idea developed itself into that of Work as it now exists, with the British excavator for the central group, as the outward and visible type of Work. (Codell 1998)

The contrast between the work of the navvies with the idleness of passers-by, including members of the gentry, is clear. At the time, essential work was being undertaken in London to improve the water supply and sewage systems of the capital. The painting can, therefore, be read as a parable of the transformative nature of work. Marx and Engels, and Marxists since, do not emphasize the importance of work due to idealistic notions of its inherent nobility. It is rather through labour that human beings can change their world and environment. Under capitalism, they neither control their work, the form it takes, nor the use to which it is put. Nor do they control the products or commodities that are produced. According to Marx, under capitalism, labour is an alienating experience. Workers are not merely alienated from the fruits of their labour but are alienated from the species by the nature of that work itself. He specifies three forms that alienation takes in capitalist society. The first of these, he calls "the relationship of the worker to the product of labour as an alien object". This in turn has implications for the worker's relationship with the natural world, which is then experienced as "an alien and hostile world". This is alienation of the "thing" (i.e. the object, the product). The second aspect is the relationship to the act of production within labour. In this the worker is alienated from his own activity, which Marx describes as "self-alienation". He does not own his own activity and it has become alien to him. The third aspect of alienated labour lies in the fact that human beings are "species-beings".

> Since alienated labour: (1) alienates nature from man; and (2) alienates man from himself, from his own active function, his life activity; so, it alienates him from the *species*. It makes *species life* into an individual life. In the first place it alienates species-life and individual life, and secondly, it turns the latter, as an abstraction, into the purpose of the former, also in its abstracted and alienated form. (Marx [1844] 1993, 49–51; emphasis added)

At one level at least, the work of Evan Parker, Barry Guy, Maggie Nicols, Mike and Kate Westbrook, Eddie Prévost, John Stevens, Julie Tippetts and Keith Tippett confronts alienation through art. As Barry Guy notes, "But we can't do it across the whole earth." There is no suggestion that jazz or any art form can transform society. But it can present itself as a music of communication and engagement and, this is most important of all its potential functions, it can resist commodification.

In this, its British precedents lie in William Morris and John Ruskin, as well as G.D.H. Cole and William Blake. A socialist himself, Morris had read Marx and understood that the division of labour under capitalism was one significant element in the alienation of labour. He set out to reduce this within production at his company Morris & Co., and his company's failure within the late Victorian market economy encouraged rather than discouraged him in his beliefs. His vision of the future outlined in speeches and in his novel *News from Nowhere* foresaw a world where "art and literature (which included all forms of craft activity) would be at once sensuous and human" and the "division of labour would be habitually limited". As Jack Lindsay explains:

> What he insisted on was the problem would be see in a quite new perspective: what men wanted to make out of their lives in a full and free enjoyment of the earth, and what objects, tools, and machinery they needed to achieve that fullness, in which the bourgeois ideal of endlessly extended production, endlessly heaped-up objects, would have lost all its glamour (based as it was ultimately in capitalism's need for an eternally expanded amount of capital. (Lindsay 1975, 251)

Morris had, of course, been greatly influenced in his early years by the Christian Socialist, critic and writer John Ruskin. Ruskin was not the most consistent of individuals. For example, when the Paris Communards set fire to the Louvre, his righteous defence of these men and women wavered. Prior to that point, he had broken "from the chorus and hatred of his class" (Thompson 1975, 197) to defend the workers of Paris. He wrote in the seventh *Letter of Fors Clavigera*: "I am myself a Communist of the old school – reddest also of the red; and was on the very point of saying so at the end of my last letter only the telegram about the Louvre's being on fire stopped me" (quoted in Thompson 1975, 198). But his essay on political economy, *Unto This Last*, was a profound influence on Morris and others. In it, Ruskin stated his views with unusual succinctness:

> There is no wealth but life, including all its powers of love, of joy, and of admiration. That country is the richest which nourishes the greatest number of noble and happy human beings. That man is richest who has the widest helpful influence, both personal, and by means of possessions, over the life of others.
> (Quoted in Thompson 1975, 199; see also Lindsay 1975, 114–15)

That phrase, "There is no wealth but life", continued to echo for Morris. Ruskin's essay, with its distinction between "wealth" and "riches" shocked the bourgeoisie so much when its first section appeared in *Cornhill* magazine, that its editor William Makepeace Thackeray cancelled the second and third parts (Lindsay 1975, 114). In the lecture "Work" from *The Crown of Wild Olive*, Ruskin might have shocked them further, when he remarked:

> There will always be a number of men who would fain set themselves to the accumulation of wealth as the sole object of their lives. Necessarily, that class of men is an uneducated class, inferior in intellect, and more or less cowardly. It is physically impossible for a well-educated, intellectual, or brave man to make money the chief object of his thoughts; as physically impossible as it is for him to make his dinner the principle object of them.
>
> (Ruskin 1900, 46–7)

It is not necessary to claim a direct influence of Ruskin or Morris on British jazz or its musicians of the sixties. However, just as Blake resonates for Westbrook and Cole for Parker, Ruskin and Morris are part of that same British tradition that links art and politics through aesthetic and ethical reasoning. That tradition can also call upon William Cobbett, Percy Bysshe Shelley, Sidney and Beatrice Webb, F.R. Leavis, Oscar Wilde, Raymond Postgate, George Orwell, Raymond Williams, Richard Hoggart and E.P. Thompson as witnesses on its behalf. It is a rich tradition indeed and one that runs through the history of the Labour movement, and it has come to inform the environmentalist movement as well.

More than that, these ideas had percolated, if not into the mainstream, at least into academia and broader intellectual discourse during the fifties and sixties. Most notably, Anthony Crosland had acknowledged his debt to Morris, Ruskin and others in his *The Future of Socialism* (Crosland 1956). The book had a very wide currency through discussion on radio and in the newspapers (see Louvre 1992; Seed 1992). Richard Hoggart's *The Uses of Literacy* (Hoggart 1969) was also widely read. In it Hoggart was highly critical of what he saw as the drift to an amorphous, mass popular culture, which he saw as destroying an authentic British proletarian culture. Such concerns had earlier been expressed, of course, by the critic F.R. Leavis, while George Orwell had written extensively on aspects of "popular" British culture from Dickens and Kipling to boys' comics. Orwell's *The Lion and the Unicorn* was also significant in spelling out a socialist alternative. The ideas of the Webbs, the Coles, Postgate, Ruskin and Morris also informed both left and right within the Labour Party, most notably through the Fabian Society, and in government through politicians such as Aneurin Bevan and Jennie Lee. In addition, a number of works such as E.P. Thompson's *The Making of the English Working Classes* (2002) and *The Crowd in History* by George Rudé

(1964) recovered a history of dissent and protest. Running through this body of ideas is not just a concern for greater equality in life but for a greater quality of life, where beauty and play co-exist alongside work that is no longer alienated.

So, where has this discussion led us? Hopefully to a point where we can now begin to fathom those elements that might constitute the ethics and aesthetics of British jazz in the sixties. One can identify a coalescence of values around certain ideas. First, British jazz was not parochial, looking both to America and Europe as well as at traditions at home. It drew on a range of musics other than African-American jazz in its development. These included both the indigenous musics of the British Isles, the musics of the Commonwealth and of both British church and pastoral music and western European art music. I think we can say that it was at least proto-internationalist in outlook. Second, it identified a relationship between art and life in a broader sense. It recognized that art could express a range of meanings and developed new forms that allowed it to express ideas and values. In this sense it was certainly socially conscious, if not always politically so. Third, *contra* Chaney, it was anti-elitist in its desire to communicate with and its commitment to its audience. Fourth, it was ecologically minded and non-manipulative. It was not heavily reliant on technology and was neither invasive nor unnecessarily exploitative of the resources it used. Fifth, it was anti-consumerist. Its product was hard to sell to a mass market, requiring time and engagement on the part of its audience. It expressed a set of values about art, beauty and their place in life that was at odds with the philosophy of the market place. Finally, it expressed a concern and sense of responsibility to its audience and to the musical traditions it carried forward. In all these respects, British jazz of the sixties, if not all its musicians, can be seen as anti-hegemonic in its cultural stance.

We have also suggested that the music and the meanings it carried derived from both practice and theory. It was not idealistic but materialist in this regard. It developed through engagement, through work, from its class location, from the history of jazz, through struggle and from its marginal cultural–economic position in a capitalist society. But there is one more point, we need to consider now in satisfying ourselves that we have grasped these issues firmly. It derives once more from Marx and Engels and is called commodification. It is important here if we are to understand those aspects of jazz, and particularly British jazz, of the sixties that resisted commodification.

The concept is directly related to Marx's theory of alienation and he uses the term "commodity fetishism" to describe the process by which objects which have a particular use value are changed in a market context into things that have an exchange value, normally expressed in monetary terms. Money, as the song goes, changes everything. Its very dominance within the process of exchange turns the object into its price. It becomes valued not merely for its use or even exchange values but for the price for which it can be sold.

That is where the word fetishism comes in. That this can be applied not just to objects such as food, clothing, consumer goods, or whatever is made clear by Etienne Balibar:

> If commodities (food, clothing, machines, raw materials, luxury objects, cultural goods, and even the bodies of prostitutes – in short, the whole world of human objects produced or consumed) seem to *have* an exchange value, money, for its part, seems to be exchange value itself, and by the same token intrinsically to possess the power to communicate to commodities which "enter into relation with it" that virtue or power which characterizes it.
> (Balibar 2007, 59; emphasis added; also 42–79)

Jazz has at various times become a commodity. This was notably the case in Britain with the "trad boom" and in America with swing in the thirties and forties. It might also be considered according to such a term in 1920s America. Wynton Marsalis's project at the Lincoln Center can also be read as an attempt to make jazz a commodity suitable for corporate consumption along the same kind of lines as the Metropolitan Opera – or to put it another way, making jazz safe for corporate America. However, in order to achieve this, he is forced to remove from jazz elements that do not fit this criterion such as free jazz, abstraction and jazz-rock. Miles Davis up to "time, no changes" is fine, while Coltrane up to *A Love Supreme* also qualifies. Swing's the thing and, intriguingly, it is this period of commodification that Marsalis looks to in order to define his agenda.

If jazz does otherwise resist commodification, then the reason for this must lie, first, in its emphasis on improvisation and, second, in the relationship within jazz between composition and improvisation. It will be clear that I am talking primarily about modern jazz. However, were traditional and mainstream musicians to re-examine early jazz, perhaps as American composer–saxophonist Henry Threadgill has done, then the comments above would certainly include that as well.

In a recent interview, pianist Howard Riley emphasized the importance of resisting the kind of marketing of jazz that turns into a lifestyle accessory:

> It's a music of individuals and individuality. Once you get away from that ... as I've found out it takes years to find your own individuality. So, it's not easy. But all the pressure is the other way. We live in a free market society and jazz has become a bit of a brand, which is anathema to me.   (Interview with Howard Riley, April 2011)

Riley would not class himself as a radical and sees the changes in British jazz as more or less a natural evolution. His point is, nonetheless, well-made. The sense is that jazz as "a brand" of such a kind is no longer jazz. Shortly before he died, John Stevens was asked by writer Michael Hrebeniak about a collection of his work from the mid- to late seventies under the title *A Luta Continua* (Konnex CD 5056). Stevens told Hrebeniak:

> This is music as a manifestation of our artistic, philosophical and political integration... I work in a combined arts fashion. Everything is intact but integrated rather than running parallel. There is a cohesion between elements. (Hrebeniak 1994)

Jazz is certainly an integrative or syncretic musical form drawing on a wide variety of elements. Perhaps, Stevens is correct in the implied suggestion that it is this that gives it a certain plasticity and a capacity to carry multivalent meanings beyond the musical. Stevens is clearly suggesting that it can and does contain features that are critical of the existing order. The obvious place to look for guidance in this difficult area might be in the work of the philosopher and music critic, Theodor W. Adorno. Three problems exist here, however. First, Adorno hated jazz, which he saw as a debased, manufactured, artificial music. In a forthright defence of jazz and popular music against Adorno's strictures, Alan Beckett outlines Adorno's perspective quite succinctly:

> Adorno makes an overt comparison between popular and "serious" music and postulates standardization of form, detail and character as the essential characteristic of the former. In popular music, there is never a dialectical relationship between form and detail. The form remains aloof, a mere container in which the details are mechanically concatenated; it gives no ulterior logic to the details, and, in turn, is not actualized in them. Form exerts a repressive influence on detail. The detail is never allowed to develop and so becomes "a caricature of its own potentialities"; it is presented only so that its relationship to the rigid schema is clear at all times, so that it leads one back inevitably to the predictable. Popular music can never surprise, and can never be revolutionary. Already, we can discern the crux of Adorno's thesis – that popular music is mere "social cement". (Beckett 1966)

Second, Adorno decried the resort by composers such as Stravinsky to what he called "folkloric elements". The first of these is easily overcome. Adorno confused the tin pan alley pop music of his era with jazz, which he never understood as a separate category. The second, however, causes us more problems. Jazz has always drawn to a degree on folk forms. This has particularly been the case in British and European jazz, where artists such as Bobby Wellins, Lars Gullin, John Surman, Jan Garbarek and many more have utilized such idioms as a means of establishing a local identity for jazz. The third problem lies in Adorno's emphasis in his analysis of the serialist composers – primarily Arnold Schönberg, Anton Webern and Alban Berg – on the alienation of form and content within critical art. This emphasis is crucial in the theory of "negative dialectics" that Adorno developed towards the end of his life. So powerfully is this concept identified in his musical criticism with the twelve-tone approach that it is hard to see how it might be applied to jazz or other musical styles. At the same time, it is clear that this is not the same as the dialectical relationship that I have described between composition and improvisation in modern jazz. Nor is it the same as the relationship between form and content in free improvisation. In the latter content could even be said to determine form rather than vice versa.

The imperative for the members of the Frankfurt School was to discover how in a world where, as Marx and Engels put it, "The ideas of the ruling class are in every epoch the ruling ideas" the true nature of society can be understood and revealed. Bourgeois culture is seen to be immanent and all-pervading. The picture it offers of the world is that it is as it is and, within it, it is hard or even impossible to see the world as being in any way different from that dominant ruling class culture. For Adorno, a new kind of thinking was required, one which allowed the subject, the philosopher or artist, to enter the object, capitalism or the social world, on its terms but to identify the contradictions between its form and content. For his friend, the philosopher and critic, Walter Benjamin the issue was the revelation of the "truth content" of a work of art, that is those elements that identified the exploitative and alienating reality of capitalist society. Marcuse, on the other hand, referred more simply to what he called "true art". The implications of this were essentially much the same as with Adorno's "negative dialectics" or Benjamin's "truth content".

It is at this point that the liberal critic senses blood and again cries "elitist", implying that the claim made for certain artists and works of art is at the very least vanguardist, while the claim that only those able to think in a certain way can see the truth contradicts the egalitarian principles of socialism. In a sense, we find ourselves in similar difficulty in our analysis of British modern jazz and free improvisation of the late sixties and early seventies. We are making claims for it, as a marginal music, that it offers a more accurate picture of the world than other musical forms of the period. If its difficulty were one aspect of its marginality, then surely its inaccessibility must militate against it ever becoming a mass art form and therefore it remains accessible only to an elite or "specialized audience". The "truth" of any such claim lies in the fact that if ever the major corporations in the entertainment industry succeeded in marketing jazz to a mass audience it would cease to have any real critical function – a point already made eloquently by Eddie Prévost. And yet, the likelihood of this actually happening seems rather remote. British modern jazz and free improvisation of our period (not unlike dialectical materialism!) place demands upon the listener. They do not give up their secrets easily – they require effort. But in turn they reward effort. They are not the property of one class or an elite group. The culture they sustain or which sustains them is not higher or lower in any bourgeois sense. It is not even so in any sense which bourgeois aesthetics might understand as "better" or "worse". It exists, indeed it functions, as a critique of such values.

Conversely, this is the problem for the liberal jazz or art critic. She/he can only weigh works of art in terms of a set of aesthetics that conforms to rules already established for them. Any attempt at exploring broader social or cultural values beyond the music or form itself inevitably founders within those same limitations. By contrast, the function of the cultural critic is to expose those rules and their underlying social values through celebrating that art which reaches beyond those limitations.

In Adorno, we find a pessimism that for some borders on fatalism (see Harker n.d.). For others, such as Jürgen Habermas, he frustrates because of his refusal to outline his own schema of thought and its engagement with the world. For Adorno, the role of the philosopher and of negative dialectics is to rescue and reveal not to prescribe. Marcuse and (to a lesser extent) Erich Fromm were more optimistic, but it is in Benjamin that we find the clearest echo for our project. He is, in some respects, a harder figure to pin down. He was throughout his short life drawn as much to anarchism and syndicalism as to Marxism. In some respects, the structure of Marxism gave order to his analysis of capitalism, yet he remained committed to a utopian, alternative vision of society in a way that was similar to that of Morris, finding in the past a model upon which a new order might be built. Benjamin's "truth content" is less prescriptive than Adorno's "negative dialectics", though the focus remains upon art that reveals contradiction rather than that which offers an alternative. And it is precisely this, which British jazz during these turbulent years did seem to offer.

Perhaps this suggestion is an optimistic one. However, the key critical aspect of British jazz of the sixties, the one that reveals its political aspects most sharply, lies in the way it counterposes an alternative, anti-exploitative series of relationships that do not resolve the alienation of capitalist society, but suggests that reality could be otherwise. Its relationships are anti-racist, value equally the collective and the individual – in fact, they suggest that the individual can only truly actualize themselves (to use Maslow's phrase) within the collective. If so, this is the "truth content" of the music of Westbrook, Garrick, Collier, Tippett, Nicols, Winstone, Surman, Prévost, Parker and Stevens. It can be found in music as different as Mike Westbrook's *Marching Song*, Graham Collier's *Mosaics*, in *AMMMusic*, in Barry Guy's *Ode*, in Eddie Prévost's *Silver Pyramid* and the SME's *Karyobin*. It is there in the playing of John Surman, Michael Garrick, Harry Beckett, Shake Keane, Mike Osborne, Paul Rutherford or Joe Harriott or the voices of Norma Winstone, Maggie Nicols and Julie Tippetts. It is the sound of engagement.

Conclusion: What is this Thing Called, Love?

Now was it that both found, the meek and lofty
Did both find, helpers to their heart's desire,
And stuff at hand, plastic as they could wish;
Were called upon to exercise their skill,
Not in Utopia, subterranean fields,
Or some secreted island, Heaven knows where!
But in the very world, which is the world
Of all of us, the place where in the end
We find our happiness, or not at all!
> William Wordsworth, *The French Revolution,*
> *as it Appeared to Enthusiasts*

The jury is now out. We have marshalled our evidence and arguments. The sixties were unusual times, when many questions about how we might live on this planet were asked, if not answered or resolved. It seemed then, and still does, that those years were simultaneously fraught with doubts but rich in hope. There have been other periods in history that have seen similar intellectual and cultural turbulence – the Renaissance, the Reformation, the Romantic era, the democratic and nationalist struggles of the 1840s and perhaps also the period following the ending of the First World War and the Russian Revolution. Yet, the sixties seem unique, if only in their pace and profile – courtesy of systems of mass communication. The arts, and not least British jazz, reflected and commented upon and informed this ongoing debate.

We should not be blind to the possibility that, if you look, you will find the sixties that you seek. Some – Barry Miles, Jonathon Green and Jeff Nuttall would be among their number – would see this as an era of boldness and bravery. Others – Roger Scruton and the American New Right, for example – would argue that never was so much arrant, even dangerous nonsense spouted as in those years. And, of course, as American writer Todd Gitlin (2003) delights in pointing out, the right was as much nourished and nurtured in those heady days, as was the left. Jerry Rubin's conversion from yippie to yuppie was no accident of fate. The return to economic liberalism was a far more predictable outcome of the sixties than the prospects of an enlightened, communitarian ideal.

On balance, however, the sixties raised issues and awareness among many who went through those times. The women's movement, anti-racism, anti-sexism, the peace and environmental movements – these and many other progressive causes found expression in the 1960s. Culturally and artistically, new ideas and practices flourished and, for a time at least, an audience for a wide-ranging, open-minded aesthetic came into being. In these respects, the legacy of the sixties is a positive one and it may yet become a touchstone for new generations desirous of affecting social change. If so, hopefully they will realize, as too many of us did not, that this will take more than love, flowers and good vibes. The research projects of Stanley Milgram at Harvard in 1961 (Milgram 1974) and Philip Zimbardo at Stanford University in 1971 (Haney *et al.* 1973), and the anti-Vietnam film *Winter Soldiers* (1972), suggested a darker, more sinister trajectory for humankind.

We have argued that British jazz in this period represented a musical form and practice that embodied an aesthetic, cultural and, by implication, also a political challenge to bourgeois culture and ideology. I have sought to articulate through the comments of key musical personalities the kinds of values and assumptions that underpinned this contesting of meaning, but also have attempted to locate this within both the praxis of jazz, its history and the class position of its participants. We would certainly not propose that jazz was a "revolutionary" art form and have used the word "political" with hesitancy. Revolutionary art only occurs in revolutionary or post-revolutionary situations. At the same time, we would argue that British jazz raised cultural questioning to an extent that was radical and far-reaching.

But there is an elephant in the room and we cannot ignore it here. If British jazz was "political" in this broader sense, then is it still so today? There is not an easy answer to this question. One can certainly see in the work and broader musical and social involvement of musicians who came through in the eighties – those who played in Loose Tubes and the Jazz Warriors, for example – concerns that can only be described as "political". Similar considerations can be found in the work of many of the younger improvising musicians, most notably composer Simon Fell and multi-instrumentalist Martin Archer, and also in the endeavours of composers Colin Towns and Hans Koller.

With regard to the new generation of players, one hears and enjoys some remarkable music, complex, uplifting and sometimes brilliant. But it seems to speak of itself, its own world and those other creative worlds that touch upon it. The difference for this generation lies perhaps in a series of absences

– of questioning, of debate, of confidence, of ideas, of history, of belief. Mike Westbrook, Graham Collier, Evan Parker, John Stevens – these artists made music against a backcloth of ideas in ferment. That seems less the case today. At the same time, the socio-economic and cultural position of British jazz musicians and of British jazz remains just as ambiguous and difficult as it was for that sixties generation of players and fans.

The origin and history of this music has not changed, nor has its basis in improvisatory practice. One thing that was present in the sixties is most certainly not absent in this decade: if anything the issues about how we live together, what systems of government we have, what forms of economic production dominate and how far we share a common humanity and responsibility for each other are sharper now and will become sharper still. The potential for British jazz, and all the arts, to contribute to debate and struggle is as great now as it was then. The artists, thinkers, writers and activists among us can help to make our choices clearer, instil us with optimism and inspire us. Or they can remain quiescent. If so, then the rest truly is silence.

Appendix: 100 Essential British Jazz Records, 1957–76

AMM. 1968. *The Crypt – 12th June 1968* (Matchless MR5; MRCD05).

Ardley, Neil. 1975. *Kaleidoscope of Rainbows* (GULP1018; Dusk Fire DUSKCD101).

Barber, Chris. 1961. *At the London Palladium* (Columbia 33SX1346; Lake Records LACD210D).

Beck, Gordon. 1968. *Gyroscope* (Morgan SMJ1; Art of Life AL1003-2).

Beckett, Harry. 1971. *Flare Up* (Philips 6308026; Jazzprint JPVP124CD).

Beckett, Harry. 1971. *Warm Smiles* (RCA SF 8225; Vocalion 2CDSML8430).

Beckett, Harry. 1972. *Themes for Fega* (RCA SF 8264; Vocalion 2CDSML 8430).

Bilk, Acker. 1968. *Blue Acker* (Columbia TWO230; Lake LACD218).

Brotherhood of Breath. 1971. *Chris McGregor's Brotherhood of Breath* (Neon NE2; Fledg'ling FLED3062).

Brotherhood of Breath. 1974. *Live at Willisau* (Ogun OG100; OGCD 001).

Brown, Pete. 1970. *Things May Come and Things May Go But the Arts School Dance Goes on Forever* (Harvest SHVL768; BGOCD522).

Brown, Sandy. 1962. *The Incredible McJazz* (Columbia 33SX1509; Lake LACD229).

Brown, Sandy. 1969. *Hair at its Hairiest* (Fontana SFJL921).

Bruce, Jack. 1970. *Things We Like* (Polydor 583058; Polydor 065603-2).

Bruce, Jack. 1970. *Songs for a Tailor* (Polydor 2343033; Polydor 065604-2).

Cameron, John. 1969. *Off Centre* (Deram SML1044; Vocalion CDSML 8409).

Carr, Ian. 1972. *Belladonna* (Vertigo 6360076; BGOCD566).

Coe, Tony. 1967. *Tony's Basement* (Columbia SCX6170).

Colosseum. 1969. *Valentyne Suite* (Vertigo VO1; Sanctuary SMEDD097).

Collier, Graham. 1970. *Songs for My Father* (1970 Fontana 6309006; BGO).

Collier, Graham. 1970. *Mosaics* (Philips 6308051; BGOCD767).

Collier, Graham. 2005. *Workpoints* (Cuneiform RUNE 213/214).

Coxhill/Miller (Lol Coxhill and Steve Miller). 1973. *Miller/Coxhill* (Caroline C1503; Cuneiform RUNE 253/254).

Ken Colyer. 1961. *This is the Blues Volume I* (Columbia 33SX1363).

Dankworth, John. 1967. *The $1,000,000 Collection* (Fontana STL5445).

Dean, Elton. 1971. *Elton Dean* (CBS 64539; Cuneiform Rune 103).

D'Silva, Amancio. 1969. *Integration* (Columbia SCX6322; Universal 9866893).

Fame, Georgie. 1966. *Sound Venture* (Columbia SX6076).

Garrick, Mike. 1965. *Promises* (Argo ZDA 36; Vocalion CDSML 8440).

Garrick, Mike. 1965. *October Woman* (Argo ZDA33; Vocalion CDSML 8413).

Garrick, Mike. 1972. *Mr. Smith's Apocalypse* (Argo ZAGF1; Vocalion CDSML 8433).

Gaynair, Winton "Bogey". 1959. *Blue "Bogey"* (Tempo Tap25; Jasmine CD JM0460).

Gibbs, Mike. 1972. *Just Ahead* (Polydor 2683011; BGOCD679).

Guy, Barry and London Jazz Composers' Orchestra. 1972. *Ode* (Incus 6/7; Intakt CD041).

Harriott, Joe. 1960. *Free Form* (Jazzland JLP49; Universal 538184-2).

Harriott, Joe. 1962. *Abstract* (Columbia 33SX 1477; Universal 538 183-2).

Harriott, Joe. 1969. *Hum Dono* (Columbia SCX6345).

Harriott, Joe/Mayer, John. 1966. *Indo-Jazz Suite* (Columbia SCX6025; Rhino Records US P01692).

Harriott, Joe/Mayer, John. 1967. *Indo-Jazz Fusions* (Columbia SCX6122).

Harriott, Joe/Mayer, John. 1968. *Indo-Jazz Fusions II* Columbia SCX6215.

Hayes, Tubby. 1969. *Mexican Green* (Fontana SFJL911; Universal 9831983).

Iskra 1903. 1972. *Iskra 1903* (Incus 3/4; EMANEM 4301).

Jazz Couriers. 1958. *In Concert* (Tempo TAP 22).

Kinsey, Tony. 1961. *An Evening With...* (EmberEMB3337; Fantastic Voyage FVTD050).

Laine, Cleo. 1964. *Shakespeare and All That Jazz* (Fontana STL5209).

Lowther, Henry. 1970. *Child Song* (Deram SML1070; Vocalion CDSML 8403).

Lyttelton, Humphrey. 1960. *Blues in the Night* (Columbia 33SX1239; Lake LACD216).

Lyttelton, Humphrey. 1966. *Buck Clayton with Humphrey Lyttelton & His Band* (77 Records 77LEU 12/18; Lake LACD227).

McGregor, Chris. 1968. *Very Urgent* (1968 Polydor 184137; Fledg'ling FLED3059).

McLaughlin, John. 1969. *Extrapolation* (Marmalade 608007; Polydor 841598-2).

McLaughlin/Surman/Holland/Berger/Martin. 1971. *Where Fortune Smiles* (Dawn DNLS 3018; CMETD1433).

McNair, Harold. *The Fence* (B&C CAS1016; HUX 095).

Music Improvisation Company. 1970. *Music Improvisation Company* (ECM1005; Japo CD UCCU-9019).

New Departures Quartet. 1964. *New Departures Quartet* (Transatlantic TR134).

New Jazz Orchestra. 1969. *Déjeuener Sur L'herbe* (Verve SVLP9326).

Nucleus *Elastic Rock/We'll Talk about It Later* (Vertigo 6360008/Vertigo 6360027; BGO CD47).

NYJO. 1971. *The National Youth Jazz Orchestra* (Philips 6308067).

Osborne, Mike. 1971. *Outback* (Turtle TUR300; FMR CD07-031994).

Osborne, Mike. 1975. *All Night Long* (Ogun OG700; OGCD029).

Oxley, Tony. 1969. *Baptised Traveller* (CBS 52664; Columbia 494438 2).

Parker, Evan. 1970. *The Topography of the Lungs* (Incus 1; psi 06.05).

Pentangle. 1968. *Sweet Child* (Transatlantic TRA178).

Poetry & Jazz. 1964. *In Concert* (Argo ZDA 26/27; Vocalion 2CDSML 8416).

Prévost, Eddie & The Music Now Ensemble. 2001. *Silver Pyramid* (Matchless MRCD40).

Reece, Dizzy. 1957. *Progress Report* (Tempo TAP9; Mosaic B2-97395).

Rendell, Don. 1961. *Roarin'* (Riverside Jazzland JLP51; BGP CDBGPM166).

Rendell, Don. 1972. *Spacewalk* (Columbia SCX6491).

Rendell–Carr Quintet. 1966. *Dusk Fire* (Columbia SCX 6064; BGOCD615).

Ricotti, Frank. 1969. *Our Point of View* (CBS 52668).

Riley, Howard. 1970. *The Day Will Come* (CBS 64077).

Riley, Howard. 1971. *Flight* (Turtle TUR301; FMR).

Ross, Ronnie. 1969. *Cleopatra's Needle* (Fontana SFJL915).

Russell, Ray. 1970. *Rites and Rituals* (CBS 64271).

Russell, Ray. 1971. *Live at the ICA* (RCA SF8214; Moikai M4CD).

S.O.S. 1975. *S.O.S.* (Ogun OG400; OGCD019).

Scott, Ronnie. 1966. *The Night is Scott and You're So Swingable* (Fontana TL5332).

Scott, Ronnie and The Band. 1969. *Live at Ronnie Scott's* (CBS Realm 523661; Sony/BMG 88697072392).

Sims, Zoot. 1962. *Solo for Zoot* (Fontana 680 982TL).

Skidmore, Alan. 1969. *Once Upon a Time* (Decca Nova SDN11; Vocalion CDSML 8406).

Soft Machine. 1970. *Third* (CBS 66246; Sony BMG 82876872932).

Spontaneous Music Ensemble. 1968. *Karyobin (Are the Imaginary Birds that Live in Paradise)* (Island ILPS9079).

Stobart, Kathy. 1978. *Arbeia* (Spotlite SPJ-CD409).

Surman, John. 1969. *How Many Clouds Can You See?* (Deram SML-R 1045).

Surman, John. 1973. *Morning Glory* (Island ILPS 9237; FMR CD13-L495).

Taylor, John. 1971. *Pause, and Think Again* (Turtle TUR302; FMR CD24-L1295).

Taylor, Mike. 1965. *Pendulum* (Columbia SX6042; Sunbeam SBRCD5034).

Taylor, Mike. 1966. *Trio* (Columbia SX6137; Universal 9866894).

Tippett, Keith. 1971. *Dedicated to You But You Weren't Listening* (Vertigo 6360024; Repertoire Rep 5127).

Tippett, Keith. 1971. *Septober Energy* (RCA Neon NE9; BGOCD485).

Tippetts, Julie. 1975. *Sunset Glow* (Utopia UTS601).

Tracey, Stan. 1965. *Jazz Suite – Under Milk Wood* (Columbia E33SX17741970; Resteamed RSJ101).

Tracey, Stan. 1970. *Seven Ages of Man* (Columbia SCX6413).

The Trio. 1970. *The Trio* (Dawn DNLS 3006; Sanctuary CMETD1433).

Welsh, Alex. 1968. *At Home With … Alex Welsh and His Band* (Columbia SX6213).

Westbrook, Mike. 1969. *Marching Song* (Deram SML 1047/1048; PSALM2312).

Westbrook, Mike. 1971. *Metropolis* (RCA Neon NE10; BGOCD 454).

Westbrook, Mike. 1975. *Citadel/Room 315* (RCA SF8433; BGOCD 713).

Wheeler, Kenny. 1968. *Windmill Tilter* (Fontana STL5494; BGO CD944).

Wheeler, Kenny. 1973. *Song for Someone* (Incus 10; psi 04.01).

Winstone, Norma. 1971. *Edge of Time* (Argo ZDA148).

Bibliography

Abrams, M. A. 1959. *The Teenage Consumer*. London: London Press Exchange.

Abrams, M. A. 1960. *Must Labour Lose?* Harmondsworth: Penguin.

Adams, R., S. Gibson and S. Muller Arisona. 2008. *Transdisciplinary Digital Art*. Berlin: Springer.

Aitken, J. 1967. *The Young Meteors*. London: Secker & Warburg.

Arieti, S. 1981. *Understanding and Helping The Schizophrenic: A Guide for Family and Friends*. London: Pelican.

Ash, V. with S. Spillett and H. Ash. 2006. *I Blew It My Way: Bebop, Big Bands and Sinatra*. London: Northway.

Attali, J. 1985. *Noise: The Political Economy of Music*. Minneapolis, MN: University Of Minnesota Press.

Bailey, D. 1992. *Improvisation: Its Nature and Practice in Music*. Cambridge, MA: Da Capo Press.

Balibar, E. 2007. *The Philosophy of Marx*. London: Verso.

Banks, O. 1981. *Faces of Feminism: A Study of Feminism as a Social Movement*, Oxford: Oxford University Press.

Baraka, A. 1998. *Black Music*. Cambridge, MA: Da Capo Press.

Barthes, R. 1981. *Mythologies*. St Albans: Granada.

Becker H, 1963. *Outsiders*. New York: Free Press.

Beckett, A. 1966. "Popular Music: Basic Assumptions and Background". *New Left Review* I(39) September/October: 87–90.

Bell, C. 1999. "History of the LMC". *Variant* 8, Summer, www.variant.org.uk/8texts/Clive_Bell.html.

Berg, L. 1969. *Risinghill: Death of a Comprehensive School*. Harmondsworth: Penguin.

Berlin, I. 1969. *Two Concepts of Liberty: Four Essays on Liberty*. Oxford: Oxford University Press.

Birch, B. 2010. *Keeper of the Flame: Modern Jazz in Manchester 1946–1972*. Cleckheaton: Amadeus Press.

Bird, C. 1967. "McGregor: The New 'Boss' Man From Cape Town". *Melody Maker* 15 July: 6.

Black, L. 2006. "'Not only a source of expenditure but a source of income': The Creative Industries and Cultural Politics in Britain from the 1960s to Cool Britannia". In

Cultural Industries: The British Experience in International Perspective. C. Eisenberg, R. Gerlach and C. Handke (eds). Berlin: Humboldt University.

Blake, W. 1804 Untitled verses (now commonly known as "Jerusalem") from the Preface to *Milton: a Poem*. See www.blakearchive.org/exist/blake/archive/work.xq?workid= milton&java=yes.

Boulton, D. 1958. *Jazz in Britain*. London: W.H. Allen.

Boyd, J. 2006. *White Bicycles: Making Music in the 1960s*. London: Serpent's Tail.

Brand, P. 1960. "Beaulieu: R.I.P. Jazz Succumbs to the Hooligans". *Melody Maker* 5 August: 2–3.

Brooke, H. 1964. "Operation of the Immigration Control under the Commonwealth Immigrants Act". Cabinet Paper CP (64) 89, 22 April.

Brown, J. R. 2007. "Dankworth at 80". *Jazz Review* 83, August–September: 13–17.

Brown, R. 1974. "Ian Carr Interviewed". *Into Jazz* February: 7–11.

Brown, T. 1960. "Jazz under Fire: Fans Must Fight to End Smear Campaign". *Melody Maker* 20 August: 2–3.

Burman, M. 1958. "Ronnie Scott Says: 'Our Critics Are at Fault'". *Melody Maker* 23 August: 5.

Byrne, P. 1997. *Social Movements in Britain*. London: Routledge.

Callaghan, T. 2000. Sleevenotes to *Septober Energy*. BGOCD485.

Capel, M. 1961. "The Metamorphosis of Orpheus". *Jazz Monthly* January: 2–6, 12.

Capel, M. 1962. "Fight For Equality: A Reply to G.E. Lambert". *Jazz Monthly* 7(12): 26.

Carr, I. 1971. "The State of British Jazz Part 2: the Audience". *Melody Maker* 30 October: 24.

Carr, I. 2008. *The Music Outside*. London: Northway.

Carr, I., D. Fairweather and B. Priestley. 1987. *Jazz: The Essential Companion*. London: Grafton.

Carter, A. 1978. *The Sadeian Woman and the Ideology of Pornography*. New York: Pantheon.

Case, B., S. Britt and C. Murray. 1986. *The Illustrated Encyclopedia of Jazz*. London: Salamander.

Caute, D. 1988. *Sixty-Eight Years of the Barricades*. London: Hamish Hamilton.

Chambers, I. 1993. *Popular Culture: The Metropolitan Experience*. London: Routledge.

Chaney, D. 1994. *The Cultural Turn: Scene-setting Essays on Contemporary Cultural History*. London: Routledge.

Chapman, R. 2010. *Syd Barrett: A Very Irregular Head*. London: Faber.

Clark, T. J. 2012. "For a Left with No Future". *New Left Review* 74, www.newleftreview. org/?page=article&view=2954.

Clements, S. 2008. "Feminism, Citizenship and Social Activity: The Role and Importance of Local Women's Organisations, Nottingham 1918–1969". PhD thesis, University of Nottingham.

Cockburn, A. and R. Blackburn. 1970. *Student Power*. Harmondsworth: Penguin.

Cockburn, A. and J. St Clair. 1991. *Whiteout: The CIA, Drugs and the Press*. London: Verso.

Codell, J. F. 1998. "Ford Madox Brown, Carlyle, Macaulay and Bakhtin: The Pratfalls and Penultimates of History". *Art History* 21(3): 324–66.

Cohen, S. 1972. *Folk Devils and Moral Panics: Creation of Mods and Rockers*. London: MacGibbon & Kee.

Cole, G. D. H. and W. Mellow. 1918. *The Meaning of Industrial Freedom*. London: George Allen & Unwin.

Coleman, R. 1961. "Trad: a Taste of Money." *Melody Maker* 23 December: 3, 13.

Collier, G. 1970. Sleevenotes to *Songs For My Father*. Fontana SFJL922.

Collier, G. 2004 Sleevenotes to *Workpoints* CD. RUNE 213/214.

Collier, L. 1978. *The Making of Jazz: A Comprehensive History*. London: Papermac.

Conway, D. 2007. *A Nation of Immigrants?: A Brief Demographic History of Britain*. London: Civitas.

Cook, R. and B. Morton. 2000. *The Penguin Guide to Jazz on CD*. 5th Edition. London: Penguin.

Cooper, C. 1998. "Obituary: Ivor Mairants". *Independent* 26 February, www.independent. co.uk/news/obituaries/obituary-ivor-mairants-1147017.html

Copasetic, J. 1972. "Johnny Cool and the Island of the Sirens". In *Rock File*, C. Gillett (ed.). London: Pictorial.

Courtwright, D. 2001. *Forces of Habit: Drugs and the Making of the Modern World*. Cambridge, MA: Harvard University.

Cox, B., J. Shirley and M. Short. 1977. *The Fall of Scotland Yard*. Harmondsworth: Penguin.

Creasy, M. 2007. *Legends on Tour: The Pop Package Tours of the 1960s*. Stroud: History Press.

Crosland, A. 1956. *The Future of Socialism*. London: Jonathan Cape.

Crossman, R. 1979. *The Crossman Diaries*. London: Methuen.

Crouch, C. 1970. *The Student Revolt*. London: Bodley Head.

Dankworth, J. 1950. "Johnny Dankworth". *Jazz Illustrated* May: 2–3.

Dankworth, J. 1998. *Jazz: In Revolution*. London: Constable.

Davidson, M. 1997a. Sleevenotes to *Withdrawal*. EMANEM 4020.

Davidson, M. 1997b. "John Stevens: An Appreciation". *Jazzlive* 114: 24–5.

Davidson, M. 2001. Sleevenotes to SME *Challenge*. EMANEM 4053.

Dawbarn, B. 1960. "The Next Step?". *Melody Maker* 10 September: 12.

Dawbarn, B. 1961a. "Something's Got to Happen ...". *Meolody Maker* 18 November: 7.

Dawbarn, B. 1961b. "What Happended? Screams Bob Dawbarn". *Melody Maker* 18 November: 15.

Dawbarn, B. 1962a. "British Modern Scene is at Its Lowest Ebb". *Melody Maker* 7 January: 9.

Dawbarn, B. 1962b. "Eric Dolphy's Out There". *Melody Maker* 21 April: 7.

Dawbarn, B. 1962c. "You Have to Work Harder in the States: Says Tubby Hayes". *Melody Maker* 7 July: 9.

Dawbarn, B. 1964. "The Four Altos Of Joe Harriott". *Melody Maker* 8 August: 10.

Dawbarn, B. 1968. "Agony of Tubby Hayes". *Melody Maker* 12 September: 16.

Denselow, R. 1990. *When The Music's Over: The Story of Political Pop*. London: Faber.

Donnelly, M. 2005. *Sixties Britain*. London: Pearson Longman.

Ehrenreich, B. and J. Ehrenreich. 1979. "The Professional-Managerial Class." In *Between Labour and Capital*, P. Walker. (ed.). Brighton: Harvester.

Eisenberg, C., R. Gerlach and C. Handke. (eds). 2006. *Cultural Industries: The British Experience in International Perspective*. Berlin: Humboldt University.

Fairclough, A. 1983. "Was Martin Luther King a Marxist?" *History Workshop* 15: 117–25.

Farbey, R. 2010. *The Music of Ian Carr: A Critical Discography*. London: Farbey.

Fordham, J. 1986. *Let's Join Hands and Contact the Living*. London: Elm Tree.

Fox, C. 1972. *The Jazz Scene*. London: Hamlyn.

Fraser, R. 1988. *1968: A Student Generation in Revolt*. London: Pantheon.

Freeguard, J. 2004. "It's Time for the Women of the 1950s to Stand Up and Be Counted". Unpublished DPhil thesis, University of Sussex.

Frith, S. 1975. "You Can Make It If You Try: The Motown Story" In *The Soul Book*, I. Hoare (ed.). London: Methuen.

Frith, S. 2007. "Is Jazz Popular Music?" *Jazz Research Journal* 1(1): 7–23.

Fussell, P. 2000. *The Great War and Modern Memory*. London: Sterling.

Gabbard, K. 1996. *Jammin' At the Margins: Jazz and the American Cinema*. Chicago, IL: University of Chicago Press.

Gelder, K. and S. Thornton. 2007. *Subcultures: Cultural Histories and Social Practice*. London: Routledge.

Gillett, C. 1972. *Rock File*. London: Pictorial.

Gillett, C. 1975. *Making Tracks*. London: Panther.

Gitlin, T. 2003. *The Whole World is Watching: Mass Media in the Making and Unmaking of the New Left*. Berkeley, CA: University of California Press.

Glyn, S. and Booth, A. 1996. *Modern Britain: An Economic and Social History*. London: Routledge.

Godbolt, J. 1986. *A History of Jazz in Britain 1919–50*. London: Paladin.

Godbolt, J. 1989. *A History of Jazz in Britain 1950–70*. London: Quartet.

Goldthorpe, J. and D. Lockwood. 1968. *The Affluent Worker: Industrial Attitudes and Behaviour*. Cambridge: Cambridge University Press.

Goldthorpe, J. and D. Lockwood. 1969. *The Affluent Worker in the Class Structure*. Cambridge: Cambridge University Press.

Goode, C. and R. Cotterell. 2003. *Bass Lines*. London: Northway.

Green, B. 1962. *The Reluctant Art*. London: MacGibbon & Kee.

Green, J. 1998a. *Days in the Life: Voices from the English Underground 1961–71*. London: Pimlico.

Green J. 1998b. *All Dressed Up: The Sixties and the Counterculture*. London: Jonathan Cape.

Gregg, P. 1968. *The Welfare State: An Economic and Social History of Great Britain from 1945 to the Present Day*. London: Harrap.

Grimes, K. 1979. *Jazz at Ronnie Scott's*. London: Robert Hale.

Hallward, P. 2006. "Staging Equality: On Rancière's Theatrocracy". *New Left Review* 37: 109–29.

Halsey, A. H. [1958] 1977. "Genetics, Social Structure and Intelligence". In *Heredity and Environment*, A. H. Halsey. (ed.). London: Methuen.

Halsey, A. H. (ed.) 1972. *Trends in British Society since 1900: A Guide to the Changing Social Structure of Britain*. Basingstoke: Macmillan.

Halsey, A. H. 1978. *Change in British Society*. Oxford: Oxford University Press.

Halsey, A. H., A. F. Heath and J. M. Ridge. 1980. *Origins and Destinations: Family, Class, and Education in Modern Britain*. Oxford: Clarendon Press.

Haney, C., W. C. Banks and P. G. Zimbardo. 1973. "Study of Prisoners and Guards in a Simulated Prison". *Naval Research Reviews* 9: 1–17.

Harker, D. 1980. *One for the Money: Politics and Popular Song*. London: Hutchinson.

Harker, D. n.d. "In Perspective: Theodor Adorno". Humbolt University Paper, www2. hu-berlin.de/fpm/textpool/texte/harker_in-perspective-theodor-adorno.htm.

Harris, R. 1961. *Enjoying Jazz*. London: Jazz Book Club.

Harrison, M., E. Thacker and S. Nicholson. 2000. *The Essential Jazz Records Volume 2: Modernism to Postmodernism*. London: Mansell.

Haycock, D. B. 2009. *A Crisis of Brilliance*. London: Old Street.

Hebdige, D. 1980. *Subculture: The Meaning of Style*. London: Methuen.

Heckstall-Smith, D. 1989. *The Safest Place in the World*. London: Quartet.

Heffley, M. 2000. "Jazz in German Eyes". http://mheffley.web.wesleyan.edu/almatexts/almamusicology/German%20Free%20Jazz%20in%20German%20Eyes.pdf.

Heining, D. 1997a. "Is This Man Britain's Greatest Living Composer?" *Avant* 1: 22–3.

Heining, D. 1997b. "'Pathfinder' Surman". *Avant* 2: 4–7.

Heining, D. 2000. "Annie Whitehead: Before We Knew". *Avant* 17: 10.

Heining, D. 2001a. "Prime Direction". *Jazzwise* 40: 26–9.

Heining, D. 2001b. "Song of a Smaller World". *Jazz UK* 40: 11–12.

Heining, D. 2001c. "Blazing Horns". *Jazzwise* 44: 40–2.

Heining, D. 2001d. "Wide Open Spaces". *Jazzwise* 46: 36–8.

Heining, D. 2003a. "Milestone Man". *Jazz UK* 55: 19.

Heining, D. 2003b. "Soft Machine Way Ahead". *Jazzwise* 67: 28–33.

Heining, D. 2004a. "Flash Back". *Jazzwise* 71: 36–8.

Heining, D. 2004b. "Miles Ahead". *Jazz UK* 58: 14–15.

Heining, D. 2004c. "Shy Guy". *Jazzwise* 90: 34–7.

Heining, D. 2005a. "Parallel Universe". *Jazz UK* 64: 16–17.

Heining, D. 2005b. "Alive in Every Moment". *Jazz UK* 66: 16–17.

Heining, D. 2006a. "Tempus Fugit". *Jazzwise* 102: 34–5.

Heining, D. 2006b. "The Big Picture". *Jazzwise* 103: 35–6.

Heining, D. 2006c. "The Outsider". *Jazzwise* 95: 40–1.

Heining, D. 2006d. "Standard Time". *Jazzwise* 104 : 36–9.

Heining, D. 2006e. "Duet for One". *Jazz UK* 70: 19.

Heining, D. 2006f. "A Critical Light on Project Jazz". *Jazz UK* 68: 16–17.

Heining, D. 2007a. "Big It Up". *Jazzwise* 105: 36–8.

Heining, D. 2007b. "The Tipping Point". *Jazzwise* 109: 28–32.

Heining, D. 2007c. "Changing Man". *Jazzwise* 111: 30–3.

Heining, D. 2007d. "Human Nature". *Jazzwise* 113: 24–8.

Heining, D. 2007e. "The Strange Life and Death of Mike Taylor". *Jazzwise* 115: 42–5.

Heining, D. 2008a. "Free Spirit". *Jazzwise* 122: 34–7.

Heining, D. 2008b. "The Calling". *Jazzwise* 123: 33–5.

Heining, D. 2008c. "Bass Instinct". *Jazzwise* 124: 20–4.

Heining, D. 2008d. "An Audience With the Jazz Royals". *Jazz UK* 82: 22–4.

Heining, D. 2008e. "Mixing It". *Jazzwise* 125: 26–8.

Heining, D. 2009a. "Cry Freedom". *Jazzwise* 126: 40–43.

Heining, D. 2009b. "Old Flames New Flames". *Jazz UK* 87: 20–23.

Heining, D. 2009c. "An Englishman Abroad". *Jazzwise* August: 18–21.

Heining, D. 2010a. "Standard Time". *Jazzwise* 140: 32–3.

Heining, D. 2010b. "Days of Thunder". *Jazz UK* 94: 18–22.

Heining, D. 2010c. "Drumming to a Different Beat". *Jazzwise* 147: 30–32.

Heining, D. 2010d. *George Russell: The Story of an American Composer*. Lanham, MD: Scarecrow.

Hennessey, M. 1999. Sleevenotes to *Celebration*. Universal reissue 844852-2.

Hensman, C. R. 1975. *Rich and Poor*. Harmondsworth: Penguin.

Hill, P. 1992. "Chronochromie". www.philharmonia.co.uk/messiaen/music/chrono.html.

Hoare, I. (ed.). 1975. *The Soul Book*. London: Methuen.

Hobsbawm, E. 1990. *Industry and Empire*. Harmondsworth: Penguin.

Hobsbawm, E. 2010. "Diary: My Days as a Jazz Critic". *London Review of Books* 32(10): 41.

Hoggart, R. 1965. "The Culture Confusion". *Focus* March: 33–4.

Hoggart, R. 1969. *The Uses of Literacy*. Harmondsworth: Pelican.

Hollis, P. 1997. *Jennie: A Life*. Oxford: Oxford University Press.

Hornsey College of Art Students and Staff. 1969. *The Hornsey Affair*. Harmondsworth: Penguin.

Horrocks, R. 1995. *Male Myths and Icons*. Basingstoke: Macmillan.

Houston, B. 1963. "We're Getting There Says Joe Harriott". *Melody Maker* 23 February: 15.

Houston, B. 1965. "Harriott in High Spirits". *Melody Maker* 22 February: 14.

Houston, B. 1966. "'The Indo-jazz Gap is Closing Rapidly". *Melody Maker* 23 April: 12.

Houston, B. 1967. "Another Fruitful Trip Down that Old Indo-Jazz Trail". *Melody Maker* 15 April: 14.

Houston, B. 1968. "The Sextet: The McGregor Legend on Record at Last". *Melody Maker* 1 June: 14.

Houston, B. 1969. "Westbrook Surman". *Melody Maker* 8 February: 21.

Hrebeniak, M. 1994. Sleevenotes to *A Luta Continua*. Konnex KCD5056.

Hunt, K. 2004. "Obituary: John Mayer Composer Who Successfully Fused Indian and Western Music". *Guardian* 13 March, www.guardian.co.uk/news/2004/mar/13/guardianobituaries.artsobituaries1.

Jackson, J. H. 2003. *Making Jazz French: Music and Modern Life in Interwar Paris*. Durham, NC: Duke University Press.

Jewell, D. 1971. Sleevenotes to *NYJO*. Philips 6308 067.

Jones, M. 1962. "Rhythm & Blues Boom Hits London Clubs but Blues Inc Korner the Market". *Melody Maker* 25 August: 8–9.

Jones, M. 1966. "Harriott Yielding Ground to the East". *Melody Maker* 2 April: 4.

Kater, M. H. 2003. *Different Drummers: Jazz in the Culture of Nazi Germany*. New York: Oxford University Press.

Kemp, T. 1985. *Industrialization in Nineteenth Century Europe*. London: Longman.

Keynes, J. M. 1945. *The Listener* 12 July.

Kilmuir. 1957. "Colonial Immigrants: Report of the Committee of Ministers". Cabinet Paper C (57) 162, 12 July.

Kuhn, T. 1996. *The Structure of Scientific Revolutions*. Chicago, IL: University of Chicago Press.

Labour Party. 1959. "Leisure for Living: Labour Party Policy Statement". London: Transport House.

Laing, D. 1972. "Roll Over Lonnie (Tell George Formby the News)". In *Rock File*. C. Gillett (ed.). London: New England Library.

Lambert, G. E. 1962. "Random Reflections". *Jazz Monthly* 7(12): 13.

Larkin, P. 1985. *All What Jazz*. London: Faber.

Lart, R. 1992. "Changing Images of the Addict and Addiction". *International Journal on Drug Policy* 1: 118–25.

Le Gendre, K. 1998. "Too Good to Be Forgotten" *Independent* 13 November, www.independent.co.uk/arts-entertainment/music-too-good-to-be-forgotten-1184552.html

Levin, R. 1962. Sleevenotes to Dizzy Reece *Asia Minor* CD release. OJCCD-1806-2.

Levy, S. 2003. *Ready Steady Go!: Swinging London and the Invention of Cool*. London: Fourth Estate.

Lindsay, J. 1975. *William Morris*. New York: Taplinger.

Litweiler, J. 1990. *The Freedom Principle: Jazz After 1958*: London: Da Capo Press.

Lock, G. 1985a. "Sweet Thunder". *The Wire* April: 10–15.

Lock, G. 1985b. "Save the Wail". *The Wire* April: 34–7.

Long, M. A. 1998. "From Scooter to Scooterist: A Cultural History of the Italian Motor-scooter". Senior thesis presented to Prof. Anne Cook Saunders on 17 December 1998, www.vespaclubvolos.com/Scooter_History_1_.pdf

Lott, E. 1993. *Love and Theft: Blackface Minstrelsy and the American Working Class*. New York: Oxford University Press.

Lotz, R. E. 1997. "Amerikaner in Europa". In *That's Jazz: Der Sound Des 20. Jahrhunderts*. K. Wolbert (ed.). Darmstadt: Jürgen Häusser.

Louvre, A. 1992. "The New Radicalism: The Politics of Culture in Britain, America and France, 1956–73". In *Cultural Revolution? The Challenge of the Arts in the 1960s*. B. Moore-Gilbert and J. Seed (eds). London: Routledge, 45–70.

Lydon, M. 1969. "Rock for Sale". Originally published in *Ramparts Magazine*. Republished in J. Eisen. 1969. *The Age of Rock 2: Sights and Sounds of the American Cultural Revolution*. New York: Vintage.

Lyttelton, H. 1957. *I Play as I Please: The Memoirs of an Old Etonian Trumpeter*. London: Jazz Book Club.

Lyttelton, H. 1969. Sleevenotes for *Our Point of View*. CBS Realm Jazz Series 52668.

MacDonald, I. 1995. *Revolution in the Head*. London: Fourth Estate.

MacInnes, C. 1960. *Absolute Beginners*. London: MacGibbon & Kee.

MacInnes, C. 1966. *England, Half English*. Harmondsworth: Penguin.

Mager, F. 1967. *Was Wollen Die Studenten?* Frankfurt: Fischer.

Mailer, N. 1968. *The Armies of the Night*. Harmondsworth: Penguin.

Marcuse, H. 1969. *An Essay on Liberation*. Boston, MA: Beacon Hill.

Marcuse, H. 1970. *One Dimensional Man*. London: Sphere.

Marcuse, H. 1973. *Eros and Civilisation*. London: Abacus.

Martin, T. E. 1965. "Joe Harriott". *Jazz Monthly* January: 2–4.

Marwick, A. 1996. *British Society Since 1945*. Harmondsworth: Penguin.

Marwick, A. 1998. *The Sixties*. Oxford: Oxford University Press.

Marx, K. [1844] 1993. *Economic and Philosophical Manuscripts of 1844*. Marx/Engels Internet Archive, http://marxists.org, 49–51.

Marx, K. 1969. *Theories of Surplus Value*. London: Lawrence & Wishart.

Marx, K. and F. Engels. 1970. *The German Ideology*. London: Lawrence & Wishart.

Maslow, A. 1954. *Motivation and Personality*. New York: Harper.

Massarik, J. 2005. "Mr. 100 Percent". *Jazzwise* 90: 34–7.

Masters, B. 1985. *The Swinging Sixties*. London: Constable.

McCoy, A. W. 1991. *The Politics of Heroin: Central Intelligence Agency Complicity in the Global Drug Trade*. Brooklyn, NY: Lawrence Hill.

McGregor, M. 1995. *Chris McGregor and the Brotherhood of Breath*. Flint, MI: Bamberger Press.

McKay, G. 2005. *Circular Breathing: The Cultural Politics of Jazz in Britain*. London: Duke University Press.

Mead, M. 1969. *Coming of Age in Samoa: A Study of Adolescence and Sex in Primitive Society*. Harmondsworth: Pelican.

Melly, G. 1970. *Revolt into Style*. Harmondsworth: Allen Lane.

Melly, G. 1974. *Owning Up*. Harmondsworth: Penguin.

Melody Maker. 1958. "Race Riots". 6 September: 1 and 16.

Melody Maker. 1960. "Round the Jazz Clubs". 3 September: 13.

Melody Maker. 1962. "Raver". 4 August: 5.

Melody Maker. 1965. "Here Comes Them". 10 April: 8.

Melody Maker. 1968. 3 February: 14.

Mezzrow, M. and B. Wolfe. 1959. *Really the Blues*. London: Jazz Book Club.

Miles, B. 2004. *Hippie*. London: Cassell Illustrated.

Miles, B. 2006. *Pink Floyd: The Early Years*. London: Omnibus.

Milgram, S. 1974. *Obedience to Authority: An Experimental View*. London: HarperCollins.

Minnion J. and P. Bolsover. 1983. *The CND Story*. London: Allison & Busby.

Mold, A. N. 2004. "Dynamic Dualities: The British System of Heroin Addiction Treatment 1965–87". PhD thesis, Birmingham University, http://etheses.bham.ac.uk/75/1/Mold04PhD.pdf.

Moore, B. 2005. "British Perceptions of Italian Prisoners of War, 1940–7". In *Prisoners of War, Prisoners of Peace: Captivity, Homecoming and Memory in World War II*. B. Moore and B. Hately-Broad (eds). Oxford: Berg.

Moore, H. 2007. *Inside British Jazz: Crossing Borders of Race, Nation and Class*. Farnham: Ashgate.

Moore, B. and B. Hately-Broad (eds). 2005. *Prisoners of War, Prisoners of Peace: Captivity, Homecoming and Memory in World War II*. Oxford: Berg.

Moore-Gilbert, B. and J. Seed (eds). 1992. *Cultural Revolution? The Challenge of the Arts in the 1960s*. London: Routledge.

Morgan, K. O. 1997. "The Wilson Years: 1964–1970". In *From Blitz to Blair*, N. Tiratsoo (ed.) London: Weidenfeld & Nicolson.

Morton, A. L. 1969. *The English Utopia*. London: Lawrence & Wishart.

Morton, J. 2001. *Bent Coppers: Survey of Police Corruption*. London: Warner.

Murphy, R. and S. Roe. 2007. *Drug Misuse Declared: Findings from the 2006/07 British Crime Survey England and Wales*. London: Home Office Statistical Bulletin.

Musicians' Union and The Labour Party. 1963. *Jazz 1963 Souvenir Programme Royal Festival Hall Concert*.

Myrdal, G. 1944. *An American Dilemma: The Negro Problem and Modern Democracy*. New York: Harper & Bros.

Newton, F. 1960. *The Jazz Scene*. London: MacGibbon & Kee.

Nicholson, S. 2005. "Flash-back". *The Observer Music Monthly*, 19 June.

Nuttall, J. 1970. *Bomb Culture*. London: Paladin.

O'Brian, L. 2002. *She-Bop II*. London: Continuum.

O'Brien, L. 1995. *She-Bop: The Definitive History of Women in Rock, Pop and Soul*. Harmondsworth: Penguin.

O'Brien, R., D. Sheppard, A. H. Halsey *et al*. 1985. *Faith in the City: A Call for Action by Church and Nation: Report of the Archbishop of Canterbury's Commission on Urban Priority Areas*. London: Church House Publishing.

Oldham, A. L. 2000. *Stoned*. London: Secker & Warburg.

Oliver, P. 1962. *Blues Fell This Morning*. London: Jazz Book Club.

Orwell, G. 1941. *The Lion and the Unicorn*. London: Secker & Warburg.

Overmans, R. 2005. "The Repatriation of Prisoners of War Once Hostilities Are Over: A Matter of Course?" In *Prisoners of War, Prisoners of Peace: Captivity, Homecoming and Memory in World War II*, B. Moore and B. Hately-Broad (eds). Oxford: Berg.

Parkin, F. 1968. *Middle Class Radicalism: The Social Bases of the Campaign for Nuclear Disarmament*. Manchester: Manchester University Press.

People Band. 2004. Sleevenotes to EMANEN 4102 CD, reissue of original Transatlantic LP release.

Phillips, M. and T. Phillips. 1999. *Windrush: The Irresistible Rise of Multi-Racial Britain*. London: HarperCollins.

Pointon, M. and R. Smith. 2010. *Goin' Home: The Uncompromising Life and Music of Ken Colyer*. London: Ken Colyer Trust.

Postgate, J. 1963. "Jazz and Race". *Jazz Monthly* 19(10): 2–4.

Prévost, E. 1992. Sleevenotes to *The Crypt*. MRDCD05 taken from Cardew, C. 1967. "Towards an Ethic of Improvisation". www.ubu.com/papers/cardew_ethics.html.

Prévost, E. 1995. *No Sound is Innocent*. Harlow: Copula.

Priestley, B. 1971. "Ardley's Arranging". *Melody Maker* 21 August: 12.

Priestley, B. 1988. *Jazz on Record*. London: Elm Tree.

Priestley, J. B. 1937. *The Arts under Socialism*. London: Turnstile.

Race, S. 1960. "In My Opinion". *Jazz Journal* January: 7–8.

Rancière, J. 2011. *The Politics of Aesthetics: The Distribution of the Sensible*. London: Continuum.

Renaud, P. 1995. *Simply Not Cricket: Catalogue Du Jazz Britannique 1964–1994*. France: Philippe Renaud.

Reynolds, S. and J. Press. 1995. *The Sex Revolts: Gender, Rebellion and Rock 'n' Roll* London: Serpent's Tail.

Rickert, J. 1986. "The Fromm-Marcuse Debate Revisited". *Theory and Society* 15(3): 351–400.

Ritter, D. 2008. "The Ethics of Aesthetics". In *Transdisciplinary Digital Art*, R. Adams, S. Gibson and S. Müller Arisona (eds). Berlin: Springer.

Robertson, A. 2003. *Fire in His Soul*. London: Northway.

Robertson, A. 2011. *Fire in His Soul*. Second edition. London: Northway.

Rosen, A. 2003. *The Transformation of British Life 1950–2000 (A Social History)*. Manchester: Manchester University Press.

Rudé, G. 1964. *The Crowd in History: A Study of Popular Disturbances in France and England, 1730–1848*. London: Wiley & Sons.

Ruskin, J. 1900. *The Crown of Wild Olive*. London: Harrap.

Rye, H. 1990. "Fearsome Means of Discord: Early Encounters with Black Jazz". In *Black Music in Britain: Essays on the Afro-Asian Contribution to Popular Music*, P. Oliver (ed.). Milton Keynes: Open University.

Sadler, R. Undated. "England and Wales". www.answers.com/topic/england-and-wales.

Sandbrook, D. 2006. *Never Had It So Good*. London: Abacus.

Sandbrook, D. 2008. *White Heat: A History of Britain in the Swinging Sixties*. London: Abacus.

Santosuosso, L. and C. Casanova. 2011. "Sessantotto e jazz: la parola ai testimony". http://italia.allaboutjazz.com/php/article.php?id=6567.

Savage, M. 2005. "Revisiting Classic Qualitative Studies". *FQS Forum: Qualitative Social Research* 6(1), http://nbn-resolving.de/urn:nbn:de:0114-fqs0501312.

Savage, M. 2010. *Identities and Social Change in Britain Since 1940: The Politics of Method*. Oxford: Oxford University Press.

Schonfield, V. 1967. Sleevenotes to original release *Celebration*. Deram DML 1013.

Schonfield, V. 1992. British National Sound Archive John Stevens Interview: Oral History of Jazz in Britain. Ref: C122/158-160, December.

Schwarz, B. 1990. *Tubby Hayes: A Discography*. Zurich: Blackpress.

Scott, R, with M. Hennessey. 1979. *Some of My Best Friends are Blues*. London: W. H. Allen.

Searle C. 2008. *Forward Groove*. London: Northway.

Seed, J. 1992. "Hegemony Postponed: The Unravelling of the Culture of Consensus in Britain in the 1960s". In *Cultural Revolution? The Challenge of the Arts in the 1960s*, B. Moore-Gilbert and J. Seed (eds). London: Routledge, 15–44.

Shapiro, H. 1997. *Alexis Korner: The Biography*. London: Bloomsbury.

Shapiro, H. 1999. *Waiting for the Man: The Story of Drugs and Popular Music*. London: Helter Shelter.

Shapiro, H. 2005. *Graham Bond: The Mighty Shadow*. Oxford: Crossroads.

Shapiro, H. 2010. *Jack Bruce Composing Himself*. London: Jawbone.

Shera, M. 1966. "Mike Westbrook and His Orchestra". *Jazz Journal* January: 10–11.

Shera, M. 1967. "Review of Celebration". *Jazz Journal* December: 36.

Shipton, A. 2001. *A New History of Jazz*. London: Continuum.

Shipton, A. 2006. Sleevenotes to *Citadel/Room 315*. BGOCD713.

Shipton, A. 2007. Sleevenotes to *Down Another Road/Songs for My Father/Mosaics*. BGOCD767.

Shipton, A. 2010. Sleevenotes to *Windmill Tilter*. BGOCD944.

Simons, A. 2001. Sleevenotes to *Black British Swing*. Topic 781.

Simons, A. 2010. *Black British Swing: The African Diaspora's Contribution to England's Own Jazz of the 1930s and 1940s*. London: Northway.

Smart, C. 1984. "Social Policy and Drug Addiction: A Critical Study of Policy Development". *British Journal of Addiction* 79: 31–49.

Smart, C. 1985. "Social Policy and Drug Dependence: An Historical Case Study". *Drug and Alcohol Dependence* 16: 169–80.

Smith, G. 1994. Interview with Stan Tracey, BBC Radio Three, 12 January.

Stanbridge, A. 2008. "From the Margins to the Mainstream: Jazz, Social Relations, and Discourses of Value". *Critical Studies in Improvisation/Etudes Critiques En Improvisation* 4.

St Ives Times and Echo. 1971. "Jazz Musician Attacked Girl in Host's Home". 26 February: 1.

Stanford, C. V. and G. Shaw. 1905. *National Song Book: A Complete Collection of the Folk-Songs, Carols and Rounds suggested by the Board of Education*. London: Boosey.

Sudhalter, R. M. 1974. "Patient Healthy: Prognosis Uncertain". *Into Jazz* February: 34–5.

Tannahill, J. A. 1958. *European Volunteer Workers in Britain*, Manchester: Manchester University Press.

Taylor, D. "British Modern Jazz: From the 1940s Onwards". http://vzone.virgin.net/davidh.taylor/bebop.htm.

This Is London. 2007. "Lord Montagu on the Court Case Which Ended the Legal Persecution of Homosexuals". thisislondon.co.uk, *The Evening Standard*, 14 July.

Thomas, R. 2003. *Twentieth Century Military Recording Project: Prisoner of War Camps (1939–1948)*. Swindon: English Heritage.

Thompson, E. P. 1975. *William Morris: Romantic to Revolutionary*. New York: Pantheon.

Thompson, L. with J. Green. 2009. *Swing from a Small Island*. London: Northway.

Thompson, E. P. 2002. *The Making of the English Working Class*. Harmondsworth: Penguin.

Thornton, S. 1995. *Club Cultures: Music, Media, and Subcultural Capital*. Cambridge: Polity.

Tiratsoo, N. (ed.). 1997. *From Blitz to Blair: a New History of Britain Since 1939*. London: Weidenfeld & Nicolson.

Tomkins, L. 1974. "The Kathy Stobart Story". *Crescendo* March: 14–15.

Toscano, R. 2005. "Isaiah Berlin's *Two Concepts of Liberty*". *Pace Diritti Umani/Peace Human Rights* 2: 63–8.

Tracy, S. 1997. *Talking Swing*. Edinburgh: Mainstream.

Traill, S. and G. Lascelles. (eds). 1957. *Just Jazz*. London: Peter Davies.

Under Milk Wood. 1993. Sleevenotes to Blue Note 789449.

Valentine, D. 2006. *The Strength of the Wolf*. London: Verso.

Vaughan Williams, R. and A. L. Lloyd. 1959. *Penguin Book of English Folk Songs*. Harmondsworth: Penguin.

Voce, S. 1964. "It Don't Mean a Thing". *Jazz Journal*, August: 8–9.

Voce, S. 2010. "Harry Beckett: Highly respected Trumpeter Who Worked with Mingus, Scott, Dankworth and Tracey". *The Independent* 24 August.

Walsh A. 1966. "An Avant Gardist Loose With Manfred". *Melody Maker* 23 April: 14.

Walvin, J. 1984. *Passage to Britain: Immigration in British History and Politics*. Harmondsworth: Penguin.

Warburton, D. 2001. *Paris Transatlantic Magazine* January, http://www.paristransatlantic.com/magazine/interviews/rowe.html.

Wastell, M. 1998. "Unsung Hero Paul Rutherford". *Avant* 5: 16–17.

Watson, B. 2004. *Derek Bailey and the Story of Free Improvisation*. London: Verso.

Welch, C. 1965a. "The Brain Drain! The Men Jazz Lost to Pop". *Melody Maker* 23 January: 10.

Welch, C. 1965b. "Last of the R&B Groups?" *Melody Maker* 12 June: 8.

Welch, C. 1965c. "… If The Animals Get Too Far Out?" *Melody Maker* 14 August: 3.

Welch, C. 1965d. "Manfred Wants More Men: Modern Jazz Group Within the Group". *Melody Maker* 30 October: 1.

Whent, C. 1961. "Phenomenon of Jazz". *Jazz Monthly* March–May: 9–14.

White Paper Cmnd. 2601. 1965. "A Policy for the Arts: the First Steps". London: HMSO, February.

Wickes, J. 1999. *Innovations in British Jazz*. Chelmsford: Soundworld.

Williams, R. 1971. "Centipede's Energy". *Melody Maker* 16 October: 37.

Williams, R. 1972. "Review of Mike Westbrook *Metropolis*". *Melody Maker* 26 February: 32.

Wilmer, V. 1968. "Workpoints: Graham Collier Purcell Room, London". *Down Beat* 16 May 16: 36–9.

Wilmer, V. 1982. "Kathy Stobart: Music in My Blood". *Jazz Forum* 76, 43–6.

Wilmer, V. 1986. "Leslie Thompson: A Pioneer Remembers". *The Wire* 25: 16–19, 52.

Wilmer, V. 1989. "Burning 'Speare". *Wire* 68, September.

Wilmer, V. 1991. *Mama Said There'd Be Days Like This*. London: Women's Press.

Wilmer, V. 1992. "Blue Bogey". *Jazz FM* 10: 40–3.

Wilson, C. 1956. *The Outsider*. London: Gollancz.

Wilson, H. C. 2002. "How the Child Poverty Action Group Came Into Being". *Poverty* 113, www.childpoverty.org.uk/about/history/poverty113-history.htm

Wilson, P. 2002. "John Stevens' Discography". http://efi.group.shef.ac.uk/mstevens.html.

Winnick, C. 1961. "The Taste of Music: Alcohol, Drugs and Jazz". *Jazz Monthly* October: 8–11, November: 10–12.

Wright, E. O. 1978. *Class, Crisis, and the State*. London: New Left Books.

Young, J. 1971. "The Role of Police as Amplifiers of Deviancy, Negotiators of Reality and Translators of Fantasy". In *Images of Deviance*, S. Cohen (ed.). Harmondsworth: Penguin.

Zwerin, M. 1985. *La Tristesse De Saint Louis: Jazz Under the Nazis*. New York: Quartet.

Interviews

Alexander, Gill, February 2009

Ashton, Bill, February 2009

Baker, Ginger, August 2009

Ball, Kenny, May 2008

Barber, Chris, February 2008

Bayley, Gary, via e-mail, April 2011

Beckett, Harry, June 2008

Bilk, Acker, February 2008

Bruce, Jack, October 2007

Bryars, Gavin, November 2010

Carr, Ian, May 2004

Charles, Goudie, February 2008

Collier, Graham, November 2004

Dankworth, John, February 2008

Dee, Brian, March 2008

Dunbar, John, April 2011

Eden, Peter, February 1996

Fairweather, Digby, July 2010

Fame, Georgie, April 2009

Foster, George, March 2009

Garrick, Michael, March 2003

Goode, Coleridge, May 2008

Guy, Barry, November 2010

Henderson, Russell, March 2012

Hiseman, Jon, October 2007

Hiseman, Jon, May 2009

Holder, Frank, March 2012
Holland, Dave, January 2009
Hopper, Hugh, via e-mail, June 2003
Horovitz, Michael, February 2009
Jack, John, June 2008
Kilby, Jak, via e-mail, January 2011
Laine, Cleo, February 2008
Mayer, John, June 2001
Miller, Hazel, June 2008
Moholo-Moholo, Louis, June 2008
Moholo-Moholo, Louis, September 2008
Morgan, Laurie, February 2012
Nicols, Maggie, October 2010
Oxley, Tony, April 2010
Palmer, Louis, June 2008
Palmer, Tony, via e-mail, July 2010
Parker, Evan, September 2008
Parker, Evan, April 2009
Riley, Howard, May 2006
Robson, Jeremy, April 2009
Rubin, Ron, October 2007
Shapiro, Harry, April 2009

Shipton, Alyn, via e-mail, May 2011
Skidmore, Alan, July 2009
Stobart, Kathy, March 2009
Surman, John, June 2008
Surman, John, November 2008
Thompson, Barbara, March 2010
Thompson, Danny, February 2009
Tippett, Keith, March 2004
Tippetts, Julie, September 2008
Tomlin, Dave, October 2007
Tracey, Clark, February 2011
Tracey, Stan, December 2009
Wellins, Bobby, September 2009
Westbrook, Mike, January 2006
Westbrook, Mike, November 2008
Westbrook, Mike, May 2011
Westbrook, Mike, via e-mail, July 2011
Westbrook, Mike, August 2011
Wheeler, Kenny, October 2005
Winstone, Norma, December 2010
Winstone, Norma, May 2006
Wyatt, Robert, June 2003

Index

Breath 256, 269; with Kathy Stobart 256, 280; *All Night Long* soundtrack 254–5, 260; Barry Guy *Ode* 342; contribution to British jazz 256, 269–70, 444; Mike Westbrook *Metropolis* 387; with John Surman 256, 392; New Jazz Orchestra 370

Bell, Maggie 282, 301

Benjamin, Walter 2, 308, 423, 443, 444

Bennett, Richard Rodney 110, 253, 258, 284

Benson, Ivy 279, 300

Berendt, Joachim 8, 9, 133, 288

Berklee School of Music 78, 175, 260, 358

Berlin, Isaiah, concepts of freedom 306–7

Bevan, Aneurin 356, 440
    opposes unilateral nuclear disarmament 353, 408

Big Three 126, 416

Bilk, Acker 7, 18, 21, 26, 44, 115, 125, 214, 407
    with Ken Colyer 18; chart success 29, 30, 31, 32; *Blue Acker* 22–3, 25, 33; Stan Tracey *We Love You Madly* 25; on modern jazz 24–5; trademark bowler 31; Beaulieu riot 52–3, 54–5; on rise of beat groups 127; *Stranger On The Shore* in US charts 97

Biscoe, Chris, NYJO 89, 90

Blain, Brian 88, 134, 390, 404, 412

Blair, Eddie 242, 243, 253

Blair, Tony 276

Blake, Cyril "Happy" 223

Blake, William, and Mike Westbrook 379, 384, 432, 435, 438, 439

Blakey, Art 66, 98, 117, 136, 142, 194, 314

Blue Note (record company) 95, 232, 420

Blue Notes 398, 414
    impact of 92–3, 104, 247, 261–6; The Old Place 100; inspiration for Keith Tippett 178; Musicians' Union and 261–2, 265; disintegration 264; Joe Boyd and 262–4; reaction of younger musicians to 265–6; deaths of members of 266, 269; contribution to British jazz 266, 270; *see also* Chris McGregor; Brotherhood Of Breath

Bond, Edward 276, 352

Bond, Graham 228, 244, 364
    Don Rendell *Roarin'* 67, 158, 190; move

from jazz to R&B 124, 145, 146, 148, 155, 156, 158; club success 144, 159, 416; *Sound Of Bond, There's A Bond Between Us, Solid Bond, Holy Magick, We Put Our Magic on You* 158–60; Jon Hiseman on 159, 160; Ginger Baker on 202; influence on other groups 160–62; with Pete Brown 160, 172; drug use 158, 191, 194, 202; Brian Dee on 184, 191–2; Jack Bruce on early Organization 158, 209; Mike Taylor and 210

Boyle, Gary
    and Brian Auger 158; with Mike Westbrook 386, 387; Isotope 158, 173

Braine, John 13

Branscombe, Alan 169
    Beatles' sessions 148; drug use 184, 194; *The Day I Met The Blues* 194; Harold McNair *Affectionate Fink* 260; Cosmic Eye 233

Brecht, Bertolt 384

British Broadcasting Corporation *see* BBC

Britten, Benjamin 107, 143, 361, 375

Brooks, Elkie 282, 301

Broonzy, Big Bill 20, 21, 33

Brotherhood of Breath 256, 259, 261, 317, 374
    Chris Barber on 33; Joe Boyd and 92, 263, 265; *Eclipse At Dawn* 263; attitude of British musicians to 178, 265–8; *Brotherhood Of Breath/Brotherhood* 268–9; Evan Parker on 266–8; John Surman on 268; Hazel Miller on 265–6; *Kongi's Harvest* 266; *Live At Willisau* 256, 269; Anti-Apartheid Movement 412; *see also* Blue Notes; Chris McGregor

Brown, Ford Madox 13
    "Work" 436–9

Brown, James 151, 165, 417

Brown, Pete
    New Departures 78, 79, 81, 362, 363, 364; from jazz to rock 145; and Graham Bond 160; Cream, Jack Bruce and 170; Battered Ornaments 172, 175; Piblokto *Things May Come and Things May Go* 172; counter culture and 406

Brown, Sandy 45, 50, 223
    Fairweather-Brown band 19, 21, 23, 24, 32, 127; *Incredible McJazz* 23, 34;